Communities Directory

A Comprehensive Guide
to Intentional Communities
and Cooperative Living

Communities Directory

*A Comprehensive Guide
to Intentional Communities
and Cooperative Living*

᮪

2005 Edition

Published by
The Fellowship for Intentional Community
Rutledge, Missouri

How to Use This Directory

Looking for Basic Information on Community?
Check out our Articles section. Be sure to use the Article Index in the Appendix if you're looking for information on a specific concept.

Looking for a Community?
The most direct path to choose in using this directory will depend on:
- what you already know about (or seek in) a community,
- whether you're looking for a specific group (one you already know something about), or
- if you're interested in any group that satisfies a number of characteristics.

Do You Know the Name?
Look for a description in the Community Listings (p. 89), and in the Cross-Reference Charts (sorted alphabetically by community name). You can also look in the Short Listings Section (p. 273) where we have basic contact info for communities found in previous editions of the *Directory* that did not fill out a questionnaire for this edition.

Do You Know the Geographic Region?
Look at the Maps (p. 37) to locate the North American groups in this directory. For all communities worldwide you can check the Key to Communities by Country/State/Province (p. 49).

Do You Know Some Defining Characteristics?
Examine the Cross-Reference Charts (p. 57). Hopefully, the specific characteristics you're seeking are among those reviewed in the chart. If a desired characteristic does not appear in the chart, try locating relevant keywords in the Community Listings Keyword Index (p. 291) in the Appendix.

Still Can't Find It?
If you followed the steps outlined above and were not successful, we suggest you write or call the Fellowship for Intentional Community (FIC), publishers of this *Directory*, with your specific request. The FIC's database of intentional communities is quite extensive—not all choose to list in the Directory. Plus, the FIC has file cabinets full of resource information. Contact information for the FIC can be found on page 35.

Want to make sure you have the most current information possible?
The most current *Communities Directory* information can be found at the FIC's *Communities Directory* website at *directory.ic.org*. Communities are constantly updating their listings on our site and new ones are added all the time.

We hope to print a new edition of this book approximately every year or two, so if you want the latest but don't want it on the web, don't despair. New editions should be coming soon, so you will have the best information we can provide.

Finally, you may have information about a group that we don't know about. If so, please let us know! We'd like to invite their participation in future printings. Please use the form on the last page of the book to share any new leads you have, or email us at *directory@ic.org*. Thanks!

A note on web and email addresses

Web addresses within the articles are listed in italics. For example: *directory.ic.org*. If your web browser requires, you may need to add "http://" to the beginning of these addresses, but you should not add "www" as this would have been included if it were necessary.

Email addresses are also listed in italics. For example: *directory@ic.org*. Email addresses can be distinguished from web addresses by the presence of an @ symbol.

A note on telephone numbers

For communities outside the US and Canada, phone numbers are listed such that they can be called from any country. An example for a German community would be +49-(0)1234-56789. The plus sign indicates that one must start with your country's International Direct Dialing (IDD) prefix for any call abroad (011 is the IDD for the US and Canada). The next numerals (up to the dash) are the country code, which is also necessary for international calls (in the example 49 is the country code for Germany). In parenthesis, you will find the National Direct Dialing (NDD) prefix which is the number one would dial within the country before dialing the actual phone number (in the US and Canada the NDD is 1; in Germany it is 0) and which is not necessary when dialing from outside the country. After that is the complete phone number including any area, region, or city codes. Thus for the above example, if calling from the US one would dial 011-49-1234-56789 but if calling within Germany one would dial 0-1234-56789.

Table of Contents

What This *Directory* Is and Isn't

WITHIN THIS DIRECTORY you will find listings from hundreds of intentional communities located in North America and overseas. For the most part, included communities are open to being contacted by individuals or other communities interested in what they are doing. Some are actively seeking new members, while others wish to build inter-community ties. Some are just willing to share their example—to be a source of information or inspiration.

The FIC worked to generate high community participation, but given limited production time there are certainly many groups not listed in this book who would like to be.

Who Qualifies for Listing as an "Intentional Community"

In general, the information you will find in this directory was gathered through our questionnaire, which we offer at the *Online Communities Directory* website, *directory.ic.org*. Interested communities also responded by email or over the phone.

Using this method, the FIC chooses to let communities define themselves. Participating communities wrote their own descriptions for the Communities Listings section. This means the FIC avoided arbitrarily excluding anyone through an overly narrow definition of what it means to be a community. However, it also means that any group of two or more adults that considered itself a community was welcome to participate. Even one adult with a vision for starting a community was able to place a listing.

That said, the same basic screening process used for previous editions is still in place. Specifically, the FIC asked communities to participate only if they do not advocate violent practices and if they do not interfere with members' freedom to leave their group at any time.

To the extent possible, all communities listed met those two basic criteria. However, readers should be aware that the FIC does not yet have the staff time to examine each community firsthand. As the FIC has not independently assessed the accuracy of community statements and representations, we encourage individual fact-checking and urge reasonable caution.

When a Community is Categorized as "Forming"

As mentioned previously, a community with as few as one adult member still qualifies to appear in the directory. However, that community will have a "forming" label in our listings. Listing forming communities is an important service, as it helps those groups find the new members they need.

Because forming communities have a much greater tendency to change in a short period of time, it can be challenging to include them in book format. We do apologize for any information that becomes out of date due to these changes, but feel that the benefit of including these communities outweighs the possible inconvenience.

Deciding which communities are classified as forming can prove to be a delicate task as well. To provide clarity, the policy that the FIC has been using for several years is listed below:
- any community that labels itself as such,
- any community with fewer than four adult members, or
- any group that has not lived together for at least a year.

"Forming" communities are often, but are not always, brand new. Some older existing communities go through periods of reorganization or upheaval in which their populations drop to "forming" levels. Others have held steady with a small number of members for some time.

Differences Between Ideology and Daily Reality

Communities are often inspiring and caring places to live, but—like any human undertaking—they are not perfect. As stated above, communities write their own descriptions, and naturally groups want to describe themselves at their best.

En route to fulfilling these visions of what they want their community to be, they sometimes go through the same rough spots human groupings everywhere experience, such as power struggles, miscommunication, and unrealistic expectations. Readers should be prepared to empower themselves to assess the information describing each group. Attempting to identify which statements are part of a long-term vision and which reflect day-to-day life can be an interesting process, as well as a prudent one.

How the FIC Handles Complaints About Listed Communities

You may wonder what the FIC does when someone visits a community and finds it quite different from what was written in its listing. Based on experience with the previous three editions of the book, users were overwhelmingly pleased with what they found.

However, very occasionally we receive a complaint that a community has seriously misrepresented itself in the directory. In response to this, the FIC makes an effort to open constructive dialog between the community and the person with the complaint, to see what kind of understanding can be reached. If no resolution is found, the FIC brings into play its system called "Feedback Files." All points of view in the disagreement are written up and placed in a file about that community. These files are kept in the FIC office. The contents of the files can be summarized upon request, with a processing fee of $1 per community to compensate for the time. Please see the Feedback piece in the Appendix for information on where to send feedback or how to request information from Feedback Files.

Reasons You Might Not Find a Community Listed Here

Readers should be aware that there are hundreds, if not thousands, of communities that are not listed in this directory. There are many communities about which the FIC simply has not yet heard. Additionally, although email has significantly decreased the cost and amount of time needed for worldwide communication, language barriers sometimes impede communication with international communities.

Some communities may also receive our survey but choose not to list. Reasons for this choice could include the following:

- they're worried that listing would attract attention they don't want;
- networking within the Communities Movement does not appeal to them;
- they don't want any new members and also don't wish to handle visitors or inquiries;
- they're looking to generate a very specific type of membership, and this directory has too broad a readership base; or
- they prefer to attract visitors to their community through word of mouth.

As well, sometimes communities move, and we aren't able to discover their new location to send them a survey.

Some communities didn't return their surveys in time to list in this edition, but can be found on the *Online Communities Directory (directory.ic.org)* and will be contained in future editions of the book.

More Than Community Listings . . .

Before you begin searching the Community Listings, please take time to read through the included articles. They contain important basic information about intentional communities.

If you are planning to visit communities, especially consider reading "Red Carpets and Slammed Doors: Visiting Communities," by Geoph Kozeny. He has been visiting communities for more than 17 years, and has packed this piece with helpful advice.

Much thanks for your interest in community. Enjoy!

Other Communities Directories

Diggers and Dreamers
The definitive directory of intentional communities in the United Kingdom.

http://www.diggersanddreamers.org.uk
Diggers & Dreamers, c/o Edge of Time Ltd
BCM Edge, London, WC1N 3XX, UK
info@diggersanddreamers.org.uk

Eurotopia
Directory of European intentional communities available in German, English and Spanish.

http://www.eurotopia.de
Oekodorf Sieben Linden, 38486 Bandau, Germany
+49-(0)39000-90621
info@eurotopia.de

History of the *Directory* and Acknowledgments

by Tony Sirna
Directory Project Coordinator

THE FIC'S *COMMUNITIES DIRECTORY* has changed a lot since our first edition was published in 1990. Back then, desktop publishing was in its infancy, email was something only a few people had, and the world wide web was only a gleam in some computer geek's eye.

The first three editions of this book all came about through multi-year, Herculean efforts of dedicated volunteers and a few paid staff. Communities were contacted by mail and phone, and only more recently via email. It took years to collect all the data and collate it into the amazing reference book the *Communities Directory* came to be.

However, it has become increasingly obvious each year that the internet has become the main conduit for the sharing of reference information. Sales of our book have slowed while the number of visits to our website goes up and up. Thus in 2004 the FIC made the leap, launching the *Online Communities Directory*, a fully searchable database available for free to the world at *directory.ic.org*.

Not only did the web allow the information to be more easily searched, it also allowed it to be more easily updated. We've created a system in which communities can update their listings themselves, as often as they like, directly on our website. This means more up-to-date information for those searching and less data collection work for the FIC. We were pleasantly surprised when, within a few months of our public launch, hundreds of communities had updated their listings themselves. We still had to make a lot of phone calls to get the data presented in this book, but I'm told it was nothing compared to the past.

So why print a book when the web is the place to be? Well, despite some pundits' predictions, the web has not made books obsolete. We knew that for dozens of reasons some people would still want a tangible, hard copy version of the *Communities Directory*. So, in addition to our ever-updating website, we hope to publish a new edition of the *Communities Directory* approximately every year or two based on the data submitted to our website.

This book is the first *Communities Directory* produced with this new method. As such, it is an experiment and, in some ways, a first draft. Our new *Online Directory* went public in October of 2004, leaving only 6 months for communities to update and add listings. Surprisingly, despite the short production time we have as many listings as the last edition! Unfortunately, there were many communities that did not update their listings and, consequently, we have also included a section of abbreviated listings from our 2000 edition that are believed to still be active. You can always visit our website, *directory.ic.org*, to check for more recently updated listings.

As always, the FIC only prints listings from communities that have asked to appear in one of our *Communities Directories*. There are hundreds, if not thousands, of communities out there not listed in our book, only some of which we are even aware of. If there are communities you know of that don't appear in our book or website, let them know about us and encourage them to be listed. And let us know so we can be better aware of the breadth of the Communities Movement.

You may also notice that this *Directory* is slimmed down from previous editions. We have cut back on the number of articles, including only what we felt were the most essential pieces covering the basics of community. We also left out the resources section and the reading list found in our last edition. While it's sad to see these sections go, that type of information is now more widely available on the web. The articles from our last book are on our website: *www.ic.org*. If you are looking for books on community check out our Community Bookshelf at *store.ic.org*.

The slimmer book has its advantages. For one, this new book (when purchased directly from FIC) has a lower price than our third edition from five years ago. Further, a simpler book allows us to have a quicker production cycle. We hope this will lead to better quality information for what, at root, the directory is all about—the community listings. And we bet it will fit better in a community visitor's backpack!

Funding

In the past the *Communities Directory* has been able to pay for itself, and even be a money-making venture for the FIC, with proceeds going to further our other movement work such as Communities Magazine. But, as sales slowed over the past few years, we realized that it might no longer be able to fund itself.

As a result, we sought out donors willing to support this keystone of our work and, in turn, support the larger Communities Movement. Through donations we were able to develop the initial version of the *Online Communities Directory* and to get the basic systems in place for producing a book from our online data. Now the *Communities Directory* book need only make enough money to cover production and printing expenses, allowing it to cost less and be a viable enterprise for our chronically under-funded nonprofit (see sidebar p. 35 for more information on the *Directory* Endowment).

The Intentional Community Data Collective

While the *Communities Directory* is published and produced by the FIC, it is certainly produced with much cooperation from other Communities Movement organizations.

For years the FIC has been working with the Cohousing Association of the United States (Coho/US)—a networking organization—and its predecessors, to share data and information management systems. We recently dubbed this cooperative effort The Intentional Communities Data Collective (ICDC) and are inviting other community networking organizations to join us.

The *Online Communities Directory* is the first major effort of the ICDC. Information submitted on directory.ic.org is also used to update the Coho/US listing of cohousing communities at *www.cohousing.org*. Soon, Coho/US will have a similar system for allowing cohousing communities to update their information, and data will flow both ways between the organizations.

We are very grateful to Coho/US for their help and collaboration in spreading the word about community, and in helping to maintain this valuable database.

Acknowledgments

First I want to thank all the people who worked on previous editions of the Communities Directory for laying the groundwork for this edition. I'd especially like to thank Elph Morgan and Jillian Downey of Great Oak Cohousing, who were the editors of the 2000 edition on which this book is largely based. And while I'm at it, I'll thank them and Michael McIntyre of Sunward Cohousing for their years of work shepherding the Intentional Communities website at *www.ic.org* and the Intentional Communities List, the precursor to the *Online Communities Directory*.

Next, I thank all those who helped with the development of the online directory. Ofek for creating the ICDB (Intentional Communities Data Base) and allowing us to work from his code in developing our system; Charles uchu Strader of Sirius for providing hosting, technical support, and systems design; Michael McIntyre who supported the cohousing end of things and had great ideas for interface design; and McCune Renwick-Porter of Twin Oaks for his years of service in the FIC office, his work maintaining the Communities Database for the past few years, and his help in testing, promoting, and maintaining the new website.

Much of the work for this edition was done by myself and other members of Skyhouse Community at Dancing Rabbit Ecovillage. I was the lead programmer for the *Online Communities Directory* and coordinator for the production of this book. Amy Seiden of Skyhouse did the graphic design for the website, and also the layout and design for the book, including the cover. Jeffrey Harris and Cecil Scheib, both of Skyhouse, provided much needed technical support and emergency bug fixing. (Special thanks to all in Skyhouse for allowing me the flexibility to do this kind of work.) Laura Jaworski and Tereza Brown, both of Dancing Rabbit, deserve thanks for copyediting and proofreading. Without their meticulous eyes I'd be embarrassed to have you read this.

I also want to thank Diana Christian of Earthaven for her tremendous work selling advertisements, Harvey Baker of Dunmire Hollow for helping to collate articles, Deborah Altus for her work as part of the ERB, and Debby Bors of Twin Oaks Indexing for the indexes in the appendix.

I especially want to thank Laird Schaub of Sandhill Farm for his tireless energy given toward all FIC work, and particularly this project. Thanks for the articles, the editing, the fundraising, the contacting communities, and your support and mentoring throughout the years.

Thanks go to my partner Rachel Katz for her help with the maps and for suffering through my late nights at the computer as deadlines approached.

I want to thank all those who donated money to help launch the *Online Communities Directory* and those who have donated (and those who will!) to the *Communities Directory* endowment. We couldn't do it without your support.

And of course I want to thank all those who work with and have worked with the FIC over the years. This book wouldn't be possible without all of you and neither would the wonderful community life I live.

In Community, Intentionally

by Geoph Kozeny

"*I* WANT MORE OF A SENSE OF COMMUNITY in my life." It seems like you hear people saying that all the time these days. What's remarkable is that this inspiration is not coming only from folks that might be called alternative—I hear it from people representing a wide spectrum of values, ideals, and lifestyles.

Not surprisingly, intentional communities also represent a wide spectrum of values and ideas. For thousands of years people have been coming together to share their lives in creative and diverse ways. Today is no different; efforts to create new lifestyles based on shared ideals are as common as ever.

Pursuing Dreams

All intentional communities have idealism in common—each one was founded on a vision of living in a better way, usually in response to something perceived as lacking in the broader culture. Many communities aspire to provide a supportive environment for the development of members' awareness, abilities, and spiritual growth. Most seek to create a life that will satisfy shared human cravings: security, family, relationship, fellowship, mutual cooperation, creativity and self-expression, as well as a sense of place, a sense of belonging.

Typically, today's intentional communities are melting pots of ideals and issues that have been in the public spotlight over the decades: equality and civil rights, women's liberation, antiwar efforts, ecology and conservation, alternative energy, sustainable agriculture, co-ops, worker-owned businesses, personal growth, and spirituality. Some

An Intentional Community ...

"is a group of people who have chosen to live or work together in pursuit of a common ideal or vision. Most, though not all, share land or housing. Intentional communities come in all shapes and sizes, and display an amazing diversity in their common values, which may be social, economic, spiritual, political, and/or ecological. Some are rural; some urban. Some live all in a single residence; some in separate households. Some raise children; some don't. Some are secular, some are spiritually based, and others are both. For all their variety though, the communities featured in our magazine hold a common commitment to living cooperatively, to solving problems nonviolently, and to sharing their experience with others."

—*Communities* magazine

groups focus on only one or a few of these areas, while others try to integrate them all into a coherent whole. (You can get a good overview of how broadly groups in this directory focus their vision by using the cross-referencing charts that precede the listings.)

Although intentional communities are usually on the fringes of mainstream culture, the everyday values and priorities of community members are surprisingly compatible with those of their less adventurous counterparts. Both tend to assign value to providing a stable home and good education for their children, finding meaningful and

Geoph Kozeny has lived in various kinds of communities for 33 years, and has been on the road for the past 17 years—visiting, studying, facilitating, and consulting for intentional communities all across North America. He asks about their visions and realities, takes photos, and gives multi-media shows about the diversity and vitality of the Communities Movement. He was a core staff member for the first two editions of the *Communities Directory*, and is a regular columnist for *Communities* magazine. In 2002, he released "Visions of Utopia," a full-length video documentary on intentional communities and is presently editing footage for a second volume. He can be reached via email at *geoph@ic.org*, or write Community Catalyst Project, c/o 1531 Fulton Street, San Francisco CA 94117, USA.

Michael McIntyre – Sunward Cohousing

"Communities value providing a stable home and good education for their children, finding meaningful and satisfying work, and living in a safe neighborhood and an unpolluted environment."

satisfying work, living in a safe neighborhood and an unpolluted environment, and participating in local organizations and activities. For many, finding a spiritual path is also important as it can provide a context for the other goals and a basis for making decisions in times of uncertainty. The main difference is that most community members are not satisfied with the status quo. Intentional communities are testing grounds for new ideas about how to maintain more satisfying lives that enable people to actualize more of their untapped potential.

Time Is Not Standing Still

Most communities sound very clear and confident when describing their values, goals, and practices, but such things inevitably evolve over time. When you come across a documentary or a directory listing that profiles a community, I suggest thinking of the description as a snapshot in their family scrapbook. Most of the images—the people, the buildings, the activities, the priorities, even the visions—are subject to change over time.

I'm amazed at the number of times I've heard someone say, "I couldn't live in a community without this," or "I could never live in a community that did that"—only to interview them several years later and discover that they were happily living without the former and with the latter. I suspect this lack of wisdom about what we really need and want is due, in part, to the fact that society does not adequately teach us to explore this type of question.

⑥

After living in six communities over 15 years, I thought I knew what worked best— wrong!

Obviously, people's needs change over time as well. On the individual level, needs change as a person matures. On a societal level cultural values and norms shift for many, often inter-related, reasons.

Major changes do occasionally occur overnight in communities. However, it is far more common for large shifts to happen over a more extended period of time. For example, I've visited at least a dozen communities that were radically political in their early years, usually with a population of members mostly in their twenties. Within twenty years, the members— now in their forties—had shifted their focus to improving the quality of their kids' schools, worrying about health concerns, and making plans for their old age.

A Unique Experience

Contrary to popular stereotypes, every branch of the family portrayed in the "scrapbook" is unique. Just as no two brothers, sisters, aunts, uncles, or cousins lead identical lives, no two communities offer precisely the same experience. In the Catholic Worker network, for example, all the houses are based on a core philosophy that was articulated in the 1930s, yet no two are the same. Each community varies according to the number and ages of members, the projects emphasized, local laws and customs, and the cultural backgrounds and personalities of their members.

Likewise, the level of affluence in intentional communities runs the gamut from urban poor, to suburban and rural middle class, to quite well-heeled. Not surprisingly, there is a prevalence of nuclear families, single-parent families, and singles roughly proportionate to what you'd find in the mainstream.

Although there's a full range of ages among the people living in communities—from newborns to those well into their 90s—that diversity does not numerically reflect the demographics of the mainstream. Instead, there is a disproportionate representation of people in the 25- to 50-year-old age range, with the balance skewed toward the older end. Likewise, many cultures and ethnic groups are represented in North American intentional communities, but the well-educated white middle class is represented in proportions greater than in the mainstream.

What Works

After living in six communities over 15 years, I thought I knew what worked best—wrong! Since then I've visited over 300 communities to talk with members and ex-members about their experiences, and to observe what seemed to work and not work. My revised opinion about which structures and decision-making processes work best: whatever the members wholeheartedly believe in.

I've seen reasonably well-functioning examples of communities using consensus, majority voting, inspired anarchy, and benevolent dictatorships. I've also seen examples of each of those styles that seemed dysfunctional and disempowering. Sometimes the same community covered both ends of the spectrum, depending on the issue at hand

Flavors of Community

While every community is unique, there are broad ways we can categorize some communities that share important characteristics. Hopefully these definitions can help in our understanding of community, as long as we remember that even within categories communities will vary widely.

Cohousing: Though there is no precise definition, cohousing communities have a variety of typically shared characteristics. Cohousing can appear similar to some mainstream housing developments, but incorporates ideals of participation, cooperation, sharing, and knowing one's neighbors. Most cohousing communities have considerable resident input into the design process as it unfolds, and resident management of the community after it is built. The architectural design generally clusters the housing, with cars de-emphasized and pedestrian/play areas enhanced, to promote frequent and spontaneous human contact. Cohousing communities have a common house, a building/space with a large kitchen and dining room, as well as a range of other facilities desired by the residents. This is intended to act as an extension of the individual private homes, allowing them to be smaller than their non-community counterparts. Most operate by consensus. Work is shared, though work systems vary widely.

Ecovillages: The concept of ecovillage is a vision, an ideal. It combines the principles of ecology (understanding the complex effects of human activities on the environment around us, integration of multiple natural and human systems, sustainability into the indefinite future) and the idea of village (human scaled, with all features needed to meet the basic physical and social needs of its residents). In the real world, an ecovillage is a process toward this general vision. Ecovillages make a commitment to explore various physical and social technologies, and implement those that can move them closer to their vision of this ideal. People from many countries and from many cultures are taking up this challenge. They start from where they are, with widely differing levels of technology and other resources available to them. Each ecovillage asks "How can we use what is available to us to move closer to the ecovillage ideal? What are our strengths that we can share with other ecovillage projects? What do we need that others can help us with?" Each ecovillage finds different answers to these questions, and is at a different point on the path toward its vision.

Kibbutzim: There are 285 kibbutzim (communal settlements) in Israel today. Though most are not religiously focused, a few are. The vast majority are affiliated with the Kibbutz Movement, a pluralistic umbrella organization. While all are more or less politically left wing, kibbutzim have diverged widely from the high level of similarity and centralized economies that characterized the movement just a generation ago. In response to intense economic, political, and generational pressures, most groups have become less communal and allow much more individual choice around finances and job selection. It remains to be seen whether this trend toward diversification and privatization will ultimately produce a stronger, more resilient movement.

and what side of the bed community members got out of that day. No amount of theory, dogma, or peer pressure can eliminate the need for clarity of vision, open mindedness, personal integrity, good communication, compassion, the spirit of cooperation, and common sense.

The structure a group uses is merely a tool; how it's applied is what's important. Strong leadership can prove to be inspirational and empowering, or it can prove to be dogmatic and repressive—and the same is true of decentralized individualism. What counts most is a collective sense of well-being, empowerment, and community.

The more egalitarian the group's vision, the more likely that there will be subtle internal power dynamics that go unnoticed, unacknowledged, or are outright denied. This observation is not intended to imply that hierarchies have no inherent problems, including those that produce power struggles, rather that the way they describe their own decision-making process is normally closer to the truth than those groups who aspire to equality. (See Joreen Freeman's article, "The Tyranny of Structurelessness," in the second edition of the *Communities Directory* for a more detailed exploration of this tendency.[1])

While a sense of unity is typically one of the fundamental goals of intentional communities, it is a quality often lacking—sometimes existing only in theory, or deferred as a long-range goal that will be achieved only when the community becomes more "evolved." Unfortunately, we are quite capable of imagining a glorious utopian future without having yet developed many of the skills required to live up to our own high expectations.

Religious/Spiritual Communities: In this category, the variety is quite large. Communities range from long-standing Catholic monasteries and nunneries to the newest New Age groups. Some have a very unified practice, with all in the community sharing a single practice while others have members following a variety of paths. The main thing they all have in common is that they tend to use community as a tool to further their spiritual agenda, rather than as an end in itself. Being gathered into a community allows participants to separate from the temptations and diversions of the outside world, and provides more intense reinforcement for living the focused life of the religious aspirant. We can view spiritual community as a cauldron that creates an intense, focused heat not easily found elsewhere. Many spiritual leaders have recommended or even required that their followers live in a community of believers, as a way to deepen their spiritual life and promote the internal changes that move them closer to the ideal. If you choose to enter the life of a religious community, it is important that you accept the religious practice of the group, without thinking that it will be perfect once you get them to change one or several aspects you don't agree with.

Egalitarian Communities: Some communities explicitly adopt a list of agreements that promote the equality of their members. One group of such communities that is very active in the US Communities Movement is the Federation of Egalitarian Communities (FEC). Each member community agrees to four principal values: egalitarianism, income sharing, cooperation, and non-violence. Each member has equal access to the decision-making process, and to the resources of the community.

FEC communities range in size from family size groups to village size, with their decision-making and resource-allocation systems generally becoming more structured and complex as their size increases. Because of the large overlap of shared values, the FEC communities have been able to create and maintain a variety of inter-community connections and projects, including a work exchange program, joint businesses, and a major medical insurance fund.

Student Co-ops: Student housing co-ops are associated with a number of colleges and universities, providing a low-cost alternative to dorms, apartments, fraternities, and sororities. Students often choose co-ops initially for the lower cost, and only discover the interpersonal benefits after they move in. For many young people, student co-ops provide them with their first taste of intentional community. Houses range in size from small houses with a handful of residents, to large buildings that house over a hundred co-opers. Some co-ops restrict members to students while others draw members from the broader community. Student co-ops generally subscribe to the principles of the Co-op Movement, known as the Rochdale principles, written down by a group of weavers in Rochdale, England in 1844. In brief, these are: 1) voluntary and open membership; 2) democratic member control; 3) member economic participation; 4) autonomy and independence; 5) cooperation among cooperatives; and 6) concern for community. The North American Students of Cooperation (NASCO) is the organizational voice of the student Co-op Movement. It provides education, training, networking, and development assistance to existing and new student housing, dining, and business co-ops.

Michael McIntyre – Sunward Cohousing

"Cohousing design generally clusters the housing, with cars de-emphasized and pedestrian/play areas enhanced, to promote frequent and spontaneous human contact."

Novelty and Neighbors

One of the problems with pushing the envelope of mainstream society is running up against laws and regulations that make innovation either illegal, or full of bureaucratic hoops to jump through. Innovative construction styles such as strawbale, cob, and earthships, as well as greywater systems, composting toilets, and organic farming technologies, have until recently been so far outside the norm that local inspectors rarely have a clue about such techniques. As a result, government officials regularly erect hurdles and walls in the path of such alternatives. Fortunately, the innovators have persisted, and local and national codes are slowly embracing alternative technologies.

Zoning regulations, in particular, have proved challenging at times. Numerous cities have laws that prohibit more than three—or in some cases, up to five—unrelated adults from living together in one household. Although such laws were ostensibly instituted to protect neighborhoods from an excess of noise and cars, frequently they are enforced to protect against neighbors displaying nontraditional values and lifestyles. Some of these laws have been overturned in court, but many still exist, and don't usually draw much attention because enforcement is often very lax or nonexistent.

Another set of legal obstacles surfaces around the ownership and financing of commonly held property. Many communities seek to place ownership of their property

⑥

Many community groups are unaware of this history and end up starting the community-building process from scratch.

into a land trust for reasons of affordability, equality, and land stewardship. Land trust philosophy has come a long way over recent decades, but much work has yet to be done before it will be an easily available option in a culture geared toward the sanctity of the individual.

This is also true with funding. It is rare to find a banker who understands and appreciates cooperation and shared ownership, and that makes financing community-held property difficult. For example, a lack of interim construction financing delayed the start of the Cohousing Movement by several years. It is much easier to secure such funding now that there are nearly five dozen existing prototypes to point to.

Further, because social innovations are often more threatening than technological and economic innovations, relations with neighbors are often hugely challenging. The way neighbors perceive the community—and more importantly, how they interact with it—can run the gamut from generic mistrust and violent hostility to hearty appreciation and mutual cooperation.

When there is a media "cult" scare in the news, some communities—most notably the secretive or isolated groups—experience unfavorable rumors and critical scrutiny from their neighbors. On the other hand, those deeply involved in local activities (thereby having regular face-to-face encounters with folks living nearby) typically experience very little change in their neighborly interactions and the degree of local acceptance.

This variance reflects the tendency in our culture to mistrust strangers and anyone "different from us." Thus when a community settles into a new area, the usual default mode is that the locals will eye the newcomers with suspicion until the newcomers have "proven themselves."

This guilty-until-proven-innocent mentality has been fed by the media since the inception of the tabloid, and probably longer. The prevailing attitude among mainstream publishers is simple: sensational news is what sells newspapers and magazines. Yet, for some reason it seems that most readers fail to take that—and the cultural biases automatically built into so-called objective reporting—into account when assessing what coverage to believe.

As a result, it is the communities that are on familiar and friendly terms with their neighbors that fare the best during times of widespread paranoia. When facts are scarce, the tendency is to fill the gaps with imagination. Unfortunately, these projections do not often give newcomers the benefit of the doubt.

Reinventing Wheels

Most of these "unique new ideas" are neither new, nor unique. They seem so to us only because they're not commonly discussed or covered in standard history texts or daily news. People throughout the world have been trying out similar—if not identical—ideas over many centuries, often bucking resistance and persecution.

Many community groups are unaware of this history and end up starting the community-building process from scratch. There is also a tendency to resist advice from outside experts, usually because of a mistrust of outsiders, or a diehard sense that "We need to be able to do this for ourselves if our model is to be self-sufficient and sustainable." The reality is that the insights of an outsider—someone experienced with the issues at hand, but not caught up in the internal dynamics of the community—can often provide the exact piece of information or insight needed to break through an impasse and move the community toward a constructive resolution.

One way around this tendency toward isolation is to develop sister communities and networks built around common ideals and interests—the raison d'être for the FIC and this directory. Communities in close association with one another can share ideas, resources, and mutual support, thereby benefiting from each other's assets and experience. In addition, community networks can create common funds to do outreach, develop community-based business ventures, and cover medical emergencies (in lieu of expensive insurance policies that drain working capital out of the movement).

It Ain't Easy

Over the centuries well-intentioned attempts to live in community have generated a huge list of casualties. Countless thousands of folks have been inspired by a vision of a better world, and eventually ended up completely frustrated by the discrepancy between the vision and the reality.

At first glance this might seem peculiar, but it's exactly what should be expected, as most of us are products of an imperfect, overly competitive, alienating society. Although we tend to be aware of some of our negative conditioning, most of it is beyond the grasp of our limited worldview. If we're serious about creating a better world, we need to start with ourselves.

If you should happen to hear a glowing report about the perfect community somewhere, one with no rough edges, presume you're not getting the whole story. There's probably a shadow side somewhere that's unexplored and needs to be acknowledged before the members will be able to work through, rather than avoid, the underlying issues.

Conflict is inevitable, and traditionally it is handled so poorly that many of us have learned to dread it and avoid it. However, conflict is a useful indicator of points of non-alignment. Working creatively with these points usually results in tremendous positive growth spurts for everyone involved, both individually and collectively. The key to using conflict constructively is to get the affected parties to believe that a solution is possible, and to commit their best effort to finding a solution that works for all.

Every one of us brings along our own baggage wherever we go, and a supportive cooperative environment is the best possible place for us to explore our personal growing edge. It will prove to be the most challenging and frustrating inner work we've ever attempted, but if we pick the right people to work with, and approach it with the right attitude, it's entirely worth it—the best path available for actualizing our full potential.

Endnotes

1. Joreen Freeman's article from the second edition of the *Communities Directory*, "The Tyranny of Structurelessness," is also available on the Web, at http://www.ic.org/pnp/cdir/1995/23joreen.html

> ⑥
> Communities in close association with one another can share ideas, resources, and mutual support, thereby benefiting from each other's assets and experience.

State of the Communities Movement

Getting Hitched

by Laird Schaub
Executive Secretary, Fellowship for Intentional Community

*M*ANY PEOPLE LIKEN LIVING IN intentional community to a marriage (yes, it can be that exciting, that complicated, and that big a part of your life), so playing on that theme...

Welcome to the Fellowship for Intentional Community's 4th edition *Communities Directory*, the comprehensive reference that'll tell you who's doing what and where. (If you want to know who's doing what with whom, you'll need a different book.)

Whether you've already made your community vows, just going steady, or thinking about setting up a fun community weekend, we'll try to help you out.

Every five years—whenever we produce a new *Directory*—we offer a reflection on the State of the Communities Movement. Here's our 2005 status report.

Snapshot of a Moving Target

For a variety of reasons—I'll give you five—it's difficult to draw firm conclusions about what's happening in the Communities Movement today, and how that compares with prior trends.

1. Foremost, the revitalization of the FIC in 1986 marked the beginning of an ecumenical organization attempting to collect and maintain information about all North American intentional communities. Thus, communities today are almost certainly better chronicled than they were prior to 1986.
2. The people who comprise the FIC are mostly from the secular side of the movement. That is, our best connections are with groups that do not make spiritual orientation a condition of membership. Both because it is easier to collect information from those one knows best, and because spiritual groups tend to consider their community life secondary to their spiritual pursuit, we believe that spiritual groups are undercounted.
3. Intentional communities can be sorted into those that include outreach to the wider culture as part of their purpose, and those that are focused more internally. Naturally, the former are more motivated than the latter to answer inquiries about what they are doing and to be included in surveys.
4. There is a soft boundary between group house and intentional community, and between retreat center as business or as community. Some groups dance back and forth between the two, and whether they are counted as a community in any given survey depends greatly on when they were asked and which individual responded.
5. It is important to understand the wide variance in what people mean by the label "intentional community." At Ganas in New York City, the norm for many years was to meet for five or more hours every day to explore interpersonal and group dynamics; there are other groups that gather only once a month for a potluck dinner. Obviously the expectations about living together are completely different for members of groups at opposite ends of the engagement spectrum—yet all identify as intentional communities.

Laird Schaub helped found Sandhill Farm, a small agricultural income-sharing community in Rutledge, Missouri, in 1974, and has lived there ever since. He has been integrally involved with the FIC since its revitalization in 1986, and has served as its chief administrator since 1995. He was Managing Editor for the first two editions of the *Communities Directory*, and has become a nationally recognized expert on consensus and meeting facilitation since starting a career as a group process consultant in 1987. He can be contacted at *laird@ic.org*.

Altogether, the FIC listed 304 North American communities in its first edition of the *Communities Directory* in 1990; 565 in the 1995 edition; 585 in the 2000 edition; and 614 with full listings in the book you now hold. Despite all the caveats posted in the paragraphs above, we're pretty confident that these numbers accurately reflect a steady, gradual increase in the number of North American communities.

But let's not get carried away. North Americans living in intentional community represent only a tiny fraction of the total population. In fact, there are not enough people living this way in the United States to even be a category on census forms. Though the Israeli population living on kibbutzim averaged about 3 percent in the 20th century, in North America it's debatable if 0.03 percent of the population—roughly 100,000 people—live in some form of intentional community, even with the most liberal definition of the term.

If you do the math, you'll notice that the total population of the groups listed in this *Directory* does not come close to totaling 100,000. That's because only about 30 percent of the groups in our database chose to be included (see "What this Directory Is and Isn't" p. 8 for possible reasons).

Counting both start-ups and groups we discover only after they've been around for a while, the FIC learns about new communities at a rate of about one per week. Taken all together, it's a fluid field of information, and slippery to pin down. Nonetheless, there are trends....

Something Old

While there are many ways in which the community environment today is unique, some challenges in cooperative living are timeless. All groups still have to get the dishes done, decide what to do with barking dogs, and determine what latitude to give adults disciplining children not their own. No matter how times change, at its core, community is still about how people get along with one another.

People seek community for a variety of reasons. For some it's about getting away from a world that doesn't work and creating a sanctuary where it does. For others it's about building a base from which to experiment with innovative relationships to place, to sustainable technologies, or to money (such as income-sharing communities or those pioneering alternative currencies). Others focus on spirit, which can be subdivided into those asking members to align with an articulated spiritual path and those asking only that members support each other's individual pursuit of spiritual inquiry.

Most communities explicitly name diversity as a root value, and are thus compelled to wrestle with the question of how much of it they can support without being

⑥

North Americans living in intentional community represent only a tiny fraction of the total population.

stretched too far. How much deviance from an exact value match is desirable? How much is tolerable?

In general, community membership comprises people raised in the mainstream culture, which is predominantly competitive and hierarchic—reinforced by the top-down power structures of family, school, church, and government. Many come to intentional community seeking an alternative to the mainstream, and bring with them heavy scarring around power abuse. Once in community, they are caught in the dilemma of requiring healthy leadership to manifest their dreams, yet having knee-jerk suspicions about its potential misuse. At what point does the questioning of leaders pass from constructive reflection into paralyzing paranoia? There are a number of high-profile groups that have struggled with replacing charismatic leaders whose leadership was embattled, or whose stepping down left an awkward void.

Something New

While the challenges and questions may look familiar, there is nonetheless a lot that's new about the Communities Movement today, especially in contrast with the surge of a generation ago, in 1965–75.

Foremost is the ubiquity of computers, which has led to an explosion of electronic information. This has opened up choices in community location because it's more possible to satisfy baseline needs and desires without being tied to geography. Relationships that rely on electronic communication can flourish anywhere and, with the advent of telecommuting, it's possible for rural groups (which constitute about two-thirds of the movement today) to benefit from city wages and rural costs of living—if you have marketable skills that can be delivered electronically. Similarly, rural groups are less isolated from resources today because they can shop online and have just about anything shipped to their doors.

For those interested in how the experience of others can help guide new starts, it is much easier to find out what others have learned, and this has coincided with a shift in the willingness of groups to ask for help. While there was no one advertising services as a professional consultant on group process or community building skills in the 1990 edition of *Communities Directory*, there were ten in the 2000 edition, and 30 offer their services on our website today (see *fic.ic.org/process.html*).

Something else that's different is the steady effort to control growth and protect property values through increased adoption of zoning and building codes. Not surprisingly, this is coupled with spiraling land costs, which adds up to a double whammy for new communities. Not only does it cost more to get into the game, but development is typically much slower as groups pursue variances from conservative building codes, or have to convince traditional lending sources that their unfamiliar development is an acceptable risk. In the case of Dancing Rabbit, for example, its plans for ecological design and construction were so radical (featuring strawbale housing and off-grid electricity) that they gave up trying to cope with skyrocketing land costs and building restrictions in California when looking for land in the mid-90s. They moved to rural Missouri instead, where they found much cheaper land, no zoning, and at the same time retained access to web-based jobs with California wages.

There is also something about demographics that has shifted. Where community living was overwhelmingly a young person's itch in the 60s and 70s, there are increasing numbers of people over 50 trying intentional community for the first time. With their families grown and their careers already established, they now have time to explore an old curiosity about a different, perhaps better way to live. Many are drawn to the cohous-

⑥

> *Where community living was overwhelmingly a young person's itch in the 60s and 70s, there are increasing numbers of people over 50 trying intentional community for the first time.*

Will communities pioneer meaningful alternatives for the growing population of older adults?

Michael McIntyre – Sunward Cohousing

ing model, and others are taking advantage of today's better information about community choices to investigate groups that were started more than 20 years ago, figuring that communities so long established are bound to have members their age already in residence.

Something Borrowed

Cohousing as a style of intentional community is a Danish import, brought over to North America in the late 80s by Berkeley-based architects Katie McCamant and Chuck Durrett. The basic cohousing concept is clustered, compact housing (minimum footprint) oriented toward each other, with a common house centrally located for social functions; parking on the perimeter and pedestrian-only traffic in the middle; land held in common, with houses owned by individuals or families; multigenerational; and, at least for the first residents, the chance to be integrally involved in the designing of the community.

Popular right from the start, by early 2005 there were about 90 cohousing communities built in North America and another 150 in various stages of development or construction. While there are a number of successful communities built prior to the 1980s that employed a design evocative of what's labeled cohousing today (Shannon Farm in Virginia and Miccosukee in Florida are two examples), the significant thing about cohousing is that it has been marketed successfully to a new segment of the population—the liberal, professional middle class with no particular background in cooperative living. The early cohousing projects struggled to secure the support of financial institutions, who were reluctant to lend to this unfamiliar form of housing development. But the success of first investments has substantially overcome that resistance and today there's little difficulty finding banks willing to loan to these projects.

While most cohousing communities are located in urban or suburban areas and most are new construction, there are notable exceptions. N Street in Davis, California was one of the first cohousing communities. It got its start with a group house whose members were looking to expand and started acquiring the neighboring property, one house at a time. Pretty soon they had a community. Doyle Street in Emeryville, California was built by retrofitting an old warehouse.

Nomad in Boulder, Colorado is one of the smallest cohousing communities. Only 11 households, it was shoehorned into a tiny site adjacent to a 50-year-old playhouse which is still active—in fact, the community common space is shared with the theater on opening nights.

Monterey Cohousing in Saint Louis Park, Minnesota is a unique blend of a retrofitted Edwardian mansion and newly constructed adjacent townhouses.

In the family of intentional communities, cohousing is the newest form, and arguably the one that looks most like traditional middle class housing. While cohousing demonstrates a marked savings in resource use and ecological impact when compared with other tract housing, it is—with rare exceptions—the most high-end form of intentional community extant (some projects have no units priced under $200,000). Cohousing is noteworthy as it is introducing many people to a first taste of community living and a practical application of resource sharing. However, because it has so far been sold mainly to people who have already succeeded financially in the mainstream, cohousing's potential for addressing issues of affordable housing has been little tested.

Something Blue

Do contemporary communities attract blue bloods or blue collar members? Mostly not. The Communities Movement is overwhelmingly white and middle class. It tends to be well educated, pro-environment and politically liberal. While most communities aspire to embrace diversity on some level, they tend to most readily attract new members like themselves. It's difficult for people of privilege to walk away from the advantages of money and class and share power gracefully with others (hence few blue bloods); it is also challenging for communities created in the image of white collar educated folks to do the work needed to make blue collar (working class) members feel that it can be their home also. There are notable exceptions to this—Padanaram in Indiana is a place that has focused on opportunities for people from working class backgrounds, and the many Catholic Worker Houses often draw members from that class. Differences in styles of communication can be larger hills than many wish to climb.

> ☯
>
> *While most communities aspire to embrace diversity on some level, they tend to most readily attract new members like themselves.*

Why Everyone Isn't Married to Community

In observing the flow of inquiries for all kinds of information about intentional communities, some recurring questions stand out because the Communities Movement does not as yet have many answers:

Networks of Intentional Communities

Cohousing Association of the United States (Coho/US)
Promotes and encourages the cohousing concept and cohousing communities in the US.
http://www.cohousing.org • 314-754-5828 • 4676 Broadway, 2nd floor, Boulder, CO 80304,USA

Canadian Cohousing Network
Promotes and facilitates cohousing in Canada.
http://www.cohousing.ca • #24 - 20543 96th Ave, Langley, BC V1M 3W3, Canada • info@cohousing.ca

Ecovillage Network of the Americas (ENA)
The western hemisphere's node for GEN, ENA promotes ecovillages throughout North and South America.
http://ena.ecovillage.org • Regional contacts available on website • ena@ecovillage.org

Federation of Egalitarian Communities (FEC)
Network of secular, income-sharing communities throughout the US.
http://thefec.org • 206-324-6822 ext. 2 • 1309 13th Ave S, Seattle, WA 98144, USA • secretary@thefec.org

Global Ecovillage Network (GEN)
Supports the development of ecovillages and sustainable communities around the world. Divided into three regions for the Americas, Europe/Africa, and Oceania/Asia.
http://gen.ecovillage.org • Regional contact available on website.

North American Students of Cooperation (NASCO)
A voice for campus, student and community cooperatives in the US and Canada.
http://www.nasco.coop • 734-663-0889 • PO Box 7715, Ann Arbor, MI 48107, USA • info@nasco.coop

Northwest Intentional Community Association (NICA)
Network of intentional communities in the pacific northwest region of the US and Canada.
http://www.ic.org/nica • 9132 Ravenna Ave NE, Seattle, WA 98115, USA • nica@ic.org

Opportunities for people with disabilities

When the United States government undertook in the 1980s a massive program of de-institutionalizing people with disabilities, the Communities Movement made no effort to pick up the slack. With the exception of Los Horcones (Mexico), Innisfree (Virginia), Gould Farm (Massachusetts), the Camphill Villages (there are six in North America) based on the teachings of Rudolf Steiner, and the L'Arche communities (there are 110 worldwide and several in North America) based on the teachings of Jean Vanier, there are almost no communities which categorically welcome people with disabilities. People with Multiple Chemical Sensitivity (MCS), in particular, have reported to us that they have had difficulty finding communities that can meet their needs to avoid most synthetic chemicals. While many communities have modified local customs and practices to meet the needs of members with mild cases of MCS, we know of no established community today which specializes in helping members with severe cases.

Opportunities for older adults

As the Baby Boomers reach retirement age, North America will face the challenge of integrating into its population the largest ever percentage of people over 65. So far, the response of intentional communities has been on the immediate level—providing adequate housing and lifestyle opportunities for the aging members they already have. With the notable exception of Elder Spirit (Virginia) and Silver Sage (a forming cohousing community in Colorado) there has been little attempt to develop communities expressly for people over 50. It is not clear if intentional communities will attempt to pioneer any kind of meaningful alternative to the typical warehousing of those who lack the resources needed to buy better care.

Opportunities for community where you are

It is clear that there is a broad-based hunger in North America for a greater sense of community in one's life. Many recall a childhood with greater safety and sense of place than they have today and yearn for a return to that quality of connection. Despite this, intentional communities are unlikely to attract more than a slim slice of the population. The movement's contribution to society is more likely to lie in its ability to supply the tools and inspiration of community, than in convincing increasing numbers to forsake private property.

I've been wedded to community for 31 years, and they really have been the best years of my life. While the FIC can't promise that you'll find your cooperative living soul mate using this *Directory*, we produced it because it's possible that you will.

Dancing Rabbit Ecovillage

"No matter how times change, at its core, community is still about how people get along with one another."

Organizations Studying or Supporting Community

Communal Studies Association
An organization that promotes the study and understanding of communal societies, both past and present.

http://www.communalstudies.info
PO Box 122, Amana, IA 52203, USA
319-622-6446 • csa@netins.net

International Communal Studies Association
Promotes scholarly exchange regarding communes, intentional communities, collective settlements, and kibbutzim around the world.

http://www.ic.org/icsa
Yad Tabenkin, Ramat Efal 52960, Israel
+972-(0)35344458 • rsoboly-t@bezeqint.net

Community Services, Inc.
Dedicated to the development, growth and enhancement of small, local communities.

http://www.smallcommunity.org
PO Box 243, Yellow Springs, OH 45387, USA
937-767-2161 • csi@communityservice.net

Red Carpets and Slammed Doors
Visiting Communities
by Geoph Kozeny

HOPING TO VISIT A COMMUNITY? The good news is that most communities welcome visitors, and a majority of those are open to new members. The bad news? Because so many community seekers want to visit, many communities at some point experience visitor overload and feel burned out from the seemingly never-ending flow of strangers. The best news: if you're considerate and persistent, the odds are good that you'll be able to arrange a visit and have a great experience.

An essential element of planning a satisfying visit is getting really clear about exactly what you want from a community. In other words, what is the purpose of your visit? You'll save considerable time and effort if you can learn to intuit how well any given community's reality will match with the picture you've envisioned. There's definitely an art to this prescreening process, as it's based solely on information from written materials, letters, phone calls, emails, and perhaps a website—nothing physical that you can actually see, touch, smell, or taste.

While you're exploring communities from a distance, it also pays to sort through, point by point, all the different characteristics you think you want. Ask yourself: which attributes are mandatory, which are strong preferences, and which are nice but not necessary? This *Directory* is probably the best resource you'll find to aid in wrapping your mind around the possibilities. Carefully study each group's entry in the cross-reference chart and its written description in the listings section. With practice you can learn to use that information to spot potential incompatibilities in visions, values, and social norms. And please, don't assume that the community welcomes visitors just because they're listed in this book. Be sure to check out the "Visitors Accepted" column in the charts.

Even under stress, many overloaded communities will agree to host more visitors, usually due to a sense of mission or obligation, but beware: often it is only the visitor coordinators and a few others who are enthusiastic about the idea. Some community members, typically acting from instinct rather than clarity, will go about their daily lives while keeping a low profile and acting distant in a weary, mostly subconscious attempt to minimize interactions with the newest batch of "tourists"—which might turn out to be you. Try not to take it personally.

Introductions and First Impressions

Usually the best line of first contact is through a friend who knows the community and is willing to give you a personal referral. If you don't have a friend with direct connections, friends-of-friends can prove just as effective.

Use your network of friends and acquaintances creatively. Let it be known that you're interested in visiting certain communities, and ask your friends if they—or anyone they know—has a connection to those groups. If through correspondence, or especially through a visit, you make a connection with a member of one community, ask that person if they can recommend an especially good contact at the other communities you hope to visit. If your feelers yield a connection, be sure to open your introductory letter or phone call by saying "So-and-so over at Community X referred you to me." On the other hand, avoid giving the impression that you're a name-dropper, or that you're trying to do an end-run around their official channels. Alienating the community's designated visitor coordinator is far from being the optimal way to start a visit.

If no leads materialize, there's still a reasonably good chance of making a fruitful connection through self-introduction. Avoid sending an email or letter that poses a long list of questions about the community, but provides little or no information about who you are and what you're seeking. Although there's a wide range of styles that can work well in a letter of inquiry, a good general formula is to give approximately equal emphasis to: (1) describing what you're looking for, how you heard about them, and why they interest you; (2) telling about your history, skills, and special needs; and (3) posing questions about their community and their visiting protocols.

Your letter should be short, to the point, and engaging—if you send a long letter, you run the risk of overwhelming them right off the bat, or of having your letter shunted to the needs-to-be-answered-but-requires-a-lot-of-time-and-energy-to-deal-with pile. Such letters, unfortunately, only occasionally make it back to the top of the priority pile. Usually a one-page letter (or the equivalent in email) is best, and two pages should be the absolute maximum—anything longer than that reduces your chances of getting a prompt response. If you want to be remembered, enclose a photo, artwork, doodles, an interesting article, or something else eye-catching to make your letter stand out in the crowd (but please—no confetti, glitter, or other mess-making surprises). And, if you are sending a paper letter, be sure to include a self-addressed stamped envelope (SASE).

You may also want to consider first visiting one or more groups located in your region. Even if they are not likely candidates for where you'll finally want to settle, you can hone your visitor skills. The fact that they're relatively easy to get to means you can get some visiting experience under your belt without a large investment of your time or resources. It can be pretty devastating to use up all your precious vacation traveling cross-continent to visit your dream community, only to discover that it's not at all what you had in mind (which is fairly common, by the way). Instead, go through the steps face-to-face with real people, and get comfortable doing the interviews, the work, and the socializing.

Following Up

The sad truth is that many groups don't respond to correspondence in a timely fashion, in spite of good intentions. The reality is that living in community can be very demanding—there's always so much to be done—and answering a stack of correspondence doesn't usually rank as high on the chore list as milking the cows, supervising the kids, taking out the recycling, or building the new community center.

If your letter or email has received no response after two to four weeks, try a follow up. If you still receive no response a short phone call is probably in order. Try to pick a time when folks are likely to be around and not otherwise busy. Often early evenings, or right before or after a meal, are good times to call. If you reach an answering machine, identify yourself, leave your number, and ask them to call you back at their convenience. Suggest times when you're most reachable, and explain that when they do get through, you'll be happy to hang up and call them right back on your dime.

When you reach a live person, first introduce yourself—mentioning your referral if you have one—and explain that you're interested in visiting. Be sure to note that you've already sent a letter. Ask whoever answers if he or she is a good person to talk with about visiting and arrangements, and verify that this is a good time to talk. If the time's not right, make a date to call back at a better time. If they suggest you talk with someone else, note the new name, and ask for suggestions about how and when to reach the identified contact person. When you do finally connect with your contact person, be sure to verify up-front all the details related to visiting (see sidebar on p. 29).

If you wrote and got no response, it's usually far better to call first rather than show up unannounced. However, if they have no phone listing in the *Directory*, if their line's always busy, or if their published number has been disconnected and the community has no listing in Directory Assistance, then an exploratory "Hello" might be in order. If you've tried well in advance to reach a community but received no reply, it may work to "drop by" for a few minutes to introduce yourself—but be sensitive to their energy levels. Be prepared to find accommodations elsewhere, and arrange to come back when it's convenient for them. A 10- or 15-minute visit may be all that's appropriate if you catch them in the middle of something—but if your timing's good, you might get the deluxe two-hour tour right on the spot, plus get invited to dinner. Be flexible.

Drop-in visitors can be especially awkward for groups that are far off the beaten path, but in most cases you can locate a park or a campground within commuting distance. If they remember your letter, they'll know you made a bona fide effort to set up a visit and that they were the ones to drop the ball by not responding—so make your letter memorable.

Fitting In

Always remember: the community you want to visit is also somebody's home, so plan on using the same standards you would use if visiting a hometown friend or relatives you see only occasionally.

Often it's helpful to figure out why they're open to visitors in the first place. They may be: seeking new members, needing help with the work, wanting the stimulation of meeting new people, and/or spreading their vision (e.g., egalitarianism, ecovillages) or religion (including the promotion of "community").

What will they gain from your stay? There are infinite ways to plug in and make yourself useful. Pitch in with everyday chores such as gardening, farm work, construction projects, bulk mailings, cooking, cleaning, dishes, or

❦

Always remember: the community you want to visit is also somebody's home...

childcare. You may gain "Much Appreciated Guest" status if you have special skills to offer: layout or graphic design (newsletters), computer skills, meeting facilitation, storytelling, music, or massage. One fellow I met is a chiropractor who plies his trade for free at each community he visits. A woman therapist offers private and group counseling sessions to community members. Another fellow built a solar oven at each community he visited. Alternative building technologies, permaculture, and composting toilet expertise are all skills generally in high demand. Often, however, the most appreciated contribution is your willingness to pitch in to help with whatever boring chore needs doing at the moment.

Some groups are not organized in a way that lets them take advantage of visitor labor, and your desire to pitch in can actually become more of a headache for them than a help. Use your intuition in such situations. Make suggestions, but be open—offer, but don't push too hard. If they aren't able to involve you in the work and don't have much time to spend with you, be prepared to entertain yourself: bring books, tapes, musical instruments, etc.

Some groups use a buddy system for orienting visitors, pairing each visitor with a community member who can serve as a guide and a liaison. Having an identified support person to turn to is often helpful. If the community you are visiting doesn't use such a system, you might look around for someone willing to fill that role.

It's important to be clear about your underlying motives so that both your expectations and the community's are realistic. Are you seeking a community to join, or gathering ideas about how groups deal with various issues so you can start your own? Perhaps you are just curious about shared living options and open to being inspired. Perhaps you're looking for a love affair or relationship. That may, in fact, be a possibility, but usually you'll alienate community members who sense you're on the prowl for romance rather than looking for community. What you're most likely to get in those situations is the hot seat, the cold shoulder, an invitation to leave, or some unpleasant combination of the three.

Sometimes awkward situations will come up, and it can take fairly sophisticated interpersonal skills to set things straight with your hosts. After all, many people have been conditioned to be stoic, and your hosts may be reluctant to say anything "impolite" about something you're doing that's bothering them. In those cases it's up to you to initiate the process of exploring any concerns or annoyances that they're sitting on, and it's much

> ✆
>
> Often, however, the most appreciated contribution is your willingness to pitch in to help with whatever boring chore needs doing at the moment.

"What will they gain from your stay? There are infinite ways to plug in and make yourself useful. Pitch in with everyday chores such as gardening, farm work, construction projects, bulk mailings, cooking, cleaning, dishes, or childcare."

Albert Bates – The Farm

better to get those things out in the open early in your visit, before unexpressed resentments fester. Gracefully facing awkward issues head-on will give you the option to work on them and to develop a rapport with your hosts. Ignoring the tension will usually feed the sense of alienation or mistrust, and prompt your hosts to close up a bit more with every interaction.

It's a warm and wonderful feeling to be included by the group and to experience a sense of "being in community" during your first visit, but don't count on it. Deep connections often take time, and sometimes come only after mutual trust and friendship have been solidly established.

Beyond First Impressions

"Being human" implies that we all bring along some baggage from our conditioning, and that we are seldom capable of living up to our own high standards. The discrepancy between our visions of an ideal world and the reality of our daily lives is probably the most common catalyst underlying the creation of new intentional com-

⑥

Deep connections often take time, and sometimes come only after mutual trust and friendship have been solidly established.

munities. As a result, what we say we're going to do, both as individuals and as communities, is usually a lot more grandiose than what we actually accomplish. Keeping that perspective in mind while visiting communities can help keep your expectations in line with probabilities, and may ultimately help you avoid setting yourself up for a lot of unnecessary disappointment.

Visiting communities is much like dating—people have a tendency to put their best foot forward and try to hide what they consider to be weaknesses. It's helpful to fine-tune your eyes and ears to pick up pieces of the hidden story, and to sensitize yourself to what kinds of conversations and interactions will give you an accurate sense of the underlying day-to-day realities. Remember, undesirable habits are easily obscured when members are on their best behavior. If you visit at least a handful of communities, you can compare and contrast their strengths and weaknesses. There's no better way than visiting to learn what to look for and where to find it.

Resources For Starting Your Own Community

One of the best ways to prepare yourself to start your own community is to learn about communities that already exist, especially ones similar to what you would like to create. What do they look and feel like? How are they organized? How do they make decisions? How do they own their property?

One way to answer these questions is by in-person visits, of course, and this *Communities Directory* can help you find and contact them. Each community you visit will give you ideas about what you do and don't want in your own community. You can also—if you're polite and respectful of people's time—ask questions. How did the founders start up the community? What are they really glad they did? Do they recommend that you do the same? On the other hand, what do they wish they'd never done and suggest you not do?

Another way to "visit" communities is to watch Geoph Kozeny's *Visions of Utopia* video documentary, parts one and two (available at *store.ic.org*). Each video profiles a wide range of communities—from urban group households to rural ecovillages, service-oriented communities, spiritual communities, and cohousing neighborhoods. You'll get a lot of good ideas from listening to members of these communi-

ties give their opinions on a variety of topics.

Browsing the Internet is also a good way to learn about communities. Look for community vision and purpose statements, community goals, visitor policies, documents and bylaws. You can get great ideas about your forming community's agreements and policies just by reading what hundreds of communities are happy to share publicly on their own websites. The FIC's websites at *www.ic.org* and *directory.ic.org* are great places to start, but you can also see the list of Networks of Intentional Communities (p. 21) for more websites.

Reading stories about how different communities have faced and resolved challenges is another excellent way to prepare. Of course, we recommend the FIC's quarterly *Communities* magazine, where you'll find articles on ecovillages, cohousing neighborhoods, as well as rural, urban, income-sharing, and spiritual communities. Among other topics, there are often special articles on communication and process skills, membership issues, and sustainability projects. For sample issues, back issues, and subscriptions visit *store.ic.org*. Read about starting up and living in cohousing communities in *Cohousing* magazine, online at *www.cohousing.org/magazine*.

To dig deeper, learn how to ask friendly but penetrating questions. After you've gotten to know a new group well enough to get more personal, try posing such open-ended queries as:

- What are some of the things you like best about living here? The least?
- What's the most difficult issue your community has had to deal with in the last year, or in the last five years?
- How many members have left in the past year or two, and why did they leave?
- How has the community changed over the years? What changes would you like to see in the future?
- What are some of the big challenges your community is facing now?
- How has living here contributed to your personal growth and happiness?

If the community members perceive you as being sincere, interested, and open-minded, most will be willing to engage with you in a thoughtful dialogue. However, if they sense that you've already made up your mind about what's right—and are likely to pass judgment on them—not much information will be forthcoming.

The best way to learn about yourself, and about the communities themselves, is to visit.

Avoid stereotypes of how you think communities should be. If you assume they will have any particular standard or feature you associate with "communities"—things like art facilities, organic gardens, health food, homeschooling, sexual openness—you're asking for disappointment. Many will have at least a few of those features, but few will have them all. Being outspoken or opinionated about the "shoulds" is an easy way to wear out your welcome fast—or to not get invited in the first place, if it shows up during the introductory phase. If something you value highly seems to be missing, ask them about it. Would they be open to it in the future? Would there be room and support for you to introduce it? Present your concern as, "Is it likely the group would be open to this?" rather than, "I couldn't live here unless."

While probing for deeper understanding, be sensitive to members' needs for privacy and quiet time, and to what kind of energy you're putting out. If you make a good personal connection, chances are good that they'll be happy to offer you hospitality. Otherwise, hosting you tends to become a chore for them, or worse, an annoyance.

The FIC also hosts one- or two-day-long Art of Community gatherings in various regions of North America. You can take workshops by some of the most experienced community founders and veterans in the Communities Movement, and meet like-minded souls from your region. You might discover co-creators for your own community project sitting across from you at lunch. Other organizations also host communities conferences and workshops on community. For schedules and more information see our online events calendar at *www.ic.org/events*.

When you want to get down to the nuts and bolts of starting a new community, we recommend *Creating a Life Together: Practical Tools to Grow Ecovillages and Intentional Communities*, written by *Communities* magazine editor Diana Leafe Christian (New Society Publishers, 2003). Diana spent years learning everything she could from community founders about what does and doesn't work when starting a new community. Chapters cover typical timeframes and costs, characteristics of community founders, tips on getting started as a group, crafting vision and purpose documents, decision making and governance, finding and financing land, neighbors and zoning, legal structures, site planning, communication and process, and selecting new people.

You can also gain valuable information by reading a how-we-did-it story by community founder Liz Walker in *EcoVillage At Ithaca: Pioneering a Sustainable Culture* (New Society Publishers, 2005). Liz takes you step by step through the joys and challenges of the community-building process—the firsthand experience of folks who did it, and did it successfully. EcoVillage at Ithaca is both an ecovillage and two clustered cohousing communities, so you'll learn about the start-up issues of both kinds of projects.

Another helpful guide is *The Cohousing Handbook, Second Edition*, by Chris and Kelly ScottHanson (New Society Publishers, 2004). It contains information that would benefit people starting non-cohousing, as well as cohousing, communities. Areas of focus include: forming the core group, buying land, the design process, legal issues, finance and budget, and marketing and membership.

For more ideas on cohousing communities, see *Cohousing: A Contemporary Approach to Housing Ourselves, Second Edition*, by Kathryn McCamant, Charles Durrett, and Ellen Hertzman (Ten Speed Press, 1994). If you are specifically interested in community design, see *Rebuilding Community in America*, by Ken Norwood and Kathleen Smith (Shared Living Resource Center, 1995). All books are available from the FIC's Community Bookshelf at *store.ic.org*.

What's Really Important?

Having talked to thousands of community seekers over several decades, I am convinced that most of us do not truly know what would make us happy, nor do we see how habits we've developed over the decades stand in the way of our accomplishing the things we say we want. It's only after we've tried something a time or two that we really understand how important, or not, that thing is to our happiness. For example, I've witnessed dozens of back-to-the-land dreamers who moved to the country to do gardening, raise livestock, chop wood, and carry water—only to discover that those things are hard work that cause calluses, sunburn, mosquito bites, sore backs, and are subject to the harsh unpredictabilities of nature. Many of those dreamers adapt to the reality and subsequently thrive in that environment, but nearly as many decide to move back to a more urban, less physically demanding lifestyle.

Real-life experience can be similarly eye-opening for folks with visions of a community based on shared ownership, cooperative businesses, and consensus decision making. Living that way can certainly be inspiring and fulfilling, but because most of us have grown up in a society that emphasizes individualism and competition, we are often surprised by how challenging and frustrating the cooperative life can be. Often we fail to see how our attitudes and actions are contributing to the problems rather than generating solutions.

One problem stems from the fact that we conduct mostly mental research and don't get nearly enough hands-on experience. The best way to learn about yourself, and about the communities themselves, is to visit. In that context you can experiment with balancing work involvement with social involvement, and experience how easy (or not!) it is for you to adapt to a new culture.

Love at First Sight?

Investigating communities that are based on the idea of creating a better life can be very refreshing. However, be warned: there is a tendency to fall in love with the first group visited. It usually pays to check out a few more anyway. Your first impression may be based on the excitement of discovering the many ways the group's vision matches your own, but be sure that you also look for the differences. For a good match, both you and the community need to be able to tolerate each other's rough edges.

There may have been some common interactions that you missed. Did you get to see the group go through a

Living in intentional community is a lot of hard work, but it's a noble undertaking that offers great rewards for those with enough vision and perseverance to stick with it.

meeting process? Did you watch them deal with a challenging issue? People's rough edges are most likely to show up when they're under heavy stress, so unless you saw them under pressure, you'll probably leave with an incomplete picture of how well they fare when dealing with interpersonal tensions. If you do witness them working on a conflict, try to hear both sides and watch to see if they approach differences with an open mind.

If you develop closeness with folks in one subgroup, you will most likely see and hear an incomplete picture of the issues and norms in question. Seek out members holding an opposing point of view, and see if you can understand their side of the issue. It's also possible that a few influential members are away, and the vibe at the community may be very different when they're home—more supportive if it's a primary nurturer/diplomat who's absent, or more strained if it's the chief skeptic/troublemaker who's gone. Additionally, there may be other visitors present whose issues or energy affect the dynamics.

You can learn a lot from other visitors, and from folks living in other communities. Both groups have a perspective that's somewhat detached from the hubbub of the everyday reality, and it's quite possible that they've witnessed the group under stress. Ex-members are also a great source of perspective on what tensions might be lurking below the surface, and how deep they're submerged.

It's usually a good idea to let your first impressions percolate before deciding to make a commitment to join a community. After a first visit, spend some time away from the group to see how well your initial impression holds up when you're no longer being influenced by their energy and enthusiasm. It's especially interesting and informative to listen to yourself handle questions about the community posed by your pre-community friends and acquaintances.

A Never-Ending Quest

No two communities are identical and, in fact, no community is the same today as it was five years ago—nor will it be the same five years hence. Visions change, priorities change, the cast of characters change, people get older, the weather gets colder. This ever-evolving nature makes the search for a community to join both interesting and challenging. What you experience during a first visit is unlikely to remain static, yet you must decide based on that initial impression. And you must be prepared to adapt to the shifts in values and priorities that will inevitably come with the passage of time.

With that in mind, pay careful attention to the ideas

and interactions that feel best to you, noting whether it's the philosophy, the lifestyle, the place, or the people that touch you at the deepest level. If you feel yourself drawn most energetically to a group whose stated philosophy isn't very well aligned with your own, it will probably not work out for you to be there for the long haul. However, if they're open to it, consider spending more time with them in order to explore what makes it work for you on the energetic level. Similarly, for a community with ideals matching yours but a shortage of group chemistry, try spending enough time with them to learn about what's either lacking or overdone—what's getting in the way of the synergy?

Sorting through all the complexities can be overwhelming, and the best thing you can do to gain perspective and solace is to connect with others who can relate to what you're going through. If you know of friends who are also on a community quest, consider creating a support group to share experiences, insights, and leads. Scan the ads in the alternative press and on the bulletin boards of nearby co-ops

and health food stores, looking for announcements of support groups and networking opportunities. Check out the Intentional Communities Web site, *www.ic.org*, and follow the links from there. Or participate in one of the FIC's community conferences, a veritable cornucopia of seekers, networkers, and communitarians coming together to share information on the hows, whys, and wheres of shared living. It's a special opportunity to learn a lot in a few days about a number of communities from a wealth of experienced communitarians, all in an atmosphere of community.

Living in intentional community is a lot of hard work, but it's a noble undertaking that offers great rewards for those with enough vision and perseverance to stick with it. The first step in that process is finding a group compatible with your vision of a better world, and the rest of the work—for the rest of your life—will require an open mind, creativity, flexibility, commitment, integrity, common sense, and a lot of heart. Daunting? Yes, but worth it.

⑥

It's usually a good idea to let your first impressions percolate before deciding to make a commitment to join a community.

Get Things Clear Up Front

- Confirm that the community allows visitors, and that you'll be welcome to visit.
- Do they have particular times when visitors are welcome, regular visitor days, or a visitor program? Plan to be flexible to accommodate their scheduling needs.
- Do they have written Visitors' Guidelines that they could send you? Do they have policies or agreements about smoking, drugs, alcohol, diet, kids, pets, nudity, celibacy, quiet hours, etc. that you need to know about in advance? Usually it's best to leave pets at home.
- Do they have any literature about themselves that you can read in the meantime? Brochures? Copies of articles written about them? A website?
- Are there any costs involved (visitor fees, utilities, food)?
- Verify length of stay, and any work that will be expected of you. If no work is expected, ask if you'll be able to help them with their work projects. (This is one of the best ways to get to know individual members as well as to learn about the community's daily life.)
- Confirm what you will need to bring: bedding, towels, shampoo, rain gear, work clothes and gloves, special foods, etc. Inform them of any unusual needs you may have (diet, allergies, medications). To the extent possible, plan to cover for yourself so that meeting your special needs doesn't become a burden on the community.
- Let them know if you can provide your own accommodation, such as a tent, RV, or a van to sleep in. Sometimes, if they're feeling overwhelmed with visitors, being self-sufficient in that way will increase your chances of getting invited.
- If you are traveling by public transportation and need to be picked up, try to arrange a convenient time and place of arrival. If a special trip is required to pick you up, reimburse the community for their travel costs.
- Even if a community requires no visitor fees, offer to pitch in a few bucks for food and utility costs. Especially when visiting small communities, I like to bring a special treat for the members—a bag of fruit, almonds, gourmet coffee, ice cream (or non-dairy desserts for the vegans).
- If you need to alter your dates or cancel the visit, please inform the community immediately. They may have turned away other visitors in order to make room for you.

"Cults" and Intentional Communities

Working Through Some Complicated Issues

by Tim Miller

A FAIR NUMBER OF PEOPLE BELIEVE our society is swarming with dangerous cults, religious (and sometimes political or social) organizations that are terribly destructive to their members and a real danger to society at large. For better or worse, intentional communities are often drawn into the "cult" controversy. Communities, after all, in many cases do have features that many consider cultic. Individual will sometimes takes the back seat for the good of the group. Some communities have strong-minded leaders. Commitment to the group can run high. Because of these similarities, communitarians cannot altogether escape the great American cult controversy.

While off-course groups and dysfunctional—or even outright evil—individuals may exist, my own conclusion is that, by and large, the cult scare is seriously overblown. To say the least, many of the most frequent allegations about cult activities don't hold up under scrutiny. Groups that represent a real threat to the public do not number many thousands, nor do their members number hundreds of thousands, or even millions, as some anti-cult activists assert. Unless, of course, one preposterously considers every Hindu temple, Muslim mosque, and intentional community a dangerous "cult."

Equally erroneous is the assertion that the cult menace is growing. Religions with unconventional appeal have been around as long as civilization, and the fear of the different is just as ancient as those alternative pathways. While not all traditions, groups, and persons are wholesome, most are relatively innocuous. One wishes that the generalized anti-cult denunciations that are so easy to throw around were based on real case-by-case evidence, not the sort of spectral hysteria that fueled the Salem witch trials.

If I could choose just one step forward in the cult controversy, it would consist of the abandonment of the term "cult" itself. As Catherine Wessinger once wrote in *Communities* magazine, "The word 'cult,' which formerly referred to an organized system of worship, is now a term that slanders any religion that you don't know about and don't like." And that does matter; when a society tolerates pejorative language, it announces that some people are marginal, even subhuman.

Hateful thought, we have painfully learned, can lead to hateful acts. The widespread belief that destructive cults are proliferating and posing a grave danger to society has led to atrocities. Many who have studied the Waco siege and fire believe that the federal agents at the scene badly overestimated the danger that the Branch Davidians posed to society. There was very little understanding about just who the Davidians were and what they believed, which contributed to a situation in which several dozens of innocent people—many of them children—were killed.

People who see these shadowy groups as a major social menace often draw up lists of generalizations by which a savvy observer should be able to identify out-of-control groups. The problem is that the items on those lists almost always apply just as fully to good, healthy groups as to problematic ones. Consider these items from the typical cult-hazard list:

"A cult has a strong, powerful, dominant leader." But

Tim Miller teaches in the Department of Religious Studies at the University of Kansas, where he specializes in alternative religions and intentional communities. He is the editor of *America's Alternative Religions* and author of *The Quest for Utopia in Twentieth-Century America* and *The 60s Communes*. He may be reached at the Department of Religious Studies, University of Kansas, 1300 Oread St, Lawrence KS 66045, USA. Email: *tim@ic.org*.

that doesn't identify inherently dangerous situations. Alan Greenspan, the head of the Federal Reserve System, is enormously powerful and makes decisions that deeply affect the lives of all of us, so is he automatically a cult leader?

"A cult works extremely zealously to attract new members." But missionary zeal is a crucial element of Christianity, Islam, and other religions the world over. Most religions are always very happy to receive new members. You can believe that you know the ultimate truth and work hard to get others to accept your version of truth without deserving to be considered a social menace.

"A cult is preoccupied with getting money." A lot of groups sure do want your money—from religious groups to an array of nonprofits, and back again. While it is sad that our social institutions seem so uniformly thirsty for cash, it clearly shows the situation is not unique to cults.

"Cults suppress questioning and doubt." Many religious sects believe that they embody the truth, and urge followers to promulgate that truth, rather than seriously debate it.

"Indoctrination techniques help keep people involved in the group." Most groups have rituals and practices that push members to stay involved. It's possible (at a stretch) to see things like meditation, chanting, speaking in tongues, and group yoga as manipulative, but they don't cause otherwise sane people to lose their free will.

"A cult imposes major lifestyle restrictions on members, sometimes telling them what clothes to wear, how to raise their children, and even whom to marry." Most groups are not all that restrictive, but a few, indeed, are. Hardly any, however, are more restrictive than a Catholic religious community that tells its members they can't marry, can't have much money, and must follow a strict code of conduct. Most people wouldn't choose that, but those who voluntarily choose a restricted, guided lifestyle often find it empowering. Ask any nun about that.

"Cult members often cut off ties with their birth families and old friends in favor of total dedication to the cult." Actually, that's just what Jesus advised his followers to do; see Matthew 19:29 and Luke 14:26.

"Cult members are asked to give huge amounts of their time to the group." All religions and most social groups urge their members to be highly dedicated to group purposes. Hard workers are prized. And what's so bad about working hard for a cause in which one believes? Building community isn't easy, and the most dedicated are the ones who make it happen.

All of that is not to say that abuses don't occur, that people don't get hurt. People do get exploited, and well-intentioned people get taken advantage of in every corner of our society—in child care, in schools, in religious organizations, in offices and businesses, in intentional communities, and everywhere else. What's unfair is singling out small religious organizations and intentional communities for special persecution just because they happen to fit someone's preconceptions about cults. People have the right to basic freedoms as long as they're not hurting others, and they should be regarded as innocent until proven guilty. When truly abusive situations do occur, call the police. Short of that, friendly dialogue is usually possible if one retains an open mind.

The average person encounters thousands of individuals, groups, and communities in a lifetime, and inescapably has to work through a never-ending process of making judgments about them. If you encounter an intentional community or a religious group you need to evaluate, I would suggest keeping precepts like these in mind:

⑥
Different is not always pathological, and normal is not always safe.

• Different is not always pathological, and normal is not always safe. Some groups can be wildly unconventional yet utterly harmless; others can look very normal, superficially, and still be deeply flawed.

• People have different needs. One person's great communitarian or religious experience can be another's worst nightmare.

• Double standards are unfair. Small, offbeat groups should have the same rights and privileges as large, well-established ones. Lots of groups of all sizes and types are eagerly looking for new members, for example, and it is not any more wrong for a small, unconventional community to urge you to join than it is for the biggest church or social club in town to do so.

• One should take responsibility for one's own actions. One of the most frequent allegations against cults is that they engage in brainwashing of prospective members. Actually, there is no definitive scientific evidence that brainwashing really exists. Most people under most circumstances are capable of making decisions that are right for them and usually have mainly themselves to blame when they make unwise ones.

• The nature of personal relations is subtle and never the same twice. One individual may encounter a given group and find it the best thing that ever happened to him or her; another person may find the same group disgusting. People need to find their own congenial relationships. Joining a group is rather like romance—the chemistry that makes it magical is different in every case.

Behaviors often criticized as signs of abusive situations do not necessarily identify a dysfunctional religious group or community. What, then, should a prospective communitarian do to avoid falling in with a bad crowd?

The basic answer is eternal vigilance. One should be on the lookout all the time—and probably more so in regular, daily life than in a communal situation. Keep both eyes open, and don't let emotion get in the way of common sense. Be wary of persons who are both authoritarian and convinced that they have all the answers. Most communities are wonderful, uplifting places that provide their members with good, meaningful lives, but a few fall short of the mark. If you'll indulge me in one last list, here are a few final tips on staying centered in life:

- Trust your instincts. If you don't feel good about a person or situation, remain skeptical until your doubts have been resolved.
- Don't give your money away unless you are willing to let it go unconditionally and never see it again.
- Remember that things are not always what they initially seem; keep your options open even as you begin to take steps toward serious commitment.
- Question authority.
- Stay away from people who have guns.
- Remember that life goes on; if you make a mistake, extract yourself from it and get on with things.

Communities, on the whole, are the greatest! With a bit of prudent common sense, living in the company of others can be the best experience life has to offer.

Jillian Downey

"With a bit of prudent common sense, living in the company of others can be the best experience life has to offer."

Resources/Notes

Many calm and reflective books on nonmainstream religions provide a useful counterpoint to the rather sensational array of popular volumes that have contributed so heavily to the widespread public fear of the influence and growth of cults.

All of the works of the British sociologist of religion Eileen Barker offer useful insights; perhaps the most direct is *New Religious Movements: A Practical Introduction* (Unipub, London, 1989).

John A. Saliba, a Jesuit priest, knows a lot about disciplined community living; his books, especially *Understanding New Religious Movements* (Grand Rapids, Michigan, 1995), are fair, measured, and quietly rational.

Mariana Caplan, who lives in the Hohm Community in Arizona, offers solid personal insights into the stresses that occur in families when children make religious or personal choices not pleasing to their parents in her book *When Sons and Daughters Choose Alternative Lifestyles* (Hohm Press, Prescott, Arizona, 1996), and offers practical suggestions for getting beyond hostility and stereotyping in the generational conflict.

A website that seeks to provide dispassionate inofrmation about a wide array of groups is the *Religious Movements* homepage, *www.religiousmovements.org*. In the interest of full disclosure, I am one of the editors of that website.

My own perspectives on cult issues are elaborated at greater length in a theme section on "Intentional Communities and 'Cults'" that I edited for *Communities* magazine, No. 88, Fall 1995.

About the
Fellowship for Intentional Community

by Laird Schaub
Executive Secretary, Fellowship for Intentional Community

OR NEARLY TWO DECADES the Fellowship for Intentional Community—publisher of this *Directory*—has been promoting cooperative living in a world awash in competition and hierarchy.

FIC is a nonprofit dedicated to providing the tools and inspiration of community to the widest possible audience. We're making available the basic learnings of intentional communities to people hungry for positive alternatives to a mainstream culture of isolation and alienation.

Our work is based on four common values: cooperation, nonviolence, inclusivity, and unrestricted freedom to leave a group at any time.

To promote these values, the Fellowship pursues three main goals:

1. To act as a clearinghouse for up-to-date information about intentional communities, including referrals to match groups seeking new members with people in search of a group. This work occasionally leads to receiving critical feedback. When it does, we try to promote dialog and resolution between communities and dissatisfied members or visitors.

2. To build familiarity and trust among communities by encouraging communication, visits, and joint activities. In addition, we facilitate exchange of skills, technical information, and practical experience among both well-established and newly forming communities.

3. To broaden the wider culture's awareness of cooperative alternatives and make accessible the nuts-and-bolts of how to live cooperatively. We regularly explain the potential and reality of community choices to both the press and the public at large.

How Do We Do It?

Publications

The Fellowship's first major project was creating the 1990/91 *Directory of Intentional Communities*, which took more than two years to compile. We sold out three printings and 18,000 copies, and then produced a second edition in 1995 and a third in 2000. This book is our fourth edition. Over the last 15 years the *Directory* has become the benchmark reference for North American options in intentional community.

Encouraged by the *Directory's* success, we negotiated in 1992 to become the publishers of *Communities* magazine. Launched in 1972, the magazine had run out of gas by the late 80s, and we got it up and running again as an 80-page quarterly under the able direction of Editor Diana Christian. Each issue is organized around a theme and offers up a smörgåsbord of insightful stories about how people create community and what they're learning along the way.

In 1995 we made our debut on the Internet at *www.ic.org*. In the ten years since, our online presence has grown enormously—from a modest start as an electronic novelty we've become a robust interactive site serving 9000 pages daily. Today it's our number one conduit for delivering information about community. Go to any search engine, type in "intentional community," and our site will be the first URL you'll see.

In addition to info about the FIC, our website includes a vast array of attractive features:

- Events Calendar, a list of upcoming community-related events (see *www.ic.org/events*);
- Reachbook, where people looking for community and groups looking for members can find each other (see *reach.ic.org*);
- Community Bookshelf, a mail-order book-selling business specializing in titles about cooperative living, sustainability, and right livelihood (see *store.ic.org*);
- *Communities* magazine archive, where you can look up and purchase any of the 125+ issues in the magazine's history (see *fic.ic.org/cmag*);
- Process Clearinghouse, a listing of group process consultants who approach their work from a community

orientation (see *fic.ic.org/process.html*); and,

- *Online Communities Directory,* a searchable database of community listings that provides the source material for this book (see *directory.ic.org*).

Events

In 1993, the FIC produced the Celebration of Community. With 1,000 participants from all over the world, it was the largest community-focused event ever held. There were more than 200 workshops spread out over six days.

In 1997, the Fellowship pioneered Art of Community weekend conferences where people could get practical information about community living, while getting a bit of the feel of community living. Building on our event experience—and taking advantage of how much fun it is—in recent years we've become a popular junior partner for events sponsored by other organizations. Our cadre of presenters and community veterans show up as a party in a box, ready to raise energy and talk community from the moment they arrive on site until the last song is sung.

Fellowship Organizational Meetings

The Fellowship is administered by a board of directors, which gathers twice yearly for three-day meetings with as many of the staff as can come. In an attempt to make meetings accessible to participants from all corners of the continent, the location is rotated from region to region. While the board sessions focus on values and policy questions, committee meetings happen around the edges, providing a rich ferment of ideas and program initiatives. These meetings are open to all, and operate by consensus in a way that encourages input from all who attend. There is no better way to meet the folks who make the FIC go, to find out what's going on, and to find where your energy might fit in.

As we work together, we work things out. In the process, we deepen understanding and trust, and Fellowship meetings and projects become important personal experiences—not just occasions for doing business. We don't just talk community; we try to live community. Each meeting becomes a time to renew old friendships and establish new ones, expanding the personal connections that are the ultimate wealth of our organization.

Who Are These People?

Taking a page from Margaret Mead, we are a small group of dedicated individuals trying to change the world. While it hasn't always been the same small group, year-in-and-year-out there are about 20-25 major enthusiasts who comprise the vibrant core of the Fellowship. As a decentralized organization, tasks are managed from a variety of locations, and it's common for a project team to

have members working across the continent. Generally we are concentrated in geographic nodes, where it's possible to find face-to-face sustenance for the work (email is a wonderful tool, but sharing a stream of electrons is not the same as breathing the same air).

We do the work with the people who show up. Anyone interested in supporting the Communities Movement and the vision of the Fellowship is welcome to join the party. For those with time and skills, it usually works best to attend an organizational meeting and meet the family—to see if we're your kind of people, and find out where your offerings best intersect with our needs. For those with other resources—such as contacts or funding—you can help by lending a hand with invitations and hosting when the FIC circus comes to your area, or by becoming a donor.

In addition, we invite you to become a member: either as an individual, as a community, or as a supporting organization. FIC members receive copies of the periodic newsletter, invitations to all organizational meetings and events, and discounts on all our products. Most importantly, your annual dues help keep the ship of cooperation afloat.

> ☯
> Our cadre of presenters and community veterans show up as a party in a box.

What We've Done for You Lately

While we're always cooking up new ways to promote community, here are highlights of four recent developments that help illustrate the many fronts of our work:

- FIC's online store *store.ic.org* was unveiled January 2002, offering the convenience of unified purchasing and one-stop shopping for all FIC products. Thus we are working to become more user friendly.
- Geoph Kozeny's *Visions of Utopia, volume 1* (available both as a video and DVD) came out in spring 2002, offering a 94-minute introduction to contemporary communities. Thus we are taking our community promotion work into new media.
- In 2004, we made our primary product—the *Communities Directory*—available free online. For the first time all our listing information was presented in a searchable database. This was a daring step given that profits from book sales have been a traditional mainstay for FIC budgets. Now we're depending on a successful fundraising campaign to create a *Directory* Endowment, the interest from which will pay for the labor needed to keep the information comprehensive and current. (see sidebar on the following page) Thus we're working to make our products as accessible as possible.
- In 2006, we are gearing up to host a summit of nonprofits that share a core value of community, to explore the opportunities for cooperation among those dedicated to cooperation. Let's see how far we can walk that talk. Thus we're working to expand the base of cooperation.

For many of us, the Fellowship is the realization of a long-sought vision: a continental association dedicated to nurturing and promoting a greater sense of community everywhere, and to helping people find the right home in community for themselves and their families. This dream can grow only as fast as people feel the call to come together and do the work. If you're inspired to participate in the Intentional Communities Movement, please get in touch. We'd love to hear from you.

The FIC welcomes your input and can be reached via the following contact information:

Fellowship for Intentional Community
RR 1, Box 156
Rutledge, MO 63563
660-883-5545 (phone & fax)
fic@ic.org
www.ic.org

Why the *Directory* is now free online (and why we need your help to pay for it)

On a snowy New Hampshire day in 1988, I was in the room when the fledgling FIC committed to the ambitious idea of publishing a new *Communities Directory*—bigger and better than any that had come before. It was the Fellowship's first project.

Seventeen years and 45,000 copies later, you're now holding a copy of our 4th edition. Over the years we've learned the importance of this book, both to communities and to a public hungry for comprehensive, objective, and up-to-date information about who's doing what and where. We've proven that nobody collects and delivers this better than the FIC.

We have never charged for a basic listing in our *Directory*, and we still don't. We are committed to minimizing barriers to this information—both for communities trying to tell their story, and for people eager to hear it. At the same time, there are costs to getting this done, and we're asking for your support.

Years ago we could sell the book at a modest profit. Today that is no longer the case. While we sold 18,000 copies each of our 1990 and 1995 editions, we sold only half that number of the 2000 version, and the book barely paid for its production costs—despite being our best *Directory* of the three. The trend was clear. There has been no decline in demand for information about community living, but the Internet has increased resistance to paying for reference material.

Swallowing hard, we abandoned our model of supporting our work solely through product sales and committed to a daring plan—we'd continue to collect the information, and then make it available at no charge on our website, as well as making it available as a book (We figure sales are still strong enough to cover printing costs, but not the costs of gathering the information). We unveiled the free *Online Directory* in October 2004, and people loved it. Now we have to pay for it all.

Our funding plan is simple. We're going to raise the money to capitalize a *Directory* Endowment, the interest from which will pay for the labor it takes to keep the data perpetually fresh and organized. We are doing this through a two-year capital campaign.

We figure an endowment of $250,000 will be enough to keep the *Directory* going. If we can raise $400,000 we'll be able to go beyond that and pay for ongoing improvements to our website—the mode by which information is often sought and delivered in today's world.

We're asking you—a member of our main constituency and someone who appreciates the value of the *Directory*—to support the organization that supports you. If the purchase price of the book is all you can afford, we understand. If however, you can give more, now is the time we need your help.

On page 312 there is a reply form that lists categories of support. In addition to writing a check for the *Directory* Endowment (which is tax deductible), you can help by becoming an FIC member, subscribing to *Communities* magazine, or purchasing a few other goodies for your community library.

While we don't do it for the money, we can't do it without the money. Please give as generously as you can.

Laird Schaub

Laird Schaub
FIC Executive Secretary

Albert Bates – The Farm

About the Maps

This section contains maps showing community locations in North America. The United States maps are spread out over the next 10 pages. The maps of Canadian and Mexican communities are on page 48. Unfortunately, we were not able to include maps of any additional countries in this edition.

We have split the United States maps into regions based on some obvious groupings and on how well the various sections fit on a page. Some pages will seem somewhat sparse and others a bit crowded, and some community names are abbreviated to allow them to fit. See the key at the bottom of the Charts section for standard abbreviations. In addition to community names, the maps also show major cities, which we hope will be helpful.

The community locations are somewhat approximate. The placement is based on the postal zip code, so with rural locations the dot can be quite far removed—these maps are meant to be rough guides only. If you are going to visit some communities, please contact each community ahead of time for detailed directions.

Some communities did not list a specific location. Some do not yet have a site, while others chose not to for other reasons. These communities do not appear on the maps. A few communities have more than one location and are found on multiple maps.

Following the maps you will find a list of communities by country and state/province. Communities which did not specify a site should all be listed there, even if they are not on the maps.

Communities in grey do not have full descriptions, as they did not fill out a questionnaire in time for this edition, and are found in the Short Community Listings section on page 273. Communites in black have full descriptions and are found in the Communites Listing section and in the Cross-Reference Charts.

Finally, help keep us accurate—if you notice errors please email us at *directory@ic.org*.

Communities Directory

United States Maps

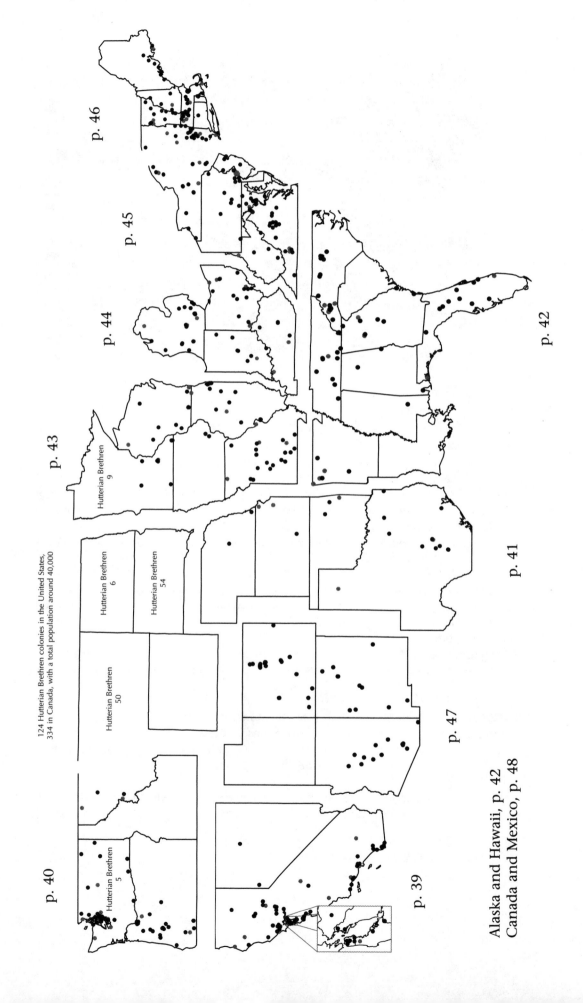

124 Hutterian Brethren colonies in the United States,
334 in Canada, with a total population around 40,000

Hutterian Brethren 9

Hutterian Brethren 6

Hutterian Brethren 54

Hutterian Brethren 50

Hutterian Brethren 5

p. 46

p. 45

p. 44

p. 43

p. 42

p. 41

p. 40

p. 39

p. 47

Alaska and Hawaii, p. 42
Canada and Mexico, p. 48

38

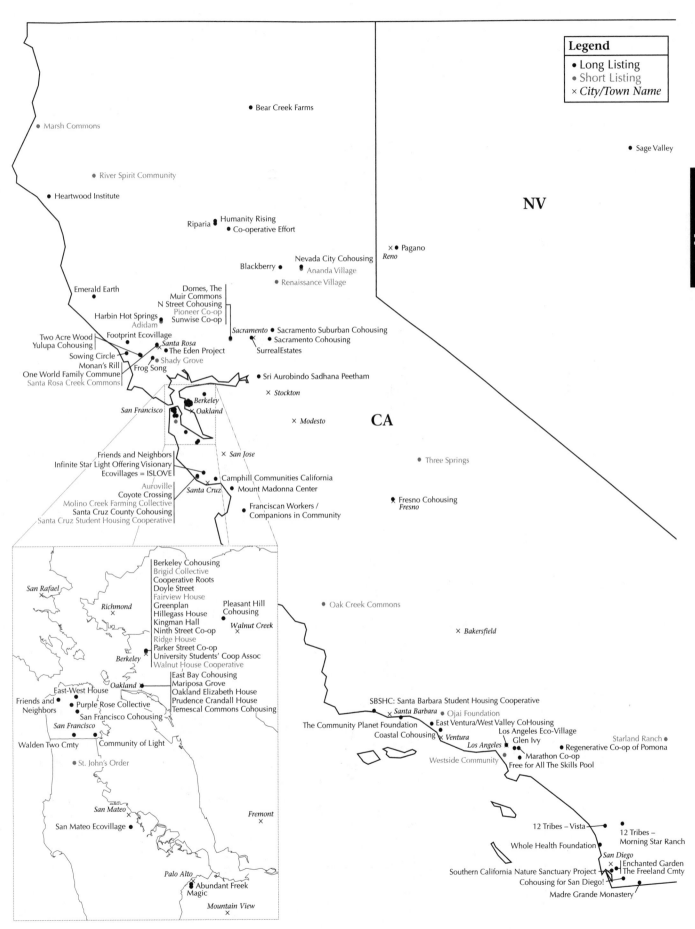

Legend
- Long Listing
- Short Listing
× City/Town Name

Bear Creek Farms

Marsh Commons

Sage Valley

River Spirit Community

Heartwood Institute

NV

Riparia • Humanity Rising
• Co-operative Effort

× • Pagano
Reno

Nevada City Cohousing
Blackberry • • Ananda Village
• Renaissance Village

Emerald Earth
Domes, The
Muir Commons
N Street Cohousing
Pioneer Co-op
Harbin Hot Springs Sunwise Co-op
Adidam
Two Acre Wood Footprint Ecovillage
Yulupa Cohousing
Sowing Circle *Santa Rosa* • Sacramento Suburban Cohousing
Monan's Rill • The Eden Project *Sacramento* • Sacramento Cohousing
One World Family Commune Shady Grove SurrealEstates
Santa Rosa Creek Commons Frog Song

• Sri Aurobindo Sadhana Peetham

San Francisco × *Stockton*

Berkeley
× *Oakland*

× *Modesto*

CA

Friends and Neighbors
Infinite Star Light Offering Visionary × *San Jose*
Ecovillages = ISLOVE • Three Springs

Auroville
Coyote Crossing • Camphill Communities California
Molino Creek Farming Collective *Santa Cruz* • Mount Madonna Center
Santa Cruz County Cohousing
Santa Cruz Student Housing Cooperative • Franciscan Workers /
Companions in Community
• Fresno Cohousing
Fresno

Berkeley Cohousing
Brigid Collective
Cooperative Roots
San Rafael Doyle Street
× Fairview House
Richmond Greenplan Pleasant Hill
× Hillegass House Cohousing
Kingman Hall
Ninth Street Co-op *Walnut Creek*
Ridge House ×
Parker Street Co-op
Berkeley University Students' Coop Assoc • Oak Creek Commons
Walnut House Cooperative

East Bay Cohousing × *Bakersfield*
Oakland Mariposa Grove
Oakland Elizabeth House
East-West House Prudence Crandall House
Purple Rose Collective Temescal Commons Cohousing
Friends and
Neighbors San Francisco Cohousing SBSHC: Santa Barbara Student Housing Cooperative
San Francisco × *Santa Barbara*
Walden Two Cmty Community of Light • Ojai Foundation
The Community Planet Foundation • East Ventura/West Valley CoHousing
St. John's Order Coastal Cohousing Los Angeles Eco-Village
× *Ventura* Glen Ivy Starland Ranch
Los Angeles • Regenerative Co-op of Pomona
Westside Community • Marathon Co-op
Free for All The Skills Pool

San Mateo
× *Fremont*
San Mateo Ecovillage ×
12 Tribes – Vista • • 12 Tribes –
Morning Star Ranch
Whole Health Foundation •
San Diego
Palo Alto Southern California Nature Sanctuary Project × • Enchanted Garden
Abundant Freek • The Freeland Cmty
Magic Cohousing for San Diego!
Mountain View Madre Grande Monastery
×

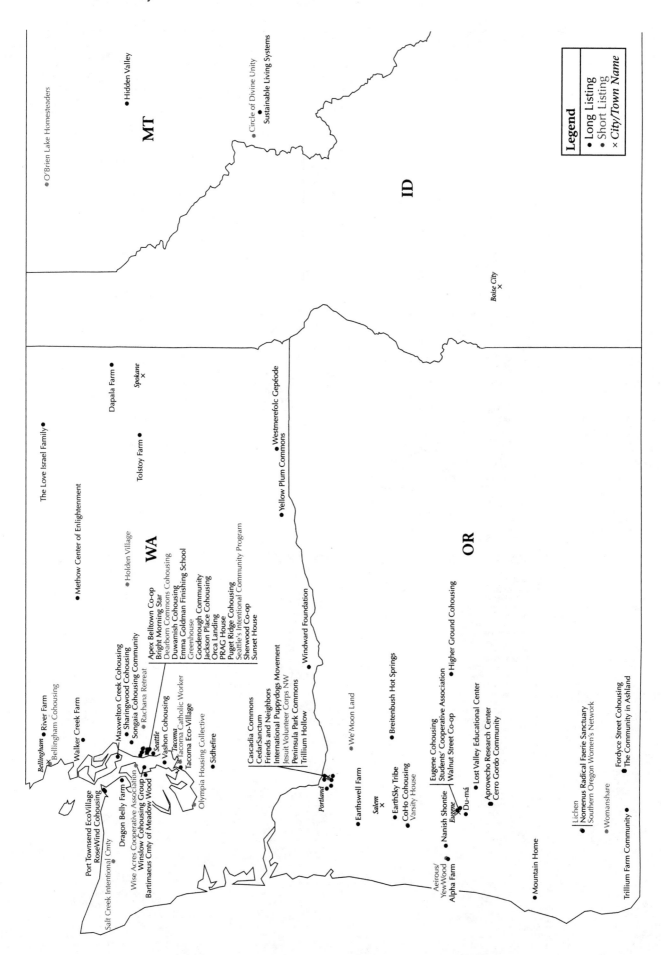

Legend
• Long Listing
• Short Listing
× *City/Town Name*

MT

ID

WA

OR

• O'Brien Lake Homesteaders

• Hidden Valley

• Circle of Divine Unity
• Sustainable Living Systems

× *Boise City*

• Dapala Farm

× *Spokane*

• The Love Israel Family
• Methow Center of Enlightenment
• Holden Village
• Tolstoy Farm

• Westmerefolc Gepéode
• Yellow Plum Commons

Maxwelton Creek Cohousing
Sharingwood Cohousing
Songaia Cohousing Community
Rachana Retreat

Apex Belltown Co-op
Bright Morning Star
Dearborn Commons Cohousing
Duwamish Cohousing
Emma Goldman Finishing School
Greenhouse
Goodenough Community
Jackson Place Cohousing
Orca Landing
PRAG House
Puget Ridge Cohousing
Seattle's Intentional Community Program
Sherwood Co-op
Sunset House

Seattle
Tacoma
Vashon Cohousing
Tacoma Catholic Worker
Tacoma Eco-Village

Cascadia Commons
CedarSanctum
Friends and Neighbors
International Puppydogs Movement
Jesuit Volunteer Corps NW
Peninsula Park Commons
Trillium Hollow

Windward Foundation

Windward Foundation

• Bellingham × • River Farm
Bellingham Cohousing
• Walker Creek Farm

Olympia Housing Collective
• Sidhefire

Port Townsend EcoVillage
RoseWind Cohousing
Dragon Belly Farm
Wise Acres Cooperative Association
Winslow Cohousing Group
Bartimaeus Cmty of Meadow Wood
Salt Creek Intentional Cmty

• We'Moon Land
• Breitenbush Hot Springs
• Higher Ground Cohousing

Portland

• Earthswell Farm
× *Salem*
• EarthSky Tribe
CoHo Cohousing
Varsity House
Eugene
Eugene Cohousing
Students' Cooperative Association
Walnut Street Co-op
• Nanish Shontie
Du-má
• Lost Valley Educational Center
Aprovecho Research Center
Cerro Gordo Community

Aeirous/
YewWood
Alpha Farm

• Mountain Home

Lichen
• Nomenus Radical Faerie Sanctuary
Southern Oregon Women's Network
• Womanshare

• Fordyce Street Cohousing
• The Community in Ashland

Trillium Farm Community

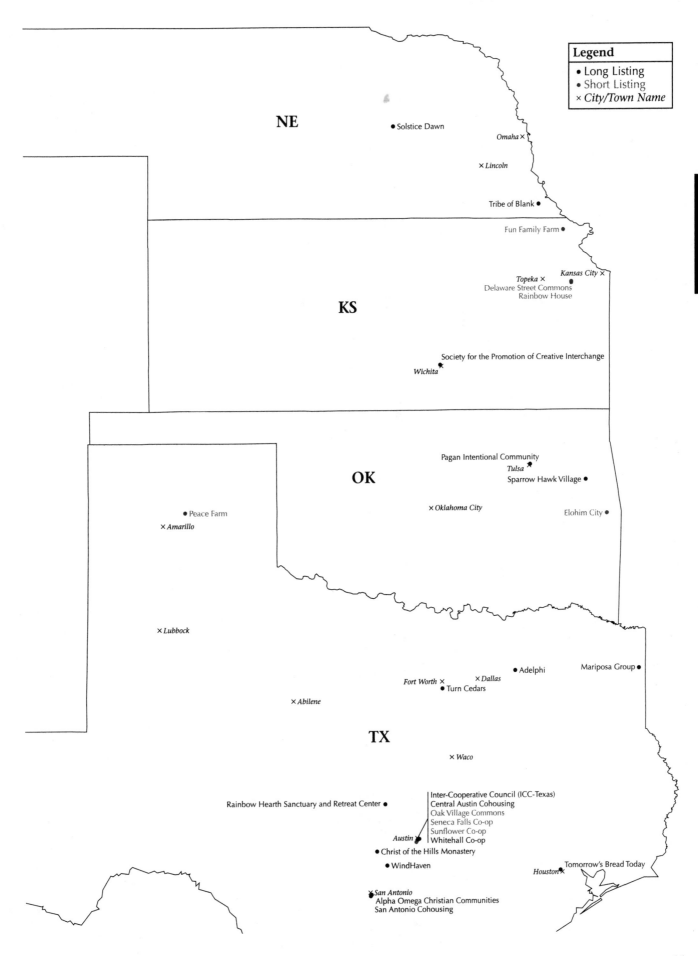

Legend
- Long Listing
- Short Listing
× City/Town Name

NE

• Solstice Dawn

Omaha ×

× *Lincoln*

Tribe of Blank •

Fun Family Farm •

Topeka ×   *Kansas City* ×
Delaware Street Commons •
Rainbow House

KS

Society for the Promotion of Creative Interchange
Wichita ×

Pagan Intentional Community
Tulsa ×

OK

Sparrow Hawk Village •

• Peace Farm

× *Oklahoma City*

Elohim City •

× *Amarillo*

× *Lubbock*

• Adelphi   Mariposa Group •

Fort Worth ×   × *Dallas*
• Turn Cedars

× *Abilene*

TX

× *Waco*

Inter-Cooperative Council (ICC-Texas)
Central Austin Cohousing
Rainbow Hearth Sanctuary and Retreat Center •   Oak Village Commons
Seneca Falls Co-op
Sunflower Co-op
Austin ×   Whitehall Co-op
• Christ of the Hills Monastery

• WindHaven

Tomorrow's Bread Today
Houston ×

× *San Antonio*
Alpha Omega Christian Communities
San Antonio Cohousing

41

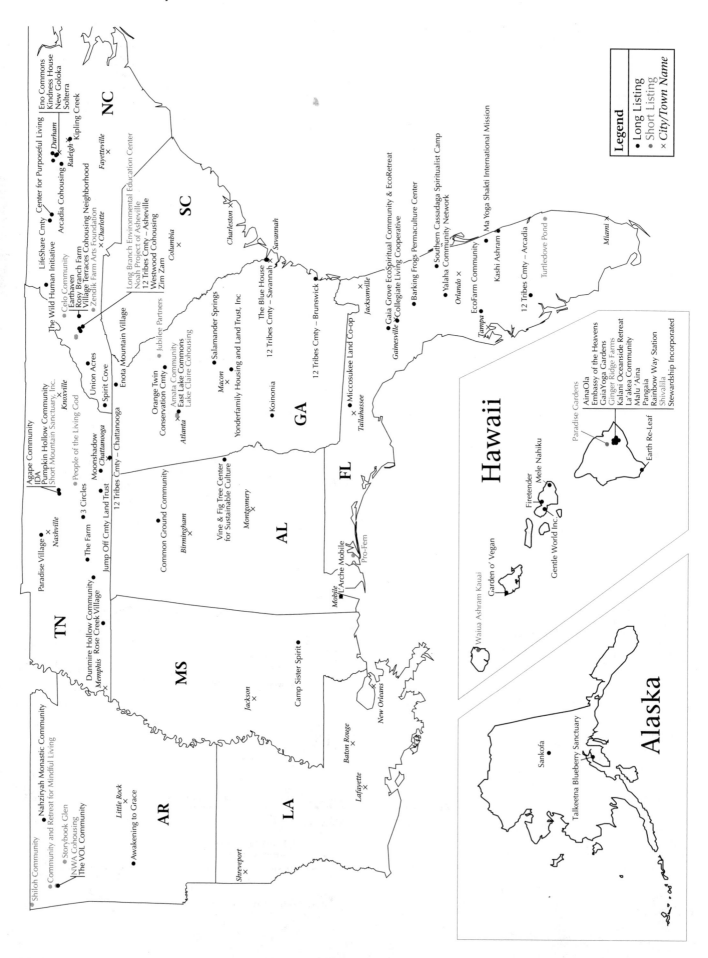

Legend

- ● Long Listing
- ○ Short Listing
- × *City/Town Name*

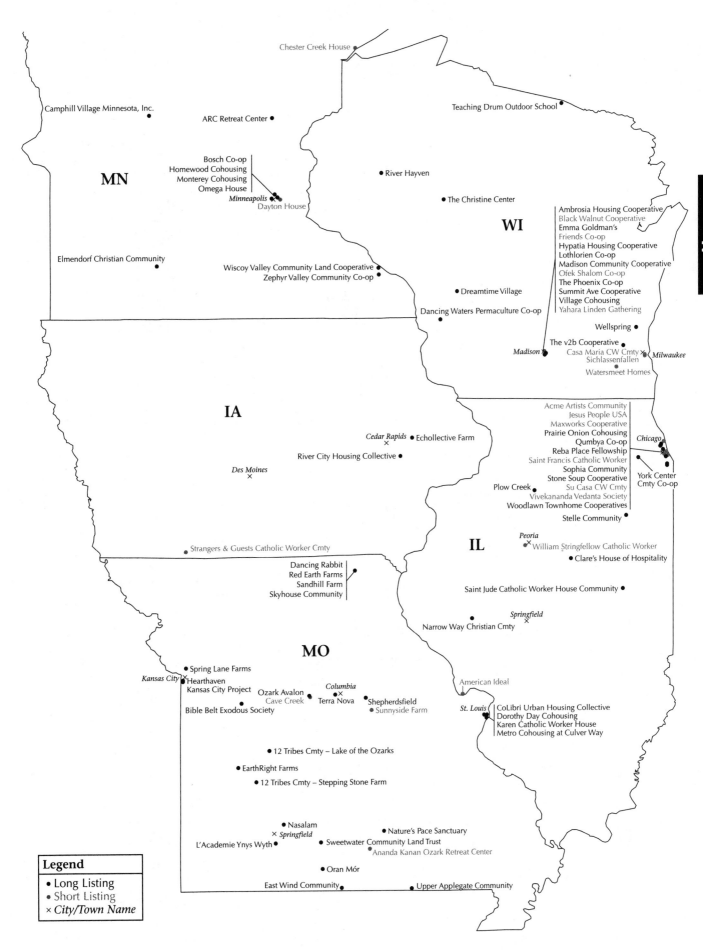

Chester Creek House

Teaching Drum Outdoor School

Camphill Village Minnesota, Inc.

ARC Retreat Center

MN

Bosch Co-op
Homewood Cohousing
Monterey Cohousing
Omega House
Minneapolis
Dayton House

River Hayven

The Christine Center

WI

Ambrosia Housing Cooperative
Black Walnut Cooperative
Emma Goldman's
Friends Co-op
Hypatia Housing Cooperative
Lothlorien Co-op
Madison Community Cooperative
Ofek Shalom Co-op
The Phoenix Co-op
Summit Ave Cooperative
Village Cohousing
Yahara Linden Gathering

Elmendorf Christian Community

Wiscoy Valley Community Land Cooperative
Zephyr Valley Community Co-op

Dreamtime Village

Wellspring

Dancing Waters Permaculture Co-op

The v2b Cooperative
Madison
Casa Maria CW Cmty × *Milwaukee*
Sichlassenfallen
Watersmeet Homes

IA

Acme Artists Community
Jesus People USA
Maxworks Cooperative
Prairie Onion Cohousing
Qumbya Co-op
Chicago
Reba Place Fellowship
Saint Francis Catholic Worker
Sophia Community
Stone Soup Cooperative
Su Casa CW Cmty
Vivekananda Vedanta Society
Woodlawn Townhome Cooperatives

York Center
Cmty Co-op

Cedar Rapids × Echollective Farm

River City Housing Collective

Des Moines ×

Plow Creek

Stelle Community

Strangers & Guests Catholic Worker Cmty

IL

Peoria
× William Stringfellow Catholic Worker

Clare's House of Hospitality

Dancing Rabbit
Red Earth Farms
Sandhill Farm
Skyhouse Community

Saint Jude Catholic Worker House Community

Springfield
×

Narrow Way Christian Cmty

MO

American Ideal

St. Louis
CoLibri Urban Housing Collective
Dorothy Day Cohousing
Karen Catholic Worker House
Metro Cohousing at Culver Way

Spring Lane Farms
Kansas City ×
Hearthaven
Kansas City Project
Ozark Avalon
Columbia
Cave Creek Terra Nova
×
Shepherdsfield
Bible Belt Exodus Society
Sunnyside Farm

12 Tribes Cmty – Lake of the Ozarks

EarthRight Farms

12 Tribes Cmty – Stepping Stone Farm

Nasalam
× *Springfield*
L'Academie Ynys Wyth
Nature's Pace Sanctuary
Sweetwater Community Land Trust
Ananda Kanan Ozark Retreat Center

Oran Mór

East Wind Community

Upper Applegate Community

Legend
• Long Listing
• Short Listing
× *City/Town Name*

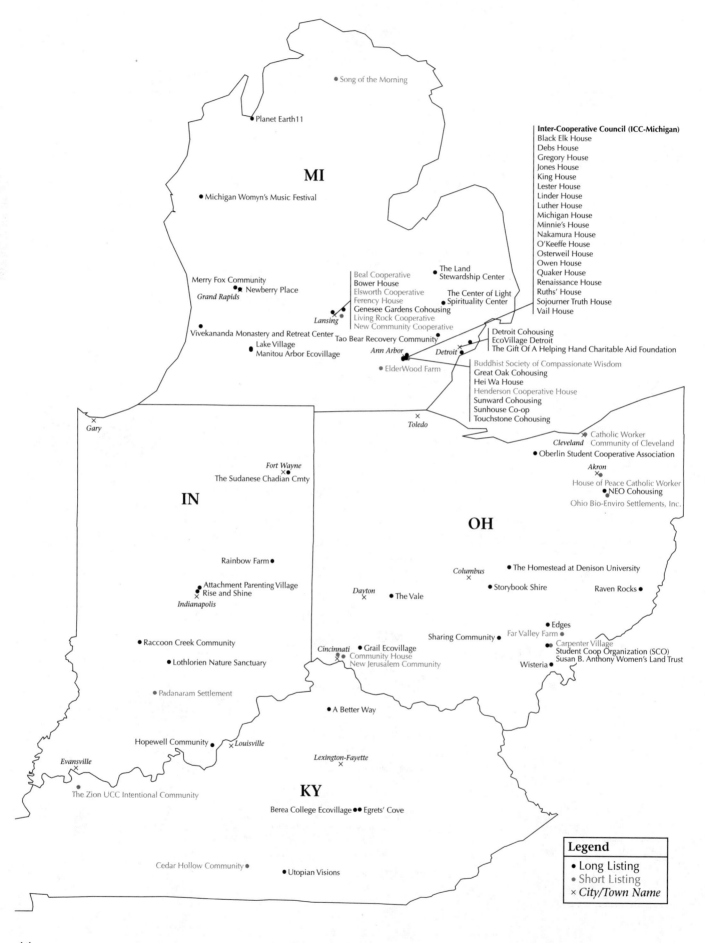

● Song of the Morning

● Planet Earth11

MI

● Michigan Womyn's Music Festival

Inter-Cooperative Council (ICC-Michigan)
Black Elk House
Debs House
Gregory House
Jones House
King House
Lester House
Linder House
Luther House
Michigan House
Minnie's House
Nakamura House
O'Keeffe House
Osterweil House
Owen House
Quaker House
Renaissance House
Ruths' House
Sojourner Truth House
Vail House

Merry Fox Community
● Newberry Place
Grand Rapids

● The Land Stewardship Center

Beal Cooperative
Bower House
Elsworth Cooperative
Ferency House
Genesee Gardens Cohousing
Living Rock Cooperative
New Community Cooperative

The Center of Light
● Spirituality Center

Lansing

● Vivekananda Monastery and Retreat Center
Tao Bear Recovery Community
● Lake Village
● Manitou Arbor Ecovillage

Ann Arbor

× *Detroit*

Detroit Cohousing
EcoVillage Detroit
The Gift Of A Helping Hand Charitable Aid Foundation

● ElderWood Farm

Buddhist Society of Compassionate Wisdom
Great Oak Cohousing
Hei Wa House
Henderson Cooperative House
Sunward Cohousing
Sunhouse Co-op
Touchstone Cohousing

× *Toledo*

● Catholic Worker Community of Cleveland
Cleveland
● Oberlin Student Cooperative Association

× *Gary*

Akron ×
House of Peace Catholic Worker
● NEO Cohousing
Ohio Bio-Enviro Settlements, Inc.

Fort Wayne ×
● The Sudanese Chadian Cmty

IN

OH

● Rainbow Farm

● The Homestead at Denison University
Columbus ×

● Attachment Parenting Village
× Rise and Shine
Indianapolis

● Storybook Shire
● Raven Rocks

Dayton ×
● The Vale

● Raccoon Creek Community

● Edges
Sharing Community ● Far Valley Farm ●

● Lothlorien Nature Sanctuary

Cincinnati
● Grail Ecovillage
Community House
New Jerusalem Community
Carpenter Village
Student Coop Organization (SCO)
Susan B. Anthony Women's Land Trust
● Wisteria

● Padanaram Settlement

● A Better Way

Hopewell Community ●
× *Louisville*

Evansville ×

Lexington-Fayette ×

KY

● The Zion UCC Intentional Community

Berea College Ecovillage ●● Egrets' Cove

Cedar Hollow Community ●
● Utopian Visions

Legend
● Long Listing
● Short Listing
× *City/Town Name*

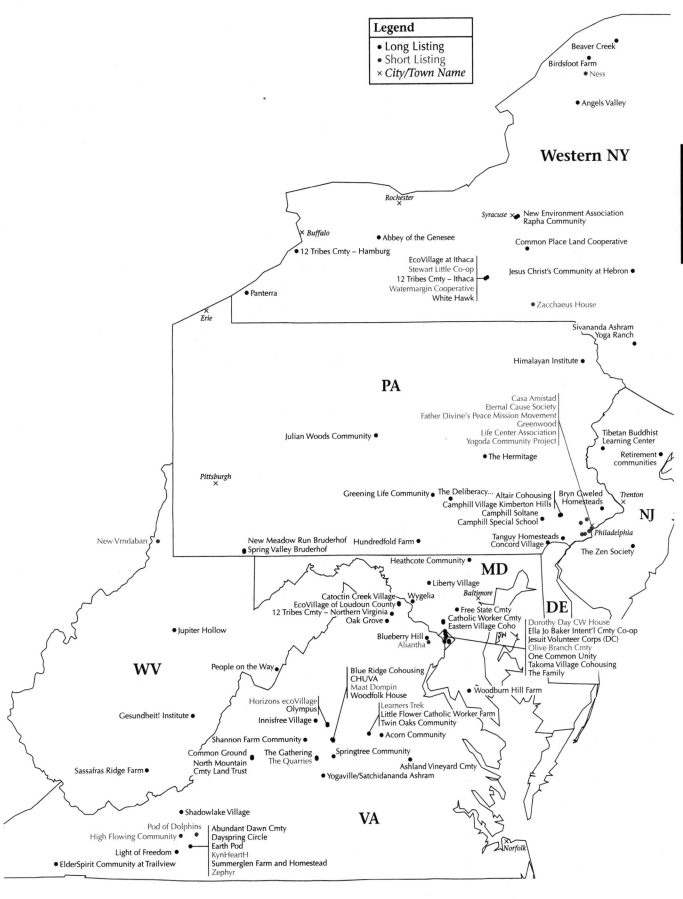

Legend
- Long Listing
- Short Listing
× *City/Town Name*

Western NY

Beaver Creek
Birdsfoot Farm
Ness
Angels Valley

Rochester ×

Syracuse × New Environment Association
Rapha Community

× *Buffalo* • Abbey of the Genesee
• 12 Tribes Cmty – Hamburg

Common Place Land Cooperative

EcoVillage at Ithaca
Stewart Little Co-op
12 Tribes Cmty – Ithaca
Watermargin Cooperative
White Hawk

Jesus Christ's Community at Hebron

• Panterra

• Zacchaeus House

× *Erie*

Sivananda Ashram
Yoga Ranch

Himalayan Institute

PA

Casa Amistad
Eternal Cause Society
Father Divine's Peace Mission Movement
Greenwood
Life Center Association
Yogoda Community Project

Tibetan Buddhist
Learning Center

Julian Woods Community •

Retirement
communities

• The Hermitage

Pittsburgh ×

Greening Life Community • The Deliberacy...
Altair Cohousing
Camphill Village Kimberton Hills
Camphill Soltane
Camphill Special School

Bryn Gweled
Homesteads

Trenton ×

NJ

New Vrndaban •

New Meadow Run Bruderhof
• Spring Valley Bruderhof

Hundredfold Farm •

Tanguy Homesteads
Concord Village

Philadelphia

The Zen Society

Heathcote Community •

MD

• Liberty Village

Baltimore ×

DE

Catoctin Creek Village •
EcoVillage of Loudoun County •
12 Tribes Cmty – Northern Virginia •
Oak Grove •

Wygelia

• Free State Cmty
• Catholic Worker Cmty
• Eastern Village Coho

Dorothy Day CW House
Ella Jo Baker Intent'l Cmty Co-op
Jesuit Volunteer Corps (DC)
Olive Branch Cmty
One Common Unity
Takoma Village Cohousing
The Family

• Jupiter Hollow

Blueberry Hill
Aliantha

WV

People on the Way •

Blue Ridge Cohousing
CHUVA
Maat Dompin
Woodfolk House

• Woodburn Hill Farm

Gesundheit! Institute •

Horizons ecoVillage
Olympus

Learners Trek
Little Flower Catholic Worker Farm
Twin Oaks Community

Innisfree Village •

• Acorn Community

Shannon Farm Community •

Common Ground
North Mountain
Cmty Land Trust

The Gathering
The Quarries

Springtree Community •

Ashland Vineyard Cmty

Sassafras Ridge Farm •

• Yogaville/Satchidananda Ashram

• Shadowlake Village

VA

Pod of Dolphins
High Flowing Community •

Abundant Dawn Cmty
Dayspring Circle
Earth Pod
KynHeartH
Summerglen Farm and Homestead
Zephyr

× *Norfolk*

Light of Freedom •

• ElderSpirit Community at Trailview

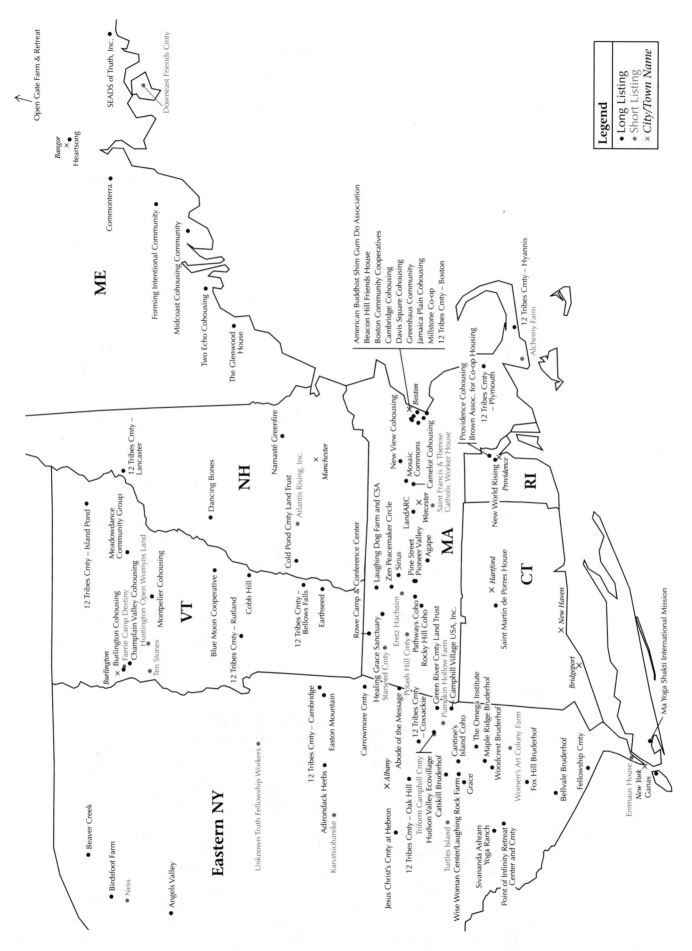

Legend
- Long Listing
- Short Listing (grey dot)
× *City/Town Name*

Open Gate Farm & Retreat

SEADS of Truth, Inc.

Downeast Friends Cmty

Bangor × Heartsong

Commonterra

ME

Forming Intentional Community

Midcoast Cohousing Community

Two Echo Cohousing

The Glenwood House

Namasté Greenfire

12 Tribes Cmty – Lancaster

Dancing Bones

Cold Pond Cmty Land Trust

Atlantis Rising, Inc.

Manchester ×

NH

12 Tribes Cmty – Island Pond

Meadowdance Community Group

Burlington × Burlington Cohousing
Faerie Camp Destiny
Champlain Valley Cohousing
Huntington Open Womyns Land
Ten Stones
Montpelier Cohousing

VT

Blue Moon Cooperative

Cobb Hill

12 Tribes Cmty – Rutland

12 Tribes Cmty – Bellows Falls

Earthseed

Rowe Camp & Conference Center

American Buddhist Shim Gum Do Association
Beacon Hill Friends House
Boston Community Cooperatives
Cambridge Cohousing
Davis Square Cohousing
Greenhaus Community
Jamaica Plain Cohousing
Millstone Co-op
12 Tribes Cmty — Boston

Boston ×

New View Cohousing

Mosaic Commons

Camelot Cohousing

Saint Francis & Therese
Catholic Worker House

Laughing Dog Farm and CSA

Zen Peacemaker Circle

Sirius

Pine Street
Pioneer Valley

LandARC

Worcester ×

Agape

MA

Providence Cohousing
Brown Assoc. for Co-op Housing

12 Tribes Cmty – Plymouth

12 Tribes Cmty – Hyannis

Alchemy Farm

New World Rising

Providence ×

RI

Beaver Creek

Birdsfoot Farm

Ness

Angels Valley

Eastern NY

Unknown Truth Fellowship Workers

Carrowmore Cmty

Healing Grace Sanctuary

Starseed Cmty

Eretz Hachaim

Potash Hill Cmty

Pathways Coho
Rocky Hill Coho

Green River Cmty Land Trust

Pumpkin Hollow Farm

Camphill Village USA, Inc.

The Omega Institute

Maple Ridge Bruderhof

Woodcrest Bruderhof

Saint Martin de Porres House

Hartford ×

CT

New Haven ×

Bridgeport ×

12 Tribes Cmty – Cambridge

Adirondack Herbs

Easton Mountain

Kanatsiohareke

Albany ×

Abode of the Message

12 Tribes Cmty – Coxsackie

Jesus Christ's Cmty at Hebron

12 Tribes Cmty – Oak Hill

Triform Camphill Cmty

Hudson Valley Ecovillage

Catskill Bruderhof

Cantine's Island Coho

Grace

Turtles Island

Wise Woman Center/Laughing Rock Farm

Sivananda Ashram
Yoga Ranch

Point of Infinity Retreat
Center and Cmty

Women's Art Colony Farm

Fox Hill Bruderhof

Bellvale Bruderhof

Fellowship Cmty

New York Ganas

Emmaus House

Ma Yoga Shakti International Mission

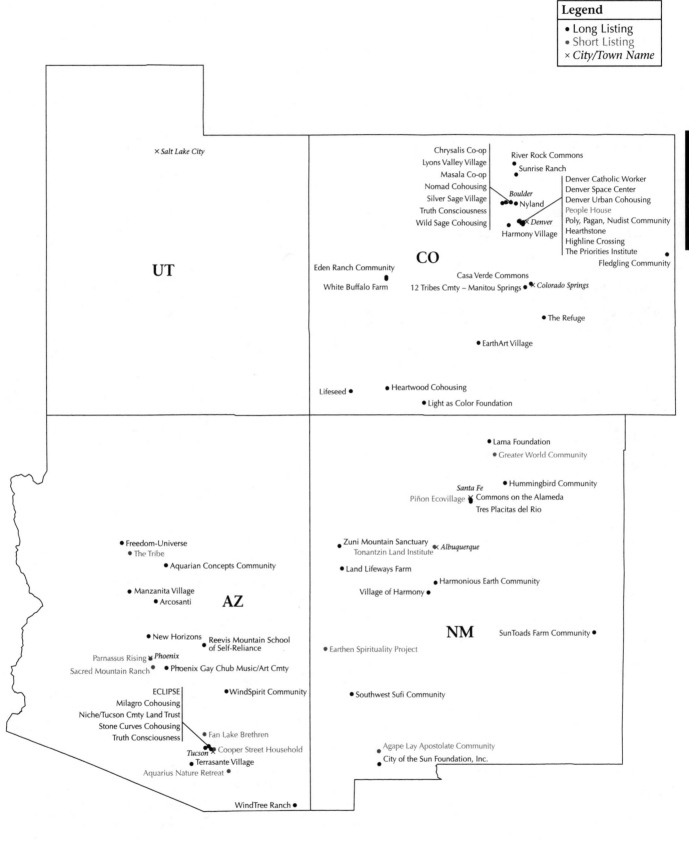

Legend
- Long Listing
- Short Listing
× City/Town Name

UT

× Salt Lake City

CO

Chrysalis Co-op
Lyons Valley Village
Masala Co-op
Nomad Cohousing
Silver Sage Village
Truth Consciousness
Wild Sage Cohousing

River Rock Commons
Sunrise Ranch

Boulder
Nyland

Denver Catholic Worker
Denver Space Center
Denver Urban Cohousing
People House
Poly, Pagan, Nudist Community
Hearthstone
Highline Crossing
The Priorities Institute

× Denver
Harmony Village

Fledgling Community

Eden Ranch Community
White Buffalo Farm

Casa Verde Commons
12 Tribes Cmty – Manitou Springs
× Colorado Springs

The Refuge

EarthArt Village

Lifeseed
Heartwood Cohousing
Light as Color Foundation

Lama Foundation
Greater World Community

Santa Fe
Piñon Ecovillage ×

Hummingbird Community
Commons on the Alameda
Tres Placitas del Rio

Zuni Mountain Sanctuary
Tonantzin Land Institute
× Albuquerque

Land Lifeways Farm
Village of Harmony

Harmonious Earth Community

NM

SunToads Farm Community

Earthen Spirituality Project

Southwest Sufi Community

Agape Lay Apostolate Community
City of the Sun Foundation, Inc.

AZ

Freedom-Universe
The Tribe
Aquarian Concepts Community

Manzanita Village
Arcosanti

New Horizons
Reevis Mountain School
of Self-Reliance
Parnassus Rising × Phoenix
Sacred Mountain Ranch
Phoenix Gay Chub Music/Art Cmty

ECLIPSE
Milagro Cohousing
Niche/Tucson Cmty Land Trust
Stone Curves Cohousing
Truth Consciousness

WindSpirit Community

Fan Lake Brethren

Tucson × Cooper Street Household
Terrasante Village
Aquarius Nature Retreat

WindTree Ranch

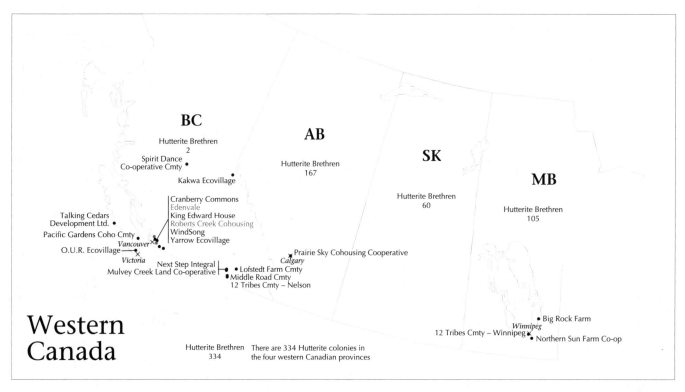

BC

AB

SK

MB

Hutterite Brethren
2

Spirit Dance
Co-operative Cmty •

Kakwa Ecovillage •

Hutterite Brethren
167

Hutterite Brethren
60

Hutterite Brethren
105

Cranberry Commons
Edenvale
King Edward House
Roberts Creek Cohousing
WindSong
Yarrow Ecovillage

Talking Cedars
Development Ltd. •

Pacific Gardens Coho Cmty •

O.U.R. Ecovillage ✕

Vancouver ✕

Victoria ✕

Next Step Integral
Mulvey Creek Land Co-operative

• Lofstedt Farm Cmty
• Middle Road Cmty
12 Tribes Cmty – Nelson

• Prairie Sky Cohousing Cooperative
Calgary ✕

• Big Rock Farm
Winnipeg
12 Tribes Cmty – Winnipeg ✕
• Northern Sun Farm Co-op

Hutterite Brethren
334

There are 334 Hutterite colonies in
the four western Canadian provinces

Western
Canada

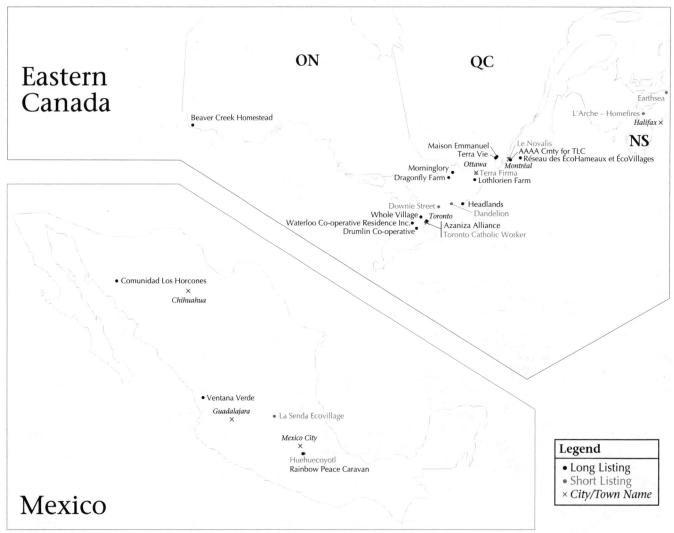

Eastern
Canada

ON

QC

• Beaver Creek Homestead

Maison Emmanuel
Terra Vie
• AAAA Cmty for TLC
Le Novalis
• Réseau des ÉcoHameaux et ÉcoVillages
Montréal ✕

Morninglory •
Dragonfly Farm •

Ottawa ✕

✕ Terra Firma
• Lothlorien Farm

Earthsea •
L'Arche – Homefires
Halifax ✕

NS

Downie Street •
Whole Village •
Waterloo Co-operative Residence Inc. •
Drumlin Co-operative •

• Headlands
Dandelion
Toronto ✕
Azaniza Alliance
Toronto Catholic Worker

Mexico

• Comunidad Los Horcones
✕
Chihuahua

• Ventana Verde

Guadalajara
✕

• La Senda Ecovillage

Mexico City
✕

Huehuecoyotl
Rainbow Peace Caravan

Legend	
•	Long Listing
•	Short Listing
✕	*City/Town Name*

Key to Communities by Country/State/Province

What follows is a list of the communities in this book alphabetized by state or province within each country. Following each community name is a city name in parenthesis, if one is given (if not you'll see a dash '—'). In addition to the United States, Canada, and Mexico there are 40 other countries represented.

Communities in grey do not have descriptions, as they did not fill out a questionnaire in time for this edition, and are found in the Short Community Listings section on page 273. Communites in black have full descriptions and are found in the Communites Listing section and in the Cross-Reference Charts.

There are eight communities within the United States that did not list a specific state and are listed under "No State" at the end of the US listings. Similarily there is one community listed under "No Location" at the very end of the list.

Maps

United States

AL-Alabama
Common Ground Community (Blountsville)
L'Arche Mobile (Mobile)
Vine & Fig Tree Center for Sustainable Culture (Lanett)

AK-Alaska
Sankofa (Ester)
Talkeetna Blueberry Sanctuary (Talkeetna)

AZ-Arizona
Aquarian Concepts Community (Sedona)
Aquarius Nature Retreat (Vail)
Arcosanti (Cordes Lakes)
Cooper Street Household (Tucson)
ECLIPSE (Tucson)
Freedom-Universe (Ash Fork)
Manzanita Village (Prescott)
Milagro Cohousing (Tucson)
New Horizons (Phoenix)
Niche / Tucson Community Land Trust (Tucson)
Parnassus Rising (Phoenix)
Phoenix Gay Chub Music/Art Community (Phoenix)
Reevis Mountain School of Self-Reliance (Roosevelt)
Sacred Mountain Ranch (Phoenix)
Stone Curves Cohousing (Tucson)
Terrasante Village (Tucson)
The Tribe (Paulden)
Truth Consciousness (Desert Ashram, Tucson)
WindSpirit Community (Winkelman)
WindTree Ranch (Douglas)

AR-Arkansas
Awakening to Grace (Mt. Ida)
Community and Retreat for Mindful Living (Fayetteville)
Nahziryah Monastic Community (Yellville)
NWA Cohousing ---
Shiloh Community (Sulphur Springs)
Storybook Glen (Pettigrew)
The VOL Community (Fayetteville)

CA-California
Abundant Freek (Palo Alto)
Adidam (Middletown)
Ananda Village (Nevada City)
Auroville (Santa Cruz)
Bear Creek Farms (Fall River Mills)
Berkeley Cohousing (Berkeley)
Blackberry (near North San Juan)
Brigid Collective (Berkeley)
Camphill Communities California (Soquel)
Co-operative Effort (Chico)
Coastal Cohousing (Ventura)
Cohousing for San Diego! (San Diego County)
Community of Light (San Francisco)
The Community Planet Foundation (Santa Barbara)
Cooperative Roots (Berkeley)
Coyote Crossing (Santa Cruz)
Domes, The (Davis)
Doyle Street (Emeryville)
East Bay Cohousing (Oakland/Berkeley)
East Ventura/West Valley CoHousing (Ventura)

East-West House (San Francisco)
The Eden Project (Mendocino County)
Emerald Earth (Boonville)
Enchanted Garden (San Diego)
Fairview House (Berkeley)
Footprint Ecovillage (Guerneville)
Franciscan Workers / Companions in Community (Salinas)
Free for All The Skills Pool (Los Angeles)
The Freeland Community (San Diego)
Fresno Cohousing (Fresno)
Friends and Neighbors (San Francisco)
Friends and Neighbors (San Lorenzo Valley)
Frog Song (Cotati)
Glen Ivy (Corona)
Greenplan (Berkeley)
Harbin Hot Springs (Middletown)
Heartwood Institute (Garberville)
Hillegass House (Berkeley)
Humanity Rising (Chico)
infinite star Light offering visionary ecovillages = isLove (Santa Cruz county)
Jesus Christians (Los Angeles)
Kingman Hall (Berkeley)
Los Angeles Eco-Village (Los Angeles)
Madre Grande Monastery (Dulzura)
Magic (Palo Alto)
Marathon Co-op (Los Angeles)
Mariposa Grove (Oakland)
Marsh Commons (Arcata)
Molino Creek Farming Collective (Davenport)
Monan's Rill (Santa Rosa)
Mount Madonna Center (Watsonville)
Muir Commons (Davis)
N Street Cohousing (Davis)
Neo Hippie Haven —
Nevada City Cohousing (Nevada City)
Ninth Street Co-op (Berkeley)
Oak Creek Commons (Paso Robles)
Oakland Elizabeth House (Oakland)
Ojai Foundation (Ojai)
One World Family Commune (Santa Rosa)
Parker Street Co-op (Berkeley)
Pioneer Co-op (Davis)
Pleasant Hill Cohousing (Pleasant Hill)
Prudence Crandall House (Oakland)
Purple Rose Collective (San Francisco)
Regenerative Co-op of Pomona (Pomona)
Renaissance Village (Penn Valley)
Ridge House (Berkeley)
Riparia (Chico)
River Spirit Community (Mad River)
Sacramento Cohousing (Sacramento)
Sacramento Suburban Cohousing (Fair Oaks)
San Francisco Cohousing (San Francisco)
San Mateo Ecovillage (San Mateo)
Santa Cruz County Cohousing (Santa Cruz)
Santa Cruz Student Housing Cooperative (Santa Cruz)
Santa Rosa Creek Commons (Santa Rosa)
SBSHC: Santa Barbara Student Housing Cooperative (Isla Vista)
Shady Grove (Penngrove)
Soma - The SOMA Project (Southern CA)

Southern California Nature Sanctuary Project (San Diego)
Sowing Circle (Occidental)
Sri Aurobindo Sadhana Peetham (Lodi)
St. John's Order (South San Francisco)
Starland Ranch (Yucca Valley)
Sunwise Co-op (Davis)
SurrealEstates (Sacramento)
Temescal Commons Cohousing (Oakland)
Three Springs (North Fork)
Twelve Tribes Community at the Morning Star Ranch (Valley Center)
Twelve Tribes Community in Vista (Vista)
Two Acre Wood (Sebastopol)
University Students' Coop Assoc (Berkeley)
Walden Two Community California (San Francisco)
Walnut House Cooperative (Berkeley)
Westside Community (Los Angeles)
Whole Health Foundation (Cardiff by the Sea)
Yulupa Cohousing (Santa Rosa)

CO-Colorado
Ascension Point —
Casa Verde Commons (Colorado Springs)
Chrysalis Co-op (Boulder)
Denver Catholic Worker (Denver)
Denver Space Center (Denver)
Denver Urban Cohousing (Denver)
EarthArt Village (Moffat)
Eden Ranch Community (Paonia)
Fledgling Community (Burlington)
Harmony Village (Golden)
Hearthstone (Denver)
Heartwood Cohousing (Durango)
Highline Crossing (Littleton)
Lifeseed (Mancos)
Light as Color Foundation (Pagosa Springs)
Lyons Valley Village (Lyons)
Masala Co-op (Boulder)
Nomad Cohousing (Boulder)
Nyland (Lafayette)
People House (Denver)
Poly, Pagan, Nudist Community (Denver Area)
The Priorities Institute (Denver)
The Refuge (Pueblo)
River Rock Commons (Fort Collins)
Silver Sage Village (Boulder)
Sunrise Ranch (Loveland)
Truth Consciousness (Boulder)
Twelve Tribes Community in Manitou Springs (Manitou Springs)
White Buffalo Farm (Paonia)
Wild Sage Cohousing (Boulder)

CT-Connecticut
Saint Martin de Porres House (Hartford)

DC-District Of Columbia
Dorothy Day Catholic Worker House (Washington)
Ella Jo Baker Intentional Community Co-op (Washington)
The Family (Washington)
Jesuit Volunteer Corps (Washington)
Olive Branch Community (Washington)
One Common Unity (Washington)
Takoma Village Cohousing (Washington)

FL-Florida
Barking Frogs Permaculture Center (Sparr)
Central Florida Cohousing (looking for property near Disney)
Collegiate Living Cooperative (Gainesville)
EcoFarm Community (Plant City)
Emerald Coast Village (Panhandle of Florida)
Everything is Related (no specific location picked at this time)
Gaia Grove EcoSpiritual Community & EcoRetreat (near Gainesville)
Kashi Ashram (Sebastian)
Ma Yoga Shakti International Mission (Palm Bay)
Miccosukee Land Co-op (Miccosukee CPO)
Pro-Fem (Pensacola)
Southern Cassadaga Spiritualist Camp (Cassadaga)
Turtledove Pond (Jupiter)
Twelve Tribes Community in Arcadia (Arcadia)
Yalaha Community Network (Yalaha, Lake County)

GA-Georgia
Amata Community (Atlanta)
The Blue House (Savannah)
East Lake Commons (Decatur)
Enota Mountain Village (Hiawassee)
Jubilee Partners (Comer)
Koinonia (Americus)
Lake Claire Cohousing (Atlanta)
Orange Twin Conservation Community (Athens)
Salamander Springs (Milledgeville)
Twelve Tribes Community in Brunswick (Brunswick)
Twelve Tribes Community in Savannah (Savannah)
Yonderfamily Housing and Land Trust, Inc (Jeffersonville)

HI-Hawaii
AinaOla (Kapoho area, Pahoa town, Puna County)
Earth Re-Leaf (Naalehu)
Embassy of the Heavens (Pahoa)
Firetender (Paia)
GaiaYoga Gardens (Pahoa)
Garden o' Vegan (Laupahoehoe)
Gentle World Inc. (Kapaau)
Ginger Ridge Farms (Pahoa)
Kalani Oceanside Retreat (Pahoa)
La'akea Community (Pahoa)
Malu 'Aina (Ola`a (Kurtistown))
Mele Nahiku (Hana)
New Earth Cooperative —
Pangaia (Pahoa)
Paradise Gardens (Hilo)
Rainbow Way Station (Kurtistown)
Shivalila (Pahoa)
Stewardship Incorporated (Mountain View)
Waiua Ashram Kauai (Kapaa)

IL-Illinois
Acme Artists Community (Chicago)
American Ideal (Golden Eagle)
Clare's House of Hospitality (Bloomington)
Jesus People USA (Chicago)
Maxworks Cooperative (Chicago)
Narrow Way Christian Community (Chapin)
Plow Creek (Tiskilwa)
Prairie Onion Cohousing (Chicago)
Qumbya Co-op (Chicago)
Reba Place Fellowship (Evanston)
Saint Francis Catholic Worker (Chicago)
Saint Jude Catholic Worker House Community (Champaign)
Sophia Community (Chicago)
Stelle Community (Stelle)
Stone Soup Cooperative (Chicago)
Su Casa Catholic Worker Community (Chicago)
Vivekananda Vedanta Society (Chicago)
William Stringfellow Catholic Worker (Peoria)
Woodlawn Townhome Cooperatives (Chicago)
York Center Community Co-op (Lombard)

IN-Indiana
Attachment Parenting Village (Indianapolis)
Hopewell Community (Lanesville)
Lothlorien Nature Sanctuary (Bloomington)
Padanaram Settlement (Williams)
Raccoon Creek Community (between Spencer and Bloomington)
Rainbow Farm (Selma)
Rise and Shine (Indianapolis)
The Sudanese Chadian Community in NE Indiana (Fort Wayne)

IA-Iowa
Echollective Farm (Mechanicsville)
River City Housing Collective (Iowa City)
Strangers & Guests Catholic Worker Community (Blockton)

KS-Kansas
Delaware Street Commons (Lawrence)
Fun Family Farm (Robinson)
Kansas City Project (Kansas City)
Rainbow House (Lawrence)
Society for the Promotion of Creative Interchange (Wichita)

KY-Kentucky
A Better Way (Williamstown)

Berea College Ecovillage (Berea)
Cedar Hollow Community (Edmonton)
Egrets' Cove (Big Hill)
Utopian Visions (Jamestown)
The Zion UCC Intentional Community (Henderson)

LA-Louisiana
Oceanic Ecovillage —

ME-Maine
Coastal Cohousing —
Commonterra (Monroe)
Downeast Friends Community (Bar Harbor)
Forming Intentional Community (Appleton area)
The Glenwood House in Portland (Portland)
Heartsong (Orono)
Midcoast Cohousing Community (Damariscotta)
Open Gate Farm & Retreat (West Chapman)
SEADS of Truth, Inc. (Harrington)
Two Echo Cohousing (Brunswick)

MD-Maryland
Catholic Worker Community (Silver Spring)
The Deliberacy... (Hagerstown)
Eastern Village Cohousing (Silver Spring)
Free State Community (Howard County)
Heathcote Community (Freeland)
Liberty Village (Libertytown)
Woodburn Hill Farm (Mechanicsville)
Wygelia (Adamstown)

MA-Massachusetts
Agape (Ware)
Alchemy Farm (East Falmouth)
American Buddhist Shim Gum Do Association (Brighton)
Beacon Hill Friends House (Boston)
Boston Community Cooperatives (Somerville)
Cambridge Cohousing (Cambridge)
Camelot Cohousing (Berlin)
Community in Plymouth (Plymouth)
Davis Square Cohousing (Cambridge/Somerville)
Eretz Hachaim (Sunderland)
Greenhaus Community (Jamaica Plain, Boston)
Healing Grace Sanctuary (Shelburne Falls)
Jamaica Plain Cohousing (Boston)
Komaja (Beverly)
LandARC —
Laughing Dog Farm and CSA (Gill)
Millstone Co-op (Somerville)
Mosaic Commons (MetroWest)
New View Cohousing (Acton)
Pathways CoHousing (Florence)
Pine Street (Amherst)
Pioneer Valley (Amherst)
Potash Hill Community (Cummington)
Rocky Hill Cohousing (Northhampton)
Rowe Camp & Conference Center (Rowe)
Saint Francis & Therese Catholic Worker House (Worcester)
Sirius Community (Shutesbury)
Starseed Community (Savoy)
Twelve Tribes Community in Boston (Dorchester)
Twelve Tribes Community in Hyannis (Hyannis)
Zen Peacemaker Circle (Montague)

MI-Michigan
Beal Cooperative (East Lansing)
Black Elk House (Ann Arbor)
Bower House (East Lansing)
Buddhist Society of Compassionate Wisdom (Ann Arbor)
The Center of Light Spirituality Center (Oxford)
Debs House (Ann Arbor)
Detroit Cohousing (Detroit)
EcoVillage Detroit (Detroit)
ElderWood Farm (Manchester)
Elsworth Cooperative (East Lansing)
Ferency House (East Lansing)
Genesee Gardens Cohousing (Lansing)
The Gift Of A Helping Hand Charitable Aid Foundation (Detroit)
Great Oak Cohousing (Ann Arbor)
Gregory House (Ann Arbor)

Hei Wa House (Ann Arbor)
Henderson Cooperative House (Ann Arbor)
Inter-Cooperative Council (ICC-Michigan) (Ann Arbor)
Jones House (Ann Arbor)
King House (Ann Arbor)
Lake Village (Kalamazoo)
The Land Stewardship Center (Columbiaville)
Lester House (Ann Arbor)
Linder House (Ann Arbor)
Living Rock Cooperative (East Lansing)
Luther House (Ann Arbor)
Manitou Arbor Ecovillage (Kalamazoo)
Merry Fox Community (Grand Rapids)
Michigan House (Ann Arbor)
Michigan Womyn's Music Festival (Walhalla)
Minnie's House (Ann Arbor)
Nakamura House (Ann Arbor)
New Community Cooperative (East Lansing)
Newberry Place: a Grand Rapids Cohousing Community (Grand Rapids)
O'Keeffe House (Ann Arbor)
Osterweil House (Ann Arbor)
Owen House (Ann Arbor)
Planet Earth11 (Traverse City)
Quaker House (Ann Arbor)
Renaissance House (Ann Arbor)
Ruths' House (Ann Arbor)
Sojourner Truth House (Ann Arbor)
Song of the Morning (Vanderbilt)
Sunhouse Co-op (Ann Arbor)
Sunward Cohousing (Ann Arbor)
Tao Bear Recovery Community (Farmington Hills)
Touchstone Cohousing (Ann Arbor)
Vail House (Ann Arbor)
Vivekananda Monastery and Retreat Center (Fennville)

MN-Minnesota
ARC Retreat Center (Stanchfield)
Bosch Co-op (Minneapolis)
Camphill Village Minnesota, Inc. (Sauk Centre)
Chester Creek House (Duluth)
Dayton House (Saint Paul)
Elmendorf Christian Community (Mountain Lake)
Homewood Cohousing (Minneapolis)
Monterey Cohousing (Minneapolis)
Omega House (Minneapolis)
Order of Saint Benedict (Collegeville)
Wiscoy Valley Community Land Cooperative (Winona)
Zephyr Valley Community Co-op (Rushford)

MS-Mississippi
Camp Sister Spirit (Ovett)

MO-Missouri
Ananda Kanan Ozark Retreat Center (Willow Springs)
BBES (Bible Belt Exodous Society) (Warrensburg)
Cave Creek (Boonville)
CoLibri Urban Housing Collective (Saint Louis)
Dancing Rabbit (Rutledge)
Dorothy Day Cohousing (St. Louis)
EarthRight Farms (Osceola)
East Wind Community (Tecumseh)
Hearthaven (Kansas City)
Kansas City Project (Kansas City)
Karen Catholic Worker House (Saint Louis)
L'Academie Ynys Wyth (Springfield)
La Familia Arbo Komunumo —
Metro Cohousing at Culver Way (St. Louis)
Nasalam (Fair Grove)
Nature's Pace Sanctuary (Hartshorn)
Oran Mór (Squires)
Ozark Avalon (Columbia/Boonville)
Red Earth Farms (Rutledge)
Sandhill Farm (Rutledge)
Shepherdsfield (Fulton)
Skyhouse Community (Rutledge)
Spring Lane Farms (Kansas City)
Sugar Mountain —
Sunnyside Farm (Mokane)
Sweetwater Community Land Trust (Mansfield)

Maps

Terra Nova (Columbia)
Twelve Tribes Community At Stepping Stone Farm (Weaubleau)
Twelve Tribes Community on the Lake of the Ozarks (Warsaw)
Upper Applegate Community (Couch)

MT-Montana
Circle of Divine Unity (Victor)
Hidden Valley (Bigfork)
O'Brien Lake Homesteaders (Eureka)
Sustainable Living Systems (Corvallis)

NE-Nebraska
Pioneer Trails Institute —
Solstice Dawn (Belgrade)

NV-Nevada
Pagano (Sparks)
Sage Valley (Battle Mountain)

NH-New Hampshire
Atlantis Rising, Inc. (Bradford)
Cold Pond Community Land Trust (Acworth)
Dancing Bones (Wentworth)
Namasté Greenfire (Center Barnstead)
Tribe of Dirt —
Twelve Tribes Community in Lancaster (Lancaster)

NJ-New Jersey
Garden State Cohousing —
Retirement communities (Kenilworth)
Tibetan Buddhist Learning Center (Washington)
The Zen Society (Shamong/Southampton)

NM-New Mexico
Agape Lay Apostolate Community (Deming)
Albuquerque Urban Ecovillage (Albuquerque)
City of the Sun Foundation, Inc. (Columbus)
Commons on the Alameda (Santa Fe)
Earthen Spirituality Project (Reserve)
Greater World Community (Taos)
Harmonious Earth Community (Belen)
Hummingbird Community (Mora)
Lama Foundation (San Cristobal)
Land Lifeways Farm (Pinehill)
Piñon Ecovillage (Santa Fe)
Southwest Sufi Community (Silver City)
SunToads Farm Community of New Mexico USA (Elida)
Tonantzin Land Institute (Albuquerque)
Tres Placitas del Rio (Santa Fe)
Village of Harmony (Veguita/Bosque)
Zuni Mountain Sanctuary (Ramah)

NY-New York
Abbey of the Genesee (Piffard)
Abode of the Message (New Lebanon)
Adirondack Herbs (Galway)
Angels Valley (Harrisville)
Beaver Creek (Winthrop)
Bellvale Bruderhof (Chester)
Birdsfoot Farm (Canton)
Camphill Village USA, Inc. (Copake)
Cantine's Island Cohousing (Saugerties)
Carrowmore Community (Petersburgh)
Catskill Bruderhof (Elka Park)
Common Place Land Cooperative (Truxton)
EcoVillage at Ithaca (Ithaca)
Emmaus House (New York)
Fellowship Community (Spring Valley)
Fox Hill Bruderhof (Walden)
Ganas (Staten Island)
Grace (Bearsville)
Green River Community Land Trust (Hillsdale)
Hudson Valley Ecovillage (Hudson Valley)
Jesus Christ's Community at Hebron (Jefferson)
Kanatsiohareke (Ga na jo ha lay gay) (Fonda)
Ma Yoga Shakti International Mission (New York)
Maple Ridge Bruderhof (Ulster Park)
Ness (Hermon)
New Environment Association (Syracuse)
The Omega Institute for Holistic Studies (Rhinebeck)
Panterra (Westfield)

The Point of Infinity Retreat Center and Community (Greenfield Park)
Pumpkin Hollow Farm (Craryville)
Rapha Community (Syracuse)
Sivananda Ashram Yoga Ranch (Woodbourne)
Stewart Little Co-op (Ithaca)
Triform Camphill Community (Hudson)
Turtles Island (Pine Hill)
Twelve Tribes Community in Cambridge (Cambridge)
Twelve Tribes Community in Coxsackie (Coxsackie)
Twelve Tribes Community in Hamburg (Lake View)
Twelve Tribes Community in Ithaca (Ithaca)
Twelve Tribes Community in Oak Hill (Oak Hill)
Unknown Truth Fellowship Workers (Warrensburg)
Watermargin Cooperative (Ithaca)
White Hawk (Ithaca)
Wise Woman Center/Laughing Rock Farm (Woodstock)
Women's Art Colony Farm (Poughkeepsie)
Woodcrest Bruderhof (Rifton)
Zacchaeus House (Binghamton)

NC-North Carolina
Arcadia Cohousing (Carrboro)
Celo Community (Burnsville)
Center for Purposeful Living (Winston-Salem)
Earthaven (Black Mountain)
Eno Commons (Durham)
Kindness House (Mebane)
Kipling Creek (Raleigh)
LifeShare Community (Winston-Salem)
Long Branch Environmental Education Center (Leicester)
New Goloka (Hillsborough)
Noah Project of Asheville (Leicester)
Rosy Branch Farm (Black Mountain)
Solterra (Durham)
Spirit Cove (Murphy)
Spirit Cove —
Twelve Tribes Community in Asheville (Asheville)
Union Acres (Whittier)
Village Terraces Cohousing Neighborhood (Black Mountain)
Westwood Cohousing (Asheville)
The Wild Human Initiative (Boone/Asheville)
Zim Zam (Asheville)

OH-Ohio
Carpenter Village (Athens)
Catholic Worker Community of Cleveland (Cleveland)
Community House (Cincinnati)
Edges (Glouster)
Far Valley Farm (Amesville)
Grail Ecovillage (Loveland)
The Homestead at Denison University (Granville)
House of Peace Catholic Worker (Akron)
Knowledge Farm —
NEO Cohousing (Akron/Canton)
New Jerusalem Community (Cincinnati)
Oberlin Student Cooperative Association (Oberlin)
Ohio Bio-Enviro Settlements, Inc. (Canton)
Raven Rocks (Beallsville)
Sharing Community (South Bloomingville)
Storybook Shire (Pickerington)
Student Coop Organization (Athens)
Susan B. Anthony Women's Land Trust (Athens)
The Vale (Yellow Springs)
Wisteria (Miegs County)

OK-Oklahoma
Elohim City (Muldrow)
Pagan Intentional Community (Tulsa)
Sparrow Hawk Village (Tahlequah)

OR-Oregon
Aeirous / YewWood (Deadwood)
Alpha Farm (Deadwood)
Aprovecho Research Center (Cottage Grove)
Breitenbush Hot Springs (Detroit)
Cascadia Commons (Portland)
CedarSanctum (Portland)
Cerro Gordo Community (Cottage Grove)
CoHo Cohousing (Corvallis)
The Community in Ashland (Ashland)

Du-má (Eugene)
EarthSky Tribe (Independence)
Earthswell Farm (McMinnville)
Eugene Cohousing (Eugene)
Fordyce Street Cohousing (Ashland)
Friends and Neighbors (Portland)
Higher Ground Cohousing (Bend)
International Puppydogs Movement (Portland)
Jesuit Volunteer Corps NW (Portland)
Lichen (Wolf Creek)
Lost Valley Educational Center (Dexter)
Mountain Home (Coquille)
Nanish Shontie (Blachly)
Nomenus Radical Faerie Sanctuary (Wolf Creek)
Pagano (Pagano)
Peninsula Park Commons (Portland)
Southern Oregon Women's Network (Wolf Creek)
Students' Cooperative Association (Eugene)
Trillium Farm Community (Jacksonville)
Trillium Hollow (Portland)
Varsity House (Corvallis)
Walnut Street Co-op (Eugene)
We'Moon Land (Estacada)
Womanshare (Grants Pass)

PA-Pennsylvania
Altair Cohousing (Phoenixville)
Bryn Gweled Homesteads (Southampton)
Camphill Soltane (Glenmoore)
Camphill Special School (Glenmoore)
Camphill Village Kimberton Hills (Kimberton)
Casa Amistad (Philadelphia)
Concord Village —
Empty Nest Cohos (near or in town west of Philadelphia)
Eternal Cause Society (Philadelphia)
Father Divine's Peace Mission Movement (Gladwyne)
Greening Life Community (Shermans Dale)
Greenwood (Lansdowne)
The Hermitage (Pitman)
Himalayan Institute (Honesdale)
Hundredfold Farm (Gettysburg area)
Julian Woods Community (Julian)
Life Center Association (Philadelphia)
New Meadow Run Bruderhof (Farmington)
Spring Valley Bruderhof (Farmington)
Tanguy Homesteads (Glen Mills)
Yogoda Community Project (Philadelphia)

RI-Rhode Island
Brown Assoc. for Coop Housing (Providence)
New World Rising (Providence)
Providence Cohousing (Providence)

SD-South Dakota
Voice for the Voiceless —

TN-Tennessee
Agape Community (Liberty)
Dunmire Hollow Community (Waynesboro)
The Farm (Summertown)
IDA (Dowelltown)
Jump Off Community Land Trust (Sewanee)
Moonshadow (Whitwell)
Paradise Village (Whites Creek)
People of the Living God (McMinnville)
Pumpkin Hollow Community (Liberty)
Rose Creek Village (Selmer)
Short Mountain Sanctuary, Inc. (Liberty)
3Circles Community (Shelbyville)
Twelve Tribes Community in Chattanooga (Chattanooga)

TX-Texas
Adelphi (Quinlan)
Alpha Omega Christian Communities for the Chemically Injured (San Antonio area)
Central Austin Cohousing (Austin)
Christ of the Hills Monastery (Blanco)
Inter-Cooperative Council (Austin)
Mariposa Group (Bivins)
Oak Village Commons (Austin)
Peace Farm (Panhandle)

Rainbow Hearth Sanctuary and Retreat Center (Burnet)
San Antonio Cohousing (San Antonio)
Seneca Falls Co-op (Austin)
Sunflower Co-op (Austin)
Tomorrow's Bread Today (Houston)
Turn Cedars (Fort Worth)
Whitehall Co-op (Austin)
WindHaven (Pipe Creek)

UT-Utah
Utah United Order (West Box Elder)

VT-Vermont
Blue Moon Cooperative (South Strafford)
Burlington Cohousing (Burlington)
Champlain Valley Cohousing (Charlotte)
Cobb Hill (Hartland)
Earthseed (Putney)
Faerie Camp Destiny (Winooski)
Huntington Open Womyns Land (Huntington)
Meadowdance Community Group (Walden)
Montpelier Cohousing (Montpelier)
Ten Stones (Charlotte)
Twelve Tribes Community in Bellows Falls (Bellows Falls)
Twelve Tribes Community in Island Pond (Island Pond)
Twelve Tribes Community in Rutland (Rutland)

VA-Virginia
Abundant Dawn Cmty (Floyd)
Acorn Community (Mineral)
Aliantha (Vienna)
Ashland Vineyard Community (Ashland)
Blue Ridge Cohousing (Charlottesville)
Blueberry Hill (Vienna)
Catoctin Creek Village (Taylorstown)
CHUVA - Co-Operative Housing at the University of Virginia (Charlottesville)
Common Ground (VA) (Lexington)
Dayspring Circle (Floyd)
Earth Pod (Floyd)
EcoVillage of Loudoun County (Taylorstown)
ElderSpirit Community at Trailview (Abingdon)
The Gathering (Schuyler)
High Flowing Community (Riner)
Horizons ecoVillage (Nellysford)
Innisfree Village (Crozet)
KynHeartH (Floyd)
Learners Trek (Louisa)
Light Morning —
Light of Freedom (Willis)
Little Flower Catholic Worker Farm (Louisa)
Maat Dompin (Charlottesville)
North Mountain Community Land Trust (Lexington)
Oak Grove (Round Hill)
Olympus (Charlottesville)
Pod of Dolphins (Check)
The Quarries (Schuyler)
Shadowlake Village (Blacksburg)
Shannon Farm Community (Afton)
Springtree Community (Scottsville)
Summerglen Farm and Homestead (Floyd)
Twelve Tribes Community in Northern Virginia (Hillsboro)
Twin Oaks Community (Louisa)
Woodfolk House (Charlottesville)
Yogaville/Satchidananda Ashram (Buckingham)
Zephyr (Floyd)

WA-Washington
Apex Belltown Co-op (Seattle)
Bartimaeus Community of Meadow Wood (Bremerton)
Bellingham Cohousing (Bellingham)
Bright Morning Star (Seattle)
Dapala Farm (Elk)
Dearborn Commons Cohousing (Seattle)
Dragon Belly Farm (Pt. Ludlow)
Duwamish Cohousing (Seattle)
Emma Goldman Finishing School (Seattle)
Fan Lake Brethren (Elk)
Goodenough Community (Seattle)
Greenhouse (Seattle)
Holden Village (Chelan)

Hutterian Brethren (Reardan)
Ishayas (Stanwood)
Jackson Place Cohousing (Seattle)
The Love Israel Family (Kettle Falls)
Maxwelton Creek Cohousing (Whidbey Island)
Methow Center of Enlightenment (Twisp)
Olympia Housing Collective (Olympia)
Orca Landing (Seattle)
Port Townsend EcoVillage (Port Townsend)
PRAG House (Seattle)
Puget Ridge Cohousing (Seattle)
Rachana Retreat (Redmond)
River Farm (Deming)
RoseWind Cohousing (Port Townsend)
Salt Creek Intentional Community (Port Angeles)
Seattle's Intentional Community Program (Seattle)
Sharingwood Cohousing (Monroe, Snohomish County)
Sherwood Co-op (Seattle)
Sidhefire (Yelm)
Songaia Cohousing Community (Bothell)
Sunset House (Seattle)
Tacoma Catholic Worker (Tacoma)
Tacoma Eco-Village (Fircrest/Olympia)
Tolstoy Farm (Davenport)
Vashon Cohousing (Vashon)
Walker Creek Farm (Mount Vernon)
Westmerefolc Gepéode (Walla Walla)
Windward Foundation (Klickitat)
Winslow Cohousing Group (Bainbridge Island)
Wise Acres Cooperative Association (Indianola)
Yellow Plum Commons (Kennewick)

WV-West Virginia
A Better Way —
Gesundheit! Institute (Hillsboro)
Jupiter Hollow (Weston)
New Vrndaban (Moundsville)
People on the Way (Brandywine)
Sassafras Ridge Farm (Hinton)
Zendik Farm Arts Foundation (Marlinton)

WI-Wisconsin
Ambrosia Housing Cooperative (Madison)
Black Walnut Cooperative (Madison)
Casa Maria Catholic Worker Community (Milwaukee)
The Christine Center (Willard)
Dancing Waters Permaculture Co-op (Gays Mills)
Dreamtime Village (La Farge)
Emma Goldman's (Madison)
Friends Co-op (Madison)
Hypatia Housing Cooperative (Madison)
Lothlorien Co-op (Madison)
Madison Community Cooperative (Madison)
Ofek Shalom Co-op (Madison)
The Phoenix Co-op (Madison)
River Hayven (Colfax)
Sichlassenfallen (Milwaukee)
Summit Ave Cooperative (Madison)
Teaching Drum Outdoor School (Three Lakes)
The v2b Cooperative (Waukesha)
Village Cohousing (Madison)
Watersmeet Homes (Mukwonago)
Wellspring (West Bend)
Yahara Linden Gathering (Madison)

No State
Buddhist CoHousing (Unsited)
Chaneeg Channesch —
Everett (Southwest)
Gaia University —
Infinite StarLight Offering Visionary Ecovillages (Hawaii, Mexico, California, etc.)
Rewilding Community —
Tribe of Blank —
Twelve Tribes —
Buddhist CoHousing —

Åland Islands
Meridiana —

Argentina
Chacra Millalen (Chubut)
Ecovilla Asociación GAIA (Navarro)
Twelve Tribes Comunidad en Buenos Aires (General Rodriguez)

Australia
Backyard Tech (Macleay Island, QLD)
Canberra Cohousing (Canberra)
Cascade Cohousing (South Hobart)
Cennednyss Community —
Central Coast Community (Central Coast)
The Change (Glenorchy)
Co-ordination Co-op (Near Nimbin, NSW)
Cohousing Research and Education (Brisbane)
Crossroads Medieval Village (Yass, NSW)
Crystal Waters Permaculture Village (Conondale, QLD)
Danthonia Bruderhof (Inverell)
Earth First Australia (Norseman)
Freestone Hill Community (Warwick)
Gondwana Sanctuary (Tyagarah)
Hope Hill Community (Hobart)
Jesus Christians (Newcastle, NSW)
Jindibah (Bangalow, NSW)
Komaja (Bowral)
Kookaburra Park Eco-Village (Gin Gin/Bundaberg)
Melbourne Cohousing Network (Melbourne)
Molloy Ashram Retreat —
Mt. Murrindal Cooperative (W Tree Via Buchan, VIC)
Osho Mevlana Residential Community (Myocum)
Rosneath Farm (Dunsborough)
Shambala (Bellingen, NSW)
Somerville Ecovillage (Chidlow)
Sunrise Farm Community (W Tree Via Buchan, VIC)
THiNC (Tasmania)
Twelve Tribes Community at Peppercorn Creek Farm (Picton, NSW)
Twelve Tribes Community in Katoomba, Blue Mountains (Sydney)
Twelve Tribes Community in Oatlands (Oatlands, Sydney)
Village Community (Perth)

Austria
Familien-Gemeinshaft Rat & Tat (Frauendorf)
Keimblatt Oekodorf (Riegersburg)
Komaja (Vienna)
Lebensraum (Gänserndorf)

Belgium
Cohousing.be (Gent)
Communauté de la Vieille Voie (Liège)
De Regenboog (Brussels)
Samenhuizing West-Brabant (near Brussels)

Belize
La Flor del Agua Community (San Ignacio)
Namaste'... Multi-Cultural, Sustainable Living Community of Belize C.A., -

Bolivia
Comunidad Planetaria Janajpacha —

Brazil
Lothlorien - Centro de Cura e Crescimento (Palmeiras, BA)
Twelve Tribes Comunidade de Curitiba (Curitiba)
Twelve Tribes Comunidade de Londrina (Londrina)
Twelve Tribes Comunidade de Osório (Osório)

Canada
Alberta
Prairie Sky Cohousing Cooperative (Calgary)

BC-British Columbia
Cranberry Commons (North Burnaby)
Edenvale (Abbotsford)
Kakwa Ecovillage (McBride)
King Edward House (Vancouver)
Lofstedt Farm Community (Kaslo)
The Middle Road Community (Nelson)
Mulvey Creek Land Co-operative (Slocan)
Next Step Integral (Winlaw)
O.U.R Ecovillage (Shawnigan Lake)
Pacific Gardens Cohousing Community (Nanaimo)
Roberts Creek Cohousing (Roberts Creek (Sunshine Coast))

Spirit Dance Co-operative Community —
Talking Cedars Developments Ltd. (Tofino)
Twelve Tribes Community in Nelson (Nelson)
WindSong (Langley)
Yarrow Ecovillage (Chilliwack)

MB-Manitoba
Big Rock Farm (River Hills)
Northern Sun Farm Co-op (Sarto)
Twelve Tribes Community in Winnipeg (Winnipeg)

NS-Nova Scotia
Earthsea (Riverport)
L'Arche - Homefires (Wolfville)

ON-Ontario
Azania Alliance (Toronto)
Beaver Creek Homestead (Nolalu)
Dandelion Community Co-op, Inc. (Enterprise)
Downie Street Collective (Peterborough)
Dragonfly Farm (Lake Saint Peter)
Drumlin Co-operative (Brantford)
Headlands (Stella)
Lothlorien Farm (Ompah)
Morninglory (Killaloe)
Terra Firma (Ottawa)
Toronto Catholic Worker (Toronto)
Waterloo Co-operative Residence Inc. (Waterloo)
Whole Village (Caledon)

QC-Quebec
AAAA Cmty for Tender Loving Care (Montreal)
Le Novalis (Auteuil, Laval)
Maison Emmanuel (Val Morin)
Réseau des ÉcoHameaux et ÉcoVillages du Québec (Wotton)
TerraVie (Saint-Sauveur-des-Monts)

Colombia
Atlantis (Belen)

Costa Rica
H.O.M.E. Heaven On Mother Earth (Costa Rica)

Croatia
Komaja (Zagreb)

Denmark
Andelssamfundet i Hjortshøj (Hjortshoj)
Hertha (Galten)
Hesbjerg (Blommenslyst)
Ibsgården (Roskilde)
Mørdrupgård (Lynge)
Svanholm (Skibby)
Udgaarden (Sabro)
Valsølillegård (Jystrup)

Ecuador
Hospital Comunitario Waldos (Sangolqui)
Los Visionarios (Vilcabamba)
Sacred Suenos (Near Villcabamba, Loja)

France
Communauté de L'Arche (Roqueredonde)
Communaute du Pain de Vie (Valenciennes)
Dharma House Community Project —
Projetorgone (Neuilly sur marne)
Taizé Community (Taizé)
Twelve Tribes Communauté de Heimsbrunn (Heimsbrunn)
Twelve Tribes Communauté de Sus (Sus-Navarrenx)

Germany
Bread and Roses - Base community (Hamburg)
Bruderhof-Haus Holzland (Bad Klosterlausnitz)
Bruderhof-Haus Sannerz (Sinntal-Sannerz)
Dolphin Community (Herrischried-Niedergebisbach)
Ecovillage Sieben Linden —
Freie Christliche Jugendgemeinschaft (Lüdenscheid)
Kana-Gemeinschaft (Dortmund)
Komaja (Gottmadingen)
Komaja (Cologne)
Lebensgarten Steyerberg (Steyerberg)
Niederkaufungen (Kaufungen)

Projekt Eulenspiegel (Wasserburg/Bodensee)
ProWoKultA (Frankfurt)
Tribe of Likatien (Füssen)
Troubadour Märchenzentrum (Vlotho)
Twelve Tribes Gemeinschaft in Klosterzimmern (Deiningen)
UFA-Fabrik (Berlin)
Wawavox (Berlin)
WOGENO München eG (München)
ZEGG - Centre for Experimental Cultural Design (Belzig)
ÖkoLeA - Klosterdorf (Klosterdorf)

Greece
New Humanity Centre (Kalamata)

India
Atmasantulana Village (Maharashtra)
Auroville (Auroville)
Kerala Commune (Thavalam P.O.)

Ireland
Komaja (Limerick)

Israel
Hanoar Haoved Vehalomed - Tnuat Habogrim - Adult movement (Kibbutz Ravid)
International Communes Desk - ICD —
Kibbutz Ketura (Eilot)
Kibbutz Lotan (Southern Arava)
Kibbutz Migvan (Sderot)
The Kibbutz Movement —
Kibbutz Neot Semadar (Eilot)
Kibbutz Tamuz (Beit Shemesh)
Kvutsat Yovel
Ma'agal Hakvutzot (Nationwide)
Neve Shalom/Wahat al-Salam - Oasis of Peace (Doar Na Shimshon)

Italy
Arcobaleno Fiammeggiante - Tribe (Napoli)
Damanhur (Baldissero Canavese, Torino)
Hairakhandi Love Center (Pietralunga (PG))
Nomadelfia (Grosseto, GR)
Order of Saint Benedict (Rome)
Osho Miasto ---
Torri Superiore Ecovillage (Ventimiglia)
Utopiaggia (Montegabbione (TR))

Japan
Ittoen (Yamashina-ku, Kyoto)
Yamagishi-kai (Ayama-gun Mie Prefecture)

Kenya
Jesus Christians (Nairobi)

Macedonia, The Former Yugoslav Republic of
Komaja (Skopje)
Komaja (Ohrid)

Malta
Komaja (Sliema)

Mexico
Comunidad Los Horcones (Hermosillo)
Huehuecoyotl (Morelos)
La Senda Ecovillage (San Miguel de Allende, GTO)
Rainbow Peace Caravan —
Ventana Verde (Lo de Marcos)

Netherlands
CW Lismortel (Eindhoven)
De Hobbitstee (HW Wapserveen)
Dutch Cohousing Association - LVCW (Utrecht)
Elim (Evangelische Leefgemeenschap Immanuël) (RA Doorn)
Emmaus Haarzuilens (SJ Haarzuilens)
Gemeenschappelijk Wonen Nieuwegein (Nieuwegein)
Het Carre (Delfgauw)
Het Huis van Antonia ---
In Planning "Ecovillage" (Zuidbroek)
Komaja (HR Den Haag)
Landelijke Vereniging Centraal Wonen (HE Utrecht)
Vlierhof —
The Weyst (SV Handel)

Maps

Communities Directory

New Zealand
Anahata Community (Auckland)
Awaawaroa Bay Eco-Village (Waiheke Island)
Cambridge Terrace Community (Gisborne)
Chippenham Community (Christchurch)
Creekside Community (Christchurch)
Earthsong Eco-Neighbourhood (Waitakere)
Gricklegrass (Oxford)
Heartwood Community Incorporated Te Ngakau O Te Rakau (Christchurch)
Otamatea Eco-Village (Kaiwaka)
Rainbow Valley (Takaka)
Riverside Community (Nelson, South Island)
Shambala Eco-Resort & EcoVillage Community Project New Zealand —
Tararu Valley Sanctuary (Thames)
Tui Land Trust (Takaka)

Nicaragua
Abundance Farm (Nicaragua)

Nigeria
Federation of Arts for the Youth of Our Nation – Foundation (Lagos)
Palmgrove Christian Community (Abak, AKS)

Panama
Finca Buena Vida (Bocas del Toro)

Philippines
7th Millennium Community (somewhere in Maasin City)

Poland
Association for the Earth (Staroscin)

Portugal
Chumbaria (Central Portugal - Beiras Region)
Tamera - Healing Biotope I (Colos)

Romania
Ecotopia Romania (Stanciova, Timis)

Russian Federation
Aleskam (Razdolny Setl, Kamchatka)
Grishino Community (Leningradskaya oblast')
Kitezh Children's Eco-Village Community (Baryatinsky)

Serbia and Montenegro
Komaja (Novi Beograd)

South Africa
The Blue Crane —
Khula Dhamma —

Spain
El Bloque (La Nucia)
El Semillero (Valdeavero, Madrid)
Finca Luna (La Palma)
Guayrapá (Montral (Tarragona))
Twelve Tribes Community in Irún (Irún)
Twelve Tribes Community in San Sebastian (San Sebastian)
Walden Community (Madrid)

Sweden
Ekobyn Bålarna (Bergsjö)
Kadesh-biyqah (Arvika)
Lindsbergs Kursgård (Falun)
Stiftelsen Stjärnsund (Stjärnsund)
Tullstugan Collective Housing Unit (Stockholm)
Vialen —
Wäxthuset Väddö (Väddö)

Switzerland
Center of Unity Schweibenalp —
Komaja (Gersau)
Monte Vuala (Walenstadtberg)
Zentrum Waldegg (Wengen)

Turkey
Dedetepe Eco-farm (Canakkale)
Komun (Istanbul)

United Kingdom

England
Anarres Ecovillage (Northampton)

Ashram Community (Sheffield)
The Barn (Devon)
Beech Grove Bruderhof (Nonington)
Beech Hill Community (Devon)
Birchwood Hall Community (Worcs)
Canon Frome Court Community (Ledbury)
CoFlats Stroud (Stroud)
Cohousing Bristol (Bristol)
Community Forming (King's Somborne)
The Community Project (Lewes)
Corani Housing and Land Co-op (Leicester)
Cornerstone Housing Cooperative (W Yorkshire)
Darvell Bruderhof (Robertsbridge)
Earthworm Housing Co-op (Shropshire)
Frankleigh Co-Flats (Bradford on Avon, Wiltshire)
The Grail Community (Middx)
Grimstone Community (Devon)
Gwerin Housing Association (W Midlands)
Hockerton Housing Project (Southwell)
Jesus Christians (London)
Keveral Farm Community (Cornwall)
Komaja (Brighton)
Lee Abbey Aston Household Community (Birmingham)
Little Grove Community (Bucks)
Losang Dragpa Buddhist Centre (Todmorden)
Love & Nonviolence Commune (London)
Monkton Wyld Court (Dorset)
New Creation Christian Community (Northampton)
New Creation Christian Community (Birmingham)
New Creation Christian Community (Leicester)
New Creation Christian Community (Coventry & Warwickshire)
New Creation Christian Community (Milton Keynes)
New Creation Christian Community (Oxford)
New Creation Christian Community (London)
New Creation Christian Community (Brighton & Hove)
New Creation Christian Community (Bristol)
New Creation Christian Community (Liverpool)
New Creation Christian Community (Sheffield)
New Creation Christian Community (Leeds)
New Creation Christian Community (Preston)
The Othona Community (Essex)
Oxford Community (Oxford, Oxon)
Pathfinder Fellowship (London)
Pennine Camphill Community (W Yorkshire)
Plants for a Future (Blagdon Cross, Ashwater, Beaworthy)
Plants for a Future (The Field, Higher Penpol, Lostwithiel)
Redfield Community (Buckinghamshire)
Simon Community (London)
Springhill Cohousing Community (Stroud)
Stepping Stones Housing Co-op (Yeovil)
Town Head Collective (Sheffield)
Twelve Tribes Community at Stentwood Farm (Devon)
Two Piers —
The Well at Willen (Milton Keynes)

N. Ireland
Clanabogan Camphill Community (County Tyrone)
Columbanus Community of Reconcillation (Belfast)
Mourne Grange Camphill Village Community (County Down)
New Creation Christian Community (Belfast)

Scotland
Beannachar Camphill Community (Aberdeen)
Camphill Village, Newton Dee (Aberdeen)
Findhorn Foundation and Community (Findhorn)
Iona Community (Glasgow)
Isle of Erraid (Argyll)
Laurieston Hall (Castle Douglas)

Wales
Brynderwen Vegan Community (Swansea)
Centre for Alternative Technology – CAT (Powys)
Chicken Shack Housing Cooperative (Gwynecki)
Fox Housing Cooperative (Carmarthen Dyfed)
New Creation Christian Community (Swansea)

No Location
Welcome Here - Circle of Light Community Network – Rainbow Tribes (World Wide)

Jillian Downey – Great Oak Cohousing

About the Cross-Reference Charts

The data for the cross-reference charts was collected at the *Online Communities Directory* at *directory.ic.org* starting in October of 2004. It was initially populated with the data from last edition of the *Directory*. Communities were allowed to answer a series of questions and in most cases to comment on their answers. Unfortunately, there is not space in this book to include all such commentary but it is available on our website.

For each entry, the date that the community submitted their questionnaire is indicated. Some information (such as total population) may be outdated quickly, while other figures (such as year founded) are stable. Other information (such as diet) can be misleading in its simplicity when the reality is usually very complex. As mentioned before, tbe FIC is not in a position to verify the data each community submitted. We suggest using the data as a guide while keeping in mind that this is just a snapshot of how that community (or more precisely the person filling out the questionnaire) presented itself at the date listed.

An empty space by a community name indicates that they did not answer the given question.

A key to all abbreviations is found at the bottom of each page.

Name	State/Province	Country	Forming	Year Formed	Visitors Accepted	Open to More Adults	Open to More Children	Total Population	# Adults	# Children (<19yrs)	Percentage Women	Identified Leader	Leadership Core Group	How are Major Decisions Made	Join Fee	Income Shared/Indep.	Labor Required	Who Owns Land	Uses Cohousing Model	Survey Date
AAAA Cmty for Tender Loving Care	QC	Canada	F	2005		Y	y					Y	Y	C	Y	O	Y	clt		Mar05
Abbey of the Genesee	NY	USA		1951	Y	Y		35	35		0	Y	Y	L	N	S		cmty		Jan05
Abode of the Message	NY	USA		1975	Y	Y	y	62	50	12	55	Y	Y	O	Y	I	Y	other		Jan05
Abundance Farm		Nicaragua	F	2004	Y	Y	y	4	4				Y	O		P	Y	subgrp		Jan05
Abundant Dawn Cmty	VA	USA		1994	Y	Y	y	6	6	0	66			C	Y	O	Y	cmty		Mar05
Abundant Freek	CA	USA	F	1998	Y	Y	y	0						C		O	Y			Mar05
Acorn Community	VA	USA		1993	Y	Y	y	20	16	4	52	N	N	C		S	Y	cmty		Mar05
Adelphi	TX	USA																		Mar05
Adirondack Herbs	NY	USA		1990	Y	Y	y	9	8	1	33		Y		O	I	Y	other		Mar05
Agape	MA	USA		1982	Y	Y	y	9	5	4		Y	Y	C			Y	indiv		Mar05
Agape Community	TN	USA		1972	Y	Y	y						Y	C	N	O		cmty		Jan05
AinaOla	HI	USA	F	1999	Y	Y	y	1	1	0	0	Y		C	Y	I	Y	indiv		Jan05
Albuquerque Urban Ecovillage	NM	USA	F	2003	Y	Y	y	15	12	3	50			C	Y	I	Y	other	Y	Mar05
Alpha Farm	OR	USA		1972	Y	Y	y	6	4	2	33		Y	C		S	Y	cmty		Nov04
Alpha Omega Christian Communities F...	TX	USA	F			Y	y					Y	Y		O	Y	I	Y			Oct04
Altair Cohousing	PA	USA		1999															Y	Feb05
Ambrosia Housing Cooperative	WI	USA	F	2004	Y	Y	y	27	25	2	50				O	I	Y	nonprft		Mar05
American Buddhist Shim Gum Do Assoc...	MA	USA		1978	Y	Y	y	42	12	30	45	Y	Y		Y	O	Y	other		Mar05
Anahata Community		NewZealand		2000	Y	Y	y	31	21	10	40		Y	C		I	Y	nonprft		Mar05
Anarres Ecovillage		UK	F		Y	Y	y							C		O	Y	clt	Y	Jan05
Angels Valley	NY	USA	F	2000	Y	Y	y	1	1	0		Y			O	S	N	indiv		Nov04
Apex Belltown Co-op	WA	USA		1982	Y	Y	y	22	21	1	42		Y		Y	I	Y	cmty		Mar05
Aprovecho Research Center	OR	USA		1976	Y			16	14	2	43			C		I	Y	ind-lt	Y	Feb05
Aquarian Concepts Community	AZ	USA		1989	Y	Y	y	110	82	28	50	Y	Y		O	Y	O	Y	cmty		Mar05
ARC Retreat Center	MN	USA																		Mar05
Arcadia Cohousing	NC	USA		1991	Y	Y	y	60	44	16	66		Y	C		I	Y	cmty	Y	Feb05
Arcosanti	AZ	USA		1970	Y	Y	y	62	60	2	45	Y	Y		O	Y	I	Y	other		Nov04
Ascension Point	CO	USA	F	2005		Y	y	3	3					C			N			Mar05
Ashland Vineyard Community	VA	USA		1983		Y	y	14	12	2	58			C		O	Y	indiv		Feb05
Ashram Community		UK		1967	Y	Y		40	40		55	Y	Y	C	N	O		cmty		Mar05
Atlantis		Colombia		1970	Y	Y	y	25	13	12	50	Y	Y	C M L G O	N	SO	Y	cmty		Mar05
Attachment Parenting Village	IN	USA	F	2004	Y	Y	y	4	2	2	50			C			N			Oct04
Awaawaroa Bay Eco-Village		NewZealand		1994	Y			38	24	14	45			C	Y	I	Y	cmty		Mar05
Awakening to Grace	AR	USA	F	2005	Y	Y	y	2	2	0	50			C		I	Y	indiv	Y	Feb05
Azania Alliance	ON	Canada	F	2004	Y		y	7	6	1	80		Y	C		P	Y		Y	Feb05
Barking Frogs Permaculture Center	FL	USA	F	1997	N	Y	n	2	2			N	Y	C	O	IO		indiv		Mar05
The Barn		UK		1980								Y			O			nonprft		Mar05
Bartimaeus Community of Meadow Wood	WA	USA		2002	Y	Y	y	19	14	5	50			C	Y	I	Y	cmty	Y	Jan05
BBES (Bible Belt Exodus Society)	MO	USA	F	2004	Y			4	4	0	75	Y		C	Y	O	Y			Dec04
Beacon Hill Friends House	MA	USA		1954	Y	Y		20	20					C			N			Jan05
Bear Creek Farms	CA	USA	F	1985	Y	Y	y	4	4		50			O	Y	O	Y	other		Mar05
Beaver Creek	NY	USA	F	2004	Y	Y	y	4	2	2	25	Y	Y		Y	P	Y	indiv		Nov04
Beaver Creek Homestead	ON	Canada	F	2004	Y	Y	y	2	2	0	50	Y		C		I	Y	indiv		Feb05
Beech Grove Bruderhof		UK		1995	Y								Y	C		S	Y			Feb05
Beech Hill Community		UK		1994	Y	Y	y	12	11	1	75			C		I	Y	clt		Mar05
Bellvale Bruderhof	NY	USA																		Feb05
Berea College Ecovillage	KY	USA		2001	Y	Y	y									I	Y	nonprft	Y	Mar05
Berkeley Cohousing	CA	USA		1992	Y			28	23	5	72		Y	C		I	Y	cmty	Y	Feb05
A Better Way	WV/KY	USA	F	2004	Y	Y	y	5	2	3	50			C		P	N	cmty		Jan05

KEY *General:* Cmty = Community, Co-op = Cooperative, Coho = Cohousing
Canadian Provinces: AB = Alberta, BC = British Columbia, MB = Manitoba, NS = Nova Scotia, ON = Ontario, QC = Quebec
Country: Russian Fed = Russian Federation, UK = United Kingdom, USA = United States of America
Decisions: C = Consensus, M = Majority, L = Leader, G = Group of leaders or elders, O = Other.
Income: S = Members Share Income, I = Independently Handle Own Finances, P = Partial Income Sharing, O = Other.
Labor required: Members are expected to regularly contribute labor to the group.
Who Owns Land: clt = community land trust, cmty = community, indiv = individual, ldlord = landlord, subgrp = subgroup of members.
Survey Date: Date shown is when online questionnaire was completed or last updated by community.

Community Name	Eat Together How Frequently	What % of Own Food Is Grown	Common Diet	Dietary Practice	Alcohol Use	Tobacco Use	Education	Rural, Urban, etc.	# of Residences	Acres of Land	LGBT Memb Welcome	Spiritual Path	Primary Purpose and/or Focus
AAAA Cmty for Tender…	2–5 times/week		R	prim raw	seldom	prohib	C	R			Y	Y	love, eco/alt-tech, soul, healing
Abbey of the Genesee	Nearly all dinners	1–5%			occais	prohib		R				Y	Catholic monks contemplative
Abode of the Message		21–50%	O	prim veg	seldom	seldom	O	R		400	Y	Y	spiritual, retreat
Abundance Farm	Nearly all meals	21–50%	I	omni	seldom	seldom		R	3	346	Y	N	international, education, nature
Abundant Dawn Cmty	2–5 times/week	6–20%	I	other	occas	seldom		R	6	90	Y	N	loving and sustainable culture
Abundant Freek				omni	occas	occais		R		0	Y	N	independence via co-operation
Acorn Community	Nearly all dinners	21–50%	I	omni	seldom	seldom	H	R	3	72	Y	N	egalitarianism, process
Adelphi													
Adirondack Herbs	2–5 times/week	6–20%	I	omni	seldom	often		R	7	210	Y	N	conservation, tolerance
Agape	Nearly all meals	over 50%	C	prim veg	occas	prohib	O	R	2	32	N	N	prayer, simplicity, nonviolence
Agape Community	2–5 times/week	1–5%		omni			H	R	6	400		Y	
AinaOla	2–5 times/week	over 50%	C	raw only	seldom	prohib	H	R	10	3		N	sustainable primal diet/lifestyle
Albuquerque Urban Ecovill…			I	omni	seldom	seldom		U	16		Y	N	urban ecovillage/spirit/cohousing
Alpha Farm	Nearly all dinners	21–50%	I	omni	occais	seldom	Pb	R	4	280	Y	N	
Alpha Omega Christia…								O	0	0	N	Y	Christian MCS healing
Altair Cohousing										10			
Ambrosia Housing Co-op	Nearly all dinners	none	I	omni	occas	occas	Pb	U	1	0	Y	N	housing, food, family-friendly
American Buddhist Shim…	Nearly all dinners	1–5%	I	omni	seldom	prohib	O	U	1	1	Y	Y	Zen Buddhism / martial arts
Anahata Community	Nearly all dinners	1–5%	I	omni	occas	occas	Pr	S	15	30	Y	N	harmoniously living together
Anarres Ecovillage		over 50%	I	prim vegan	occas	occas	H	R			Y	N	ecological
Angels Valley		1–5%	I	omni	occas	occas	Pb	R	1	58	N	N	help cure suffering children
Apex Belltown Co-op	1–3 times/month	1–5%	I	omni	occas	occas		U	1		Y	N	affordable community living
Aprovecho Research Center	Nearly all dinners	over 50%	I	prim veg	occas	seldom		R	4	40	Y	N	sustainable living education
Aquarian Concepts Cmty	Nearly all dinners	6–20%	I	omni	prohib	prohib	C	O	23	25	N	Y	spiritual unity/global change
ARC Retreat Center													
Arcadia Cohousing	1 time/week	1–5%	I	omni	occas	seldom	Pr Pb	S	33	16	Y	N	cohousing
Arcosanti	Nearly all meals	21–50%	I	omni	occas	occas	O	T	12	4000	Y	N	building a prototype urban lab
Ascension Point			I		occas						Y	Y	conscious creation
Ashland Vineyard Cmty	1 time/week	1–5%	I	omni	occas	seldom	Pb	R	6	40	Y	Y	Quaker-oriented family cmty
Ashram Community	1–3 times/month		I					U	4		Y	Y	
Atlantis	Nearly all meals	over 50%		prim veg	prohib	prohib		R	5	175	N	Y	organic self-sufficient ecological
Attachment Parenting…			I	omni		prohib	O			0	Y	N	family focused
Awaawaroa Bay Eco-Village	1–3 times/month	6–20%	I		often	occas	O	R	15	420	Y	N	restoration & conservation
Awakening to Grace	2–5 times/week	6–20%	R	veg only	seldom	seldom		R	2	7	Y	Y	peaceful rural forest home
Azania Alliance	2–5 times/week	none	I	omni	occas	often	H	U	5	0	Y	N	dialogue, critical, radical
Barking Frogs Permaculture…	Nearly all dinners	6–20%	I	omni	occas	prohib		R	1.5	16			
The Barn	Nearly all dinners	21–50%		prim veg				R		15		Y	
Bartimaeus Community…	1–3 times/month	1–5%	I	omni	occas	seldom	H Pb	O	25	7	N	Y	faithbased missional community
BBES (Bible Belt Exodus…	1–3 times/month		I	omni	occas	occas		U				Y	sustainable urban community
Beacon Hill Friends House													
Bear Creek Farms	Nearly all meals	over 50%	R	other	prohib	prohib	H C Pr	O		26	Y	N	diet fitness organic creative
Beaver Creek	Nearly all dinners	6–20%	I	omni	occas	seldom	H C Pb	R	1	5	N	N	renewable & sustainable energy
Beaver Creek Homestead	Nearly all meals	over 50%	R	prim veg	seldom	seldom	H	R	3	65	Y	N	sustainability and learning
Beech Grove Bruderhof								R			N	N	spiritual revolution
Beech Hill Community	Nearly all meals	21–50%	I	omni	occas		Pb	R		7	Y	N	environmentally sustainable
Bellvale Bruderhof													following Jesus' teachings
Berea College Ecovillage								T	33	2	Y	N	ecological design
Berkeley Cohousing	2–5 times/week	1–5%	I	omni	often	seldom	Pr Pb	U	15	1	Y	N	
A Better Way	1–3 times/month	21–50%	I	omni	seldom	seldom	H C	S		50	Y	N	

KEY *Common Diet:* I = up to each individual, C = community shares a common diet, R = diet is somewhat restricted, O = Other
Dietary Practice: omni = omnivorous, prim = primarily, veg = vegetarian, raw = raw foods.
  Note: Some communities list omni and provide vegan options, some list vegan yet allow personal food without restriction. Take the label as a rough guideline.
Alcohol/Tobacco: occas = occasionally, prohib = prohibited
Education: System(s) used for childhood education. Pb = Public School, Pr = Private School, C = Private School at the Community, H = Homeschool, O = Other
Rural, Urban, etc. : R = Rural, U = Urban, S = Suburban, T = Small Town, O= Other
LGBT Memb Welcome: The community indicated that lesbians, gay men, bisexuals or transgendered people are welcome as members.
Spiritual Path: The community indicated it has a primarily spiritual or religious focus.

Charts

Communities Directory

Name	State/Province	Country	Forming	Year Formed	Visitors Accepted	Open to More Adults	Open to More Children	Total Population	# Adults	# Children (<19yrs)	Percentage Women	Identified Leader	Leadership Core Group	How are Major Decisions Made	Join Fee	Income Shared/Indep.	Labor Required	Who Owns Land	Uses Cohousing Model	Survey Date
Big Rock Farm	MB	Canada	F	1999	Y	Y	y	3	3	0	33			C		P	Y	indiv		Oct04
Birdsfoot Farm	NY	USA		1972	Y	Y	y	11	6	5	50	N	N	C	N	O	Y	cmty		Mar05
Black Elk House	MI	USA		1986	Y							Y	Y							Mar05
Blackberry	CA	USA		1988	Y	Y	y	8	5	3	80			C		P	Y	indiv		Jan05
The Blue Crane		South Africa	F		Y	Y	y	8	5	3	50			C	Y	I	Y	indiv		Oct04
The Blue House	GA	USA		2000	Y	Y		8	8	0	25	Y			Y	P	N	ldlord	Y	Nov04
Blue Moon Cooperative	VT	USA		1983				17	9	8	50			C	Y	I	N	cmty		Mar05
Blue Ridge Cohousing	VA	USA	F	2005	Y	Y	y				50			C		I	N		Y	Feb05
Blueberry Hill	VA	USA		1994	Y	Y	y	60	35	25	60		Y	C		I	Y	cmty	Y	Feb05
Bosch Co-op	MN	USA		1982	Y	Y		5	5	0	60			C		I	Y	cmty		Mar05
Boston Community Cooperatives	MA	USA		1999	Y	Y	y	9	9	0				C	Y	I	Y			Mar05
Bower House	MI	USA		1950	Y	Y	n	17	17		59	N	Y		Y		Y	cmty		Jan05
Breitenbush Hot Springs	OR	USA		1977	Y	Y	y	33	30	3	50		Y		Y	O	N	cmty		Mar05
Bright Morning Star	WA	USA		1979	Y			7	6	1	50			C		I	Y	indiv		Jan05
Brown Assoc. for Coop Housing (BACH)	RI	USA		1970	Y	Y	n	27	27		69	Y	Y	C	N	O	Y	cmty		Mar05
Bruderhof Communities, The					Y															Feb05
Bruderhof-Haus Holzland		Germany																		Feb05
Bruderhof-Haus Sannerz		Germany																		Feb05
Bryn Gweled Homesteads	PA	USA		1940	Y	Y		43		43	54				Y	IO		cmty		Mar05
Brynderwen Vegan Community		UK		2002	Y	Y	y	4	4	0	25			C		I	Y	indiv		Feb05
Buddhist CoHousing			F	2000		Y	y										N		Y	Feb05
Burlington Cohousing	VT	USA	F	2000	Y	Y	y						Y	O	Y	I	Y	nonprft	Y	Mar05
Cambridge Cohousing	MA	USA		1995	Y	Y	y	92	66	26	53		Y	C	Y	I	Y	cmty	Y	Mar05
Cambridge Terrace Community		NewZealand	F	2003	Y	Y	y	21	11	10	51		Y	C		I	Y	indiv		Mar05
Camelot Cohousing	MA	USA	F	2003		Y	y	28	23	5		Y	Y	C	Y	I	Y	cmty	Y	Jan05
Camp Sister Spirit	MS	USA	F	1993	Y	Y	y	4	3	1	80	Y	Y	C		I	Y	nonprft	Y	Jan05
Camphill Communities California	CA	USA		1998	Y	Y		29	28	1	49	Y				O	Y	cmty		Dec04
Camphill Soltane	PA	USA		1988	Y	Y		84	75	9	50	Y	Y	C		S	N	cmty		Jan05
Camphill Special School	PA	USA		1963	Y	Y		75	51	24	55		Y	C		S	N	cmty		Feb05
Camphill Village Kimberton Hills	PA	USA		1972	Y	Y	y	109	87	22	66			C		O	Y	other		Feb05
Camphill Village Minnesota, Inc.	MN	USA		1980	Y	Y	y	46	44	2	43		Y	C		O	Y	cmty		Mar05
Camphill Village USA, Inc.	NY	USA		1959	Y	Y	y	275	240	35	50		Y	C		O	Y	cmty		Feb05
Camphill Village, Newton Dee		UK		1960	Y	Y	y				43			C		S	Y	nonprft		Mar05
Canon Frome Court Community		UK		1979	Y	Y	y	45	30	15				C		I	Y	cmty		Oct04
Cantine's Island Cohousing	NY	USA		1990	Y	Y	y	28	18	10	61	N	N	C	Y	IO	Y	cmt-ind	Y	Feb05
Carrowmore Community	NY	USA	F																	Jan05
Casa Verde Commons	CO	USA		1997	Y	Y	y	71	53	18	60		Y	C		I	Y	cmty	Y	Jan05
Cascade Cohousing		Australia		1990	Y			34	20	14	55			C		I	Y	other	Y	Jan05
Cascadia Commons	OR	USA		1992	Y	Y	y	45	37	8	57			C		I	Y	cmty	Y	Mar05
Catholic Worker Community	MD	USA	F	1995	Y	Y		2	2		50			C			N			Jan05
Catoctin Creek Village	VA	USA		2000															Y	Feb05
Catskill Bruderhof	NY	USA																		Feb05
CedarSanctum	OR	USA	F	2000	Y	Y		4	4	0	25	Y				I	Y	indiv		Feb05
Center for Purposeful Living	NC	USA		1986	Y							Y				I	Y	cmty	Y	Oct04
The Center of Light Spirituality Ce...	MI	USA	F	1995	Y			2	2		50			Y C	Y	I	Y	nonprft	Y	Mar05
Central Austin Cohousing	TX	USA	F	2000	Y	Y	y				50		Y	C	Y	I	Y		Y	Nov04
Central Coast Community		Australia	F		Y	Y	y						Y	C	Y		N			Oct04
Central Florida Cohousing	FL	USA	F	2004		Y	y							C	Y	I	Y		Y	Dec04
Cerro Gordo Community	OR	USA		1970	Y	Y	y	42	37	5	35	N	N		Y	I		subgrp		Mar05

KEY *General:* Cmty = Community, Co-op = Cooperative, Coho = Cohousing
Canadian Provinces: AB = Alberta, BC = British Columbia, MB = Manitoba, NS = Nova Scotia, ON = Ontario, QC = Quebec
Country: Russian Fed = Russian Federation, UK = United Kingdom, USA = United States of America
Decisions: C = Consensus, M = Majority, L = Leader, G = Group of leaders or elders, O = Other.
Income: S = Members Share Income, I = Independently Handle Own Finances, P = Partial Income Sharing, O = Other.
Labor required: Members are expected to regularly contribute labor to the group.
Who Owns Land: clt = community land trust, cmty = community, indiv = individual, ldlord = landlord, subgrp = subgroup of members.
Survey Date: Date shown is when online questionnaire was completed or last updated by community.

Community Name	Eat Together How Frequently	What % of Own Food Is Grown	Common Diet	Dietary Practice	Alcohol Use	Tobacco Use	Education	Rural, Urban, etc.	# of Residences	Acres of Land	LGBT Memb Welcome	Spiritual Path	Primary Purpose and/or Focus
Big Rock Farm	Nearly all meals	6–20%	I	omni	seldom	seldom	H	R	6	80	Y	N	permaculture/human relationships
Birdsfoot Farm	Nearly all dinners	21–50%	I	prim veg	seldom	seldom	C	R	5	73	Y	N	learn/grow good food and friends
Black Elk House	Nearly all dinners	1–5%	C	veg only							Y	N	
Blackberry	Nearly all dinners	1–5%	I	prim veg	seldom	seldom	H	R	6	50	Y	N	ecology, homeschool, activist
The Blue Crane	2–5 times/week	none	C	other	occas	occas	C	O	4	2	Y	Y	alternative education
The Blue House	1 time/week	1–5%	I	other	prohib	occas		U	1		Y	N	affordable community living
Blue Moon Cooperativ...	1–3 times/month	1–5%	I	other			PrPb	R	5	165	Y	N	cooperation and conviviality
Blue Ridge Cohousing			I	omni			HCPrPb				Y	N	Charlottesville cohousing
Blueberry Hill	2–5 times/week	none	I	omni	occas	seldom	Pb	S	19	7	Y	N	neighborly living
Bosch Co-op	1–3 times/month	none	R	prim veg	seldom	prohib		U	1	0		N	cooperative community house
Boston Community Co-op	2–5 times/week	1–5%	R	prim veg	occas	prohib		U	1		Y	N	affordable community housing
Bower House	Nearly all dinners	1–5%		prim veg	prohib			O	1		Y		live cooperatively
Breitenbush Hot Springs	2–5 times/week	none	I	prim veg	seldom	seldom	O	R	35	155	Y	N	service health growth
Bright Morning Star	Nearly all dinners	1–5%	I	prim vegan	seldom	seldom	H	U	1		Y	N	supportive gay-friendly family
Brown Assoc. for Co-op	Nearly all dinners	1–5%		prim veg	often	often		U	2				to live cooperatively
Bruderhof Communities													sermon on the mount
Bruderhof-Haus Holzland													fighting selfishness
Bruderhof-Haus Sannerz													sermon on the mount
Bryn Gweled Homesteads	1–3 times/month	1–5%	I				Pr Pb	O	74	240	Y		cherish diversity neighborhood
Brynderwen Vegan Cmty	2–5 times/week	1–5%	C	vegan only	occas	prohib			1	1	Y	N	ethical veganism
Buddhist CoHousing								O			Y	Y	
Burlington Cohousing								U	32	6	Y	N	urban cohousing in Vermont
Cambridge Cohousing	2–5 times/week	1–5%	I	omni	occas	prohib	Pb	U	41	1	Y	N	
Cambridge Terrace Cmty	2–5 times/week	1–5%	I	omni	occas	seldom	Pb	T	5	3	Y	Y	faith indigenous families
Camelot Cohousing								T			Y	N	cohousing
Camp Sister Spirit	Nearly all meals	6–20%	I	omni	prohib	prohib	O	R	10	120	Y	Y	education, rental, events
Camphill Communities CA	Nearly all meals	1–5%	I	omni	prohib	occas	Pr	S	3	5	Y	Y	developmentally disabled
Camphill Soltane	Rarely	1–5%	I	omni	prohib	occas	Pr	S	8	50	Y	Y	sharing life with disabled
Camphill Special School	Rarely	1–5%	I	omni	prohib	seldom	Pr	R	11	70		Y	
Camphill Village Kimberton...	Rarely	21–50%	I	omni	seldom	seldom	C Pr	R	20	430	Y	Y	anthroposophy / lifesharing
Camphill Village MN	1 time/week	over 50%	I	omni	seldom	occas	H Pb	R	7	470	Y	Y	live with special needs adults
Camphill Village USA, Inc.	1–3 times/month	21–50%	I	omni	prohib	seldom	Pr	R	20	600	Y	Y	celebrating the human spirit
Camphill Village, Newton...	Nearly all meals	6–20%	I	omni	prohib		Pr	O	0	170	N	Y	anthroposophical community
Canon Frome Court Cmty	1 time/week	over 50%	I	omni			Pb	R	18	40	Y	N	farming, food and fellowship
Cantine's Island Cohousing	2–5 times/week	1–5%	I	omni	often	prohib	H Pr Pb	U	12	9	Y		private homes and shared cmty
Carrowmore Community													practical needs
Casa Verde Commons	2–5 times/week	1–5%	I	other	often	seldom	Pb	S	34	4	Y	N	cohousing community
Cascade Cohousing	2–5 times/week	1–5%	I	omni	occas		Pr Pb	S	14	2	N	N	coho to develop sense of cmty
Cascadia Commons	2–5 times/week	1–5%	I	omni	occas	prohib	O	S	26	3	Y	N	sharing, caring community
Catholic Worker Cmty		none						U			N	N	
Catoctin Creek Village									18	164			
Catskill Bruderhof													love your neighbor as yourself
CedarSanctum	2–5 times/week	6–20%	R	omni	seldom	prohib		U	1		Y	Y	co-creative Inspirators
Center for Purposeful...	1–3 times/month	none	O	prim veg	prohib	prohib	H	U	2	15	Y	Y	service & community
The Center of Light...	1 time/week	6–20%	I	omni	seldom	occas	Pb	R	3	52	Y	Y	spiritual ecovillage
Central Austin Cohousing	2–5 times/week	none	I		occas	occas		U	36	2	Y	N	cohousing
Central Coast Community						seldom		R			Y	N	community, ecology, education
Central Florida Cohousing								S			Y	N	building community
Cerro Gordo Community	Rarely	1–5%	I				Pb	R	13	1186			ecological cmty sustainability

KEY *Common Diet:* I = up to each individual, C = community shares a common diet, R = diet is somewhat restricted, O = Other
Dietary Practice: omni = omnivorous, prim = primarily, veg = vegetarian, raw = raw foods.
   Note: Some communities list omni and provide vegan options, some list vegan yet allow personal food without restriction. Take the label as a rough guideline.
Alcohol/Tobacco: occas = occasionally, prohib = prohibited
Education: System(s) used for childhood education. Pb = Public School, Pr = Private School, C = Private School at the Community, H = Homeschool, O = Other
Rural, Urban, etc. : R = Rural, U = Urban, S = Suburban, T = Small Town, O= Other
LGBT Memb Welcome: The community indicated that lesbians, gay men, bisexuals or transgendered people are welcome as members.
Spiritual Path: The community indicated it has a primarily spiritual or religious focus.

Charts

Communities Directory

Community	State/Province	Country	Forming	Year Formed	Visitors Accepted	Open to More Adults	Open to More Children	Total Population	# Adults	# Children (<19yrs)	Percentage Women	Identified Leader	Leadership Core Group	How are Major Decisions Made	Join Fee	Income Shared/Indep.	Labor Required	Who Owns Land	Uses Cohousing Model	Survey Date
Chacra Millalen		Argentina		1990	Y			5	4	1	20	N	N	C		N	I	Y	indiv		Mar05
Champlain Valley Cohousing	VT	USA	F	2000	Y	Y	y					Y	Y		O	Y	I	Y	cmty	Y	Oct04
Chaneeg Channesch		USA																			Mar05
The Change		Australia	F	2004	Y	Y	y	2	2	0	50	Y				Y	S	Y	indiv		Feb05
Chippenham Community		NewZealand		1970	Y	Y	y	12	9	3	40			C			I	Y	nonprft		Mar05
Christ of the Hills Monastery	TX	USA		1968	Y	Y		7	7	0	0	Y	Y	L		S	Y	cmty		Oct04
The Christine Center	WI	USA		1980	Y	Y		8	6	2	67	Y		O		I	Y	nonprft		Feb05
Chrysalis Co-op	CO	USA		1998	Y	Y	y	11	10	1	60			C		I	Y	nonprft		Feb05
CHUVA (Co-Operative Housing at the …	VA	USA		2003	Y	Y		10	10		40				Y	I	Y	ldlord		Nov04
City of the Sun Foundation, Inc.	NM	USA		1972	Y	Y	y	29	25	4	51	Y			Y	I	N	other		Mar05
Clare's House of Hospitality	IL	USA	F	1977	Y	Y	y	2	2	0		Y		C	N		Y	cmty		Feb05
Co-operative Effort	CA	USA	F	2004	Y	Y	y	4	3	1				C		P	Y	nonprft		Jan05
Coastal Cohousing	CA	USA	F			Y	y												Y	Feb05
Coastal Cohousing (Maine)		USA	F	2005		Y	y										N		Y	Jan05
Cobb Hill	VT	USA		1996	Y	Y	y	53	37	16	60			C		I	Y	cmty	Y	Feb05
CoFlats Stroud		UK	F	2005		Y	y	16	16		50			C	Y	I	Y	cmty	Y	Mar05
CoHo Cohousing	OR	USA	F	2002	Y	Y	y							C	Y	I	N		Y	Oct04
Cohousing Bristol		UK	F	2001		Y	y				46			C		I	Y		Y	Mar05
Cohousing for San Diego!	CA	USA	F	2004	Y	Y	y	28	28			Y		C	Y	I	N		Y	Oct04
Cold Pond Community Land Trust	NH	USA		2000	Y	Y	y	12	8	4	51	Y		C		I	Y	clt		Mar05
CoLibri Urban Housing Collective	MO	USA		1996	Y	Y	y	12	12		50			C	Y	I	Y	cmty		Feb05
Collegiate Living Cooperative	FL	USA		1931	Y			68	68		36	Y	Y		Y	I	Y	cmty		Mar05
Common Ground (VA)	VA	USA	F	1980	Y	Y	y	7	7		57			C	Y	I	Y	clt		Mar05
Common Ground Community	AL	USA		1980	Y			14	11	3	46			O		O	Y	other		Nov04
Common Place Land Cooperative	NY	USA		1980	Y	Y	y	24	13	11	48			C	Y	I	N	ind-lt		Mar05
Commons on the Alameda	NM	USA		1990	Y	Y	y	80	60	20	62	Y	Y	C		I	Y	indiv	Y	Dec04
Commonterra	ME	USA																		Mar05
Community of Light	CA	USA	F	1999		Y	y				55	Y	Y	C		O	N	cmty		Jan05
The Community Planet Foundation	CA	USA	F																	Oct04
The Community Project		UK		1999															Y	Mar05
Comunidad Los Horcones		Mexico		1973	Y	Y	y	24	19	5	32			O		S	N	indiv		Oct04
Comunidad Planetaria Janajpacha		Bolivia			Y	Y	y	100	100									other		Feb05
Concord Village	PA	USA	F	2002	Y	Y	y					Y		C	Y	I	N		Y	Jan05
Cooperative Roots	CA	USA		2003	Y	Y	y	15	15	0	50			C		I	Y	nonprft		Mar05
Corani Housing and Land Co-op		UK		1978	Y	Y	y	6	4	2	50			C		P	Y	other		Mar05
Cornerstone Housing Cooperative		UK		1993	Y	Y	y	12	12	0	50			C	Y	I	Y	cmty		Oct04
Coyote Crossing	CA	USA																	Y	Mar05
Cranberry Commons	BC	Canada		1992	Y	Y	y	48	36	12	58			C	Y	I	N	cmty	Y	Mar05
Crystal Waters Permaculture Village		Australia		1985	Y	Y	y	230	150	80	69	Y		O		O	Y	other		Mar05
CW Lismortel		Netherlands		1977	Y	Y	y	115	75	40	55					I	N		Y	Feb05
Dancing Bones	NH	USA		1997	Y	Y	y	7	7	0	58			C		I	N	other		Mar05
Dancing Rabbit Ecovillage	MO	USA		1993	Y	Y	y	23	23		48			C		I	Y	clt		Mar05
Dancing Waters Permaculture Co-op	WI	USA		1982	Y			12	9	3	55			C	Y	O	Y	cmty		Feb05
Danthonia Bruderhof		Australia																		Feb05
Dapala Farm	WA	USA	F	1990	Y	Y	y	2	2	0	50			C	Y	I	Y	indiv		Mar05
Darvell Bruderhof		UK																		Feb05
Davis Square Cohousing	MA	USA	F	2004															Y	Dec04
Dayspring Circle	VA	USA	F	1994	Y	Y	y	3	3	0	66			C	Y	I	Y	cmty		Mar05
Debs House	MI	USA		1967	Y							Y	Y							Mar05

KEY *General:* Cmty = Community, Co-op = Cooperative, Coho = Cohousing
Canadian Provinces: AB = Alberta, BC = British Columbia, MB = Manitoba, NS = Nova Scotia, ON = Ontario, QC = Quebec
Country: Russian Fed = Russian Federation, UK = United Kingdom, USA = United States of America
Decisions: C = Consensus, M = Majority, L = Leader, G = Group of leaders or elders, O = Other.
Income: S = Members Share Income, I = Independently Handle Own Finances, P = Partial Income Sharing, O = Other.
Labor required: Members are expected to regularly contribute labor to the group.
Who Owns Land: clt = community land trust, cmty = community, indiv = individual, ldlord = landlord, subgrp = subgroup of members.
Survey Date: Date shown is when online questionnaire was completed or last updated by community.

Community Name	Eat Together How Frequently	What % of Own Food Is Grown	Common Diet	Dietary Practice	Alcohol Use	Tobacco Use	Education	Rural, Urban, etc.	# of Residences	Acres of Land	LGBT Memb Welcome	Spiritual Path	Primary Purpose and/or Focus
Chacra Millalen	Nearly all meals	21–50%		prim veg	seldom	seldom	Pb	R	5	30			human relationships & ecology
Champlain Valley Cohousing			I	other				O	R	26	125	Y	N	rural cohousing near city
Chaneeg Channesch													
The Change	Nearly all meals	over 50%	R	prim vegan	prohib	prohib	H	O	0	222	Y	Y	self-empowerment life-centered
Chippenham Community	Nearly all dinners	1–5%	I	omni	occas	occas	Pb	U			Y	N	cooperative lifestyle
Christ of the Hills Monastery	Nearly all meals	6–20%	C	prim veg	occas	prohib	O	R	32	105	N	Y	prayer of the heart
The Christine Center	Nearly all meals	1–5%	C	prim veg	seldom	seldom	Pb	R	15	120	Y	N	private, group retreats
Chrysalis Co-op	Nearly all dinners	none	R	veg only	occas	seldom		U	1		Y	N	good food and kindness
CHUVA (Co-Operative…	1 time/week	none	I		occas	prohib		U	2		Y	N	student housing cooperative
City of the Sun Foundation…		1–5%	I	omni	often	often	Pb	R	30	157	Y	Y	independence
Clare's House of Hospitality	Nearly all meals	6–20%			occas	prohib		U	1			Y	to serve those in need
Co-operative Effort	Nearly all dinners		I		occas	seldom	H	R	0	16	Y	N	ecological community
Coastal Cohousing						prohib					Y	N	
Coastal Cohousing (Maine)								S			Y	N	cohousing south coastal Maine
Cobb Hill	2–5 times/week	6–20%	I	omni	occas	seldom	O	R	14	260	Y	N	sustainability, environment
CoFlats Stroud	2–5 times/week	none	I	omni	occas	seldom		T	14	0	Y	N	cohousing, consensus
CoHo Cohousing								T		7	Y	N	
Cohousing Bristol								U		2	Y	N	urban ecovillage
Cohousing for San Diego											N	N	cohousing
Cold Pond Cmty Land Trust	1 time/week	over 50%	I	omni	occas	seldom	H	R	5	275	Y	N	
CoLibri Urban Housing…	Nearly all dinners	6–20%	R	prim veg	occas	often		U	2		Y	N	affordable environmentally
Collegiate Living Co-op	Nearly all meals	none						U	2	1	Y	N	housing for UF Students
Common Ground (VA)	Rarely	over 50%	I	omni	occas	seldom	C	R	8	80	Y	N	homestead/cooperation/ecology
Common Ground Cmty	1–3 times/month	6–20%	I				PrPb	R	7	80	Y	N	community ecology humor
Common Place Land Co-op	1–3 times/month	6–20%	I	omni	occas	seldom	HPb	R	12	432	Y	N	stewarding trusterty consensus
Commons on the Alameda	2–5 times/week	none	I	omni	occas	prohib	PrPb	S	28	4	Y	N	enjoying our neighborhood
Commonterra													
Community of Light		over 50%		other				O	R			Y	N	peace, food, right livelihood
The Community Planet…													
The Community Project										23			
Comunidad Los Horcones	Nearly all meals	21–50%	C	omni	occas	prohib	H	R	12	240	N	N	
Comunidad Planetaria…									10	17			
Concord Village							HPb	T			Y	N	small town cohousing
Cooperative Roots	Nearly all dinners	1–5%	R	veg only	occas	occas		U	2		Y	N	
Corani Housing and Land…	2–5 times/week	1–5%	I	omni	occas	prohib	Pb	U	2		Y	N	cooperative housing
Cornerstone Housing Co-op	Nearly all dinners	1–5%	I	prim vegan	occas	occas		U	2		Y	N	direct action & mutual aid
Coyote Crossing										5			
Cranberry Commons	1 time/week	none	I	omni	often	prohib	Pb	U	22	0	Y	N	balance privacy and community
Crystal Waters Permaculture…	1–3 times/month	21–50%	I	omni	often	occas	Pb	R	83	640	Y	N	permaculture, educational tour
CW Lismortel	1–3 times/month	none	I	prim veg	occas	occas	Pb	U	60	5	Y	N	cohousing
Dancing Bones	2–5 times/week	1–5%	I		occas	seldom		R	4	40	Y	N	simple living, rural ecovillage
Dancing Rabbit Ecovillage	2–5 times/week	21–50%	I	omni	occas	seldom	O	R	12	280	Y	N	ecologically sustainable town
Dancing Waters Permacult…	1–3 times/month	6–20%	I	omni	occas		Pb	R	4	130	Y	Y	cooperative rural community
Danthonia Bruderhof													following Jesus' teachings
Dapala Farm	1 time/week	over 50%	I	prim veg	seldom	prohib	Pb	R	1	16	Y	N	education, co-op community
Darvell Bruderhof													fighting selfishness
Davis Square Cohousing								U		1	Y	N	urban cohousing
Dayspring Circle	2–5 times/week	6–20%	I	omni	occas	seldom		R	3	90	Y	N	stewardship and friendship
Debs House	Nearly all dinners		I	prim veg							Y	N	

KEY *Common Diet:* I = up to each individual, C = community shares a common diet, R = diet is somewhat restricted, O = Other
Dietary Practice: omni = omnivorous, prim = primarily, veg = vegetarian, raw = raw foods.
    Note: Some communities list omni and provide vegan options, some list vegan yet allow personal food without restriction. Take the label as a rough guideline.
Alcohol/Tobacco: occas = occasionally, prohib = prohibited
Education: System(s) used for childhood education. Pb = Public School, Pr = Private School, C = Private School at the Community, H = Homeschool, O = Other
Rural, Urban, etc. : R = Rural, U = Urban, S = Suburban, T = Small Town, O= Other
LGBT Memb Welcome: The community indicated that lesbians, gay men, bisexuals or transgendered people are welcome as members.
Spiritual Path: The community indicated it has a primarily spiritual or religious focus.

Charts

Communities Directory

	State/Province	Country	Forming	Year Formed	Visitors Accepted	Open to More Adults	Open to More Children	Total Population	# Adults	# Children (<19yrs)	Percentage Women	Identified Leader	Leadership Core Group	How are Major Decisions Made	Join Fee	Income Shared/Indep.	Labor Required	Who Owns Land	Uses Cohousing Model	Survey Date
Dedetepe eco-farm		Turkey	F	2002	Y	Y	y	2	2		50			C		I	Y	subgrp		Oct04
The Deliberacy…	MD	USA	F	2005		Y	y					Y		L	Y	P	Y	indiv		Mar05
Denver Catholic Worker	CO	USA		1978	Y	N	n	5	5	0	62	N	N	C	N	O	Y	ldlord		Mar05
Denver Space Center	CO	USA		1977	N			4	4		50	Y		C		O	Y	indiv		Mar05
Denver Urban Cohousing	CO	USA	F	2004		Y	y							C		I	Y		Y	Jan05
Detroit Cohousing	MI	USA	F	2002															Y	Mar05
Dharma House Community Project		France	F	2004	Y	Y	y									I	Y	other		Oct04
Dolphin Community		Germany		1995	Y	Y	y	8	6	2	50		Y	C		P	N	subgrp		Jan05
Domes, The	CA	USA		1972	Y	Y		28	28	0				C		O	Y	other		Mar05
Dorothy Day Cohousing	MO	USA																	Y	Mar05
Doyle Street	CA	USA		1990	Y			27	19	8	63			C		I	Y	cmty	Y	Mar05
Dragon Belly Farm	WA	USA	F	1989	Y	Y	y	6	4	2	50	Y			Y	I	Y	indiv		Feb05
Dragonfly Farm	ON	Canada		1971	Y	Y	y	4	4		25			C	Y	O	N	cmty		Feb05
Dreamtime Village	WI	USA		1991	Y	Y	y	13	9	4	22		Y	C		I	Y	clt		Jan05
Drumlin Co-operative	ON	Canada		1988									Y		Y	I	Y			Feb05
Du-má	OR	USA		1988	Y	Y	y	7	7		57	Y		C	Y	I	Y	other		Dec04
Dunmire Hollow Community	TN	USA		1973	Y	Y	y	7	6	1	33			C	Y	I	Y	other		Oct04
Dutch Cohousing Association (LVCW)		Netherlands																		Mar05
Duwamish Cohousing	WA	USA		1996	Y	Y	y	55	35	20	60	Y		C		I	Y	cmty	Y	Oct04
Earth First Australia		Australia	F	1995	Y	Y	y					Y		C		I	N	cmty		Oct04
Earth Pod	VA	USA	F	1991	Y	Y	y	2	2	0	50			C	Y	I	Y	cmty		Mar05
Earth Re-Leaf	HI	USA	F	1982	Y	Y	y	1	1	0				C		I	N	clt		Feb05
EarthArt Village	CO	USA	F	1998	Y	Y	y	3	3	0	33	Y		C	Y	O	Y	cmty		Jan05
Earthaven Ecovillage	NC	USA		1990	Y	Y	y	65	60	5	48			C	Y	I	Y	cmty		Mar05
EarthRight Farms	MO	USA	F	2000	Y	Y		2	2	0	0	Y		O	Y	P	Y	indiv		Mar05
Earthseed	VT	USA		1994	Y	Y	y						Y	C		I	N			Oct04
EarthSky Tribe	OR	USA	F		Y									C		O	Y			Jan05
Earthswell Farm	OR	USA	F	2004	Y	Y	y	2	2	0	66			C	Y	I	Y	cmty	Y	Nov04
East Bay Cohousing	CA	USA	F	1998	Y	Y	y				65	Y		C	Y	I	Y		Y	Oct04
East Lake Commons	GA	USA		1997	Y	Y	y	149	114	35	65			C		I	Y	cmty	Y	Mar05
East Ventura/West Valley CoHousing	CA	USA	F	2005	Y	Y											N		Y	Feb05
East Wind Community	MO	USA		1970	Y	Y	y	75	64	11	40					S	Y	cmty		Dec04
East-West House	CA	USA		1957	N	Y	y	13	13		50			C	Y	O	Y	ind-lt		Mar05
Eastern Village Cohousing	MD	USA		2002	Y	Y	y	90	76	14	66	Y		C		I	Y	indiv	Y	Jan05
Easton Mountain	NY	USA		2000	Y	Y		15	15		0	Y								May05
Echollective Farm	IA	USA	F	2003	Y	Y	y	5	4	1	75			C			N			Mar05
ECLIPSE	AZ	USA	F	2004	Y	Y	y										N			Jan05
EcoFarm Community	FL	USA																		Feb05
Ecotopia Romania		Romania	F	2000	Y	Y	y	5	4	1				C			O	Y	other		Jan05
Ecovilla Asociación GAIA		Argentina	F	1996	Y	Y	y	11	9	2	40			C		S	Y	cmty		Jan05
EcoVillage at Ithaca	NY	USA		1992	Y	Y	y	162	102	60	55			C	Y	I	Y	nonprft	Y	Mar05
EcoVillage Detroit	MI	USA	F	2003	Y							Y		O		I	Y	indiv		Mar05
EcoVillage of Loudoun County	VA	USA	F	1990	Y	Y	y	19	15	4	60	Y	Y	O	Y	IO	Y	other		Mar05
Ecovillage Sieben Linden		Germany		1989	Y	Y	y	71	47	24	52				Y	I	Y	cmty		Mar05
The Eden Project	CA	USA	F		Y	Y	y					Y	Y	C	Y	I	Y	nonprft		Oct04
Eden Ranch Community	CO	USA	F		Y	Y	y	2	2			Y	Y	C	Y	I	Y	cmty		Mar05
Edges	OH	USA		1992	Y	Y	y	13	8	5	62	N	N	C	Y	O	Y	clt		Mar05
Egrets' Cove	KY	USA																		Nov04
El Semillero		Spain	F	1993	Y	Y	y	5	4	1	44	N	Y		N	S	Y	other		Mar05

KEY *General:* Cmty = Community, Co-op = Cooperative, Coho = Cohousing
Canadian Provinces: AB = Alberta, BC = British Columbia, MB = Manitoba, NS = Nova Scotia, ON = Ontario, QC = Quebec
Country: Russian Fed = Russian Federation, UK = United Kingdom, USA = United States of America
Decisions: C = Consensus, M = Majority, L = Leader, G = Group of leaders or elders, O = Other.
Income: S = Members Share Income, I = Independently Handle Own Finances, P = Partial Income Sharing, O = Other.
Labor required: Members are expected to regularly contribute labor to the group.
Who Owns Land: clt = community land trust, cmty = community, indiv = individual, ldlord = landlord, subgrp = subgroup of members.
Survey Date: Date shown is when online questionnaire was completed or last updated by community.

Community Name	Eat Together How Frequently	What % of Own Food Is Grown	Common Diet	Dietary Practice	Alcohol Use	Tobacco Use	Education	Rural, Urban, etc.	# of Residences	Acres of Land	LGBT Memb Welcome	Spiritual Path	Primary Purpose and/or Focus
Dedetepe eco-farm	Nearly all meals	6–20%	C	veg only	prohib	prohib		R	3	3	Y	N	ecology and organic farming
The Deliberacy…	Nearly all meals	over 50%	I	omni	occas	seldom	H	T	1		N	N	super low impact 5-level build
Denver Catholic Worker	Nearly all meals	1–5%	I	omni	prohib	seldom		U	1		Y	Y	hospitality and simplicity
Denver Space Center	1–3 times/month	1–5%						U	1				good friends, interesting comp
Denver Urban Cohousing	Nearly all dinners	none	I					U			Y	N	Denver urban cohousing
Detroit Cohousing								U					affordable urban cohousing
Dharma House Community…	1 time/week	1–5%	C	veg only	prohib	prohib	Pb	R	5		Y	Y	Buddhist, eco, community
Dolphin Community	2–5 times/week	1–5%	R	veg only	prohib	prohib	Pr Pb	R	1	2	N	Y	helping others finding God
Domes, The	2–5 times/week	6–20%	I	prim veg				O	14	3	Y	N	student sustainable living
Dorothy Day Cohousing													hospitality, social justice
Doyle Street	2–5 times/week	none	I	omni	occas		Pr	U	2	0	Y	N	cohousing intentional neighbor
Dragon Belly Farm	1 time/week	21–50%	R	prim veg	occas	prohib	Pb	R	1	39	Y	N	sustainable living
Dragonfly Farm	Rarely	1–5%	I	omni	seldom	seldom		R	6	248	Y	N	provide alternatives
Dreamtime Village	1–3 times/month	6–20%	I	omni	occas	occas	H	R	4	80	Y	N	permaculture hypermedia
Drumlin Co-operative													affordable housing, community
Du-má	Nearly all dinners	1–5%	R	prim veg	seldom	prohib		U	1		Y	N	intentional/urban
Dunmire Hollow Community	1 time/week		I		occas	seldom	Pb	R	10	163	Y	N	small, rural, land stewardship
Dutch Cohousing Assoc…													cohousing
Duwamish Cohousing	2–5 times/week		I	omni	occas	seldom	H Pr Pb	U	23	3	Y	N	sharing neighbors
Earth First Australia	1–3 times/month	none	R	prim veg	prohib	prohib	C	T	10	30	Y	N	sustainable development
Earth Pod		21–50%						R		90	Y	N	
Earth Re-Leaf	Rarely	over 50%	I	prim vegan	seldom	seldom	HCPrPb	R	4	3	Y	Y	consensus, sustain., spiritual
EarthArt Village	2–5 times/week	21–50%	I	omni	occas	occas		R	1	480	Y	N	wholistic sustainability
Earthaven Ecovillage	Nearly all dinners	1–5%	I	omni	occas	occas	H O	R	30	320	Y	N	learning sustainable culture
EarthRight Farms	2–5 times/week	6–20%	I	prim veg	occas	often		R	1	80	Y	N	self- sustainability
Earthseed	Rarely	1–5%	I		seldom		Pr	R			Y	N	space for healing/connection
EarthSky Tribe					occas	often					Y	Y	rainbow family
Earthswell Farm	1 time/week	21–50%	I	omni	occas	seldom	Pr Pb	R	3	123	Y	N	live sustainably in community
East Bay Cohousing	1–3 times/month		I	omni	seldom	seldom		U			Y	N	make/find coho Berkley/Oakland
East Lake Commons	2–5 times/week	6–20%	I	omni	occas	seldom	H Pr Pb	U	67	20	Y	N	cohousing; organic gardens
East Ventura/West Valley Coho													creating a cohousing community
East Wind Community	Nearly all meals	21–50%	I	omni	occas	often	H Pb	R	15	1045	Y	N	cooperation and sharing
East-West House	Nearly all dinners	1–5%	I	prim veg	occas	prohib	O	U	1		Y	N	low income collective living
Eastern Village Cohousing	1 time/week	none	I	omni		prohib	Pr Pb	U	56	1	Y	N	cohousing
Easton Mountain				omni	seldom	prohib		R		175	Y	Y	
Echollective Farm	2–5 times/week	21–50%	I	prim vegan	occas			R		53	Y	N	sustainable farming & housing
ECLIPSE											N	N	lifestyle activist students
EcoFarm Community													
Ecotopia Romania	1–3 times/month	6–20%	I	omni	occas	occas	Pb	R	1	1	Y	N	model of sustainable living
Ecovilla Asociación GAIA	Nearly all meals	21–50%	C	veg only	prohib	seldom	H	R	6	46	Y	N	education & permaculture
EcoVillage at Ithaca	2–5 times/week	21–50%	I	prim veg	seldom	seldom	H Pr Pb	O	60	175	Y	N	ecological cohousing village
EcoVillage Detroit	Rarely	1–5%	I	omni	occas	seldom	O	U	3		Y	N	urban sustainable neighborhood
EcoVillage of Loudoun County	2–5 times/week		I	omni	occas	seldom	H	R	70	180		N	environmentalism, cohousing
Ecovillage Sieben Linden	Nearly all dinners	21–50%	R	prim veg	occas	occas	Pr	R	5	104	Y	N	ecology, communication
The Eden Project	2–5 times/week	over 50%	I	omni	occas	seldom	H	R	70	2240	Y	Y	sustainable ecovillage
Eden Ranch Community	2–5 times/week	6–20%	I	prim veg	seldom	seldom	H	R	1	65	Y	N	responsible stewardship
Edges	1–3 times/month	6–20%	I	omni	seldom	prohib	Pb	R	4	94	Y	N	permaculture alt energy balance
Egrets' Cove													ecological lifestyle
El Semillero	Nearly all dinners	21–50%			prohib	prohib	C	R	1	5	Y		sharing simple conscious

KEY *Common Diet:* I = up to each individual, C = community shares a common diet, R = diet is somewhat restricted, O = Other

Dietary Practice: omni = omnivorous, prim = primarily, veg = vegetarian, raw = raw foods.

   Note: Some communities list omni and provide vegan options, some list vegan yet allow personal food without restriction. Take the label as a rough guideline.

Alcohol/Tobacco: occas = occasionally, prohib = prohibited

Education: System(s) used for childhood education. Pb = Public School, Pr = Private School, C = Private School at the Community, H = Homeschool, O = Other

Rural, Urban, etc. : R = Rural, U = Urban, S = Suburban, T = Small Town, O= Other

LGBT Memb Welcome: The community indicated that lesbians, gay men, bisexuals or transgendered people are welcome as members.

Spiritual Path: The community indicated it has a primarily spiritual or religious focus.

Charts

Community	State/Province	Country	Forming	Year Formed	Visitors Accepted	Open to More Adults	Open to More Children	Total Population	# Adults	# Children (<19yrs)	Percentage Women	Identified Leader	Leadership Core Group	How are Major Decisions Made	Join Fee	Income Shared/Indep.	Labor Required	Who Owns Land	Uses Cohousing Model	Survey Date
ElderSpirit Community at Trailview	VA	USA	F	1999	Y	Y		36	36	0	81			C		I	Y	cmty	Y	Mar05
Elim (Evangelische Leefgemeenschap …		Netherlands		1975	Y			7	5	2	40			C		S	Y	clt		Feb05
Ella Jo Baker Intentional Community Co-op	DC	USA		2000	Y	Y	y	22	15	7	95				Y	I	Y	nonprft		Feb05
Elmendorf Christian Community	MN	USA		1994	Y	Y	y	125	50	75	52	Y	Y	C		S	Y	cmty		Mar05
Embassy of the Heavens	HI	USA	F	1998	Y	Y	y	5	5	0	40	Y	Y		Y	O	Y	nonprft		Nov04
Emerald Coast Village	FL	USA	F	2005		Y	y										Y			Feb05
Emerald Earth	CA	USA		1989		Y	y	15	11	4	50	N	N	C	Y	I	Y	nonprft		Dec04
Emma Goldman Finishing School	WA	USA		1996		Y	y	11	11	0	55			C		P	Y	clt		Oct04
Emma Goldman's	WI	USA		1996	Y	Y	y	15	15	0	55			C	Y	I	Y	cmty		Feb05
Empty Nest Cohos	PA	USA	F	2004	Y	Y	y							C		I	Y		Y	Nov04
Enchanted Garden	CA	USA		1980	Y			8	8		50	Y	Y	L		I	Y	other		Mar05
Eno Commons	NC	USA		1992	Y	Y	y	55	36	19	61			O		I	Y	other	Y	Mar05
Enota Mountain Village	GA	USA		1998	Y	Y	y	13	10	3	60	Y				O	Y	ind-lt	Y	Mar05
Eugene Cohousing	OR	USA	F	2003															Y	Jan05
Everett		USA	F	2005	Y			0	0					O		P	Y		Y	Feb05
Everything is Related	FL	USA	F	2004	Y	Y	y	2	2	0	50	Y		C		O	Y	other		Mar05
The Family	DC	USA		1968	Y	Y	y	15	12	3	40	Y				S	Y	other		Mar05
The Farm	TN	USA		1970	Y	Y	y	1175	1155	20	55	Y			Y	O	N	ind-lt	Y	Mar05
Federation of Arts for the Youth of…		Nigeria		1995	Y	Y	y	28	16	12	30					O	Y			Jan05
Fellowship Community	NY	USA		1966	Y	Y	y	150	120	30	70	Y		C		O	Y	cmty	Y	Feb05
Finca Buena Vida		Panama		1998	Y	Y	y	6	6	0	40	Y		O		I	N	indiv		Feb05
Finca Luna		Spain	F																	Mar05
Findhorn Foundation and Community		UK		1962	Y	Y	y	149	121	28	67	Y	Y	O		I	Y	other		Mar05
Firetender	HI	USA	F	2005	Y	Y	y	8	8	0	60	Y		C		I	Y	ldlord		Mar05
Fledgling Community	CO	USA	F	2004	Y	Y	y	1	1	0	25	Y		O		O	Y	indiv		Oct04
Footprint Ecovillage	CA	USA	F	2004		Y	y	1	1								N			Dec04
Fordyce Street Cohousing	OR	USA	F	2002		Y	y	16	11	5	70			C	Y	I	Y	other	Y	Jan05
Forming Intentional Community	ME	USA	F	2005		Y	y										Y			Mar05
Fox Hill Bruderhof	NY	USA																		Feb05
Fox Housing Cooperative		UK		1998	Y	Y	y	14	7	7	50	Y		C		I	Y	cmty		Feb05
Franciscan Workers / Companions in Cmty	CA	USA	F	1982	Y	Y	y	6	4	2	75	Y		C		O	Y	nonprft		Mar05
Frankleigh Co-Flats		UK		1995	Y	Y	y	28	13	15	54			C	Y	I	N	cmty		Mar05
Free for All The Skills Pool	CA	USA		1975	Y	Y	y				55	Y		L		I	N	other		Feb05
Free State Community	MD	USA	F	2005		Y	y	0	0	0				C	Y	I	Y	indiv	Y	Jan05
Freedom-Universe	AZ	USA	F	2004	Y	Y		1	1	0	0	Y		C		S	Y	cmty		Mar05
The Freeland Community	CA	USA	F	2004		Y	y	5	3	2	67	Y		C		S	Y			Nov04
Freestone Hill Community		Australia		1981	Y	Y	y	125	55	70	60	Y		O		I	Y	other		Mar05
Fresno Cohousing	CA	USA	F	2004		Y	y					Y				I	Y		Y	Jan05
Friends and Neighbors	OR/CA	USA	F	2004	Y	Y	y	2	2	0	50	Y	Y	O	Y	O	N	clt	Y	Oct04
Frog Song	CA	USA		1998	Y			72	50	22	60			C		I	Y	indiv		Mar05
Gaia Grove EcoSpiritual Cmty & Ecoretreat	FL	USA	F	1997	Y	Y	y	16	12	4	50			C	Y	P	Y	other		Mar05
Gaia University		USA	F	2004	Y	Y						Y			Y		N			Mar05
GaiaYoga Gardens	HI	USA	F	2003	Y	Y	y	2	2		50			C		O	Y	indiv		Mar05
Ganas	NY	USA		1978	Y	Y	y	91	88	3	49	Y		C		O	Y	subgrp		Mar05
Garden o' Vegan	HI	USA		1999	Y	Y	y	7	5	2	40	Y		C		I	Y	indiv		Mar05
Garden State Cohousing	NJ	USA	F	2003		Y	y	10	8	2	50			C	Y	I	Y		Y	Oct04
The Gathering	VA	USA	F	1972	Y	Y	y	7	7		60	Y	Y	C		P	Y	indiv		Mar05
Gemeenschappelijk Wonen Nieuwegein		Netherlands																	Y	Mar05
Genesee Gardens Cohousing	MI	USA		2003	Y	Y	y	14	8	6	50			C		I	Y	indiv	Y	Jan05

KEY *General:* Cmty = Community, Co-op = Cooperative, Coho = Cohousing
Canadian Provinces: AB = Alberta, BC = British Columbia, MB = Manitoba, NS = Nova Scotia, ON = Ontario, QC = Quebec
Country: Russian Fed = Russian Federation, UK = United Kingdom, USA = United States of America
Decisions: C = Consensus, M = Majority, L = Leader, G = Group of leaders or elders, O = Other.
Income: S = Members Share Dincome, I = Independently Handle Own Finances, P = Partial Income Sharing, O = Other.
Labor required: Members are expected to regularly contribute labor to the group.
Who Owns Land: clt = community land trust, cmty = community, indiv = individual, ldlord = landlord, subgrp = subgroup of members.
Survey Date: Date shown is when online questionnaire was completed or last updated by community.

Community Name	Eat Together How Frequently	What % of Own Food Is Grown	Common Diet	Dietary Practice	Alcohol Use	Tobacco Use	Education	Rural, Urban, etc.	# of Residences	Acres of Land	LGBT Memb Welcome	Spiritual Path	Primary Purpose and/or Focus
ElderSpirit Community…								T	30	4			mutual help in retirement
Elim (Evangelische…	2–5 times/week	none	I	omni	occas	seldom	Pb	T	3	3	N	Y	Christian community-life
Ella Jo Baker Intentional…	Rarely	none	I	omni	occas	seldom	Pb	U	6		Y	N	activists
Elmendorf Christian Cmty	Nearly all meals	over 50%	C	omni	seldom	prohib	C	R	20	2000	N	Y	evangelistic anabaptist
Embassy of the Heaven	2–5 times/week	1–5%	I	omni	occas	seldom	H	R	2	86	Y	Y	heavenly souls visiting earth
Emerald Coast Village								S		15	Y	N	green building village setting
Emerald Earth	Nearly all meals	6–20%	I	prim veg	occas	seldom	H	R	6	189	Y	N	getting in the mud
Emma Goldman Finishing…	Nearly all dinners	1–5%	I	veg only	occas	prohib		U	1	0	Y	N	social justice activism
Emma Goldman's	Nearly all dinners	1–5%		prim veg	seldom	seldom		U	1		Y	N	activist cooperative
Empty Nest Cohos		none						S		4	N	N	individuals or small families
Enchanted Garden	Rarely	1–5%	R	prim veg	prohib	prohib		U	1	0	Y	N	seed dreams grow here
Eno Commons	2–5 times/week	1–5%	I	omni	occas	seldom	Pr Pb	O	22	11	Y	N	being a good neighbor
Enota Mountain Village	Nearly all meals	21–50%	C	prim veg	prohib	prohib	Pb	R	27	60	Y	Y	conservation, education, love
Eugene Cohousing													
Everett			C			prohib		O	R			Y	Y	children community
Everything is Related	Nearly all meals	21–50%	O	omni	seldom	seldom	O	R	0	0	Y	Y	health, free time
The Family	Nearly all meals	none	C	omni	occas	prohib	H	U	1			N	Y	non-conventional Christians
The Farm	1 time/week	1–5%	I	prim vegan	seldom	seldom	H C Pb	R	60	1750	Y	Y	spiritual growth, nonviolence
Federation of Arts…					prohib	prohib	O	O			N	N	building lives through art
Fellowship Community	Nearly all meals	21–50%	C	prim veg	prohib	seldom	Pr	R	10	80	Y	Y	intergenerational elder care
Finca Buena Vida	Rarely	21–50%	I	prim veg	occas	seldom	H	R	3	102	Y	N	holistic health & the arts
Finca Luna													
Findhorn Foundation & Cmty	Nearly all meals	21–50%	I	prim veg	occas	prohib	O	R	70	30	Y	N	love all, serve all
Firetender	2–5 times/week		I	omni	occas	seldom		T	2	1	Y	N	healer community on Maui
Fledgling Community	Rarely	over 50%	I	omni	prohib	prohib	H C	R	2	90	Y	N	small animal & veggie farming
Footprint Ecovillage					prohib	prohib		R		25	Y	N	carrying capacity
Fordyce Street Cohousing	2–5 times/week	1–5%	I	omni	occas	prohib	O	T	13	1	Y	N	
Forming Intentional Cmty			I	prim veg	seldom	prohib		R			Y	N	community, sustainability
Fox Hill Bruderhof													following Jesus
Fox Housing Cooperative	Nearly all dinners	6–20%	R	prim vegan	occas	prohib	H	R	3	70	Y	Y	ecological/social change
Franciscan Workers…	2–5 times/week	1–5%	I	prim veg	occas	seldom	Pr	U	5		Y	N	hospitality and youth
Frankleigh Co-Flats	Rarely	none		omni	occas		H	R	6	8	Y	N	consensus, mutual respect
Free for All The Skills Pool	Rarely	none	I	omni	seldom	seldom	O	U	0	0	Y	N	share services
Free State Community		none	I		seldom	seldom	Pb	S	50	5	Y	N	affordable cohousing/community
Freedom-Universe	Nearly all meals	none	I	other	seldom	prohib	O	R	2	40	Y	Y	egalitarian cooperation
The Freeland Community	Nearly all meals		C			prohib	H	R			Y	Y	loving children above all else
Freestone Hill Community	Rarely	none	I	omni	seldom	seldom	C	T	42	15	N	Y	education school rural
Fresno Cohousing								U		2	Y	Y	cohousing, environment
Friends and Neighbors	Rarely	6–20%	I	omni	often	occas	C	O	4		Y	Y	yuppy and hippie friendly
Frog Song	2–5 times/week	1–5%	I	omni	occas	seldom	O	O	30	2	Y	N	cohousing community
Gaia Grove EcoSpiritual…	Nearly all dinners		O		occas	seldom	H	R		102	Y	Y	eco global health all-inclusive
Gaia University								O			Y	N	global learning community
GaiaYoga Gardens	Nearly all meals	6–20%	R	other	seldom	prohib	H	R	2	18	Y	Y	sustainable & holistic living
Ganas	Nearly all dinners	1–5%	I	omni	occas	seldom	Pr Pb	U	10	2	Y	N	love dialogue group wisdom
Garden o' Vegan	Nearly all meals	1–5%	C	vegan only	seldom	prohib	H	R	1	57	N	N	cruelty-free self-sufficiency
Garden State Cohousing											Y	N	NJ cohousing community
The Gathering	Nearly all dinners	none	I	prim veg	seldom	prohib		R	2	10	Y	Y	spiritual advancement
Gemeenschappelijk Wonen…													
Genesee Gardens Cohousing	2–5 times/week	1–5%	I	omni	occas	seldom		U	8				a retrofit cohousing community

KEY *Common Diet:* I = up to each individual, C = community shares a common diet, R = diet is somewhat restricted, O = Other

Dietary Practice: omni = omnivorous, prim = primarily, veg = vegetarian, raw = raw foods.

   Note: Some communities list omni and provide vegan options, some list vegan yet allow personal food without restriction. Take the label as a rough guideline.

Alcohol/Tobacco: occas = occasionally, prohib = prohibited

Education: System(s) used for childhood education. Pb = Public School, Pr = Private School, C = Private School at the Community, H = Homeschool, O = Other

Rural, Urban, etc. : R = Rural, U = Urban, S = Suburban, T = Small Town, O= Other

LGBT Memb Welcome: The community indicated that lesbians, gay men, bisexuals or transgendered people are welcome as members.

Spiritual Path: The community indicated it has a primarily spiritual or religious focus.

Charts

Community	State/Province	Country	Forming	Year Formed	Visitors Accepted	Open to More Adults	Open to More Children	Total Population	# Adults	# Children (<19yrs)	Percentage Women	Identified Leader	Leadership Core Group	How are Major Decisions Made	Join Fee	Income Shared/Indep.	Labor Required	Who Owns Land	Uses Cohousing Model	Survey Date
Gentle World Inc.	HI	USA		1970	Y	Y	y	10	10	0	54	Y	Y	O	Y	O	Y	cmty		Mar05
Gesundheit! Institute	WV	USA		1972	Y			9	9		44	Y	Y	O		O	Y	cmty		Mar05
The Gift Of A Helping Hand Charitable…	MI	USA		2002	Y	Y		500	200	300	60	Y	Y		Y	P	Y	clt		Nov04
Glen Ivy	CA	USA		1977	Y	Y	y	28	27	1	60	Y	Y	O		I	Y	other		Mar05
The Glenwood House in Portland, Maine	ME	USA	F	2004	Y	Y	y	11	9	2	50			O		I	N	other		Dec04
Gondwana Sanctuary		Australia		1986	Y	Y	y	15	12	3	57			C	Y	I	Y	other		Jan05
Goodenough Community	WA	USA		1981	Y	Y	y	40	30	10	60		Y	C		O	Y	indiv		Mar05
Grace	NY	USA	F		Y									C	Y	I	Y	cmty	Y	Nov04
Grail Ecovillage	OH	USA	F		Y							Y	Y		Y		Y	nonprft		Mar05
Great Oak Cohousing	MI	USA		2001	Y	Y	y	98	64	34	59			C		I	Y	cmty	Y	Oct04
Green River Community Land Trust	NY	USA	F	2005	Y	Y	y				66			C		I	N	clt		Mar05
Greenhaus Community	MA	USA		2003	Y			23	14	9	58		Y	C		I	Y	indiv		Feb05
Greening Life Community	PA	USA		1972	Y			11	11		45	Y	N	C	Y	IO	Y	cmty		Feb05
Greenplan	CA	USA	F	1994	Y	Y	y							O	Y	I	Y			Jan05
Gregory House	MI	USA		1995	Y	Y		23	23			Y	Y		Y	O	Y	cmty		Mar05
Gricklegrass		NewZealand		1973	Y	Y	y	10	6	4	67			C		P	Y	clt	Y	Dec04
Gwerin Housing Association		UK		1979	Y	Y	y	12	9	3	40			C	Y	O	N	cmty		Jan05
H.O.M.E. Heaven On Mother Earth		Costa Rica	F	2004																Oct04
Hanoar Haoved Vehalomed - Tnuat Hab…		Israel	F	1982	Y	Y					45			C		S	Y	cmty	Y	Mar05
Harbin Hot Springs	CA	USA		1972	Y	Y	y	162	150	12	51	Y	Y	C		I	N			Mar05
Harmonious Earth Community	NM	USA	F																	Mar05
Harmony Village	CO	USA		1992	Y	Y	y	62	44	18	66		Y	C		I	Y	cmty	Y	Mar05
Headlands	ON	Canada		1971	Y			5	5		40	N	N			I	N	other		Oct04
Healing Grace Sanctuary	MA	USA	F		Y	Y		1	1	0				C	O		N			Mar05
Hearthaven	MO	USA		1988	Y			6	6	0	50			C		O	Y	cmty		Feb05
Hearthstone	CO	USA		1998	Y	Y	y	72	53	19	55			C			Y	cmty	Y	Jan05
Heartsong	ME	USA	F	1999	Y	Y	y	6	6		33	Y	Y	L		I	N			Mar05
Heartwood Cohousing	CO	USA		1994	Y	Y	y	65	43	22	53		Y	C	Y	I	Y	cmty	Y	Oct04
Heartwood Institute	CA	USA		1978	Y	Y		103	100	3	60	Y	Y			O	N	ldlord		Feb05
Heathcote Community	MD	USA		1965	Y	Y		18	12	6	46	N	N	C	Y	O	Y	ind-lt		Mar05
Hei Wa House	MI	USA		1985	Y	Y	y	10	8	2	50			C		O	Y	subgrp		Feb05
The Hermitage	PA	USA	F	1987	Y	Y		2	2				Y			P	Y	cmty		Jan05
Hertha		Denmark	F	1993	Y	Y	y	45	33	12	67		Y	C		I	N	clt		Mar05
Het Carre		Netherlands		2002	Y	Y	y	107	69	38	65		Y	C		I	N	nonprft	Y	Oct04
Hidden Valley	MT	USA	F		Y	Y	y						Y	O		P	Y	clt		Mar05
Higher Ground Cohousing	OR	USA		1992	Y	Y	y	88	61	27	60		Y	O		I	Y	cmty	Y	Mar05
Highline Crossing	CO	USA		1991	Y	Y	y	75	53	22	65	N	Y	C		I	Y	indiv	Y	Feb05
Hillegass House	CA	USA		1979	Y	Y		9	8	1	50			C		O	Y	nonprft		Mar05
Himalayan Institute	PA	USA																		Mar05
Hockerton Housing Project		UK	F	1994	Y			20	9	11	44			C		P	Y	indiv		Jan05
The Homestead at Denison University	OH	USA		1976	Y	Y		12	12	0	50			O	Y	I	Y	nonprft		Feb05
Homewood Cohousing	MN	USA	F	1996	Y	Y	y	5	3	2	50			O		I	N	indiv	Y	Mar05
Hope Hill Community		Australia	F	2000	Y	Y	y	10	6	4		Y	Y	L		S	Y	ind-lt		Mar05
Hopewell Community	IN	USA	F	1996	Y	Y	y	2	2	0	50		Y	C	Y	I	N	cmty		Mar05
Hospital Comunitario Waldos		Ecuador		1996	Y								Y	C		P	Y			Mar05
Hudson Valley Ecovillage	NY	USA	F	2004		Y	y				55			C		I	N	cmty	Y	Mar05
Humanity Rising	CA	USA	F	1992	Y	Y	y		0	0	40	Y		C		I	Y	other		Mar05
Hummingbird Community	NM	USA		1986	Y	Y		12	12	0	45		Y		O	I	Y	cmty		Mar05
Hundredfold Farm	PA	USA	F	1998	Y	Y	y	18	13	5	50			C	Y	I	N	cmty	Y	Mar05

KEY *General:* Cmty = Community, Co-op = Cooperative, Coho = Cohousing
Canadian Provinces: AB = Alberta, BC = British Columbia, MB = Manitoba, NS = Nova Scotia, ON = Ontario, QC = Quebec
Country: Russian Fed = Russian Federation, UK = United Kingdom, USA = United States of America
Decisions: C = Consensus, M = Majority, L = Leader, G = Group of leaders or elders, O = Other.
Income: S = Members Share Income, I = Independently Handle Own Finances, P = Partial Income Sharing, O = Other.
Labor required: Members are expected to regularly contribute labor to the group.
Who Owns Land: clt = community land trust, cmty = community, indiv = individual, ldlord = landlord, subgrp = subgroup of members.
Survey Date: Date shown is when online questionnaire was completed or last updated by community.

Community Name	Eat Together How Frequently	What % of Own Food Is Grown	Common Diet	Dietary Practice	Alcohol Use	Tobacco Use	Education	Rural, Urban, etc.	# of Residences	Acres of Land	LGBT Memb Welcome	Spiritual Path	Primary Purpose and/or Focus
Gentle World Inc.	Nearly all dinners	21–50%	C	vegan only	prohib	prohib		R			N	Y	love sun nature integrity
Gesundheit! Institute	Nearly all dinners	6–20%	I	omni	seldom	seldom		R	3	310	Y	N	social justice, joy of service
The Gift Of A Helping…	Nearly all meals	none	R	prim veg	prohib	prohib	H	U	50	2	Y	N	economically disadvantaged
Glen Ivy	Nearly all meals	6–20%	I	omni	occas	seldom	Pb	R	19	70	Y	Y	intentional spiritual community
The Glenwood House…	1–3 times/month	none	I	omni	seldom	prohib	Pb	S	2	0	Y	N	holistic, urban haven
Gondwana Sanctuary	1 time/week	6–20%	I	prim veg	occas	occas	Pr Pb	R	11	100	Y	Y	meditation
Goodenough Community	1 time/week	6–20%	I	omni	occas	occas	Pr	O	10	60	Y	Y	a demonstration of transformation
Grace	Nearly all dinners	over 50%	R	veg only	prohib	prohib	HC	R		50	Y	N	non-violence, joy, authentic
Grail Ecovillage								O					ecological community
Great Oak Cohousing	2–5 times/week	1–5%						R	37	7	Y	N	
Green River Cmty Land Trust			I	prim veg	seldom	seldom		R	5	12		N	remove land from the market
Greenhaus Community	1 time/week	1–5%	I	omni	seldom	seldom	O	U	3	0	N	Y	Christian Jesus church gospel
Greening Life Community	1–3 times/month	6–20%	I	prim veg	seldom	seldom		R	8	136			growth in spirit; balance
Greenplan				prim vegan							Y	N	pacifist sustainable land reform
Gregory House	Nearly all dinners	none			prohib	prohib		U	1				student cooperative housing
Gricklegrass	Nearly all dinners	21–50%	C	omni	occas	seldom	O	R	1	28	Y	N	simple living, small farming
Gwerin Housing Association	1–3 times/month	1–5%	I	omni	often	often	O	O	5		Y	N	mutual support by consent
H.O.M.E. Heaven On…											Y	N	heaven on mother earth
Hanoar Haoved Vehalo…	1 time/week	none			occas		Pb				Y	N	socialist educational movement
Harbin Hot Springs	1–3 times/month	1–5%	I				H Pr Pb	R	50	1700	Y	Y	heart consciousness
Harmonious Earth Cmty													heart-centered, sustainability
Harmony Village	1 time/week	1–5%	R	omni	occas	seldom	Pr Pb	T	27	5	Y	N	cooperative sustainable living
Headlands	Rarely	21–50%	I	omni	occas	seldom	Pb	R	2	350			cooperative living and farming
Healing Grace Sanctuary	Nearly all dinners	over 50%		omni	prohib	prohib		R		85	Y	Y	spirit-led tribal village
Hearthaven	1 time/week	none	R	prim veg	occas	prohib		U	1		Y	Y	environment, reflection
Hearthstone	2–5 times/week		O	omni	occas		O	U	34	2	Y	N	
Heartsong				other	prohib	prohib		R		0	N	N	relationship, communication
Heartwood Cohousing	2–5 times/week	6–20%	I	omni	occas	seldom	H Pb	R	24	250	Y	N	cmty w/ people and nature
Heartwood Institute	Nearly all meals	1–5%	I	prim veg	seldom	seldom	H Pb	R	30	200	Y	N	education planetary healing
Heathcote Community	Nearly all dinners	6–20%		prim veg	seldom	prohib	H Pr Pb	R	8	112	Y		sustainable cooperative living
Hei Wa House	Nearly all dinners	1–5%	R	prim veg	seldom	prohib		U	2		Y	N	affordable cooperative housing
The Hermitage	Nearly all dinners	6–20%	C	prim veg	seldom	seldom		R	2	63	Y	N	queer creativity
Hertha	Nearly all dinners	over 50%	I				Pr	R	18	40	N	Y	
Het Carre								S	49		Y	N	ecology, cmty, spirituality
Hidden Valley	2–5 times/week	over 50%	O	other	seldom	seldom	C	R			Y	Y	self-sufficient
Higher Ground Cohousing	2–5 times/week	1–5%	I	omni	occas	seldom	Pb	S	37	7	Y	N	strong core group
Highline Crossing	2–5 times/week	1–5%	I				Pr Pb	S	40	4			learning to live as friends
Hillegass House	2–5 times/week	1–5%	I	omni	occas	prohib	Pb	U	3		Y	N	consensual group living
Himalayan Institute													
Hockerton Housing Project	Rarely	over 50%	I	omni	often	seldom	Pb	R	5	20	N	N	sustainable development
The Homestead at Denison…	Nearly all dinners	6–20%	I	prim veg	occas	occas		T	3	10	Y	N	sustainability and community
Homewood Cohousing	Rarely	1–5%	I	omni	occas		Pb	U	2	0	Y	N	
Hope Hill Community	Nearly all meals	over 50%	R	other	occas	prohib	H	R	4	200	N	Y	Amish-style community
Hopewell Community	Rarely	6–20%	I	prim veg	seldom	seldom	Pb	R	1	16	Y	N	community ecology
Hospital Comunitario Waldos								T					healthcare
Hudson Valley Ecovillage											Y	N	sustainable living&permaculture
Humanity Rising	Rarely	none	I		prohib	prohib		R		0	Y	Y	manifest spiritual principles
Hummingbird Community	2–5 times/week	1–5%	I	omni	seldom	seldom		R	6	486	Y	Y	co-creation and education
Hundredfold Farm	1–3 times/month		I	omni	occas		H	R	1	80	Y	N	

Charts

KEY *Common Diet:* I = up to each individual, C = community shares a common diet, R = diet is somewhat restricted, O = Other
Dietary Practice: omni = omnivorous, prim = primarily, veg = vegetarian, raw = raw foods.
   Note: Some communities list omni and provide vegan options, some list vegan yet allow personal food without restriction. Take the label as a rough guideline.
Alcohol/Tobacco: occas = occasionally, prohib = prohibited
Education: System(s) used for childhood education. Pb = Public School, Pr = Private School, C = Private School at the Community, H = Homeschool, O = Other
Rural, Urban, etc. : R = Rural, U = Urban, S = Suburban, T = Small Town, O= Other
LGBT Memb Welcome: The community indicated that lesbians, gay men, bisexuals or transgendered people are welcome as members.
Spiritual Path: The community indicated it has a primarily spiritual or religious focus.

Name	State/Province	Country	Forming	Year Formed	Visitors Accepted	Open to More Adults	Open to More Children	Total Population	# Adults	# Children (<19yrs)	Percentage Women	Identified Leader	Leadership Core Group	How are Major Decisions Made	Join Fee	Income Shared/Indep.	Labor Required	Who Owns Land	Uses Cohousing Model	Survey Date
Hutterian Brethren	WA	USA		1528	Y	Y	y	40000	40000			N	Y		N	S		cmty		Mar05
Hypatia Housing Cooperative	WI	USA		1963		Y		14	14	0	50			C	Y	I	Y	cmty		Oct04
Ibsgården		Denmark		1980	Y	Y	y	55	34	21	53		Y	C	Y	I	Y	cmty	Y	Oct04
IDA	TN	USA		1993	Y	Y	y	8	8		40			C		O	Y	ldlord		Mar05
In Planning "Ecovillage"		Netherlands	F		Y	Y	y							C		S	Y	cmty		Oct04
infinite star Light offering visionary…	CA	USA	F	1965	Y	Y	y	55	55		50	Y	Y	L		O	N	other		Mar05
Innisfree Village	VA	USA		1971	Y	Y	y	75	68	7	54	Y	Y	C M L G	Y	I	Y	other		Mar05
Inter-Cooperative Council (ICC-Mich)	MI	USA		1932	Y	Y	y	560	560	0	43	Y	Y		Y	I	Y	cmty		Mar05
Inter-Cooperative Council (ICC-Texas)	TX	USA		1937	Y	Y		187	187	0	50	Y	Y		Y	O	Y	cmty		Oct04
International Communes Desk (ICD)		Israel																		Mar05
International Puppydogs Movement	OR	USA	F	1993	N	Y	n	4	4		0	N	N	C	N	I				Feb05
Iona Community		UK		1938	Y	Y		28	23	5	57	Y	Y		O	I	N			Jan05
Jackson Place Cohousing	WA	USA		1996	Y	Y	y	61	45	16	62			C		I	Y	cmty	Y	Oct04
Jamaica Plain Cohousing	MA	USA		1999	Y	Y	y	55	42	13	60		Y	C		I	Y	cmty	Y	Mar05
Jesus Christ's Community at Hebron	NY	USA			Y	Y	y	12	9	3			Y	C		S	Y	cmty		Mar05
Jesus Christians(UK, USA, Kenya, Australia)	CA	Various		1980	Y	Y	y	26	23	3	33	Y		O	Y	S	Y	other		Oct04
Jindibah		Australia		1994	Y	Y	y	8	7	1	39		Y	C		I	N	other		Oct04
Jones House	MI	USA			Y			42	42	0		Y	Y				N			Mar05
Julian Woods Community	PA	USA		1970	Y	Y	y	19	16	3	33		Y	C	Y	O	N	clt		Mar05
Jump Off Community Land Trust	TN	USA		1990	Y			12	10	2	50			C	Y	I	Y	ind-lt		Mar05
Jupiter Hollow	WV	USA		1976	Y	Y	y	4	4	0	50				Y	O	Y	other		Mar05
Kakwa Ecovillage	BC	Canada	F	2003	Y	Y	y							C	Y				Y	Mar05
Kalani Oceanside Retreat	HI	USA		1973	Y	Y		40	40	0	57	Y	Y		Y	I	Y	other		Mar05
Kansas City Project	KS/MO	USA	F			Y	y	1	1				Y	C		I	Y	indiv		Jan05
Karen Catholic Worker House	MO	USA		1977	Y	Y	y	8	8		80		Y	C		O	Y	other	Y	Mar05
Kashi Ashram	FL	USA		1976	Y	Y	y	87	76	11	71	Y	Y			I	Y	cmty		Mar05
Keimblatt Oekodorf		Austria	F	2001	Y	Y	y	2	2	0	0			C		S	Y	cmty		Mar05
Kerala Commune		India	F		Y															Jan05
Khula Dhamma		South Africa	F	2003	Y	Y	y	4	3	1	34			C	Y	P	Y	cmty		Mar05
Kibbutz Lotan		Israel		1983	Y	Y	y	100	50	50	50					S	Y	cmty		Mar05
Kibbutz Migvan		Israel		1987																Mar05
The Kibbutz Movement		Israel																		Mar05
Kibbutz Tamuz		Israel		1987	Y	Y	y	61	26	35	48			C		S	N	cmty		Mar05
Kindness House	NC	USA		1993	Y	Y	y	14	12	2	57	Y	Y			O	Y	nonprft		Feb05
King Edward House	BC	Canada		1974	Y	Y		6	6	0	50			C		I	Y	ldlord		Mar05
King House	MI	USA			Y	Y		8	8		0	Y	Y		Y		Y	cmty		Mar05
Kingman Hall	CA	USA		1977	Y	Y		50	50	0	50		Y		Y	I	Y	other		Mar05
Kipling Creek	NC	USA	F	2005	Y	Y	y						Y		Y	I	Y	indiv	Y	Mar05
Kitezh Children's Eco-Village Community		Russian Fed		1992	Y	Y	y	55	22	33	50	Y	Y	C	N	S				Mar05
Knowledge Farm	OH	USA	F	2004	Y	Y	y							C		O	Y	nonprft		Jan05
Koinonia	GA	USA		1942	Y	Y	y	33	27	6	52	Y	Y			P	Y	cmty		Mar05
Komaja	MA	USA/Various		1978	Y	Y	y	300	260	40	50	Y	Y			I	Y	nonprft	Y	Mar05
Komun		Turkey		2001	Y	Y		14	14					C		P	Y	other	Y	Nov04
Kookaburra Park Eco-Village		Australia	F	2003	Y	Y		80	55	25	50		Y		Y	I	N	indiv		Oct04
Kvutsat Yovel		Israel		1999	Y	Y								C		S	N			Jan05
L'Academie Ynys Wyth	MO	USA	F	1996		Y	y	0	0	0										Mar05
L'Arche Mobile	AL	USA		1974	Y	Y		44	40	4	50	Y	Y			I	Y	cmty		Mar05
La Flor del Agua Community		Belize	F	1982	Y	Y	y	4	4	0	43	Y	Y	C	Y	I	Y	subgrp		Feb05
La'akea Community	HI	USA	F	2005	Y	Y	y	7	6	1	57			C	Y	P	Y	cmty		Mar05

KEY *General:* Cmty = Community, Co-op = Cooperative, Coho = Cohousing
Canadian Provinces: AB = Alberta, BC = British Columbia, MB = Manitoba, NS = Nova Scotia, ON = Ontario, QC = Quebec
Country: Russian Fed = Russian Federation, UK = United Kingdom, USA = United States of America
Decisions: C = Consensus, M = Majority, L = Leader, G = Group of leaders or elders, O = Other.
Income: S = Members Share Income, I = Independently Handle Own Finances, P = Partial Income Sharing, O = Other.
Labor required: Members are expected to regularly contribute labor to the group.
Who Owns Land: clt = community land trust, cmty = community, indiv = individual, ldlord = landlord, subgrp = subgroup of members.
Survey Date: Date shown is when online questionnaire was completed or last updated by community.

Community Name	Eat Together How Frequently	What % of Own Food Is Grown	Common Diet	Dietary Practice	Alcohol Use	Tobacco Use	Education	Rural, Urban, etc.	# of Residences	Acres of Land	LGBT Memb Welcome	Spiritual Path	Primary Purpose and/or Focus
Hutterian Brethren	Nearly all meals	over 50%		omni	occas	prohib		C	R			Y	Christian community
Hypatia Housing Co-op	2–5 times/week	1–5%	I	other	occas	occas	O	U	1		Y	N	affordable co-op living
Ibsgården	2–5 times/week	1–5%	R	omni	occas		Pb	S	2	1	Y	N	sociality
IDA	Nearly all meals	6–20%		prim veg	occas	occas	Pb	R	4	250	Y	N	art, ecology, queer revolution
In Planning "Ecovillage"		over 50%	R	omni	occas			C	R			Y	N	ecovillage in planning
infinite star Light…	Rarely	21–50%	R	vegan only	prohib	prohib	H C O	R			N	Y	pure vegan sans pet-animals
Innisfree Village	2–5 times/week	1–5%		omni	occas	occas	Pr Pb	R	12	600			
ICC – Michigan	Nearly all dinners	none	I	omni	occas	occas		U	18		Y	N	affordable quality housing
ICC – Texas	Nearly all dinners	1–5%	I	omni	often	occas		U	9		Y	N	affordable student housing
International Communes Desk													
International Puppydogs…	2–5 times/week	none	I		occas			U			Y		extended intimate family
Iona Community	Nearly all meals	1–5%		omni	seldom	seldom	Pb	R	6		Y	Y	sharing common life
Jackson Place Cohousing	2–5 times/week	1–5%		omni	occas	seldom		U	27	1	Y	N	meaningful life for all
Jamaica Plain Cohousing	2–5 times/week	1–5%	I	omni	occas	seldom	O	U	1	1	Y	N	urban cohousing near train
Jesus Christ's Community…	Nearly all dinners	6–20%	O	omni	prohib	prohib	Pb	R	3	26	N	Y	living in God's purpose
Jesus Christians	Nearly all meals	none	I	omni	occas	seldom	H	U	4		N	Y	faith, love, Jesus, sincerity
Jindibah	1–3 times/month	1–5%	I	omni			O	R	12	113	Y	Y	triple bottom-line balance
Jones House													
Julian Woods Community	1–3 times/month	6–20%	I				Pb	R	12	140	Y	N	
Jump Off Community Land…	1–3 times/month	6–20%		omni	occas	seldom	H	R	10	1100	Y	N	sustainable/eco stewardship
Jupiter Hollow	Rarely	1–5%	I			seldom	O	R	5	177	Y	N	neighbors and friends
Kakwa Ecovillage		6–20%	I	omni	occas	prohib		R	4	540	Y	N	multicultural ecovillage
Kalani Oceanside Retreat	Nearly all meals	1–5%	I	prim veg	seldom	seldom		R	23	113	Y	N	Hawaii, nature, culture, wellness
Kansas City Project					seldom	prohib		U	1	0	Y	N	social and political projects.
Karen Catholic Worker House	2–5 times/week	1–5%	I	prim veg	seldom	seldom	Pb	U	1		Y	Y	Catholic worker house
Kashi Ashram	2–5 times/week	none	R	veg only	prohib	prohib	C Pr Pb	T	5	80	Y	Y	spirituality, service, education
Keimblatt Oekodorf	Nearly all dinners	none	I	prim vegan	seldom	seldom	O	R	1	1	Y	N	peaceableness, sustainability
Kerala Commune													social upliftment
Khula Dhamma	Nearly all meals	6–20%	R	veg only	prohib	prohib	H	R	3	741	Y	Y	living the practice
Kibbutz Lotan	Nearly all meals	6–20%	I	kosher	seldom	seldom	C Pr Pb	R	54	143	Y	Y	Jewish ecological cooperative
Kibbutz Migvan													
The Kibbutz Movement													communal living
Kibbutz Tamuz	1 time/week	none	I	omni	occas	seldom	Pb	U	24		N	Y	communal involved socialist
Kindness House	Nearly all meals	21–50%	C	prim veg	prohib	prohib	H	R	7	68	Y	Y	spiritual practice and service
King Edward House	Nearly all dinners	1–5%	C	prim veg	occas	prohib		U	1		Y	N	cooperative living
King House	Rarely							U	1				
Kingman Hall	Nearly all dinners	1–5%	I	prim veg	occas	occas	O	U	1	0	Y	N	cooperative living
Kipling Creek			I					O		110	Y	N	cluster village
Kitezh Children's Eco…	Nearly all meals	21–50%	I	omni	seldom	seldom	C Pb	R	10	90		Y	noncommerical partnership
Knowledge Farm		over 50%					H C	R	0	75	Y	N	dissemination of knowledge
Koinonia	Nearly all dinners	1–5%	I	omni	prohib	occas	O	R	10	573	Y	Y	spirituality farming outreach
Komaja	2–5 times/week	1–5%	C	veg only	prohib	prohib	O	O	12	25	Y	Y	self-realization, radiant love
Komun	Nearly all dinners	none	I	other	occas	often		U	1		Y		anarchism, relationships
Kookaburra Park Eco-Village	1–3 times/month	1–5%	I	omni	occas	seldom	Pb	T	38	465	N	N	mainstream community
Kvutsat Yovel	Nearly all dinners	none	I					U	3		Y	Y	
L'Academie Ynys Wyth													Prytani Blue Star Paganism
L'Arche Mobile	1–3 times/month	none	I	omni	seldom	seldom	Pr	U	5		Y	Y	Christian community for mental
La Flor del Agua Community	1–3 times/month	1–5%	I	omni	seldom	prohib	H	R	0	9	Y	N	organic, tropical, living
La'akea Community	Nearly all dinners	over 50%	I	prim veg	seldom	seldom	O	R	7	23	Y	N	health, ecology, intimacy

KEY *Common Diet:* I = up to each individual, C = community shares a common diet, R = diet is somewhat restricted, O = Other

Dietary Practice: omni = omnivorous, prim = primarily, veg = vegetarian, raw = raw foods.

　Note: Some communities list omni and provide vegan options, some list vegan yet allow personal food without restriction. Take the label as a rough guideline.

Alcohol/Tobacco: occas = occasionally, prohib = prohibited

Education: System(s) used for childhood education. Pb = Public School, Pr = Private School, C = Private School at the Community, H = Homeschool, O = Other

Rural, Urban, etc. : R = Rural, U = Urban, S = Suburban, T = Small Town, O= Other

LGBT Memb Welcome: The community indicated that lesbians, gay men, bisexuals or transgendered people are welcome as members.

Spiritual Path: The community indicated it has a primarily spiritual or religious focus.

Charts

	State/Province	Country	Forming	Year Formed	Visitors Accepted	Open to More Adults	Open to More Children	Total Population	# Adults	# Children (<19yrs)	Percentage Women	Identified Leader	Leadership Core Group	How are Major Decisions Made	Join Fee	Income Shared/Indep.	Labor Required	Who Owns Land	Uses Cohousing Model	Survey Date
Lama Foundation	NM	USA		1968	Y	Y	y	10	10	0	40		Y	C		O	Y	nonprft		Mar05
Land Lifeways Farm	NM	USA	F	2003	Y	Y	y	2	2	0	50	Y	Y			I	Y	indiv		Mar05
The Land Stewardship Center	MI	USA	F	1991	Y	Y	y	3	3	0	33			C		I	N	ind-lt		Mar05
LandARC	MA	USA	F	2003	Y	Y	y				50			C	Y	I	Y	cmty		Feb05
Landelijke Vereniging Centraal Wonen		Netherlands																		Feb05
Laughing Dog Farm and CSA	MA	USA	F	2000	Y	Y	y	5	4	1	50	Y	Y	C		I	Y	indiv		Jan05
Lebensraum		Austria		2001	Y	Y	y	76	50	26	65		Y		Y	I	Y	indiv	Y	Mar05
Lester House	MI	USA			Y			15	15			Y	Y				N			Mar05
Liberty Village	MD	USA		1989	Y	Y	y	39	29	10	54		Y	C		I	Y	cmty	Y	Mar05
Lifeseed	CO	USA	F	1999	Y								Y		O	Y	I	Y	cmty	Feb05
LifeShare Community	NC	USA	F	2005		Y	y	1	1	0	100			C		S	Y	cmty		Mar05
Light as Color Foundation	CO	USA	F	1997	Y	Y	y	2	2	0	100	Y		C		I	Y	indiv		Nov04
Light Morning	VA	USA		1973	Y	Y	y	11	8	3	50		Y	C		I	Y	clt		Mar05
Light of Freedom	VA	USA	F	1993	Y	Y	y	6	6		50		Y	C		I	Y	cmty		Nov04
Linder House	MI	USA		1989	Y	Y		20	20			Y	Y			I	Y			Mar05
Little Flower Catholic Worker Farm	VA	USA		1996	Y	Y	y	8	5	3	50			C		S	Y	clt		Feb05
Lofstedt Farm Community	BC	Canada	F	1984	Y	Y	y	9	6	3	50	Y	Y	L	Y	I	Y	indiv		Mar05
Los Angeles Eco-Village	CA	USA		1993	Y	Y	y	36	35	1	50		Y	C	Y	I	Y	nonprft	Y	Feb05
Los Visionarios		Ecuador	F	1996	Y	Y	y	3	2	1	50			C	Y	P	Y	other		Mar05
Lost Valley Educational Center	OR	USA		1988	Y	Y	y	24	18	6	50		Y	C	Y	O	Y	nonprft		Mar05
Lothlorien Co-op	WI	USA		1973	Y	Y	y	32	32	0	50			C	Y	I	Y	cmty		Mar05
Lothlorien Farm	ON	Canada		1972	Y	Y	y	6	6	0	50			C	Y	I	N	cmty		Oct04
Lothlorien Nature Sanctuary	IN	USA		1983	Y	Y	y						Y		Y	I	N	cmty		Jan05
Love & Nonviolence Commune		UK	F		Y	Y	y	1	1	0				C			Y			Feb05
The Love Israel Family	WA	USA	F	1968	Y	Y	y	13	13	0	40	Y	Y			S	Y	indiv		Mar05
Luther House	MI	USA			Y	Y		50	50			Y	Y		Y		Y			Mar05
Lyons Valley Village	CO	USA	F	2004	Y	Y	y							C	Y	I	Y	cmty	Y	Jan05
Ma Yoga Shakti International Mission	NY/FL	USA		1979	Y	Y							Y		O	O	N	other		Jan05
Ma'agal Hakvutzot		Israel																		Mar05
Madison Community Cooperative	WI	USA		1968	Y	Y	y	215	200	15	50		Y	C	Y	I	Y	cmty		Oct04
Madre Grande Monastery	CA	USA	F	1975	Y	Y	y	2	2		60	Y	Y			O	Y	nonprft		Mar05
Magic	CA	USA		1972	Y	Y	y	17	14	3	50		Y	C		O	Y	nonprft		Jan05
Maison Emmanuel	QC	Canada		1982	Y	Y	y	50	40	10	54		Y	C		O	Y	cmty		Feb05
Malu 'Aina	HI	USA		1979	Y	Y		4	4	0	50	Y	Y	C			Y	cmty		Mar05
Manitou Arbor Ecovillage	MI	USA	F																Y	Feb05
Manzanita Village	AZ	USA		1994	Y	Y	y	24	18	6	50	N	Y	C	Y	IO	Y	other	Y	Mar05
Maple Ridge Bruderhof	NY	USA																		Feb05
Marathon Co-op	CA	USA		1988	Y	Y	y								Y	I		cmty		Mar05
Mariposa Group	TX	USA	F	1984	Y	Y	y	8	6	2	50	Y			O	Y	I	Y	indiv	Y	Jan05
Mariposa Grove	CA	USA		1999	Y	Y	y	12	9	3	56			C	Y	I	Y	ind-lt	Y	Jan05
Masala Co-op	CO	USA		1999	Y	Y	y	11	11		55	N	N	C	Y	I		nonprft		Mar05
Maxwelton Creek Cohousing	WA	USA		1992	Y		y	19	12	7	58			C		I	Y	cmty	Y	Mar05
Meadowdance Community Group	VT	USA		1997	Y	Y		13	6	7	67			C		P	Y	cmty		Jan05
Melbourne Cohousing Network		Australia	F																Y	Oct04
Mele Nahiku	HI	USA		2001	Y			6	4	2	50			C		S	Y	indiv		Mar05
Meridiana		Åland Islands	F	2004		Y	y													Mar05
Merry Fox Community	MI	USA		1999	Y	Y	y	6	6	0	33		Y			P	Y	ldlord		Nov04
Methow Center of Enlightenment	WA	USA	F	1990		Y	y	1	1			Y								Mar05
Metro Cohousing at Culver Way	MO	USA	F	1999	Y	Y	y				59			C	Y		N	other	Y	Feb05

KEY *General:* Cmty = Community, Co-op = Cooperative, Coho = Cohousing
Canadian Provinces: AB = Alberta, BC = British Columbia, MB = Manitoba, NS = Nova Scotia, ON = Ontario, QC = Quebec
Country: Russian Fed = Russian Federation, UK = United Kingdom, USA = United States of America
Decisions: C = Consensus, M = Majority, L = Leader, G = Group of leaders or elders, O = Other.
Income: S = Members Share Income, I = Independently Handle Own Finances, P = Partial Income Sharing, O = Other.
Labor required: Members are expected to regularly contribute labor to the group.
Who Owns Land: clt = community land trust, cmty = community, indiv = individual, ldlord = landlord, subgrp = subgroup of members.
Survey Date: Date shown is when online questionnaire was completed or last updated by community.

Community Name	Eat Together How Frequently	What % of Own Food Is Grown	Common Diet	Dietary Practice	Alcohol Use	Tobacco Use	Education	Rural, Urban, etc.	# of Residences	Acres of Land	LGBT Memb Welcome	Spiritual Path	Primary Purpose and/or Focus
Lama Foundation	Nearly all meals	1–5%	I	veg only	seldom	seldom		R	10	105	Y	Y	spiritual community and school
Land Lifeways Farm	1 time/week	over 50%	I	omni	prohib	occas	O	R	3	15	Y	N	live from the land
The Land Stewardship Center	1–3 times/month	6–20%	I	prim vegan	occas	prohib	Pb	R	2	110	Y	N	land stewardship
LandARC	2–5 times/week	over 50%	I	omni	occas	occas	C	R	15	100	Y	N	community, sustainability
Landelijke Vereniging…													
Laughing Dog Farm and CSA	1–3 times/month	over 50%	C	prim veg	occas	seldom	Pr	R	2	9	Y	N	CSA, family, land stewardship
Lebensraum	1 time/week	1–5%	I	prim veg	occas	seldom	Pb	T	31	4	Y	N	cohousing
Lester House			C	veg only							Y	N	
Liberty Village	2–5 times/week	1–5%	I	omni	seldom	seldom	H Pr Pb	R	18	23	Y	N	a caring community
Lifeseed		6–20%				seldom		R		350	Y	N	creative expression
LifeShare Community	Nearly all meals	none	R	prim veg	occas	prohib	C	O		0	N	Y	
Light as Color Foundation	Rarely	21–50%	I	prim veg	occas	seldom		R	2	2	Y	N	visual arts, nature, holism
Light Morning	Nearly all meals	21–50%	C	veg only	seldom	seldom	H	R	5	150	Y	Y	transformational vortex
Light of Freedom	2–5 times/week	6–20%	I	omni	seldom	seldom		R	2	40	Y	Y	God realized oneness
Linder House	2–5 times/week		I	omni							Y	N	
Little Flower Catholic…	Nearly all meals	6–20%	I	prim veg	occas	seldom	H	R	2	17	Y	Y	radical Christian non-violence
Lofstedt Farm Community	Nearly all meals	over 50%		omni	occas	seldom	Pr	R	5	60	N	Y	biodynamic agriculture
Los Angeles Eco-Village	1 time/week	1–5%	I	prim veg	occas	prohib	Pb	U	46	0	Y	N	cooperative and ecological
Los Visionarios	Nearly all meals	21–50%	I	prim veg	occas	seldom	H	R	3	17	Y	Y	sustainable & spiritual focus
Lost Valley Educational Center	Nearly all meals	6–20%	I	prim veg	seldom	prohib	H C Pb	R	13	87	Y	N	ecology, sustainable culture
Lothlorien Co-op	Nearly all dinners	1–5%	I	veg only	occas	prohib		U	1	0	Y	N	veggie, enviro, LGBT-friendly
Lothlorien Farm	Rarely	1–5%	I	omni	occas	seldom	Pb	R	6	700	Y	N	land stewardship, friendship
Lothlorien Nature Sanctuary								O	O	109	Y	N	cooperative stewardship
Love & Nonviolence…			R	veg only	occas	seldom	H	U			Y	Y	revolutionary nonviolence
The Love Israel Family	Nearly all meals	6–20%	I	omni	occas	prohib	H	R	1	50	N	Y	manifesting love and oneness
Luther House	2–5 times/week		I	omni					2		Y	N	
Lyons Valley Village		none	I					T	18	2	Y	N	cohousing model
Ma Yoga Shakti Inter…	Rarely	none	O	veg only	prohib	prohib					N	N	teaching yoga and philosophy
Ma'agal Hakvutzot													
Madison Community Co-op	Nearly all dinners	1–5%	I	other	occas	occas	O	U	12		Y	N	affordable urban co-op housing
Madre Grande Monastery	Nearly all dinners	21–50%	I	prim veg	occas	seldom	Pb	R	10	264	Y	Y	positive spiritual path
Magic	Nearly all dinners	1–5%	I	prim veg	seldom	seldom		O	3	0	Y	Y	ecological approach to value
Maison Emmanuel	Nearly all meals	1–5%	I	omni	prohib	seldom	H	R	7	35	Y	Y	life-sharing community
Malu 'Aina	Nearly all dinners	over 50%	I	omni	occas	seldom		R	4	22	N	N	peace and justice
Manitou Arbor Ecovillage										270			
Manzanita Village	2–5 times/week	6–20%	I	omni	often	seldom	Pb	O	36	12			community
Maple Ridge Bruderhof													spiritual revolution
Marathon Co-op	Rarely	none	I				Pb	U	66				we share our housing
Mariposa Group		1–5%	I			seldom	H	R	1	3	N	Y	happiness freedom responsible
Mariposa Grove	2–5 times/week	1–5%	I	prim veg	occas	seldom		U	3	0	N	N	arts & activism
Masala Co-op	2–5 times/week	1–5%		prim veg	occas	prohib		U	1				environmental consensus driven
Maxwelton Creek Cohousing	1–3 times/month	1–5%	I	prim veg	occas	seldom	O	R	8	21	Y	N	residential
Meadowdance Community…	Nearly all meals	none	I	omni	occas	seldom	H C Pb	R	2	200	Y	N	cooperative, ecology, children
Melbourne Cohousing…													
Mele Nahiku	Nearly all meals	6–20%	I	prim veg	prohib	prohib	H	R	2	3	Y	Y	family permaculture
Meridiana													
Merry Fox Community	1 time/week	1–5%	R	veg only	occas	prohib	H	S	1	2	Y	N	sustainable, vegetarian living
Methow Center of Enlighten…		21–50%						R		88			provide community for all
Metro Cohousing at Culver…	1–3 times/month			prim veg	occas	seldom	C	U	44	1	Y	N	cohousing

KEY *Common Diet:* I = up to each individual, C = community shares a common diet, R = diet is somewhat restricted, O = Other
Dietary Practice: omni = omnivorous, prim = primarily, veg = vegetarian, raw = raw foods.
   Note: Some communities list omni and provide vegan options, some list vegan yet allow personal food without restriction. Take the label as a rough guideline.
Alcohol/Tobacco: occas = occasionally, prohib = prohibited
Education: System(s) used for childhood education. Pb = Public School, Pr = Private School, C = Private School at the Communities, H = Homeschool, O = Other
Rural, Urban, etc. : R = Rural, U = Urban, S = Suburban, T = Small Town, O= Other
LGBT Memb Welcome: The community indicated that lesbians, gay men, bisexuals or transgendered people are welcome as members.
Spiritual Path: The community indicated it has a primarily spiritual or religious focus.

Charts

Community	State/Province	Country	Forming	Year Formed	Visitors Accepted	Open to More Adults	Open to More Children	Total Population	# Adults	# Children (<19yrs)	Percentage Women	Identified Leader	Leadership Core Group	How are Major Decisions Made	Join Fee	Income Shared/Indep.	Labor Required	Who Owns Land	Uses Cohousing Model	Survey Date
Miccosukee Land Co-op	FL	USA		1972	Y	Y	y	179	140	39	54	Y	Y	C		Y	O	N	indiv		Mar05
Michigan House	MI	USA		1932	Y	Y		19	19			Y	Y			Y	O	Y	cmty		Mar05
Michigan Womyn's Music Festival	MI	USA		1976	Y	Y	y					Y	Y		L	Y	I	Y	indiv		Mar05
Midcoast Cohousing Community	ME	USA		2003		Y	y	15	14	1	70			C		Y	I	Y	subgrp	Y	Oct04
Middle Road Community, The	BC	Canada		1994	Y			46	21	25	55			C			I	N	cmty	Y	Mar05
Milagro Cohousing	AZ	USA		1994	Y	Y	y	56	48	8	70			C			I	Y	indiv	Y	Mar05
Millstone Co-op	MA	USA		1999	Y	Y		9	9					C		Y	I	Y	ldlord		Mar05
Minnie's House	MI	USA		1970	Y	Y		24	24			Y	Y					Y			Mar05
Monan's Rill	CA	USA		1972	N	Y	y	33	20	13	50	N	N	C		Y	I	Y	cmty		Dec04
Monkton Wyld Court		UK		1982	Y	Y	y	16	12	4	40		Y	C			P	Y	other		Mar05
Monterey Cohousing	MN	USA		1991	Y	Y	y	31	22	9	54			C			I	Y	cmty	Y	Mar05
Montpelier Cohousing	VT	USA	F	2004	Y	Y	y							C			N			Y	Mar05
Moonshadow	TN	USA		1971	Y			17	12	5	56	Y		C			P	Y	indiv		Feb05
Morninglory	ON	Canada		1969	Y	Y		14	9	5	55	Y		C		Y	O	N	clt		Mar05
Mosaic Commons	MA	USA		2000	Y	Y	y	46	28	18				C		Y	I	Y	cmty		Mar05
Mount Madonna Center	CA	USA		1971	Y	Y	y	96	80	16	56	Y	Y		O		O	Y	cmty		Jan05
Mountain Home	OR	USA		1989	Y	Y	y	8	4	4	40	Y	Y		O		I	Y	indiv		Mar05
Muir Commons	CA	USA		1991															cmty	Y	Mar05
Mulvey Creek Land Co-operative	BC	Canada	F	1993	Y	Y	y	10	8	2	30		Y		O	Y	O	N	cmty		Mar05
N Street Cohousing	CA	USA		1986	Y	Y	y	55	39	16	50			C			I	Y	indiv	Y	Jan05
Nahziryah Monastic Community	AR	USA		1970	Y	Y	y					Y	Y		O		O	Y	cmty		Jan05
Nakamura House	MI	USA			N	Y	n					N	Y			Y		Y	cmty		Mar05
Namasté Greenfire	NH	USA	F		Y	Y	y					N	Y	C			O	Y	indiv		Mar05
Namasté… Multi-Cultural, Sustainable…		Belize	F	2005	Y	Y	y	95	75	20	50		Y			Y	I	Y	indiv		Mar05
Nanish Shontie	OR	USA		1997	Y	Y	y	6	5	1	60	Y	Y	C			P	Y	clt		Dec04
Narrow Way Christian Community	IL	USA	F		Y	Y											N				Mar05
Nasalam	MO	USA	F	1984	Y	Y		2	2		0	Y	Y				S	Y	nonprft		Jan05
Nature's Pace Sanctuary	MO	USA		1995	Y	Y	y	5	4	1	50	Y	Y				S	Y	cmty		Oct04
NEO Cohousing	OH	USA	F	2003	Y	Y	y						Y	C			I	N		Y	Mar05
Neo Hippie Haven	CA	USA	F		Y	Y								C			S	Y			Nov04
Nevada City Cohousing	CA	USA		2003				86	56	30							N			Y	Mar05
Neve Shalom/Wahat al-Salam (Oasis of…		Israel		1970	Y	Y	y	200	100	100	50		Y		O	Y	I	N	cmty		Oct04
New Creation Christian Community		UK		1974	Y	Y	y	680	520	160	50		Y			Y	S	N	other		Oct04
New Earth Cooperative	HI	USA	F																		Dec04
New Environment Association	NY	USA		1974		Y	y						Y	C		Y	I	N			Mar05
New Goloka	NC	USA		1982	Y	Y	y	24	18	6	50	Y	Y				P	Y	nonprft		Mar05
New Horizons	AZ	USA	F	1990	Y	Y	y					Y	Y		L	Y	I	Y			Feb05
New Meadow Run Bruderhof	PA	USA																			Feb05
New View Cohousing	MA	USA		1989	Y	Y	y	83	46	37	59			C			I	Y	cmty	Y	Mar05
New World Rising	RI	USA		1986																	Mar05
Newberry Place: a Grand Rapids Coho…	MI	USA	F	2002	Y	Y	y	27	22	5	55			C		Y	I	Y	cmty	Y	Jan05
Next Step Integral	BC	Canada	F	1992	Y	Y	y	13	11	2	45		Y		O	Y	O	Y	indiv		Jan05
Niche / Tucson Community Land Trust	AZ	USA		1992	Y	Y	y	4	4	0	50			C			O	Y	ind-lt		Mar05
Niederkaufungen		Germany		1986	Y	Y	y	76	57	19	53			C		Y	S	N	cmty		Mar05
Ninth Street Co-op	CA	USA		1993				7	6	1	67		Y	C		Y	I	Y	cmty		Jan05
Nomad Cohousing	CO	USA		1994	Y			24	18	6	67			C		Y	I	Y	cmty	Y	Feb05
Nomenus Radical Faerie Sanctuary	OR	USA		1984	Y	Y		12	12		0	N	N	C		N	O	Y	nonprft		Mar05
North Mountain Community Land Trust	VA	USA	F	1972	Y	Y	y	5	3	2		N		C		Y	IO		clt		Feb05
Northern Sun Farm Co-op	MB	Canada		1984	Y	Y	y	11	7	4	40	N	N	C		Y	IO	Y	cmt/oth		Oct04

KEY *General:* Cmty = Community, Co-op = Cooperative, Coho = Cohousing
Canadian Provinces: AB = Alberta, BC = British Columbia, MB = Manitoba, NS = Nova Scotia, ON = Ontario, QC = Quebec
Country: Russian Fed = Russian Federation, UK = United Kingdom, USA = United States of America
Decisions: C = Consensus, M = Majority, L = Leader, G = Group of leaders or elders, O = Other.
Income: S = Members Share Dincome, I = Independently Handle Own Finances, P = Partial Income Sharing, O = Other.
Labor required: Members are expected to regularly contribute labor to the group.
Who Owns Land: clt = community land trust, cmty = community, indiv = individual, ldlord = landlord, subgrp = subgroup of members.
Survey Date: Date shown is when online questionnaire was completed or last updated by community.

Community Name	Eat Together How Frequently	What % of Own Food Is Grown	Common Diet	Dietary Practice	Alcohol Use	Tobacco Use	Education	Rural, Urban, etc.	# of Residences	Acres of Land	LGBT Memb Welcome	Spiritual Path	Primary Purpose and/or Focus
Miccosukee Land Co-op	1 time/week	1–5%	I	other	often	occas	O	R	100	344	Y	N	building a caring community
Michigan House	Nearly all dinners	none						U	1		Y	N	student cooperative housing
Michigan Womyn's Music…	Nearly all meals	none	I	prim veg	occas	occas		R		650	Y	N	womyn's music and culture
Midcoast Cohousing Cmty		none	I	omni				R	25	37	Y	N	building and membership
Middle Road Community	2–5 times/week	1–5%	I	omni	occas	seldom	H Pr Pb	R	11	52	Y	N	cooperative family friendly
Milagro Cohousing	1–3 times/month	1–5%	R	omni	occas	seldom	Pb	R	10	43	Y	N	arid land ecological cohousing
Millstone Co-op	Nearly all dinners	1–5%		veg only	occas	prohib		U	1		Y	N	
Minnie's House	Nearly all dinners		C	omni				U			N	N	
Monan's Rill	1–3 times/month	1–5%	I	omni	occas	seldom	Pb	R	12	440	Y	N	shared land and values
Monkton Wyld Court	Nearly all meals	6–20%	I	veg only	seldom	seldom	Pb	R	7	11	Y	N	holistic education
Monterey Cohousing	2–5 times/week	1–5%	I	omni	occas	prohib	Pr Pb	U	15	2	Y	N	a cohousing community
Montpelier Cohousing									15		Y	N	cohousing neighborhood
Moonshadow	Nearly all dinners	21–50%	I	prim vegan	occas	occas	H	R	9	340	Y	N	eco ed activist art media arch
Morninglory	1–3 times/month	21–50%	I	omni	occas	occas	O	R	9	100	Y	N	live simply, respect all life
Mosaic Commons								T		59	Y	N	cohousing
Mount Madonna Center	Nearly all meals	21–50%	O	veg only	prohib	prohib	C	R	30	355	Y	Y	yoga and service
Mountain Home	Nearly all dinners	6–20%	I	omni	occas	often	H	R	12	360	N	N	land stewardship/cooperation
Muir Commons								S	26	3			
Mulvey Creek Land Co-op	1–3 times/month	1–5%	I	prim vegan	seldom	seldom	H C Pr	R	7	240	Y	N	intentional community builders
N Street Cohousing	2–5 times/week	1–5%	I	omni	seldom	seldom	Pb	T	17	3	Y	N	sharing resources, meals, etc
Nahziryah Monastic Cmty	Nearly all meals	21–50%	C	vegan only	prohib	prohib	C	R		103	Y	Y	service toward consciousness
Nakamura House	Nearly all dinners	none	I					U	2		Y		a co-operatively run home
Namasté Greenfire	Rarely	6–20%			seldom	seldom	Pb	R	1	49		Y	family permacultural cooperation
Namasté… Multi-Cultural…	1–3 times/month	over 50%	I	prim raw	seldom	seldom	H	R	50	500	Y	Y	100% self-sustainable
Nanish Shontie	Nearly all meals	6–20%	C	omni	prohib	occas	Pb	R	3	17	Y	Y	learning, sharing native path
Narrow Way Christian Cmty	Nearly all meals	21–50%	I		prohib	prohib		R		46	N	N	live Jesus teachings, celibacy
Nasalam	Nearly all meals	6–20%	C	veg only	prohib	seldom		R	1	21	Y	Y	spritual growth
Nature's Pace Sanctuary	2–5 times/week	over 50%	R	omni	occas	prohib	H	R	3	180	Y	Y	spirituality, homestead living
NEO Cohousing	1–3 times/month	6–20%	I	omni			Pb	O			Y	N	"eco-social" sustainability
Neo Hippie Haven	Nearly all meals	over 50%	I								Y	N	neo hippie haven
Nevada City Cohousing									34	11			
Neve Shalom/Wahat…	Rarely	none	I	omni	occas	occas	C	R	50	50	Y	N	peace education
New Creation Christian Cmty	Nearly all dinners	1–5%	C	omni	prohib	seldom	Pb	O	85	200	N	Y	evangelical Christian
New Earth Cooperative													
New Environment Association	1–3 times/month	none	I	prim veg	seldom	seldom		U	0	0	Y	N	culture change
New Goloka	Nearly all meals	1–5%	C	veg only	prohib	prohib	Pr	R	2	16	Y	Y	please chant Hare Krishna
New Horizons	Rarely	1–5%	I	omni	seldom	seldom	O	O			Y	Y	sustainable living community
New Meadow Run Bruderhof													following Jesus' teachings
New View Cohousing	2–5 times/week	1–5%	I	omni	occas	prohib	H Pb	S	18	20	Y	N	respect of the earth
New World Rising													building cooperative community
Newberry Place: a Grand…	2–5 times/week	none	I	omni	occas		O	U	15	1	Y	N	urban cohousing neighborhood
Next Step Integral	2–5 times/week	6–20%	I	prim veg	occas	seldom	H	T	4	95	Y	Y	integral life, human evolution
Niche / Tucson CLT	2–5 times/week	1–5%	I	prim veg	seldom	seldom		U	3	2	Y	N	social justice
Niederkaufungen	Nearly all meals	21–50%	I	omni	occas	occas	Pb	O	7	74	Y	N	changing society / alternative
Ninth Street Co-op	Rarely	1–5%	I	omni	occas	seldom	Pb	U	5		Y	N	limited equity housing co-op
Nomad Cohousing	2–5 times/week	1–5%	I	omni	occas		Pb	U	11	1	Y	N	coho urban energy-efficiency
Nomenus Radical Faerie…	Nearly all dinners	1–5%	I	omni	occas	seldom		R	4	80	Y	Y	gay spirituality & community
North Mountain CLT	1 time/week	6–20%	I	prim veg	prohib	prohib	Pb	R	3	130			steward the land together
Northern Sun Farm Co-op	1–3 times/month	6–20%	I	omni	occas	seldom	H Pb	R	7	160	Y		living lightly on the land

KEY *Common Diet:* I = up to each individual, C = community shares a common diet, R = diet is somewhat restricted, O = Other

Dietary Practice: omni = omnivorous, prim = primarily, veg = vegetarian, raw = raw foods.

   Note: Some communities list omni and provide vegan options, some list vegan yet allow personal food without restriction. Take the label as a rough guideline.

Alcohol/Tobacco: occas = occasionally, prohib = prohibited

Education: System(s) used for childhood education. Pb = Public School, Pr = Private School, C = Private School at the Community, H = Homeschool, O = Other

Rural, Urban, etc. : R = Rural, U = Urban, S = Suburban, T = Small Town, O= Other

LGBT Memb Welcome: The community indicated that lesbians, gay men, bisexuals or transgendered people are welcome as members.

Spiritual Path: The community indicated it has a primarily spiritual or religious focus.

Charts

	State/Province	Country	Forming	Year Formed	Visitors Accepted	Open to More Adults	Open to More Children	Total Population	# Adults	# Children (<19yrs)	Percentage Women	Identified Leader	Leadership Core Group	How are Major Decisions Made	Join Fee	Income Shared/Indep.	Labor Required	Who Owns Land	Uses Cohousing Model	Survey Date
Nyland	CO	USA		1990	Y	Y	y	140	100	40	65			C		I	Y	cmty	Y	Jan05
O'Keeffe House	MI	USA			Y	Y	n	85	85		0	Y	Y		Y	I	Y	cmty		Mar05
Oak Grove	VA	USA	F	1993	Y	Y	y	1	1					C	N	IO		indiv		Mar05
Oakland Elizabeth House	CA	USA		1991	Y	Y	y	21	11	10	100	Y	Y			I	Y	nonprft		Mar05
Oberlin Student Cooperative Association	OH	USA																		Mar05
Oceanic Ecovillage (c)	LA	USA	F	2004	Y	Y	y						Y		O	Y	O	N	other		Oct04
Olympus	VA	USA	F	2005		Y		2	2	0	0		Y			I	N	subgrp		Feb05
Omega House	MN	USA		1968	Y	Y							Y	C		I	Y	cmty		Feb05
The Omega Institute for Holistic Studies	NY	USA		1977	Y	Y		200	200	0	60	Y	Y			O	Y	nonprft		Jan05
One Common Unity	DC	USA	F	2000	Y								Y	C		P	N	indiv		Oct04
One World Family Commune	CA	USA		1967	Y	Y	y	8	8	0	20	Y		C		P	Y	ldlord		Mar05
Open Gate Farm & Retreat	ME	USA	F	2004	Y	Y	y							C		P	N			Mar05
Oran Mór	MO	USA	F	2003	Y	Y	y	2	2	0	50			C		S	Y	cmty		Mar05
Orange Twin Conservation Community	GA	USA	F	2000	Y								Y	C		I	N	cmty		Dec04
Orca Landing	WA	USA		1990	Y	Y		9	6	3	67			C		I	Y	indiv		Dec04
Order of Saint Benedict		USA/Italy		530	Y	Y		35	35	0	70	Y	Y	L		S	Y	cmty		Jan05
Osho Mevlana Residential Community		Australia		1996	Y	Y	y	19	15	4	53	Y			Y	I	N			Jan05
Osterweil House	MI	USA		1946	Y	Y		13	13	0	56	Y	Y	C	Y	I	Y	cmty		Mar05
Otamatea Eco-Village		NewZealand	F	1996	Y	Y	y	27	21	6	44	N	N	C	Y	I	Y	cmty		Nov04
O.U.R. Ecovillage	BC	Canada		1990	Y	Y	y	8	4	4	67	Y	Y	L	Y	O	Y	other		May05
Owen House	MI	USA			Y	Y		24	24			Y	Y		Y		Y			Mar05
Oxford Community		UK	F	2004	Y	Y		2	2	0	50	Y		C		I	Y	ldlord	Y	Oct04
Ozark Avalon	MO	USA	F		Y							Y				I	Y	nonprft		Jan05
Pacific Gardens Cohousing Community	BC	Canada	F	1998	Y	Y	y					Y	Y	C	Y	I	Y	cmty	Y	Mar05
Pagan Intentional Community	OK	USA	F	1997	Y	Y	y				50		Y	C		O	N	cmty		Jan05
Pagano	OR/NV	USA	F	2005	Y	Y	y	4	3	1	25	Y		C		O	Y	other		Nov04
Pangaia	HI	USA	F	1991	Y	Y	y	8	7	1	50		Y	C	Y	S	Y	indiv		Mar05
Panterra	NY	USA	F	1992	Y	Y	y	2	2		50		Y	C		I	Y	subgrp		Mar05
Paradise Village	TN	USA		2002	Y	Y	y	7	6	1	43	Y	Y		O	I	Y	indiv		Jan05
Parker Street Co-op	CA	USA		1987	Y	Y	y	33	32	1	53		Y	C	Y	I	Y	cmty		Mar05
Pathways CoHousing	MA	USA		1995	Y									C		I	Y	cmty	Y	Mar05
Peninsula Park Commons	OR	USA	F	2004				8	7	1	43			C		I	Y	indiv	Y	Jan05
Pennine Camphill Community		UK		1977	Y	Y	y	40	32	8	60					S	Y	nonprft	Y	Oct04
People on the Way	WV	USA	F	2001	Y	Y	y	3	2	1	50			C		I	Y	indiv		Feb05
The Phoenix Co-op	WI	USA		1996	Y	Y		25	25	0	50	N	N	C	Y	I	Y	clt		Oct04
Phoenix Gay Chub Music/Art Communit…	AZ	USA	F	2004		Y		1	1	0	0	Y			O	Y	O	Y			Dec04
Pine Street	MA	USA																	Y	Feb05
Pioneer Trails Institute	NE	USA	F	2004	Y	Y	y	3	3	0	75		Y	C		I	N	cmty		Dec04
Pioneer Valley	MA	USA		1989	Y	Y	y	68	51	17	60			C		I	Y	cmty	Y	Feb05
Plain Anabaptist Community			F	2005	Y	Y	y						Y		O	Y	I	N	cmty		Jan05
Planet Earth11	MI	USA	F	2005				1	1			Y	Y			I	Y	indiv	Y	Feb05
Plants for a Future		UK	F	1986	Y	Y	y	5	4	1	50		Y	C	Y	I	Y	clt		Feb05
Pleasant Hill Cohousing	CA	USA		1997	Y	Y	y	71	46	25	63			C		I	Y	indiv	Y	Feb05
Plow Creek	IL	USA		1971	Y	Y	y	46	27	19	52		Y	C		P	Y	cmty		Jan05
The Point of Infinity Retreat Center & Cmty	NY	USA	F	1998	Y	Y	y	5	5		30			C		I	Y	nonprft		Mar05
Poly, Pagan, Nudist Community	CO	USA	F	2005	Y	Y	y	4	2	2	50	Y		C		I	Y	subgrp	Y	Mar05
Port Townsend EcoVillage	WA	USA	F	2004	Y	Y	y	4	4	0	50			C	Y	I	Y	other		Mar05
PRAG House	WA	USA		1970	Y	Y	y	13	11	2	63			C		P	Y	clt		Oct04
Prairie Onion Cohousing	IL	USA	F	2003		Y	y						Y	C			N		Y	Jan05

KEY *General:* Cmty = Community, Co-op = Cooperative, Coho = Cohousing
Canadian Provinces: AB = Alberta, BC = British Columbia, MB = Manitoba, NS = Nova Scotia, ON = Ontario, QC = Quebec
Country: Russian Fed = Russian Federation, UK = United Kingdom, USA = United States of America
Decisions: C = Consensus, M = Majority, L = Leader, G = Group of leaders or elders, O = Other.
Income: S = Members Share Income, I = Independently Handle Own Finances, P = Partial Income Sharing, O = Other.
Labor required: Members are expected to regularly contribute labor to the group.
Who Owns Land: clt = community land trust, cmty = community, indiv = individual, ldlord = landlord, subgrp = subgroup of members.
Survey Date: Date shown is when online questionnaire was completed or last updated by community.

Community Name	Eat Together How Frequently	What % of Own Food Is Grown	Common Diet	Dietary Practice	Alcohol Use	Tobacco Use	Education	Rural, Urban, etc.	# of Residences	Acres of Land	LGBT Memb Welcome	Spiritual Path	Primary Purpose and/or Focus
Nyland	2–5 times/week	1–5%	I	omni	occas	prohib	H Pr Pb	R	43	43	Y	N	
O'Keeffe House	Nearly all dinners			omni				U					
Oak Grove	Nearly all dinners	1–5%	I					R	1	82		Y	earth peace spirit simplicity
Oakland Elizabeth House	2–5 times/week	1–5%	I	omni	occas	often	Pr Pb	U	1		Y	Y	hospitality for homeless
Oberlin Student Co-op Assoc.													
Oceanic Ecovillage	1 time/week	21–50%	I	omni	occas	seldom	O	O			N	N	preservation of marine ecology
Olympus	Nearly all dinners	1–5%	I					R			Y	Y	pagan men
Omega House	1–3 times/month	1–5%	R	prim veg	seldom	prohib		U	1	1	Y	N	cooperative urban living
The Omega Institute…		none	O	other	occas	occas	O	R	85	82	Y	N	holistic health workshops
One Common Unity	2–5 times/week	1–5%	I	prim vegan	seldom	seldom		U	1	0	Y	N	being peace
One World Family Commune	Nearly all dinners	1–5%	C	prim veg	seldom	occas		U	1	0	Y	Y	new world sharing demonstration
Open Gate Farm & Retreat	1 time/week	over 50%	I	omni	seldom	occas	H C Pr	R			Y	Y	brotherly love farm community
Oran Mór	Nearly all meals	over 50%	O	omni	prohib	prohib	O	R	2	110	Y	Y	living close to the land
Orange Twin Conservation…								S		155			
Orca Landing	2–5 times/week	1–5%	I	prim veg	seldom	prohib	Pb	U	1	0	Y	N	
Order of Saint Benedict	Nearly all meals	6–20%	I	omni	occas	seldom		O		500	Y	Y	community religious
Osho Mevlana Residential…	Rarely	1–5%	I	prim veg	often	often	Pr Pb	R	11	400	N	Y	meditation, celebration, Osho
Osterweil House	Nearly all dinners	none		omni				U	1				affordable quality housing
Otamatea Eco-Village	1 time/week	21–50%	I	omni	occas	occas	Pb	R	13	251	Y		permaculture eco-village
O.U.R. Ecovillage	Nearly all meals	21–50%	I	prim veg	occas	seldom	H C Pr	R	2	25	Y	Y	sustainability—permaculture
Owen House	Nearly all dinners			omni									
Oxford Community	2–5 times/week	1–5%	C	veg only	occas	prohib		U			Y	N	positive vegetarian simplicity
Ozark Avalon	1–3 times/month	1–5%	I	omni	occas	occas		R	2	160	Y	Y	
Pacific Gardens Coho Cmty			I	other				O	25	4	Y	N	environmentally friendly
Pagan Intentional Cmty	2–5 times/week	over 50%	I		seldom	prohib	H	R			Y	Y	tropical pagan eco-village
Pagano	Nearly all meals	none	I	omni	occas	occas	O	R	0	80	Y	Y	virtual IC life
Pangaia	2–5 times/week	over 50%	R	omni	seldom	prohib		R	6	33	Y	Y	raw foods, permaculture, health
Panterra	Nearly all dinners	6–20%	R	prim veg	seldom	prohib		R	3	36	Y	Y	personal enrichment/awareness
Paradise Village	2–5 times/week	6–20%	I	omni	often	often	Pr	S	2	27	Y	Y	fun, harmonius spiritual life
Parker Street Co-op	1–3 times/month	1–5%	R	prim veg	seldom	prohib	Pb	U	2	0	Y	N	voluntary diverse affordable
Pathways CoHousing	Rarely	1–5%	I	omni				T	24	40	N	N	
Peninsula Park Commons		1–5%	I	omni				U	6	0	Y	N	cohousing
Pennine Camphill Cmty	Nearly all meals	over 50%	I	omni	occas	seldom	Pr Pb	S	5	35	Y	Y	Camphill cmty – anthroposophy
People on the Way	Nearly all meals	over 50%	I	omni	occas	occas	C	R	3	350	Y	Y	organic farming and community
The Phoenix Co-op	Nearly all dinners	1–5%	I	omni	often	often		U	1	0	Y		egalitarian social living
Phoenix Gay Chub Music…		none			occas	occas		U			Y	Y	art music gay Phoenix
Pine Street								R	10	7			
Pioneer Trails Institute	Nearly all meals	none	I		seldom	prohib	C	T			Y	N	renewable energy research
Pioneer Valley	2–5 times/week	1–5%	I	omni	occas			R	33	25	Y	N	
Plain Anabaptist Cmty	Rarely	over 50%	C	omni	prohib	prohib	H	R			N	Y	plain Anabaptist community
Planet Earth11	1 time/week	6–20%	I	omni	occas	seldom	Pb	T	1	2	N	Y	caring, considerate, co-op
Plants for a Future	1–3 times/month	21–50%	R	prim vegan	seldom	occas	H	R	0	100	Y	N	vegan organic permaculture
Pleasant Hill Cohousing	2–5 times/week	1–5%	I	omni	occas	seldom	O	S	32	2	Y	N	intergenerational cohousing
Plow Creek	2–5 times/week	6–20%	I	omni	seldom	seldom	H Pr Pb	R	9	189	Y	Y	to be faithful to Jesus
The Point of Infinity…	2–5 times/week	21–50%	I	prim veg	prohib	prohib	O	R	4	38	Y	Y	natural spiritual community
Poly, Pagan, Nudist Cmty	2–5 times/week	21–50%	I	omni	occas	occas	Pb	R	1	70	Y	Y	poly, pagan, nudist
Port Townsend EcoVillage	2–5 times/week	6–20%	I	omni	occas	prohib		T	3	7	Y	Y	permaculture, ecovillage, NVC
PRAG House	1–3 times/month	none	I	omni	occas	prohib	Pb	U	1		Y	N	environment, community
Prairie Onion Cohousing								U			Y	N	urban cohousing

Charts

KEY *Common Diet:* I = up to each individual, C = community shares a common diet, R = diet is somewhat restricted, O = Other
Dietary Practice: omni = omnivorous, prim = primarily, veg = vegetarian, raw = raw foods.
   Note: Some communities list omni and provide vegan options, some list vegan yet allow personal food without restriction. Take the label as a rough guideline.
Alcohol/Tobacco: occas = occasionally, prohib = prohibited
Education: System(s) used for childhood education. Pb = Public School, Pr = Private School, C = Private School at the Communities, H = Homeschool, O = Other
Rural, Urban, etc. : R = Rural, U = Urban, S = Suburban, T = Small Town, O= Other
LGBT Memb Welcome: The community indicated that lesbians, gay men, bisexuals or transgendered people are welcome as members.
Spiritual Path: The community indicated it has a primarily spiritual or religious focus.

Community	State/Province	Country	Forming	Year Formed	Visitors Accepted	Open to More Adults	Open to More Children	Total Population	# Adults	# Children (<19yrs)	Percentage Women	Identified Leader	Leadership Core Group	How are Major Decisions Made	Join Fee	Income Shared/Indep.	Labor Required	Who Owns Land	Uses Cohousing Model	Survey Date
Prairie Sky Cohousing Cooperative	AB	Canada		1995	Y	Y	y	50	36	14	50			C	Y	I	Y	cmty	Y	Mar05
The Priorities Institute	CO	USA	F	1995	Y	Y	y	3	2	1		Y		O		I	N	indiv		Mar05
Projetorgone		France	F	2004	Y	Y	y	7	5	2				C	Y	P	Y	subgrp		Mar05
Providence Cohousing	RI	USA	F	2004	Y	Y	y												Y	Jan05
Prudence Crandall House	CA	USA		1972	Y			9	8	1	89	Y	Y	C		I	Y	indiv	Y	Mar05
Puget Ridge Cohousing	WA	USA		1988															Y	Feb05
Pumpkin Hollow Community	TN	USA	F	1996	Y	Y	y	6	4	2	50			C	Y	O	Y	cmty		Mar05
Purple Rose Collective	CA	USA		1978				11	9	2	60			C		O	Y	cmty		Mar05
Quaker House	MI	USA			Y			6	6							I	Y	nonprft		Feb05
Qumbya Co-op	IL	USA		1991	Y	Y	y	51	51	0	48	Y		O	Y	O	Y	nonprft		Mar05
Raccoon Creek Community	IN	USA	F	2004	Y	Y	y				57			C	Y	I	Y	indiv	Y	Mar05
Rainbow Family Gatherings				1972	Y	Y	y							C		O	Y	other		Mar05
Rainbow Farm	IN	USA		1974	Y	Y	y	16	15	1	51	N	Y		N	I		cmty		Mar05
Rainbow Hearth Sanctuary and Retreat...	TX	USA	F	1986	Y	Y	y	2	2	0	50	Y		O		I	Y	other	Y	Oct04
Rainbow Peace Caravan		Mexico		1995	Y	Y	y	13	10	3	52			C	Y	O	Y	other		Mar05
Rainbow Valley		NewZealand		1974	Y	Y	y	20	12	8	50	N	N	C M	Y	I	Y	cmty		Feb05
Rainbow Way Station	HI	USA	F	2004	Y	Y							Y	O		I	N	indiv		Oct04
Rapha Community	NY	USA		1971	Y	Y		31	24	7	55	N	N	C	N	O	Y	other		Feb05
Raven Rocks	OH	USA		1970		Y	y	11	11	0	0			C	N			cmty		Mar05
Reba Place Fellowship	IL	USA		1957	Y	Y	y	50	38	12	0	Y	Y	C		S	N	cmty		Dec04
Red Earth Farms	MO	USA	F	2005	Y	Y	y	4	4	0	50			C	Y	I	N			Mar05
Redfield Community		UK		1978	Y	Y	y	24	15	9	50			C	Y	I	Y	cmty		Feb05
Reevis Mountain School of Self-Reliance	AZ	USA	F	1979	Y	Y		3	3	0	33	Y	Y		Y	I	Y	nonprft		Jan05
The Refuge	CO	USA	F	2004	Y	Y		1	1			Y		C		P	Y	nonprft		Mar05
Regenerative Co-op of Pomona	CA	USA		1999	Y	Y	y	16	16		50		Y	C		I	Y	indiv		Mar05
Renaissance House	MI	USA			Y	Y		66	66		0	Y	Y		Y		Y			Mar05
Réseau des ÉcoHameaux et ÉcoVillage...	QC	Canada	F	2003																Feb05
Retirement Communities	NJ	USA	F	2003	Y	Y		4	4			Y	Y	C		I	N		Y	Jan05
Rewilding Community		USA	F	2004	Y	Y	y	2	2	0	50				O		O	N	clt		Jan05
Riparia	CA	USA		1987	Y	N	n	25	14	11	57	N	Y	C	Y	I	Y	subgrp		Mar05
Rise and Shine	IN	USA	F																	Nov04
River City Housing Collective	IA	USA		1977	Y	Y	y	26	25	1	50		Y	C	Y	I	Y	cmty		Feb05
River Farm	WA	USA		1984	Y	Y	y	15	11	4	46	N	N	C	N	IO	Y	clt		Mar05
River Hayven	WI	USA		1992	Y	Y	y	8	6	2	50		Y		O	Y	I	Y	cmty		Mar05
River Rock Commons	CO	USA	F	1997															Y	Mar05
Rocky Hill Cohousing	MA	USA	F	2001	Y			83.5	48	35.5				C		I	Y	cmty	Y	Jan05
Rose Creek Village	TN	USA		1989	Y	Y	y	195	85	110	50	Y	Y			P	Y	cmty		Jan05
RoseWind Cohousing	WA	USA		1989	Y	Y	y	50	40	10	55			C	Y	I	Y	other	Y	Mar05
Rosneath Farm		Australia	F	1994	Y	Y	y	19	11	8	50	Y	Y		O	Y	O	N	cmty		Mar05
Rosy Branch Farm	NC	USA		1987	Y			18	14	4	50				Y	I	Y	indiv		Mar05
Rowe Camp & Conference Center	MA	USA		1973	Y	Y		15	15	0	70	Y	Y		O		I	Y	nonprft		Feb05
Ruths' House	MI	USA		1993	Y	Y		12	12		42	Y	Y	C	Y	I	Y	nonprft		Mar05
Sacramento Cohousing	CA	USA	F	2000	Y	Y	y						Y	C	Y	I	Y		Y	Mar05
Sacramento Suburban Cohousing	CA	USA	F	2005		Y	y						Y	C		I	N		Y	Mar05
Sacred Suenos		Ecuador	F	2001	Y	Y	y	2	2	0	50			C		O	Y	clt		Mar05
Sage Valley	NV	USA	F																	Nov04
Saint Jude Catholic Worker House Cmty	IL	USA	F	1980	Y	Y	n	3	3			N	Y	C	O	N		cmty		Mar05
Saint Martin de Porres House	CT	USA	F	1992	Y	Y	y	6	3	3		N	N	C	N	S	Y	other		Mar05
Salamander Springs	GA	USA	F	1998	Y		y	3	3	0	67		Y		O		I	Y	indiv		Mar05

KEY *General:* Cmty = Community, Co-op = Cooperative, Coho = Cohousing
Canadian Provinces: AB = Alberta, BC = British Columbia, MB = Manitoba, NS = Nova Scotia, ON = Ontario, QC = Quebec
Country: Russian Fed = Russian Federation, UK = United Kingdom, USA = United States of America
Decisions: C = Consensus, M = Majority, L = Leader, G = Group of leaders or elders, O = Other.
Income: S = Members Share Dincome, I = Independently Handle Own Finances, P = Partial Income Sharing, O = Other.
Labor required: Members are expected to regularly contribute labor to the group.
Who Owns Land: clt = community land trust, cmty = community, indiv = individual, ldlord = landlord, subgrp = subgroup of members.
Survey Date: Date shown is when online questionnaire was completed or last updated by community.

Community Name	Eat Together How Frequently	What % of Own Food Is Grown	Common Diet	Dietary Practice	Alcohol Use	Tobacco Use	Education	Rural, Urban, etc.	# of Residences	Acres of Land	LGBT Memb Welcome	Spiritual Path	Primary Purpose and/or Focus
Prairie Sky Coho Co-op	1 time/week	1–5%	I	omni	often	seldom		U	18	1	N	N	close urban community
The Priorities Institute	1–3 times/month	none	I	omni	occas	seldom	Pb	U	1	0	Y	N	intellectual stimulation
Projetorgone	Nearly all dinners	6–20%	O	other	occas	occas	Pb	R		10	N	N	
Providence Cohousing													community ecohousing
Prudence Crandall House	2–5 times/week	6–20%	R	omni	seldom	prohib	Pb	U	2		Y	N	to be an urban community
Puget Ridge Cohousing										2			
Pumpkin Hollow Cmty	2–5 times/week	1–5%	I	omni	often	often	Pb	R	4	120	Y	N	activism, art, ecology, spirit
Purple Rose Collective	Nearly all dinners	1–5%	I	prim veg	occas	prohib		U			Y	N	self-managed, anti-profit home
Quaker House	2–5 times/week		I	prim veg	seldom	prohib		T			Y	N	
Qumbya Co-op	Nearly all dinners	1–5%	I	prim veg	seldom	seldom		U	3		Y	N	cheap rent and food, fun, tofu
Raccoon Creek Community	2–5 times/week	none	I	omni	seldom	seldom	O	R		154	Y	N	living lightly on land
Rainbow Family Gatherings	Nearly all meals	none	I	prim veg	seldom	often	H Pb O	R			Y	N	we gather to pray for peace
Rainbow Farm	Rarely	1–5%	I	omni	occas	seldom		R	9	326	Y	Y	sacred space provider
Rainbow Hearth Sanctuary...	Nearly all dinners	6–20%	R	prim veg	seldom	prohib	Pb	R	5	9	Y	Y	retreat center
Rainbow Peace Caravan	Nearly all meals	1–5%	O	prim veg	occas	seldom	H	O			Y	N	ecology, arts, indigenous
Rainbow Valley	1–3 times/month	6–20%	I	omni	occas	occas	Pb	R	10	100	Y	N	extended family, love of land
Rainbow Way Station	Rarely		I	prim veg				R	0	3	N	N	ecology, earth spirituality
Rapha Community	1–3 times/month	none	I			prohib	Pb	U	0			Y	family on a spiritual journey
Raven Rocks								R		1047			education, ecology, sharing
Reba Place Fellowship	1–3 times/month	1–5%	I	omni	seldom	seldom	H Pr Pb	U	20		N	Y	radical discipleship, service
Red Earth Farms	Nearly all dinners	6–20%	I	prim vegan	occas	seldom	H	R	0	0	Y	N	eco-sustainable lifestyles
Redfield Community	Nearly all dinners	6–20%	O	prim veg	often	often	O	T	1	17	Y	N	co-operative living
Reevis Mountain School...	Nearly all meals	over 50%	C	omni	prohib	prohib	H	R	11	13	N	Y	live what you love
The Refuge	Nearly all meals	1–5%	C	omni	occas	prohib		R		30	N	Y	healing spirit, soul & body
Regenerative Co-op ...	Nearly all dinners	1–5%	R	prim veg	occas	prohib	Pb	S	3	1	Y	N	enviromental housing
Renaissance House	Nearly all dinners			omni									
Réseau des ÉcoHameaux...													démarrage d'écohameaux
Retirement Communities								U			Y	N	retire to urban college areas
Rewilding Community	Nearly all dinners	none	C	omni	prohib	prohib	H	R			Y	Y	hunting/gathering healing
Riparia	1–3 times/month	21–50%	I	prim veg	seldom	seldom	H Pr Pb	R	8	12			peace and social justice issues
Rise and Shine													animal sanctuary seeking land
River City Housing Collective	Nearly all dinners	1–5%	I	prim veg	occas	occas	Pb	U	2	0	Y	N	education ecology diversity
River Farm	1 time/week	21–50%	I	omni	occas	occas	Pb	R	7	80	Y	N	land stewardship & consensus
River Hayven	Nearly all meals	over 50%	C	prim raw	seldom	seldom	H Pb	R	4	250	Y	N	ecological and spiritual life
River Rock Commons										3			
Rocky Hill Cohousing								O	28	28	Y	N	
Rose Creek Village	Rarely	1–5%	I	omni	occas	prohib	H	R	20	100	N	Y	follow Christ, God's son
RoseWind Cohousing	2–5 times/week	1–5%	I	omni	occas	seldom	H Pr Pb	T	24	9	Y	N	cohousing
Rosneath Farm	1–3 times/month	over 50%	I	omni	occas	occas		T	71	365	Y	Y	permaculture village and farm
Rosy Branch Farm	1–3 times/month	1–5%	I	other	occas	occas	O	R	8	50	Y	N	modeling cooperative options
Rowe Camp & Conference...	Nearly all meals	none	I	prim veg	seldom	seldom		R	4	45	Y	N	personal & spiritual growth
Ruths' House	2–5 times/week	none	I	omni	seldom	seldom		U	1		Y		affordable student housing
Sacramento Cohousing			I					U			Y	N	cohousing
Sacramento Suburban Coho			I					S	30	5	Y	N	friendly community
Sacred Suenos	Nearly all meals	1–5%	R	prim veg	occas	seldom	H	R	1	25	Y	N	sustainable agriculture
Sage Valley													earth living in balance
Saint Jude Catholic Worker...	Nearly all meals	1–5%			prohib			U	2		Y	Y	works of mercy
Saint Martin de Porres House	Nearly all dinners	1–5%	I	omni	often	prohib	Pb	U				Y	poverty relief peacework
Salamander Springs	Nearly all dinners	6–20%	I	other	occas	seldom	O	R	6	80	Y	N	sustainability; planetary healing

KEY *Common Diet:* I = up to each individual, C = community shares a common diet, R = diet is somewhat restricted, O = Other
Dietary Practice: omni = omnivorous, prim = primarily, veg = vegetarian, raw = raw foods.
Note: Some communities list omni and provide vegan options, some list vegan yet allow personal food without restriction. Take the label as a rough guideline.
Alcohol/Tobacco: occas = occasionally, prohib = prohibited
Education: System(s) used for childhood education. Pb = Public School, Pr = Private School, C = Private School at the Communities, H = Homeschool, O = Other
Rural, Urban, etc. : R = Rural, U = Urban, S = Suburban, T = Small Town, O= Other
LGBT Memb Welcome: The community indicated that lesbians, gay men, bisexuals or transgendered people are welcome as members.
Spiritual Path: The community indicated it has a primarily spiritual or religious focus.

Charts

Name	State/Province	Country	Forming	Year Formed	Visitors Accepted	Open to More Adults	Open to More Children	Total Population	# Adults	# Children (<19yrs)	Percentage Women	Identified Leader	Leadership Core Group	How are Major Decisions Made	Join Fee	Income Shared/Indep.	Labor Required	Who Owns Land	Uses Cohousing Model	Survey Date
Samenhuizing West-Brabant		Belgium	F	2000	Y	Y	y	41	23	18	48			C	Y	I	Y	cmty	Y	Feb05
San Antonio Cohousing	TX	USA	F	2005	Y	Y	y									I	N		Y	Jan05
San Francisco Cohousing	CA	USA	F	2004		Y	y	28	12	16				C	Y	I	Y			Dec04
San Mateo Ecovillage	CA	USA	F	1998	Y	Y	y	10	10		50	Y		C		I	Y	subgrp	Y	Feb05
Sandhill Farm	MO	USA		1973	Y	Y	y	6	5	1	40			C		S	N	cmty		Feb05
Sankofa	AK	USA	F	2004	Y	Y	y	4	2	2	50			C			Y			Mar05
Santa Cruz County Cohousing	CA	USA	F			Y	y							C					Y	Mar05
Sassafras Ridge Farm	WV	USA		1972	Y			24	17	7	30		Y	C		I		indiv		Mar05
SBSHC: Santa Barbara Student Housing...	CA	USA		1976	Y	Y		71	71		48	Y	Y		Y	I	Y	cmty		Mar05
SEADS of Truth, Inc.	ME	USA	F	1979	Y	Y	y	3	2	1		N	Y	C G	Y	IO	Y	other		Mar05
7th Millennium Community		Philippines	F	1992	Y	Y	y						Y			P	Y	nonprft		Mar05
Shadowlake Village	VA	USA		1998	Y	Y	y	63	43	20	63		Y	C		I	Y	indiv	Y	Feb05
Shambala Eco-Resort & EcoVillage Cmty...		NewZealand	F	2004	Y	Y	y						Y	O		I	N	indiv	Y	Feb05
Shannon Farm Community	VA	USA		1972	Y	Y	y	93	62	31	49			C		O	Y	clt		Feb05
Sharing Community	OH	USA		1999	Y	Y		5	5	0	60		Y	C		I	N	indiv		Mar05
Sharingwood Cohousing	WA	USA		1984	Y	Y	y	85	50	35	55			C		I	Y	indiv	Y	Oct04
Shepherdsfield	MO	USA		1979	Y	Y	y	95	57	38	0	Y	Y	C		S	N	cmty		Mar05
Sherwood Co-op	WA	USA		1935	Y	Y		14	14		43			C	Y	I	Y	other		Mar05
Sidhefire	WA	USA	F	2002	Y	Y		3	3	0	33	Y	Y	C	Y	P	Y	indiv		Feb05
Silver Sage Village	CO	USA		2003	Y	Y		12	12	0	75		Y	C	Y	I	N	cmty	Y	Jan05
Sirius Community	MA	USA		1978	Y	Y	y	38	30	8	0	Y		O		O	Y	other		Mar05
Sivananda Ashram Yoga Ranch	NY	USA		1974	Y	Y	y	15	12	3	50	Y	Y	L		S	Y	cmty		Mar05
Skyhouse Community	MO	USA		1996	Y	Y	y	5	5		40			C		S	Y	ind-lt		Mar05
Society for the Promotion of Creative...	KS	USA	F	1987	Y	Y		2	2	0	50			C		P	Y	ldlord		Oct04
Sojourner Truth House	MI	USA			Y	Y		53	53		35	Y	Y		Y	I	Y	cmty		Mar05
Solstice Dawn	NE	USA	F	1999	Y	Y	y	3	2	1	50			C		S	Y	cmty	Y	Mar05
Solterra	NC	USA		1993	Y	Y	y	75	53	22	60	Y	Y	C		O	Y	indiv	Y	Nov04
Soma - The SOMA Project	CA	USA	F	2004	Y	Y	y	2	1	1	0	Y	Y	C	Y	O	Y	other		Jan05
Somerville Ecovillage		Australia	F	2000	Y	Y	y						Y		Y	I	N	cmty		Jan05
Songaia Cohousing Community	WA	USA		1987	Y	Y	y	36	25	11	50		Y	C		I	Y	indiv	Y	Jan05
Sophia Community	IL	USA		1993	Y	Y		8	7	1	50			C		I	Y	nonprft		Mar05
Southern California Nature Sanctuary...	CA	USA	F	2004		Y	y				50	Y	Y	C	Y		Y	clt		Dec04
Southern Cassadaga Spiritualist Camp	FL	USA		1894	Y	Y	n						N	O	Y	IO		cmty		Mar05
Southwest Sufi Community	NM	USA	F	1995	Y	Y	y	3	3	0	67	Y	Y	C	Y	I	Y	cmty		Feb05
Sowing Circle	CA	USA		1994	N		n	19	17	2	41	N	Y	C	Y		Y	clt		May05
Sparrow Hawk Village	OK	USA		1981	Y	Y	y	80	73	7	68	Y		O		I	Y	indiv		Mar05
Spirit Cove	NC	USA	F	2004	Y	Y	y							C		I	N	other		Jan05
Spirit Dance Co-operative Community	BC	Canada	F	2000	Y	Y	y	11	10	1	60		Y	C	Y	P	Y	nonprft		Feb05
Spring Lane Farms	MO	USA	F	2004	Y	Y	y					Y	Y	C		I	N	cmty		Feb05
Spring Valley Bruderhof	PA	USA																		Feb05
Springhill Cohousing Community		UK	F	2000	Y	Y	y	79	52	27	64			C	Y	I	Y	cmty	Y	Feb05
Springtree Community	VA	USA		1971	Y	Y		4	4		50					S	Y	cmty		Feb05
Sri Aurobindo Sadhana Peetham	CA	USA	F	1993	Y	Y		4	4		25	Y			Y	O	Y	cmty		Feb05
Stelle Community	IL	USA		1963	Y	Y	y	90	60	30	50					I	N	other		Jan05
Stewardship Incorporated	HI	USA	F			Y	y					Y	Y				Y		Y	Oct04
Stone Curves Cohousing	AZ	USA	F	2001	Y	Y	y							C		I	N	nonprft	Y	Oct04
Stone Soup Cooperative	IL	USA		1997	Y	Y	y	39	38	1	50			C	Y	I	Y	cmty		Jan05
Storybook Shire	OH	USA	F	2004	Y	Y	y							C	Y	I	Y	indiv		Dec04
Student Coop Organization (SCO)	OH	USA		1990	Y	Y	y	8	8	0	37			C	Y	I	Y	nonprft		Nov04

KEY *General:* Cmty = Community, Co-op = Cooperative, Coho = Cohousing
Canadian Provinces: AB = Alberta, BC = British Columbia, MB = Manitoba, NS = Nova Scotia, ON = Ontario, QC = Quebec
Country: Russian Fed = Russian Federation, UK = United Kingdom, USA = United States of America
Decisions: C = Consensus, M = Majority, L = Leader, G = Group of leaders or elders, O = Other.
Income: S = Members Share Dincome, I = Independently Handle Own Finances, P = Partial Income Sharing, O = Other.
Labor required: Members are expected to regularly contribute labor to the group.
Who Owns Land: clt = community land trust, cmty = community, indiv = individual, ldlord = landlord, subgrp = subgroup of members.
Survey Date: Date shown is when online questionnaire was completed or last updated by community.

Community Name	Eat Together How Frequently	What % of Own Food Is Grown	Common Diet	Dietary Practice	Alcohol Use	Tobacco Use	Education	Rural, Urban, etc.	# of Residences	Acres of Land	LGBT Memb Welcome	Spiritual Path	Primary Purpose and/or Focus
Samenhuizing West-Brabant	Nearly all dinners	1–5%	I	prim veg	occas	seldom	Pb	R	20	3	Y	N	cohousing, ecology
San Antonio Cohousing								U			Y	N	to create community in S.A.
San Francisco Cohousing								U			Y	N	community with heart
San Mateo Ecovillage	1 time/week	6–20%	I	prim veg	occas	prohib	Pb	S	2		Y	N	sustainability / social change
Sandhill Farm	Nearly all meals	over 50%	C	prim veg	occas	prohib	H	R	4	135	Y	N	organic, equality, dialog, fun
Sankofa		6–20%	C	omni	seldom	prohib	H	R	0	0	Y	N	low-tech, low-energy lifestyle
Santa Cruz County Coho											Y	N	
Sassafras Ridge Farm	Rarely	6–20%	I				H Pb	R	10	400	Y	Y	cooperative farm neighborhood
SBSHC: Santa Barbara Stud…	2–5 times/week	1–5%	I	omni	occas	seldom		U	4		Y	N	co-op living for students
SEADS of Truth, Inc.	Rarely	1–5%	I	omni	seldom	prohib	Pb	R	3	60			solar environment peace ed
7th Millennium Cmty	Nearly all dinners	21–50%	R	prim veg	seldom	prohib	Pr	T			N	Y	self-sufficient community
Shadowlake Village	2–5 times/week	1–5%		omni	occas	seldom	O	O	33	33	Y	N	to live together in community
Shambala Eco-Resort…		over 50%	I	veg only	seldom	prohib	C	R		0	Y	N	holistic, non-violence
Shannon Farm Community	1 time/week	6–20%	I	omni	occas	occas	O	R	35	520	Y	N	cooperative rural lifestyles
Sharing Community	2–5 times/week	21–50%		omni	occas	seldom		R	3	60	N	N	environmental stewardship
Sharingwood Cohousing	2–5 times/week	1–5%	I	omni	occas	seldom	H Pr Pb	R	25	40	Y	N	rural cohousing, large greenbelt
Shepherdsfield	Nearly all meals	1–5%			seldom	prohib	C	R		200	N	Y	to follow the way of Christ
Sherwood Co-op	Nearly all dinners	1–5%	I	prim veg	occas	seldom		U	1	0	Y	N	cooperative student housing
Sidhefire	2–5 times/week	6–20%	I	prim veg	occas	occas		R	1	2	Y	Y	sustainability
Silver Sage Village		none						U	16	1	Y	N	proactive adult community
Sirius Community	Nearly all dinners	21–50%		prim veg	seldom	seldom	H Pb	R	8	90	Y	Y	spiritual education ecology
Sivananda Ashram Yoga…	Nearly all meals	21–50%	C	prim veg	prohib	prohib	Pr	R	5	77	Y	Y	practice & teach yoga & Vedanta
Skyhouse Community	Nearly all dinners	21–50%	I	prim vegan	occas	seldom		R	2	1	Y	N	social change ecology equality
Society for the Promotion…	Nearly all dinners	1–5%	C	veg only	seldom	prohib	O	U	1	0	N	Y	promoting creative interchange
Sojourner Truth House	Nearly all dinners	none		omni	often	often		U	1			Y	affordable student housing
Solstice Dawn	Nearly all meals	6–20%	I	omni	seldom	prohib	Pb	R	1	20	Y	Y	sustainable living
Solterra	2–5 times/week	1–5%	I	omni	occas	occas	H Pr Pb	U	30	20	Y		green, community meals peace
Soma – The SOMA Project	1 time/week	6–20%	R	other	seldom	prohib	H	R	0	0	N	Y	community
Somerville Ecovillage	Rarely		I	other	occas	occas	O	O	2	399	Y	N	ecovillage Perth, Australia
Songaia Cohousing Cmty	2–5 times/week	6–20%		other	occas	prohib	H Pr Pb	S	13	11	Y	Y	earth-centered cohousing
Sophia Community	2–5 times/week	1–5%	I	prim veg	occas	prohib		U	1	0	Y	Y	intentional community
Southern California Nature…							H Pb				Y	Y	spiritual reverence of nature
Southern Cassadaga Spirit…	1–3 times/month	none					Pb	R		57		Y	belief that life is continuous
Southwest Sufi Cmty	1 time/week	1–5%	I	prim veg	occas	seldom	O	R	1	1500	Y	Y	wilderness retreat center
Sowing Circle	Nearly all dinners	21–50%		prim veg	seldom	seldom		R	12	80	Y		community, ecology, education
Sparrow Hawk Village	1 time/week	1–5%	I		occas	occas	Pb	R	52	440	Y	Y	spiritual community
Spirit Cove	1–3 times/month	none	I	omni	occas	seldom	Pb	O	13	25	Y	Y	harmony with nature
Spirit Dance Co-op Cmty			I	omni	occas	seldom		R			Y	Y	
Spring Lane Farms								T		85	Y	N	sustainable living
Spring Valley Bruderhof													spiritual revolution
Springhill Cohousing Cmty	2–5 times/week	none	R	veg only	occas	occas	H	T	35	2	Y	N	cohousing and consensus
Springtree Community	Nearly all meals	21–50%	R	veg only	often	prohib		R	2	100	Y	N	sharing and cooperation
Sri Aurobindo Sadhana…	Nearly all meals	1–5%	C	prim veg	prohib	prohib		R	2	3	N	Y	Sri Aurobindo's Yoga Ashram
Stelle Community	Rarely	6–20%	I	omni	seldom	seldom	Pb	R	40	40	Y	N	wholistic living
Stewardship Incorporated			O		prohib	prohib					Y	N	stewardship
Stone Curves Cohousing								U	48	5	Y	N	
Stone Soup Cooperative	2–5 times/week	1–5%	I	prim veg	occas	occas		U	3		Y	N	joy and justice
Storybook Shire	1 time/week	21–50%	I	omni	occas	seldom	Pr	R		10	Y	N	self sustainability, cottages
Student Co-op Organization	2–5 times/week	1–5%	I		occas	seldom	O	T	1		Y	N	

KEY *Common Diet:* I = up to each individual, C = community shares a common diet, R = diet is somewhat restricted, O = Other
Dietary Practice: omni = omnivorous, prim = primarily, veg = vegetarian, raw = raw foods.
    Note: Some communities list omni and provide vegan options, some list vegan yet allow personal food without restriction. Take the label as a rough guideline.
Alcohol/Tobacco: occas = occasionally, prohib = prohibited
Education: System(s) used for childhood education. Pb = Public School, Pr = Private School, C = Private School at the Community, H = Homeschool, O = Other
Rural, Urban, etc. : R = Rural, U = Urban, S = Suburban, T = Small Town, O= Other
LGBT Memb Welcome: The community indicated that lesbians, gay men, bisexuals or transgendered people are welcome as members.
Spiritual Path: The community indicated it has a primarily spiritual or religious focus.

Charts

	State/Province	Country	Forming	Year Formed	Visitors Accepted	Open to More Adults	Open to More Children	Total Population	# Adults	# Children (<19yrs)	Percentage Women	Identified Leader	Leadership Core Group	How are Major Decisions Made	Join Fee	Income Shared/Indep.	Labor Required	Who Owns Land	Uses Cohousing Model	Survey Date
Students' Cooperative Association	OR	USA		1935	Y	Y		74	74	0	50		Y	C		Y	I	Y	cmty		Mar05
The Sudanese Chadian Community in...	IN	USA	F	2003	Y	Y	y	428	400	28	20	Y	Y				I	N	other		Mar05
Sugar Mountain	MO	USA		1998				28	18	10	50	Y	Y			Y	I	Y	indiv		Jan05
Summerglen Farm and Homestead	VA	USA	F	1999	Y	Y	y	2	2	0	50	Y		C			I	Y	indiv		Oct04
Summit Ave Cooperative	WI	USA		1970	N	Y		17	17		50	N	N	C M	O	Y	O	Y	cmty		Mar05
Sunhouse Co-op	MI	USA	F	1997	Y	Y		3	3	0	50			C			I	Y	cmty		Mar05
Sunrise Ranch	CO	USA		1945	Y	Y	y	98	83	15	55	Y	Y				I	Y	cmty		Mar05
Sunset House	WA	USA		1978	Y	Y		6	6	0	50			C			I	Y	clt		Nov04
SunToads Farm Community of New Mexico	NM	USA		1999	Y	Y	y	6	6	0	50	Y	Y		L		I	Y	other		Nov04
Sunward Cohousing	MI	USA		1994	Y	Y	y	88	65	23	59		Y	C		Y	I	Y	cmty	Y	Mar05
Sunwise Co-op	CA	USA		1978	Y	Y		8	8	0	70	Y	Y	C		Y	I	Y	nonprft	Y	Mar05
SurrealEstates	CA	USA	F	1992	Y	Y	y	15	13	2	25	Y	Y	C		Y	I	Y	indiv		Jan05
Susan B. Anthony Women's Land Trust	OH	USA		1979	Y	Y		5	5	0	100			C		Y	I	Y	clt		Mar05
Sustainable Living Systems	MT	USA	F	2000	Y	Y	y	13	5	8	40	Y	Y	C			O	Y	clt		Mar05
Svanholm		Denmark		1977	Y	Y	y	100	65	35	60			C		Y	P	Y	cmty		Feb05
Sweetwater Community Land Trust	MO	USA		1981	Y	Y	y	10	6	4	50	N		C		Y	I	N	clt		Feb05
Tacoma Eco-Village	WA	USA	F	2005	Y	Y	y							C			I	N	other		Mar05
Takoma Village Cohousing	DC	USA		1998	Y	Y	y	78	59	19	59			C			I	Y	indiv	Y	Jan05
Talkeetna Blueberry Sanctuary	AK	USA	F	2001	Y	Y	y	13	6	7	50	Y	Y	C		Y	I	Y	cmty		Feb05
Talking Cedars Developments Ltd.	BC	Canada	F	1988	Y	Y	y	6	6		40		Y		O	Y	O	N	indiv	Y	Feb05
Tamera - Healing Biotope I		Portugal		1995	Y	Y	y	105	90	15	53				O	Y	O	Y	clt		Mar05
Tanguy Homesteads	PA	USA		1945	Y	Y	y	98	67	31	54	Y		C		Y	O	Y	other		Feb05
Tao Bear Recovery Community	MI	USA	F			Y	Y	y						C			I	Y			Nov04
Tararu Valley Sanctuary		NewZealand	F	2004	Y	Y	y				50		Y	C		Y	P	Y	clt		Oct04
Teaching Drum Outdoor School	WI	USA		1989	Y	Y	y	8	7	1	50				O		I	Y	other		Jan05
Temescal Commons Cohousing	CA	USA		1996	Y	Y	y	25	15	10	40		Y	C			I	Y	cmty	Y	Jan05
Terra Nova	MO	USA	F	1995	Y			3	3		20			C		Y	P	N	subgrp		Mar05
Terrasante Village	AZ	USA	F	2004	Y	Y	y	15	12	3	50		Y	C		Y	I	Y	clt		Dec04
TerraVie	QC	Canada											Y	C							Mar05
3Circles Community	TN	USA	F	2005	Y	Y	y	2	2		50	Y					I	N	indiv		Feb05
Tibetan Buddhist Learning Center	NJ	USA		1958	Y												O				Jan05
Tolstoy Farm	WA	USA		1963				48	33	15	53				O		O	N	indiv		Mar05
Tomorrow's Bread Today	TX	USA	F	1995	Y	Y	y	8	5	3	60	Y	Y				S	N	cmty		Jan05
Torri Superiore Ecovillage		Italy		1989	Y	Y	y	16	11	5	50		Y	C		Y	P	Y	subgrp		Jan05
Touchstone Cohousing	MI	USA	F	2001		Y	y	28	23	5				C		Y	I	Y	cmty	Y	Oct04
Tres Placitas del Rio	NM	USA		1996	Y	Y	y	22	14	8	57			C		Y	I	Y	cmty	Y	Jan05
Tribe of Blank		USA	F	2004	Y	Y	y	3	2	1				C				N		Y	Jan05
Tribe of Dirt	NH	USA	F	2001	Y	Y	y	3	2	1	0		Y	C			S	Y	ind-lt		Mar05
Tribe of Likatien		Germany		1974	Y	Y	y	253	104	149	49	Y	Y	C			P	N	cmty	Y	Mar05
Trillium Farm Community	OR	USA	F	1976	Y	Y	y	2	2		65		Y	C		Y	I	Y	clt		Mar05
Trillium Hollow	OR	USA		1991	Y	Y	y	42	35	7	63			C			I	Y	cmty	Y	Mar05
Truth Consciousness	AZ/CO	USA		1974	Y	Y							Y			N					Oct04
Tullstugan Collective Housing Unit		Sweden		1994	Y			52	35	17	56	Y	Y			Y	I	Y	other	Y	Feb05
Turn Cedars	TX	USA	F	1980	Y	Y	y	2	2	0	50	Y	Y	C			P	Y	indiv	Y	Mar05
Twelve Tribes		USA		1972	Y	Y	y						Y				S	Y	indiv		Mar05
Twelve Tribes Communauté de Heimsbr...		France			Y	Y	y						Y		O		O	N			Mar05
Twelve Tribes Communauté de Sus		France		1983	Y	Y	y						Y		O		O	Y	indiv		Mar05
Twelve Tribes Cmty at Peppercorn Creek...		Australia		1987	Y	Y	y	51	24	27	50		Y				S	Y	indiv		Mar05
Twelve Tribes Cmty at Stentwood Farm		UK		1997	Y	Y	y					N	Y		O	N	SO	Y	indiv		Mar05

KEY *General:* Cmty = Community, Co-op = Cooperative, Coho = Cohousing
Canadian Provices: AB = Alberta, BC = British Columbia, MB = Manitoba, NS = Nova Scotia, ON = Ontario, QC = Quebec
Country: Russian Fed = Russian Federation, UK = United Kingdom, USA = United States of America
Decisions: C = Consensus, M = Majority, L = Leader, G = Group of leaders or elders, O = Other.
Income: S = Members Share Income, I = Independently Handle Own Finances, P = Partial Income Sharing, O = Other.
Labor required: Members are expected to regularly contribute labor to the group.
Who Owns Land: clt = community land trust, cmty = community, indiv = individual, ldlord = landlord, subgrp = subgroup of members.
Survey Date: Date shown is when online questionnaire was completed or last updated by community.

Community Name	Eat Together How Frequently	What % of Own Food Is Grown	Common Diet	Dietary Practice	Alcohol Use	Tobacco Use	Education	Rural, Urban, etc.	# of Residences	Acres of Land	LGBT Memb Welcome	Spiritual Path	Primary Purpose and/or Focus
Students' Co-op Association	Nearly all dinners	none	R	other	occas	occas		U	3	1	Y	N	student democratic co-op
The Sudanese Chadian…	1 time/week	none	O	kosher	prohib	often	C	O			N	N	supporting refugees/immigrants
Sugar Mountain	1–3 times/month	21–50%	I	omni	seldom	often	Pb	R	10	56	N	N	homesteading/preparedness
Summerglen Farm and…	2–5 times/week	over 50%	I	omni	prohib	prohib	O	R	4	110	N	Y	primitive homesteading
Summit Ave Cooperative	Nearly all dinners	1–5%			seldom	seldom		U	1			Y	residential housing and meals
Sunhouse Co-op	2–5 times/week			prim veg	occas	prohib		S	1	20	Y	N	creating great collective home
Sunrise Ranch	Nearly all meals	6–20%	I	omni	occas	seldom	Pr Pb	R	35	360	Y	Y	radiant expression of divine
Sunset House	1–3 times/month	1–5%	I	prim veg	occas	prohib		U	1	1	Y	N	promote cmty development
SunToads Farm Community…	1–3 times/month	over 50%	I	omni	seldom	prohib	O	R	6	160	Y	N	privacy, keep your own income
Sunward Cohousing	2–5 times/week	1–5%	I		occas	prohib	H Pr Pb	O	40	20	Y	N	cohousing, stewardship of land
Sunwise Co-op	2–5 times/week	21–50%	R	veg only	often	seldom	O	T	2	0	Y	N	cheap sustainable solar house
SurrealEstates	Rarely	none	I	other			Pb	U	11	1	Y	N	artist live/work community
Susan B. Anthony Women's…	Rarely	6–20%	I	omni	occas	often		R	4	150	Y	N	feminist education
Sustainable Living Systems	2–5 times/week	over 50%	I	omni	prohib	prohib	H	R	3	10	Y	N	sustainable living systems
Svanholm	Nearly all meals	over 50%	O	omni	occas	occas	Pr Pb	R	12	1000	N	N	sharing and ecological living
Sweetwater Community…	Rarely	6–20%	I	omni	seldom	seldom	H Pb	R	6	480	Y	N	rural / land stewardship
Tacoma Eco-Village			I	prim veg	occas	occas	H	O			Y	Y	spiritual path peace community
Takoma Village Cohousing	1 time/week	none	I	omni	occas	seldom	Pr Pb	U	43	1	Y	N	an urban community
Talkeetna Blueberry…	1–3 times/month	1–5%	I	omni	often	seldom	Pb	R	2	240	Y	N	caring, family, pool resources
Talking Cedars Devel…	1 time/week	1–5%	I	prim veg	occas	seldom	C	T	2	17	Y	Y	community ecology spiritual
Tamera – Healing Biotope I	Nearly all meals	6–20%		prim veg	occas	occas	H	R	15	330	Y	Y	future, community, peace model
Tanguy Homesteads	1–3 times/month		I				Pr Pb	S	38	100	Y	N	diverse cooperative community
Tao Bear Recovery Cmty			I	omni	prohib	occas		S			Y	Y	recovery taoism healing
Tararu Valley Sanctuary	2–5 times/week	6–20%	I	prim veg	occas	seldom	Pb	R	5	1500	N	N	active ecosystem guardianship
Teaching Drum Outdoor…	Nearly all dinners	none	C	omni	prohib	prohib	Pb	R	4	80	Y	Y	native-earth balanced lifeway
Temescal Commons Coho	2–5 times/week	1–5%	I	omni	occas	prohib	Pb	U	9	0	N	Y	
Terra Nova	Nearly all dinners	6–20%	I	omni	seldom	prohib		U	2	1	Y	N	making town life sustainable
Terrasante Village	1 time/week	1–5%	I	prim veg	occas	occas	Pb	R	5	25	Y	N	health, harmony, creativity
TerraVie											Y	N	ecologically viable community
3Circles Community	1–3 times/month		I	omni	seldom	seldom	O	R			N	N	Christ Centered non-traditional
Tibetan Buddhist Learning…													
Tolstoy Farm	1 time/week	over 50%	I	omni	occas	occas	H Pr Pb	R	27	200	Y	N	decentralized rural living
Tomorrow's Bread Today	Nearly all meals	none	I	omni	seldom	prohib	Pb	O	2	5	N	Y	community with surplus to poor
Torri Superiore Ecov…	Nearly all meals	6–20%	C	omni	often	occas	Pb	R	22	5	Y	N	ecovillage and sustainable cmty
Touchstone Cohousing								S	46	6			cohousing
Tres Placitas del Rio	1 time/week	1–5%	I	omni	occas	prohib	Pb	U	9	2	Y	N	caring home creating awareness
Tribe of Blank	Nearly all meals	over 50%	I	omni			H				Y	N	independent tribalism
Tribe of Dirt	Nearly all meals	1–5%	I	omni	occas	occas	H	O			Y	N	making a living together
Tribe of Likatien	Nearly all meals	21–50%	I	prim veg	occas	seldom	H	U	25	198	Y	N	tribe, sustainability, lively
Trillium Farm Community	2–5 times/week	6–20%	O	prim veg	occas	seldom	H Pb	R	10	82	Y	N	love, harmony and beauty
Trillium Hollow	2–5 times/week	1–5%	I	omni	occas	occas	Pb	S	3	4	Y	N	cohousing community
Truth Consciousness	2–5 times/week	1–5%		veg only	prohib							Y	truth consciousness
Tullstugan Collective…	Nearly all dinners	none	I	omni	occas	seldom	Pb	U	21	0	Y	N	sharing meals
Turn Cedars	Nearly all meals	6–20%	R	prim veg	occas	prohib	O	S	1	2	Y	Y	supporting one another fairly
Twelve Tribes	Nearly all meals		C	other	prohib	prohib	H					Y	establish the twelve tribes
12Tribes Heimsbrunn	Nearly all meals	1–5%	C	omni	prohib	prohib	H	T				Y	
12Tribes de Sus	Nearly all meals	6–20%		omni	prohib	prohib	H	R				Y	establish the twelve tribes
12Tribes Peppercorn Creek…	Nearly all meals	21–50%	C	omni	prohib	prohib	H	R	3	22		Y	establish the twelve tribes
12Tribes Stentwood Farm	Nearly all meals	1–5%		omni	prohib	prohib	H	R		4		Y	establish the twelve tribes

KEY *Common Diet:* I = up to each individual, C = community shares a common diet, R = diet is somewhat restricted, O = Other

Dietary Practice: omni = omnivorous, prim = primarily, veg = vegetarian, raw = raw foods.

Note: Some communities list omni and provide vegan options, some list vegan yet allow personal food without restriction. Take the label as a rough guideline.

Alcohol/Tobacco: occas = occasionally, prohib = prohibited

Education: System(s) used for childhood education. Pb = Public School, Pr = Private School, C = Private School at the Community, H = Homeschool, O = Other

Rural, Urban, etc. : R = Rural, U = Urban, S = Suburban, T = Small Town, O= Other

LGBT Memb Welcome: The community indicated that lesbians, gay men, bisexuals or transgendered people are welcome as members.

Spiritual Path: The community indicated it has a primarily spiritual or religious focus.

Charts

Community	State/Province	Country	Forming	Year Formed	Visitors Accepted	Open to More Adults	Open to More Children	Total Population	# Adults	# Children (<19yrs)	Percentage Women	Identified Leader	Leadership Core Group	How are Major Decisions Made	Join Fee	Income Shared/Indep.	Labor Required	Who Owns Land	Uses Cohousing Model	Survey Date
Twelve Tribes Cmty at Stepping Stone Farm	MO	USA		2003	Y	Y	y	12	10	2	40	Y				S	Y	indiv		Mar05
Twelve Tribes Cmty at the Morning Star…	CA	USA		2003	Y	Y	y	70	40	30	40	Y				S	Y	indiv		Mar05
Twelve Tribes Cmty in Arcadia	FL	USA		2002	Y	Y	y	24	14	10	50	Y				S	Y	indiv		Mar05
Twelve Tribes Cmty in Asheville	NC	USA	F	2005	Y	Y	y	20	10	10	50	Y				S	Y	indiv		Mar05
Twelve Tribes Cmty in Ashland	OR	USA	F	2004	Y	Y	y	10	6	4		Y	Y		Y	S	Y	cmty		Jan05
Twelve Tribes Cmty in Bellows Falls	VT	USA		1984	Y	Y	y	40	20	20	40	Y				S	Y	indiv		Mar05
Twelve Tribes Cmty in Boston	MA	USA		1981	Y	Y	y					Y				S	Y	indiv		Mar05
Twelve Tribes Cmty in Brunswick	GA	USA	F	2001	Y	Y	y	40	30	10	50	Y				S	Y	indiv		Mar05
Twelve Tribes Cmty in Cambridge	NY	USA		1997	Y	Y	y					Y		O		O	Y	indiv		Mar05
Twelve Tribes Cmty in Chattanooga	TN	USA		1971	Y	Y	y	45	30	15	50			O		S	N	indiv		Mar05
Twelve Tribes Cmty in Coxsackie	NY	USA		1997	Y	Y	y					Y			N	SO	Y	indiv		Mar05
Twelve Tribes Cmty in Hamburg	NY	USA		1993	Y	Y	y	36	20	16	50	Y				S	Y	indiv		Mar05
Twelve Tribes Cmty in Hyannis	MA	USA		1991	Y	Y	y					Y				O	Y	indiv		Mar05
Twelve Tribes Cmty in Irún		Spain		1999	Y	Y	y	45	27	18	50	Y				S	Y	other		Mar05
Twelve Tribes Cmty in Island Pond	VT	USA		1978	Y	Y	y					Y		O		S	Y	indiv		Mar05
Twelve Tribes Cmty in Ithaca	NY	USA		2001	Y	Y	y	55	35	20	50	Y				S	Y	indiv		Mar05
Twelve Tribes Cmty in Katoomba, Blue Mtn		Australia		2002	Y	Y	y	17	10	7	50	Y				S	Y	indiv		Mar05
Twelve Tribes Cmty in Lancaster	NH	USA		1988	Y	Y	y	80	40	40	50	Y		O		S	Y	indiv		Mar05
Twelve Tribes Cmty in Manitou Springs	CO	USA		1972	Y	Y	y	40	25	15	50	Y		O		S	Y	indiv		Mar05
Twelve Tribes Cmty in Nelson	BC	Canada		2000	Y	Y	y	32	24	8	50	Y				S	Y	indiv		Mar05
Twelve Tribes Cmty in Northern Virginia	VA	USA		2003	Y	Y	y	45	25	20	50	Y	Y			S	Y	cmty		Mar05
Twelve Tribes Cmty in Oak Hill	NY	USA		1997	Y	Y	y	80	40	40	45	N	Y	O	N	SO	Y	indiv		Mar05
Twelve Tribes Cmty in Oatlands		Australia		2001	Y	Y	y	21	16	5	40	Y				S	N	other		Mar05
Twelve Tribes Cmty in Plymouth	MA	USA	F	1999	Y	Y	y	65	45	20	40	Y				S	Y	indiv		Mar05
Twelve Tribes Cmty in Rutland	VT	USA		1993	Y	Y	y	45	24	21	50	Y				S	Y	indiv		Mar05
Twelve Tribes Cmty in San Sebastian		Spain		1994	Y	Y	y	25	15	10	50	Y			Y	S	Y	indiv		Mar05
Twelve Tribes Cmty in Savannah	GA	USA		2002	Y	Y	y	34	20	14	50	Y				S	Y	indiv		Mar05
Twelve Tribes Cmty in Vista	CA	USA		2002	Y	Y	y	30	20	10	30	Y				S	Y	indiv		Mar05
Twelve Tribes Cmty in Winnipeg	MB	Canada		1983	Y	Y	y					N	Y	O	N	SO	Y	indiv		Mar05
Twelve Tribes Cmty - Lake of the Ozarks	MO	USA		1997	Y	Y	y				50	Y				S	Y	cmty		Mar05
Twelve Tribes Comunidad en Buenos Aires		Argentina		1997	Y	Y	y	45	30	15	45	Y				S	Y	indiv		Mar05
Twelve Tribes Comunidade de Curitiba		Brazil		1997	Y	Y	y	47	30	17	47	Y				S	Y	indiv		Mar05
Twelve Tribes Comunidade de Londrina		Brazil		1989	Y	Y	y	100	100		45	Y				O	Y	indiv		Mar05
Twelve Tribes Comunidade de Osório		Brazil	F	2004	Y	Y	y	17	11	6	50	Y				S	N	indiv		Mar05
Twelve Tribes Gemeinschaft Klosterzimmern		Germany		2001	Y	Y	y	120	60	60	50	Y				S	Y	indiv		Mar05
Twin Oaks Community	VA	USA		1967	Y	Y		100	85	15	50	Y		O		S	Y	cmty		Feb05
Two Acre Wood	CA	USA		1994	Y	Y	y	35	25	10	60	Y	C		Y	I	Y	indiv	Y	Feb05
Two Echo Cohousing	ME	USA		1991	Y	Y	y	80	50	30	55		C		Y	I	Y	cmty	Y	Mar05
UFA-Fabrik		Germany		1976	Y			38	30	8	50		C			P	N	other		Mar05
Union Acres	NC	USA		1989	Y	Y	y	34	22	12	53	Y	C			I	Y	indiv		Nov04
University Students' Co-op Association	CA	USA		1933	Y			1250	1250	0	50	Y	Y		Y	I	Y	other		Jan05
Upper Applegate Community	MO	USA	F	1998	Y	Y	y	20	15	5	34	Y	Y			O	Y	nonprft		Jan05
Utah United Order	UT	USA	F	2005	Y	Y	y					Y	C		Y	I	Y	indiv		Mar05
Utopiaggia		Italy		1975	Y	Y	y	18	15	3	56		C		Y	I	Y	cmty		Mar05
Utopian Visions	KY	USA	F	2004	Y	Y	y	1	1	0	0	Y		L		I	Y	other	Y	Nov04
The v2b Cooperative	WI	USA	F	2004	Y	Y	y	20	18	2	50		C			I	N	other		Feb05
Vail House	MI	USA		1960	Y	Y		23	23			Y	Y		Y		Y			Mar05
The Vale	OH	USA		1960	Y	N	n	40	22	18	50	N	Y	C		IO	Y	ind-lt		Feb05
Vashon Cohousing	WA	USA		1989	Y														Y	Oct04

KEY *General:* Cmty = Community, Co-op = Cooperative, Coho = Cohousing
Canadian Provinces: AB = Alberta, BC = British Columbia, MB = Manitoba, NS = Nova Scotia, ON = Ontario, QC = Quebec
Country: Russian Fed = Russian Federation, UK = United Kingdom, USA = United States of America
Decisions: C = Consensus, M = Majority, L = Leader, G = Group of leaders or elders, O = Other.
Income: S = Members Share Dincome, I = Independently Handle Own Finances, P = Partial Income Sharing, O = Other.
Labor required: Members are expected to regularly contribute labor to the group.
Who Owns Land: clt = community land trust, cmty = community, indiv = individual, ldlord = landlord, subgrp = subgroup of members.
Survey Date: Date shown is when online questionnaire was completed or last updated by community.

Community Name	Eat Together How Frequently	What % of Own Food Is Grown	Common Diet	Dietary Practice	Alcohol Use	Tobacco Use	Education	Rural, Urban, etc.	# of Residences	Acres of Land	LGBT Memb Welcome	Spiritual Path	Primary Purpose and/or Focus
12Tribes Stepping Stone Farm	Nearly all meals	21–50%	O	kosher	prohib	prohib	H	R	2	100		Y	spiritual unity
12Tribes the Morning Star…	Nearly all meals	6–20%	C	other	prohib	prohib	H	R	5	67		Y	establish the twelve tribes
12Tribes Arcadia	Nearly all meals	1–5%	C	kosher	prohib	prohib	H	T	3	27		Y	learning to love
12Tribes Asheville			O	kosher	prohib	prohib	H					Y	fulfilling our created purpose
12Tribes Ashland	Nearly all meals	none	C	omni	occas	prohib	C	O	1	20		Y	the restoration of all things
12Tribes Bellows Falls	Nearly all meals	6–20%	C	other	prohib	prohib	H	R	1	120		Y	establish the twelve tribes
12Tribes Boston	Nearly all meals	none	C	omni	prohib	prohib	H	U				Y	establish the twelve tribes
12Tribes Brunswick	Nearly all meals		C		seldom		H		2			Y	the expression of God's love
12Tribes Cambridge	Nearly all meals	1–5%		omni	prohib	prohib	H	R		112		Y	establish the twelve tribes
12Tribes Chattanooga	Nearly all meals	none	C	kosher	prohib	prohib	H	S	3	5		Y	disciples of Yahshua
12Tribes Coxsackie	Nearly all meals	none		omni	prohib	prohib	H	U	2			Y	establish the twelve tribes
12Tribes Hamburg	Nearly all meals	1–5%		omni	prohib	prohib	H	T	1	7		Y	attain to perfect love
12Tribes Hyannis	Nearly all meals	1–5%	C	omni	prohib	prohib	H	U	3	1		Y	establish the twelve tribes
12Tribes Irún	Nearly all meals	21–50%		omni	prohib	prohib	H	R	1	5		Y	
12Tribes Island Pond	Nearly all meals	none		omni	prohib	prohib	H	U				Y	establish the twelve tribes
12Tribes Ithaca	Nearly all meals		C	omni	prohib	prohib	H	S	1	1		Y	loving God & one another
12Tribes Katoomba, Blue Mtn	Nearly all meals	none	C	omni	prohib	prohib	H	U	1			Y	
12Tribes Lancaster	Nearly all meals	1–5%	C	other	prohib	prohib	H	T	4	3		Y	establish the twelve tribes
12Tribes Manitou Springs	Nearly all meals	1–5%	C	other	prohib	prohib	H	T	2	3		Y	love, mercy, friendship
12Tribes Nelson	Nearly all meals	6–20%	C	omni	prohib	prohib	H	O		130		Y	manifest kingdom of God
12Tribes Northern Virginia	Nearly all meals	1–5%	C	kosher	prohib	prohib	H	R	3	11		Y	loving God / loving man
12Tribes Oak Hill	Nearly all meals	6–20%	C	omni	prohib	prohib	H	R				Y	establish the twelve tribes
12Tribes Oatlands	Nearly all meals	none	C	omni	prohib	prohib	H	S	1			Y	to build up the twelve tribes
12 Tribes Plymouth	Nearly all meals	none	C	other	prohib	prohib	H	S	3	5		Y	twelve tribes community
12Tribes Rutland	Nearly all meals	1–5%	R	omni	prohib	prohib	H	U	3	3		Y	establish the twelve tribes
12Tribes San Sebastian	Nearly all meals	1–5%	O	omni	prohib	prohib	H	O	1	1		Y	establish the twelve tribes
12Tribes Savannah		none	C	kosher	prohib	prohib	H	U	3			Y	fulfilling our created purpose
12Tribes Vista	Nearly all meals	none	C	omni	prohib	prohib	H	S	1	2		Y	establish the twelve tribes
12Tribes Winnipeg	Nearly all meals	none	C	omni	prohib	prohib	H	O				Y	establish the twelve tribes
12Tribes Lake of the Ozarks	Nearly all meals	6–20%	C	omni	prohib	prohib	H	T	2	5		Y	establish the twelve tribes
12Tribes Buenos Aires	Nearly all meals	21–50%	C	omni	prohib	prohib	H	R	5	15		Y	establish the twelve tribes
12Tribes Curitiba	Nearly all meals	6–20%	C	omni	prohib	prohib	H	O		59		Y	establish the twelve tribes
12Tribes Londrina	Nearly all meals	1–5%	C	omni	prohib	prohib	H	O		37		Y	establish the twelve tribes
12Tribes Osório	Nearly all meals	1–5%	C	omni	prohib	prohib	H	R	1	111		Y	establish the twelve tribes
12Tribes Klosterzimmern	Nearly all meals	over 50%	C	prim veg	prohib	prohib	H	R	3	69		Y	
Twin Oaks Community	Nearly all meals	over 50%	I	omni	seldom	seldom	H Pb	R	8	450	Y	N	egalitarianism, income-sharing
Two Acre Wood	1 time/week	1–5%	O	prim veg	often	seldom	Pr Pb	T	14	2	Y	N	community oriented living
Two Echo Cohousing	1–3 times/month	1–5%	I	omni	occas	prohib	Pb	R	27	94	Y	N	cohousing
UFA-Fabrik	Nearly all dinners	none	I	omni	occas	occas	Pr	U	3	4	N	N	culture ecology social welfare
Union Acres	1–3 times/month	6–20%	I	omni	occas	prohib	H Pb	R	15	80	Y	Y	
University Students' Co-op…	Nearly all dinners	none		omni	seldom	seldom		U	20		Y	N	student housing (university)
Upper Applegate Cmty	Nearly all meals	over 50%	R	prim veg	prohib	prohib	H	R	3	42	N	Y	Christian community, campouts
Utah United Order	1–3 times/month	over 50%	I	omni	seldom	prohib	H C Pb	R	250	0	N	Y	self sufficiency living
Utopiaggia	Nearly all dinners	6–20%	O	omni	occas	occas	Pb	R	3	247	Y	N	egalitarian, self-organized
Utopian Visions	Nearly all meals	over 50%	I				O	O	1	0	Y	N	zero impact aquatic living
The v2b Cooperative	1 time/week	6–20%	I	other	occas	occas	O	U	1	0	Y	N	live/work artists artisans
Vail House	Nearly all dinners			omni				U					
The Vale	1–3 times/month	6–20%	I	omni	occas	prohib	Pr Pb	R	11	40	Y		relieve loneliness
Vashon Cohousing										12			cohousing community

KEY *Common Diet:* I = up to each individual, C = community shares a common diet, R = diet is somewhat restricted, O = Other
Dietary Practice: omni = omnivorous, prim = primarily, veg = vegetarian, raw = raw foods.
 Note: Some communities list omni and provide vegan options, some list vegan yet allow personal food without restriction. Take the label as a rough guideline.
Alcohol/Tobacco: occas = occasionally, prohib = prohibited
Education: System(s) used for childhood education. Pb = Public School, Pr = Private School, C = Private School at the Community, H = Homeschool, O = Other
Rural, Urban, etc. : R = Rural, U = Urban, S = Suburban, T = Small Town, O= Other
LGBT Memb Welcome: The community indicated that lesbians, gay men, bisexuals or transgendered people are welcome as members.
Spiritual Path: The community indicated it has a primarily spiritual or religious focus.

Charts

Name	State/Province	Country	Forming	Year Formed	Visitors Accepted	Open to More Adults	Open to More Children	Total Population	# Adults	# Children (<19yrs)	Percentage Women	Identified Leader	Leadership Core Group	How are Major Decisions Made	Join Fee	Income Shared/Indep.	Labor Required	Who Owns Land	Uses Cohousing Model	Survey Date
Ventana Verde		Mexico	F	2003										C		I	N	other		Mar05
Village Cohousing	WI	USA		1992	Y	Y	y	35	28	7	71		Y	C	Y	I	Y	cmty	Y	Nov04
Village of Harmony	NM	USA	F	1993	Y	Y	y	8	8	0	50			C		I	Y	indiv		Mar05
Village Terraces Cohousing Neighborhood	NC	USA		2000	Y	Y	y	9	5	4	50			C	Y	I	Y	cmty	Y	Mar05
Vine & Fig Tree Center for Sustainable…	AL	USA	F	1986	Y	Y	y				50	N	N			O	N			Mar05
Vivekananda Monastery and Retreat Center	MI	USA		1960	Y	Y		7	7		29	Y	Y	L	N	IO	Y	other		Feb05
Vlierhof		Netherlands		2002	Y	Y	y	10	10	0	50			C		P	N	indiv		Jan05
Voice for the Voiceless	SD	USA	F	2005		Y	y							O		S	Y			Feb05
The VOL Community	AR	USA		1978	Y	Y	y	4	4	0	25				Y	O	Y	other		Oct04
Walden Two Community California	CA	USA	F	2005		Y			0	0	0		Y		O	Y	S	Y	clt		Feb05
Walker Creek Farm	WA	USA		1975	Y			14	7	7	58			C	Y	I	Y	other		Oct04
Walnut Street Co-op	OR	USA		2000	Y	Y	y	9	9	0	67		Y	C		I	Y	cmty		Oct04
Waterloo Co-operative Residence Inc.		Canada																		Mar05
Welcome Here - Circle of Light Cmty…				1972	Y	Y	y							C		O	N	other		Oct04
Wellspring	WI	USA		1982	Y	Y		5	5	0	55	Y	Y	C		I	Y	nonprft		Feb05
Westmerefolc Gepéode	WA	USA	F	1999		Y	y				50	Y	Y	C		I	N	indiv		Mar05
Westwood Cohousing	NC	USA		1992	Y	Y	y	50	38	12	60			C		I	Y	cmty	Y	Jan05
White Buffalo Farm	CO	USA		1975	Y	Y	y	18	16	2	42	Y	Y			I	Y	indiv		Dec04
White Hawk	NY	USA	F	2004	Y	Y	y	10	8	2	50		Y	C	Y		N			Mar05
Whitehall Co-op	TX	USA		1949	Y	Y	y	13	13	0	49			C	Y	I	Y	cmty		Mar05
Whole Health Foundation	CA	USA		1972	Y	Y		12	12	0	25	Y	Y	C	Y	I	Y	indiv		Jan05
Whole Village	ON	Canada	F	1995	Y	Y	y	28	20	8	56		Y	C	Y	I	Y	clt	Y	Jan05
The Wild Human Initiative	NC	USA	F	2004	Y	Y	y	36	12	24	50	Y	Y		O	P	Y	subgrp		Feb05
Wild Sage Cohousing	CO	USA		2000	Y	Y	y						Y	C	Y	I	Y	cmty	Y	Jan05
WindHaven	TX	USA	F	2005	Y	Y	y				60			C			Y	indiv		Feb05
WindSong	BC	Canada		1996	Y	Y	y	90	60	30	60			C		I	Y	cmty	Y	Mar05
WindSpirit Community	AZ	USA		1993	Y	Y	y	8	7	1	40		Y	C	Y	I	Y	cmty		Mar05
WindTree Ranch	AZ	USA	F	1989	Y	Y	y	3	3		70	Y	Y		Y	O	Y	nonprft		Mar05
Windward Foundation	WA	USA		1977	Y	Y	y	12	10	2	60	N	Y			I	Y	nonprft		Jan05
Winslow Cohousing Group	WA	USA		1989	Y	Y	y	78	50	28	52			C	Y	I	Y	other	Y	Jan05
Wiscoy Valley Community Land Co-op	MN	USA		1975	Y			26	25	1	50			C	Y	I	Y	cmty		Feb05
Wise Woman Center/Laughing Rock Farm	NY	USA	F	1982	Y	Y	n	9	8	1	100	Y		C L	O	IO	Y	indiv		Mar05
Wisteria	OH	USA		1996				38	22	16	55	Y	Y			I	Y	cmty		Jan05
Woodburn Hill Farm	MD	USA		1975	Y	Y	y	13	10	3	60	N	Y	C	N	IO	Y	cmty		Feb05
Woodcrest Bruderhof	NY	USA																		Feb05
Woodfolk House	VA	USA		1999	Y			8	8	0	50			C			Y	indiv		Dec04
Woodlawn Townhome Cooperatives	IL	USA	F	2004															Y	Mar05
Wygelia	MD	USA		1985	Y	Y	y	6					Y	C		SI	Y	indiv		May05
Yalaha Community Network	FL	USA	F	2003	Y	Y	y				55		Y	C		I	Y			Nov04
Yarrow Ecovillage	BC	Canada		2002	Y	Y	y	27	27		50			C	Y	I	Y	cmty	Y	Mar05
Yellow Plum Commons	WA	USA	F	2001	Y	Y	y	40	25	15				C	Y	I	Y	indiv	Y	Jan05
Yogaville / Satchidananda Ashram	VA	USA		1966	Y	Y	y	230	200	30	60	Y	Y		O	N	IO	Y	nonprft		Feb05
Yonderfamily Housing and Land Trust, Inc.	GA	USA	F	1967	Y	Y	y						Y		O	O	Y	clt		Feb05
York Center Community Co-op	IL	USA		1944								Y	Y		Y	O	N	cmty		Feb05
Yulupa Cohousing	CA	USA	F	2000		Y	y							C		I	N	cmty	Y	Jan05
Zen Peacemaker Circle	MA	USA		2003	Y	Y	y					Y	Y			I	N			Feb05
The Zen Society	NJ	USA		1985	Y	Y		4	4	0	50	Y	Y			I	Y	indiv	Y	Feb05
Zephyr Valley Community Co-op	MN	USA		1993	Y	Y	y	23	13	10	55			C	Y	I	Y	cmty	Y	Mar05
Zim Zam	NC	USA	F	1996	Y	Y	y	4	4		25	N	N	C		I	Y	indiv		Mar05
Zuni Mountain Sanctuary	NM	USA		1995	Y	N	n	8	8	0		N	N	C		N	S		cmty		Feb05

KEY *General:* Cmty = Community, Co-op = Cooperative, Coho = Cohousing
Canadian Provinces: AB = Alberta, BC = British Columbia, MB = Manitoba, NS = Nova Scotia, ON = Ontario, QC = Quebec
Country: Russian Fed = Russian Federation, UK = United Kingdom, USA = United States of America
Decisions: C = Consensus, M = Majority, L = Leader, G = Group of leaders or elders, O = Other.
Income: S = Members Share Income, I = Independently Handle Own Finances, P = Partial Income Sharing, O = Other.
Labor required: Members are expected to regularly contribute labor to the group.
Who Owns Land: clt = community land trust, cmty = community, indiv = individual, ldlord = landlord, subgrp = subgroup of members.
Survey Date: Date shown is when online questionnaire was completed or last updated by community.

Community Name	Eat Together How Frequently	What % of Own Food Is Grown	Common Diet	Dietary Practice	Alcohol Use	Tobacco Use	Education	Rural, Urban, etc.	# of Residences	Acres of Land	LGBT Memb Welcome	Spiritual Path	Primary Purpose and/or Focus
Ventana Verde	Rarely	none	I	other				R	5	4	N	N	escape from LA
Village Cohousing	2–5 times/week	1–5%	R	omni	often	seldom	Pb	U	18	1	Y	N	community, service, nurture
Village of Harmony	Rarely	6–20%	I	omni	seldom	seldom	Pb	R	8	10	Y	Y	simplicity, harmony
Village Terraces Cohousing...	2–5 times/week	6–20%	I	omni	seldom	seldom	C	R	4	20	Y	Y	extended-family cohousing pod
Vine & Fig Tree Center...							O	R	1	60	Y	N	food & energy self-sufficiency
Vivekananda Monastery...	2–5 times/week	1–5%		prim veg	prohib	seldom		R	12	105		Y	spiritual development
Vlierhof	Nearly all meals	6–20%	C	prim veg	occas	seldom	O	R	2	4	Y	Y	spirituality, autonomy
Voice for the Voiceless				veg only	prohib	prohib		T			N	Y	animal rights advocacy
The VOL Community	Nearly all meals	21–50%	C	prim veg	occas	occas	H	R	2	49	Y	N	self-realization
Walden Two Community...	Rarely	none	I	omni	prohib	prohib	C	R	10	10	Y	N	radical behaviorism
Walker Creek Farm	1–3 times/month	6–20%	I	omni	occas	seldom	H Pr Pb	R	4	20	Y	N	
Walnut Street Co-op	2–5 times/week	1–5%	I	prim veg	seldom	seldom		U	1	0	Y	N	
Waterloo Co-op Residence...													affordable student housing
Welcome Here – Circle...				prim veg	seldom	often	O	O			Y	N	freedom assemblies, community
Wellspring	2–5 times/week	over 50%	I	prim veg	prohib	prohib		R	3	31	Y	Y	education gardening environment
Westmerefolc Gepéode	1–3 times/month		I		occas		H	R	5		N	Y	heathen tribal community
Westwood Cohousing	2–5 times/week	1–5%	I	omni	occas	seldom	H Pb	U	24	4	Y	N	
White Buffalo Farm	Nearly all dinners	over 50%	I	omni	prohib	occas	H Pb	R	7	60	Y	Y	natural mysticism
White Hawk							H	R	25	120	Y	N	natural building, organic farm
Whitehall Co-op	2–5 times/week	none	R	prim veg	occas	prohib		U	1		Y	N	independence within community
Whole Health Foundation	1–3 times/month	21–50%	R	prim veg	prohib	prohib		U	1	0	N	N	
Whole Village	Nearly all meals	21–50%	I	omni	occas	seldom	H Pb	R	2	200	Y	N	coho biodynamic farm ecovillage
The Wild Human Initiative	Nearly all dinners	21–50%	C	omni	occas	occas	H	T	10	10	Y	Y	music, unschooling, grassroots
Wild Sage Cohousing	2–5 times/week	none	I	omni	occas	seldom	O	U	34	2	Y	N	environmental sustainability
WindHaven	Nearly all meals	21–50%	I	omni	occas	occas	HCPrPb	R		27	Y	N	psychology sustainability
WindSong	1 time/week	1–5%	I	omni	occas	seldom	Pb	S	34	6	Y	N	semi-rural, family-oriented
WindSpirit Community	2–5 times/week	21–50%	R	prim veg	occas	occas	H Pb	R	7	16	Y	N	organic permaculture God in all
WindTree Ranch	Nearly all meals	6–20%	R	veg only	occas	prohib	C	R	5	1227	Y	Y	land preserve devoted children
Windward Foundation	Nearly all dinners	6–20%		omni	occas	occas	H Pb	R	10	111	Y	Y	stewardship self-reliant
Winslow Cohousing Group	2–5 times/week	1–5%	I	omni	seldom	seldom	H Pr Pb	T	30	5	Y	N	cohousing village
Wiscoy Valley Community...	1–3 times/month	21–50%	I	omni	occas	occas	Pb	R	13	358	N	N	consensus, organic, rural
Wise Woman Center/Laugh...	Nearly all dinners	21–50%		omni	seldom	seldom		R	3	55	Y	Y	woman spirit, herbal medicine
Wisteria	1–3 times/month	1–5%	I	omni	occas	occas	H Pb	R	6	622	Y	N	land stewardship event site
Woodburn Hill Farm	2–5 times/week	21–50%	I	omni	seldom	seldom	H Pb	R	5	128			earth based
Woodcrest Bruderhof													following Jesus
Woodfolk House	2–5 times/week	6–20%	O	prim veg	occas	occas		U	1		Y	N	environment, activism, crazy
Woodlawn Townhome Co-op													
Wygelia	Nearly all meals	6–20%		omni	prohib	occas		R	1	65	Y		empowerment of creativity
Yalaha Community Network	1–3 times/month	1–5%	I	omni	occas	seldom	H	R			Y	N	eco, self sufficient sustainable
Yarrow Ecovillage	1–3 times/month	6–20%	I	prim veg	occas	seldom	O	R	2	25		N	linking community with nature
Yellow Plum Commons	2–5 times/week	1–5%						S	18	2	Y	N	
Yogaville / Satchidananda...	Nearly all dinners	21–50%		veg only	prohib	prohib	HCPrPb	R	50	700	Y	Y	spiritual vegetarian group
Yonderfamily Housing...	1–3 times/month	6–20%	I	other			HCPbO	R		100	Y	Y	social eco-logical harmony
York Center Cmty Co-op	Rarely						Pr Pb	T	78	104			living in a tranquil oasis
Yulupa Cohousing								U	29	2	Y	N	urban cohousing
Zen Peacemaker Circle								O			Y	N	spirituality and social action
The Zen Society	Nearly all meals	1–5%	I	prim veg	occas	prohib	Pb	R	2	50	Y	Y	community is the spirit
Zephyr Valley Cmty Co-op	1 time/week	6–20%	I	omni	occas	seldom	Pb	R	7	550	Y	N	rural cohousing community
Zim Zam	1 time/week	1–5%	R	prim vegan	seldom	prohib		U	1	1	Y	N	eco, forest grdn, no owned animals
Zuni Mountain Sanctuary	Nearly all meals	1–5%		prim veg	occas	often		R	2	315	Y	Y	rural radical faeries

KEY *Common Diet:* I = up to each individual, C = community shares a common diet, R = diet is somewhat restricted, O = Other
Dietary Practice: omni = omnivorous, prim = primarily, veg = vegetarian, raw = raw foods.
   Note: Some communities list omni and provide vegan options, some list vegan yet allow personal food without restriction. Take the label as a rough guideline.
Alcohol/Tobacco: occas = occasionally, prohib = prohibited
Education: System(s) used for childhood education. Pb = Public School, Pr = Private School, C = Private School at the Community, H = Homeschool, O = Other
Rural, Urban, etc. : R = Rural, U = Urban, S = Suburban, T = Small Town, O= Other
LGBT Memb Welcome: The community indicated that lesbians, gay men, bisexuals or transgendered people are welcome as members.
Spiritual Path: The community indicated it has a primarily spiritual or religious focus.

Charts

Dianne Brause – Lost Valley Educational Center

About the Community Listings

The Community Listings contain descriptions of over 730 intentional communities around the world, with contact information when provided, including addresses, email, phone numbers, and web addresses.

At the beginning of each listing, we have included some helpful descriptive data from our questionnaire. The categories are as follows: year began, population, forming or reforming, dietary habits, urban/rural, and whether the community feels it has a primarily spiritual or religious focus.

A community's listing is where you'll get a sense of how the group sees itself—its vision, history, and daily life. Hopefully these descriptions will give you a feeling for each community, to complement the facts and figures listed in the Charts.

At the end of each listing we note the date the listing was updated. You will also notice that some listings have a scissors symbol [✂] indicating that they were edited by the *Directory* editors for length and that longer descriptions are present on our website at *directory.ic.org*.

A few general disclaimers: First, we can't guarantee that the information in the Charts and Community Listings is accurate—each community decided what to say about itself. We edited lightly, and only for length and clarity. We caution each reader to verify information before getting involved with any of the groups listed. Second, these listings should be viewed as a "snapshot" of how each community saw itself at the time they wrote their listing. You may visit the community and view it differently. In addition, communities change. Information becomes outdated. Some groups wrote about their plans for the future, but others did not. Third, community descriptions may vary depending on who wrote the description; each person brings their own unique perspective.

A note on telephone numbers

For communities outside the US and Canada, phone numbers are listed such that they can be called from any country. An example for a German community would be +49-(0)1234-56789. The plus sign indicates that one must start with your country's International Direct Dialing (IDD) prefix for any call abroad (011 is the IDD for the US and Canada). The next numerals (up to the dash) are the country code, which is also necessary for international calls (in the example 49 is the country code for Germany). In parenthesis, you will find the National Direct Dialing (NDD) prefix which is the number one would dial within the country before dialing the actual phone number (in the US and Canada the NDD is 1; in Germany it is 0) and which is not necessary when dialing from outside the country. After that is the complete phone number including any area, region, or city codes. Thus for the above example, if calling from the US one would dial 011-49-1234-56789 but if calling within Germany one would dial 0-1234-56789.

AAAA COMMUNITY FOR TENDER LOVING CARE

Norm or Nachum
Montreal, QC
CANADA

514-342-9414
nfinkelstein_tlc@hotmail.com
normfinntlc@videotron.ca

Began: 2005 | Forming | Spiritual
Rural | Diet: Primarily raw foods

Shalom. AAAA=Association for the Advancement of Absolute Altruism Community for Tender Loving Care/Total Life Concepts. Jewish/others who relate, universal spiritual intentional rural community is forming. One hour to Montreal at new urban home center for all Jews and others. Virgin land, 100s to 1000s of acres with ecovillage single homes; cohousing; 24-hour: kitchen/grocery, library, gym/co-op sports, social, audio/visual, health center; small/large commerce/industry employee-owned ecobusiness; organic farm; third of land preserved; use of: dowsing, sacred math/pyramidology, feng shui, etc. Energy will be 100% alternative self-reliant. There will be: only natural products, fully recyclable, no chemicals and no EMF/microwave; Gaia sensitive. Education will be local Montessori/Waldorf/Jewish. Ecokosher, organic, live-food, vegan. It will have Orthodox area; total openness and respect and will study all traditions, but non-evangelical/fundamentalist. Join via consensus, vision attuned to our concepts. We go deep into Kabbala, psi, new/old sciences, healing frontiers via spiritual masters, medical and alternative doctors, scientists, Nobel laureates, applied uses. Wise seniors, mental/physical challenged, Tsedaka/charity via nonprofit tax exempt are involved. The center has Friday Onegs, services, havdala/mela malka/parties-music, dance, creativity to end Shabbat, Sunday business meals. Our focus is love/tender loving care/being childlike/altruism/play/laughter. Lehetraot/Until we meet.Contact to become part of initial formation of community [Mar2005]

ABBEY OF THE GENESEE

Br. Anthony Weber
3258 River Rd
Piffard, NY 14533

585-243-0660, 585-243-0661
anthonyweber@geneseeabbey.org
community@geneseeabbey.org

http://www.geneseeabbey.org

Began: 1951 | Pop. 35 | Spiritual | Rural

A Roman Catholic community of monks wholly ordered to contemplation belonging to the Cistercian Order of the Strict Observance, more commonly known as Trappists. The monks are dedicated to the worship of God in a hidden life within the monastery following the Rule of St. Benedict. They lead a life of solitude and silence, prayer and penance in a joyful spirit of faith. The monastic community supports itself by the common work of baking Monks' Bread. In addition, the brothers help out on the farm and with cooking, laundry, cleaning, hospitality, formation of new members, and care of the sick and elderly of the community. The community is cloistered and has no outside ministry. Guests are received for quiet, private retreats at the retreat house. The monastic day begins with vigils at 2:25 am and ends with compline at 6:40 pm. Throughout the day there is a good balance between prayer, reading, and work, all lived in fraternal love and support. Silence is practiced seriously. The brothers speak only when necessary and then as briefly as possible. Some of the brothers are priests; most are not. At the end of their formation program candidates take the monastic vows and remain with the community for the rest of their lives.

Visitors Accepted: The reception room is open from 2:00 am until 7:00 pm. Visitors are welcome anytime. They may visit the Abbey Church, our bookstore and our Monks' Bread outlet. [Jan2005]

ABODE OF THE MESSAGE

5 Abode Rd
New Lebanon, NY 12125

518-794-8090, 518-794-8095
live@theabode.net
programsoffice@theabode.net

http://www.theabode.net

Began: 1975 | Pop. 62 | Spiritual
Rural | Diet: Primarily vegetarian

An intentional spiritual community in upstate New York, the primary residential community of the Sufi Order International.

We are dedicated to honoring unity, truth, and wisdom of all the world's religions.

A vital conference/retreat center, a school of esoteric study, and a residential community are all parts of the Abode.

There are many ways to be here: a service-study program, short- or long-term residency, b&b, personal retreats, attending conferences, classes and Universal Worship.

Visitors Accepted: See website for info; call for information and reservation; long-term visit or residency requires application (found on website). [Jan2005]

ABUNDANCE FARM

Peter Christopher
Finca La Abundancia
Apdo Postal 36
Diriamba - Carazo
NICARAGUA

+505-(0)866-3982 (Nicaraguan cellular)
contact@abundancefarm.com

http://abundancefarm.com

Began: 2004 | Pop. 4
Rural | Diet: Omnivorous

We are a group of friendly, hard-working people living the good life in a pleasant place. We work hard to achieve our dreams. This is our mission statement:

1. To develop a place where work and play are in balance and enjoyed; where basic needs are met with local resources when reasonable; where democratic education is practiced to develop curiosity, engagement with the world, and a life-long learning habit; where international exchanges occur for the goal of global harmony; and where honesty and kindness are supremely valued.
2. To research and develop psychology, knowledge, and practices that are necessary to socially and ecologically sustainable lifestyles.

Visitors Accepted: Read the relevant pages of our website and contact us in accordance with those directions. [Jan2005]

Scissors [✂] at the end of a listing indicate that it was edited for length by the Directory *editors and a longer description can be found at* directory.ic.org.

ABUNDANT DAWN COMMUNITY

PO Box 433
Floyd, VA 24091

540-745-5853
info@abundantdawn.org

http://www.abundantdawn.org

Began: 1994 | Pop. 6 | Rural | Diet: Other

Abundant Dawn is a rural community in southwest Virginia, USA. We are made up of small subgroups, which we call pods. We are just a few members and two pods now, and intend to grow to 40-60 members in 4-5 pods in the course of time.

Floyd County, in the Blue Ridge Mountains of Virginia, is our home. We are the stewards and grateful residents of 90 acres in a horseshoe bend of a river, with mountain vistas, peaceful forests and grassy meadows. The community moved here in May 1997.

We range in age from 30s to 60s. We include single, partnered, and married people, with a variety of spiritual and sexual orientations. Most of us had significant community living experience before coming to Abundant Dawn, and most of us are self-employed.

The whole community eats together several times per week, making use of our ample supply of home grown vegetables. Members range from mostly vegan to omnivorous. We tend to have elaborate holiday meals and occasional low key rituals drawing from eclectic traditions. We have weekly business meetings, and meet three times a year for three days in "congresses," in which we address longer-term issues, policies, and vision.

All community members are members of a pod. Each pod has 1-2 acres designated for its use and control. Within the guidelines of our vision statement, land plan, ecological guidelines, and other broad agreements, pods are encouraged to develop their own ways of living together.

Visitors Accepted: Please email us with some information about yourself and your interest in living in community. We'll respond with some information about our visitor program. If email is not available, please write to the postal address—response is likely to be less prompt. Phoning is not recommended as an initial point of contact. [Mar2005]

ABUNDANT FREEK

160 Lincoln Ave
Palo Alto, CA 94301

650-327-0367
christopherbalz@yahoo.com
musicglenn@yahoo.com

http://fmrfreek.best.vwh.net/
    personalSite.d/secondLayer.d/
    aF.html

Began: 1998 | Forming
Rural | Diet: Omnivorous

The Abundant Freek community-in-formation is specifically conceived of as a co-community. This means that it is attuned to addressing the challenge of enabling other pre-existing communities of people in their quest to find more equitable ways to live. We aim to only need about 10 acres of good farmland, in a location such as Blue Lake, California, USA. By effective tractor and hand cultivation of the land, we will be in a position to offer biodynamic bulk produce to the core and related community in exchange for any hand weeding needed and the picking labor. By making equipment shop facilities available to responsible parties, we will enable members of the community to own low-cost, functional trucks, etc. By keeping our land open to all enthusiastic people, we will enable people to find their own relationship to the land. By providing community facilities, we will enable people to find their own relationship to each other. By offering a very low-cost but abundant lifestyle, we will enable people to find out what cultural-economic ("culturonomic") change is about.

Visitors Accepted: There is one member of this community-forming who currently lives in an established residential cooperative and is open to visits regarding Abundant Freek. [Mar2005]

ACORN COMMUNITY

1259 Indian Creek Rd
Mineral, VA 23117

540-894-0595
acorn@ic.org

http://www.ic.org/acorn

Began: 1993 | Pop. 20
Rural | Diet: Omnivorous

Acorn is a young community seeking ways of living that are cooperative, caring, and

Listings

Additions and corrections: email: directory@ic.org, web: directory.ic.org, mail: RR 1 Box 156-D, Rutledge MO 63563, USA.

91

ecologically sustainable. Our ideals embrace a diverse, egalitarian society that welcomes feminism, multiculturalism, varied sexual and relationship orientations, and personal growth. Our members include equal numbers of vegans, vegetarians, and omnivores. We value energy spent on improving interpersonal communication. Our decisions are made by consensus. We currently have about 20 members. Our ages range from 2 months to over 50. Our beautiful 72 acres border on the South Anna River. Our two main residences are a white clapboard farmhouse built in 1908 and a community center with a dozen bedrooms. Acorn's money and resources are held in common. We give "labor credit" for community work, such as building, gardening, cooking, cleaning, etc., whether or not it produces income. Members usually work around 40 hours per week. Our main businesses at this time are tinnery crafts (made from recycled cans) and our seed business, Southern Exposure Seed Exchange. Groups may gather for swimming in the river, folksinging, videos, jam sessions, drum circles, gaming, art parties, dances, yoga class, poetry readings, and hot-tubbing. In addition, many members take advantage of cultural opportunities at Twin Oaks Community, in the college town of Charlottesville, or in Washington, DC. We are actively seeking new members.

Visitors Accepted: Write a detailed letter or email telling us about you, your reason for an interest in Acorn, how long you might want to stay, and what you might be looking for in a visit. We decide by consensus if we are all comfortable with a visit, or if we feel we have room for a visitor at that time. [Mar2005]

The members of Acorn Community.

ADELPHI

The Adelphi Organization
PO Box 2423
Quinlan, TX 75474

972-563-1346

Adelphi is an intentional community, founded by the author of the book *The Ultimate Frontier*. It is a place for those people interested in the philosophy presented in that book to live and interact with others of like mind. The book gives an intelligent explanation of the mysteries of human existence, and provides a practical approach to spiritual growth. Many readers said it tied together the many pieces of their own philosophy they had already learned through living. The book's philosophy is centered on the idea that the purpose of life is personal growth in psychological and emotional maturity. The pursuit of ever-greater matu-

rity is a continuous challenge with great rewards, and it is the ultimate frontier.

Learning about the community and becoming a member and resident begins with reading *The Ultimate Frontier*. Adelphi is a place where conscious, deliberate effort to achieve ever-greater maturity is our purpose, and members work to create a culture that supports that goal. Come live, learn, and grow with us. [Mar2005]

ADIRONDACK HERBS

7295 Fish House Rd
Galway, NY 12074

518-762-8082, 518-883-3453
herb@klink.net

http://www.aherbs.org

Began: 1990 | Pop. 9
Rural | Diet: Omnivorous

Three farms 30 miles apart in the Adirondacks near Sacandaga Lake; 210 acres. We grow medicinal herbs, produce tea bags, sell to health-food stores, build wood-fired water heaters. Minimum 17 hours work/week; additional optional work counts toward land ownership; profit shares. Option to start your own business here.

We have a good library, piano, sailboats, Windsurfer, soon a hang glider or an ultra-light. We are very interested in bees, fly-wheels, alternative-energy vehicles, small airships, steel-fiber-reinforced ferro-cement, aquaculture, winter ice refrigeration. We prefer using dumped or surplus material, such as paper, envelopes, lumber, steel, bananas with brown spots. We'd rather pick firewood at the town dump than cut down

Scissors [✂] at the end of a listing indicate that it was edited for length by the Directory editors and a longer description can be found at directory.ic.org.

trees. We respect all religions/spiritual paths, propose herbal medicine as an adjuvant rather than an alternative to modern medicine. We take very seriously environmental degradation, the destruction of indigenous cultures, cruelty against humans and animals, television, waste, war, peace, and science. We take a bit less seriously astrologers, therapists, political correctness, the New Age, disco, and the New World Order, by which we mean that astrologers, numerologists, iridologists, kinesiologists, and even phrenologists ought to expect some good-humored kidding if they come here.

Visitors Accepted: Read our website, then email or write. [Mar2005]

AGAPE

Suzanne and Brayton Shanley
2062 Greenwich Rd
Ware, MA 01082

413-967-9369
Peace@agapecommunity.org
http://www.agapecommunity.org

Began: 1982 | Pop. 9 | Rural | Diet: Primarily vegetarian

Founded in 1982, Agape is a lay Catholic nonviolent community dedicated to prayer, poverty, nonviolent education, and ministry and witness in the world. We are ecumenical and interfaith in orientation.

We accept volunteers for any length of time to work in our garden and assist with homesteading, including maintenance of our two buildings, St. Francis House and St. Brigid House, a strawbale house with solar energy and a composting toilet.

We welcome interns for stays of three months to a year. We live on 32 acres of land in the Quabbin Reservoir in central Massachusetts.

We support ourselves through a nonviolent education ministry, donations and grants, which includes outreach to inner-city youths and adults, and retreats and other programs at the community. We host a variety of educational groups who are interested in sustainability. We drive a grease car, which is of considerable interest to many groups.

We pray together, study Scripture, and witness out of this base against all forms of violence.

We welcome people who have a yearning for a community life based on prayer, simplicity, and nonviolence. No TV or commercial radio but lots of music and a definite love of art in all its forms.

Those drawn to Agape will interact with hundreds of people throughout the year, including college students who attend Agape's twice yearly retreats. Office work, computer assistance, gardening, homesteading of all kinds, and public witness and outreach are a part of our lives, as is contact with children.

Visitors Accepted: People wishing to visit may call, email or write. We will arrange a mutually compatible time for a visit. [Mar2005]

AGAPE COMMUNITY

1180 Orthodox Way
Liberty, TN 37095

615-536-5239
info@sjkp.org
frgregory@kronstadt.org

Began: 1972 | Spiritual
Rural | Diet: Omnivorous

Agape Community is a residential settlement of the Russian Orthodox Church outside of Russia. It is located in a remote rural area of mountain hollows some 60 miles

---

HELP WANTED

We are searching for intelligent, enthusiastic, highly motivated, hard working people willing to dedicate their brilliant minds to challenging work in the space age setting of Adirondack Herbs. What follows are job descriptions for positions we must urgently fill. If you feel that you might qualify, please send us your resume.

A: Firewood Reader

B: "New Science" Officer--must be a person of Atlantian background, familiar with ancient technologies of free energy and perpetual motion

C: Multimedia Analyst--must be able to spend multi-hours(a minimum of 8) daily,analyzing television. Will submit detailed quarterly reports.

D: Curriculum Director--for our own Horizontally Challenged Studies Institute, dedicated to the study of afternoon sleep disorders.

E: Meteorological Officer--must observe work from a reclining position and promptly warn workers if it starts to rain.

F: Stove Leaner-- consideration for this position will be given only to persons qualified to make split-second decisions, the briefest delay in distancing posterior from stove may have dire consequences.

G: Triage Specialist--scientifically determines which vehicle or piece of equipment ought to be decommissioned and promptly breaks it.

H: Slow Motion Researcher--must be qualified to move small objects very slowly from one place to another for no apparent reason.

Adirondack Herbs ~~~~~~~~~~518-883-3453

---

southeast of Nashville. Permanent residence is open to those who share fully with the community in the faith, either as landholders purchasing neighboring property or as leaseholders on community-owned property.

Temporary residence on community property is possible for those who seriously seek instruction in the faith. Visitors who seek information concerning the Orthodox Christian faith and an experience of a life centered therein are welcome for short periods of time by prior arrangement, but should be prepared for primitive living conditions and a diet and daily life conditioned by the discipline of the church.

The community operates a small religious press and publishes a bimonthly magazine, *Living Orthodoxy*, at $20/year (US). For further written information and recent issue, send $5 to cover the cost of response. Our resources are severely limited.

Visitors Accepted [Jan2005]

AINAOLA

Chitta
RR 2 Box 3344
Pahoa, HI 96778

808-965-7704
ainaola2@aloha.net

Began: 1999 | Pop. 1
Rural | Diet: Raw food only

AinaOla means "Land of Aliveness." We are located on the big island of Hawaii, and our vision is to create a sustainable, exclusively raw-food, tribal homestead. For us, this begins with actively growing our own organic, raw foods and animals using efficient permaculture systems. But that's just the start. The AinaOla vision also encompasses truly human sustainability through shared responsibility; consensus decision making; egalitarian, tribal social structure; open and honest, nonviolent communication; and real commitments to personal, family, and community growth, and spiritual awakening. We're also exploring how to live our sexuality with freedom, responsibility, and sanity, such that it strengthens and enriches our community. And our vision is open to change and growth as new folks arrive.

So far, our greatest mastery has been in the homesteading and raw-food realms. Creating an intimate, stable, bonded core family is taking more time. We've definitely found that humans are the toughest crop of all, but we like 'em, so we're not giving up.

Is our vision compellingly attractive to

Additions and corrections: email: directory@ic.org, web: directory.ic.org, mail: RR 1 Box 156-D, Rutledge MO 63563, USA.

93

you? Let's talk. (If you think you could live another way, we're probably not your community.)

Aloha, from AinaOla.

Visitors Accepted: Email, phone, or show up...all of these could work. [Jan2005]

ALBUQUERQUE URBAN ECOVILLAGE

**Zaida Amaral and Sharon McLaren
Albuquerque, NM**

**505-410-4611, 505-991-0839
info@createvolution.net
avatar@ic.org**

Began: 2003 | Pop. 15 | Forming
Urban | Diet: Omnivorous

We are a forming group working to create an urban ecovillage near downtown Albuquerque. One of our goals is to create a visible model of sustainable development that can be a source of inspiration for the city as a whole, especially regarding water use. We are interested in following a cohousing style model for building (or renovations work) and having an emphasis on

personal growth and responsibility, and spiritual exploration. Our ecological values are influenced by permaculture and other ecovillage projects we have connections with, as well as our desert environment. We are actively pursuing training to use consensus for effective decision making.

We have a committed core group ranging in ages from the mid-30s to early 60s, plus kids. We are a mix of urban professionals. We'd like to integrate at least some of our work lives onto our land as well, and envision an arts and performance center, ecovillage training center and cool neighborhood coffee shop as some of the work scene available on the land. We are also looking at properties that put us within walking distance of downtown and on the bus line.

Our spiritual practices are varied and non-dogmatic. What these paths have in common is explorations for how to do life with a sense of deliberate sacredness.

Community membership options include both renting and owning, and we invite a diversity of identities to come play. We also have a sister ecovillage project in Brazil, so native Portuguese speakers may find a good

match with us, if the other areas we are pursuing are of interest.

Visitors Accepted: Contact us first via phone or email. [Mar2005][✂]

ALPHA FARM

**92819 Deadwood Creek Rd
Deadwood, OR 97430**

**541-964-5102 (Farm),
541-268-4311 (Alpha-Bit)
alpha@pioneer.net
alinst@pioneer.net**

**http://www.pioneer.net/~alpha/
index.htm**

Began: 1972 | Pop. 6
Rural | Diet: Omnivorous

Alpha Farm is an extended-family-style community on 280 acres in the Coast Range of Oregon. Consensus, our decision-making process, is also a metaphor for the ideal world we seek to create here—and so help create in the larger world. We seek to honor and respect the spirit in all people and in nature; to nurture harmony within ourselves, among people, and with the Earth;

Scissors [✂] at the end of a listing indicate that it was edited for length by the Directory editors and a longer description can be found at directory.ic.org.

and to integrate all of life into a balanced whole. We value service and work as love made visible. Group process is a strong point; we meet regularly for business and sharing.

Founded in 1972, we average 10–15 adults and 4–6 children. New people participate in an internship of 3 or 6 months followed by a year as residents (trial members) before becoming eligible for membership. Members and residents work primarily on the farm or in community-owned businesses (a cafe-bookstore-gift shop, contract mail delivery, and a consensus and facilitation training/consulting practice) or occasionally in paid work off the farm. All income and resources are held in common. We are experimenting with different housing patterns, particularly for families; individuals have private rooms, while other living space is common; evening meals are communal.

We are open to new residents; visitors are welcome for a three-day initial visit. Please call well ahead to arrange dates.

Visitors Accepted: Please call to book a visit at 541-964-5102. [Nov2004]

ALPHA OMEGA CHRISTIAN COMMUNITIES FOR THE CHEMICALLY INJURED

Kiri Hyatt
PO Box 71
San Antonio, TX 78291
ao_communities@yahoo.com

http://www.aocommunities.org

Forming | Spiritual

We are a nonprofit ministry and are looking for individuals who are committed to serving God by living in community and volunteering time toward the creation of larger communities for individuals who have multiple chemical sensitivity/environmental illness and related diseases. This first community will be located in or near the San Antonio, Texas, area.We are still seeking funds to purchase land. There is no property to visit. Anyone interested in working toward starting this community please dialogue. [Oct2004]

ALTAIR COHOUSING

13 East Morgan St
Phoenixville, PA 19460

Joel Bartlett
610-917-3648
Altaircohousing1@verizon.net

John Pittock
610-827-1486
rninercsp@hotmail.com

http://www.altaircohousing.com

Began: 1999

Altair has been active for over five years and currently consists of four families who have invested in Cohousing. We follow the traditional model, looking to build 30-40 units ranging in size from studios to four bedrooms. A unique feature: we are looking to an architecture influenced by the work of Rudolf Steiner. We are looking for a site within a ten-mile radius of the Phoenixville/Kimberton area. Possibilities include urban infill, brownfields, suburban or rural sites.

Upon an agreement of sale, we anticipate having a design retreat for our expanded membership: site, common house, and units. We have several professionals actively interested: civil engineer, green developer, cohousing developer, and architect.

We seek people of all ages and income levels. You can visit our website or contact us by emailing Joel at altairchousing1@verizon.net or calling at 610-917-3648. [Feb2005]

AMBROSIA HOUSING COOPERATIVE

225 E Lakelawn Pl
Madison, WI 53703

608-256-3503

http://madisoncommunity.coop

Began: 2004 | Pop. 27
Urban | Diet: Omnivorous

Ambrosia is the latest cooperative incarnation to appear in this huge house on the shores of Lake Mendota. The co-op was founded in August of 2004, and our lakeside mansion has 27 rooms, five bathrooms, a music room, a sauna, an office, a kids' playroom, three porches, and a dock on the lake. We aim to be a family friendly house, which means we reserve certain larger rooms for members with children and we aim to create an environment where children can thrive. We are a diverse group of people coming from many different walks

Additions and corrections: email: directory@ic.org, *web:* directory.ic.org, *mail: RR 1 Box 156-D, Rutledge MO 63563, USA.*

95

of life, but united in our effort to make this house a great place for everyone to live.

We are a part of the Madison Community Cooperative (MCC), which includes 11 houses and has over 200 members, and we share their vision of encouraging community interest in affordable housing alternatives.

Visitors Accepted: We'd love if you'd come by. We have dinner every week day at 6:00, so give us a call to let us know you are coming. To membership you must attend three meals and then have a membership meeting. [Mar2005]

AMERICAN BUDDHIST SHIM GUM DO ASSOCIATION

Mary J. Stackhouse
Abbot and USA Head Master
203 Chestnut Hill Ave
Brighton, MA 02135

617-787-1506
info@shimgumdo.org
http://www.shimgumdo.org

Began: 1978 | Pop. 42 | Spiritual
Urban | Diet: Omnivorous

Shim Gwang Sa (Mind Light Temple) is the main teaching center of the American Buddhist Shim Gum Do Association which teaches the Zen martial art called Shim Gum Do, which means "Mind Sword Path." The Founding Master of Shim Gum Do is enlightened Zen Master Chang Sik Kim. Master Kim had his formal Zen training at the Hwa Gye Temple of the Chyoge order of Zen Buddhism in Seoul, Korea where he entered the temple at the age of 13. At the age of 21, Master Kim underwent a 100-day retreat. During this time he discovered Shim Gum Do through his meditation and he attained enlightenment. Shim Gum Do is a Zen practice which brings together the mind and body through dynamic practice of the forms of Shim Gum Do and meditation. Shim Gum Do includes the study of sword and other weapons and also Shin Boep which means 'Body Dharma' which is weaponless. The practice of Shim Gum Do emphasizes attaining a clear mind, clear thinking, and clear action. Shim Gum Do is an authentic original art, still taught in its original form. Students have the opportunity to study directly under Shim Gum Do's Founding Master, Great Zen Master Chang Sik Kim. Shim Gwang Sa offers ongoing classes in Shim Gum Do and meditation. Great Zen Master Chang Sik Kim gives regular Dharma Talks. Shim Gwang Sa has a residential program for those who are interested in a more intensive study of Shim Gum Do and traditional Zen practices.

Visitors Accepted: Visitors are welcome during our class time, the current schedule is listed on our website. The 1st Friday of each month is an open meditation session and Dharma Talk from 6–7:30 pm. Please call if this date falls on a holiday. [Mar2005]

ANAHATA COMMUNITY

PO Box 258
Albany Village
North Shore City
NEW ZEALAND

+64-(0)9-415-9468
inquiries@anahata.org.nz
http://www.anahata.org.nz

Began: 2000 | Pop. 31
Suburban | Diet: Omnivorous

Anahata Community is located in the northern suburbs of North Shore City, about 15 km north of downtown Auckland, New Zealand. Anahata occupies about 30 acres in a small, secluded valley with two streams running through it. The extensive infrastructure includes a central community building with large kitchen and dining area, numerous bedroom blocks, an automotive workshop, crafts buildings, garden areas, tennis courts, a hot tub, and an olympic size swimming pool.

Anahata has a unique lifestyle which could perhaps be summarized as "socially communal, financially independent." Each resident has a private room for sleeping quarters. However, all other facilities—kitchen, dining room, laundry, showers, workshops—are shared by all the residents. Residents of Anahata contribute 7 hours of labor a week and make a weekly board payment to support the community. This covers the land lease, utilities, maintenance, and the common food supply. All other expenses—clothing, transportation, medical care, education, etc.—are the responsibility of the individual or family concerned.

What is required of residents is the desire and ability to live harmoniously with others in a situation involving the sharing of most of the physical infrastructure of everyday home life. Over the past several years the population at Anahata has fluctuated between 20 and 30 residents. Since the facilities were built to handle a substantially larger population, Anahata is open to new residents; singles, couples, and families.

Visitors Accepted: Please contact us several days in advance (preferably by email) to determine if space is available for overnight stays and to find out current costs. Day visits are easier to arrange. [Mar2005]

ANARRES ECOVILLAGE

24 St. Michaels Ave
Northampton NN1 4JQ England
UNITED KINGDOM
blackcurrent@members.v21.co.uk
http://www.anarres.info

Forming | Rural | Diet: Primarily vegan

This community is in the process of finding some land in Europe.

We are intending to:
• live from the land, eventually growing all our own food and materials,
• use ecological building techniques,
• demonstrate that people can exist happily and healthily without degrading the environment,
• develop an extensive natural woodland,
• take part in direct action and demonstrations, against capitalism and war, for example.

Anarres will have the following rules which everyone living in the village agrees to live by:
• no sale of produce and plants, minerals, or water from the land,
• no pets or livestock,
• no motor vehicles within the village,
• no toxic chemicals,
• one third of land to be kept wild and undisturbed,
• all growing to be done vegan organically.

Visitors Accepted: Contact first by letter or email, explaining why you would like to come. [Jan2005]

ANGELS VALLEY

Filip Marceron
PO Box 600
Harrisville, NY 13648

315-543-0025
filip@curedisturbancesinchildren.org
http://www.curedisturbancesinchildren.org

Began: 2000 | Pop. 1 | Forming
Rural | Diet: Omnivorous

Angels Valley is a nonprofit rural therapeutic foster home designed to cure children suffering from mental disturbances (autism, schizophrenia, mental retardation, epilepsy) or physical illnesses (cancer, diabetes, obesity, asthma) when caused by deeply repressed emotional issues. The project is based on psychoanalysis, psychosomatics,

---

Scissors [✁] at the end of a listing indicate that it was edited for length by the Directory editors and a longer description can be found at directory.ic.org.

and Bruno Bettelheim's milieu therapy. It is kept to a family size with only a few children to be the best efficient model for cure at lowest cost, so that it can be duplicated everywhere else needed.

The way of life of the team then has to be modest and no salaries are likely to be offered.

The relationships for all are non-directive, allowing everyone small or big to find one's own rhythm in life. Thus children lead all the way to their recovery.

The project includes diversified reality-oriented activities like growing a vegetable garden, improving the place, making and selling handicrafts. This helps mediatize relationships and also helps the project keep self-sufficient for independence's sake.

Team members can have their own income-making activities outside, as well as own their own home independently, and can choose how much time and energy they want to spend with the project.

Guidelines on paper can be sent by mail to those who want to know more.

Visitors Accepted: To not miss you when you come, better let us know in advance. Also let us know if you'd like to have overnight accommodation. First see our website. You can ask for the guidelines on paper to know more before you visit. Anyone is welcome to stop by unannounced anyway, but our availability is not certain. [Nov2004]

APEX BELLTOWN CO-OP

2225 1st Ave
Apt 207A
Seattle, WA 98121

206-956-0275
thekaypex@yahoo.com
sweetfigs@hotmail.com
apex@speakeasy.org

http://www.speakeasy.org/~apex

Began: 1982 | Pop. 22
Urban | Diet: Omnivorous

The Apex is a limited-equity housing cooperative located at First Avenue and Bell Street in Seattle's Belltown district. Apex provides its members with affordable housing and community facilities on a nonprofit basis. Apex seeks diversity of all types in its members and caters especially to people eligible for low-income housing.

We Own It!

Apex members (there are about 25 of us) collectively own and operate 35% of the building (the owner of Egbert's owns the remaining portion). This ownership trans-

lates to a lot of freedom, responsibility and community involvement on the part of members.

Visitors Accepted: Please call or email us several days in advance for a tour, or to attend our open-house potlucks that take place the 3rd Sunday of each month. Thanks! [Mar2005]

APROVECHO RESEARCH CENTER

80574 Hazelton Rd
Cottage Grove, OR 97424

541-942-8198, 541-942-0761
apro@efn.org

http://www.aprovecho.net

Began: 1976 | Pop. 16
Rural | Diet: Primarily vegetarian

The mission that inspires our community is to provide a basis for scientific research on appropriate technologies and techniques for simple and cooperative living, and to serve an educational role in disseminating information on such technologies and techniques. Our initial mission has expanded somewhat, to emphasize sustainable forestry, food production, and related skills as well as appropriate technology, but the spirit of our work remains unchanged: to learn how to live together sustainably and ecologically and to help others to do the same, in this and other countries. Our sustainable forestry research focuses on selective thinning as an alternative to clear-cutting, low impact methods of timber removal (such as horse logging), planting, cultivation, and use of non-timber forest products. Our appropriate technology research concentrates on developing energy-efficient, nonpolluting, renewable technologies that reflect current research but which are designed to be made in most any country. Our designs use readily available materials, many of them considered trash, to create devices that can improve the quality of life while lessening environmental degradation. In our acre-plus organic garden, we grow the great majority of fresh produce we consume year round.

We currently offer a 10 week internship program where we teach up to 14 interns about sustainable forestry, appropriate technology, organic gardening, and other sustainable living skills. Contact us if you are interested.

Visitors Accepted: Please contact us by phone or email if you are interested in coming for a visit. Normally we have an Open House the first Sunday of every month.

There are self-guided tours at the entrance of Aprovecho. [Feb2005]

AQUARIAN CONCEPTS COMMUNITY

PO Box 3946
Sedona, AZ 86340

928-204-1206
info@aquarianconceptscommunity.org

http://www.aquarianconcepts community.org

Began: 1989 | Pop. 110 | Spiritual
Diet: Omnivorous

Aquarian Concepts Community, a nonprofit in Sedona, Arizona, was founded by Gabriel of Sedona and Niann Emerson Chase, who share the Mandate of the Bright and Morning Star. All facets of the community are based on teachings in *Fifth and Continuing Fifth Epochal Revelation*, *The Urantia Book* and *Cosmic Family* volumes, with an emphasis on expanded information on Jesus, known as Christ Michael. The Starseed and Urantian Schools of

Additions and corrections: email: directory@ic.org, web: directory.ic.org, mail: RR 1 Box 156-D, Rutledge MO 63563, USA.

Melchizedek for children, teens, and adults provide unique information.

Living in divine pattern, service to others, and soul growth are emphasized. Healing incorporates spiritual and scientific techniques of Tron therapy (an advanced form of energy transference), personal transmissions (past lives, wrong thinking, and destiny purpose), morontia counseling, and Reiki.

Members gain experiential training and expand skills and talents in organic gardening at Avalon Gardens; in landscaping, stone masonry and carpentry through Planetary Family Services; and by many avenues of services, including: the Soulistic Medical Institute, recording studio, Global Change Video and DVD Productions, art studio and gallery, spiritual touring company, lodge and retreat center, legal services, and publishing company, which includes a bi-monthly periodical, "Alternative Voice." Vocational training and apprenticeships run year-round; weekend seminars are held bi-monthly.

Openings for members available. Visitors welcome by appointment.

Visitors Accepted: Please call, email, or write to arrange your visit. [Mar2005][✂]

ARC RETREAT CENTER

1680 373rd Ave NE
Stanchfield, MN 55080

763-689-3540
arcretreat@hotmail.com

http://www.arcretreat.org

ARC (action, relection, celebration) is an ecumenical Christian community of 5-7 persons dedicated to the ministry of contemplative prayer and hospitality. We serve groups and individuals seeking time apart, rest and spiritual renewal. ARC is located on 92 acres of beautiful pine woods forest and wetlands about 6 miles north of Cambridge, Minnesota. Founded by Ruth and Loren Halvorson in 1977, ARC's cornerstone expresses the ARC way of life as "joyful, simple, merciful." Homestyle meals are lovingly prepared for guests, and the community's daily worship is open to all.

Individuals make a covenant from year to year, based on discernment between the community member, the Director and the community. General areas of work involve welcoming guests, meal preparation, spiritual direction, retreat leadership, laundry, cleaning, gardening, trail development, maintenance, volunteer coordination, worship leadership, and computer and office tasks.

Small stipends, room and board, and medical insurance are provided as needed. Short-term volunteers are also welcomed into the community. [Mar2005]

ARCADIA COHOUSING

134 Circadian Way
Carrboro, NC 27516

Julie DeCamp Palmer
palmer4888@bellsouth.net

Began: 1991 | Pop. 60
Suburban | Diet: Omnivorous

Arcadia is a pedestrian-oriented residential cohousing community on sixteen acres of wooded land. The thirty-three individually-owned homes are clustered on five acres around the centrally-located common house. The remaining land is held in common, including woods, pond, stream, organic gardens, outdoor playspaces, and the common house, with kitchen, dining area, guest rooms, playroom, office, laundry room, and storage areas. The majority of homes have a passive solar design and the common areas are handicapped accessible. We are located near rural areas about 3 miles from the towns of Carrboro and Chapel Hill.

Visitors Accepted: Contact a member of the community to arrange a tour or to join us at a scheduled meal. [Feb2005]

ARCOSANTI

HC 74 Box 4136
Mayer, AZ 86333

928-632-6217 (gallery),
928-632-6222 (public relations)
info@arcosanti.org
pr@arcosanti.org

http://www.arcosanti.org

Began: 1970 | Pop. 62
Small Town | Diet: Omnivorous

Arcosanti is an experimental architectural project of the Cosanti Foundation, a non-profit educational foundation. As a construction site our goal is to build a prototype structure called an "Arcology." Arcology (architecture as ecology) is a concept developed by founder and chief architect Paolo Soleri. When complete Arcosanti will rise 25 stories on approximately 30 acres of land in a complex, three-dimensional, energy-efficient, pedestrian configuration of integrated living/working/social spaces for about 5,000 people of all ages.

As it is now, we serve as a learning center,

offering five-week workshops in which over 6,000 students and people of all interests have come to participate. All of our residents, volunteers, and interns come in through our five-week workshops. After completing the workshop, you have the option to become a resident or volunteer. We offer many areas of interest, including construction, planning, bronze foundry, woodworking, landscaping, and agriculture. We offer a gallery, bakery and cafe open to the public, as well as guided tours from our gallery seven days a week from ten until four. We do welcome visitors and have overnight accommodations available. Closed Christmas and Thanksgiving. Call for details.

Visitors Accepted: Anyone can visit for one or several days staying in our lean accommodations at a great price. We offer very delicious food, tours, an immense local ecology untouched by callous human hands in the last 2000 years, and more hiking than a long vacation could accomplish. [Nov2004]

ASCENSION POINT

BJ Harris
Englewood, CO

303-789-4544, 720-289-8443
info@ascensionpoint.org

http://www.ascensionpoint.org

Began: 2005 | Pop. 3 | Forming | Spiritual

Mission Statement: To construct a community of dedicated, powerful people focused on creating from within a new paradigm of living, where each individual is honored and valued as part of the whole and where Universal Laws of truth are understood and practiced. [Mar2005]

ASHLAND VINEYARD COMMUNITY

12456 Ashland Vineyard Ln
Ashland, VA 23005
poneill@vcu.edu

Began: 1983 | Pop. 14 | Spiritual
Rural | Diet: Omnivorous

Ashland Vineyard Community is an intentional community of six families sharing 40 acres of land, of which over 30 are held in common. We are a Quaker-oriented community, although not all of us are Quaker. Thus we make our decisions using consensus, and we incorporate the Friends' traditions of silence and attentiveness to the spirit in our routine business. Our purpose

---

Scissors [✂] at the end of a listing indicate that it was edited for length by the Directory *editors and a longer description can be found at* directory.ic.org.

is to foster an environment where our families may live simply in an atmosphere that encourages personal growth, inward spiritual insight, and outward expression of commitment. We maintain separate family households, but we share meals, chores, transportation, and equipment we use to maintain the gravel road, fields, pond, and woods. We have only one rule, the "no gossip rule." This means that "we aspire to speak of others without malice or self-serving interest and to speak directly and lovingly with each other about concerns." This rule has deeply enriched our lives together by building trust and safety. With the knowledge that we always know when there is a problem and we always work it out, we have been able to form deeply satisfying relationships. The community is restricted to six family units by county zoning law. Openings are available when a family leaves. There have been 2 openings since the community began in 1986. Contact us by email. [Feb2005]

ASHRAM COMMUNITY

178 Abbeyfield Rd
Sheffield 54 7AY England
UNITED KINGDOM

+44-(0)1142-436688
ashramcommunity@hotmail.com

http://www.ashram.org.uk

Began: 1967 I Pop. 40 I Spiritual I Urban

A relaxed community of individual radical Christians of all and no denominations who support each other in individual and corporate lifestyle issues, including joint projects and community houses.

Current projects include inner-city houses, a whole-foods shop and cooperative, homes with some income sharing. Publications include *Radical Theology, Lifestyle, Neighbourhood Community, Ecological Urban Living.*

Visitors Accepted [Mar2005]

ATLANTIS

Belen, Huila
COLOMBIA
atlantiscol@hotmail.com

http://www.afan.org.uk

Began: 1970 I Pop. 25 I Spiritual
Rural I Diet: Primarily vegetarian

Atlantis is a gutsy tribe of three generations, mainly English, Irish, Colombian; 10 adults; 10 kids; hundreds of visitors. Dedicated to

bypassing "civilization," 30 years old, we have lived on deserted islands and in mountain forests in Ireland and Colombia, developing creative ways of relating cooperatively with full self-expression.

Our kids are self-reliant, happy, hardworking, and talented, brought up with physical freedom but not allowed to piss the adults off! They have no formal education but masses of practical skills.

We're vegetarian, atheist, and politically revolutionary. Own food organically grown. We began as a therapeutic community. Our free expression can shock some people. No drugs; alternative medicine; 100 percent ecological lifestyle; no electricity; we reject twentieth-century values. One hundred seventy-five hectares of forest, caves, streams, waterfalls; 5,000-foot mild climate. Hard physical work, lots of fun, theater, music; we write songs, plays, books; do psychic work, dancing, sports, yoga. We run a traveling "Green Theatre."

Nonsmoking visitors welcome any time; must have sense of humor and willingness to express feelings. We are not "politically correct"! Donations of seeds for our tree-saving, organic-farming campaign among Colombian peasants welcome. This is a guerrilla area (calm).

Visitors Accepted [Mar2005]

ATTACHMENT PARENTING VILLAGE

Chris or Mary
5510 Rue Marceau
Indianapolis, IN 46220

317-205-9502
indywhited@yahoo.com

http://groups.yahoo.com/group/
Indy_AP_IC

Began: 2004 I Pop. 4 I Forming
Diet: Omnivorous

Seeking eco-conscious, attachment parenting families for discussion and planning of an intentional community in the greater Indianapolis area. Ideally members should be practitioners or supporters of attachment parenting and should be committed to nonviolence in general, and positive (non-punitive and non-corporal) discipline specifically.

We are seeking several families with similar priorities of respecting ourselves, our children and our planet. We seek a lifestyle that allows small group support for families and a pooling/better use of planetary resources. We're into "green" building materials, home/unschooling, on-site organic

farming, homebirthing suites, meeting rooms for area eco/family activists...

We envision 3 to 4 families coming together to share space (to be determined by group), chores, childcare, laughter, tears, expenses (potentially), and generally to fight the isolationist tendencies of the modern nuclear family model.

Visitors Accepted: Contact via phone or email to schedule. [Oct2004]

AWAAWAROA BAY ECO-VILLAGE

RD 1, Waiheke Island
NEW ZEALAND
awaeco@netscape.net
http://pl.net/~simong

Began: 1994 I Pop. 38 I Rural

Awaawaroa Bay Eco-Village owns 169 hectares (420 acres). There is a large wetland and estuarine system and a number of large pockets of regenerating bush. More than 50 percent of the bush is covenanted with DOC.

To protect the wildlife there are currently no cats or dogs on the property. Nontoxic and energy-efficient building materials and methods are required. An internal building code is in place. Most families use alternative power systems. We aim for a chemical-free environment with all land-use practices to be organic.

Our community vision statement is as follows:

"We live in community, creating a safe, sustainable environment that encompasses and enhances wholesome relationships with each other and the land.

All land use is organic, encouraging biodiversity.

We protect and enhance eco-systems and natural habitats.

Our community is based on cooperation, honesty and consensus.

We have a willingness to balance individual needs with the greater good of the community, while also valuing people's diversity.

We are a community who understands that our actions and behaviours influence the world of the future."

As of March 2005 there are no shares available for sale.

A communal tractor shed/barn has been built. The building of a multi-purpose mud-brick Community Building is well under way and should be completed in 2005.

Visitors Accepted: Email and find out if someone is willing to host you. Will be required to do some work in exchange. [Mar2005]

Listings

Additions and corrections: email: directory@ic.org, *web:* directory.ic.org, *mail:* RR 1 Box 156-D, Rutledge MO 63563, USA.

99

AWAKENING TO GRACE

Sharon
84 Holly Ridge
Mt. Ida, AR 71957

870-867-3465, 870-867-7337
sharon@healthpositive.com

Began: 2005 | Pop. 2 | Forming | Spiritual
Rural | Diet: Vegetarian only

We are two adults looking for spiritually-minded community partners. We're situated on seven acres with a three bedroom home and a cottage, on two live streams, in the National Forest near Mt. Ida, Arkansas. We're only one mile from a large lake, one of the cleanest in the US.

We've already started organic gardens and a small orchard and we want to move out of our current homes and build earth bag domes. We're seeking partners who want to either use our existing homes and share our land or co-create a new place in this vicinity. For more info, call.

Visitors Accepted: Please call us to arrange to visit. [Feb2005]

AZANIA ALLIANCE

512-650 Dupont St
Toronto, ON M6G 4B1
CANADA

416-703-5488
azanialliance@yahoo.ca

http://www.darkdaughta.com/
azania.html

Began: 2004 | Pop. 7 | Forming
Urban | Diet: Omnivorous

We are a people of colour driven, matriarchal, intergenerational, mixed-class, queer dominated, polyfidelitous, cooperative, grassroots coalition of womyn and willingly conscientizing patriarchs grounded in the principles of anti-oppression and collectivity.

Our formation has been heavily influenced and informed by the dystopic writings of notable Black science fiction author Octavia Butler and her books "The Parable of The Sower" and "The Parable of The Talents," and by Starhawk's "The Fifth Sacred Thing."

We are an intentionally and rigorously built community grounded in a shared belief that combines political consciousness, radical truth telling, creating home, and maintaining food security and abundance. This is a powerful gathering of differently located community members who are involved in creative, spiritually and emotionally grounded, activism-oriented, politicized, intentional community building.

As people of colour who very often find it difficult to have our issues addressed in any meaningful way through available community services, the Azania Alliance is also significant in that it's members are developing emotional/ psychological/ social supports through a web of community/peer support that will sustain us and our families, our intimate relationships, our children (present and future), our animal companions, our allies and our friends as we continue to pursue meaningful activism-based cooperative work.

Visitors Accepted: You are invited to read the Azania description, and then send us an email describing your understanding of yourself in relation to a community of queered, matriarchal, politically radical, ableism-questioning people of colour. [Feb2005][✂]

Visions of Utopia:
Experiments in Sustainable Culture

Geoph Kozeny, a core staff member of the first two editions of the *Communities Directory* and a featured columnist in *Communities* magazine, spent 4 years creating this documentary about intentional communities. Now you can actually see how some communities look "up close" while you listen to community members tell their stories in their own words. Featuring:

• A brief history of 2500 yrs of shared living
• Profiles of 7 very diverse communities
   Camphill Special School ('61, PA) , Twin Oaks ('67, VA), Ananda Village ('69, CA), Breitenbush Hot Springs ('77, OR), Purple Rose Collective ('78, CA) Earthaven ('92, NC)
• Insights about what works and what doesn't
• 90 minutes of information & inspiration!

"Outstanding Project of the Year Award"
–Communal Studies Association, Oct 2003

$33 Postpaid: FIC Video • 138-V Twin Oaks Rd, Louisa VA 23093 • (800)995-8342 • Online info & orders: http://store.ic.org/products/visions-of-utopia-video.html For progress reports email <geoph@ic.org>.

Ordinary people doing extraordinary things.

BARKING FROGS PERMACULTURE CENTER

PO Box 52
Sparr, FL 32192
YankeePerm@aol.com

Began: 1997 | Pop. 2 | Forming
Rural | Diet: Omnivorous

The major thrust of Barking Frogs Permaculture Center is permaculture.

Permaculture design brings our lives back into participation with the Earth. Permaculturists and other environmentalists warn of global destruction unless we learn to live with the Earth rather than continuing to prey upon her. Permaculture trusts that the Earth shows us solutions to halt the destruction of the biosphere while sustaining ourselves in wholesome and fulfilling ways.

Permaculture design integrates people into nature's design for the bioregion as a whole so that it is respected, enhanced, and

Scissors [✂] at the end of a listing indicate that it was edited for length by the Directory *editors and a longer description can be found at* directory.ic.org.

strengthened. People receive shelter, energy, food, water, income, community, and aesthetic as well as spiritual fulfillment as part of the permaculture design, all within a balanced biological community. Permaculture-design students learn to make practical recommendations to develop the natural potential of a site. They also learn to identify the source and availability of every resource required to implement the permaculture design. A timetable for orchestrating the unfolding of the design and using each stage of implementation to prepare for the next helps to assure practical and efficient results. Thus the design integrates the goals of the Earth and the people in that place.

Visitors Not Accepted [Mar2005]

THE BARN

Lower Sharpham Barton
Ashprington, nr. Totnes
Devon TQ9 7DX England
UNITED KINGDOM

+44-(0)1803-732661
barn@sharphamcollege.org

http://www.sharpham-trust.org/
barn.htm

Began: 1980 | Spiritual
Rural | Diet: Primarily vegetarian

The Barn is a rural retreat center offering an integrated lifestyle combining meditation practice, mindfulness work practice on the land, and community living. Uniquely located, we overlook the beautiful River Dart. Accommodations are singles, and there is guidance from experienced meditation teachers. Our aim is to live simply and be as self-sufficient as possible. We have extensive vegetable gardens, polytunnels, woodland, ducks, chickens, and geese. Please contact us for further information. [Mar2005]

BARTIMAEUS COMMUNITY OF MEADOW WOOD

1172 NE Fairgrounds Rd
Bremerton, WA 98311

Nancy Conrad
360-779-4644
nancyconrad@sprintmail.com

Barbara Buckham
360-692-8064
bbuckham@earthlink.net

Guy Coe
360-692-2310
christinecoe1@msn.com

http://www.bartcommunity.org

Began: 2002 | Pop. 19 | Spiritual
Diet: Omnivorous

Bartimaeus Cohousing, L.L.C. presents: "Meadow Wood."

"Our mission is to create a safe residential neighborhood for people to substantially grow into the whole, healthy, unique persons God intended."

This distinctive neighborhood in Bremerton, Washington offers quality affordable living in a spectacular waterfront and mountain setting, an hour away by ferry from Seattle. The community of Meadow Wood is reminiscent of a New England village, nestled in a gently sloping pasture, bordered by a creek, surrounded by tall trees and nature trails. Yet it is ideally located for "modern living," less than 10 minutes from two urban centers.

The site balances a desire for personal privacy with the social dynamics of a friendly, intergenerational community. We're dedicated to bringing out the best in each other, through active listening, mutual respect, an appreciation of differences, and honest caring. Community decisions are made by consensus. There is no single leader, no pooled incomes, or other required communal practices. This is a unique neighborhood, not a commune or church.

While most Meadow Wood residents will share an active Christian faith perspective, we also include those who agree with the values of the mission, as outlined on the website. Visitors who may not agree with all these values are nevertheless welcomed.

A guest house is reserved for people or a family going through difficult circumstances to stay in while seeking life skills enhancement, and living within a safe and healthy community of people. They will be considered carefully for suitability by the residents.

Visitors Accepted: Please contact us by email, and expect humorous, welcoming responses. After receiving your request to visit, we will work together to accommodate those requests. [Jan2005]

BBES (BIBLE BELT EXODUS SOCIETY)

216 W Culton
Warrensburg, MO 64093

816-405-6904
bohemianrathole@yahoogroups.com

Began: 2004 | Pop. 4 | Forming
Urban | Diet: Omnivorous

WHO: We are an open-minded accepting family dedicated to sharing our ideas, goals, talent, and assets in order to continually grow personally and as a community.

WHAT: We will strive to create a holistic, peaceful, happy home where we pool our creative and intellectual talents in order to better ourselves and our surrounding community while encouraging every advantage through our collective and communal co-existence.

WHY: We wish to create a society that values cooperation over competition through a supportive network of friends.

If this seems vague, it is because we are a bunch of idealistic college students who have no idea what we're going to run into along the way. We're still in the process of discovering who we are as a group, so it's a little hard to tell what we are going to become. Currently we are twelve members strong, with backgrounds in theatre, film, photography, sociology, music education, carpentry, landscaping, and automechanics. We realize that we would have a much more satisfying, comfortable, post-collegiate life working together rather than individually pursuing our goals. To anyone with expertise concerning forming intentional communities in urban areas: We are all ears, please help, S.O.S.

Side note: We're not English majors, so please excuse any grammatical errors.

Visitors Accepted: Drop us an email or call to set up a visiting time. [Dec2004]

BEACON HILL FRIENDS HOUSE

6 Chestnut St
Boston, MA 02108

617-227-9118
directors@bhfh.org

http://www.bhfh.org

Began: 1954 | Pop. 20

Beacon Hill Friends House is:
• a center for Quaker educational activities,

Additions and corrections: email: directory@ic.org, *web:* directory.ic.org, *mail: RR 1 Box 156-D, Rutledge MO 63563, USA.*

• the home of Beacon Hill Friends Meeting, and

• a cooperative residence for those interested in community living.

Beacon Hill Friends House is located on historic Beacon Hill in Boston, Massachusetts, a few blocks from the State House. The building was originally built in the early 1800's. Since being given to the Religious Society of Friends (Quakers) in 1954, the building has became a center for the growing Quaker community in Boston.

Mission: "To embody the Quaker principles of faith, simplicity, integrity, community, and social responsibility in order to nurture and call forth the Light in all of us."

Beacon Hill Friends House fulfills its mission by:

• providing a center where Friends and others can meet, worship and study,

• advancing and fostering the principles of the Religious Society of Friends,

• offering opportunities for the development of leadership, and

• maintaining a diverse, ecumenical, residential community guided by Friends' principles.

Visitors Accepted: We have two guest rooms that are available for short-term stays. [Jan2005]

BEAR CREEK FARMS

Bill Brunner (SASE)
PO Box 1049
Deaf Mule Trail
Fall River Mills, CA 96028

530-336-1010, 530-336-5414

Began: 1985 | Pop. 4 | Diet: Other

Couples and homeschooled children in wholistic resolve! No pacifist, religious guru, racist, dopers, TV, caffeine, booze, sugar, or paramilitary types. We're happy in the 16th century and prepared with high tech in town apartments over our health food store, martial arts and gym. We enjoy a pristine aquifer, abundant solar, family wholesome videos, and a huge library of alternative medical books. We own the ultimate tools, equipment, blacksmithing, timber-framing, and construction items necessary. Our strictly organic orchard-refuge sanctuary is in a million acre private timber preserve, off the electric grid. We're into Amish buggies, non-electric items, and ready for when "Mad Max" strikes. We enjoy 4,300 miles of Pacific Ocean that purifies our air at 3,400 ft elevation set in neat meadows—ideal for: alpacas, horses, cats, dogs, all the critters for gardening. Accomplished artists, craftsmen, and writers will marvel at how well set up our studios are for such. A concise rundown on your individual spirituality is a must, together with what you'll bring that will enhance this micro community. Best to come with a self-contained home on wheels and be ready to assist in finalization of our huge community structure (half completed). Don't call if your divorce from the city isn't finalized! SASE resume required.

Visitors Accepted: SASE resume. Phone conversation with all prospective members. Must have established an outside time table for relocation, with a resolute divorce from outside affiliations such as city employment. We are not set up to accommodate the curious. Only serious contenders. Workshops and seminars when community is established. [Mar2005]

Scissors [✂] at the end of a listing indicate that it was edited for length by the Directory *editors and a longer description can be found at* directory.ic.org.

BEAVER CREEK

Steve Spence
93 Sheldon Rd
Winthrop, NY 13697

315-328-5726
sspence@green-trust.org

http://www.green-trust.org

Began: 2004 | Pop. 4 | Forming
Rural | Diet: Omnivorous

A fledgling community in upstate New York, our focus is renewable energy and permaculture research and development. Organic gardening and farmsteading with up to 10 families on 5 existing acres, with agriculture privileges on 10 more. Housing is insulated geodesic quonset home/greenhouses. Power is solar, wind, and vegetable oil powered diesel generator. Biodiesel, ethanol, and bio-methane projects are in development. Wholistic education projects where subjects are weaved into life, instead of life into subjects.

Visitors Accepted: Please send an email to make appointment. [Nov2004]

BEAVER CREEK HOMESTEAD

Brad Neufeld
RR 2
Nolalu, ON P0T 2K0
CANADA

425-481-7633
neufeldb4@yahoo.com
bradneufeld@myrealbox.com

http://www.bradneufeld.com

Began: 2004 | Pop. 2 | Forming
Rural | Diet: Primarily vegetarian

This homestead is just starting and is fairly primitive as of yet, but is loaded with possibilities. The objective is to make a largely self-sufficient, eco-friendly, cooperative commune that will be sustainable for many generations. The core values are longevity, learning, and liberty—although the actual constitution is still being drafted (feedback appreciated).

We have 65 acres, an older home, a sauna, and a pond. We are building an in-ground passive solar home that combines cob, strawbales, solar energy and as many natural building techniques as we can incorporate. It is still a very young "commune" as there are only 2 members, but we have big plans.

There is no specific religious agenda and no political affiliations. We are a ways out of town and people must be comfortable in a wilderness setting if they are interested in joining us.

Inquiries and visitors are more than welcome.

Cheers.

Visitors Accepted: Give me a call, drop me a line, or send me a letter and I will be happy to tell you how to get here. Be prepared for a "camping" kind of experience, although much more comfortable. There is a nearby full service boarding home/restaurant in case you would like to be a bit more comfortable. [Feb2005]

BEECH GROVE BRUDERHOF

**http://www.beechgrovebruderhof
.co.uk**

Began: 1995 | Rural

Beech Grove Bruderhof in Nonington, Kent was founded in 1995 at the site of a former sports college.

The Peace Garden at Beech Grove is a popular local attraction. In 1997, the area behind the community's school was a tangle of nettles and giant stumps. Today it has grown and blossomed into a garden for peace. Sculptures, trees, a splashing waterfall, flowerbeds and sparkling tear-drop mirrors remind us of the many places where peace is still needed.

Visitors Accepted: In general, we encourage first-time visitors to come for a short stay—overnight or for a few days. We are not a retreat center, so expect to join us in our work, communal meals, and other activities during your stay. If possible, please contact us in advance to work out the details. [Feb2005]

BEECH HILL COMMUNITY

Morchard Bishop
Crediton
Devon EX17 6RF England
UNITED KINGDOM

+44-(0)1363-877228
+44-(0)1363-877587
SJBUNKER@aol.com
kjo@premier.co.uk

Began: 1994 | Pop. 12
Rural | Diet: Omnivorous

We live in a large country house in the rolling Devon Hills. Accommodation is both rented and leasehold, in converted outbuildings and in the main house. On our seven acres of land we grow organic fruit and vegetables. We have a paddock with three sheep and chickens, an orchard, a vineyard, a walled garden, a swimming pool, composting toilets, and a reed-bed sewage system. Together we run a course center and spend the income on community projects. We share responsibility for our home and the land on which we live. We have shared meals most evenings and at least 20 birthdays a year (cake, candles, and song). We participate in the wider community, promoting awareness of everyone's impact on the environment, through the local recycling scheme and community open days. Individuals earn their income in the wider world in journalism, education, recycling, complementary health and alternative ceremonies; some work from home. We do not want our community to be a place of dogmatism, judgment, or preaching. We value our diversity and flexibility. We aim to care for one another and enjoy life as it happens. We welcome each other's differences and enjoy visitors and volunteers.

Visitors Accepted: Please contact us first. We welcome WWOOFers and volunteers if we can host you. We run "visitor weekends" every six weeks or so for those interested in community living. [Mar2005]

BELLVALE BRUDERHOF

http://www.bellvalebruderhof.com

Bellvale is one of the newest Bruderhof communities. In 2001, the Bruderhof movement as a whole was growing and straining the capacity of existing settlements. We considered how to expand in a manageable way, the idea being to move into existing campuses and buildings and use them as they were, with a minimum of renovation and construction.

So properties were looked at with a view to their suitability for communal living and their readiness and availability to be moved into and lived in at short notice. We also reminded ourselves that in a small community we get to know each other better, so there was no need for a new Bruderhof to accommodate up to 400 people, as some of our existing communities do.

The campus of Pope Pius XII School in Chester, New York, was chosen as the site for the new Bruderhof. The school had been closed for a number of years, but was in a repairable state. Renovation began, and immediately families from other Bruderhof communities moved in. Bellvale was officially founded on November 3, 2001.

Today, about 120 people live at Bellvale. The property, which includes a fairly large lake, lies in a lovely rural valley surrounded

Listings

Additions and corrections: email: directory@ic.org, *web:* directory.ic.org, *mail:* RR 1 Box 156-D, Rutledge MO 63563, USA.

by wooded hills, perfect for hiking and our children's love of nature and play. [Feb2005]

BEREA COLLEGE ECOVILLAGE

Richard Olson
CPO 1921
Berea, KY 40404

859-985-3593
richard_olson@berea.edu

http://www.berea.edu/sens/
ecovillage

Began: 2001 | Small Town

An ecologically- and socially-sustainable residential and learning complex designed to meet the housing needs of Berea College students, principally those who are married or single parents, in a manner that supports their academic, labor and family responsibilities.

In addition to 32 new units of family housing and a new state-of-the-art child development and daycare center, the complex includes a commons house, a Sustainability and Environmental Studies (SENS) demonstration house, and site and landscaping features such as vegetable gardens, fruit trees, a greenhouse and a wetland.

Stringent performance goals for the Ecovillage include: reduction of energy use by 75%; generation of 10% of the Ecovillage's electricity on-site from renewable sources; reduction of per capita water use by 75%; treatment of sewage and wastewater on-site to swimmable quality; and recycling, reusing or composting at least 50% of waste. To accomplish these and other goals, the Ecovillage incorporates a wide range of "green design" elements including passive solar heating, and alternative energy production. On-site treatment of waste is accomplished using composting toilets and a "living machine," which converts sewage to swimmable quality water. Roof-top capture of rainwater contributes to irrigation and production of fruits and vegetables in local gardens and greenhouses.

Visitors Accepted: Just contact us as far in advance as possible. [Mar2005]

BERKELEY COHOUSING

Berkeley, CA 94702
berkcoho-info@ebcoho.org

Began: 1992 | Pop. 28
Urban | Diet: Omnivorous

Berkeley's first and only cohousing community.

Visitors Accepted: Contact us well in advance to make arrangements; fees apply for guestroom use. [Feb2005]

A BETTER WAY

Dena Flege
Barnes Rd
Williamstown, KY 41097

859-823-8111
fleges50@aol.com

Began: 2004 | Pop. 5 | Forming
Suburban | Diet: Omnivorous

We are a group that is forming an intentional living community in the KY/WV area. We share no spiritual paths and are mostly interested in escaping from the historical ways things are done in this country.

Visitors Accepted: Please contact us via email or phone to schedule a visit to one of our monthly meetings. [Jan2005]

BIG ROCK FARM

Box 82
River Hills, MB R0E 1T0
CANADA

204-345-4258, 204-878-4320
linsea_mccoy@yahoo.ca

Began: 1999 | Pop. 3 | Forming
Rural | Diet: Omnivorous

We are a five year old ecovillage in the making. Our focuses are living permaculture principals and healthy human relationships.

Visitors Accepted: Please write an email or call requesting a visit. In letters, include a brief description of yourself, your interests and why you would like to come. [Oct2004]

BIRDSFOOT FARM

1263 County Rte 25
Canton, NY 13617

315-386-4852
steve@littleriverschool.org

Began: 1972 | Pop. 11
Rural | Diet: Primarily vegetarian

Birdsfoot Farm is a consensus-based agricultural community founded in 1972. Our farm is located where the St. Lawrence River Valley meets the foothills of the Adirondack Mountains. Though the area is quite rural, the presence of four colleges nearby brings cultural diversity we appreciate.

Our 73-acre farm has fertile loam soil, woods, a stream, a large community house,

three comfortable homes, a schoolhouse, two barns and some seasonal housing.

Members share monthly living expenses, purchase equity in the property, and participate in community work projects. We care a lot about each other and find time for many kinds of sharing. Each person follows their own spiritual path. Individuals are active in social and environmental issues. The new-member process includes a one-year trial period. We welcome new members, including children and elders.

Our vegetable business grows two acres of certified organic vegetables for the community, wholesale, CSA, and farmers market using low input techniques, intensive spacing and cover cropping.

Little River Community School now serves 23 students in grades K-12 with three full time teachers. The school is founded on the belief that children are inherently motivated to learn about their world and should be allowed to proceed at their own rate (http://www.littleriverschool.org).

The farm and school provide income to some community members and others work off the farm. Each year the veggie business and school seek interns.

For more information about our community, or internship programs, please send a letter.

Visitors Accepted [Mar2005][✂]

BLACK ELK HOUSE

902 Baldwin Ave
Ann Arbor, MI 48104

734-930-2684

http://www.icc.coop

Began: 1986 | Diet: Vegetarian only

We are a socially conscious community of vegetarians and vegans who live, play, work, discuss, perform, and create together. We eat and socialize on our two wooden porches, in the warmth of the study's fireplace, and in our spacious kitchens and living room. Our property includes a bountiful organic garden, several fruit and nut trees, a performance space, and a sweet tree swing. We have a VCR and TV in the basement (with no cable or TV reception) as well as wireless internet. The Elk is a queer-friendly environment with a special focus on local and global activism, nutritious gourmet meals, and rockin' theme parties!

Visitors Accepted: Contact House President. [Mar2005]

Scissors [✂] at the end of a listing indicate that it was edited for length by the Directory *editors and a longer description can be found at directory.ic.org.*

BLACKBERRY

PO Box 208
North San Juan, CA 95960
janiekess@hotmail.com

Began: 1988 | Pop. 8
Rural | Diet: Primarily vegetarian

Blackberry is a close-knit intentional family committed to living, working, learning, and growing together in the Sierra Foothills north of Nevada City, California. We place much value on raising our children and ourselves in a nonviolent, emotionally and physically healthy environment.

We intend to become an income-sharing group, working toward perfecting an egalitarian, collective economic system. All our decisions are made by consensus. In our daily lives we like to experiment with various forms and rituals gleaned from many sources. We share an Earth-based spirituality, celebrating the seasons together.

A main focus of our community is responsible stewardship of the Earth, starting with this piece of the forest. We intend to develop sustainable cottage industries here, perhaps using renewable materials gathered from our land.

We see ourselves being active in local and global issues of health, peace, and the environment. Underlying all this is the desire to be deeply involved in each other's lives, to be sources of inspiration and learning, and to grow older and wiser together.

Visitors Accepted: Please tell us lots about yourself, including your background and experiences with, and/or visions of, living in community. Then, if it seems appropriate, we will send you more information about ourselves and invite you to visit. [Jan2005]

THE BLUE CRANE

http://thebluecrane.com

Pop. 8 | Forming | Spiritual | Diet: Other

The Blue Crane Centre was started to provide a exciting, safe, healthy and inspiring environment for over 15's and beyond who have been democratically homeschooled, unschooled, or non-coercively educated.

A place to continue their interests into secondary, tertiary and lifelong learning, or simply to live in a democratic, self sustaining, ecologically aware, coeducational, multi-cultural residential community and enjoy life!

The centre is run on a non-hierarchical democratic system. Based around a core of 20/25 resident students and up to 20 day students, the centre will remain a small replicable unit.

The Blue Crane Centre will however serve as a social and training centre for the local population, so aspects of the centre will create a large temporary influx of visitors.

There is no fixed dogma or curricula attached to the Blue Crane. It is a place where one can study in any given subject even if there are no existing recognized qualifications, such as it was ICT 20 years ago. Courses from Permaculture farming/gardening to motor mechanics can be arranged as required. On the question of physical activity—if you can think of it, you can do it here!

Extreme surfing, horse riding, trekking, bungee jumping, if you want it, here it is.

The Blue Crane will use state of the art communication systems to maintain and develop relationships with global academic and practical science institutions. It will also use "state of the art" social skills to maintain and develop relationships with the local communities.

Visitors Accepted: Email [Oct2004][✂✂]

THE BLUE HOUSE

Paul Schwartzkopf
410 W Duffy St
Savannah, GA 31401

912-233-4461
pschwa20@student.scad.edu

Began: 2000 | Pop. 8 | Urban | Diet: Other

The Blue House is a cooperative living community in the urban context of Savannah, Georgia. Individual rooms are rented and common space is shared. We host free, open dinners every Thursday night and feed the homeless on Sundays. We also help to maintain a local community garden.

Visitors Accepted: People who wish to visit The Blue House can call, or they can just show up on the doorstep. The best time to visit would probably be during the open dinners on Thursday nights which start at 8:00. Travellers passing through Savannah are welcome to stay up to two weeks in exchange for work trade. [Nov2004]

BLUE MOON COOPERATIVE

Jim Schley
24 Blue Moon Rd
South Strafford, VT 05070
jschley@sover.net

Began: 1983 | Pop. 17 | Rural | Diet: Other

This cooperative neighborhood on a gorgeous old farmstead in central Vermont was established by a group of friends who met in the early 1980s while working together in regional antinuclear, feminist, and disarmament coalitions. Initially we gathered as an informal study group to learn about land trusts and collective living. We spoke with people who had lived in communes and collectives, and began to explore alternative legal and financial structures with a lawyer who specializes in cooperatives and worker-owned businesses. Our goal was simplicity, fairness, and flexibility. Fortunately, it meanwhile took us more than two years to find land that we could afford, by which time we had a strong basis of understanding among our members (during those two years we met together at least monthly), as well as a solid set of bylaws. Being a cooperative instead of a land trust has been important to all of us; also important has been the fact that we "live off the grid"—our homes are powered by solar and/or wind energy. Our present shared projects include woodland stewardship and building a community sauna. We're a musical, good-humored group, very tuned into our kids. [Mar2005]

Additions and corrections: email: directory@ic.org, *web:* directory.ic.org, *mail:* RR 1 Box 156-D, Rutledge MO 63563, USA.

BLUE RIDGE COHOUSING

PO Box 72
Charlottesville, VA 22902

571-212-1678
info@blueridgecohousing.org
http://www.blueridgecohousing.org

Began: 2005 | Forming | Diet: Omnivorous

We are a group of families committed to establishing multi-generational cohousing around Charlottesville, Virginia. We are currently looking for land and for new members. Ultimately, we look to develop a neighborhood of between 25 and 35 households.

We represent a diversity of ages, backgrounds and experiences, including families with small children and retirees.

Several families have a wealth of experience in cohousing and intentional communities. Blue Ridge Cohousing has strong ties with cohousing professionals and existing cohousing neighborhoods, and will not hesitate to use these experts for advice and consultation.

Visitors Accepted: Please email us.
[Feb2005]

BLUEBERRY HILL

9684 Farmside Pl
Vienna, VA 22182

info@blueberryhill.org

Dee Dishon
703-759-9501
ddishon@erols.com

Hana Newcomb
9697 Farmside Pl
Vienna, VA 22182
703-759-2109
jonahana@aol.com

http://www.blueberryhill.org

Began: 1994 | Pop. 60
Suburban | Diet: Omnivorous

Blueberry Hill is a cohousing community of 19 houses in Northern Virginia, 20 miles from DC. We are closely connected to the vegetable farm next door—the farmers instigated the community and several of the family members live at Blueberry Hill. We are self-developed, and the only cohousing community in Fairfax County. We own a Common House together (where we eat 2–3 times a week, not including parties) and we maintain our commonly owned outdoor spaces. Our membership is diverse—in age, profession, place of origin, family size, and religious affiliation. We strive to maintain our relationships by working together on community projects, eating together often, watching movies, meeting as a full group once a month, having parties, and through many chance meetings along the greenway.

Visitors Accepted: Contact us through the website and we will respond with offers of a guide or dinner. A week or more warning is helpful. [Feb2005]

BOSCH CO-OP

Bruce Blacher
1823 15th Ave S
Minneapolis, MN 55404

612-871-2835
blacherbruce@hotmail.com

Janet Johnson
612-871-4260
janetltbo@hotmail.com

Began: 1982 | Pop. 5
Urban | Diet: Primarily vegetarian

Bosch Co-op is an age/gender/orientation diverse community of five adults (age 20s–40s) living in an old Victorian house in an urban inner-city neighborhood of Minneapolis, Minnesota. We are all left-oriented progressives with concerns for social

and economic justice. We are queer friendly, tolerant, inclusive, and affirming of each other's lifestyles. Living in an economically depressed and under-served neighborhood that faces many of the difficulties of urban blight, we have focused energy into community justice and revitalization issues. This has included organizing a block group and helping to develop a community garden. We share vegetarian and organic food and are active members of our local food co-op. We make decisions by consensus and all contribute labor into keeping our house and our community going. We're all friendly, down-to-earth folks; feel free to contact or visit us.

Visitors Accepted: Please contact us via phone if you're located in the US, or snail-mail or email if visiting from abroad. [Mar2005]

BOSTON COMMUNITY COOPERATIVES

102 Morrison Ave Apt 2
Somerville, MA 02144

617-718-9285
bcc@bostoncoop.net
bcc-housing@bostoncoop.net

http://www.bostoncoop.net/bcc

Began: 1999 | Pop. 9
Urban | Diet: Primarily vegetarian

Boston Community Cooperatives (BCC) is a 501(c)3 organization formed to build community through cooperative living, member education, neighborhood improvement and collective action. Members participate in a no-equity model of communally owned, democratically controlled, affordable residential cooperatives.

Currently, BCC has one rental co-op (BCC rents from a landlord), the Millstone Co-op in Somerville, Massachusetts. Millstone is an 8 person vegetarian household.

BCC is in the middle of purchasing a house in Fields Corner, Dorchester, which would be a 12-person cooperative (yet unnamed). If this exciting project goes through, there will be a number of openings in both of the BCC houses in the spring of 2005.

Visitors Accepted: Please contact us at bcc-housing@bostoncoop.net, or contact one of our member houses directly. If you contact BCC, we will try to put you in touch with a member house. Different houses may have different policies or expectations regarding guests. Please respect any

Scissors [✂] at the end of a listing indicate that it was edited for length by the Directory editors and a longer description can be found at directory.ic.org.

guidelines set up in the BCC houses you visit. [Mar2005]

BOWER HOUSE

127 Whitehills Dr
East Lansing, MI 48823

517-351-4490

http://www.msu.edu/user/coop/
houses/bower.htm

Began: 1950 | Pop. 17
Diet: Primarily vegetarian

Our house is a cooperative that is part of Student Housing Organization (12 houses total). We are the only vegetarian house, full of creativity, passion, and fire. We have a beautiful garden that we grow every summer, full of organic goodies. There are many activities that most members participate in together. These include camping, potlucks, initiatives, and many other things. Our house is full of love and happiness.

Visitors Accepted [Jan2005]

BREITENBUSH HOT SPRINGS

PO Box 578
Detroit, OR 97342

503-854-3321 (Retreat Center)
office@breitenbush.com

http://www.breitenbush.com

Began: 1977 | Pop. 33
Rural | Diet: Primarily vegetarian

We are an intentional community and worker-owned cooperative that operates Breitenbush Hot Springs Retreat and Conference Center, hosting 25,000 guests annually. Sixty miles east of Salem, Oregon, Breitenbush sits on 155 acres in ancient forests of the Cascades. Our community ranges from 50 to 90 adults and children. We are off the grid using hydro and geothermal, and practice low-impact Earth stewardship.

The members of the worker-owned cooperative make major decisions about community and business affairs at annual meetings, and elect the Board of Directors from their midst to oversee operations. The Business, Financial and Marketing Directors all work as a team and report to the Board. To be a worker-owner, a community member must be employed for one year, be an employee in good standing, and purchase a membership share of $500.

The community lives across the river from the retreat center in an ecovillage setting. We have regular community Sharings,

and three times a year we close for a 4-day community renewal where we join together for training, fun, and community building.

We live a rich, full life here. We delight in an abundance of diverse people, innovative ideas, healing practices, friendships and challenges.

From our credo: "Our primary service is to provide a healing retreat and conference center that promotes holistic health and spiritual growth. We mutually support and respect each person's dignity, and awaken to the Spirit within each of us that acknowledges we are all One. . . . It is our hope that the thriving Community which we create will be an inspiration to others in their exploration of lifestyle and community. We also extend ourselves to the greater society in which we live, the world community, and commit ourselves to being socially, spiritually, politically, and environmentally responsible."

Visitors Accepted: Call for reservations. [Mar2005]

BRIGHT MORNING STAR

302 NW 81st St
Seattle, WA 98117

206-782-9305
jbetzzall@yahoo.com

http://www.ic.org/nica/
communities/bms.htm

Began: 1979 | Pop. 7
Urban | Diet: Primarily vegan

Bright Morning Star is a small urban cooperative, formed to support our members in their social change and artistic pursuits. Located in Seattle, we enjoy many benefits of city living, including a wide range of friends and interests outside our home: Quaker meeting, opera, environmental and social justice organizations, and the Northwest Intentional Community Association, among others. We are especially proud to be gay and straight together. We share food, mostly vegetarian meals, and chores, and meet regularly, making decisions by consensus. Our workdays honor the continued well-being of our home, and our celebrations recognize the Light within each of us. Occasionally one of us spontaneously bursts into song. We began in Philadelphia in 1979 via the Life Center as two couples (gay and straight) combining incomes and coparenting three children. In 1985 we moved to Seattle and eventually bought a large, airy house. Although members have come and gone over the years, we are still committed to

maintaining a pleasant, cooperative, and nurturing environment for personal growth and social activism. Invited guests are welcome. Advance notice required.

Visitors Accepted: Write at least two weeks in advance, either by email or with a SASE. All visitors are approved by the group, so tell us something substantial about yourself, particularly your purpose in visiting. We are small in size and short on time and energy to share with visitors, but welcome those who may share our interests. [Jan2005]

BROWN ASSOCIATION FOR COOPERATIVE HOUSING (BACH)

PO Box 2562
Eastside Post Office
Providence, RI 02906

401-453-6836
bach@brown.edu
Joseph_Miri@brown.edu

http://www.brown.edu/
Students/BACH

Began: 1970 | Pop. 27 | Urban | Diet: Primarily vegetarian

The Brown Association for Cooperative Housing (BACH) is a nonprofit student-run housing cooperative in Providence, Rhode Island. Since 1971 it has dedicated itself to providing affordable housing and a sense of community to the students, faculty, administration, and employees of Brown University.

Each house runs its own food cooperative, allowing its members and others to discover the joys of bulk orders and cooking enough for 25 at a time. BACH is run entirely by its members. It is governed by a board of directors that takes responsibility for day-to-day operations as well as long-term projects of the corporation. There are currently two houses, Finlandia and Watermyn, housing a total of 27 people.

While every house makes its own rules, every BACH member is expected to behave and interact according to certain cooperative principles. Central to cooperative living is the idea of consensus that we use at the board and in the houses.

Visitors Accepted [Mar2005]

THE BRUDERHOF COMMUNITIES

contact@bruderhof.com

http://www.bruderhof.org

The Bruderhof is a faith-based intentional community movement with branches in

Listings

the United States, England, Germany and Australia.

In a world of loneliness and discord, countless people long for community, and our life together is an expression of that longing. Our goal is to overcome the isolation and fragmentation that mark our time by fighting their root cause—selfishness—in ourselves.

Working and eating communally, sharing houses and cars, raising our children together, and helping each other in the care of disabled and aged loved ones, we seek to live an organic life that addresses the needs of every individual yet still serves a greater common good.

We come from a wide spectrum of backgrounds—large cities and family farms, various religious (and non-religious) traditions, the working class and the Ivy League, and more than a dozen different nationalities. But we have a common basis: the teachings of Jesus and, even more important, the example of his life.

Visitors Accepted: In general, we encourage first-time visitors to come for a short stay—overnight or for a few days. We are not a retreat center, so expect to join us in our work, communal meals, and other activities during your stay. If possible, please contact us in advance to work out the details. [Feb2005]

BRUDERHOF-HAUS HOLZLAND

http://www.holzlandbruderhof.de

Bruderhof community house in Germany. [Feb2005]

BRUDERHOF-HAUS SANNERZ

http://www.sannerzbruderhof.de

Community house in central Germany. [Feb2005]

BRYN GWELED HOMESTEADS

1805 Meadow Rd
Southampton, PA 18966

215-953-8884
info@bryngweled.org
decentralist@comcast.net

http://www.BrynGweled.org

Began: 1940 | Pop. 43

A residential community just north of Philadelphia on 240 acres including 75 homesteads on 2 acre lots, community cen-

ter, recreational facilities, and 45 wilderness acres eased to a local conservancy. Member families own their home and lease their lot. We consider applicants for membership in a fair and friendly process whereby all have the opportunity to judge quality of fit. BG is not "low cost," but the land has not changed ownership since purchased in 1940 for $18,000. We value diversity and seek to increase it, not only in race, sexual orientation, ethnicity and religion, but in outlook and opinion, as much as possible within the framework of cooperation and neighborliness that is the strength of our community. Our management style consists of numerous committees, a board of directors, and monthly membership meetings where lively debate is often heard. Prohibitions include hunting, snowmobiles, ATVs, fences except for livestock/gardens, and alcohol on common land.

Visitors Accepted [Mar2005]

BRYNDERWEN VEGAN COMMUNITY

Malcolm Horne
Brynderwen, Crymlyn Rd,
Llansamlet
Swansea SA7 9XT Wales
UNITED KINGDOM

+44-(0)1792-792442
vegancom@btinternet.com

http://www.veganviews.org.uk/
brynderwen

Began: 2002 | Pop. 4 | Diet: Vegan only

Brynderwen is a spacious 4-5 bedroom house on the outskirts of Swansea in South Wales. There is a terraced garden, and a huge double garage which could be converted to further accommodation, or to a workshop, or both.

We're involved with local vegan/ vegetarian groups, and we run the Vegan Summer Gathering (a one week national event).

The aim over the next few years is to expand and to attract others (with or without capital, and of any age), either joining us in our projects or developing their own.

Some people live at Brynderwen, others live independently nearby. See our website for photos and more details.

Visitors Accepted: Read our website then contact us by email, letter or telephone. [Feb2005]

BUDDHIST COHOUSING

Unsited

Tim Clark
gsadix@earthlink.net

http://groups.yahoo.com/group/
BuCoHo

Began: 2000 | Forming | Spiritual

This is a parking lot for people interested in forming a cohousing sangha. [Feb2005]

BURLINGTON COHOUSING

344 North St #1
Burlington, VT 05401

802-863-8755
bcoho@sover.net

Began: 2000 | Forming | Urban

Burlington Cohousing is community in the heart of the city. We are creating an urban community grounded in the principles of cohousing. We see a path to a sustainable future that includes affordable living, decreased automobile dependence, and harmonious sharing of resources, along with ample opportunities for privacy.

We have recently gained control of an open site near the University of Vermont and walking distance from downtown. The group works closely with selected professionals and the City of Burlington, forming a dynamic development team. At this time, we are going through the permitting process. Move-in day may be as soon as fall 2005.

Construction plans include 32 private homes in several multi-unit buildings. We are a mixed income community; half of our living units will be subsidized; the remaining units will sell at market rate. There will be a community building for optional group meals and many other uses. A large outdoor area (about 5 acres) will be used for outdoor play, socializing, and gardening. The land borders a large conserved natural area with hiking trails through a mature forest.

Community "governance" and tasks will be managed by the residents. All aspects of being neighbors who own and use some shared spaces will be taken care of by committees. Everyone will be expected to participate on some level. (Our website is undergoing revisions; therefore please contact us directly to learn more.)

Visitors Accepted: To see our building site or meet some of the members, please contact us. [Mar2005]

Scissors [✂] at the end of a listing indicate that it was edited for length by the Directory *editors and a longer description can be found at* directory.ic.org.

CAMBRIDGE COHOUSING

175 Richdale Ave
Cambridge, MA 02140

617-661-1682
info@cambridgecohousing.org
webmaster@cambridgecohousing.org

http://www.cambridgecohousing.org

Began: 1995 | Pop. 92
Urban | Diet: Omnivorous

Cambridge Cohousing is a community-designed and -developed housing project in Cambridge, Massachusetts. We are a group of people of diverse ages, backgrounds, abilities, professions and lifestyles. We are committed to creating a neighborly and cooperative community in which we know and care about one another. Children can play safely, surrounded by neighbors, and residents know that caring friends are close by. We are committed to the vitality, convenience and diversity that is Cambridge.

Visitors Accepted: Please contact us well in advance. Tours may be scheduled in advance by contacting: tours-info@cambridgecohousing.org. [Mar2005]

CAMBRIDGE TERRACE COMMUNITY

Manu Caddie
23 Cambridge Terrace
Kaiti
Gisborne, Aotearoa 3802
NEW ZEALAND

manucaddie@hotmail.com

Began: 2003 | Pop. 21 | Forming | Spiritual
Small Town | Diet: Omnivorous

A collection of households nextdoor to each other in Gisborne/Turanganui-a-Kiwa, Aotearoa/NZ.

We have agreed that the community is at this stage a collective of homes connected through a mutual commitment to:

• take practical steps to live by and measure the values we agree upon;
• provide an increasing level of accountability on a day-to-day basis;
• live close to each other and share daily tasks, family, celebrations and goals;
• support each other through life's struggles and hard decisions;
• develop our capacity to love others and serve the wider community;
• encourage and acknowledge the good things about the wider body of Christ and those things that bring life to our neighbourhood and the wider society;
• challenge and work for healing in aspects that are sick in the wider body of Christ and our society;
• promoting *te reo me ona tikanga* in our homes, family life and work places;
• meeting together weekly to do Bible Study, share meals and pray together;
• opening our homes to others to share *kai, korero* and *karakia* on a regular basis; and
• find ways to resolve problems and differences that are fair and just and which encourage reconciliation, healing and restored relationships.

Our vision for the community:

A place for people to: identify areas for development; find support; be challenged; find restoration and healing; grow and change; support others; move on to new things.

Visitors Accepted: Email us with a description of who you are, why you would like to visit and how long you can stay for. We can provide meals and accommodation in exchange for work around the properties. [Mar2005][✂<]

CAMELOT COHOUSING

http://www.camelotcohousing.com

Began: 2003 | Pop. 28 | Forming
Small Town

We are a group of people from the Boston, Massachusetts area that is developing a 30-unit cohousing site. Right now, we are looking for land for our community to build on. We usually have about 25 people at our meetings—including our equity members, associate members and observers.

We are searching for land to the west of Boston, in the area bounded by I-495 (on the west), I-95 (on the east), I-90 (on the south) and Rte 2 (on the North).

We hope to complete construction and move in around 2006-2007. Contact Kathy@camelotcohousing.com. [Jan2005]

CAMP SISTER SPIRIT

Andie Gibbs
PO Box 12
Ovett, MS 39464

601-344-1411, 601-645-6479
sisterspir@aol.com

http://www.campsisterspirit.com

Began: 1993 | Pop. 4 | Spiritual
Rural | Diet: Omnivorous

We welcome group/individual rental for retreat and gatherings. We have a bunkhouse and 7 small cabins, RV hook-ups and 120 acres of tent space! We welcome visitors/volunteers for $15 to $25 per night, per-person sliding scale, access to our large kitchen (bring your own food) and our hot water shower house. We produce the LGBT and Allies Statewide Summit (other states welcome). We produce the Gulf Coast Womyn's Sister Camp. We host several spirituality gatherings and more each year. Check our website for more info.

We have several ongoing projects: antipoverty, sharing resources and skills, educational program here and in Mexico.

We faced great opposition to our presence in this community but have worked hard to earn our rightful space here, and the opposition has been quiet since we won our lawsuit.

Men who are allies are welcome to visit this space. At least three days notice needed before you visit. You must preregister. We need self-motivated volunteers who are willing to learn and work. No illegal drugs or alcohol. No violence. Pets considered with prior approval. The land is home to many pets!

Visitors Accepted: Contact us via email. [Jan2005]

CAMPHILL COMMUNITIES CALIFORNIA

Sirleen Ghileri
PO Box 1272
Soquel, CA 95073

831-476-7194
sirleen@camphillca.org
info@camphillca.org

http://www.camphillca.org

Began: 1998 | Pop. 29 | Spiritual
Suburban | Diet: Omnivorous

Located in Soquel, California on five acres overlooking Monterey Bay, Camphill Communities California is a residential care

Listings

Additions and corrections: email: directory@ic.org, web: directory.ic.org, mail: RR 1 Box 156-D, Rutledge MO 63563, USA.

109

community for adults with developmental disabilities. This exciting new venture opened in 1998 and has attracted wide interest and acclaim for its high standards, social innovation and organizational acumen. Well integrated in a region famous for its rich social, cultural and recreational opportunities, Camphill California is breaking new ground in interdependent community living.

An interdependent community, in which caregivers who are volunteers live and work in extended family settings with those with special needs, promotes social cooperation between individuals of different abilities. Such cooperation creates a rich cultural, social, and vocational life, which includes opportunities for all to celebrate and learn. It seeks to support the unfolding of individual development on the basis of a social context that emphasizes giving as well as receiving.

Camphill Communities California provides residential, vocational, social, recreational, and cultural services to meet the individual and collective needs of residents. Activities include baking, fiber arts, gardening, art, music, recreational and social excursions, cultural and community events, and ongoing training in life skills and communication.

Visitors Accepted: Email or telephone Sirleen Ghileri. [Dec2004]

CAMPHILL SOLTANE

**224 Nantmeal Rd
Glenmoore, PA 19343**

**610-469-0933, 610-469-1054
info@camphillsoltane.org**

http://www.camphillsoltane.org

Began: 1988 | Pop. 84 | Spiritual
Suburban | Diet: Omnivorous

Camphill Soltane is a lifesharing intentional community based on Anthroposophy, as developed by the Austrian educator Rudolf Steiner. Soltane is part of the International Camphill movement, with 90 locations worldwide. We share our lives and work with young adults with developmental disabilities (students), on 50 acres in a beautiful part of Pennsylvania, one hour west of Philadelphia. We have biodynamic orchards and gardens, a pottery studio, and facilities for baking, painting, singing, drama, and many arts and crafts, which we employ in building community together with our students. Ours is a spiritual and service community with a reverence for life, for cooperation, and for celebration. Our program features a strong emphasis on advocacy, and supporting students to make their own life choices.

Approximately 85 people live and work together, including several families with children. Most children attend the local Waldorf School, for which Camphill Soltane pays the tuition. Two other Camphill communities are located close by, providing many social and cultural opportunities.

Those seeking long-term involvement are encouraged to make a one-year commitment to get to know us, our students, and the Camphill way of living and working. Many people come from different countries, bringing a unique and lively atmosphere to Soltane. Altogether, this is a high energy, full, and busy life—especially the very demanding but rewarding work with our students with disabilities. See our website, then give us a call, write, or (best) visit!

Visitors Accepted: Email or call, preferably a month in advance, and tell us the specific dates you'd like to visit. [Jan2005]

CAMPHILL SPECIAL SCHOOL

**1784 Fairview Rd
Glenmoore, PA 19343**

**610-469-9236, 610-469-9758 (fax)
BRvolunteer@aol.com
csproll@aol.com**

http://www.beaverrun.org

Began: 1963 | Pop. 75 | Spiritual
Rural | Diet: Omnivorous

Camphill Special Schools, Inc., is a residential community of 150 people; almost half are developmentally disabled children and adolescents living with trained curative educators and their families. Called "Beaver Run," this children's village is located on 77 woodland acres in Chester County, one hour west of Philadelphia, Pennsylvania. The campus includes 11 custom-built family homes for the special children and those who work with them, a schoolhouse, a cultural hall, space for group and individual therapeutic treatments, a medical care unit, a craft house with a store and workshop, a stable for therapeutic riding, and various auxiliary buildings.

Camphill's educational philosophy, called "Curative Education," is based on

Scissors [✂] at the end of a listing indicate that it was edited for length by the Directory editors and a longer description can be found at directory.ic.org.

the social, educational, and spiritual insights of Rudolf Steiner, an Austrian scientist and philosopher, and aims for a more complete understanding and appreciation of man's spiritual nature and destiny. The school offers a four-year training for qualified adults in Curative Education that combines conceptual academic course work with hands-on practical experience. Life is intense and demanding here but very enriching. American applicants can participate in the Americorps program, which offers a bonus award program toward payment of student loans or further education.

Please contact us for further information. **Visitors Accepted** [Feb2005]

Trying to run a meeting?

FIC has some tools you need—the best books around on consensus facilitation.

http://consensusbooks.ic.org

CAMPHILL VILLAGE KIMBERTON HILLS

Nell Hazinski
PO Box 1045
Kimberton, PA 19442

610-935-3963, 610-935-0300
information@camphillkimberton.org

http://www.camphillkimberton.org

Began: 1972 | Pop. 109 | Spiritual
Rural | Diet: Omnivorous

Camphill Village of Kimberton Hills is one of eight North American communities in the Camphill movement—each one unique, yet all with similar purposes. We seek to create a renewed village life and to establish healthy social forms of human interdependence. Our approach is a nondenominational Christian way of life based on the inspirations of Rudolf Steiner's anthroposophy, which allows each person to evolve to their potential as a respected individual.

Started in 1972, our 430-acre agricultural and crafts community is run by 87 members, including some with developmental disabilities. We have 12 houses that shelter "extended families" who work in the dairy, CSA garden,

herb garden, orchard, bakery, fiber workshop, wood workshop, and cafe. We have a strong cultural life that integrates art and music into our lives. Volunteers are welcome to share in our life and work for a year, or perhaps a lifetime. Our community sponsors an apprenticeship program in biodynamic agriculture, and training in fabric arts. Contact us for more information by phone or email.

Visitors Accepted: Contact us by phone or email. [Feb2005]

CAMPHILL VILLAGE MINNESOTA, INC.

Laura Briggs
15136 Celtic Dr
Sauk Centre, MN 56378

320-732-6365
cvmn@rea-alp.com

http://www.camphillvillage-minnesota.org

Began: 1980 | Pop. 46 | Spiritual
Rural | Diet: Omnivorous

Camphill Village Minnesota is one of 105 Camphill Communities around the world.

Additions and corrections: email: directory@ic.org, web: directory.ic.org, mail: RR 1 Box 156-D, Rutledge MO 63563, USA.

Listings

We are a spiritually striving intentional community of approximately 45 people including adults with disabilities.

Our Village is nestled amongst 470 acres of gently rolling forested hills and sparkling lakes and waterways in the beautiful heartland of America.

The life, work, and celebrations of our community are based on the strong belief that every individual, regardless of ability, is an independent spiritual being.

Developmental disabilities are treated not as illnesses, but as a part of the fabric of human experience, worthy of recognition, respect, and honor.

We live together in the quest to bring the needs of the land, people, and animals into harmony with the needs of the Spirit.

Our community has a strong agricultural component with biodynamic farming and gardening and a small beef- and goat-herd.

Our Craft Shops include a bakery, weavery, woodworking shop, card shop, and a food processing and cheese making kitchen.

All members of the community are cared for within the context of healthy home environments and an active village life in which the dignity of humanity is enkindled and nurtured collectively and individually.

Camphill was founded in 1939 in Scotland by Austrian born Karl Koenig MD, and a small group of enthusiastic people whose aim was to live together in shared responsibility, caring for each other's needs, and creating a healing environment for the education of and life with disabled children and adults.

Visitors Accepted: We are open to new members as space is available. Please inquire by email, letter or phone. Contact Laura Briggs. [Mar2005][✂]

CAMPHILL VILLAGE USA, INC.

Joanne S. Gambino
84 Camphill Rd
Copake, NY 12516

518-329-4851
camphill@taconic.net

http://www.camphillvillage.org

Began: 1959 | Pop. 275 | Spiritual
Rural | Diet: Omnivorous

Camphill Village USA is a community of 240 people, some with special needs, caring for each other and for the earth and working together for the renewal of social, economic, and cultural life. Daily life is based on an active affirmation of the dignity, spiritual integrity, and valued contribution of each individual by providing extended family homes; meaningful, creative work; and a fulfilling cultural life with opportunities for further education, artistic expression, and personal growth. The village is comprised of 29 houses, barns and storage sheds for the biodynamic farm, 8 workshops, the Bakery, the Village Green Cafe, and Foutain Hall—our community cultural center—all on 600 pastoral acres of wooded hills, pastures, ponds, and gardens.

Visitors Accepted: Telephone Liz Hamann to arrange a tour or email her at cvvolunteer@taconic.net. [Feb2005]

CAMPHILL VILLAGE, NEWTON DEE

Newton Dee Village
Bieldside
Aberdeen AB15 9DX Scotland
UNITED KINGDOM

+44-(0)1224-868701
info@newtondee.org.uk

http://www.newtondee.org.uk

Began: 1960 | Spiritual | Diet: Omnivorous

Newton Dee Village is one of 90 Camphill communities around the world. We are a semirural community of around 200 people, 93 of whom are adults with learning disabilities. Our striving is based on anthroposophy, formulated by Rudolf Steiner. We work out of Christianity and celebrate the festivals of the year.

We live and work together in 21 households on a 170-acre estate. The products of our village workshops include toys, metalwork, and bakery and confectionery goods. In addition, we have a cafe, gift shop, and grocery store and also two farms and gardens that are run using biodynamic methods.

We receive no salaries, and our needs are met by the community. Our workforce is based on volunteers, with young people (minimum age 19) from Britain and abroad joining us for a minimum of one year. We are open to new members as space is available.

Visitors Accepted: Please inquire by letter or phone to: The Reception Group, Newton Dee Village. [Mar2005]

Scissors [✂] at the end of a listing indicate that it was edited for length by the Directory *editors and a longer description can be found at* directory.ic.org.

CANON FROME COURT COMMUNITY

Attn: Membership Secretary
Canon Frome
Ledbury, Herefordshire
HR8 2TD England
UNITED KINGDOM

+44-(0)870-765-0711
membership@canonfromecourt.org.uk

Attn: WWOOF Coordinator
+44-(0)870-765-0713
wwoof@canonfromecourt.org.uk

http://www.canonfromecourt.org.uk

Began: 1979 | Pop. 45
Rural | Diet: Omnivorous

Canon Frome Court is an intentional farm community founded in 1979. We have about 30 adults (from about 30 to 70 years old) and 15 children, on 40 acres.

We run a mixed farm with cows, goats, sheep, chickens, a walled garden, and arable fields.

Visitors Accepted: Contact the Membership Secretary or WWOOF coordinator. [Oct2004]

CANTINE'S ISLAND COHOUSING

Unit 6 Cantine's Island Ln
Saugerties, NY 12477

Michael Compain
845-246-3271
mcompain@hvc.rr.com

http://cantinesisland.home.att.net

Began: 1990 | Pop. 28
Urban | Diet: Omnivorous

Recently completed cohousing community of 16 modest private houses and common house built on 3 acres of an 9-acre property, with one-quarter mile frontage on the Esopus, a deep-water creek, between the falls over Barclay's Dam and the Hudson River. Saugerties is a friendly provincial town, near Woodstock and the city of Kingston. Our uniquely lovely property is the largest in the village, offering the convenience of town living and a nice degree of privacy. We worked long and hard to achieve our success, and in so doing came to know each other as trusted partners. We're all delighted to be living here!

We are looking for one or two more households to join us, who will be able to engage in an abbreviated version of the development phase that we went through, building on lots contiguous to or near the main site and joining as equal partners in this warm, well-functioning community. We will offer support and guidance, but we can't do it for you, because the growth into community life comes with the commitment to do it! Cohousing embodies an ideology of sharing, balanced with respect for privacy. We are egalitarian, tolerant, open to alternative lifestyles. Only a few of us are vegetarians, but most of the food we serve in the common house is vegetarian or vegan.

Visitors Accepted [Feb2005]

CARROWMORE COMMUNITY

homewright@taconic.net

http://www2.taconic.net/homewright

Forming

Carrowmore Community would like to attract individuals and families who wish to build environmentally considerate and economically affordable housing. We emphasize working together to provide basic necessities (housing; organic gardening; recreation: XC skiing, hiking, sailing, etc.; shared transportation; etc.)

Our vision for community emphasizes low environmental impact; economic frugality and resource sharing, to reduce the necessity for wage earning; organic gardening, community-built housing; egalitarian decision making and shared property interest.

The scale of the community would include three to four households, of varying sizes and composition, housed in community designed and built housing.

At a minimum, community members would be expected to be non-smokers, vegetarians, and have the ability to cover their expenses. This is a great opportunity to live a lifestyle that will afford time for personal/family growth and well being, while deriving the economic and social benefits of living in community. [Jan2005]

CASA VERDE COMMONS

1355 Lindenwood Grove
Colorado Springs, CO 80907
info@casaverde.us

http://www.colospringscohousing.com

Began: 1997 | Pop. 71
Suburban | Diet: Other

Visitors Accepted: Contact members@colospringscohousing.com and give contact information, approximate date of visit, and purpose of visit; wait for confirmation. [Jan2005]

CASCADE COHOUSING

Ian Higginbottom
South Hobart, Tasmania 7004
AUSTRALIA

+61-(0)3-6223-4405
ian@sonardata.com

http://www.sonardata.com/cascade cohousing

Began: 1990 | Pop. 34
Suburban | Diet: Omnivorous

Cascade Cohousing is a cohouse modeled on the Danish and US experiences described in the book *Cohousing* by McCammant and Durret.

We have a strong focus on the sharing of meals as a catalyst of "sense of community" and have three common meals per week available in our common house. The community has a concern to reduce environmental impact of our lifestyles, and individuals generally choose their own paths. We have a strong emphasis on both community and privacy. Half the group are vegetarian. We have common gardens, a workshop, children's areas, guest room, video room, and the like. We enjoy working and playing together. We lack a common ideology other than wanting to live this type of lifestyle. Our children love living at Cascade Cohousing.

Visitors Accepted: Contact the community and arrange a date/time to visit. We do not have fixed visiting times or days. We welcome visitors subject to a host being available to meet the visitor. [Jan2005]

CASCADIA COMMONS

4377 SW 94th Ave
Portland, OR 97225

503-650-7169
cccoho@easystreet.com

http://www.cascadiacommons.com

Began: 1992 | Pop. 45
Suburban | Diet: Omnivorous

Cascadia Commons Cohousing is a community of 26 homes and a common house located in a pleasant suburb 6 miles southwest of the center of Portland, Oregon. We were self-developed over the period from 1995-2004, with construction completed in 2001.

We occupy 2.9 acres of land, of which approximately half is legally designated wet-

Listings

Additions and corrections: email: directory@ic.org, *web:* directory.ic.org, *mail:* RR 1 Box 156-D, Rutledge MO 63563, USA.

113

lands and wetlands buffer that is required to be maintained in a natural state. Our homes are a mix of renovated townhouses, newly constructed flats, and townhouses.

We are a quarter of a mile from good bus service to the center of Portland, a 35 minute ride. It takes about 10-15 minutes by car.

Our current residents range in age from one to 81. We are a mix of singles, single moms, couples, and families. We are ecumenical as to religion or lack thereof, philosophy, sexual orientation, dietary preferences, and—at least in principle—politics. We share green values of caring for the earth and its creatures.

We are egalitarian in our governance, using consensus decision making, with legally required provision for breaking impasses, as required by Oregon's condominium law.

Visitors Accepted: Contact us by email or telephone. Explain interest and reason for visit. A host will be assigned to work out details. [Mar2005]

CATHOLIC WORKER COMMUNITY

**15405 Short Ridge Ct
Silver Spring, MD 20906**

**301-598-5427
cathwkr@aol.com**

http://www.angelfire.com/un/cw

Began: 1995 | Pop. 2 | Urban

The Silver Spring Catholic Worker gives hospitality on a small scale to seniors and those who come to Washington, DC for demonstrations, lobbying and studying. We are located in a three-bedroom house and garage which is at Leisure World, Maryland. This is fifteen miles north of downtown Washington, DC. At the house is a desktop publishing cooperative. Its name is CWP and its website is at www.angelfire.com/un/cwp. We are self-supporting and do not need financial or other contributions. When we started about ten years ago, we had ambitions of re-establishing the pre-trial house that used to exist at Fourteenth and N St NW, Washington, DC from the late 1960s to the mid-1980s. But because we have had to take care of our

own family members, this larger project is on hold.

Visitors Accepted: Best to contact us beforehand. [Jan2005]

CATOCTIN CREEK VILLAGE

**41298 Yakey Ln
Taylorstown, VA 20180**

**Lauranne Oliveau
703-346-3071
LauranneOliveau@aol.com**

**Kevin Oliveau
703-453-0487
oliveau@aol.com**

http://www.catoctincreekvillage.com

Began: 2000

[Feb2005]

CATSKILL BRUDERHOF

http://www.catskillbruderhof.com

Catskill Bruderhof is a Christian intentional community located on the site of a former

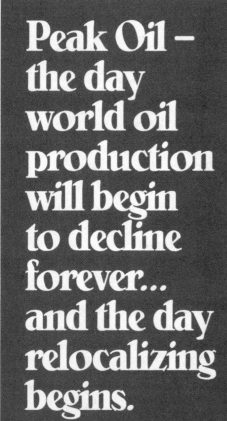

Scissors [✂] at the end of a listing indicate that it was edited for length by the Directory editors and a longer description can be found at directory.ic.org.

New York State Police Camp in Elka Park, New York in the midst of the scenic Catskill mountains. [Feb2005]

CEDARSANCTUM

Jef and Stacy Murphy
3508 NE Simpson
Portland, OR 97211

503-284-1160
cedarsanctum@comcast.net

http://www.cedarsanctum.net

Began: 2000 | Pop. 4 | Forming | Spiritual
Urban | Diet: Omnivorous

A beautiful shared home in NE Portland with an organic garden, hot tub, tree house, and other amenities. The house has three bedrooms and has four members with many visitors, family and friends. We share meals, starting with silent grace, and make most decisions by consensus.

CedarSanctum hosts monthly Creativity Sharing Circles, House Concerts, and an Open Dialogue About Community. Our mission is to encourage creativity and provide a forum where people can share and celebrate.

Visitors Accepted: Please contact us ahead of time by email. [Feb2005]

CENTER FOR PURPOSEFUL LIVING

Joanna White
3983 Old Greensboro Rd
Winston-Salem, NC 27101

336-761-8745, 336-595-8889
jwhite@ufhg.org
inquiry@ufhg.org

http://www.ufhg.org

Began: 1986 | Spiritual
Urban | Diet: Primarily vegetarian

Do you have an inquiring mind? Are you open to change? Would you like to make a difference in the world? Do you believe that practical "hands-on service" can be a path to personal transformation? The Soul Centered Education (SCE) Program for a Lifetime builds common sense, clear thinking, freedom from barriers, and a sense of life purpose. Learn practical life skills that will prepare you to pursue any endeavor with confidence and competence. Students of all ages and backgrounds are learning how to translate their good visions, ideas, aspirations and knowledge into practical, useful, "real world" application. The CPL offers its programs at no charge and is

staffed entirely by unpaid volunteers who have been working as a cohesive group since 1986.

The SCE program is a one-year commitment that includes 6 hours of classes and 45 hours of practical service per week, where theories about good human relations and cooperative teamwork are put into practice. Admission is open all year. Contact the Dean of Admissions with requests.

Upcoming events include our "Come & See Preview" weekends for interested individuals and prospective students/community members. Experience the community's environment. Meet students and faculty. Registration required. Room and board provided at a nominal fee. See firsthand what it is like to be a student/community member and the growth that is possible.

Visitors Accepted: Please call Joanna White or Penelope Kilpatrick to schedule a tour and/or visit at 336-761-8745. [Oct2004]

THE CENTER OF LIGHT SPIRITUALITY CENTER (OXFORD, MICHIGAN)

Revs. Annette or Edward Jones
5898 Baldwin Rd
Oxford, MI 48371

248-236-0432, 248-236-0431
annette@centeroflight.us
edward@centeroflight.us

http://www.centeroflight.us

Began: 1995 | Pop. 2 | Forming | Spiritual
Rural | Diet: Omnivorous

The Center of Light fellowship shares a common dream, a vision of a new paradigm lifestyle. We live gently upon the land. The land has the beauty and sacredness of a nature retreat. The Center of Light is an ecclesiastical corporation formed in 1995, providing Interfaith Sunday services, classes, workshops and events. Three years ago we moved to this location and began to expand the use of the facility by adding a tipi, medicine wheel, sweatlodge, Geodesic dome, and spiritual gardens. We are very much a community of teachers and healers. The property already has roads, water system, 2 large ponds with a bridge and boardwalks with night lighting and children's play area. There are also picnic and camping areas, trails through the woods, tennis courts, shuffleboard, horseshoe pits, volleyball and basketball courts. The facility offers a laundromat, shared shower house, a large clubhouse with dining facility, sauna, swimming pool and hot tub. There is also a pole barn totally equipped to run a resort facility. We

Listings

Additions and corrections: email: directory@ic.org, *web:* directory.ic.org, *mail: RR 1 Box 156-D, Rutledge MO 63563, USA.*

115

were divinely led to be here and are in research and development phases for completion of the business plan for fundraising and acquisition of the complete facility. We currently lease and have already come to terms with the owner for purchase. Private housing to be built, looking at very energy efficient dwellings (Rd. cordwood and geodesic domes, earth sheltered when possible). Our spirituality is simple...We believe there are many paths to the same place, all are honored, but not obtrusive.

Visitors Accepted: Call on phone. [Mar2005]

CENTRAL AUSTIN COHOUSING

c/o Becky Weaver
3814 Halfpenny Rd
Austin, TX 78722

512-478-7321
info@austincohousing.org
beckyweaver@swbell.net

Jessica Arjet
jessica@arjet.net

http://www.austincohousing.org

Began: 2000 | Forming | Urban

We are currently in the land acquisition phase of building our cohousing community. We envision an urban intentional neighborhood of 30-40 households. We practice consensus decision making and wish to appeal to a wide range of household types and ages. We have no ideological viewpoint other than a wish to live in a close-knit and interdependent community.

Visitors Accepted: Contact info@austin-cohousing.org or call. Normally we have potluck suppers the second and fourth Sundays of every month. [Nov2004]

CENTRAL COAST COMMUNITY

PO Box 585
Woy Woy, NSW 2256
AUSTRALIA

+61-(0)2-4342-5333
mark@cooperative.cc

http://www.cooperative.cc

Forming | Rural

We aim to buy property of around 80-120 hectares in the NSW Central Coast hinterland (Australia) to create a community with between 80 and 100 adults and their children.

Ideally, it would be partly bush, partly farmland. Houses would be built in seven to 10 clusters as hamlets around a village centre. Each hamlet would take no more than 0.5 hectare and accommodate 10 to 15 adults each. The whole village would be less than eight hectares in area.

Visitors Accepted: Open meetings are held on the third Sunday of the month. [Oct2004]

CENTRAL FLORIDA COHOUSING

c/o Dave Finnigan
402 Elderberry Ct
Celebration, FL 34747

407-566-0381, 770-329-1152
davefinnigan@yahoo.com

http://groups.yahoo.com/group/
centralfloridacohousing

Began: 2004 | Forming | Suburban

We are just getting started. Please join the Yahoo group and help us with planning and decision making. We want to get 30 to 40 households of all sorts together to build a community that is non-sectarian and provides an alternative to the "cookie-cutter" developments here in Central Florida. [Dec2004]

CERRO GORDO COMMUNITY

PO Box 569
Cottage Grove, OR 97424

541-942-7720
cerrogordo@igc.org

http://www.cerro-gordo.org

Began: 1970 | Pop. 42 | Rural

Our goal is a symbiosis of village, farm, and forest for up to 2,500 people on 1,200 acres—a whole valley on the north shore of Dorena Lake, near Eugene, Oregon. Homes, businesses, and community facilities are being clustered in and near a pedestrian solar village, preserving over 1,000 acres of forest and meadow.

We're planning a self-supporting settlement, with organic agriculture, sustainable forestry, and a variety of small businesses on-site. While homes and businesses are privately owned, all residents are members of the nonprofit Cerro Gordo Cooperative, which owns community land and utilities and facilitates democratic self-government. We're seeking to create a life-enhancing community that reintegrates the human community and our inner selves with the larger community of the biosphere. We invite you to join our extended community

of residents, future residents, and supporters who are working together to create Cerro Gordo as a prototype symbiotic community and to network with ecovillage and ecocity projects worldwide. For more information, contact the Cerro Gordo Forum.

Visitors Accepted [Mar2005]

CHACRA MILLALEN

El Hoyo
9211 Chubut
ARGENTINA

+54-(0)2944-471569
millalen@red42.com.ar

http://welcome.to/millalen

Began: 1990 | Pop. 5
Rural | Diet: Primarily vegetarian

Millalen is a learning center situated in southwest Argentina at the foot of the Andes. We are dedicated to promoting peace by learning to live together—with each other and with nature. In our experience, listening, communication, and mutual agreement provide a path toward healthy relationships. In the principles of ecology, we have found valid criteria for our relationship with nature. As a learning center, each year we offer a program of gatherings and retreats, which include personal-growth exercises, self-discovery games, circle dances, and meditation.

Apart from these programs, we also receive visitors, who join in our daily life in a more informal way. There is opportunity to assist with organic gardening, home food preservation, bread making, and vegetarian cooking. For much of the year our work is centered in the practical tasks of caring for the land, maintaining and expanding the garden (using a biointensive method), construction projects, and the daily work in the kitchen and in maintenance. Spanish is our common language, but members of the group also read and write English, French, German, and Italian. Please feel welcome to contact us for more information.

Note: No longer accepting members. Land ownership is single family, not a "mix" as described in Directory 2000.

Visitors Accepted: Please write or phone in advance. [Mar2005]

Scissors [✂] at the end of a listing indicate that it was edited for length by the Directory *editors and a longer description can be found at* directory.ic.org.

CHAMPLAIN VALLEY COHOUSING

14 Moss Glen Ln
Charlotte, VT 05403

802-425-5030
info@champlainvalleycohousing.org
http://www.champlainvalleycohousing
.org

Began: 2000 | Forming | Rural | Diet: Other

Champlain Valley Cohousing will be a cluster of townhouses and building lots on 10 of our 125 rural acres, with the rest preserved for agriculture, woodlands, and wildlife corridors. Twenty-six households will garden, play, eat, and labor together mindful of the need for personal and environmental sustainability. Lively, artsy Burlington is only 12 miles away with theaters, colleges, airports, and hospital readily available. The international city of Montreal is an easy two hour drive north. The Green Mountains, Lake Champlain, and the rugged wildness of the Adirondack Mountains are close by. Construction anticipated in summer of 2005; 1/3 of spaces already reserved. Champlain Valley Cohousing combines the best of a vigorous, simple, rural lifestyle with convenient access to both city and wilderness experiences within 1/2 hour drive.

Visitors Accepted: Land tour available by contacting Debbie Ramsdell at number above. [Oct2004]

CHANEEG CHANNESCH

Sunshine, WA

360-658-7668
owlchild@hotmail.com

We are a small intentional community, called Chaneeg Channesch. We hold a land base for a larger part of our membership. On the land, we have space for a couple renters and we have a space available... If you know of someone who would like the experience of living in an intentional community for a while without the need of a lifetime commitment, please have him or her call us. Our place is on the res very near Marysville and on a bus line...we are close to all types of shopping, yet have a country feel on our little farm with organic gardens, range-fed chickens and rabbits and a sheep. Participation on the land is voluntary and negotiable, maybe even for part of the rent fee of $350 a month, which gives the person their own private bedroom and access to all the shared spaces of the community house and gardens. [Mar2005]

THE CHANGE

PO Box 380
Glenorchy, Tasmania 7010
AUSTRALIA

tyler@earthsociety.org
brionyturtle@earthsociety.org
http://www.earthsociety.org/civs/
change

Began: 2004 | Pop. 2 | Spiritual
Diet: Primarily vegan

We are a new permaculture community in Tasmania as of 2005. We have over 200 acres, mostly light native forest and we have begun building on the land. We are seeking visitors, WWOOFers, and any potential members. Our philosophy comes from a wide range of books by authors like Daniel Quinn, Ayn Rand, B.F. Skinner, Sun Tzu, Plato, John Robbins, Gene Roddenberry, Robert Heinlein, Frank Herbert, and Issac Asimov. However, mentioning one of these authors shouldn't lead one to assume we agree fully with them. Please visit our website for a more detailed description.

Visitors Accepted: Visits are arranged via email (thechange@earthsociety.org) or via regular mail. Each visitor must submit a letter to us detailing their background and desire for coming to visit. No drop-ins! If you turn up without an invitation you will be turned away. Pick-up from Hobart is very possible, just let us know when and where. [Feb2005]

CHIPPENHAM COMMUNITY

Christchurch
NEW ZEALAND

+64-(0)3-355-4746,
+64-(0)3-355-4004
dave.chipnaway@inet.net.nz

Began: 1970 | Pop. 12
Urban | Diet: Omnivorous

Chippenham Community is an urban intentional community in Christchurch, New Zealand sharing a large old historic house (1862) on a beautiful tree lined section. We are part of Heartwood Community Te Ngakau O te Rakau, an umbrella organisation for three shared-house communities, first founded in 1970 (under a different name). Our community has maintained a strong ethos of equality and democratic participation across 34 years.

Visitors Accepted: We are a busy house and welcome visitors, when and if we can. However we need to be contacted several weeks in advance. [Mar2005]

CHRIST OF THE HILLS MONASTERY

PO Box 1049
Blanco, TX 78606

830-833-5363
newsarov@moment.net
http://omna.nettinker.com/
chrsthil.htm

Began: 1968 | Pop. 7 | Spiritual
Rural | Diet: Primarily vegetarian

The monastic life is very serious—in fact, it's the hardest thing a person can do, but the rewards are spiritual and produce great peace. We are a loving and open family of monks who struggle to develop oneness of mind, and the Prayer of the Heart, as we follow the path of ancient Christianity, preserved in the sacred Tradition of the Eastern Orthodox Church. The life is rugged, but physical handicaps are not an impediment. All that is needed is the will to persevere, and a willingness to listen to the still, small voice of God.

Visitors Accepted: Day visitors are welcome between 10 am and 6 pm every day except Tuesday and Wednesday. Overnight or long-term guests should call or email beforehand to make a reservation. [Oct2004]

THE CHRISTINE CENTER

W8303 Mann Rd
Willard, WI 54493

715-267-7507
christinecenter@tds.net
http://www.christinecenter.org

Began: 1980 | Pop. 8
Rural | Diet: Primarily vegetarian

The Christine Center is a locus for meditation, spiritual transformation, group and private retreats. This not-for-profit organization, which embraces the mystical aspect of spirituality, welcomes all spiritual traditions. The mission of the Center is the promotion of individual and global spiritual transformation. Toward this end the center offers seminars, retreats, bodywork, whole foods meals, and spiritual guidance. It is located on 120 acres of tranquil forestland with abundant wildlife to nurture the re-creation of body, mind, and spirit. Begun in 1980 as a place for solitude, meditation, and spiritual studies, the Center welcomes groups, writers, musicians, sabbatical, work study, and volunteer persons.

Visitors Accepted: Call or email. [Feb2005]

Additions and corrections: email: directory@ic.org, *web:* directory.ic.org, *mail: RR 1 Box 156-D, Rutledge MO 63563, USA.*

117

Listings

CHRYSALIS CO-OP

2127 16th St
Boulder, CO 80302

303-440-1233

Began: 1998 | Pop. 11
Urban | Diet: Vegetarian only

Chrysalis is full of intention. We are all trying to be better listeners, givers, lovers, friends, cooks and more. We make some yummy yummy food and our kitchen is the heart of the house.
Visitors Accepted [Feb2005]

CHUVA (CO-OPERATIVE HOUSING AT THE UNIVERSITY OF VIRGINIA)

1900 Jefferson Park Ave #11
Charlottesville, VA 22903

434-245-7083
chuvachair@virginia.edu

http://www.student.virginia.edu/
~chuva

Began: 2003 | Pop. 10 | Urban

CHUVA: "We create good places to live!"
We are a housing cooperative for both students and non-students. We serve very low, low, and moderate income people by providing occupant-managed housing that is as low-rent and high-quality as possible. In the houses, we share some meals, some groceries, and chores are assigned. We maintain a quiet but friendly atmosphere. CHUVA has been in existence since early 2003, and we currently rent two houses near UVA. We are hoping to buy a house in the next few years.
Visitors Accepted [Nov2004]

CITY OF THE SUN FOUNDATION, INC.

Maya, Secretary
PO Box 370
Columbus, NM 88029

505-531-2637, 505-531-2337
mayanolastname@hotmail.com
maya.nolastname@gmail.com
july@vtc.net

Began: 1972 | Pop. 29 | Spiritual
Rural | Diet: Omnivorous

Founded in 1972. Located on 157 acres of land in Luna County, New Mexico adjacent to the Village of Columbus (pop. 1600+). Columbus is located on Highway 11, 31 miles south of Deming (off I-10) and three miles north of Palomas, Mexico (pop. est. 14,000+).
Our goal is to live and work in mutual cooperation, respecting Unity in our Diversity. Spiritual beliefs vary, all beliefs (for the good, of course) welcome. We have Sufi, Pagan, Christian, Native American, to name a few. We offer workshops in the fall relating to spiritual practices, alternative healing, Dances of Universal Peace, and alternative housing. We have a designated off-the-grid area for alternative housing, solar, and composting. We have an EPA-approved lagoon, at least for the next 4 years, and two domestic wells, but we are required to use Village water. Some use solar water distillers. Due to lack of jobs in the area, residents must be self-sufficient or very creative. We would welcome people who know how to operate an incorporated foundation (i.e., office work, paperwork, fundraising, finances). Please email, write, or call the secretary and leave a message.
Visitors Accepted: Check in at our community center, or call for sponsorship to stay a bit, or for an escort so that you may, with permission, visit alternative houses and walk in the desert and get to know the community. [Mar2005]

CLARE'S HOUSE OF HOSPITALITY

703 E Washington St
Bloomington, IL 61701

309-828-4035
birdcls@aol.com

Began: 1977 | Pop. 2 | Spiritual | Urban

Clare House is a Catholic Worker house that offers hospitality to homeless women and their children. We also have a food pantry at the house where we hand out approximately 150 bags of food a week. At a local church we operate a soup kitchen two days a week. The house was opened in 1978 and has a good support community. Live-in community receives room and board and a small stipend.
Visitors Accepted [Feb2005]

CO-OPERATIVE EFFORT

Chico, CA 95928
rabbitseffort@yahoo.com
rabbit801@hotmail.com

http://www.co-operativeeffort.com

Began: 2004 | Pop. 4 | Forming | Rural

Located in the Sierra Nevada Foothills, 40 minutes away from Paradise, California, we are in the process of acquiring 15.7 acres of beautifully forested virgin land. Our goal is to build a self-sustaining community of like-minded individuals with a common focus in mind.
Another important aspect to our community will be to produce enough organic vegetables, fruits and nuts to support us for health and financial gain to further our project. Selling our goods at farmers markets or roadside stands will be some ways to make this and other cottage industries happen.
Members of the community will be expected to commit to group meetings, work schedules, and offer up ways to be more efficient.
A nightly dinner together is something we will strive for because it helps to keep the sense of true family relationships alive.
We will strive to limit unnecessary bad language, drug and alcohol abuse, and all other negatively impacting activities. Together we can create the eco-utopia that we desire.
Visitors Accepted: If you would like to contribute to the formation of our community or are interested in joining please email us. [Jan2005][✂]

COASTAL COHOUSING

c/o George Naugles
PO Box 4974
Ventura, CA 93007

805-647-4907
gnaugles@yahoo.com

Forming

[Feb2005]

COASTAL COHOUSING (MAINE)

Gregg Dinino
info@coastalcohousing.org

http://www.coastalcohousing.org

Began: 2005 | Suburban

We are hoping to develop a cohousing community in Kennebunk, Maine. At this point we are simply trying to educate the public about what cohousing is, and gauge interest. Also, we hope that our website will attract landowners interested in possibly selling us suitably zoned land. We hope to offer twenty percent of the homes as "affordable" housing. [Jan2005]

Scissors [✂] at the end of a listing indicate that it was edited for length by the Directory *editors and a longer description can be found at* directory.ic.org.

COBB HILL

Judith Bush
28A Linden Rd
Hartland, VT 05048
802-436-1488
jbush@together.net

Beth Sawin
802-436-1393
bethsawin@vermontel.net

http://www.cobbhill.org

Began: 1996 | Pop. 53
Rural | Diet: Omnivorous

Cobb Hill is a 23 unit cohousing community on 260 acres of farm and forest land in Hartland, Vermont. Construction of homes and a common house was completed in 2002. We formed as an intentional community with a focus on finding ways to live sustainably, to support local farm enterprises, and to understand our impacts on the environment. We make efforts to learn from our experiments, having used a number of new technologies in the home building and shared infrastructure here.

Visitors Accepted: Contact a current member or Judith Bush (802-436-1488) and Marie Kirn (802-436-1036) can arrange for a contact person for the visit. [Feb2005]

COFLATS STROUD

David Michael
16 Springhill Cohousing
Uplands
Stroud GL5 1TN England
UNITED KINGDOM

+44-(0)1453-766466

http://www.coflats.com

Began: 2005 | Pop. 16 | Forming
Small Town | Diet: Omnivorous

Coflats is similar to cohousing but it's just flats (apartments).

Coflats Stroud is being converted from a large old church in the centre of Stroud. It is due to be complete in April 2006. Stroud is in the west of England and is the location of the first new build cohousing in Britain. Stroud has 4 organic cafes, great shops, art venues, community assisted agriculture and the only Green Town Council.

Coflats will be 14 self contained units or studios. There will be a small "common house" with a kitchen, dining area and two washing machines.

We will have two shared electric G-wizz cars, running on renewable power, parked in the driveway. These will be part of the town wide Car Share Club which includes

another three ordinary cars. All members of Coflats are obliged to be members of the car share club and undertake not to own a private car. Photovoltaic roof tiles are planned to power the Common House.

Coflats is a three minute walk to the town centre, where there is a 90 min train service to London and local bus and train connections.

There is a courtyard and small garden with secure parking for 20 bicycles.

The building is a beautiful old Unitarian Church, built in about 1835.

Members will make decisions by consensus. However, the development company is separate from the members and so is a departure from cohousing. [Mar2005]

COHO COHOUSING

321 SW 9th St
Corvallis, OR 97333
info@cohousing-corvallis.com

Karen Heilesen
541-758-3347

Bruce Hecht
541-754-3028
brucehe@peak.org

http://www.cohousing-corvallis.com

Began: 2002 | Forming | Small Town

Visitors Accepted [Oct2004]

COHOUSING BRISTOL

20 Cornwall Rd
Bristol BS7 8LH England
UNITED KINGDOM

+44-(0)117-9422569
+44-(0)117-9048611
abigail@spring96.freeserve.co.uk
nw007@blueyonder.co.uk

Neil Whitehead
38 Brendan Rd
Windmill Hill
Bristol BS3 4PL England
UNITED KINGDOM

http://www.cohousing.co.uk/bristol.htm

Began: 2001 | Forming | Urban

We are an embryonic cohousing group that has been meeting since June 2001. We intend to purchase land within a 15-mile radius of Bristol, large enough to accommodate up to 35 households. We are currently a mixture of households with and without children, singles and couples. We actively encourage people of

all ages and backgrounds to be part of our group, and join our monthly meetings, which deal with business and also offer the opportunity for people to get to know each other better. Our intention is to build or convert individual properties (low impact and energy efficient) that can be owned, rented or part-owned/part-rented, depending on individual choice and the availability of partnership funding. There will be a communal building with shared resources. We want the main area of the site to be vehicle-free, with green space for children to roam freely and safely. Some of us are keen to grow vegetables, keep animals, set up cooperative businesses and provide workshop space to rent. We want to be outward-looking and seek ways to involve and engage with the wider community. [Mar2005][✄]

COHOUSING FOR SAN DIEGO!

Alan Ridley
1380 Montera St
Chula Vista, 91913

858-883-7314
cohousingforsd@cox.net

Donee Krause
619-640-2210

Laura Rosenbluth
619-838-1727

http://www.cohousingforsandiego.org

Began: 2004 | Pop. 28 | Forming

We are a local organization committed to supporting efforts to build cohousing communities in the County of San Diego.

Cohousing core groups are now active and thriving for the areas of North County (i.e., north of Pacific Beach) and Central County (i.e., north of National City and south of La Jolla). Please contact us for information about how to join and receive news from the local Core Group that interests you.

A Core Group consists of individuals and families who have decided to live in the same cohousing community and are in the process of deciding upon suitable sites, purchasing the site, and building or converting the site into housing that suits their needs.

Membership in Cohousing for San Diego! is open to all people interested in supporting the development of cohousing in San Diego County.

Benefits of membership include:
1. The opportunity to network and cooperate with like-minded people to design, develop and complete neighborhood-friendly cohousing projects in San Diego County through the support of specific Core

Additions and corrections: email: directory@ic.org, *web:* directory.ic.org, *mail:* RR 1 Box 156-D, Rutledge MO 63563, USA.

119

Listings

Groups for projects and in areas agreed upon by the Core Group members.

2. Voting rights-consensus model will be used first and issues that cannot be so resolved will be submitted for a simple majority vote.

3. Ability to help refine the purpose, mission and vision of the organization.

4. Ability to serve on the Board of Directors or Coordinating Council.

5. Free attendance at all general membership meetings.

Non-members will be asked to join after two meetings.

Visitors Accepted [Oct2004][✂]

COLD POND COMMUNITY LAND TRUST

PO Box 212
Cold Pond Rd
Acworth, NH 03601

603-835-2403, 603-835-2556
CPCLT1@email.com
sorlando@newport.lib.nh.us

http://www.sover.net~cpclt

Began: 2000 | Pop. 12
Rural | Diet: Omnivorous

Formed in May, 2000, Cold Pond Community Land Trust (CPCLT) is an organization in which the resources of our forest and farmland, watershed, wildlife habitat, and open space are made available to residents and community members. Our non-profit status assures that our 275 acres can be kept available for current and future residents to live on and enjoy. Strengthening the local community and protecting the environment are of paramount importance to the land trust.

CPCLT is governed by two primary objectives:

To provide an opportunity for low and moderate income people to derive a livelihood from farming in a community setting.

To serve as an education resource for sustainable and regenerative agriculture.

Visitors Accepted: Contact us by telephone, email, or post to get more information and set up a visit date. [Mar2005]

COLIBRI URBAN HOUSING COLLECTIVE

Saint Louis, MO 63104

314-773-2842, 314-772-0322
vince@ic.org

Began: 1996 | Pop. 12
Urban | Diet: Primarily vegetarian

Colibri is an activist community in the heart of St. Louis City. We provide affordable housing for those who share in our vision of living socially and ecologically responsible lifestyles. Our group reflects a wide array of interests including human rights, animal rights, concern for our earth, physical well-being, and supporting those in need. Colibri is a two house community with a garden nestled between them. We have cozy bedrooms, common spaces, active kitchens, a fire ring, and whatever else we desire to create. Members gather most Sunday evenings for a common meal and a community meeting to discuss activities and concerns. There is a mediation procedure for resolving interpersonal conflicts. All people, from small to big to furry, are welcome here.

We are into gardening, biking, and living the revolution. We like eating together and playing together and creating together. We are into hands-on affection and respecting other's boundaries. We like to educate ourselves and everyone else, and that happens through direct communication. We are eccentric, artists, queer, or all three. We get wild ideas and try to make them happen. Explore our space, join our fun, and add your special flavor to our sauce. Spicy and sweet, yours for the revolution…Colibri.

Visitors Accepted: Please call to arrange a visit. Groups are welcome as well, provided the timing's right and the space is available. Quite often there is a Saturday night fire all are welcome to. [Feb2005]

COLLEGIATE LIVING COOPERATIVE

117 NW 15th St
Gainesville, FL 32603

352-377-4269
clo@grove.ufl.edu

http://grove.ufl.edu/~clo

Began: 1931 | Pop. 68 | Urban

Providing inexpensive housing for University of Florida students since 1931, the Collegiate Living Organization, also known as CLO, is student run and offers a diverse and supportive environment for students. We elect our leaders from among our members to govern the corporation. Members also share in the work to keep CLO operating. Please contact us either by phone or email, or send letters care of the Secretary. [Mar2005]

COMMON GROUND (VA)

Glen Leasure
109 Broad Wing Trl
Lexington, VA 24450

540-463-4493, 540-463-1070
ritajane@rockbridge.net
herb@rockbridge.net

http://www.people.virginia.edu/ ~was/CGHmpg.html

Began: 1980 | Pop. 7
Rural | Diet: Omnivorous

Common Ground, a homesteading intentional cooperative community, holds a perpetual lease on 77 acres of land owned by the School of Living—a regional community land trust. Members hold lifetime subleases. Each household has use rights to two acres or so. The community exists and operates for the mutual benefit of its members, to help one another become established on the land while conserving, protecting, and improving the environment.

Members follow their own spiritual and dietary leadings. Currently we have five households. To date, all our children have been homeschooled. Members work together in our organic gardens, on community-building or maintenance projects. We build shared facilities through group planning, joint and individual labor. We are now planning our new community center, which will help us realize a goal of becoming an educational center.

We seek members with homesteading skills, commitment to ecological land use, goodwill and initiative, good communication skills, and the ability to work cooperatively and enthusiastically with others.

Our membership process is extensive, lasting from 6 to 21 months. Full membership is by consensus. The membership fee is $1,750. Members finance, own, and maintain their "improvements." Each household is responsible for their own income.

Visitors are welcome weekends upon pre-arrangement. Tenting, camping spaces, and a few rooms are available. Learn more about us at the School of Living website: http://www.schoolofliving.org.

Visitors Accepted: Call or write and arrange a visit. Glen is usually home and reliable. As a last resort you can email Rita Jane Leasure at ritajane@rockbridge.net but expect delays in response time. [Mar2005][✂]

Scissors [✂] at the end of a listing indicate that it was edited for length by the Directory editors and a longer description can be found at directory.ic.org.

COMMON GROUND COMMUNITY

442 Red Maple Rd
Blountsville, AL 35031

205-429-3088, 205-429-3090

Began: 1980 | Pop. 14 | Rural

We are 11 like-spirited adults and 5 children. Our purpose includes harmony with our environment, nurturance, celebration of spiritual diversity, and social change. The community leases 80 acres of farmland from Gaia Land Trust, created in 1980, and members sublease holdings. The trust's purpose is to own and preserve land and improvements, promote community, honor ecosystems, and prevent abuse of resources. The community pays monthly rent to the trust. Community members pay dues and rent equally, and in-kind service is an option. Each member is economically independent. The trust pays taxes, fire protection, maintenance, etc. With no community members, the land would devolve to a party committed to preservation.

We gather monthly for a day of work, play, and business (using modified consensus). Working through difficult decisions and writing our guidelines have developed deep trust and extended family. In 17 years as a community, only one full member has left. We dream of all being on the land full-time, and most of us are now. We live in owner-built structures heated with wood and solar, passively cooled. Power varies from solar to conventional to mixed, but conservation is key in all. We enjoy visitors, but our membership is closed. Visitors must write in advance.

Visitors Accepted [Nov2004]

COMMON PLACE LAND COOPERATIVE

Alison Frost
4211 State Rte 13
Truxton, NY 13158

607-842-6799

Began: 1980 | Pop. 24
Rural | Diet: Omnivorous

Common Place Land Cooperative is a 432-acre rural land trust located in the rolling hills of central New York State. We are currently 15 adults and 11 children, and we are actively seeking new members. We expect to evolve into a small-scale community of 35-40 households, aiming at greater food and energy self-sufficiency. Eleven homesteads have been created on the land, and the farmhouse serves as transitional housing and as a community building.

Over 25 years, we have come to agreement on 11 core ideals that define and guide our community, including land stewardship and trust, economic self-reliance, diversity, consensus decision making, community participation, and voluntary simplicity. Members have diverse views and interests. As a community we are not affiliated with any political or religious organization. Our varied individual interests include organic gardening and homesteading, organic farming, perennial garden design and maintenance, livestock fence installation, alternative energy, attachment parenting, homeschooling, the arts and music, natural healing, activism, spirituality, home birth, and writing.

Our decision-making process consists of two meetings per month. We are working to create a cohesive community that inhabits the land, preserving its integrity and resources. For more information send a SASE and a short description of yourself and your interests in community.

Visitors Accepted: Call Alison to set up a workable date and to discuss any details. [Mar2005]

COMMONS ON THE ALAMEDA

2300 W Alameda, Unit D4
Santa Fe, NM 87507

505-471-4764
info@santafecohousing.org

http://www.santafecohousing.org

Began: 1990 | Pop. 80
Suburban | Diet: Omnivorous

The Commons on the Alameda is an adobe-style cohousing community on five acres in the outskirts of Santa Fe. Construction began in 1991 and the last homes were completed in 1997. There are 28 houses clustered around four beautifully landscaped placitas (courtyards). The common house and home businesses surround the main plaza. We have communal organic meals Mondays and Thursdays with produce from the kitchen garden. Residents cook/clean for one meal per month and put the remaining of their eight hour/month labor commitment into building and grounds work.

Managers (kitchen, guest room, grounds, compost) orchestrate much of the nitty-gritty. We have two community meetings/month—one to discuss and make consensus-based decisions on business items and the other to consider, "What's on your mind?" Every fall we celebrate our feast day with tree planting, horse rides, cider making, clown/jugglers, green chili stew, and dancing.

Visitors Accepted: Please contact Marion Seymore at 505-438-9693 to arrange visits. [Dec2004]

COMMONTERRA

127 Stovepipe Alley
Monroe, ME 04951

207-525-7740
invert@acadia.net

Commonterra (est. '77) is five households, total population 10 adults, living on 150 acres held in common through a community land trust. Not currently open to new members. Individual families own their own houses, and are responsible for their own finances and domestic arrangements; community decisions are by consensus. [Mar2005]

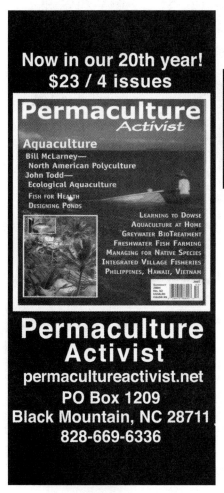

Additions and corrections: email: directory@ic.org, *web:* directory.ic.org, *mail: RR 1 Box 156-D, Rutledge MO 63563, USA.*

121

COMMUNITY OF LIGHT

creative1@creativeideasforyou.com

http://www.creativeideasforyou.com/commune_land.html

Began: 1999 | Forming | Rural | Diet: Other

We are a forming community. We intend to grow much of the food we'll enjoy, to work cooperatively and make decisions by consensus. We will honor the essence of religion by providing a place where we will share and honor each other's paths.

We will provide for ourselves through community projects, such as providing retreat space, relaxation opportunities, while individuals might create cottage industries, projects or programs that would enhance the viability of our community.

We will explore right livelihood, peaceful existence, and reach out to the greater community and world to provide what we can to help others in whatever way we come to feel is meet with the community's ability and desire. [Jan2005]

THE COMMUNITY PLANET FOUNDATION

Jack Reed
1611 Olive St
Santa Barbara, CA 93101

805-962-2038
jackreed@communityplanet.org

Forming

The mission of the Community Planet Foundation is nothing less than transforming the planet. We are not an existing community, but we are working on creating a demonstration community on the level of 400 to 500 people that will redefine how we as people live together on the planet. We realize that the way we live together and relate together in community is the basic building block that is needed to change the world. The creation of a large-scale egalitar-

ian, sustainable community that utilizes the latest technology will enable others to see how we can all cooperate and enjoy a happier and healthier standard of living. With media exposure, millions will be able to see and hear about a lifestyle that they too can enjoy. Given the current status of our planet, at this point in our history nothing less is called for and nothing less will work.

For a complete description of our project, you may purchase our book, *The Next Evolution: A Blueprint for Transforming the Planet* by Jack Reed. Please order by email. [Oct2004]

THE COMMUNITY PROJECT

Lewes, England
UNITED KINGDOM

+44-(0)1323-815725
newmembers@thecommunityproject.com

Angela Rogers
angela@laughtonlodge.org

Melanie Nock
mel@laughtonlodge.org

http://www.cohousing.co.uk/cmtyproj.htm

Began: 1999

[Mar2005]

COMUNIDAD LOS HORCONES

Apartado Postal #372
Hermosillo, Sonora 83000
MEXICO

+52-(01)662-2147219,
+52-(01)662-2638308
walden2@loshorcones.org.mx

http://www.loshorcones.org.mx

Began: 1973 | Pop. 24
Rural | Diet: Omnivorous

Los Horcones began in 1973. It is located on 250 acres in Sonora, Mexico, below Arizona. Our basic objectives are to design a society where people cooperate for a common good, share property, and reinforce egalitarian pro-ecological and pacifist behaviors. Los Horcones is an ecological- and self-sufficient-oriented community.

However, we devote most of our resources in the area of human behavior (education, human relationships, and behavioral research). We have communal child rearing. We have our own school. Students learn personal and social behaviors (self-knowl-

edge, interpersonal skills, etc.) as well as academics.

We have an experimental approach to the design of a community, basing our cultural practices on scientific research, not on personal beliefs. We are deeply concerned with personal growth and interpersonal relationships. We are a "Walden Two" community in the sense that we apply behavioral principles in our daily life to learn communitarian behaviors. Being a "Walden Two" does not mean we are inspired by or follow the novel *Walden Two* (Skinner) but rather that we apply the science of behavior on which *Walden Two* was based.

Los Horcones is an income-sharing community. We earn income from various sources—selling natural food products, special education, summer camps, and consulting. We value the participation of all members in decision making. We call our organization "personocracy." We are open to new members or visitors. Please write or call in advance.

Visitors Accepted: We ask that you contact us by email, ordinary mail or telephone. We also ask that you visit our web page. [Oct2004]

COMUNIDAD PLANETARIA JANAJPACHA

Lizeth Santana
BOLIVIA

+591-4-426-1234, +591-4-426-4324
Janajpacha@uevn.org
fle@albatros.cnb.net

http://www.chamalu.com

Pop. 100

Es un mandala etno ecologico, con arquitectura Chipaya, un pueblo indigena del Altiplano sur de Bolivia, en una parte tenemos 8 casas circulares y un Templo Inca al centro y a parte tenemos otras casas y habitaciones.

Estamos asentados en un espacio de 7 hectareas, con tres dedicadas a la agricultura y el resto jardines y espacios recreativos.

Nosotros somos muy conocidos a nivel de varios paises, debido a que el Fundador de Janajpacha, Chamalu a viajado durante 24 años, a mas de 500 ciudades del mundo y publicado 40 libros, varios de ellos traducidos a varios idiomas, esa es la razon por la que antes no hemos hecho gran difusion via internet, porque hay mucha gente que nos conoce y visita.

Visitors Accepted: Email or call us first. We have a hotel on the property where you can stay. [Feb2005]

Scissors [✂] at the end of a listing indicate that it was edited for length by the Directory *editors and a longer description can be found at* directory.ic.org.

CONCORD VILLAGE

Tom Hammer
227 Meredith St
Kennett Square, PA 19348

610-444-2382
thammer302@yahoo.com

Howard Porter
308 Meredith St
Kennett Square, PA 19348

610-925-2950
muscadyne@aol.com

http://www.concordvillage.org

Began: 2002 | Forming | Small Town

Concord Village envisions 30 to 40 environmentally friendly homes, clustered around a central walkway, with a lively, well-used common house. We are actively seeking children and diversity. One of our distinguishing features is our goal of being within walking distance of a thriving small town.

Visitors Accepted: Contact us by email or phone. [Jan2005]

COOPERATIVE ROOTS

Fort Awesome
3090 King St
Berkeley, CA 94703

510-486-8222
cooperativeroots@yahoo.com
coop4life@barringtoncollective.org

http://barringtoncollective.org/
roots/about.html

Began: 2003 | Pop. 15
Urban | Diet: Vegetarian only

Visitors Accepted: Email or call, if you would like to spend a few nights with us please ask at least one week in advance. If you'd just like to check it out and see the place, just ring the bell, or holler at the gate. [Mar2005]

CORANI HOUSING AND LAND CO-OP

12 Bartholomew St
Leicester LE2 1FA England
UNITED KINGDOM

+44-(0)116-254-5436
+44-(0)533-541403
info@corani.org

Began: 1978 | Pop. 6
Urban | Diet: Omnivorous

There are two adjoining Corani houses in Leicester where six to eight of us live collectively and that act as a center for the other Some People in Leicester network activities. Housing is flexible and need not be collective. Homes are urban terraces at present. We work allotments, and we own one in Leicester that is becoming a forest garden. Capital is not essential to join, but those who have it are asked to deposit some with Corani. Most members income pool.

Decision making is essentially pragmatic: by consensus where all are concerned and otherwise with sensitive autonomy. We welcome, by arrangement, visitors who will help out or participate while with us. We probably have one or two room spaces for new members. Alternatively, we have been known to accept people and their houses! Corani is a non-equity-sharing, fully mutual body IE commonwealth.

We are a city-based cooperative network with a variety of practical activities: vehicle pool, organic gardening, income pooling, cooperative housing, capital pooling.

We feel it is vital that local groups do not exist in isolation but are involved in wider struggles and broader visions. We are members of Radical Routes Secondary Co-op—a network of radical housing and worker co-ops.

We welcome visitors by arrangement and are looking for more people to get involved.

Visitors Accepted: Write, phone, or email us. [Mar2005]

CORNERSTONE HOUSING COOPERATIVE

16 Sholebroke Ave
Chapeltown, Leeds
W Yorkshire LS7 3HB England
UNITED KINGDOM

+44-(0)113-262-9365
cornerstone@gn.apc.org

http://www.cornerstonehousing.org.uk

Began: 1993 | Pop. 12
Urban | Diet: Primarily vegan

Cornerstone has two large shambolic Victorian houses in Chapeltown, an ethnically diverse and run-down part of Leeds. Both houses need a lot of maintenance, but have large gardens front and back, where the odd co-op member does their best to create beautiful and productive landscapes. Each house has space for seven members and there are often short and long-term visitors swelling our numbers. Both houses have office space and computer facilities, enabling us to run campaigns, produce newsletters, zines, catalogues, and create and maintain websites. We also run a worker co-op (footprint) from the cellar of one of the houses.

Cornerstone is a member of Radical Routes, the secondary co-op and ethical investment fund promoting cooperation and working for social change.

Visitors Accepted: Phone or email us if you want to visit. Please bear in mind that we are inner city based and most of us have jobs/projects that we work on during the day that you may not be able to help with so don't necessarily expect to be given something to do. If you want to experience a wholesome community, and help tend the fields and make timber frame buildings, etc., then you'd best go elsewhere :-) [Oct2004]

COYOTE CROSSING

Santa Cruz, CA

Kristina Mutén
kmuten@coho.org

Steven Mentor
cybunny@coho.org

http://www.coho.org

[Mar2005]

CRANBERRY COMMONS

#100 - 4272 Albert St
North Burnaby, BC V5C 2E8
CANADA

Dan 604-294-1225
dhill@cranberrycommons.ca

http://www.cranberrycommons.ca

Began: 1992 | Pop. 48
Urban | Diet: Omnivorous

Cranberry Commons Cohousing is in an "urban village" setting. We wanted housing that would support greater social interconnectedness while making efficient use of resources. With the support and services of our selected professional team, we managed the challenges of the development process: securing a site, negotiating with the regulatory authorities for development approvals, securing the financing, building membership, and creating an organizational structure that allowed for an effective and timely consensus decision making process. We formed a development corporation and acted as the developer to complete a 22-home multi-family residential building with 3400 square feet of common amenity area. Construction was completed in October of 2001.

Each household at Cranberry Commons

Additions and corrections: email: directory@ic.org, web: directory.ic.org, mail: RR 1 Box 156-D, Rutledge MO 63563, USA.

123

privately owns a complete, self-contained home. Community connection is supported by the physical layout of our site and by the involvement of all members in the development and operation of the community using consensus decision making.

In addition to its social focus, Cranberry Commons holds respect for the environment as one of its highest values. We have attempted to incorporate sustainability into every aspect of the community design, starting with the selection of the site right up to the solar hot water panels that were installed on the roof.

Visitors Accepted: Contact the persons whose names are on the website and they will let you know when and if it is convenient for you to visit. [Mar2005]

CRYSTAL WATERS PERMACULTURE VILLAGE

59 Crystal Waters
65 Kilcoy Ln
Conondale, Queensland 4552
AUSTRALIA

+61-(0)7-5494-4620,
+61-(0)7-5494-4741
lindegger@gen-oceania.org
office@ecologicalsolutions.com.au

http://gen.ecovillage.org

Began: 1985 | Pop. 230
Rural | Diet: Omnivorous

Crystal Waters has been designed from inception according to the principles of permaculture by Max Lindegger, Robert Tap, Barry Goodman and Geoff Young. A wildlife sanctuary where dogs and cats are banned and people really do try to live in harmony with nature. Eighty percent of the 640 acres are owned in common, and these are a mix of terrains: the clear waters of the Mary River, serene lakes, open grasslands, timbered hills and gullies, and increasingly, pockets of rain-forest trees planted as part of the community's passion for reforestation. The idea was that people should be able to operate from home, and many businesses operate from here, e.g., foresters; mail-order businesses—books, organic gardening supplies; carpenters; builders; electricians; permaculture course providers and consultants; nurseries; caterers; craftspeople; architects; entertainers; baker; bed-and-breakfast accommodation; furniture manufacturers; ecovillage designer and also the base for the Oceania/Asia secretariat of the Global Ecovillage Network. Crystal Waters won an award in the 1996 World Habitat Awards and was a finalist in the 1998 Best Practices

Awards. Many innovative ideas in building, wastewater, water, agriculture, and nature conservation are evident. The model has proved attractive to the relatively mainstream as well as an alternative market. Crystal Waters is the home of the award-winning Eco Center. About 240 live now in the village. A short video is available from the GEN Oceania/Asia office (see www.ecologicalsolutions.com.au).

Visitors Accepted: Write, ring. Don't bring a dog, please. Visitors are requested to make prior arrangements before visiting. [Mar2005]

CW LISMORTEL

Tourslaan 22
Eindhoven, 5627 KX
NETHERLANDS
info@cwl.antenna.nl

http://www.cwl.lvcw.nl

Began: 1977 | Pop. 115
Urban | Diet: Primarily vegetarian

CW Lismortel is one of the larger cohousing projects in The Netherlands with about 60 households.

The project consists of 10 groups (clusters).

For the whole project there is a central building for all kind of meetings.

The Dutch name for cohousing is "centraal wonen" (CW).

Visitors Accepted: Twice a year we have an "open day;" if you want to be invited send a mail. [Feb2005]

DANCING BONES

PO Box 232
Wentworth, NH 03282

603-764-9844
dancingbones@eagle1st.com
evbull17@hotmail.com

Began: 1997 | Pop. 7 | Rural

We are co-creating a rural ecovillage of small cabins, and sharing life day to day. We advocate living a simple and sustainable life in full harmony with the Earth. A community land trust holds the land in perpetuity. Major decisions are made with full consensus.

The proposed 22 cabins will be privately owned, some with electricity/water. Composting toilets prevail. A 16'x16' cabin now provides shared kitchen, laundry and showers. As our numbers increase, a larger amenities building is planned. There is an outside 48'x48' dance platform and tent platforms for an annual week long circle dance camp. Some community members plan to circle dance on a regular basis throughout the year.

Ours is a rugged, heavily wooded site of 40 acres on the edge of the White Mountain National Forest—close to Appalachian Trail, mountains, and lakes. Low-impact, low-cost living, mindfulness in nature.

Visitors Accepted: Call or email to set up a time that works for us all. [Mar2005]

DANCING RABBIT ECOVILLAGE

1 Dancing Rabbit Ln
Rutledge, MO 63563

660-883-5511
dancingrabbit@ic.org

http://www.dancingrabbit.org

Began: 1993 | Pop. 23
Rural | Diet: Omnivorous

At Dancing Rabbit Ecovillage (DR), we understand how hard it is to live sustainably and responsibly within the framework of US culture. We believe that we can build a healthy, vibrant alternative—a social structure that is nonexploitative, supportive, and vibrant.

In 1997 the Dancing Rabbit Land Trust purchased 280 acres in northeastern Missouri. We are now busy constructing buildings and developing community systems, with a goal of creating a village of up to 1,000 people.

Ecological sustainability is our primary focus. Many of us are dedicated to eating local, organic, and in-season foods. We build our homes using alternative techniques such as strawbale and cob. All electricity comes from renewable sources. Vehicles are powered by biodiesel and owned by a co-op, rather than privately.

We strive to be good stewards of our land. To support increased biodiversity, we are reintroducing native plants. Much of our land is reserved as wildlife habitat.

Our village is composed of individuals, family units, and an income-sharing community (see Skyhouse listing). To allow for economic diversity and simple living, we have kept lease rates and membership dues low, with no buy-in fee. We encourage the development of cohousing and cooperatives.

Scissors [✂] at the end of a listing indicate that it was edited for length by the Directory editors and a longer description can be found at directory.ic.org.

Outreach and education are integral to our mission. Besides being a wonderful home, DR acts as a model for social change.

If you are interested in Dancing Rabbit, write us to arrange a visit or to receive our newsletter. We are actively seeking new members to share our lives and goals. We also often host interns in the warmer months.

Visitors Accepted: Write us a letter or email and our visitor team will help schedule you. As spots fill up quickly, please contact us at least one month in advance. We ordinarily accept visitors mid-March to mid-November, and first-time visitors usually come for one week. See our website for more information. [Mar2005]

DANCING WATERS PERMACULTURE CO-OP

Lynda Schaller
43188 Guthrie Rd
Gays Mills, WI 54631

608-872-2407, 608-872-2498
rickspix@mwt.net

Began: 1982 | Pop. 12 | Spiritual
Rural | Diet: Omnivorous

Dancing Waters Permaculture Co-op is on 130 acres in the beautiful hills and hollows of southwestern Wisconsin. We are nine adults and three children, owning land and buildings in common. Primary focuses include annual and perennial communal gardening, house building, and learning how to live in long-term harmony with each other and with the land. We use the ideas of permaculture in our building, gardens, hayfields, orchard, and woodlots.

We gather twice monthly for a potluck and meeting. Decisions are made by consensus. Individual and family housing units are clustered so we bump into each other as we go about our daily lives—sharing food, meals, work, childcare, song, and spirit on an informal basis.

Individuals follow a variety of spiritual paths and diets. Some individuals make their incomes at home. Some have jobs off the land. Income is not shared. Each adult pays a monthly fee for group expenses. We are surrounded by an extensive alternative community, including food co-ops, community building, a Waldorf school, extensive alternative healing community, and the headquarters of the USA's largest producer owned organic food pool (Organic Valley). This wider community helps us create a home that is more than a refuge from the mainstream. We are blessed with a stable membership but have occasional openings.

Visitors Accepted: Visitors are required to make advance arrangements. [Feb2005]

DANTHONIA BRUDERHOF

http://www.bruderhof.com.au

Danthonia Bruderhof is a growing community of families and singles located in Inverell Shire, New South Wales. We seek to follow the teachings of Jesus, and to "share all things in common" as the first Christians did. [Feb2005]

DAPALA FARM

Daniel and Patti Christman
E 15014 Laurel Rd
Elk, WA 99009

509-292-0423
Twoearthandsky@aol.com

http://www.ic.org/nica/
communities/dap1.htm

Began: 1990 | Pop. 2 | Forming |
Rural | Diet: Primarily vegetarian

Dapala Farm is a Sustainable Technologies Educational Center which has taught food and energy self-reliance skills since 1990. We're long time students of Helen and Scott Nearing and have lived and evolved applications of their examples since the 70's.

Our goal is to form a cooperative community to share our lifestyle and the growing, processing and storage of our mutual year around food supply, and for the further development of our educational services to help others achieve the same.

To a couple, family, or small group who seek intentional community we offer to sell 8 acres of undeveloped land bordering our own 8 acres. This land has a year around stream running through it, and its own deed. Those purchasing this land must have the resources and abilities to build upon it on their own. Open to those without the resources to purchase is space on our land to build low-cost shelters.

For cottages industry there are opportunities to develop and teach classes related to our educational center. We've also established infrastructures for CSA and produce stand sales and have an opening for an experience organic grower. We also need people with building trade skills.

At Dancing Rabbit we're building a rural ecovillage, learning about sustainable living while we educate others. We're open to all kinds of individuals, families, and groups, who, like us, are committed to sustainability, cooperation, feminism, and building for the future.

Mission Statement:

To create a society, the size of a small town or village, made up of individuals and communities of various sizes and social structures, which allows and encourages its members to live sustainably.

To encourage this sustainable society to grow to have the size and recognition necessary to have an influence on the global community by example, education, and research.

Dancing Rabbit Ecovillage
1 Dancing Rabbit Lane
Rutledge, MO 63563
660-883-5511
dancingrabbit@ic.org
www.dancingrabbit.org

Dancing Rabbit
E C O V I L L A G E
Building Sustainable Community

Additions and corrections: email: directory@ic.org, *web:* directory.ic.org, *mail: RR 1 Box 156-D, Rutledge MO 63563, USA.*

Listings

The Deliberacy...
Taking Deliberate Measures to Benefit All!

*B*ased on my books "Conceptual Communal Home Design" and "Environmental Practices: From Living Simply to Global Advancements" (Available at Trafford.com) I am hoping to build **THE MOST** environmentally friendly and fully-featured communal home you'll ever hope to find: a five-level, sixteen-bedroom facility, with **75 to 85**% less land use than an equivalent number of single-family homes! Such a low-impact facility (now being planned for Hagerstown, Maryland) also offers several "hard-to-believe" features that actually improves upon a middle-class standard-of-living:

Care to avoid traffic and earn a living at home? This home would have 912 square ft. of street-level office space as well as a reception desk and waiting area for multiple private practices. The garage can hold ambulance-sized work trucks, and there is 2,236ft^2 of **Votech-quality shop space** for crafts and light manufacturing. A year-round hydroponics greenhouse with 2,300ft^2 of usable surface area would further complement the home's self-sufficiency.

Aside from having four living rooms, a large rooftop balcony, and a living room-sized exercise/weight room, the home will have an open 18x19 martial arts area, a 13x23 10-seat home schooling/craft room, two music rooms, a bike shed, and even a multi-purpose **RACQUETBALL COURT** that's convertible to a game room/sports bar! Try finding that in your average Common House!

Instead of forcing newcomers into an estranged new lifestyle that they aren't used to (like bathrooms without doors and bedrooms without closets) such a home would offer "office-style" men's and women's bathrooms with segregated shower, toilet stall, and sink areas. There would also be the equivalent of an 8x10 wardrobe room PLUS 68ft^2 of bulk storage space available PER BEDROOM!

To eliminate any points-of-contention, the home's dining, living, and kitchen areas would all be separated, hallways would be wider, modern appliances would meet or exceed demands, and a commercial 32-line telephone system would be utilized.

On top of these hard-to-beat features, Hagerstown is itself very nice! It is located on the Appalachian foothills a mere ten minutes from the Appalachian Trail. There are seven State and National Forests within 20 miles, as well as the historic Antietam and Monocacy Civil War Battlefields to visit. Gettysburg, Washington DC, Baltimore, and the scenic Skyline Drive are one hour away! There is a community college, sports complex, Potomac river attractions, and no major threats from natural disasters.

Basically, this home is meant for professionals and tradespeople working at the edge of their fields: a SLICE of average middle-class Americas just wanting to be more efficient and smarter about life. Costs to join are on par with owning a home. However, when tailors, carpenters, mechanics, lawyers, teachers, martial arts instructors, and alternative healthcare professionals stand shoulder-to-shoulder in mutual support of one another, they become near independent of corporate downsizing and secure a quality-of-service not seen in this country since the 50's! So disconnect yourself from the '**lottery mentality**' of foolishly thinking you can '**win**' your way to a better life and see what **TRUE** communal living has to offer! Check out the books mentioned above and join this ground-breaking new community! For more information contact:

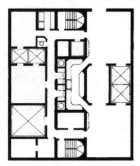

The Deliberacy...
Post Office Box 4314
Harrisburg, Pennsylvania 17111-0314
E-Mail: Function_First@Hotmail.com

Please share with us your bios and aspirations.

Visitors Accepted: There is much we'll all need to learn about one another and make clear about our compatibilities on goals and other factors before arranging a visit. We seek people whose response to our community goal is a strong and clear "Yes!" We need to be inspired by knowing you are inspired. [Mar2005]

DARVELL BRUDERHOF

http://www.darvellbruderhof.co.uk

Christian community in Robertsbridge, East Sussex. [Feb2005]

DAVIS SQUARE COHOUSING

Cambridge/Somerville, MA

781-769-9220
info@davissquarecohousing.com
chris@cohousingresources.com

http://www.davissquarecohousing.com

Began: 2004 | Forming | Urban

- A Cohousing neighborhood at Davis Square, Somerville, Massachusetts
- Construction underway now!
- Completion and move in during 2005
- Prices start from $300,000 (averaging $470,000)
- The project site is one block west of the Davis Square T station along the Millennium Trail bike path.
- Currently the site is under construction, with the concrete underground parking garage underway. [Dec2004]

DAYSPRING CIRCLE

PO Box 433
Floyd, VA 24091
info@abundantdawn.org
velma@abundantdawn.org

http://www.abundantdawn.org/
index.html#ThePods

Began: 1994 | Pop. 3
Rural | Diet: Omnivorous

Dayspring Circle is a subgroup (pod) of Abundant Dawn Community, founded in 1994.

At present we are three adults, good friends in our 50s and 60s, who keep separate incomes but work and play together frequently. We are committed to living thoughtfully, with beauty, economy, conviviality and care.

We live on a south-facing hillside in a meadow, with woods on three sides. We have three homes here, including a "guest cottage" which is available for temporary housing for new members. We attempt to practice environmentally sound building methods, use composting toilets, and have built a constructed wetland for our graywater output.

Flowers are important to us here, and the birds and wildlife.

We anticipate 2-3 more houses in our circle, the center of which will eventually have a solar-powered fountain and a flowering park.

Current members support themselves with computer programming and web development, work in the communities movement, a bakery, and local property management.

Dayspring member Velma Kahn created the online store of community products at communitymade.com, as well as the FIC's online store at store.ic.org.

Visitors Accepted: Please see visitor information under Abundant Dawn Community. [Mar2005]

DEBS HOUSE

House President
909 E University Ave
Ann Arbor, MI 48104

734-996-5962

http://www.icc.coop

Began: 1967 | Diet: Primarily vegetarian

Debs Co-op is a fun, cozy, queer-friendly haven for artists, writers, musicians, activists, and anyone else who likes to meet diverse people and live and grow cooperatively. We eat dinners with our friends at nearby Lester House, and both houses make a concerted effort to buy organic and local foods. We buy only vegetarian food, but members are not restricted as to what foods they may bring into the house. Debs has a study/guest room, a piano, 6+ parking spaces, a 15-space bike shed, a VCR, a computer and the Internet, several portraits of our namesake, and a huge Mother Earth sculpture. Currently, we do not allow cats. Stop by anytime!

Visitors Accepted: Contact House President. [Mar2005]

DEDETEPE ECO-FARM

http://www.dedetepe.com

Began: 2002 | Pop. 2
Rural | Diet: Vegetarian only

Erkan (32) and Tamahine (28) bought three acres of land two years ago and have recently created an eco-farm, which is an official ecological site registered with GEN Europe. The farm produces an average of 50 kgs of olives and 600 kgs of olive oil each year. Tamahine is a yoga teacher and runs workshops on the land, which the volunteers will be able to join in on.

The accommodation is a range of native tents such as tipis and Indian tents. All the farm food is vegetarian and cooked on natural fire, and meals are held together in a food circle around a fireplace. They target minimum waste through minimum consumption and proper division of waste. All food waste is suitably composted. No chemicals are used on the site; natural soaps are used for cleaning. The farm is not connected to city electric, electricity is produced by solar panels and a small wind generator.

The environment is gradual sloping countryside with a high rate of oxygen.

There are great views and a biological richness that supports much wildlife, such as squirrels, hawks and many smaller birds, deer, tortoises, mice, rabbits and hedgehogs, fish, frogs and crabs, as well as snakes and scorpions; and village animals such as sheep, goats, donkeys, horses and chickens.

Visitors Accepted: Email us one week before your visit. [Oct2004]

THE DELIBERACY...

Christopher Eldridge
23 Westwood Ct
Enola, PA 17025

717-728-0681, 717-433-1753
Function_First@Hotmail.com

http://www.Trafford.com/
robots/03-2197.html

Began: 2005 | Forming
Small Town | Diet: Omnivorous

Please check out our full-page ad! Our five-level, 16-bedroom communal home will be the most environmentally friendly and yet fully-featured home you'll ever hope to find in a community; racquetball anyone? Such low-impact (85% less than that of contemporary homes) does require, however, vehicle sharing, staggered meal periods, and a ban on non-functional luxury/sports cars. With 3,140 sq ft of Votech-quality office and shop space, we hope to attract professionals and tradespeople that want to work from home in the mutual support of one another! Costs would be on par with owning a home.

Basically, we are a slice of middle

Additions and corrections: email: directory@ic.org, *web:* directory.ic.org, *mail: RR 1 Box 156-D, Rutledge MO 63563, USA.*

127

America, just wanting to be more efficient and smarter about life! As such, we want to maintain an atmosphere of normalcy that everyone can find acceptable. Nudity, poor hygiene, group sing-a-longs, and religious extremes are unwelcome. There is a dress code and a "don't ask—don't wish to know" policy towards sexual preferences, where romantic displays are kept private. TVs/PCs are welcome, and all a-typical holidays like Christmas are celebrated! [Mar2005]

DENVER CATHOLIC WORKER

2420 Welton St
Denver, CO 80205
denvercw@juno.com

Began: 1978 | Pop. 5 | Spiritual
Urban | Diet: Omnivorous

We are a faith community committed to voluntary simplicity and hospitality. Our group is currently five members, and we live with temporary guests (numbering an average of 10–12) who join us based on their financial and housing needs. Food and household goods are received through donations, and our extended community joins our hospitality efforts. We welcome new members who are serious about living a lifestyle committed to service. If so, please write, email, or call about arranging a trial visit.

Visitors Accepted [Mar2005]

DENVER SPACE CENTER

3450 Marion St
Denver, CO 80205
mquesting@aol.com

Began: 1977 | Pop. 4 | Urban

We are an urban cooperative household established in 1979—more intentional than a boarding house, less intense than a commune; more civilized than a fraternity, less crowded than a dormitory. We have relatively few rules, though relatively much experience in this lifestyle. We share the rent, the common spaces, the housework, a piano, and a big yard with gardens, and make decisions by consensus when possible. We encourage friendships, good company, interesting conversations, aesthetic ruminations, and connections to a developing circle of friends. We have a nonbiological resemblance that eludes prosaic description.

Visitors Not Accepted [Mar2005]

DENVER URBAN COHOUSING

Ted Pearlman
519 Lafayette St
Denver, CO 80218

720-934-2474
ted.pearlman@gmail.com

http://denverurbancohousing
.blogspot.com

Began: 2004 | Forming | Urban

[Jan2005]

DETROIT COHOUSING

c/o Greater Corktown
Development Corporation
2411 14th St, Suite 200
Detroit, MI 48216

313-965-5853
info@detroitcohousing.org

http://www.adamah.org/cohousing

Began: 2002 | Forming | Urban

We are a cohousing community located in the city of Detroit. We are building our community to include affordable housing, environmentally-friendly design, and urban gardening. [Mar2005]

DHARMA HOUSE COMMUNITY PROJECT

thedharmahouse@yahoo.co.uk

http://groups.yahoo.com/group/
DharmaHouse

Began: 2004 | Forming | Spiritual
Rural | Diet: Vegetarian only

Hello friends in the Dharma!

We are the Dharma House Community Project. We are looking to find people interested in setting up a Buddhist community, preferably in France but we are still open to finding the right property at this stage. We have set up a Yahoo group to discuss our ongoing progress. We would also like this group to be a discussion forum for the issues relating to setting up various types of Dharma community. People from all over the world are invited to join us to share their vision of community living. Maybe you live in one already? Maybe a few different visions of community will arise so then a few different communities could form, or maybe even a network of communities?

Let's discover possibilities...! Be wonderful, have Metta and love the world!

Visitors Accepted: Please contact us via email. [Oct2004]

DOLPHIN COMMUNITY

Alpenblickstr. 12
Herrischried, D-79737
GERMANY

+49-(0)7764-933999,
+49-(0)7764-933225
meyer@gemeinschaften.de
gemeinschaften@gmx.net
oekodorf@gemeinshaften.de

http://www.gemeinschaften.de/
delphingemeinschaft.htm

Began: 1995 | Pop. 8 | Spiritual
Rural | Diet: Vegetarian only

In Native American mythology, the dolphin represents the combination of heaven and Earth, spirituality and matter, vision and realization. In this sense, we are already living communally without having a communal home, through spiritual diversity (within the limits of the ancient rules of the great religions of the world), communal singing, eating, hiking, baby-sitting, decision making by consensus, solving conflicts. We are learning from the experiences of older communities and are passing on our own experiences through the Ökodorf Institute. Service to fellow human beings: at the moment we are supporting the establishment of free health care for poor people in India. We are friends with several dozen local residents and are in friendly contact with the others. South Black Forest considers itself something like a melting pot since southern and eastern Europeans have been working in the textile industry here for over 150 years. In the long run, we would like to establish a spiritual-ecological village in addition to being integrated in the existing village and region. We would like to build the village together with the regional network of friends of our community. As a first step in this direction, we have established a local labor-exchange system and ARTABANA-health-community instead of health insurance.

We trust that God/inner voice will guide us in deciding what to do next, just as we have been guided so well since 1995. People interested in joining should first send us a few pages about themselves and their vision. We will then send more information about ourselves as well.

Visitors Accepted: Please write one page about you and why you want to visit us. The best times to visit are our monthly seminars for searching and founding communities. The dates are in our email newsletter. [Jan2005][✂]

Scissors [✂] at the end of a listing indicate that it was edited for length by the Directory *editors and a longer description can be found at* directory.ic.org.

DOMES, THE

The Domes, Baggins End
6 Baggins End
Davis, CA 95616

530-754-1450, 530-754-1111
webmaster@thedomes.org
domies@ucdavis.edu

http://www.thedomes.org

Began: 1972 | Pop. 28
Diet: Primarily vegetarian

Commonly known as "the domes," Baggins End is a community of 28 students housed in fourteen double occupancy dome-shaped buildings.

Constructed in 1972, Baggins End is situated on the northwest sector of the campus adjacent to the Sustainable Research Area and includes approximately three acres of garden space. The living environment of the domes emphasizes community, cooperation, and responsibility. Residents make a significant contribution to the care of their surroundings and program administration, including selection of occupants.

Visitors Accepted: To visit the domes, just come by! We have community dinners at 6 or 7 pm, Sunday through Thursday. We also have work parties at 10 am and meetings at 4 pm, every other Sunday. Or send an email to the current webmaster, or give us a call at any of the numbers listed. [Mar2005]

DOROTHY DAY COHOUSING

Karen House
1840 Hogan St
St. Louis, MO 63106

314-621-4052

Teka Childress
314-436-0277
teka10@juno.com

Dorothy Day Cohousing is a community of families who have lived at Karen House Catholic Worker (offers hospitality for homeless women and children) and other catholic workers who want to share their lives and resources. This is a long-term community that follows the tradition of the Catholic Worker Movement. [Mar2005]

DOYLE STREET

5514 Doyle St
Emeryville, CA 94608

http://www.emeryville-cohousing.org

Began: 1990 | Pop. 27
Urban | Diet: Omnivorous

Small urban cohousing community, 12 units plus common house. All units (condominiums) currently owner occupied. Units recently sold at $325,000 to $450,000. Group formed in 1990. Project completed and first occupied in spring 1992. Second cohousing project built in North America. Ask to be put on mailing list if you want to be notified when a unit is for sale.

Visitors Accepted: Visit us by signing up for a tour through the Cohousing Association of the United States http://www.cohousing.org/news/tours.html. [Mar2005]

DRAGON BELLY FARM

3882 Larson Lake Rd
Pt. Ludlow, WA 98365

360-732-4855

Sanda Everette
3329 Los Prados St
San Mateo, CA 94403

650-574-7155
sanda@cohousing.org

http://www.greensolutions.org/dbf.htm

Began: 1989 | Pop. 6 | Forming
Rural | Diet: Primarily vegetarian

We wish to build intentional community amid the greater community in Jefferson County on 39 acres, 17 miles south of Pt. Townsend, 30 miles and a ferry northwest of Seattle on the Olympic Peninsula. The land has a variety of ecosystems, about half forest, some of which is wetlands; a quarter meadow on glacial moraine; and a quarter pasture on wetter bottom land. There are two creeks and two ponds. We expect land to be owned in common, with some form of private ownership of home and homesite. We prefer environmentally sensitive, ecologically sustainable building materials and design. Current growth limitations may require multifamily housing with shared kitchen.

Our values include sustainable organic agriculture, conscious eating of a natural-foods diet, a recognition of how dietary choices involve/affect planetary economics and the environment. We prefer open communication with regular community meetings and other shared rituals, shared activities, shared reality.

We still envision community on this land, but the form and timing have changed. Owners are currently living in California, building urban community, accumulating capital, seeking partners, and probably waiting until retirement to return full-time. There are caretakers on the land.

If we are able to find partners for this project, we will return to DBF at least part-time when we retire in a couple of years. This would require partners with capital to own and build. We have also considered building it more as a retreat/resort center as an alternative community if a residential community does not manifest.

Visitors Accepted: Email me and then I will email Michael, the caretaker of the land, if a visit seems appropriate to all of our goals. [Feb2005]

DRAGONFLY FARM

Gen Del
Lake Saint Peter, ON K0L 2K0
CANADA

613-338-3421, 613-338-3316
edenvick@resist.ca

Began: 1971 | Pop. 4
Rural | Diet: Omnivorous

Situated just east of Algonquin Park amid the rolling, pre-Cambrian hills of the Canadian Shield is Dragonfly Farm. Our small collection of people persists on 250 acres of trees, marginal agricultural land, and beaver pond. Our seasonal businesses include a commercial greenhouse offering a variety of flowers, organic vegetable and herb starts and a mobile sawmill that custom cuts local people's logs. Our gardens provide us joy and bounty.

We welcome visitors, especially those from foreign lands who wish to experience rural Canada and need a place to stay. Accommodations are primitive. We heat with wood, have electricity, and use an outhouse since there is no indoor running water. In the summer months, camping is available at the conference site. Donations of money from visitors go toward taxes, etc. A few hours of assisting in farm activities is welcomed.

Here at Dragonfly the "politics of anarchy" rule within a sense of "communal individualism." Communication is preferred before arrival.

Visitors Accepted [Feb2005]

Additions and corrections: email: directory@ic.org, web: directory.ic.org, mail: RR 1 Box 156-D, Rutledge MO 63563, USA.

129

DREAMTIME VILLAGE

10375 County Hwy A
La Farge, WI 54639

608-625-4619 (office),
608-625-2412 (hotel)
dtv@mwt.net

http://www.dreamtimevillage.org

Began: 1991 | Pop. 13
Rural | Diet: Omnivorous

Dreamtime Village (DTV) is emerging as an experiment in ecovillage design whose mission is to create new planetary culture. By consciously drawing from the more biodiverse and imaginative resources of present-day and ancient cultures, we garden the complex interface between plant, animal, and human worlds. Our challenge is to design a landscape that is functional, alive, and phantasmagorical, while simultaneously serving as an ecovillage demonstration and a hands-on learning environment for people of all ages. We delight in discovery, innovation, and experimentation.

We lean toward open systems and self-organization, allowing the ecovillage to grow as an organism. A diversity of DTV residents and visitors tends to create an eclectic mix; folks are drawn here through a broad variety of channels. Studios, woods, wetlands, gardens, orchards, a huge 1920's brick school building, five other buildings, and 80 acres of land form the facility for DTV workshops, gatherings, retreats, and more. Our focus is on permaculture and "hypermedia" (a term we use to expand on common notions of "art" and "media"). Dreamtimers past or present have been involved in pottery, yoga, musical improvisation and instrument making, wood turning, gourds, herbs, computers, natural building, bookmaking, etc.

Visitors Accepted: We like visitors, and are content to show you around, answer questions, feed you, inspire you, and put a shovel in your hand. We ask for a donation of $8 per night, which helps with our expenses (but we don't turn people away for lack of funds). We discourage people arriving unannounced, so please write, call or email ahead of time. [Jan2005]

DRUMLIN CO-OPERATIVE

drumlin.co-op@sympatico.ca

http://www3.sympatico.ca/
drumlin.co-op

Began: 1988

Drumlin Co-op is a 91-unit housing cooperative located in Brantford, Ontario, Canada. Brantford is located centrally in southwestern Ontario, about an hour's drive from Toronto and London, and about three hours from the borders at either Windsor or Fort Erie. Drumlin was first established in September of 1988 and first occupied in 1989. The co-op consists of 2, 3 and 4 bedroom units as well as 5 accessible units. There is a community centre and office located centrally on the co-op grounds which houses laundry, maintenance and storage facilities, along with the office. There are two staff persons available four days per week. Co-ops are one of four kinds of nonprofit housing. They are the *only* nonprofit housing that is democratically managed by the residents. The premise behind cooperative housing is to provide an affordable housing alternative for people that allows them to have some control over how their community is run. [Feb2005]

DU-MÁ

2244 Alder St
Eugene, OR 97405

541-343-5023, 541-343-1926
impact@efn.org

http://www.efn.org/~dlamp

Began: 1988 | Pop. 7
Urban | Diet: Primarily vegetarian

We are a stable urban community that formed in 1988 based on five values—ecological responsibility, personal growth, diversity, equality, and community. Daily examples of our values include growing vegetables, recycling, looking at gender and class issues, cocounseling, Naka-Ima, consensus decision making, and rituals.

Visitors remark that we are neat, well organized, and accountable to our values. We eat vegetarian meals together, nurture our relationships with one another, and share the joys and responsibilities of owning a home and yard large enough for eight people. We share expenses but not our incomes.

In 1998 we rekindled our mission "to be of service to others as an inspirational model of living and working together to create community and social change..." We are in the early stages of making our mission a reality; how it unfolds will undoubtably be an ongoing journey.

We seek members who are compatible with us, have substantial energy to contribute, are emotionally and financially stable, feel settled in Eugene, and are looking for a close group of people to grow with.

Membership process helps us determine who will thrive and be happy here.

Visitors Accepted: Please write or call us at least two weeks before you wish to visit. [Dec2004]

DUNMIRE HOLLOW COMMUNITY

2017 Dunmire Hollow Rd
Waynesboro, TN 38485

931-722-3078, 931-722-9201,
931-722-5096
harvey@ic.org

Began: 1973 | Pop. 7 | Rural

Dunmire Hollow (est. 1973) is a community of about a dozen people sharing their lives and 163 acres in a magic hollow in Tennessee. We have fields, orchards, gardens, woods, springs, creeks, a community center, a woodshop, a sauna, a food co-op, family houses, etc. Each family is economically independent; we make/have made our livings in a variety of ways—teaching, construction, woodworking, nursing, doctoring, lawyering, auto repair, sewing, truck driving, small-engine repair, crafts—and from providing for ourselves more directly through domestic economy and barter.

As individuals, we have a variety of enthusiasms that often involve us with the world and other people: organic gardening, music, crafts, environmentalism, peace work, sports, community networking, aquaculture, alternative energy, etc. Each resident adds to the diverse mix that makes up our community.

We are happy to communicate with people who are interested in rural-community living. We enjoy visitors; please write for more information or to arrange a visit.

Visitors Accepted: Please call, write, or email in advance, telling us a bit about yourself/selves, and what you are looking for and have to offer. [Oct2004]

DUTCH COHOUSING ASSOCIATION (LVCW)

Korte Elisabethstraat 13
Utrecht, 3511 JG
NETHERLANDS

+31-(0)30-2612585
info@lvcw.nl

http://www.lvcw.nl

The LVCW (Landelijke Vereniging Centraal Wonen) is the national association of cohousing projects in Holland. [Mar2005]

Scissors [✂] at the end of a listing indicate that it was edited for length by the Directory *editors and a longer description can be found at* directory.ic.org.

DUWAMISH COHOUSING

6000 17th Ave SW #24
Seattle, WA 98106

206-767-7726
outreach@duwamish.net

Wendy Walker
wendiana@duwamish.net

http://www.duwamish.net

Began: 1996 | Pop. 55
Urban | Diet: Omnivorous

Duwamish Cohousing (formerly Ciel Cohousing) is an urban cohousing community in West Seattle, about 10 minutes from downtown. We moved into our homes in June 2000. Our neighborhood is primarily made up of fully equipped duplex townhomes owned as condominiums and generous common facilities including large kitchen and dining spaces, two indoor and two outdoor child play areas, a woodshop, a craft studio, a laundry, an office, a sunroom/living room, sunny decks and patios, native plant landscaping, and several community gardens. Our homes line pedestrian pathways and courtyards that are all handicapped accessible. Our 2.7 acres of land are located in a multicultural neighborhood, and we value including people of many cultures and races, as well as several other types of diversity in our community. Some of our values include working cooperatively with our surrounding neighbors, using consensus, sharing work and social activities, environmental preservation, and building support and neighborliness among ourselves.

Visitors Accepted: Contact the Outreach committee at outreach@duwamish.net to set up a tour or attend a dinner. [Oct2004]

EARTH FIRST AUSTRALIA

PO Box 161
Norseman, Western Australia 6443
AUSTRALIA
efoz@earthfirst.org.au

http://www.earthfirst.org.au

Began: 1995 | Forming
Small Town | Diet: Primarily vegetarian

We have an ecovillage and city farm project on the go in Norseman, Western Australia.

We welcome new members, particularly those that wish to be part of the construction of the infrastructure.

Visitors Accepted: Write or email in the first instance. While we are still building, visitors may be accommodated in members' private residences. [Oct2004]

EARTH POD

PO Box 433
Floyd, VA 24091
info@abundantdawn.org
mark@abundantdawn.org

http://www.abundantdawn.org/
index.html#ThePods

Began: 1991 | Pop. 2 | Forming | Rural

Earth Pod is a subgroup (pod) of Abundant Dawn Community, founded in 2003.

Currently we are a provisional pod consisting of two adults, formed from a division of Tekiah into two parts (both our members are long-term community members). We hope to build off-grid dwellings, grow much of our own food, and live lightly on the land. Currently, we support ourselves through yoga teaching, working in the local CSA, and agricultural research.

Visitors Accepted: Please see visitor information under Abundant Dawn Community. [Mar2005]

EARTH RE-LEAF

PO Box 599
Naalehu, HI 96772

808-929-8003
forest@talk-story.net

http://www.lavazone2.com/forest

Began: 1982 | Pop. 1 | Spiritual
Rural | Diet: Primarily vegan

Earth Re-Leaf (continually refining) is a cooperative-consensus organic farm and nature sanctuary focusing on several areas including but not limited to: (1) refining consensus council; (2) evolving relationships; (3) responsible consensus childcare; (4) raw-foods vegan diet; (5) evolving life and language beyond polarity; (6) nonviolence; (7) self-sufficiency, sustainability, and co-op business; (8) land trust; (9) spiritual evolution.

Our foundational council agreements are: (1) short silent period before speaking; (2) all get uninterrupted three-minute speaking rotations; (3) divisions into groups of 12 or less; (4) decisions and actions based on 100 percent agreement.

A permaculture orchard plus a few small private shelters and community buildings are situated on one acre of land at 800 feet. Another two acres are nearby at 5,000 feet. We seek to attract a core group of self-reliant, grounded, country-farmer spiritual pioneers that grows and divides into supportive splinter families. Our simple council guarantees freedom from control and domination. Call, email, or write with questions.

Visitors Accepted: Email and/or check website for visitor questionnaire. [Feb2005]

EARTHART VILLAGE

64001 County Rd DD
Moffat, CO 81143

719-256-5003
info@earthart.org
linda@earthart.org

http://www.earthart.org

Began: 1998 | Pop. 3 | Forming
Rural | Diet: Omnivorous

EarthArt Village is in early formation, with intention to evolve as a model, holistic, sustainable community—living harmoniously with the Earth, sharing resources and responsibilities, and balancing the common good of the group with the well-being of each member. The purposes of this cooperative association are to:

1. Own, manage, and maintain land and facilities for the benefit, health, and well-being of the residential community and other members.
2. Cultivate lifestyles demonstrating the learning and living of cooperation, simplicity, creative expression, and respect for one another and nature. Honor, steward, protect, and enhance the natural environment.
3. Establish energy-efficient, ecologically sound living, learning, working, and playing environments, using sustainable design, methods, and materials.
4. Research, develop, and maintain alternative, off-grid, sustainable infrastructure: common food, energy, water, and waste-management systems.
5. Conduct community endeavors, such as member-managed agriculture and businesses, cooperative purchasing programs, publications, research projects, and artistic and cultural activities.
6. Provide a living context and example for educational demonstration of sustainable community living—socially, spiritually, economically, and environmentally.

Visitors Accepted: For visitor details, see our website. [Jan2005]

Listings

Additions and corrections: email: directory@ic.org, *web:* directory.ic.org, *mail: RR 1 Box 156-D, Rutledge MO 63563, USA.*

131

EARTHAVEN ECOVILLAGE

1025 Camp Elliott Rd
Black Mountain, NC 28711

828-669-3937
info@earthaven.org

http://www.earthaven.org

Began: 1990 | Pop. 65
Rural | Diet: Omnivorous

Earthaven is an aspiring ecovillage founded in 1994 on 320 acres in the mountain forests of western North Carolina, about 40 minutes from Asheville. We are spiritually diverse, and value sustainable ecological systems, permaculture design, elegant simplicity, right livelihood, and healthy social relations. We have both vegetarians and omnivores, and some of us raise livestock. We hope to become empowered, responsible, ecologically literate citizens who model bioregionally appropriate culture for our time and place.

We intend to become a village of at least 150. As of 2005, we have 60 members. While much of Earthaven is still under construction, we have built roads and bridges, community buildings, members' homes,

multi-household residences, gardens, constructed wetlands, and off-grid power and water systems.

We use consensus decision making, and own the title to our land, which is paid for. We lease homesites from the community and pay annual dues.

We are developing a small village-scale economy, and most of us work in small on-site businesses or nonprofits, including Red Moon Herbs, *Permaculture Activist* magazine, Trading Post General Store, White Owl Lodge, Useful Plants Nursery, among others, or by offering visitor lodging, carpentry and home construction, tool-rental, and solar system, electrical, and plumbing installation.

We're seeking hardworking, visionary people, including but not limited to organic growers and farmers, entrepreneurs, people with mechanical and engineering skills, healers, artists, and families with children.

Visitors Accepted: Contact information is listed above. We have regularly scheduled tours, a campground, and indoor accommodations. [Mar2005]

EARTHRIGHT FARMS

Michael Ferguson
975 SE 1041 Pvt Rd
Osceola, MO 64776
scorpio68@interlinc.net

Began: 2000 | Pop. 2 | Forming
Rural | Diet: Primarily vegetarian

This is a newly forming Farmstead community in the northern Ozarks of Missouri. We are exploring concepts of self sustainability through progressive applications of organic (certification pending) food production, xeriscaping, permaculture, and water shed management. This is a horticulturally rooted farm, meaning that the greenhouse is the heartbeat of the operation. All members must be active in all areas of the grounds, including: greenhouse work, nursery/market garden work, harvesting, pruning, landscaping, and grounds maintenance (weeding, mowing, watering, etc.). Administrative obligations (marketing, advertising, etc) will be designated to each resident member along with community duties (laundry, kitchen, hardscape maintenance, construction, etc.). We would like to find a core group of approximately ten people who are willing and wanting to settle down for the long haul. As the infrastructure becomes more established, then we will consider internships. At this time we need a permanent "seed camp." Individuals with horticultural background and/or higher education take preference, yet on-the-job training is provided.

Currently we are seeking individuals who can contribute financially to the farm to help better establish the infrastructure. We would like to keep this an adult only community at this time. All active resident members become established member/owners of the LLC business. This gives everyone executive power to craft this farmstead into the community that we envision and the ability to secure everyone's investment. The "revolving door" concept of community is counter productive for this type of establishment.

Visitors Accepted: Please contact us through email or by letter to inform us of your intent, and wait for a reply before arriving. We will respond in a timely fashion to all inquiries. [Mar2005]

EARTHSEED

PO Box 163
Putney, VT 05346

802-387-2487
earthseed@ic.org

Began: 1994 | Rural

EarthSeed is a community of people living in and near southeastern Vermont, with an ongoing web of relationships and a strong commitment to healing and activism on behalf of all life.

We meet regularly for potlucks, business/council meetings, deep personal sharing circles, Earth-based healing rituals and seasonal celebrations, and occasional weekend gatherings. Food shared at EarthSeed gatherings is free of animal products.

The consensus process is used to make decisions affecting the community.

We support each other in making and maintaining individual life choices based on self-responsibility, healing, and growth. We also support each person's lifework and creative activities.

The first EarthSeed meeting was held in October 1994, and then a meeting was held one weekend every one to two months. From September 1996 through April 1998 a group of us rented a house together in Athens, Vermont, and lived as a consensus-run household. There is currently no collective EarthSeed household.

Updates, with news of recent gatherings, meeting minutes, and announcements of upcoming events, are mailed and (preferably) emailed to people who request them. Donations toward the cost of mailing are welcomed. Many of our gatherings are open to visitors, with advance notice.

Visitors Accepted [Oct2004]

Scissors [✂] at the end of a listing indicate that it was edited for length by the Directory *editors and a longer description can be found at* directory.ic.org.

EARTHSKY TRIBE

The Medicine Man Trading Post
174 C St
Independence, OR 97351

http://www.hippieland.net

Spiritual

Earthsky tribe is a small Rainbow Family Community in Independence, Oregon.

We run a small store in old town down by the Willemete River. Circle is held every third Sunday of the month.

Our ultimate goal is to build a fully sustainable community from the ground up.

We also run an online community forum at http://www.hippieland.net

Visitors Accepted: Walk in. [Jan2005]

EARTHSWELL FARM

Amy Halloran-Steiner
McMinnville, OR

503-472-1287
aims_1972@yahoo.com

Began: 2004 | Pop. 2 | Forming
Rural | Diet: Omnivorous

We are a just-getting-starting group on 123 acres on rural land outside of McMinnville, Oregon. The land is both dry-farmed valley and oak hillside. There are three homesites available on the land, and our vision is to have several multiple-family dwellings, making up a community of up to about 16 people or so. We hope to raise goats for milk and cheese, chickens, ducks, rabbits and horses, and to live as sustainably as possible. A big garden, hiking trails, swimming pond, big old recycled barn, and potential retreat space are all visions that circulate. We welcome interested, open-minded, hard-working individuals and young families.

Visitors Accepted: Please call us and we will arrange a visit if you are serious about relocating. You can come out and camp, or if there is housing available at the time, stay in one of our mobile homes. [Nov2004]

EAST BAY COHOUSING

Oakland/Berkeley, CA
ebcoho-interest@ebcoho.org

http://www.ebcoho.org

Began: 1998 | Urban | Diet: Omnivorous

A group of households and individuals working together to create a residential community in the urban East Bay region of the San Francisco Bay area.

The mission of East Bay Cohousing is to develop a cohousing community in the urban East Bay based upon the following shared values and goals: private unit ownership with shared, smoke-free common space and common meals; desire to live in an intentional community; consideration, kindness, and respect toward other community members; willingness to compromise, cooperate, share leadership, and make decisions by consensus; desire for an environmentally sustainable lifestyle.

East Bay Cohousing has been meeting since November 1998. Our membership is dynamic and committed to creating a warm, vibrant residential community within a few years. We are currently in the planning stage and meet for monthly general meetings/potlucks and regular committee meetings. Our committees include Development, Operations, and Membership/Process.

East Bay Cohousing is currently recruiting new members. Regularly scheduled orientations are available for interested households and individuals.

Visitors Accepted: Check our calendar, RSVP, bring a potluck dish! [Oct2004]

EAST LAKE COMMONS

900 Dancing Fox Rd
Decatur, GA 30032
contactus@eastlakecommons.org

http://www.eastlakecommons.org

Began: 1997 | Pop. 149
Urban | Diet: Omnivorous

East Lake Commons is a cohousing community in Decatur, Georgia, six miles from downtown Atlanta. Completed in 2001, it includes 67 townhomes, a large common house, common green and playground. Approximately half of the 20-acre site is dedicated to an organic garden, pond, green space, and wooded areas. Cars are kept to the periphery of the site, with townhomes clustered around pedestrian courtyards and walkways.

We seek to sustain a community that nurtures children with playmates; supports teenagers with mentors and role models; provides adults with a social network and seniors with a friendly supportive community. Our members represent a rich diversity of age, religion, lifestyle, race, ethnicity, cultural background, differently abled, and economic status. Residents manage the community using the consensus decision-

making process, with the goal that everyone is heard and all needs are understood. A back-up voting procedure is in place. Critical community values also include the preservation and enhancement of the natural environment and participation in the revitalization of our surrounding neighborhoods.

Our website includes a list of homes available for sale or rent.

Visitors Accepted: First, please examine the community website to be sure of your interest. Then send us an email explaining your interest and when you might like to visit. We are not well equipped to handle casual travelers who are just looking for a place to stop over. Housing on the site is not guaranteed. [Mar2005]

EAST VENTURA/WEST VALLEY COHOUSING

Donna Freiermuth
Ventura, CA

310-455-9672
Cohousing@Organic-Design.net

http://www.ventura-county-cohousing.com

Began: 2005 | Forming

Somewhere between, say, Topanga and Santa Paula, California, a great cohousing community is waiting to be born.

This website is the first step to bring that community into being. Beginning in early 2005, a group of people willing to explore and pursue the idea can now come together.

Once that core group of serious individuals is found, we can start meeting, looking for land, thinking about building configurations and lots more.

Visitors Accepted: Arrange in advance to attend a meeting. [Feb2005]

EAST WIND COMMUNITY

HC 3 Box 3370
Tecumseh, MO 65760

417-679-4682
membership@eastwind.org
cath@eastwind.org

http://www.eastwind.org

Began: 1970 | Pop. 75
Rural | Diet: Omnivorous

We are a 75-member collective located on 1,045 acres of rural Ozark Hills in southern Missouri. We are a member of the Federation of Egalitarian Communities, and as such, we put great value in cooperation,

Listings

nonviolence, and sharing. We support ourselves through several industries: East Wind Nut Butters, East Wind Drums, Utopian Rope Sandals, and Twin Oaks Hammocks. We also strive to practice sustainability and ecological consciousness. Our membership is very diverse, we have no central leadership, and we practice democracy. Our work lives are busy and varied, but we always find time to relax and enjoy community meals, music jams, and Ozark sunsets. Our land is one of a kind, very rural, and filled with all sorts of wildlife. We encourage individuality and diversity in our members. Prospective visitors are encouraged to contact someone on our Membership Team to arrange a visit, but please call or write first, as dropping in unannounced is an unwelcome strain on our resources.

Visitors Accepted: Write us at membership@eastwind.org. [Dec2004]

EAST-WEST HOUSE

Vacancy Manager
733 Baker St
San Francisco, CA 94115
baker_street_coop@yahoo.com

Began: 1957 I Pop. 13
Urban I Diet: Primarily vegetarian

We are a 50 year old consensus-based collective of varying ages, ethnicities, sexual orientations (more than 2), genders (more than 2), etc. Our focus is sharing: food, cooking, chores, and mutual support for the thirteen member. Some of our time spent together is centered around the nightly dinners, baking for our varied diets, a shared love of bicycles, music, a beautiful garden in our backyard, and activism. We embrace the goal of creating a community based on more then just "tolerance"—one of inclusion, understanding, and support. Our house is 4 floors, 13 bedrooms, 2 permanent guest rooms, fully-stocked kitchen, dining room, pantry, 2 living rooms, small library, meditation/art room, three small porches, back yard, garden, hot tub, laundry room, six bathrooms (never wait!), guest car parking, voluminous locked bike parking, and DSL.

In the late 1950s to early 1960s a monk from Japan, Shunryu Suzuki, came to San Francisco to teach about the then unheard of religion called "Buddhism." Suzuki went on to establish what is now known as the San Francisco Zen Center and a few of his students banded together to start a dorm, dubbed "East-West House."

After over fifty years, and four locations, East-West House found a permanent home on Baker Street in the late 1980s, and cur-

rently is moving towards updating our name in order to better reflect who we are.
Visitors Not Accepted [Mar2005]

EASTERN VILLAGE COHOUSING

Katie Henry
7981 Eastern Ave #311
Silver Spring, MD 20910

301-565-9663
katie-henry@att.net

Deirdre McGlynn
7981 Eastern Ave #412
Silver Spring, MD 20910
deirdremcglynn@yahoo.com

http://www.easternvillage.org

Began: 2002 I Pop. 90
Urban I Diet: Omnivorous

Eastern Village is a 56-unit cohousing community in downtown Silver Spring, Maryland, just a few blocks from the Silver Spring metro.

EVC is a developer-driven project organized by architect/developer Don Tucker of the Eco Housing corporation (www.ecohousing.net) and cohousing consultant Ann Zabaldo.

The first organizing meetings were held in late 2002, with forty members on board within five months. Move-in started in October 2004 and is largely complete as of this writing (January 2005).

Our building is a gut rehab of an abandoned 1950s-era office building in a scruffy part of downtown Silver Spring that is benefitting from the real-estate boom in the DC area.

The EVC building incorporates a number of green building features (ground-source heat-pump system, high-efficiency central hot water, etc.) and is being submitted for LEED Silver certification.

EVC is legally structured as condominiums. Units range from one-bedroom flats to three-bedroom lofts.

Visitors Accepted: Contact Deirdre McGlynn to arrange a visit. [Jan2005]

EASTON MOUNTAIN

391 Herrington Hill Rd
Greenwich, NY 12834

518-692-8023
info@eastonmountain.com

http://www.eastonmountain.com

Began: 2000 I Pop. 15 I Spiritual
Rural I Diet: Omnivorous

Easton Mountain is home to an interfaith spiritual community of men who love men.

The community runs a retreat center that serves a variety of groups but has an emphasis on serving the spiritual development of the gay men's community. We strive to live lightly on the earth in a way that is both sustainable and joy-filled.

Currently we are 15 men ranging in age from 27-80. We are open to new members.

The current leadership consists of a core group of founding members, the executive director of the non-profit that runs the retreat center, and a board of directors consisting of both resident and non-resident community members.

All meals are served in common and we serve a variety of food types, from meat to vegan.

Alcohol is rarely consumed and no tobacco is currently used.

We are rural on 175 acres of land north of Albany, NY, and we are within three hours of NYC, Boston and Montreal.

We have several individual spiritual paths, some of which are shared by a subset of the community; we do share a weekly Quaker-style service on Sunday evenings.

LGBT members are most welcome, as are non-LGBT people.

Visitors Accepted: Visitors are welcome, please contact us to arrange a visit. [May2005]

ECHOLLECTIVE FARM

Mia Kenyon Brown
879 Echo Ave
Mechanicsville, IA 52306

563-432-7484
echofarm@netins.net

Began: 2003 I Pop. 5 I Forming
Rural I Diet: Primarily vegan

Echollective Farm is a forming community in rural Eastern Iowa on 53 acres, including a forested area with a creek and 14 acres of certified organic vegetables, herbs, flowers, and hay. Group interests center on community and sustainability. A trailer and barn are now on-site; a three-bedroom strawbale house, a yurt, and a strawbale hermitage are likely to be completed in 2005.

The garden is already an established community endeavor. Over a dozen people are involved in growing food, flowers and herbs for themselves and the community, and to be marketed through restaurants, farmer's markets and to grocery stores.

Visitors Accepted: Communicate by email or letter and describe your interests, skills, and/or community vision. [Mar2005]

Scissors [✂] at the end of a listing indicate that it was edited for length by the Directory *editors and a longer description can be found at* directory.ic.org.

ECLIPSE

207 Bio Sciences East
University of Arizona
Tucson, AZ 85721

908-295-0266
contact@eclipseovertucson.com
colepole@email.arizona.edu

http://eclipseovertucson.com

Began: 2004 | Forming

ECLIPSE is a student group created for the purpose of learning about and sharing ways to live that conserve our earth and the resources we need to survive. In addition to uniting students interested in living more sustainable and energy efficient lifestyles, ECLIPSE acts as a connection for these students to collaborate with UA administration, local businesses, and the greater Tucson community.

To actualize our mission, we plan to build a completely natural and sustainable dormitory on the UA campus. This building will feature local construction materials, solar electricity and water heating, greywater facilities, and water harvesting. The ECLIPSE dorm will serve as a place for students to learn about sustainability hands-on, a research facility for UA projects, and an introduction of sustainable technologies to the campus of the University of Arizona.

Visitors Accepted: Contact us! [Jan2005]

ECOFARM COMMUNITY

Debbie Butts
4321 Needle Palm Rd
Plant City, FL 33565

813-754-7374
debbutts@gte.net
info@ecofarmfl.org

http://www.ecofarmfl.org

[Feb2005]

ECOTOPIA ROMANIA

Stanciova, Timis, 307347
ROMANIA

+40-(0)256-330959
comunitate@yahoo.com

http://ecotopia.ngo.ro

Began: 2000 | Pop. 5 | Forming
Rural | Diet: Omnivorous

Between the stormy past of Romania and an uncertain global future, we are among those who do not just simply live, guided by unquestioned traditions or aggressive brainwash by the media, but we try to make sense of the world we live in and make choices.

Our community is made up of a diverse group of people. Some are working full time in the project, while others contribute to the project occasionally while pursuing their life in the area and beyond. Volunteers and visitors are an essential ingredient for our success. We all share a common purpose, which is to develop a model of a sustainable rural community in Stanciova. In this sense, we are an "intentional group," rather than an "intentional community" as may be seen in Western countries.

Visitors Accepted: Please check the visit us section of our website. Once you fill in the application form, we'll contact you and we'll have an informal interview face to face, by phone, or by email. The interview is designed to create a basis of communication between us, to get to know each other and identify possibilities for your visit. [Jan2005]

ECOVILLA ASOCIACIÓN GAIA

Almafuerte 1732
San Martin (CP 1650)
Buenos Aires,
ARGENTINA

+54-(0)2272-492072,
+54-(0)2227-15552554 (cell)
gaia@gaia.org.ar
gaia@wamani.apc.org

http://www.gaia.org.ar

Began: 1996 | Pop. 11
Rural | Diet: Vegetarian only

Gaia Argentina is a pioneer ecovillage project with a permaculture basis that has been

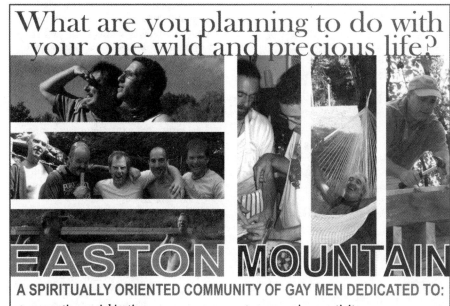
Additions and corrections: email: directory@ic.org, *web:* directory.ic.org, *mail: RR 1 Box 156-D, Rutledge MO 63563, USA.*

in development since 1996, in a rural area 120 km from Buenos Aires city.

We function as a Living and Learning Center, and we have been sharing information and inspiration for permaculture projects and ecovillage development in the southern region. We offer courses on permaculture, natural building, circle dances, and also about community building by a Findhorn member.

In March 2000, Gaia hosted the first Latin-American Permaculture Convergence with great success. We created the Argentinean Permaculture Institute (IAP) as a space for experimenting, implementing, and teaching permaculture systems. IAP is focused on research and practice of appropriate technologies adapted for local needs, to transfer them to impoverished people in our country. New members are participating in the project in many different ways, and some new businesses are starting.

Visitors Accepted: Contact us in advance to confirm details. [Jan2005]

ECOVILLAGE AT ITHACA

Anabel Taylor Hall
Cornell University
Ithaca, NY 14853

607-255-8276
ecovillage@cornell.edu
visit-coordinator@
  ecovillage.ithaca.ny.us

http://www.ecovillage.ithaca.ny.us

Began: 1992 | Pop. 162
Diet: Primarily vegetarian

Located in the beautiful rolling hills of New York's Finger Lakes region, Ecovillage at Ithaca has two thriving cohousing communities with eventual plans for a third. The village features cooperative dining in the common house, a swimming pond, gardens, hiking trails, play spaces, and sixty passive-solar, energy-efficient homes in a multigenerational community.

Our goal is to build a replicable model of a cooperative, environmentally sensitive community. The pedestrian village is surrounded by woods and open meadows. We have a 10 acre organic farm on-site that provides much of the produce for residents, and a 5 acre berry farm is being planned. Our nonprofit educational organization is affiliated with both Cornell and Ithaca College, and we teach courses in various aspects of sustainability.

Ecovillage is on 176 acres, located $1^1/_2$ miles from downtown Ithaca and $3^1/_2$ miles from Cornell University and Ithaca College.

Ninety percent of the land is preserved as green space for organic agriculture and wildlife habitat.

Visitors Accepted: People are welcome to come to our free public tour, at 3 pm on the last Saturday of each month. If that doesn't work for your schedule, you can arrange a private tour by contacting our visit coordinator at least a week or two in advance. We ask that people who take a private tour join our nonprofit educational organization, EVI, Inc. as members ($30/single, $40/household). We have some overnight accommodations available in people's homes. [Mar2005]

ECOVILLAGE DETROIT

Jacob Corvidae
2718 Rosa Parks Blvd
Detroit, MI 48216

313-961-0264
info@ecovillagedetroit.org

http://www.ecovillagedetroit.org

Began: 2003 | Forming
Urban | Diet: Omnivorous

The mission of EcoVillage Detroit is to create a living model of diverse, cooperative community building that enhances the social, economic, and environmental vitality of our neighborhood. We root our project in personal change and deep connection to our physical surroundings. We are committed to serving the wider community and being a demonstration project.

Visitors Accepted: We do not have an official visitor program. Definitely contact us ahead of time if you're interested in visiting, so we can arrange something. Our focus is less on recruiting members and more on working within our existing neighborhood. [Mar2005]

ECOVILLAGE OF LOUDOUN COUNTY

http://www.ecovillages.com

Began: 1990 | Pop. 19 | Forming
Rural | Diet: Omnivorous

Mission: EcoVillage of Loudoun County combines the cohousing ideal of people living together in community, with the ecovillage ideal of people living in harmony with Earth and its inhabitants. We aim to restore nature and expand human potential by creating a lifestyle that nurtures the human spirit and offers hope for future generations.

Ecological Goal: Preserve and restore biodiversity, quality, and abundance of natural

resources. Balance natural systems so that each generation acts to benefit future generations.

Social Goal: Maintain a community lifestyle that protects individual rights; fosters a spirit of community; and facilitates activities that benefit individuals, enrich the community, and promote positive relations with the larger world.

Visitors Accepted: Contact the EcoVillage office by phone or email. [Mar2005]

ECOVILLAGE SIEBEN LINDEN

Sieben Linden 1
Poppau, 38486
GERMANY

+49-(0)39000-51235
verein@oekodorf7linden.de

http://www.oekodorf7linden.de

Began: 1989 | Pop. 71
Rural | Diet: Primarily vegetarian

In 1997 we founded a socially and ecologically oriented settlement, an "ecovillage," where eventually 300 people could live. The village represents a holistic habitat that closely integrates and harmonizes different areas of life so that a positive human and ecological net balance and mutual resonance can develop.

We want to be an open and hospitable village, inspired by a communal culture where, within an ecological and self-organizational framework, a variety of lifestyles and convictions can become possible. We are striving for overall self-sufficiency in all areas of life: from nutrition, building, and energy all the way to our own social, medical, educational, and cultural activities. We are organizing ourselves as a village community made up of smaller living communities, which exist alongside one another in a cooperative fashion with a variety of life concepts. We seek social and cultural exchanges with our surroundings. Together with other projects and movements we are working on the development of a societal alternative: through our own example we are demonstrating that a (more) sustainable life is possible.

Until 1999 we were mainly concerned with building up communal facilities, the seminar house, and infrastructure. In 2000, the first two residential houses for 20 occupants were completed, followed by the first approved strawbale residential house in Germany, a wood workshop, and a three-story strawbale house for 18 occupants.

Visitors Accepted: You must arrange your visit in advance! [Mar2005][✂]

Scissors [✂] at the end of a listing indicate that it was edited for length by the Directory *editors and a longer description can be found at* directory.ic.org.

THE EDEN PROJECT

T McClure
PO Box 571
Kenwood, CA 95452
edenproj@yahoo.com
temeluch@yahoo.com

http://www.edenvillage.net

Forming | Spiritual
Rural | Diet: Omnivorous

The Eden Project is to create a multi-generational 2,240-acre permaculture based ecovillage community in Mendocino County in Northern California that will be able to become completely self-sustainable in food, water, energy, housing, education, and reproductive capacity.

We will each be granted one of about seventy three-acre homesteads where each can build their own passive-solar home. Each will have another two acre farm site right in front of the homestead within the good farmland in the valley for a $30,000 contribution pledge.

The Vegan Village will be a planned neighborhood of 18 homesteads that will be joined together as one.

There will also be a large community farm to create jobs and to support our own sustainable micro economy. There will also be a large central area with a strawbale roundhouse for other community uses.

We will create a market for some of the many things we will each be growing on our personal mini-farms by having our own natural-food store in town that could be called Village Foods.

Eden is child centered and for that reason it is a woman-centric community, meaning this might be just the place for the female spirit to be able to spread Her wings and fly.

Our focus is on earth stewardship in a natural learning and healing environment. Our purpose is to save the earth.

There will be low income opportunities like the no down payment pledges for one out of three homesteaders that can be paid off over time.

The *Eden Journal* is also available with maps and charts and contact resources and is only $7.00 for the next four issues.

Visitors Accepted: Come to one of our lodge meetings on the last Saturday of every January–May or September at 11am. Contact us for directions. [Oct2004][✂<]

EDEN RANCH COMMUNITY

PO Box 520
Paonia, CO 81428

970-835-8905
woodwetz@tds.net

http://www.edenranch.com

Pop. 2 | Forming
Rural | Diet: Primarily vegetarian

Forming community seeking members desiring rural, pristine environment, sharing labor and resources on 65-acre farm operating under limited-liability company and bylaws. Ultimate self-sustainability. Currently being placed in Conservation Easement.

Located on western Colorado mesa, wondrous 360 degree views. Bring your own business, or work nearby. Future community business envisioned. Diversity in thought and age; consensus decision making results from mutual respect and trust. Membership fee: $6,500 first member (prorated for additional members). Landshare fee: $15,000 (flexible terms available), plus cost of Earth-friendly home of your choice. Come meet our Llamas!

Visitors Accepted: Contact us to arrange a mutually suitable time. Generally speaking, weekends are best for us, but other times can be arranged. Seasonal camping is available at Eden Ranch; local Bed and Breakfasts and motels are also available. Maximum 2-night stay if camping, unless otherwise agreed upon. We request 2-3 hours of labor per person per day in return for your stay in the community. Please bring work clothes, work gloves, a flashlight and food to share. [Mar2005]

EDGES

10770 Hooper Ridge Rd
Glouster, OH 45732

740-448-2403, 740-448-3006
edgesfarm@aol.com

Began: 1992 | Pop. 13
Rural | Diet: Omnivorous

Edges is nestled in the foothills of the Appalachian mountains near Athens, home of progressive Ohio University. Ninety-four acres of wooded and clear hills include many "edges," hence much diversity. Seven adults and five children, ages 8 to 63, work

Additions and corrections: email: directory@ic.org, web: directory.ic.org, mail: RR 1 Box 156-D, Rutledge MO 63563, USA.

137

together to create a supportive environment, steward the land, and evolve sustainable livelihoods. One member operates a successful solar/wind design and installation business, two others operate a Bed & Breakfast and Wellness Center. Other residents work at a cooperative bakery in Athens, do book editing at home, market eco-friendly air filters, and work as a psychologist at Ohio University.

We grow and put up a percentage of our own food from several gardens, and have begun land restoration and a permaculture plan. We've held a variety of permaculture workshops and events, such as annual cider pressings and may pole dances.

Our working, playing, meeting, and eating together varies greatly as our busy schedules allow. Our vision of cooperation includes making decisions on what will work best for each and for the group as a whole. We use consensus for major decisions and, rather than emphasizing rules, prefer living by guidelines and consciousness. Everyone contributes time and money, working at projects we choose, such as gardening, ordering community food, outreach, maintenance and construction projects. We are looking for responsible, positive people dedicated to intentional community life on a land trust. Write for information, and include an introduction about yourself.

Visitors Accepted: Write or call for approval. [Mar2005][✄]

EGRETS' COVE

Dave Kennedy
Box 158
260 Radford Hollow Rd
Big Hill, KY 40405

859-986-5418
dlkennedy@acer-access.com
thildebrand@acer-access.com

Egrets' Cove is looking for two adventurous households to join the four current ones. We live on 15 wooded acres in the hills, across from a small lake near Berea, Kentucky. We are using cooperation and innovative design to significantly reduce the ecological impact and financial demands of our lives. We make decisions by consensus. Members are engaged in a range of social and appropriate-technology issues, including alternative education and food security.

Each household is building a small energy-efficient cabin while sharing the land, garden, and a community building. It's an interesting place and a great place for kids. [Nov2004]

EL SEMILLERO

La Cardosa 200
E-28816 Valdeavero Madrid
SPAIN

+34-(0)652-468685
semillero@yahoo.com

Began: 1993 | Pop. 5 | Forming | Rural

We envision a community with people of all ages and diverse interests, races, and backgrounds. In common, we are open minded, tolerant, environmentally conscious, and aware of all issues that endanger future human life and the Earth; we commit to our personal growth using all suitable tools and to learning how to work with others for the common good. Located in the countryside near Madrid, we care for an organic garden and for a few hens, and serve organic food to visitors. All this, plus facilitating our space for courses and gatherings of all kinds, keeps us in touch with our fellow humans, so increasing the chances for others to follow. We strongly believe that the right education and childcare will make a difference in the future; we will be an educational community. Our simple lifestyle allows us to carry out extraordinary lives. Masters of our days, we use them to live mindfully, renouncing only what we actually do not need. We have plenty of time for experimenting with alternate solutions in areas like health, relationships, construction, economy, and everything else. Our model communities are those that provide fertile space for many different people with diverse missions to accomplish their goals, while cooperating with all others: The Farm, Twin Oaks, and Findhorn.

Visitors Accepted [Mar2005]

ELDERSPIRIT COMMUNITY AT TRAILVIEW

Catherine Rumschlag
370 E Main St
PO Box 665
Abingdon, VA 24212

276-628-8908, 276-619-5544
espirit@preferred.com
catrkath@comcast.net

http://www.elderspirit.net

Began: 1999 | Pop. 36 | Forming
Small Town

ElderSpirit Community at Trailview is located in Abingdon, Virginia. It is a community of adults 55 and above who want to mutually support one another through the aging process. We value inner work, caring

for oneself, mutual support, service to the larger community, respect for the earth and the creative life. The cohousing neighborhood has 30 homes, a Common House where members meet and share meals, and a Spirit Center where individuals or groups can go for prayer, meditation, or meaningful celebrations and exercises. There is also a common garden and some common work space.

Visitors Accepted: Call 276-628-8908, write, or email. [Mar2005]

ELIM (EVANGELISCHE LEEFGEMEENSCHAP IMMANUËL)

Wim Dorsman
Bergweg 7
3941 RA Doorn
NETHERLANDS

+31-(0)343-417064
info@elim.nl
wdorsman@elim.nl

http://www.elim.nl

Began: 1975 | Pop. 7 | Spiritual
Small Town | Diet: Omnivorous

The community members of Elim provide for their own livelihood through full-time and part-time jobs. The community currently consists of five adults and five children. Most of the income comes from the running of a technical illustration and design bureau.

Community members live with a common purse, from which all costs are paid: rent, cars, holidays, pocket money, etc. From the circle of friends of the community, the evangelical church Elim came into being in 1985. This church has three meetings each week. One tries, both in the community and in the church, to put into practice living with God in everyday life. In addition, there are ongoing contacts with Christians in third world countries—mainly India—both with western missionaries, and with native believers.

More than sixteen years ago, Elim initiated a communities movement that now includes 35 Dutch communities. There is a work-group, a magazine, a study course, and an annual conference. With our life we hope people do discover that it is possible to live in peace and happiness through the lifegiving and transforming power of Jesus Christ, our Lord and Savior.

Visitors Accepted: Make an appointment by letter, telephone or email. [Feb2005]

Scissors [✄] at the end of a listing indicate that it was edited for length by the Directory editors and a longer description can be found at directory.ic.org.

ELLA JO BAKER INTENTIONAL COMMUNITY CO-OP

EJBICC
PO Box 34231
Washington, DC 20043

202-232-2276
ejbic_coop@yahoo.com

Began: 2000 | Pop. 22
Urban | Diet: Omnivorous

The Ella Jo Baker Intentional Community Cooperative is a limited-equity cooperative and multicultural association of activists of modest means. We have deliberately chosen to live together and work cooperatively to create a lifestyle that reflects the values of the Nguzo Saba, better known as the Kwanzaa Principles. We get our inspiration from Ella Jo Baker, who committed her life to the building of cooperation and participatory democracy for the purpose of bringing about social justice.

Visitors Accepted: Email or call first, and we'll be happy to show you around! [Feb2005]

ELMENDORF CHRISTIAN COMMUNITY

Peter Hoover
42668 600th Ave
Mountain Lake, MN 56159

507-427-2299, 507-427-2283
community@elmendorfbelievers.com
office@eccti.com

http://www.elmendorfbelievers.com

Began: 1994 | Pop. 125 | Spiritual
Rural | Diet: Omnivorous

Founded in 1994, and committed to following Jesus, Elmendorf is a community with roots in the Anabaptist (Hutterite) movement that took shape in Europe in the mid-1500s.

Whatever Jesus and his disciples did looks safe and like the right way to go for us—including what he said about giving up all our possessions to follow him. But far more than just living in community because the Bible speaks of it, or because we think we must in order to be saved, we have chosen this way because it points to the much greater reality of the Kingdom of God.

We believe all life—human, plant, and animal life—and all creation (the Earth, the heavens, the universe in its entirety) belong to God's Kingdom. So do all humans and human societies that live in the order and under the rule of God. The only thing that does not fit into God's Kingdom is rebellion against him.

Listings

Additions and corrections: email: directory@ic.org, web: directory.ic.org, mail: RR 1 Box 156-D, Rutledge MO 63563, USA.

Satan does not belong to the Kingdom. Neither does anyone else that rebels against God, breaks his rules, or hates others. Violence, war, greed, capitalism, materialistic communism, immorality, the exploitation of the poor—all forms of coercion and selfishness remain outside the Kingdom.

Our goal is to help as many as we can into God's peaceful Kingdom through our living in Christian community.

We are an English-language Anabaptist community that welcomes all visitors. We come from a wide variety of religious and geographic backgrounds, and interact with believers in many parts of North America and elsewhere.

Visitors Accepted: To visit Elmendorf write to or call addresses specified. It is helpful to acquaint oneself with the material on our website, especially "What We Believe." [Mar2005]

EMBASSY OF THE HEAVENS

808-935-5086

emary@turquoise.net

http://www.wizardofeyez.com

Began: 1998 | Pop. 5 | Forming | Spiritual
Rural | Diet: Omnivorous

"Sanctuary for all qualifying: people, plants and animals and angels as the life-forms with the volition for the service with the coming of the Kingdom on this earth." Rainforest enhancement and organic gardening of our foods and medicines. Support for healing and spiritual growth, learning and play. We must be as little children for the coming of the Kingdom, which is at hand within us. Boot camp, retreat, and home away from home for saints in training. Creating new communities and culture for surviving and thriving through 2012 and beyond, drawing on the wisdom of our traditions while nurturing our unique gifts.

Visitors Accepted: Email us. [Nov2004]

EMERALD COAST VILLAGE

Jennifer Krider
20 Harold Place
Tewksbury, MA 01876

978-851-0428

coho@krider.net

http://www.krider.net

Began: 2005 | Forming | Suburban

We have long dreamed of a village of sorts on the Emerald Coast. We want sounds of laughing children as they run through sprinklers.

We want walking and biking trails. We want potlucks, BBQs, and crawfish boils. We want to know, and like, our neighbors. We want organic gardens and lawns, free from pesticides and harsh chemicals. We want a common house for meals, parties, and hanging out on rainy days. We want music and dancing, arts and crafts, woodworking and cooking, yoga and sports. We want green building, solar and wind utilization, biodiesel. We love dolphins, and all sorts of food!

We are trying to join like-minded people from diverse backgrounds, experiences, and abilities in a beautiful area in an exciting but peaceful community. If this sounds like the start of something you would like too, let us know!

We don't have a coho site up yet, but come meet us on our own website.

-Jenn, Micah, Hayden and Carsen [Feb2005]

EMERALD EARTH

PO Box 764
Boonville, CA 95415

707-895-3302, 707-972-3096
lorax@ap.net

http://www.emeraldearth.org

Began: 1989 | Pop. 15 | Rural | Diet:
Primarily vegetarian

Emerald Earth is a 15-year-old intentional community in rural Mendocino County. We have 189 acres of mixed redwood and hardwood forest; open, south-facing meadows with majestic oaks; two springs; a pond; and a seasonal creek. The land is held in trust by a 501(c)3 nonprofit corporation.

Our values include sustainable living, simplicity, social and environmental justice, and reverence for the Earth and all living things. Our mission is to develop and demonstrate a model of living in harmony with the land and with each other. The original founding group was and is committed to developing our spiritual connection to the Earth through ritual, song, and seasonal celebrations.

We teach short workshops and longer professional trainings in natural building (including cob, strawbale, slipstraw, round pole framing, adobe floors, natural plasters, etc.) and permaculture. We are developing the infrastructure for 20 permanent residents plus guests, interns, and students. We use natural materials and our own labor to keep costs and environmental impact low. We are off-grid, with solar electricity, a cell phone, and satellite Internet. We share meals, meet, and socialize in a small common house which we hope to replace with

a larger one in a sunnier location. Each family or individual will have a small private cabin (four have been completed). We're also working on gardens, permaculture food forest, nursery, more ponds, etc.

For more information or to arrange a visit, please send a letter describing your background and interests.

Visitors Accepted: Send us a letter or email describing yourself(ves) and the reason for your interest in visiting. Ideally, give us a couple of weeks notice. [Dec2004]

EMMA GOLDMAN FINISHING SCHOOL

Outreach Coordinator
206-324-6822
egfs@riseup.net

http://egfs.org

Began: 1996 | Pop. 11
Urban | Diet: Vegetarian only

Founded in 1996, the Emma Goldman Finishing School is an intentional community in the North Beacon Hill neighborhood of Seattle. Formerly known as the Beacon Hill House, we changed our name in November 2003.

Our community is based on the principles of societal change, egalitarianism, nonviolence, ecology, simplicity, and community living. Our home is a fun and supportive place to live, and it is also an institution working to build economic, political, and cultural alternatives. We see ourselves as part of a growing infrastructure designed to oppose and replace the dominant system.

As an egalitarian community, we value our labor equally. Some of us work more hours at jobs which bring in money, others work more around the house and on community projects. Regardless, we all contribute equal time. Every member is able to have all their basic needs met by the community, including food, shelter, transportation, health care, and retirement. [Oct2004]

EMMA GOLDMAN'S

625 N Frances St
Madison, WI 53703

608-259-1976

http://www.madisoncommunity.coop/
house.cfm?HouseID=2

Began: 1996 | Pop. 15
Urban | Diet: Primarily vegetarian

Emma Goldman is the newest Madison Community Cooperatives (MCC) house,

---

Scissors [✂] at the end of a listing indicate that it was edited for length by the Directory editors and a longer description can be found at directory.ic.org.

founded in 1996, located just half a block from beautiful Lake Mendota and two blocks from the UW-Madison campus. Our house is a "safe space" for anyone interested in a more socially just society, and we strongly encourage activist endeavors of all sorts. Like Emma herself, though, we also have lots of fun! ("If I can't dance, I don't want to be part of your revolution.")

We are a dog-friendly house, and all our meals are vegetarian with vegan option. Visitors are welcome for dinner or to stay overnight anytime—just drop by or call ahead!

Visitors Accepted: If you're interested in visiting, feel free to come and have dinner with us Monday–Friday at 6:00 pm, or on Sunday at 5:30 pm! To stay overnight or longer, we would appreciate a call in advance. If you're unable to call, you can just stop by... we would then arrange a "crasher meeting" to establish an understanding of our house policies, etc., and to approve your "crasher" status. We welcome visitors!!! [Feb2005]

EMPTY NEST COHOS

610-361-0944
emptynestcohos@highstream.net

Began: 2004 | Forming | Suburban

Cohousing condo community to be built where individuals can enjoy fellowship by socializing, working and eating together some of the time, while maintaining total privacy in separately owned and occupied fully equipped condos for themselves located on same grounds. Participate in some optional shared meals in clubhouse, in some shared jobs in common areas, and interact with those that truly want to be neighborly without being intrusive. Community is ruled by consensus, where every owner has an equal say. Maintenance jobs are performed by hired outsiders if no one wants to take them on. All units will be two bedrooms, just the right size for empty nesters.

Visitors Accepted: Contact us by email. [Nov2004]

Additions and corrections: email: directory@ic.org, web: directory.ic.org, mail: RR 1 Box 156-D, Rutledge MO 63563, USA.

141

ENCHANTED GARDEN

6008 Arosa St
San Diego, CA 92115

619-582-9669
PlantYourDream@cox.net

http://www.lesliegoldman.com/
Enchanted_Garden_Intentional
_Community/index.htm

Began: 1980 | Pop. 8
Urban | Diet: Primarily vegetarian

Come, my friends,
let us taste peace in holy foods
forever; smell peace in wild baby herbs
planted where unloved weeds grow;
hear and feel its ode to joy
from the mouth of earth-like Angels
as we dare to dance with water hoses.
—Leslie Goldman
Your Enchanted Gardener

Eight of us live together on a ¹/₃-acre parcel surrounded by canyons in the state-college area of San Diego. The land exists as an oasis of green with many aromatic herbs and places to garden. The land calls for people who would like to live in an old home in the city and live as well in a natural environment suited to garden lovers.

The library houses books and materials created by Leslie Goldman, founder, and works by his mentors, Bernard Jensen, natural healing arts elder, and Edmond Bordeaux Szekely, modern Essene renaissance pioneer.

In private ownership, the house offers rental to those who would like to live as extended family and join in house meetings and shared house duties. Each person does 12 hours of work/month, or pays higher rent. Please review the profile about the Enchanted Garden Intentional Community off the link at lesliegoldman.com.

The Enchanted Garden is a name for the new Earth we can each grow one person at a time, one plant at a time, organically. Individuals who would like to live in this special environment while fulfilling their personal seed dreams and learning more about the Enchanted Garden are encouraged to be in touch.

Visitors Accepted: Give Leslie Goldman a phone call. [Mar2005]

ENO COMMONS

1 Indigo Creek Trail
Durham, NC 27712

919-309-7924
outreach@enocommons.org

http://www.enocommons.org

Began: 1992 | Pop. 55 | Diet: Omnivorous

Ours is a community of 22 households of folks who have chosen to live here because they want to know their neighbors and be involved. We have clustered our homes to free up more common spaces for play and mutual enjoyment. We have a commons house which is the focus of shared meals and activities. We have an organic vegetable garden that we share as well. We care deeply about our children and want them to grow up in a friendly and stimulating environment. We have designed our community to facilitate spontaneous interactions. For example, cars are located near the edges of the property; the space inside is reserved for people. We believe in learning through the diversity of each other.

We believe we are connected to the larger communities of our adjacent neighborhoods, our city, our county, our world. Hopefully we will make a difference in each other's lives and the life of our planet through work and play, freely given.

Visitors Accepted: Please contact us to arrange a tour ("roughly" every other Sunday) and join us at a community dinner, held almost every Tuesday and "roughly" every other Sunday. [Mar2005]

ENOTA MOUNTAIN VILLAGE

Enota Potential Member
1000 Highway 180
Hiawassee, GA 30546

706-896-9966, 800-990-6989
enota@enota.org
enota@enota.com

http://www.enota.org
http://www.enota.com

Began: 1998 | Pop. 13 | Spiritual
Rural | Diet: Primarily vegetarian

We are an aspiring community living in the beautiful Northern Georgia mountains on ancient sacred Cherokee land. We have four waterfalls, five streams, and two ponds. We are a volunteer organization that runs a special retreat center and campground. We are dedicated to conservation of the land, spiritual practice, sustainable living, raising healthy animals, organic gardening, and

Scissors [✂] at the end of a listing indicate that it was edited for length by the Directory *editors and a longer description can be found at* directory.ic.org.

creating a group of long-term members who become part of community. The work we gladly give to maintain this retreat facility and farm is greater than full-time and worth our personal dedication as we offer others a loving, memorable experience. We have diverse groups of volunteers who work here, short-term and long-term. We are aspiring/forming because we are still attracting the individuals who will become committed members of Enota. Our spiritual lives are encouraged and nourished with daily circles, prayers, and songs. We are committed to working in peaceful, loving, purposeful service for and to Mother Earth, as we see the Divine in all of humanity and in nature.

Visitors Accepted: You can visit as a paying guest or work exchange. Call us at 706-896-9966 or email to discuss a date and time. For paying guest options visit our website www.enota.com. For work exchange details visit our website www.enota.org. Cabins, retreat housing, bunkhouses, RV and tent camping are all possible. Meals can be provided. [Mar2005]

EUGENE COHOUSING

PO BOX 1558
Eugene, OR 97440

541-345-6466
henner@impartial.com

Began: 2003 | Forming

Cohousing development in downtown Eugene, Oregon—walk to everywhere—consisting of a ring of townhouses and single level apartments surrounding a large, open air plaza, located one level up and away from street noise, over-parking and some commercial. NW Corner of 11th and Lincoln Street. [Jan2005]

EVERETT

Daniel Rirdan
daniel@everettventure.com

http://www.everettventure.com

Began: 2005 | Forming | Spiritual | Rural

An ecovillage—a stand-alone community—expressly conceived for the purpose of providing a nurturing ground and home for children ages six through sixteen. The aim of this community is to help the young people realize themselves, and to support them in becoming trailblazers.

A village of a heartfelt design will be formed on privately owned land of a few hundred acres and located in an uninhabited area. It will be jointly owned by its adult population, cooperative style, and largely built by its residents.

The community would consist of an unspecified number of adults and a population of about 150 youngsters, who will reside in Everett about three quarters of the time.

The adult population would be composed of mentors, who will empower the young people in profound ways. It will also be comprised of craftsmen and tradesmen of deep integrity, who are passionate about their work, and whose presence will offer the youngsters the opportunity to acquire skills and to engage them in the pursuit of quality—by way of observation and apprenticeship.

The objective is to empower the young people to brave interactions that engage them—interactions that will bring out in them the worthy and the heartfelt. These young people will be brought up to regard their inner sense of truth as a paramount value. And operating from within this life view, they will be guided, galvanized, and spurred to express themselves heart and soul. [Feb2005]

EVERYTHING IS RELATED

Christopher Greene and
Jo Dempsey
216 Ashley St
Hawthorne, FL 32640

352-481-0275
mail@everything-is-related.info
chris_greene@highstream.net

http://www.everything-is-related.info

Began: 2004 | Pop. 2 | Forming | Spiritual Rural | Diet: Omnivorous

GOALS:
• The pursuit of health via home grown organic foods
• Maximum free time by living simply and cooperatively with each other
VALUES:
• Simple living and simple building
• Voluntary population control
• Opposition to all war
• Sharing and cooperation, yes; exploitive capitalism, no
• Dedication to an organic whole food diet
SOLUTION:
• Create a large rural cooperative community with others who share the same goals, values, and solution vision.

We want lots of free time to creatively explore our potentials and interests in life. We want to live with other people who share the same values for a cohesive community structure. We have assets to invest in community. Let's get together and make this happen!

Visitors Accepted: Please call ahead to make visiting arrangements. We expect visitors to have studied the community proposal in a careful and thorough way and to share our perception of reality. [Mar2005]

THE FAMILY

2020 Pennsylvania Ave NW PMB 102
Washington, DC 20006

202-298-0838
family@thefamily.org
PublicAffairs@thefamily.org

http://www.thefamily.org

Began: 1968 | Pop. 15 | Spiritual
Urban | Diet: Omnivorous

The Family, formerly known as the Children of God, was founded in 1968 as a fundamentalist Christian movement. The Family has been operating as a communal society for 37 years, with nearly 800 communities in over 70 countries of the world and over 9,000 full-time and associate members.

The Family's founder, David Brandt Berg, pointed members to the Book of Acts in the Bible as a blueprint of how Christ's disciples should live; sharing their earthly goods and common potting finances, abilities, and resources.

The Family's primary mission is to "preach the Gospel to every creature" by every possible means, such as personal evangelization, humanitarian aid, and the distribution of literature. Two-thirds of their membership are second-generation members, most of whom are homeschooled.

The Family's nonconventional beliefs regarding sexuality have been highlighted by the media. It is the Family's scriptural belief that God created human sexuality and that as such, when practiced as God ordained between consenting persons of the opposite sex and of legal age with the consent of all parties concerned, it is a beautiful creation of God.

In 1995 the Family adopted a governing charter, which codified the beliefs,

Additions and corrections: email: directory@ic.org, *web:* directory.ic.org, *mail:* RR 1 Box 156-D, Rutledge MO 63563, USA.

143

rights, and responsibilities of full-time Family members. The primary purpose of the Charter is to provide a well-defined governing structure. Within this structure, ample opportunity is provided for Family members to follow what they believe is God's will for them personally.

Visitors Accepted [Mar2005]

THE FARM

**34 The Farm
Summertown, TN 38483**

**931-964-3574
vickie@thefarmcommunity.com
Douglas@thefarmcommunity.com
ecovillage@thefarm.org**

http://www.thefarmcommunity.com

Began: 1970 | Pop. 1175 | Spiritual
Rural | Diet: Primarily vegan

The Farm is an intentional community of families and friends living on 1750 acres in south-central Tennessee. Since its inception in 1971, the purpose of the Farm community has been to provide a secure, ecologically healthy, commonly held land base for its members and succeeding generations. It is a place where we can relate to each other and the natural environment in a sustainable way, draw upon the collective strength of the community, and contribute to the positive transformation of the world.

Over its nearly 35 year history, The Farm community has created numerous nonprofit organizations as part of its mission: Plenty International (international aid), Kids To the Country (brings at-risk kids to the Farm), The Ecovillage Training Center (sustainability education), Swan Conservation Trust (1300 acre nature preserve), PeaceRoots Alliance (global peace movement), and More Than (students creating peace quilts sent to Afghanistan and Iraq, etc.).

The Farm is probably best known for its midwifery program. We hold the sacrament of birth as an inherent right of all women, newborns, and families.

Approximately 175 residents and over 20 Farm businesses contribute to the maintenance of the community. The Farm Education/Conference Center hosts retreats and conferences and is the umbrella organization for the Farm school which offers alternative education to both resident and neighboring school-age students.

We welcome scheduled visits and tours. Please write or call. The community is actively seeking new members and residents, especially young families. Check us out!

Visitors Accepted: We are open for visitors most days of the year. Tours available on request. The best way to visit is to participate in one of our Farm Experience Weekends, which include a history slide show, tour, community work project, workshops and entertainment. [Mar2005][✂]

FEDERATION OF ARTS FOR THE YOUTH OF OUR NATION FOUNDATION

**Mr Michael Adeyemo
99 Jebba St Ebute Meta East
Lagos, Lagos State 23401
NIGERIA**

**+234-(0)8033-74-1023
fayonfoundation@yahoo.com**

Began: 1995 | Pop. 28

Through art, we correct the social problems, ranging from human trafficking to drug abuse. We are a well known organisation in our community, and we have taken so many kids away from the streets, letting them realise their talents and use them right!

Visitors Accepted: Let us have good information about you, and we shall send you an invitation letter. [Jan2005]

FELLOWSHIP COMMUNITY

**241 Hungry Hollow Rd
Spring Valley, NY 10977**

**845-356-8494
rsffoffice@fellowshipcommunity.org**

http://www.fellowshipcommunity.org

Began: 1966 | Pop. 150 | Spiritual
Rural | Diet: Primarily vegetarian

We are an intergenerational community centered around the care of the elderly. Our administration of care extends to the land and the social process as well. As a body of

coworkers we seek to work and learn together using the spiritual science anthroposophy of Rudolf Steiner as our basis. We live on 80 acres in a suburban setting 35 miles from NYC. We farm biodynamically, growing most of our own vegetables. Our creative and practical work activities (candles, wood, metal, weavery, press, garden, medical practice, outlet store, pottery) support the community and keep the cost to the elderly reasonable. The other anthroposophical institutions in the neighborhood include Sunbridge College, Spring Valley Eurythmy School and Green Meadow Waldorf School. We are open to new coworkers and families who have an interest in learning to live in community. Currently interested in finding a new farmer, especially one with organic or biodynamic experience in growing vegetables.

Visitors Accepted: Call, write, or email your intention to visit. We give one-hour tours, usually on Saturdays. Visitors must call ahead for confirmation of tour date. We like to send out information first, so please plan to receive and read material before coming. [Feb2005]

FINCA BUENA VIDA

swanny@leisurevolution.org

http://www.leisurevolution.org

Began: 1998 | Pop. 6
Rural | Diet: Primarily vegetarian

The Finca Buena Vida Seaside Neighbourhood is located on a Caribbean island in Bocas del Toro, Panama. We operate the small scale Dolphin Bay Wellness Retreat where we offer holistic health programming and creative arts workshops. We have parcels of land for sale within the 102 acre property with approximately 35–40 acres set aside as common areas, much of it along the shores of Dolphin Bay. There are dolphins there all the time—one of only three places in the entire world where bottlenose dolphins reside permanently!!

We are seeking more neighbours (we are six at present), health practitioners, creative workshop leaders, as well as volunteers to help us continue to realize the grander vision of the project.

We are inclusive, non-judgmental, practical, fun-loving, positive folks who are living a life less ordinary and would invite you to join us.

Welcome to a different kind of comfortable! Visit our website to learn all about the project.

Visitors Accepted: Your first step would be to contact us via email. [Feb2005]

Scissors [✂] at the end of a listing indicate that it was edited for length by the Directory editors and a longer description can be found at directory.ic.org.

FINCA LUNA

info@finca-luna.com

http://www.finca-luna.com

Forming

Young project based on permaculture and co-counselling principles and practice, runs an ongoing action learning programme that involves people fully in our little community. [Mar2005]

FINDHORN FOUNDATION AND COMMUNITY

The Park, Findhorn
Forres IV36 3TZ Scotland
UNITED KINGDOM

+44-(0)1309-690311
enquiries@findhorn.org
ecovillage@findhorn.org
info@ecovillagefindhorn.com

http://www.findhorn.org

Began: 1962 | Pop. 149
Rural | Diet: Primarily vegetarian

The Findhorn Foundation is the educational heart of the spiritual community founded in 1962 by Peter and Eileen Caddy and Dorothy Maclean in Morayshire, northeast Scotland.

Our work is based on the values of living from our personal source of inner divine wisdom, cooperation with the intelligence of nature, and service to the world.

We have no formal creed or doctrine, and honour all the world's major religions as paths to our inner divinity. We believe humanity is engaged in an evolutionary expansion of consciousness, and we seek to develop new ways of living infused with spiritual values, in harmony with the earth and with each other.

We are a centre of spiritual education, offering people many ways to visit, live, and work in a transformative community environment. Over 400 people live within or are locally connected to our community.

Our residential Experience Weeks began in 1974 and provide a powerful, often heart-opening, introduction to our spiritual principles and their application in daily life, and have been attended by over 30,000 people.

The development of our ecovillage is a continuation of our work with nature and is a tangible demonstration of the links between the environment and the social, economic and spiritual aspects of life. It is a constantly evolving model. The Findhorn Foundation is a founding member of the Global Ecovillage Network and is associated with the Department of Public Information of the United Nations as a non-governmental organisation (NGO).

Visitors Accepted: By far the best way to visit is to take part in an Experience Week. They start almost every Saturday morning during the year. You need to book in advance. After Experience Week a range of options are possible; ask for our guest programmes brochure or visit our website. [Mar2005]

FIRETENDER

PO Box 790971
Paia, HI 96779
firetender@verizon.net

http://www.firetender.org

Began: 2005 | Pop. 8 | Forming | Small Town | Diet: Omnivorous

Firetender is a community of eight individuals interweaving their lives in pursuit of

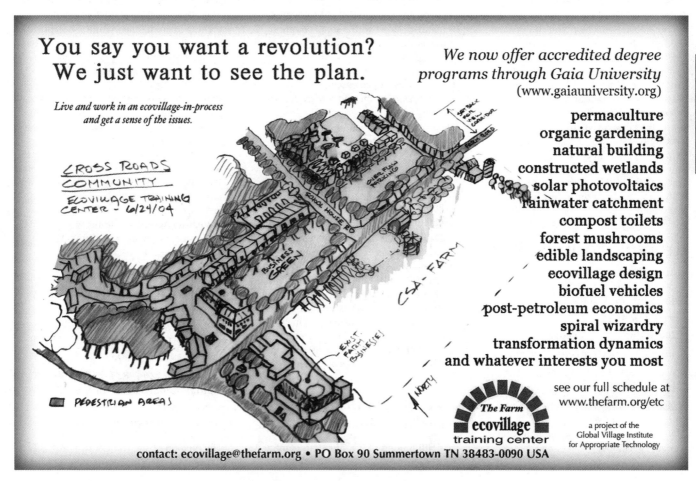
Additions and corrections: email: directory@ic.org, web: directory.ic.org, mail: RR 1 Box 156-D, Rutledge MO 63563, USA.

145

Listings

providing healing/transformational services on Maui, a premiere destination for health and wellness in the world.

A firetender's mission is to work with the fires of Spirit that live in him or herself, and others. It can take any form within the realm of the healing arts. We serve our immediate community (Paia) for free or donation, offer individual or jointly sponsored workshops to the people of the island, and develop and offer workshops that will attract attendees from around the world.

Community service, well-being meetings, spiritual diversity, ceremony, communication, touch-positive environment, ecologically aware attitude, a commitment to personal growth, and the building of satisfying and productive interpersonal relationships are values held in common. Individuals are self-supporting, and we collaborate on projects where income is shared. We're omnivorous.

We've got a three bedroom and a six bedroom home on a cul-de-sac with about 2,000 sq ft of garden space, within a few minute walk of downtown. One of the rooms is a treatment room. The open-sided garage acts as a studio/workshop space.

Our website will help you understand the focus, background, and direction of the founder. This is a sacred living space and a gathering place for people who are uniquely themselves to help others become their unique selves.

Visitors Accepted: There is a sleeping space available for visitors. $25 covers an overnight stay. Expect to be pulled in to help on some project or another. Visit if you want to participate, not be a tourist. Please write well in advance and don't plan on more than one overnight. [Mar2005]

FLEDGLING COMMUNITY

Tom Cassady
30312 Road 58
Burlington, CO 80807

719-346-7917
tcassady59@yahoo.com
http://twentyfirstcenturyfarm.org

Began: 2004 | Pop. 1 | Forming
Rural | Diet: Omnivorous

A new community (2004) centered at a farm 10 miles south of Hale, Colorado.

Visitors Accepted: Send email to Tom Cassady. [Oct2004]

FOOTPRINT ECOVILLAGE

David Grounds
14990 Outlet Dr
Guerneville, CA 95446

707-869-1652
groundsb@aol.com

Began: 2004 | Pop. 1 | Forming | Rural

Rural community forming (location TBD) based on the most recent scientific models for the human ecological footprint and environmental carrying capacity. Number of acres needed to sustain each member will depend on individual consumption standard. Typically 25 acres for US standards or as little as 12 acres for European standards. Must be committed to a scientific foundation to reduce ecological footprint and live sustainably. [Dec2004]

FORDYCE STREET COHOUSING

1338 Seena Ln
Ashland, OR 97520
sasetta@mind.net

Began: 2002 | Pop. 16 | Forming
Small Town | Diet: Omnivorous

A cohousing community of 13 townhomes is planned, along with a small common house and community garden. The homes will be passive solar and have other green building features. The members are acting as their own developer, entailing considerable commitment of time and money. [Jan2005]

FORMING INTENTIONAL COMMUNITY

Dee Clark
deeclark8997@yahoo.com

Began: 2005 | Forming
Rural | Diet: Primarily vegetarian

This community is currently being discussed. Land has not yet been purchased, but we have been looking. Please contact us if you would like to join the discussion and be part of the core group to get this started.

So far the emphasis has been on the need for community and sustainable living practices. Meetings will be scheduled soon to more formally discuss what each of us is looking for and how to make it happen. [Mar2005]

FOX HILL BRUDERHOF

http://www.foxhillbruderhof.com

Fox Hill Bruderhof is a Christian community where members share all things in common as the early Christians did.

Working and eating communally, sharing houses and cars, raising our children together, and helping each other in the care of disabled and elderly loved ones, we seek to live an organic life that addresses the needs of every individual yet still serves a greater common good. We live together to overcome the isolation and fragmentation that mark our time by fighting their root cause—selfishness—in ourselves. [Feb2005]

FOX HOUSING COOPERATIVE

Werndolau
Golden Grove
Carmarthen Dyfed SA32 8NE Wales
UNITED KINGDOM

+44-(0)1558-668798
isablelovegrove@2umail.co.uk

Began: 1998 | Pop. 14 | Spiritual
Rural | Diet: Primarily vegan

Our focus is to practically and effectively apply our values. These are broadly summarized by responsibility—to yourself, others, and the land. We are committed to living simply and lightly, home educating our children, freedom from addiction, self development, and emotional maturity. Accepting responsibility for when we fall short of our values is an important aspect of life here.

We live on a 70 acre ex-dairy farm, are involved in growing and delivering organic vegetables, agroforestry, and woodland planting. We are increasing diversity and sustainability and are developing into some kind of ecovillage.

We've got a lot to do, a lot to learn, and we're going to make mistakes and have fun. We welcome offers of both long- and short-term help. If you'd like to visit, please contact us.

Visitors Accepted: Phone, write or email. One week minimum stay. [Feb2005]

FRANCISCAN WORKERS / COMPANIONS IN COMMUNITY

Robert Smith
715 Jefferson St #1
Salinas, CA 93905

831-770-1264, 831-757-3838
imagineparadise9@neteze.com

Began: 1982 | Pop. 6
Urban | Diet: Primarily vegetarian

The mission of the Franciscan Workers and the Companions in Community is to live,

---

Scissors [✂] at the end of a listing indicate that it was edited for length by the Directory *editors and a longer description can be found at* directory.ic.org.

to love, to work together in harmony; to serve the marginalized; to create partnerships which are mutually liberating; and to pursue social justice with respect and dignity for all, in the spirit of St. Francis and Dorothy Day. Through a daily rhythm of meditation and service, community is formed, and through the practice of creative love and beauty, hope is renewed. The Franciscan Workers seek to be instruments of peace in the "ordinariness of life." We strive to follow the practices of voluntary simplicity, nonviolence, the works of mercy, contemplation, and community. Our projects include a hospitality center, a soup kitchen, a health clinic, a work co-op, a farmworker ministry, tutoring children, summer camps, immersion experiences for youth, and roundtable discussions and education. We seek a transformation of culture to one that is nonviolent and personalist. A major focus of ours is the practice of reconciliation between religions, and our members include persons of differing faiths (or no faith). We dream of a rural community to focus on nurturing children, youth, and others who find themselves marginalized. To love without limits, to receive the blessing of the poor, and to welcome children are our basic call. "Imagine paradise, practice beauty" is our sustaining vision.

Visitors Accepted: Please call to schedule your visit! [Mar2005]

FRANKLEIGH CO-FLATS

**Bradford on Avon, Wiltshire England
UNITED KINGDOM**

**+44-(0)1225-866467
info@frankleigh.com**

**David Michael
16 Springhill Cohousing
Uplands
Stroud GL5 1TN England
UNITED KINGDOM**

**+44-(0)1453-766466
david@frankleigh.com
david@ic.org**

**Frances Monte
frances@frankleigh.com**

http://www.frankleigh.com

Began: 1995 | Pop. 28
Rural | Diet: Omnivorous

Frankleigh Co-flats consists of six flats (apartments) within a large Victorian Mansion. We have 8 acres, an outside swimming pool and an orangery. There is a communal laundry and a recreation area with table tennis. We have no formal shared

meals, although we do meet informally and are often invited to each other's birthday parties and other celebrations.

We used to be part of a larger community and each family would pay equal rent for space according to their needs. We had an amicable split into two distinct communities, next door to each other. Both sides have now sold flats to residents on long leases (condominiums).

There will soon be a studio flat for sale and our long term intention is to build eco-houses in the grounds. Decision making is by consensus, or majority if deadlocked.

Visitors Accepted: Send an email. [Mar2005]

FREE FOR ALL THE SKILLS POOL

**Richard Johnson, Adm.
Los Angeles, CA**

**818-240-SAVE [7283]
communities@theskillspool.org**

**http://www.geocities.com/
theskillspool/index.html**

Began: 1975 | Urban | Diet: Omnivorous

Since 1975, Free For All has given Los Angeles area residents unlimited access to hundreds of valuable services of all kinds, supplied by the members to one another at no charge.

Services are freely shared—not traded. Each member commits to provide service upon request, up to the weekly maximum she or he stipulated upon joining. There's no maximum applying to services used.

Members offer the full gamut of services: professional, technical, creative, instructional, domestic, and blue-collar. Anything useful is welcome, as long as it's offered without charge of any kind. (Out-of-pocket expenses, if any, are paid by the receiving member.)

Visitors Accepted: Please write inquiring about the two-week trial. The trial is open to anyone in the Greater Los Angeles area, who writes us at the email address given in this listing. [Feb2005]

FREE STATE COMMUNITY

**Paul W. Woodring
pww57@hotmail.com**

Began: 2005 | Forming | Suburban

Community forming in Baltimore to Washington corridor, Maryland.

Seeking singles, couples and small families looking to found a cooperative or cohousing community aimed at working-

class people who want to own in an affordable condo style project, probably in Howard County, Maryland.

My aim is to build a community of about 50 units, priced from under 100K to max. of 200K for a family of four (max. size looking for) on about five acres. A major goal is to build a practical, but sustainable community that will enable those of modest means who work full-time but cannot afford to purchase a residence in the area to do so, and develop a place that has a great sense of participation and cohesion.

A secondary goal is to take advantage of group buying power to give residents access to health care; affordable credit and savings accounts; and secure retirement plans that many, if not most, employers no longer provide.

Other possible desirable features would /could be: fully equipped garage for working on personal vehicles, community bus for commuting to and from local transit stops/shopping, common computer lab, library, workshop, fitness room, pool, and other recreational facilities, as well as a large community room for meetings and holiday gatherings and meals. The participants will determine the final design characteristics. [Jan2005]

FREEDOM-UNIVERSE

**PO Box 1128
Paulden, AZ 86334**

**928-636-8693
freedomu@mindspring.com
kya@freedom-universe.org**

http://www.freedom-universe.org

Began: 2004 | Pop. 1 | Spiritual
Rural | Diet: Other

Freedom-Universe is an egalitarian intentional community on 40 rural acres in north central Arizona.

This community is being built on a foundation of interpersonal relationships based on shared values such as conviviality, social tolerance, equality, honesty, and nonviolence.

Environmental and economic sustainability will be pursued using renewable energy, sustainable building materials and techniques, permaculture, and organic/bio-dynamic gardening.

Greed and deception are reinforced in any system of economic hierarchy, whether it is capitalism, fascism, communism/totalitarianism, or outright dictatorship (due to the cultural conditioning that competition is the only process that creates technologi-

Additions and corrections: email: directory@ic.org, *web:* directory.ic.org, *mail:* RR 1 Box 156-D, Rutledge MO 63563, USA.

147

cal advances and improves economic prosperity). In an economic hierarchy, deception is observable in almost every marketing pitch made, where the goal is increasing consumerism, thereby redistributing the bulk of the wealth of the planet to an increasingly smaller percentage of its inhabitants. Correspondingly, this is to the economic detriment of the increasingly larger segment of the population now living below Maslow's basic hierarchy of needs, i.e., in poverty. Freedom-Universe will represent a model of egalitarian cooperation and sharing (instead of competition, greed and deception).

Visitors Accepted: Read our website, and critically analyze "The 13 Basic Behavioral Standards" for compatibility with your own individual code of ethics. If there is alignment between the two, contact us via email, PO Box, or phone to arrange a meeting either in Ash Fork or Chino Valley, Arizona. Both short term visits and internships for longer periods can be arranged. [Mar2005]

THE FREELAND COMMUNITY

Robert Freeland
Freeland Foods
6313 University Ave
San Diego, CA 92115

619-286-2446
info@goraw.org

http://progressiveparenting.org

Began: 2004 | Pop. 5 | Forming | Spiritual
Rural

Looking for others willing to do whatever it takes to achieve what is in our children's best interest.

It is the reproductive process that connects us to all living things and, in turn, the universe.

Let's create a community that honors this process by providing a foundation of structure, support, and identity that begins and ends with the welfare of our children in mind.

By working together, we can determine how to achieve to the best of our ability an optimal living environment for our children. Nothing (including faith) is to come before this most important responsibility we all share as parents and future parents.

We are a raw, organic food manufacturer and are able to provide financial support for the right group of people.

Feel free to contact us if interested.

Love your children above all else. If interested please email or call. Ask for Robert. [Nov2004]

FREESTONE HILL COMMUNITY

East Street and Freestone Rd
Warwick, Queensland 4370
AUSTRALIA

enquiries@freestonehill.org

Paul Howson
+61-(0)7-4661-7720
paul@tdgq.com.au

http://www.freestonehill.org

Began: 1981 | Pop. 125 | Spiritual
Small Town | Diet: Omnivorous

The Freestone Hill Community is located in the rural township of Warwick, in southeast Queensland, Australia. Established in 1981, the community has grown side by side with the School of Total Education (SOTE), a kindergarten to year 12 private school. Many community residents are teachers, parents, or students at the school.

The community encompasses about 40 dwellings spread over 15 acres, and includes private roads, walking tracks, barbeque areas, gardens, parkland, and bushland. It offers a positive, modern, and healthy lifestyle in a rural setting. Clean air, clean skies and a quieter pace of living.

Visitors Accepted: Email enquiries@freestonehill.org or call number above or +61-(0)7-4661-2666 for the School of Total Education. [Mar2005]

FRESNO COHOUSING

Lynette and Larry Bassman
635 East Cambridge Ave
Fresno, CA 93704

559-244-0562
lbassman@pacbell.net

http://fresnocohousing.org

Began: 2004 | Forming | Urban

We are an enthusiastic group of 15 households, and we are currently looking for land, and making offers on some parcels. We want to make this happen as quickly as we can. We are working with Katie McCamant. [Jan2005]

FRIENDS AND NEIGHBORS

Evan
San Francisco, CA 94118

415-608-0564
levisana@yahoo.com

Began: 2004 | Pop. 2 | Forming | Spiritual
Diet: Omnivorous

Basically, the purpose of this group is to live better than we could otherwise, by creating

2+ minimally-coercive, shared neighborhoods, where we can share company, common areas and resources—whatever else we may wish too—without being forced to share in anything beyond co-ownership, co-management, and commitment to making the interpersonal environment continue to prosper.

This is to be a group friendly to families and singles/couples/moresomes, structured formally to include renters, visitors, and owners, and focused on getting the most out of life: extended-family; shared child and adult education and businesses; non-coercive opportunities for shared meals, parties, and other events; building houses we each dream of (or building towards a future where we'll be financially able to); loud-and-late parties and performances (albeit probably limited to 1-2 pre-arranged dates/times a month or so, unless we have a separate sound-proof place for them); quiet campfire conversations; and general cooperative community with a bunch of other successful, growing, good-communicators.

Visitors Accepted: Call and email and see if we'll be around when you plan to come. [Oct2004]

FROG SONG

8290 Old Redwood Hwy
Cotati, CA 94931
info@cotaticohousing.org

http://www.cotaticohousing.org

Began: 1998 | Pop. 72 | Diet: Omnivorous

Our community is a part of downtown Cotati, California (population 6,700). We are a typical cohousing community in that we are not organized around any particular religious, economic, political, or lifestyle focus, other than our intention to create a neighborhood that by its physical design and social structure facilitates community.

Our community houses 30 families (including singles, couples with and without children, and single parents) in townhouse-style attached homes. Our Common House includes a kitchen, dining room, guest rooms, children's room, and a workshop.

We're a little different than many cohousing communities in that we were required by the city of Cotati to include 6700 square feet of retail space as part of our development. We decided to keep ownership of this retail space as a community. We now live next door to a handful of small businesses, which are primarily locally-owned (six out of the seven). A few of our

Scissors [✄] at the end of a listing indicate that it was edited for length by the Directory editors and a longer description can be found at directory.ic.org.

community members rent offices in this space.

Community dinners and workdays are a part of our lives. Our key policy decisions are made by consensus, and we meet twice monthly for two-hour business and community development meetings.

Our group began meeting in November of 1998, and in January 2000 we found a 2.3 acre parcel of land in downtown Cotati. With the help of the Cohousing Company (Berkeley and Nevada City, CA), and our developer, Wonderland Hill (Boulder, CO), construction was completed and residents began moving into their new homes in 2003.

Visitors Accepted: Contact us through the website or email. Drop-in visits are discouraged. [Mar2005][✄]

GAIA GROVE ECOSPIRITUAL COMMUNITY & ECORETREAT

Joanna Montana DeGaia
near Gainesville, FL 32658

561-716-8295,
386-462-9111 ext 102
GaiaGroveFL@yahoo.com

Began: 1997 | Pop. 16 | Spiritual | Rural

We are located on 102 beautiful acres 15 minutes north of Gainesville (in north central Florida where the Univ. of FL is); $1/2$ mile of Santa Fe River runs thru the land. We are seeking members to live and build organic gardens, fruit/nut orchards, homes and rustic retreats (domes, cob cottages, yurts, tree houses, indigenous "chickee" huts, teepees, etc.) using natural and recycled materials and renewable energy: solar, Tesla-technology, wind, maybe hydro, and make the community as artistic and unique as possible. We're planning to have a vehicle co-op run w/ veggie and biodiesel, electric, methane, solar power, covered pedal bikes and horse and buggies.

We will have a children's cooperative learning center (using Waldorf, Montessori and Piaget materials/methods), and in the future hope to do a traveling show in the summers with a World Culture and Ecology theme involving dance and acrobatics like Cirque du Soleil. There will also be an elder-care home, and the kids and elders will be

able to do things like art, music, and storytelling together.

Some of our businesses include a wholistic health retreat with classes/services in nutrition, herbal medicine, acupuncture, massage, meditation, qigong and yoga. We'll operate a food co-op and eventually a natural foods restaurant, and B & B and Camping Retreat. We'll offer courses on natural building, organic gardening, social justice and environmental issues, as well as world languages and religions, which will eventually be an accredited college. Another possible business is running outdoor eco-tours in Florida and around the world including kayaking, scuba diving in the N. FL caves and fresh water springs, horseback trips, biking, outdoor survival and wilderness first aid, etc. Later, we hope to have sister communities/learning centers in Latin America, Arabia and Asia.

On Saturday nights we'll have the "Gaia Gathering" which is an ecospiritual interfaith celebration open to all. We will have vegan dinners, and music and dances from different cultures (Israeli, African, Latin, Celtic) as well as Dances for Universal Peace, contra dances, and fire/drum circles. We'll also have workshops and celebrations with kid activities, and an activist project every solstice and equinox: Earth/animals/young children in spring, fire/solar and renewable energy/young adults in the summer, water/nutrition/mid adults in the fall, and air/trees/elderly in winter.

Visitors Accepted: Email. [Mar2005]

GAIA UNIVERSITY

Alejandra Liora Adler
717 Poplar Ave
Boulder, CO 80304

info@gaiauniversity.org
lioraadler@gaiau.org

http://www.gaiauniversity.org

Began: 2004 | Forming

Get credit for exploring your passion while serving the Earth!

Founded as a nonprofit corporation in 2004, Gaia University is developing a global action learning community with campuses in ecovillages, permaculture centers, holistic health centers, institutes, colleges, and other universities world-wide.

Focused on the development of world changers who are committed to earth care, people care and fair share, Gaia U is modeled on a 10 year pilot project in the UK.

Accredited to give Bachelors and Masters degrees through IMCA/Revans University and the British Accreditation Council, Gaia U will be launching its website in April, 2005 and will receive students beginning September 2005.

Please see our website for full details on how you can participate in this unique, highly flexible, learner-centered educational community.

Visitors Accepted: Please see our website. [Mar2005]

GAIAYOGA GARDENS

RR 2 #3334
Pahoa, HI 96778
aloha@gaiayoga.org

http://www.gaiayoga.org

Began: 2003 | Pop. 2 | Forming | Spiritual Rural | Diet: Other

GaiaYoga Gardens is a learning center and intentional community on Hawaii's Big Island. We're dedicated to living in harmony with the Earth, connecting with Spirit, engaging personal growth and healing, creating cooperative community, and developing holistic and sustainable life-patterns. We practice and teach permaculture, nonviolent communication, natural diet (including raw foods diet), hatha yoga, Tantra and spirituality.

Our lifestyle includes:

1) Living simply, sustainably, and close to nature through living rurally and off-grid in low-impact eco-dwellings; growing food; operating eco-businesses; and trading for goods and services.

2) Cultivating a healthy self through eating an organic diet, having an active work/service life, engaging in personal growth work, balancing autonomy and interdependence, having a life-affirming orientation toward sexuality, and being clothing-optional.

3) Establishing a land-sharing community that's intimate, caring, and feels like family. This includes practicing power-sharing, consensus decision making, and nonviolent communication; cooperating relative to resources and land development; having community businesses; sharing childrearing; and having fun together!

4) Integrating spirituality into our communal life through prayer, hatha yoga, rituals, shamanic journeying, rites of passage, and spiritual study.

Our dream is for GaiaYoga Gardens to be

Additions and corrections: email: directory@ic.org, *web:* directory.ic.org, *mail: RR 1 Box 156-D, Rutledge MO 63563, USA.*

149

a beacon of light and love, and a living example of the kind of world we want.

Visitors Accepted: People can visit us by doing a Tour-&-Project or an internship. Email us and we'll send you information and an application. [Mar2005]

GANAS

Susan Grossman
135 Corson Ave
Staten Island, NY 10301

718-720-5378
info@ganas.org

http://www.ganas.org

Began: 1978 | Pop. 91
Urban | Diet: Omnivorous

Ganas is Spanish for "motivation sufficient to act." We are 90 people who are cultivating the "ganas" to learn how to address the problems and conflicts that come from sharing our lives together. The result is a challenging, rich environment that truly embraces diversity.

Levels of participation: A core group of 14 shares income, owns and manages the

community, and is committed to open dialogue. Another 25 do not share income, but participate actively in community life and decision making. Another 50 or so are not active in governance but participate in our residential program, learning to resolve the problems of daily living. Some cover expenses through work; others pay a fee. Each morning we meet to discuss community, work and personal issues, and make most community decisions.

Our problem-solving process emphasizes personal responsibility, willingness to hear, and intention to disclose what's happening. Over the past 20 years we have established an innovative dialogue that is open, focused, penetrating, and respectful. Feedback, used with care and consent, is one of our tools.

We have ten houses in Staten Island (30 minutes by ferry from Manhattan), adorned by trees, and flower and vegetable gardens. Our used furniture and clothing stores emphasize teamwork and participatory management and are staffed by Ganas members. Encouraging reuse

and recycling is fulfilling as a way of right livelihood.

You may visit for dinner at no cost or stay with us for a reasonable fee. Depending on our needs and your skills, you may prefer to work with us for your expenses, plus a small stipend and share of profits. More info is on our website.

Visitors Accepted: Potential visitors should email Susan to set up a visit. [Mar2005]

GARDEN O' VEGAN

http://www.g0v.org

Began: 1999 | Pop. 7
Rural | Diet: Vegan only

We started because of the apparent lack of vegan communities in good locations suitable for families with children. Our aim is for a community free of drugs, alcohol, smoke, dogma, cruelty of any form, or lifestyles not suited to family units. We are, nevertheless, open to single people.

Situated on 57 acres along the Hamakua coast of the Big Island of Hawaii, we enjoy ideal growing conditions and hope to be almost completely self-sufficient in food and energy needs. We are totally vegan, with no animal products being permitted within community grounds. Pets are not desirable, but will be considered on a case-by-case basis. Our aim of building eco-friendly homes is helped by widely available materials and by not requiring substantial structures in this climate.

Due to a very profitable web-based business, we are currently able to financially compensate vegans with certain proven skills who are serious about helping out here. Our skill requirements vary from time to time, but presently include gardening/farming, construction, and computer-literacy.

Our vision for the future is a community almost completely nondependent on the outside world, and in which its members may enjoy the simple art of living.

Visitors Accepted: Please send by post or email as much relevant information about yourself as possible, including proven abilities, experience, requirements, questions, and photo(s). An application form is available on our website. Unfortunately, we do not (at time of writing) have enough time to accommodate all requests for a visit. [Mar2005]

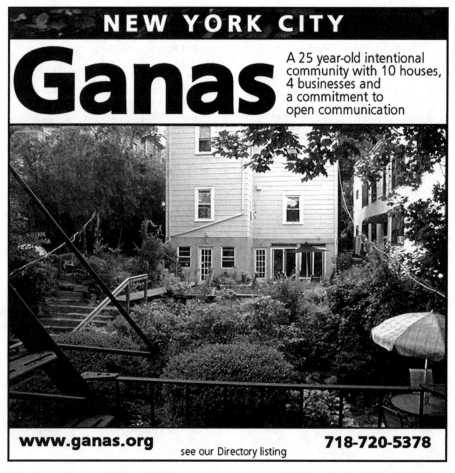

Scissors [✂] at the end of a listing indicate that it was edited for length by the Directory editors and a longer description can be found at directory.ic.org.

GARDEN STATE COHOUSING

New Jersey
GardenStateCohousing@yahoo.com

Abby Rutka
908-526-7667
stampwithabby@yahoo.com

http://www.geocities.com/
gardenstatecohousing

Began: 2003 | Pop. 10 | Forming

We are a group of people working to build a residential community in North Central New Jersey. We are a group of families with children, single people, and couples. Our goal is a supportive, friendly, inter-generational neighborhood.

Cohousing combines privacy and community in a clustered, pedestrian-oriented neighborhood. Some of the key features of cohousing are:
• Own your own home
• Shared common facilities
• Management by the residents
• Intergenerational living

Cohousing attempts to overcome the alienation of modern subdivisions in which no-one knows their neighbors, and there is no sense of community. It is characterized by private dwellings with their own kitchen, living-dining room, etc., but also extensive common facilities. The common house may include a large dining room, kitchen, lounges, meeting rooms, recreation facilities, library, workshops, and children's space. [Oct2004]

THE GATHERING

PO Box 179
Schuyler, VA 22969

434-831-2354
www@higherforces.info

http://higherforces.info

Began: 1972 | Pop. 7 | Spiritual
Rural | Diet: Primarily vegetarian

We are a spiritual group whose aim is a closer relationship with God as individuals and as a group. We came together in New York City in 1968, and began moving onto 10 acres in Virginia in 1975; at present we have seven members.

We have our own system of economics, combining elements of income sharing, as well as individual finances. We work for the refinement and uplifting of the quality of life expressed in our spiritual practices, our creative endeavors (nursing, art, carpentry, design, carving, building, medicine, etc.), the enhancement of our environment, our

relationships with each other, our economic systems, and the development of our menus and cooking practices.

Tom Ringrose is the channel of the group. He channels a group of entities who we call the Higher Forces. There are over 670 channeled session audio recordings, with over 50% transcribed. They are being made available on our website.

The website was launched in 2002, June 3rd—exactly 30 years since the first recorded session with the Higher Forces.

Think of this information as being in league with the Edgar Cayce material, but with more extensive research areas: UFOs, conspiracy, ETs, higher dimensional reality, abductions, world order, etc. in addition to the tenets of esoteric spirituality, occult science, and metaphysical study.

Visitors Accepted: Call or email us if you would like to inquire about visiting The Gathering. Thanks! [Mar2005]

GEMEENSCHAPPELIJK WONEN NIEUWEGEIN

Nieuwegein, Utrecht
NETHERLANDS

info@gwwebsite.com

http://www.gwwebsite.com

Cohousing project in Nieuwegein (Utrecht), Netherlands. Information, photos and guestbook. [Mar2005]

GENESEE GARDENS COHOUSING

Jessica Yorko
738 Bancroft Ct
Lansing, MI 48915

517-214-5684, 517-346-8594
yorko446@cs.com

Michael Hamlin
hamlinmi@math.msu.edu

Perry Godwin
715 West Genesee Street
Lansing, MI 48915

517-485-2544
peregryn2356@yahoo.com

Began: 2003 | Pop. 14
Urban | Diet: Omnivorous

We are Genesee Gardens Cohousing, formerly known as Lansing Cohousing. Genesee Gardens Cohousing is a diverse group of neighbors and friends growing a retrofit cohousing community rooted in working together, sharing resources, living

with compassion and mutual respect, actively caring for our natural and social environments, embracing peace and tolerance, and promoting the health of ourselves and our wider community. Our current membership consists of two families with children, one couple, one single parent with a child, and one single adult. Right now, we meet together regularly for common meals twice a week and a business meeting once a week.

We are a retrofit or infill type of cohousing project, using existing houses in the neighborhood to create our intentional community. Right now we have six houses that are owned by members of Genesee Gardens Cohousing. Three of these houses are in the process of being renovated, with the intention of making one of these houses the common house. There are two additional houses for sale that, once purchased, could be included as part of Genesee Gardens Cohousing. There are also options for renting, both within Genesee Gardens Cohousing and in the immediate neighborhood.

Visitors Accepted: Please get in touch with one of the contacts for Genesee Gardens Cohousing to arrange for a visit. [Jan2005][⅌<]

GENTLE WORLD INC.

PO Box 238
Kapaau, HI 96755
info@gentleworld.org

http://www.gentleworld.org

Began: 1970 | Pop. 10 | Spiritual
Rural | Diet: Vegan only

We are a nonprofit organization, educating the public as to the health, environmental, and spiritual benefits of the vegan diet and lifestyle. We publish books, and offer free cooking classes, seminars, and private consultations. We are also a community of people working together day by day to build a model world by striving to live our ideals, such as compassion, integrity, honesty, cleanliness, courage, and friendship.

Compassion as exemplified in veganism is our foundation, because we believe that it is nothing less than humanity's next evolutionary step, a step that every human being can take to help create a more peaceful, gentle world. Our founders have been vegan for 32 years. We live simply in the country.

Our headquarters is on The Big Island of Hawaii. We also own 450 acres of New Zealand countryside. There we have

Listings

planted 100 fruit trees and several veganic gardens in a beautiful valley with pristine rivers. It lives up to its name: Shangri-la. We welcome letters from love-minded people.

Visitors Accepted: Contact us first via email or letter. [Mar2005]

GESUNDHEIT! INSTITUTE

HC 64 Box 167
Hillsboro, WV 24946

gesundheitwebworker@yahoo.com

http://www.patchadams.org

Began: 1972 | Pop. 9
Rural | Diet: Omnivorous

Gesundheit Institute is a group of healers, visionaries, and clowns building a healing community based on humor, compassion, generosity, and enthusiastic hard work.

Much more than a hospital, Gesundheit seeks to be a microcosm of vibrant life, integrating art, education, fun, and friendship with health care. Gesundheit's home is 310 acres in eastern West Virginia.

With many friends we have created a four-level multipurpose building, a five-level staff dwelling with onion domes, a three-acre pond, and a ton of friendships since the land was purchased in 1980. With collaboration of people from all healing arts, we are working to build an ecologically integrated community and state-of-the-art facility. Our vision includes a 40-bed hospital where good health is a laughing matter, "patients" and "caregivers" work and play together, and the

spirit of community is itself the most potent medicine.

Patch Adams, founder, presently lectures and performs for caregivers around the world in order to raise awareness and money toward the further design and building of the Gesundheit community. The land staff stewards the property and hosts longterm volunteers and summer work camps. How can you help? Please send a silly postcard and inquire about volunteering or bringing the Gesundheit vision to your own community. Wahoo!

Visitors Accepted: Contact us about our visitor weekends. [Mar2005]

THE GIFT OF A HELPING HAND CHARITABLE AID FOUNDATION

Cathy P. Russell
1748 Waltham
Detroit, MI 48205

313-371-6631, 360-838-5162
tgoahh@hotmail.com
tgoahh@yahoo.com

http://www.tgoahh.org

Began: 2002 | Pop. 500
Urban | Diet: Primarily vegetarian

Our mission is to assist in lifting the voice of illiteracy and putting an end to homelessness.

Visitors Accepted: You can visit our community by visiting our website and you may join our e-group at http://groups.yahoo.com/group/tgoahhorg. [Nov2004]

GLEN IVY

25005 Glen Ivy Rd
Corona, CA 92883

909-277-8701
glen_ivy@emnet.org

http://www.glenivy.org

Began: 1977 | Pop. 28 | Spiritual
Rural | Diet: Omnivorous

The Glen Ivy Community thrives as a working example of the practical application of spiritual principles in everyday living. This necessitates an evolving design of community life that invites risk taking and creativity, as vision and operational practicalities come together. Community members accomplish this balance by working and learning together in an atmosphere of respect and open communication. The community values the uniqueness of each individual, recognizing that personal development is key if the collective is to flourish. Glen Ivy is also a gracious and love-filled home, both for its residents and for the many who come to visit. The activities of the Glen Ivy Community have emerged in service to its primary spiritual purpose—a collective revelation of the one spirit in form. The Glen Ivy Community was established in 1977 in accordance with the spiritual purposes of the Emissaries of Divine Light: to assist in carrying forward a work of spiritual regeneration of humanity, under the inspiration of the spirit of God.

Visitors Accepted [Mar2005]

Scissors [✂] at the end of a listing indicate that it was edited for length by the Directory editors and a longer description can be found at directory.ic.org.

THE GLENWOOD HOUSE IN PORTLAND, MAINE

Elizabeth
9 Glenwood Ave
Portland, ME 04103

207-780-8783 (Box 1)
elizff@sbcglobal.net

Began: 2004 | Pop. 11
Suburban | Diet: Omnivorous

We are a group of serious and fun students, professionals, and families who are holistically oriented, health conscious, community minded, organically inclined, and non-smoking. We are also spiritually minded and honor diverse spiritual paths and practices. Our home is located about a five to ten minute drive to downtown Portland and also a short distance to beautiful ocean coasts, spots for walking, running and biking, and universities and schools. Portland is a lively, creative city that offers wonderful culture, progressively minded friends, and wonderful bicycle trails.

The Glenwood House can sometimes accommodate shorter term stays, particularly in the warmer months or when there is an opening throughout the year. We are currently seeking longer term housemates to join us now, and may be able to accommodate a shorter term stay this winter.

Description of the home: 3 story, 5 plus bedroom, 3 bathroom duplex, washer/dryer, common furnishings, three refrigerators, DSL Internet, computer and printer use, two kitchen spaces, very spacious, lots of light, clean, hardwood floors, back deck, fenced yard, some storage and work space in the basement, nice quiet neighborhood, five minute drive to Portland. Rent is $375 to $500, including all utilities as well as unlimited US long-distance, voice mail, and DSL. Bedroom furniture may be available, if needed.

Visitors Accepted: If interested, please leave a voice mail message with Elizabeth or send an email to tell us a bit about yourself. We look forward to hearing from you. [Dec2004]

GONDWANA SANCTUARY

Mitra
Lot 1, Prestons Ln
Tyagarah, NSW 2481
AUSTRALIA

+61-(0)2-6684-7210,
+61-(0)266-848-096
gondwana@bigfoot.com

Began: 1986 | Pop. 15 | Spiritual
Rural | Diet: Primarily vegetarian

A residential community, near Byron Bay.

Visitors Accepted: Contact the phone number or email, and someone will get back to you and let you know if there is space for any visitors. Our Wednesday night community dinners are also open to visitors. Call the number to confirm that it is happening. [Jan2005]

GOODENOUGH COMMUNITY

2007 33rd Ave S
Seattle, WA 98144

206-323-4653
rebecca@goodenough.org
goodenough@aboutcommunity.org

http://www.goodenough.org

Began: 1981 | Pop. 40 | Spiritual
Diet: Omnivorous

The Goodenough Community is a 30-year-old multi-generational, multi-residential membership community with 25 adult full members. It serves 100–200 individuals and families throughout each year with programs, cultural events, retreats and daily living. The community has always intended to be both a caring, healing environment and a learning/training laboratory. The community is now seeking like-minded people to join the efforts of an intentional demonstration community—an on-going human relations laboratory for developing knowledge about community and about training leadership in service to communities.

In 2001, retreat property was acquired in Mason County, less than two hours west of Seattle. Sahale Learning Center is shared by all members and families. It is also used for retreats and workshops for other like-minded organizations. Sahale is on 65 acres of cultivated and forested land, with a river, orchards, wide vistas, and an abundance of wildlife. Internships are available in both Sahale and Seattle.

The Goodenough Community offers consultation services to other communities, cohousing groups, and other groups forming around a shared purpose. Consultants are trained and experienced leaders and teachers who have studied community organization and group dynamics for decades, both as members and leaders in the Goodenough Community and in their professional lives. For more information, call the community office.

Visitors Accepted [Mar2005][✂✁]

GRACE

Jordan Voelker
87 Cold Brook Rd
Bearsville, NY 12409

845-679-5286
Jordan@LoJoVo.net

Forming | Rural | Diet: Vegetarian only

Grace community is a dream...of a vegetarian community in a rural area of the Northeastern US. We seek to assemble a team of highly motivated folks who want to create a community grounded in nonviolence. It would be spiritually grounded in faiths that share values with the Quakers, Unitarians and others. It would be rural, have a CSA, be multigenerational, and be active in its surrounding communities. It would seek to minimize its member's impact on the planet through extensive resource sharing and implementation of permaculture, solar, and other effective means. It would strive to be a joy filled place, with a common house which regularly fills with music, dance, theater, and other participatory activities. It would be entirely drug free, including being free of any type of smoking whatsoever. It would consciously make efforts to support its members in reaching their highest potential, from supporting each other to create meaningful employment to striving to free all members of unhealthy dietary chemicals such as caffeine and refined sugars. We, as a community and as individuals, would strive for authenticity in all facets of our lives.

Visitors Accepted: Please contact Jordan to help set up introductory meetings. [Nov2004]

GRAIL ECOVILLAGE

Bonnie Hendricks
932 O'Bannonville Rd
Loveland, OH 45140

513-683-5750
bonnienit@grail-us.org

http://www.grailville.org

Forming

The Grail Ecovillage, in Loveland, Ohio, will be built on a designated part of the long-established environmental, educational, and retreat center called Grailville.

The ecovillage is a unique collaboration between future residents, the Grail, Grailville, and a development team who are meeting in monthly design "charettes" or round table planning sessions with the goal of building the village.

Listings

Additions and corrections: email: directory@ic.org, web: directory.ic.org, mail: RR 1 Box 156-D, Rutledge MO 63563, USA.

153

The Grail settled Grailville, located on 311 acres of woodlands, pastures, and organic fields, in 1944. The Grail is an international movement of women committed to spiritual search, social action, ecological sustainability, and the release of women's creative energy throughout the world.

In our ecovillage vision statement we "commit ourselves to create a diverse community of people who have a passion for an earth-harmonious, sustainable, socially equitable way of life. We seek to live the values of Grailville, which are ecological sustainability, spirituality, full empowerment of women, and social justice. We will embody a sense of life's sacredness in all our actions and gatherings."

Visitors Accepted: Contact Bonnie Hendricks. [Mar2005]

GREAT OAK COHOUSING

**500 Little Lake Dr
Ann Arbor, MI 48103**

734-929-6565
info@gocoho.org

Nick Meima
734-663-5516
nick@sunward.org

Malcolm J. Sickels
mjsickel@umich.edu

http://www.greatoakcohousing.org

Began: 2001 I Pop. 98 I Rural

Ecologically-sensitive building and site design that preserves the land's natural beauty.

An intergenerational, friendly atmosphere that is safe for children and conducive to visiting with neighbors.

A large community building, called a common house, for optional shared meals and other activities.

Scio Township location, fewer than ten minutes from downtown Ann Arbor, in the Ann Arbor School District, with city water and sewer.

Visitors Accepted: Please contact and arrange visit—no drop ins please. [Oct2004]

GREEN RIVER COMMUNITY LAND TRUST

413-0274-6950
kawms@usa.net

Began: 2005 I Forming
Rural I Diet: Primarily vegetarian

Our intent is to form a small residential community where land is removed from price escalation, and affordable housing is preserved for future generations. Members hold title to their homes, have the use of small private yards, and share gardens and open space in common.

The site has 12 acres of pine forest, with a year-round stream that feeds into the nearby Green River. There is a remote feeling to the place, although it is only a quarter of a hour from Great Barrington, MA and 25 minutes from Tanglewood. The nearest airport, Albany, is about 40 miles to the north.

The property will support four individuals or small families; at this time there is one person committed to living on the site, a retired freelance journalist. An adjoining parcel is also part of the trust, where a young architect and his family are constructing a home.

It is hoped that eventually more land will be acquired by the trust, which is modeled after similar nonprofit organizations in Massachusetts and throughout the US.

Solar energy use, water conservation and recycling will be highly valued. The intent is to live simply, strive for minimal use of the earth's resources, and share rides to town.

"Men did not make the earth...It is the value of the improvements only, and not the earth itself, that is individual property."
—Thomas Paine
Visitors Accepted [Mar2005]

GREENHAUS COMMUNITY

**71 Green St
Boston, MA 02130**

617-983-2459
info@greenhauscommunity.org

http://greenhauscommunity.org

Began: 2003 I Pop. 23 I Spiritual
Urban I Diet: Omnivorous

We're a bunch of Christians from diverse backgrounds, seeking to live the life Christ calls us to in urban Boston.

Visitors Accepted: Invite yourself to one of our open dinners. If you're really interested (and low maintenance) we might be able to host you for a night or two. Just ask! [Feb2005]

GREENING LIFE COMMUNITY

**PO Box 72
Shermans Dale, PA 17090**

717-545-4761

Began: 1972 I Pop. 11
Rural I Diet: Primarily vegetarian

Greening Life was established in 1972 on a 135-acre farm in south central Pennsylvania. We are a planned, intentional community. We built our own homes, roads, and water system. We follow organic-farming practices on our 50 acres of tillable land and in our 2-acre garden, which produces the majority of our vegetables. Our orchard is providing us with fruit.

The effort to create a balance of cooperative living, with time for individual and family has been a rewarding struggle. Growth in spirit, both individual and community, is an important part of our life together. We respect all persons and value their opinions as a voice to help guide us. We are open to share our spirit and resources with other individuals and groups.

Visitors Accepted [Feb2005]

GREENPLAN

**Sand
2124 Bonar St
Berkeley, CA 94702**

510-644-1303
b4peas@yahoo.com

http://house.4cal.org

Began: 1994 I Diet: Primarily vegan

Greenplan was started in '94 as an organizing center for rural sustainable land trust communities, with land to be financed with urban real estate equity, with no personal equity or investment required.

It is intended to prepare for the global oil shortage.

After a devastating house-fire before we could incorporate, it became very successful, mostly liquidated when the urban property skyrocketed before the group could agree on the land/structure for the first rural community. (Extensive power struggles from anarchists and homeless people.)

After downsizing, now it is time to re-form—for nonpermanent Berkeley members to live here, maintain year-round orchards/nursery/gardens, and plan/organize/network with rural ecovillages.

The lifestyle is ecology-based in almost every way, with strict protections against dishonesty and other forms of oppression/exploitation, bullying, or harassment.

A main goal is to protect members from landlord exploitation without having to be owners.

Also oriented towards vegan dinners, nonsmoking, human power, sailing, par-

Scissors [✂] at the end of a listing indicate that it was edited for length by the Directory editors and a longer description can be found at directory.ic.org.

ties, travelers, political action, music, affordability, skiing, construction, music, possibly re-opening a vegan organic community business/restaurant. (Past members: the HQ has moved since '98—email!)

Visitors Accepted: Email or call. [Jan2005]

GREGORY HOUSE

House President
1617 Washtenaw Ave
Ann Arbor, MI 48104

734-213-6816,
734-662-4414 (office)

http://www.icc.coop

Began: 1995 | Pop. 23 | Urban

Founded in 1995, Karl D. Gregory House is the newest addition to the ICC. Because our house is the only substance-free house in the ICC, we pride ourselves on a house culture quite unique from that of many other co-ops. We tend to attract friendly, slightly wacky housemates. Just because we're substance free doesn't mean we don't know how to have fun! Our house is usually quiet enough to get your work done, but there's just about always something going on, whether it be housemates goofing around in our large basement TV/recreation room, making up something tasty in our beautiful kitchen, or just hanging in our living room, enjoying a cozy fire or engaged in a death match of Twister or a philosophical discussion about the true meaning of "bologna." We pride ourselves on being one of the cleanest houses in the ICC. Most of our rooms have original hardwood floors, and we have a large number of single rooms, although new members will probably spend their first year in a double. We have house meetings every two weeks and are one of the few houses to still run on a modified-consensus system for decision making; i.e., for an important house decision to be made, 85 percent of our members must agree. Call to arrange to join us for dinner and get to know the house and its members! Gregory House is a great place to live, filled with great people. It's nice to go home after class and actually have a *home* to go to.

Visitors Accepted: Contact House President. [Mar2005]

GRICKLEGRASS

109 Woodside Rd
Oxford, Canterbury R.D.
NEW ZEALAND

+64-(0)3-3123-058
contact@gricklegrass.co.nz

http://www.gricklegrass.co.nz

Began: 1973 | Pop. 10
Rural | Diet: Omnivorous

Gricklegrass Community was founded in 1973. It has always been a community focused on sustainable farming, community life, and the development of social conscience. Throughout it's thirty years, Gricklegrass has seen many residents come and go, each person and group contributing something special and unique to the character of the farm. The challenge of living together in a rural setting has remained central to the ethos of Gricklegrass.

As a community we seek to encourage each other in our awareness of wider social issues. We hope to grow in our response to the environmental and social justice needs of this country and the world. While the development of the farm as a self-sufficient producer continues, we acknowledge our inter-dependence on the wider community for work, encouragement, and mutual support.

Visitors Accepted: Contact us by conventional mail or telephone (email is too unreliable) to arrange a convenient time to come and visit or stay. We prefer people who have the intention of staying for more than a couple of days to come to a WWOOFing arrangement with us. [Dec2004]

GWERIN HOUSING ASSOCIATION

Membership Sec.
PO Box 4169
Stourbridge
W Midlands DY8 1YF England
UNITED KINGDOM

+44-(0)7974746810
+44-(0)7793557322
gwerinhousingassociation@hotmail.com
gwerin@ironmanrecords.com

Began: 1979 | Pop. 12 | Diet: Omnivorous

Started in 1979 and located 10 minutes walk from Stourbridge town centre, Gwerin is a cooperative of five houses, four of which are part of a Victorian terrace. These large houses are shared

between members of the association. Each House is run differently, according to the individuals who live there. We have weekly meetings where the membership comes together to discuss the running of the association and a financial budget produced by rents. We are a mixture of individuals, and as a community have no particular ideological focus. Every aspect of the association is open to scrutiny by the members who, in turn, volunteer their skills to ensure that the rules of the constitution are tempered by the day-to-day reality of life in the community. Over the past 23 years Gwerin has evolved into an intentional community encouraging freedom and responsibility within a supportive and cooperative community environment. Gwerin is currently seeking new members. If you would like more information and details about how to apply to live in Gwerin, send a self-addressed envelope with a letter telling us about yourself.

Visitors Accepted: Please get in touch via post or email. [Jan2005]

H.O.M.E. HEAVEN ON MOTHER EARTH (COSTA RICA)

Peter Quilici
1625 Belford Rd
Reno, NV 89509

775-826-2125, 808-345-9940
peterquilici@hotmail.com

Began: 2004 | Forming

The H.O.M.E. project is in process of securing land near Dominical on the Pacific coast of Costa Rica—the land of Pura Vida, or Pure Life. Our mission is to find peace and love within ourselves through different spiritual practices and selfless service, and then reflect that "heaven" within on the magical land that Spirit has gifted us with. Our guidance lets us know that we will be an educational center teaching intensives on: sustainability, yoga, healing and expressive arts, dance, green building, permaculture, and all that Spirit desires of us. If you have found that "heaven" within yourself, and desire to create that with us please contact us. Love, love... [Oct2004]

Listings

Additions and corrections: email: directory@ic.org, web: directory.ic.org, *mail:* RR 1 Box 156-D, Rutledge MO 63563, USA.

155

HANOAR HAOVED VEHALOMED – TNUAT HABOGRIM (ADULT MOVEMENT)

Kibbutz Ravid
14960
ISRAEL

+972-(0)546734464,
+972-(0)46787804
tamari_a@ravid.org.il

http://noal.co.il

Began: 1982 | Forming

Our community is based on a wide network of communal groups, each consisting of between 6–30 members.

In total, our movement numbers several hundred members.

This community is synonymous with the adult movement (people aged between 20–35) that developed from the biggest Israeli youth movement: "Hanoar Haoved Vehalomed."

We have a socialist ideology, and most of the people in our movement work in educational projects within Israeli society.

These projects are possible due to the fact that we are located all over Israel, from Be'er Sheva in the south to Tiberias in the north, in Tel-Aviv, Haifa and Jerusalem.

Our aims are to make constructive changes within Israel, and to establish a new kibbutz movement.

Our central offices are located in Tel-Aviv, with a few of our communes situated nearby.

Visitors Accepted: Contact Hanoar Haoved Vehalomed from our website. [Mar2005]

HARBIN HOT SPRINGS

PO Box 782
Middletown, CA 95461

707-987-2477,
800-622-2477 (CA only)
reception@harbin.org

http://www.harbin.org

Began: 1972 | Pop. 162 | Spiritual | Rural

Harbin Hot Springs is a nonprofit retreat center owned by Heart Consciousness Church. It is operated and maintained by more than 150 members. We welcome guests from around the world who travel here to soak in our natural-spring pools, bask on our clothing-optional sun decks, receive massages or Watsu from our certified therapists, take yoga classes, hike our 1700 acres, or otherwise simply relax. Also offered are weekly dances, music events, and workshops.

Visitors Accepted: Call to make a room reservation or stop at the gate for a day visit or camping. [Mar2005]

HARMONIOUS EARTH COMMUNITY

PO 233
Belen, NM 87002

505-861-1111, 505-864-0011
harmoniousearth@aol.com
chart11@earthlink.net

http://www.harmoniousearth
communityfoundation.org

Forming

The Harmonious Earth Community is a worldwide collection of people committed to the establishment of a community based on cooperation, harmony, and sustainability —where the autonomy of the individual is valued, where diverse philosophies, abilities, and freedoms are respected, and the spirit of the land is revered. Since the early 1990s, a group of individuals and New Mexico landowners have been gathering to share a common heartfelt vision. This vision, like the community, continues to evolve and expand.

Members of the community are creating the Harmonious Earth Community Foundation Inc. (HECF). This nonprofit, 501(c)3 foundation will implement this expanding vision. The Foundation's mission is "to promote a sustainable Harmonious Earth Community through education, health, the arts, ecology, research, media communication and peaceful coexistence."

The Harmonious Earth Community Foundation will conduct various fundraising activities, solicit grants, contributions, and be the recipient of a 110-acre donation of beautiful land, on the mesa, west of Belen, New Mexico. Our intention is to be of service by living through our hearts. The Foundation is dedicated to the principles of universal responsibility, truth, joy, unconditional love and compassion. [Mar2005]

Scissors [✄] at the end of a listing indicate that it was edited for length by the Directory *editors and a longer description can be found at* directory.ic.org.

HARMONY VILLAGE

1001 Cottonwood Circle
Golden, CO 80401

John Lightburn
303-216-1140
jlnolightburn@mho.com

Ginny Cowles
303-279-3811
ginnycowles@aol.com

http://www.harmonyvillage.org

Began: 1992 | Pop. 62
Small Town | Diet: Omnivorous

Harmony Village, located at the foot of the Rockies in Golden, Colorado, is a cohousing community, dedicated to sustainable living. Our Cohousing Community opened in October 1996 and has 27 households featuring Santa Fe style, energy efficient, clustered dwellings with common facilities and open space.

Our shared mission is to create a cooperative neighborhood of diverse individuals sharing human resources within an ecologically responsible community setting.

Membership in Harmony Village spans a diversity of ages, incomes, professions, and unit sizes. The "village" features a common house with a kitchen/dining area for some regular meals together, two rooms for child care, common storage and laundry facilities, guest rooms, hot tub, and big screen TV. The common grounds include a large community garden, orchard, on-site workshop, and a river-rock labyrinth. Twenty-seven housing units are clustered around small courtyards and the common house to encourage interaction among residents. About half of the original site is reserved as open space.

High on members' priority list from the beginning has been an ecological concern. Members seek to tread lightly on the earth, and hope this small effort to conserve our land and resources will begin a reversal of the devastating effects of ill-considered land-use policy and urban sprawl. Global change occurs one neighborhood at a time. Harmony Village intends to be part of that change.

Visitors Accepted: Call John Lightburn or Ginny Cowles. [Mar2005]

Trying to run a meeting?

FIC has some tools you need—the best books around on consensus facilitation.

consensusbooks.ic.org

HEADLANDS

14775 Front Rd
Stella, ON K0H 2S0
CANADA

613-389-3444
topsyfarms@on.aibn.com

Began: 1971 | Pop. 5
Rural | Diet: Omnivorous

Headlands was founded in 1971 by five people on Amherst Island, Ontario. The commune dissolved amicably in 1975. Three communal members and a friend bought the farming assets and most of the land from the other 12 members.

We are now five adults living (somewhat) cooperatively. We are equal shareholders in Topsy Farms, which owns the real estate and a sheep flock of over 1200 ewes.

Headlands rents two homes from Topsy and charges each of us a monthly levy for accommodation. Each member is responsible for their own monthly Headlands payment. We support each other's income work.

Each house is private; those living there decide how things are done. We cooperate with each other in a spirit of mutual self-interest enriched by feelings of family and friendship. The sharing of resources and abilities allows each of us more personal freedom than we would have in more traditional living and working arrangements.

We find our land on the shores of Lake Ontario to be very beautiful. Each of us is active in the Island community (400 people) mainly by publishing a monthly newsletter, the Amherst Island Beacon.

Visitors Accepted: Write or phone and tell us why you want to visit an operating sheep farm run by (what some would call) aging hippies. [Oct2004]

HEALING GRACE SANCTUARY

34 Creamery Ave
Shelburne Falls, MA 01370

413-625-9386 (9am-9pm)

Pop. 1 | Forming | Spiritual
Rural | Diet: Omnivorous

HGS ("hugs") is 85 magical wooded acres with meadows and trails, embraced by a horseshoe bend of the Deerfield River, nestled in the Berkshire Mountains. We aim to be "in our element:" close knit family living sustainably, unplugged, mostly outdoors, immersed in nature...sanctuary from the hype of de-natured, high-tech, money driven, secular ways.

Ours is a path less traveled—we're guided by voluntary service, voluntary simplicity, and the voice of spirit. Our beliefs: the most simple, optimistic, empowering we can imagine. We aim for wholesome choices in all realms: patterned after natural systems/warm loving relationships, with all ages intermixed/an ongoing open forum where age, material wealth, and status carry no weight in whom we honor, help or invite into our midst. Push-the-envelope tools and skills are central: healthy group process, re-evolutionary education, innovative community service, social transmutation. Our unwavering focus includes:

• Empower youth
• Boost powers of mind (Prayer works! Thought creates! Mind is both camera and projector!)
• Defuse blind spots/divisiveness/one-right-way

We aim to look in the mirror often, via an enthused, open forum...avoiding the pitfalls many groups succumb to. Our pledge: humility, compassion, introspection. Rituals that strengthen us and our bonds.

Is this your heartsong? Call us! (Or write, with your enthusiasms and hugs, SASE, phone number and best time to call.) Then come intern with us in:

• Innovative service
• Rustic indigenous ways
• Paradigm shift now!

Visitors Accepted [Mar2005][✄<]

HEARTHAVEN

Maril Crabtree
3728 Tracy Ave
Kansas City, MO 64109

913-484-1733 (Maril),
913-908-5271 (Jim)
maril@prodigy.net
corestar@prodigy.net

Began: 1988 | Pop. 6 | Spiritual
Urban | Diet: Primarily vegetarian

We are an urban community of six members who seek to model a way of living from the heart that involves living responsibly, nonviolently, and ecologically. We put a high value on the practice of hospitality to all beings, and on living life out of love rather than fear. We are open to visitors, depending on schedules and needs.

Visitors Accepted: Contact us by email as far in advance as possible of desired visiting dates. [Feb2005]

Additions and corrections: email: directory@ic.org, *web:* directory.ic.org, *mail:* RR 1 Box 156-D, Rutledge MO 63563, USA.

Listings

HEARTHSTONE

Elizabeth
4700 West 37th Ave
Denver, CO 80212
info@hearthstonecohousing.com

Kathryn
303-922-2413

http://www.denvercohousing.com

Began: 1998 | Pop. 72
Urban | Diet: Omnivorous

Hearthstone Cohousing is an urban, diverse, multi-generational cohousing community located in northwest Denver. We have 33 townhomes, a common house, shared green areas, and a community garden. We are within walking distance of many locally owned businesses, including restaurants, coffee houses, and book stores, as well as public transportation. Please visit our website for more information.

Visitors Accepted: Please email and we will be happy to arrange for you to attend a common meal or another function. [Jan2005]

HEARTSONG

PO Box 227
Orono, ME 04473
mhbj8@hotmail.com

Began: 1999 | Pop. 6 | Forming
Rural | Diet: Other

We have developed a close, caring sense of community, involving a substantial sense of togetherness, as a relational "we." Our process of developing an optimal sense of harmonious community is grounded in a new understanding of optimal human relationship, interpersonal communication, and psychological growth, in which hearts, minds, and spirits are deeply connected to each other, in a state of empathic communion, or synergistic attunement. We understand the process of developing open, deeply meaningful, honest, sincere, constructive, interpersonal communication, as well as unfolding one's unique individual capabilities and natural inclinations, as one's "heart song."

We are seeking new members who are predominantly relationship-oriented, open to continued learning and growth, willing to question their own presumptions, as well as honest, warmhearted, mostly unselfish, generously giving of themselves, sincerely caring, and cooperative, rather than habitually conflictual, competitive, defensive, and selfish. Our community will serve as a model of con-

structive global transformation, grounded in psychological maturity, caring human relationships, as well as actualization of individual and relationship potentials, bringing optimal levels of holistic healings, productive functioning, and well-being.

Members are required to be financially self-supporting, and to live a wholesome, productive, lifestyle. No addictive substances or sexual promiscuity are permitted.

Visitors Accepted: Contact us first, and tell us why you are interested in Heartsong. Careful screening process required before visit can be arranged. We welcome inquiries and contact only from people who are financially self-supporting, and who are committed to living a wholesome, psychologically constructive lifestyle, free of all addictive substances and without sexual promiscuity. [Mar2005]

HEARTWOOD COHOUSING

800 Heartwood Ln #18
Durango, CO 81122

info@heartwoodcohousing.com

Alice Miller Robbins
970-884-7077
alicerobb@durango.net

Fran Hart
970-884-1139
hartmagic@frontier.net

http://www.heartwoodcohousing.com

Began: 1994 | Pop. 65
Rural | Diet: Omnivorous

Imagine a cohousing community located near Durango in Southwest Colorado, where the state's largest wilderness area and the red rock canyons of the Colorado Plateau are all close enough for a day hike.

And imagine a neighborhood of 24 homes and a deep sense of community nestled gently in 250 acres of meadow, pine forest and pasture land.

That's Heartwood Cohousing.

Our huge and easy to navigate website has lots of information, including "What's Available" (for sale or rent), so please check it out.

Visitors Accepted: Please contact us to schedule a visit and tour, especially if you want to stay over. You are welcome to attend a business meeting, common meals, or any other events that are scheduled. Please call 970-884-7577 or email info@heartwoodcohousing.com. [Oct2004]

HEARTWOOD INSTITUTE

220 Harmony Ln
Garberville, CA 95542

707-923-5000 (office),
707-923-5012 (work exchg coord)
hello@heartwoodinstitute.com

http://www.heartwoodinstitute.com/
content/living/Community.htm

Began: 1978 | Pop. 103
Rural | Diet: Primarily vegetarian

We are a unique and healing vocational school that provides a supportive community environment for staff, faculty, students, and work-study participants. We are a teaching community of dedicated individuals who care how men and women live in balance with Mother Earth, who care about the truth of our experience with one another. Basing our lives on the principles of integrity, authenticity, and truth, we see ourselves as a role model for human relationships, self-actualization, and stewardship of our planet.

As an organization, Heartwood is playing an important role as a catalyst for planetary healing through personal transformation. Vocational training in the natural healing arts, workshops, and experience in community living are our vehicle. We share three vegetarian meals a day. The resident staff members get room, board and a stipend. Work-study program participants get a discount on tuition and receive accommodations and meals in exchange for 25 hours/week of assigned work. Our land is 240 acres of mountains, meadows, and forests in the rural mountains of Northern California.

Visitors Accepted [Feb2005]

HEATHCOTE COMMUNITY

21300 Heathcote Rd
Freeland, MD 21053

410-343-DIRT
info@Heathcote.org

http://www.heathcote.org

Began: 1965 | Pop. 18
Rural | Diet: Primarily vegetarian

The adults and children of Heathcote Community strive to live in a healthy, loving, and sustainable manner. We are located on 112 acres of wooded stream valley which is part of the School of Living community land trust. We believe that we have a responsibility to care for the land and each other, treating both with dignity and respect.

Scissors [✂] at the end of a listing indicate that it was edited for length by the Directory editors and a longer description can be found at directory.ic.org.

In community we support one another in living a life that we love. We don't currently have community businesses, so each member earns income individually and makes monthly contributions. We get together for evening meals most nights, weekly community meetings, regular meetings about relationship issues, monthly community work projects, and quarterly retreats. Many of us often gather for meditation, yoga, singalongs, celebrations, house concerts, jazz jams, dances, world music drumming, and other events. All community decisions are made by consensus.

We strive to practice ever-more-sustainable ways of living. Our current projects focus on creating a living demonstration of permaculture principles and ecological sustainability, including the expansion of our organic gardens and the renovation of existing structures. We are building an alternative, energy-efficient house with individual and family units, and renovating our 150-year-old grist mill to improve our shared spaces and conference center.

We welcome inquiries from people who share our passion for creating a better world, and hope to see you at one of our monthly visitor weekends.

Visitors Accepted: Attend a visitor weekend. See the visiting page on our website. [Mar2005]

HEI WA HOUSE

530 Miller Ave
Ann Arbor, MI 48103

734-994-4937
heiwa@umich.edu
gaia@ic.org
beth@ic.org

http://www.ic.org/heiwa

Began: 1985 | Pop. 10
Urban | Diet: Primarily vegetarian

HeiWa was founded in 1985. Our current membership capacity is eight adults. We have two child members. We are a vegetarian household, and our membership tends to be environmentally conscious, politically active, lesbian/gay/bisexual/transgender celebratory, and musically inclined. Our home has often served as a meeting space for political and social-justice organizations, personal-growth groups, and community-strengthening gatherings.

Over a period of fourteen years, we lived in four consecutive rental houses. In 1999 we purchased our current house, establishing a permanent location for Hei Wa. In September of 2005, we expanded to two adjoining houses. We dream about continued growth on our block, creating a cooperative neighborhood in northwest Ann Arbor.

HeiWa's mission statement is: to provide affordable cooperative housing for a diverse membership through cooperatively owned property, communal living, and resource sharing, while upholding principles of sustainability, peace, racial and economic justice, lifelong cooperative living, and involvement in local community.

Visitors Accepted: Call or email to ask for permission to visit. People usually visit for one to three days. [Feb2005]

THE HERMITAGE

Johannes Zinzendorf
75 Grove Rd
Pitman, PA 17964

717-425-2548 (winter only)
BroJoh@yahoo.com

http://www.ic.org/thehermitage

Began: 1987 | Pop. 2
Rural | Diet: Primarily vegetarian

The Hermitage is a gay intentional community and a center for queer creativity. We offer free creative summer residencies to gay men in all fields including arts and crafts, the humanities, the sciences, spirituality, philosophy, and education. Check our website for more information and the application process.

Our workshops and gatherings are open to all people. We host summer and fall faerie gatherings, as well as workshops in traditional crafts such as flax to linen processing and sourdough bread baking in our 200-year-old outdoor brick oven.

Our emphasis is on self-reliance as well as connectedness, to each other as well as to the land and its creatures. There are two hermit caretakers who founded the Hermitage as a place of beauty and peace. We've moved more than two dozen historic log and timber-framed buildings to the site and have rebuilt them. The structures include cabins for summer residencies, as well as a community house, a variety of craft shops, plus buildings for the farm's animals and equipment. We raise hay, corn, soybeans, flax, and a variety of livestock.

We are affiliated with the Queer in Community Network.

The Hermitage is a nonprofit, tax-exempt organization operated by a board of directors as well as an advisory board. Visitors are welcome. Our newsletter, "The Flaming Faggot," is free by request.

Visitors Accepted: Contact us and we'll arrange a mutually-convenient time. [Jan2005]

HERTHA

Hertha Levefúllesskab
Landsbyvúnget 12, Herskind
DK-8464 Galten
DENMARK

+45-86954620, +45-40890383
allanelm@hotmail.com

Began: 1993 | Pop. 45 | Forming | Spiritual
Rural

Forty-five people of all ages. Practicing reverse integration with young developmentally delayed people (13 persons) on an anthroposophical basis (undogmatic). Intention is a village with about 200 persons where people help and support each other and live in a sustainable way.

Visitors Accepted: Call +45-86954520 and inquire about the possibilities. [Mar2005]

HET CARRE

Kees Voorberg
Glazenmakerstraat 19
KX-2645
NETHERLANDS

+31-(0)15-2855219
voorberg@tiscali.nl

http://www.ecodorp.carre.nl

Began: 2002 | Pop. 107 | Suburban

49 huizen, 70 volwassenen, 40 kinderen in DElfgauw bij DElft.
Uitgangspunten: ecologie, spiritualiteit, gemeenschapszin.
Visitors Accepted: Call or send email. [Oct2004]

HIDDEN VALLEY

PO Box 572
Bigfork, MT 59911
streamwalkers@yahoo.com

Forming | Spiritual | Rural | Diet: Other

Our vision of Hidden Valley: An ecologically self-sufficient multicultural mountain intentional community held in a land trust. There would be shared income; experiential homeschooling; community cooperative work with current interests in watershed rehab, stream site hatchery, organic gardening, alternative-energy healing and research, inventions, music, art, writing, theater,

Additions and corrections: email: directory@ic.org, *web:* directory.ic.org, *mail:* RR 1 Box 156-D, Rutledge MO 63563, USA.

159

draft-horse selective logging, botany, herbology, wildlife, and education.

The community of approximately 12–14 adults and beginning with 6–8 children would enjoy healthy fresh air and meals home cooked by community members in the large community lodge. There would be separate living spaces for individuals, couples, families, or roommates.

Decision making would be by timed consensus, then majority rule by rotating councils, and there would be clear rules for dealing with conflict resolution that involve Re-evaluation Counseling (RC).

Earth-centered spirituality—create our own ceremonies. Inquire and/or join us if you are respectful; a team worker; optimistic; industrious; monogamous—bi, straight, or gay; encourage parent(s) who want to raise their kids in a creative, respectful, noncompetitive, healthy home. When writing include why you desire to live in community.

Visitors Accepted: Write and tell about yourself and why you are interested in helping to form a community in Montana. [Mar2005]

HIGHER GROUND COHOUSING

1911 NE Higher Ground Ave
Bend, OR 97701

541-389-1514

Nancy Baker
541-385-9972
jnbaker@bendcable.com
jnbaker@bendbroadband.com

Mark McGarigal
541-383-5862
mooks@bendnet.com

Began: 1992 | Pop. 88
Suburban | Diet: Omnivorous

Higher Ground is comprised of 37 single family homes on seven acres, about three miles east of downtown Bend. The community was planned to provide maximum open space for meadows, play areas, pond, trails and vegetable gardens. Our Common House was the original farm house on this property, and we are just completing a large new dining/kitchen and recreation room addition. People choosing to buy or rent these homes are interested in a socially supportive environment for themselves and their families. Many homes have been constructed with innovative environmentally responsible building materials. We share general maintenance responsibilities, and

find this to be a valuable component in building community. We also take conflict resolution seriously and periodically provide positive opportunities for personal growth.

Visitors Accepted: Call or email so we can arrange a tour and hopefully you can come and share a meal with us. [Mar2005]

HIGHLINE CROSSING

1620 W Canal Ct
Littleton, CO 80120

303-347-8351

Jim Mascolo
jim@highlinecrossing.org

http://www.highlinecrossing.org

Began: 1991 | Pop. 75 | Suburban

We began forming in mid-1991. The energy-efficient, community-designed buildings were completed in stages between 1995 and 1997. Since then, we've been learning more about how to be with each other, give each other space and respect, and learn and grow together. The main challenge we confront regularly is balancing individual needs with community needs. We're an eclectic group including counselors, mediators, computer pros, lawyers, full-time parents, and much else.

Ten years have given us time for the trees to grow, and for us to grow some of our own traditions. These include annual Mardi Gras and holiday celebrations, an October Fest and St. Patrick's Day dinner, and Halloween pumpkin carving and trick-or-treating for the kids. Regular events include twice-weekly community meals or potlucks, parent-kid tea times, individual garden plots, twice-a-year workdays, and lots of cooperative child care.

Amenities include a community garden and immediate access to the Highline Canal Trail system (over 70 miles of foot/bike/horse trails, just across a footbridge). There is a wide variety of cultural and sporting activities locally. The community is less than a mile from the light rail system with easy access to downtown Denver.

Visitors Accepted [Feb2005]

HILLEGASS HOUSE

3056 Hillegass Ave
Berkeley, CA 94705

510-848-3022

Began: 1979 | Pop. 9
Urban | Diet: Omnivorous

Hillegass House is a 9-member 25-year-old collective in Berkeley. We began as a mostly

single-parent house made up of 6 adults who wanted to share the burdens and joys of parenting. The age spread of the current membership runs from the early 30s to early 70s, with the median age being mid-30s to mid-40s.

Our home is stabilized with a long term core group (one of our original members still lives in the house) but we've had several new members within the last couple of years including one baby born!

We are an exceptionally diverse group in most regards (i.e., interests, diet, spirituality, sexuality, employment, etc.). We blend together well, perhaps because we balance a strong commitment to and enjoyment of group living on the one hand, with a willingness to work through group dynamics on the other. As well, we have a healthy respect for one another's privacy.

Other factors of our success? Well, it helps that we live in a lovely house that can accommodate our number quite comfortably. Dinners are shared which builds connection. We have a large variety of gardening and creative projects and the space to do these in.

Visitors Accepted: Written inquiries only (we're sometimes slow in answering). Write with your description, desires, and why interested in us. [Mar2005]

HIMALAYAN INSTITUTE

952 Bethany Turnpike
Honesdale, PA 18431

570-253-5551, 800-822-4547
info@HimalayanInstitute.org

http://www.HimalayanInstitute.org

The Himalayan Institute is located on a beautiful, 400-acre campus near the town of Honesdale in northeastern Pennsylvania. Its rural setting in the wooded, rolling hills of the Pocono Mountains provides a wonderfully peaceful and healthy setting in which to relax and discover the best of yourself.

Founded in 1971 as a nonprofit organization, our purpose is to help people grow physically, mentally, and spiritually by combining the best knowledge of both the East and the West.

Throughout the year we offer a variety of programs in hatha yoga, meditation, yoga philosophy, psychology, holistic health and other subjects. From weekend meditation retreats and weeklong seminars on spirituality to our months-long residential programs, we attempt to provide an environment to foster gentle, inner progress.

Hatha yoga teachers' training is available

Scissors [✂] at the end of a listing indicate that it was edited for length by the Directory editors and a longer description can be found at directory.ic.org.

through the Himalayan Institute Teachers Association. Holistic health services, Ayurvedic rejuvenation programs, and pancha karma are offered through our Center for Health and Healing.

The Institute also publishes numerous books and tapes, available through the Himalayan Institute Press, and a bimonthly magazine, *Yoga International*.

The Honesdale site serves as the organization's headquarters. Institute programs are also offered at branch and affiliated centers throughout the United States, Canada, Europe, and Asia.

Membership in the Institute helps support its programs and offers members valuable benefits. [Mar2005]

HOCKERTON HOUSING PROJECT

Nick White
The Watershed, Gables Dr
Hockerton
Southwell NG25 0QU England
UNITED KINGDOM

+44-(0)1636-816902
hhp@hockerton.demon.co.uk

http://www.hockerton.demon.co.uk

Began: 1994 | Pop. 20 | Forming
Rural | Diet: Omnivorous

The Hockerton Housing Project (HHP) is an innovative residential sustainable development in the village of Hockerton near Southwell, Nottinghamshire. It was completed in September 1998 after three years of planning and 18 months of construction. Designed as one of the first zero-energy residential systems in the UK, reducing life cycle energy to a minimum, they are amongst the most energy efficient, purpose built dwellings in Europe. Maximum use of benign, organic, and recycled materials has been made in the construction, and the development is designed to be, to a large extent, self-sufficient. The houses are earth covered and have passive solar heating without a space heating system. A wind turbine and photovoltaic system provide all of the energy required to run the homes. The water and sewage system is self-contained.

The large area has allowed incorporation of features that enable the occupants to live in a sustainable and self-sufficient way. This includes crop cultivation and the rearing of small animals. It has also allowed for large water catchment for the homes and waste disposal via a reed-bed system.

In response to increasing visitors a new learning resource centre has recently been constructed by project members, which includes a dedicated audio-visual room, seminar facilities, and permanent exhibitions. The building itself is built to similar high environmental standards as the homes, including meeting the zero heating and zero CO2 standards. It also receives most of its energy from a second wind turbine recently installed.

Visitors Accepted: See website or email us. [Jan2005][✂✁]

THE HOMESTEAD AT DENISON UNIVERSITY

1385 North St
Granville, OH 43023

740-587-5679
homestead@denison.edu

http://www.denison.edu/homestead

Began: 1976 | Pop. 12
Small Town | Diet: Primarily vegetarian

The Homestead is a community offering a living alternative for students at Denison University. Started as a short experiment in living simply off the land, the Homestead has outlived its expectations and is flourishing 30 years later.

A trio of cabins about a mile from Denison's campus can house 12 students who share space with cats and dogs. We are off the grid, utilizing solar energy to pump water and to power some appliances. Cooking and heating are accomplished with wood-burning stoves.

We are striving toward sustainability but must struggle with an ever-changing population and with the balance of academic work and homestead living. We attempt to integrate the two and utilize available resources and expertise from the university, and we presently have ambitious plans for increasing efficiency and capacity.

Important aspects of homesteading include the opportunity to take responsibility for our own lives; the empowerment of admitted interdependence; the intensity of living, working, and playing together; and the opportunity to integrate lifestyle with personal ideologies. The Homestead is an amazing opportunity for students to learn far more than we could ever learn in the classroom.

Visitors Accepted: Stop on by—everyone is always welcome. Dinner is from 6-8 on weekdays and you can be assured that someone will be around during that time. Please leave your car at the gate and walk back (about .75m) to the Homestead. Come take the tour! [Feb2005]

HOMEWOOD COHOUSING

1221 Russell Ave N
Minneapolis, MN 55411

612-588-9532

Fred H. Olson
fholson@cohousing.org

http://mn.cohousing.org/homewood

Began: 1996 | Pop. 5 | Forming
Urban | Diet: Omnivorous

An intentional neighborhood-organizing effort in an existing racially mixed city neighborhood two miles from downtown.

We have cohousing-like goals. Currently rather inactive.

Visitors Accepted: Contact us [Mar2005]

HOPE HILL COMMUNITY

Edwin Morris
GPO Box 1926
Hobart, Tasmania 7001
AUSTRALIA

+61-(0)3-6297-6124
hopehillcommunity@hotmail.com

http://www.hopehill.info

Began: 2000 | Pop. 10 | Forming | Spiritual
Rural | Diet: Other

We are a small community of believers here in Tasmania, Australia, who attempt to live a simple life guided by the laws and commandments of God as best we can. We believe very strongly in good old fashioned family values, and defined roles of men and women, and believe that in today's world, in order for believing families to survive, they need to learn together. In a world full of individuals, perhaps now is the time when we all need each other most, as deep down we all long for a sense of tribal belonging.

We grow fruit and vegetables for our own use and to sell, and aim to till the soil by horse and plough, and to get back to the old ways of living, and to not be tied to our modern society any more than we have to. Although small in number at this stage, we have made much progress in this direction to date, and invite inquiries from others who love God and seek to live according to His rules among like-minded brethren.

Visitors Accepted: Please either write, email, or phone us, and get to know a bit more about us, ask us questions, and tell us a bit about yourself, and take it from there. [Mar2005]

Additions and corrections: email: directory@ic.org, web: directory.ic.org, mail: RR 1 Box 156-D, Rutledge MO 63563, USA.

161

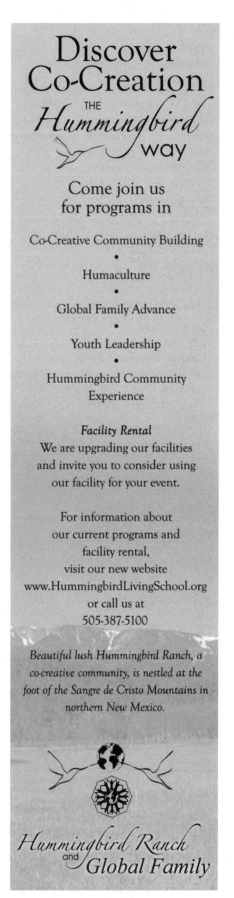
HOPEWELL COMMUNITY

Craig Butler
4645 Cliff Ave
Louisville, KY 40215

502-364-9864
factroid@insightbb.com

http://geocities.com/Heartland/
Cottage/4146

Began: 1996 | Pop. 2 | Forming
Rural | Diet: Primarily vegetarian

We have 16.5 acres (50% wooded) 18 miles from downtown Louisville Kentucky with private building sites available—wooded on three sides. Our purpose is to develop a sustainable, ecological and social community that preserves habitat and fosters democratic principles of participation, respect and responsibility. Clustered housing with partially wooded greenspace.

Visitors Accepted: Send email with phone number, or call and leave phone number. [Mar2005]

HOSPITAL COMUNITARIO WALDOS

Centro Medico Comunitario Waldos
Apartado 17-23-021
Sangolqui
ECUADOR

+593-(0)2-2-331966 (tel/fax),
+593-(0)2-2-080501
lance@waldos.org.ec

Began: 1996 | Small Town

Waldos is a medical clinic based on communitarian principles established in 1996 in Sangolqui, a green, fertile valley outside of Quito, the capital city of Ecuador. It is run by Americans and Ecuadorians. Our inspiration comes from *Walden Two* (Walden-dos hence Waldos). We are not currently living in community, but have embodied community and egalitarian principles into what we do. Our focus is providing good quality medical services to underserved populations. We have our own facility with X-ray, CT scanner and ultrasound, ER and other capabilities. We do welcome visitors but ask to please contact us first. Profesionals in the healthcare field are of course very welcome but there are many activities at Waldos not requiring healthcare training. We would be especially interested in hosting persons who can help us grow in the areas of consensus decision making and implementing community principles. Where we live in Ecuador is quite safe and we have developed a considerable local resources "net" over more than 20 years.

Foreigners are well-accepted locally and anyone coming in a visitor-working capacity would be experiencing total immersion in Latin culture.

Visitors Accepted: First contact us. Our contact person is Dr. Lance Evans. [Mar2005]

HUDSON VALLEY ECOVILLAGE

Hudson Valley, NY

212-996-1830, 917-753-8973
archiduck@verizon.net

Kevin Skvorak
k.skvorak@verizon.net

http://groups.yahoo.com/group/
HVEcovillage

http://www.hudsonvalleyecovillage.org

Began: 2004 | Forming

Mission
Our Mission is to integrate our own lives into, and facilitate others' connection with, the growing movement toward sustainable living. We will invite people to explore and learn through hands-on participation in land conservation and restoration practices, natural building methods, alternative energy production, and other permaculture practices.
Objectives
It is within the ecovillage model that we see the greatest opportunities for serving the widest range of people's needs. To house ourselves we will work together to build truly affordable, low-impact, high-efficiency shared and individual cohousing units, set within a permaculture designed community.

We plan to acquire land and hold it in a trust. The current design plan also includes long term leased lots for members to build their own homes from natural materials, and our goal is to make this as affordable as possible.

Through social innovations, such as a cooperative community investment initiatives, we seek to support and provide economic opportunities for a range of individual and cooperative projects such as: an organic farm and food processing business; a "green" design/construction company; a sustainable energy business; a retreat, seminar, and learning center; a working artists' cooperative; and others.

We are still in the early forming stages, and we welcome new members, especially those who wish to be involved in building a community with these goals from the ground up. You need not currently live in the Hudson Valley.[Mar2005][✂]

Scissors [✂] at the end of a listing indicate that it was edited for length by the Directory *editors and a longer description can be found at* directory.ic.org.

HUMANITY RISING

John Omaha, PhD
PO Box 528
Chico, CA 95927

530-899-7719
john@johnomahaenterprises.com

Began: 1992 | Forming | Spiritual | Rural

We are a clean and sober spiritual community and self-realization fellowship manifesting the principles of Humanity Rising in our daily lives. We are united by our shared oneness with the universe that is our Higher Power. We celebrate our at-oneness in the Great Mystery Lodge of Humanity Rising, a monthly sweatlodge. Our spirituality brings together many elements from the human experience, including shamanism, psychic practice, Taoism, Buddhism, psychology, cosmology, and more. Our goal is a fully realized life on a human scale. We believe we all live in both ordinary and nonordinary reality, whether we are aware of it or not. We are healers, working in both realities.

In our daily lives we live simply, organically, ecologically. Every act is a spiritual act. We strive for integrity and grace. Presently we support ourselves through counseling in recovery. One goal is to establish a rural recovery center to provide an income stream for the community. We want to be self-sustaining. We limit our reliance upon machines. We harmonize our lives psychologically through regular practice of group therapy.

If you want what we have to offer and are willing to go to any lengths to get it, contact us.

Visitors Accepted: Please call or email John Omaha to discuss your desire to join us in the Great Mystery Lodge. Dates for the lodge vary. You will need directions. [Mar2005]

HUMMINGBIRD COMMUNITY

PO Box 732
Mora, NM 87732

505-387-5100, 505-387-6440
contact@hummingbirdlivingschool
    .org

http://www.hummingbirdlivingschool
    .org

Began: 1986 | Pop. 12 | Spiritual
Rural | Diet: Omnivorous

Hummingbird Community is located on 500 acres of lush land nestled against the Sangre de Cristo Mountains of Northern New Mexico. We began as a non-local community within Global Family, bonding through our extensive international peace and educational work. Global Family, founded in 1986, is a nonprofit non-governmental organization affiliated with the United Nations, whose purpose is to support a shift in consciousness from separation and fear to unity, love and cooperation.

As social pioneers, we share a commitment to the principles and practices of co-creation. Since founding Hummingbird Ranch in 1996 we have grown into a diverse group of a dozen deeply connected core members who support one another in fulfilling our soul's purpose. We have offered an array of summer programs, which have included Permaculture Design Certification, Youth Leadership Trainings, Rites of Passage and spiritual retreats.

We are growing rapidly as several deeply resonant soul kin are currently moving here. At the center of our developing community is Hummingbird Living School, which supports us and those drawn to live and learn with us in fulfilling our vision as a co-creative ecovillage, modeling new social forms that embody an awakened, regenerative consciousness. Also in planning is a Health and Healing Retreat Center and various other conscious enterprises.

We invite others to join us in our living laboratory of discovery where source and nature guide us to co-create a new world.

Visitors Accepted: Send email to rich@globalfamily.net or call Rich at 505-387-5100 to schedule a phone conversation first. [Mar2005]

HUNDREDFOLD FARM

1668F Old Rte 30
Gettysburg, PA 17353

717-334-9426
info@hundredfoldfarm.org

Bill Hartzell
717-337-2212
rhubarb@cvn.net

Mark Knight
mmm100fold@aol.com

http://www.hundredfoldfarm.org

Began: 1998 | Pop. 18 | Forming
Rural | Diet: Omnivorous

We hope to combine a small cohousing community with an organic CSA (community supported agriculture).

Visitors Accepted: Contact the community by email or phone to let us know when you want to come. [Mar2005]

HUTTERIAN BRETHREN

3610 N Wood Rd
Reardan, WA 99029

mark@hutterites.org

http://www.hutterianbrethren.com

Began: 1528 | Spiritual
Rural | Diet: Omnivorous

The Hutterian Brethren originated in central Europe in 1528, after the Reformation. The Hutterites are a Christian church that advocates total community, spiritually and materially, which they believe fulfills the highest command of love, and they also believe that one must not only recognize Christ as Savior but also follow him. They use both the Old and New Testament in their worship services. Since they are of German descent, they still teach and use their native tongue at home and in church. Some of their history preserved and published today is in English. Each community conducts its own youth work through Sunday school and other activities. They practice adult baptism upon confession of faith, are war resisters, refuse to participate in politics, dress differently, operate their own schools, and their meals are all eaten together. The Hutterites are agriculturists by trade, some are also engaged in manufacturing, and they use modern tools to carry out these endeavors. They distribute the work among the members wherever the need arises. There are 458 colonies with close to 40,000 members in North America.

The colonies are located in Alberta (167), Manitoba (105), Saskatchewan (60), South Dakota (54), Minnesota (9), Montana (50), Washington (5), North Dakota (6), and British Columbia (2).

Visitors Accepted [Mar2005]

HYPATIA HOUSING COOPERATIVE

102 E Gorham St
Madison, WI 53703

608-257-4149
services@madisoncommunity.coop

http://www.madisoncommunity.coop

Began: 1963 | Pop. 14 | Urban | Diet: Other

Hypatia is a community of 13-17 members living in a 150-year old historic mansion with a small city park for a front yard. We are one of 12 houses that are part of the Madison Community Co-op (MCC) system. We enjoy vegetarian and/or vegan dinners, a solar electric and solar hot water system, a patio with large picnic table, and close

Additions and corrections: email: directory@ic.org, *web:* directory.ic.org, *mail: RR 1 Box 156-D, Rutledge MO 63563, USA.*

163

proximity to the Capitol, MATC-Downtown and UW-Madison. We welcome mature members who look forward to community living and participating in house dinners, meetings and labor. [Oct2004]

IBSGÅRDEN

**Ibsgården 62
DK-4000 Roskilde
DENMARK**

ibsgaarden@ibsgaarden.dk

http://www.ibsgaarden.dk

Began: 1980 | Pop. 55
Suburban | Diet: Omnivorous

Community in Roskilde, 30 km west of Copenhagen, Denmark, 21 apartments and a common house.

Visitors Accepted: Please write to our email address some weeks before your visit. We have only quite primitive facilities for overnight guests. [Oct2004]

IDA

planetida@planetida.com
http://www.planetida.com

Began: 1993 | Pop. 8
Rural | Diet: Primarily vegetarian

We are Ida, the all-purpose queer arts community tucked away on 250 acres of nature-ific loveliness in the backwoods of Tennessee. We are an ever-changing arrangement of wimmin, men, trannies and kids trying to live an alternative to consumerist, corporate-controlled spirit-numbing culture. We grow lots of vegetables, build fancy outhouses, play music, dance in caves, produce plays, agitate, bitch, kvetch, hike, and sing. We go to Dairy Queen in tattered dresses. We don't cook animals in our kitchen. We're thankful for our sweet gushing spring, crashing water-falls, and wild animals. We're hell on heels wielding chain saws for firewood. We have dozens of queer neighbors within biking distance. We are your cross-dressing, bread-baking sissy monks. We produce an annual queer music festival called Idapalooza Fruit Jam, in late September. We welcome visitors and are open to new members.

Visitors Accepted: Email or phone us and set up a visit. [Mar2005]

IN PLANNING "ECOVILLAGE"

**Lejoke
Uiterburen 36
Zuidbroek, 9636 EE
NETHERLANDS**

+31-(0)598-452180
leo.joke@tiscali.nl

Forming | Rural | Diet: Omnivorous

Planning a village of up to 150 persons in northern Spain or Portugal.

Keywords: ecological, handicrafts, own energy development, self-supporting in food, shared decisions, neighborliness in and outside the village.

Village life also means that there are animals that are part of our food.

Visitors Accepted [Oct2004]

INFINITE STAR LIGHT OFFERING VISIONARY ECOVILLAGES = ISLOVE

**Little~Star * Thakar Sevedar
PO Box 1086
Ben Lomond, CA 95005**

**831-425-3334
LordLittlestarLibertLafterLife@
yahoo.com**

http://www.infiniteStarLight.org

Bgean: 1965 | Pop: 55 | Forming | Spiritual
Rural | Diet: Vegan only

"infinite star Light offering visionary ecovillages" = "i.s.L.o.v.e." is a resource/networking center for people wishing to form/co-create and/or seek/join intentional communities that are strictly for folks who enjoy living the following simple high-minimum standard of pure 'n' healthy lifestyle: bee-vegan (no meat, fish, fowl, eggs, or dairy) and "straight-edge" (nontoxic, vital 'n' clear natural high way—no alcohol, no smoking, no drugs). This includes the rare but wonderfully excellent requirement of no pets/domestic animals!

Our name used to be Universal Residential Pure Communes Resource Manav Kendra Sant Mat Kindly International Network Divine, which all has meaning so it still helps define our efforts. Anyone who wants to sincerely know the reasons why may simply contact us, preferably if convincing you of the correct-ness of the is wisdom will result in you want-ing to join this all-important global movement!

We will assist present and future communities who sincerely want to upgrade their lifestyle as their practical sensibilities and evolution of consciousness catch up with their purported ideals! We welcome all sorts of

assistance from anyone/everyone! Please contact us for further informationand/or to help in any/every way!

Earnestly, your friends with "Love in True Knowledge 'n' Wisdom!" are happy to be assisted: please share your knowledge of existing communities we may like to visit; contact info of kindred spirits; lands being donated to us for this noble cause, such as pure houses with rooms for rent; and etc... Any and all help appreciated—be creative. Links to volunteer data-banks, etc?!

Evermore acres and many lands all round the earth are needed to save the sensitive tender angel-saints: pure health-oriented lifestyle refuge sanctuaries. Vegan / pure vegetarian sans domestic-animals, eschewing drugs/alcohol/smoking. ethical sans lie-cheat-steal-thievery; gentle sans violence/threats-of-violence. eclectic spiritual with respect for universal truth and humanistic moral character and common sense ethical codes of honor.

Please connect kindred spirits to us and us to them. we'll let you know which community lands we are aware of, many not listed with FIC. And you please let us know of all community opportunities esp. California, Hawaii, Mexico, etc.

Visitors Accepted: Land your space ship in the field near my grove of trees, or hover it over my sleeping head but first send a telepathic message that it is your gentle trustworthy space alien friends come to rescue good humans. Email me and read websites on my yahoo email auto-reply and http://www.infiniteStarLight.org etc. Call our voicemail and say your name and location and all about your purity lifestyle and first say your phone always twice or thrice clearly and slowly. [Mar2005]

INNISFREE VILLAGE

**5505 Walnut Level Rd
Crozet, VA 22932**

**434-823-5400
innisfreevillage@prodigy.net**

http://www.innisfreevillage.org

Began: 1971 | Pop. 75
Rural | Diet: Omnivorous

Nestled in the foothills of the Blue Ridge Mountains, Innisfree Village was founded in 1971 as a creative alternative for adults with mental disabilities (coworkers). We are a service-oriented community located on 550 acres about 20 miles from Charlottesville. Thirty-five adults with mental disabilities live in 10 village houses and two Charlottesville houses, along with 25 full-time volunteers. The community members live together in family-style

---

Scissors [✂] at the end of a listing indicate that it was edited for length by the Directory editors and a longer description can be found at directory.ic.org.

homes and work together in our workstations. The gardens, weavery, woodshop, kitchen, and bakery give meaning to our lives as therapeutic, as well as practical and purposeful work.

Our volunteer "staff," many of whom come from overseas, work and live together with coworkers, helping with their personal care, running a household, and working in the workstations. We ask a one-year minimum commitment for volunteers and offer room, board, medical insurance, and a monthly stipend.

Innisfree is a registered nonprofit corporation, governed by a board of directors. There is an executive director and an assistant director. There are many decisions of daily life that are made by consensus, but certain decisions are made by the board or the director. We are not an egalitarian community and our mission is to create and support a life of respect, empowerment, and creativity for persons with special needs.

If interested in becoming a volunteer, please write for more information. Visitors are welcome if arrangements are made in advance.

Visitors Accepted [Mar2005]

INTER-COOPERATIVE COUNCIL (ICC-MICHIGAN)

Director of Member Services
337 E William St
Ann Arbor, MI 48104

734-662-4414
smtubb@umich.edu

http://www.icc.coop

Began: 1932 | Pop. 560
Urban | Diet: Omnivorous

Inter-Cooperative Council (ICC) was formed in 1937 by the housing co-ops on the University of Michigan campus in order to gain greater efficiency and economy in certain functions, such as recruitment of new members, paying the taxes and mortgages, and overseeing large maintenance projects. In addition, ICC helps train new members and officers so that houses run more smoothly.

Our housing co-ops are owned and managed by the students who live in them. There are 17 group and one apartment house located on both central and north campus. The number of members in each house ranges from 13 to 150, with the aver-

age being about 33. All of our houses are co-ed. We have a substance-free house, non-smoking houses, and houses that serve vegetarian meals.

Houses are run democratically with each member having an equal voice. We rely on members to do all the work needed to run the houses (cooking, cleaning, planning, bookkeeping, etc.). Each member puts in four to six hours of work per week either at the house, ICC office, or through committee work.

Visitors Accepted [Mar2005]

INTER-COOPERATIVE COUNCIL (ICC-TEXAS)

2305 Nueces
Austin, TX 78705

512-476-1957
welcome@iccaustin.coop

http://iccaustin.coop

Began: 1937 | Pop. 187
Urban | Diet: Omnivorous

Established in 1937 and incorporated in 1970, ICC is a student housing cooperative

Listings

Additions and corrections: email: directory@ic.org, web: directory.ic.org, mail: RR 1 Box 156-D, Rutledge MO 63563, USA.

165

in Austin. Student members share the responsibility and benefits of operating our eight co-op houses, while our professional staff maintains a central office. Houses run democratically, and members do all the work to run our houses—cooking, cleaning, etc.—spending four to six hours per week on these tasks.

Our co-ed houses are walking distance to the University of Texas and house 12 to 32 students each. We offer several vegetarian and upper-division houses, and theme houses as well. Our programs and services are aimed to increase access to college education, and we operate as a nonprofit.

Members enjoy being part of local co-op community, and we are active members of NASCO, the federation of student co-ops.

Visitors Accepted: Those interested can either contact the central office to get more information, or contact the houses directly (contact info is on our website). [Oct2004]

INTERNATIONAL COMMUNES DESK (ICD)

Sol Etzioni
Secretary
Kibbutz Tzora
DN Shimshon
99803
ISRAEL

+972-(0)2-990-8365,
+972-(0)2-990-8565
solrene@tzora.co.il

http://www.communa.org.il

The ICD is a contact office between inten-

tional communities of all kinds, all over the world. It is essentially a committee of members of different types of kibbutzim, working mainly on a voluntary basis. It meets every 5 weeks or so at Efal, the kibbutz seminar centre, near Tel Aviv. The core of its work is correspondence, usually in English or Hebrew, although we are also able to translate letters written in German, French, Spanish, Dutch or Portuguese.

Founded in 1976, for the past 12 years the ICD has issued an English-language biannual journal CALL (Communes At Large Letter). It contains articles, newspaper excerpts, and various other information culled from community publications worldwide. CALL is a paper about communities, for communities and by communities. You can receive CALL free of charge, but a donation will be gratefully received, as will items for publication.

We have also set up a website devoted to the various forms of communal living around the world. The term "commune" in our name is for brevity, not exclusiveness—includes all forms of communal living.

Though originally geared to the big wide world, the ICD in recent years has become active on the Israeli scene, where there is a growing "movement" of urban communes.

We are very interested to hear from you, about life in your own community, your ideology, and aims, and your problems—if any. Through such mutual contact, we feel we can help one another by sharing our communal experiences. Any comments on our website or on CALL will be very welcome. [Mar2005][✂]

INTERNATIONAL PUPPYDOGS MOVEMENT

2808 SE 26th Ave
Portland, OR 97202

503-235-3374 (fax)

Began: 1993 | Pop. 4 | Forming | Urban

Puppydogs are known for warmth, humanity, and profoundly social patterns of living. The name "International Puppydogs Movement" comes from the fact that residents like to lie (sometimes sleep) very close together, curled up like puppies in front of the fireplace. Over time we have come to call our basic family unit the "pile," a term that stems from a complex set of overlapping philosophies. There are at least as many philosophies about the group as there are members.

We are a small number of gay and bisexual men, geographically centered in Oregon. At present, most of us own our own homes; in the future we plan to live together cooperatively. We are people attempting to love each other—willingness to accept an atmosphere of heightened communication and intimacy is perhaps the most important qualification for joining us in this search.

Becoming part of an extended intimate family necessarily takes several years of getting to know each other —it's more like falling in love and getting married than signing up for cohousing. However, we have a special interest in gay intentional communities, and can refer callers to other queer communities (e.g., if they prefer a different community type, or want to join one more quickly). We will also provide experience

Scissors [✂] at the end of a listing indicate that it was edited for length by the Directory *editors and a longer description can be found at* directory.ic.org.

and support to anyone who works to form new extended families similar to ours in spirit and vision.

Visitors Not Accepted [Feb2005]

IONA COMMUNITY

The Leader
Savoy House
140 Sauchiehall St
Glasgow G2 3DH Scotland
UNITED KINGDOM

+44-(0)141 332 6343
ionacomm@gla.iona.org.uk

http://www.iona.org.uk

Began: 1938 | Pop. 28 | Spiritual
Rural | Diet: Omnivorous

The Iona Community is an ecumenical Christian community seeking new ways of living out the Gospel in today's world. It comprises nearly 250 members, living throughout Britian and beyond, who are committed to a rule involving a spiritual and economic discipline, regularly meeting together, and action for peace and justice in society.

The community's administrative base is in Glasgow, Scotland, where outreach workers in the fields of worship and youth and the publications department are located, together with general support staff.

The community runs three residential centers (the restored medieval Benedictine monastery and Macleod Centre on the island of Iona, and Camas Adventure Centre nearby on Mull) where over 100 guests come for weeklong programs to share with the resident staff and volunteers in the building of community, and the exploration of the relevance of faith and an integrated spirituality to contemporary issues.

Visitors Accepted: Visitors can share a week with the community following specific programs relative to the concerns of the Iona Community. Details are on the website. [Jan2005]

JACKSON PLACE COHOUSING

800 Hiawatha Pl S
Seattle, WA 98144

Sylvie
206-784-5619
skashdan@scn.org

Kathy
206-522-3099
efestos@cablespeed.com

http://www.seattlecohousing.org

Began: 1996 | Pop. 61
Urban | Diet: Omnivorous

Urban cohousing community; 27 homes; 8 different types, flats and townhomes; 1.5 acres; residents ranging in age from 3 months to upper 70s; 45 adults; 16 chil-

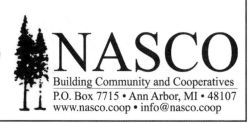
dren, at least 2 on the way; 5 renters, rest are owners.

Visitors Accepted: Contact a week in advance: Sylvie at first email or Kathy at second email. [Oct2004]

JAMAICA PLAIN COHOUSING

PO Box 420
Boston, MA 02130

617-524-6614, 617-522-2209
info@jpcohousing.org
coho@jpcohousing.org

http://www.jpcohousing.org

Began: 1999 | Pop. 55
Urban | Diet: Omnivorous

We are a mixed-income, multigenerational, urban cohousing neighborhood, within walking distance to public transportation, that is committed to being in attunement with its urban setting. As part of that commitment we plan to maintain a system of ride-matching/car-pooling, shared cars, and short-term rental cars, subsidize MBTA fare passes and maintain adequate bicycle stor-

Listings

Additions and corrections: email: directory@ic.org, web: directory.ic.org, mail: RR 1 Box 156-D, Rutledge MO 63563, USA.

167

age facilities. We use a modified consensus process to make decisions and are committed to resolving conflicts through honest, direct and respectful communication. Four hours of member work per month is expected. Participation in group meals is encouraged, but not mandated. We strive to work cooperatively for mutual benefit, while respecting personal autonomy and the privacy of one's home. We actively participate in neighborhood events and are planning to become a CSA drop-off site. We will have an organic garden with onsite composting. We are committed to conserving natural resources through environmentally-sound construction, energy conservation, recycling, and reducing consumption by sharing materials. All common areas and individual units are accessible to people with disabilities. We value diversity and welcome people from all classes, races, cultures, sexual orientations, and traditional and nontraditional families. We have two guest rooms in the common house that are available for short-term stays.

Visitors Accepted: Call on the information line (617-524-6614), send an email to info@jpcohousing.org, or fill out our web form at www.jpcohousing.org. [Mar2005]

JESUS CHRIST'S COMMUNITY AT HEBRON

http://www.jesuschrists.com

Pop. 12 | Spiritual
Rural | Diet: Omnivorous

Community (Ekklesia in Greek, the root word for church) is a calling to live as God has intended us; to have loving relationship together.

We are called by God to live by faith, a witness to Jesus in our midst, by our love for one another and for our neighbor.

We were called to serve in this locale in mid-state New York and by His calling we are a "city of refuge" awaiting His return while proclaiming life in the resurrection.

Our mission as servants is first to His body to "warn-encourage-uplift and affirm" and our witness to our neighbor is to invite you into His abiding love! Our rule is that we are held together by His love.

We are inviting all to enter into relationship with Jesus that leads to life in Him together and eternally.

How may we serve you?!

Visitors Accepted: Please contact us first... call, email or write. [Mar2005]

JESUS CHRISTIANS

Dave
Box A678
Sydney South, NSW 1235
AUSTRALIA

+61-(0)2-4954-2590
fold@idl.net.au
fold@jesuschristians.com

Casey
Box 124-L, 5221 W 102nd St
Los Angeles, CA 90045

310-527-2867
usjesuschristians@yahoo.com

Ufuoma
Box 580
Guildford GU1 1GR England
UNITED KINGDOM
ukteam@britisland.freeserve.co.uk

http://jesuschristians.com

Began: 1980 | Pop. 26 | Spiritual
Urban | Diet: Omnivorous

We sometimes refer to the "larger community" in terms of society in general. However, living in community suggests a group held together by some common unity. It could be language, geographical location, etc. Because we believe that attitudes toward money are fundamental in all human relationship, "living in community" for us means "common ownership."

Visitors Accepted: Visitors should email us, specifying which location is most convenient for them. Please visit our website (and/or request printed information about our beliefs), and then give us some indication that you understand something about what we believe and teach. Nothing quite takes the place of a personal encounter, but it could be a waste of everyone's time if we do not have a fair bit in common before you arrive. [Oct2004]

JINDIBAH

PO Box 264
Bangalow, NSW 2479
AUSTRALIA

+61-(0)2-6687-2244
ic@jindibah-community.org

http://www.jindibah-
community.org

Began: 1994 | Pop. 8 | Spiritual
Rural | Diet: Omnivorous

Welcome to our dream! Jindibah is home

to a small group of people who have turned a former dairy farm in northern New South Wales, Australia, into a small, cooperative community of 12 households. Once, most of us lived and worked in various cities around the world. Now we are re-inventing ourselves as country people, hopefully utilising our city skills to find ways to grow, maintain, share and regenerate a lovely 46ha (113-acre) coastal property, located just outside Byron Bay, Australia's most easterly point.

We are aiming to provide ourselves with a simpler, more creative and productive life, without the stresses of city living. We'd like it to be natural and real—while using the latest technology (like our community wireless broadband cooperative) to connect us with the "real world."

The property is quiet and rural, yet it's only minutes from the Pacific Highway, which runs along the entire east coast of Australia. As luck would have it, we're within easy reach of three airports, five shopping towns, private and public schools, a university and all kinds of transport—not to mention many excellent beaches where surfers share the waves with dolphins. As Byron Bay is a tourist town, we're well supplied with holiday-type ways to relax, if the pressure of growing the veggies gets too much.

We are about finding a sustainable balance between social, environmental and economic life—remembering that if it's not fun, it's probably not sustainable.

Visitors Accepted: Email us. [Oct2004]

JONES HOUSE

House President
917-923 S Forest Ave
Ann Arbor, MI 48104

734-996-2396

http://www.icc.coop

Pop. 42

We are a student cooperative house with 23 rooms, housing 42 people. We have dinner every day but Saturday, and a vegetarian option is always available. Amenities include TV, VCR, fish room, fireplace, pool table, and tire swing.

Visitors Accepted: Contact the House President. [Mar2005]

Scissors [✂] at the end of a listing indicate that it was edited for length by the Directory editors and a longer description can be found at directory.ic.org.

JULIAN WOODS COMMUNITY

Community Inquiries
215 Julian Woods Ln
Julian, PA 16844

814-355-5755, 814-355-8026
abwilken@verizon.net
fors1@mac.com

Began: 1970 | Pop. 19 | Rural

Julian Woods (established 1975) is a diverse group of 18 adults and three children on 140 acres. The common land is in a School of Living land trust. We are located 15 miles from Pennsylvania State University. Members may own or lease home lots after a capital investment. Families are autonomous, financially independent, and own their own homes. Community decisions are made by consensus. We own and operate a living machine in two greenhouses which serves as our wastewater-treatment system and provides us with some indoor, almost year-round, growing space. We have lots of gardens (and lots of deer), a recreational pond, and an interest in finding others interested in working with us to continue to build our community.

There are six artists, several carpenters and builders, an accountant, a forester and a mechanic/designer.

Tom's Community Woodworks repairs and refinishes furniture.

Barbara has created a beautiful space for meditation and yoga in O-AN Zendo.

Jean teaches PSU classes in art and deep ecology so students experience woods and pond in community.

Some of us dream of some kind of community/learning center that would serve as a gathering space.

Visitors Accepted: Call, write, or email in advance. [Mar2005]

JUMP OFF COMMUNITY LAND TRUST

1499 Tate Trail
Sewanee, TN 37375

931-598-5120

Began: 1990 | Pop. 12
Rural | Diet: Omnivorous

Our purpose is to promote and encourage environmental awareness by maintaining our land for wilderness, educational, and homestead uses; to demonstrate an ecologically sustainable lifestyle that includes affordable housing, energy efficiency, and sustainable agriculture within a cooperative community; and to host seminars, workshops, speakers, and research residencies in natural sciences, arts, spirituality, and related subjects.

We support each other in our livelihoods, spiritual growth, arts and crafts, and other projects. The land is owned in common, but we each have our own house, income, car, tools, etc.

We have 1100 acres of land, 30 acres cleared, and the balance woodland that has been protected for over 55 years. A resident member may sell, bequeath, or rent their residence subject to approval of the other members. The number of households is limited to ten and are situated around the original farm. The residents' agreement restricts toxins from being used on the land such as pesticides/herbicides. Most of the 1100 acres are left "forever wild."

Visitors Accepted: Phone or write before a visit. [Mar2005]

JUPITER HOLLOW

Kaia
2621 Keith Fork Rd
Weston, WV 26452

304-269-4207, 304-269-6034
sweetkaia@hotmail.com
kimmel4875@aol.com

Began: 1976 | Pop. 4 | Rural

We began as a community in 1976 and have progressed to now, the spring of 2005, with our focus being on friendship, neighborliness, ecological awareness, and a desire for lives in harmony with nature. At present we have four resident stockholder members and one non-stockholder resident. There is one empty house, which is available for rent and possibly sale at a later date. There is also an empty house for rent or purchase, which was formerly part of the community, but which now has a deed along with one acre.

Although we live our lives individually, we share 180 acres of beautiful wooded land and a sense of stewardship for it. The possibilities for this community's future lie in the visions of present and future participants.

Visitors Accepted [Mar2005]

KAKWA ECOVILLAGE

Russ
PO Box 725
McBride, BC V0J2E0
CANADA

info@kakwaecovillage.com

http://www.kakwaecovillage.com

Began: 2003 | Forming
Rural | Diet: Omnivorous

Kakwa Ecovillage is:
• A forming community on 540 acres in a beautiful mountain valley, on one of the best salmon rivers in the world.
• Certified as an organic farm surrounded by limitless potential for ecotourism, including great skiing.
• A place in time and a melange of current world influences dedicated to building a sustainable culture: Findhorn, Crystal Waters, and the Centre for Alternative Technology.

Values honored include: consensus decision making, right livelihood, renewable energy, world music, sacred dance, a spiritual path, alternative medicine and education.

Visitors Accepted: Email an introduction and receive a confirmation. [Mar2005]

KALANI OCEANSIDE RETREAT

Jared Sam
RR 2 Box 4500
Pahoa, HI 96778

808-965-0468 ext 117
volunteer@kalani.com

http://www.kalani.com

Began: 1973 | Pop. 40
Rural | Diet: Primarily vegetarian

Kalani is a community of long-term residents and short-term (three-month) resident volunteers, as well as others from the area, all of whom operate a not-for-profit educational conference center and retreat on a 113-acre coastal site. Kalani provides on-site visitor experiences and outreach programs that support the well-being of the local environment and communities.

Kalani is great for year-round personal getaways or group retreats (up to 125)! Kalani is the only coastal lodging facility

Listings

Additions and corrections: email: directory@ic.org, web: directory.ic.org, mail: RR 1 Box 156-D, Rutledge MO 63563, USA.

169

within the Aloha State's largest conservation area.

Kalani treats you to delicious, wholesome cuisine; comfortable, affordable accommodation options; Olympic pool/spa; massage therapies; traditional culture; and a rainbow of seminars. Kalani-sponsored seminars usually are six nights, seven days, beginning with dinner, ending with lunch.

Nearby are thermal springs, a dolphin beach, orchid farms, snorkel tidal pools, steam bathing, waterfalls, botanical gardens, historic villages, and spectacular Volcanos National Park.

Visitors Accepted: Visit our website. [Mar2005]

KANSAS CITY PROJECT

Jeff Martin
Kansas City, MO 64109

913-488-7992
dogshed@gmail.com
gbleemy@yahoo.com

Pop. 1 | Forming | Urban

I am interested in finding other people interested in sharing a house for the purposes of supporting each other in our various projects.

The first project will be remodeling the house, therefore one must be willing to live in construction dust. The house is near Linwood and Prospect in Kansas City, MO.

Please email me about yourself and your projects. [Jan2005]

KAREN CATHOLIC WORKER HOUSE

Tony Hilkin or Jenny Truax
1840 Hogan St
Saint Louis, MO 63106

314-621-4052

Began: 1977 | Pop. 8 | Spiritual
Urban | Diet: Primarily vegetarian

We are a Catholic Worker community established 27 years ago. Eight of us offer our home (an old convent) to 25-30 homeless women and children in north St. Louis.

Our main focuses are personalism and hospitality, but we also live out resistance, nonviolence, voluntary poverty, anarchism, and sustainability.

Some members have started a cohousing community with former guests of Karen House. There are currently four families and five Workers who live in apartments/houses within the Karen House neighborhood.

The Roundtable is a three-times-yearly publication produced by our community.

People who are interested in Karen House may write us a letter or call. We would of course do our best to answer any of your questions and perhaps arrange a visit.

Visitors Accepted: Call us or write us a letter. [Mar2005]

KASHI ASHRAM

11155 Roseland Rd
Sebastian, FL 32958

772-589-1403 ext 104
radhe@kashi.org
kashinfo@kashi.org

http://www.kashi.org

Began: 1976 | Pop. 87 | Spiritual
Small Town | Diet: Vegetarian only

Kashi Ashram is an interfaith spiritual community founded in 1976 by Ma Jaya Sati Bhagavati, a US-born spiritual teacher. The community embraces the sacred practices of many traditions. The essence of the teaching is based upon loving kindness, compassion, and a commitment to the truth through service to humanity and to oneself. Ma offers a spiritual path alive with color, creativity, love, service, and the rituals of many faiths.

The community stretches over 80 acres of woodlands with a number of shared residences. At the center of the ashram there is a large pond surrounded by temples and shrines to many of the world's religions. This pond symbolically represents the Ganges, the sacred river of India.

Kashi is a community of service, taking care of people in need. The River Fund, established in 1990, is dedicated to providing loving, nurturing care for people with challenging illnesses, especially people with HIV and AIDS.

In addition to serving and educating, Kashi fosters spiritual growth. People come to Kashi seeking a deeper, more meaningful, and fulfilling life. Through the uniqueness of this community many lives have been transformed. The Kashi Center for Advanced Spiritual Studies offers workshops, retreats, and intensives. Residents teach meditation, yoga, and kirtan, and facilitate workshops and seminars. Visitors are welcome—every Saturday night there is a free vegetarian dinner followed by darshan with Ma Jaya.

Visitors Accepted: Visitors are welcome. It is best to call the office beforehand to arrange for a visit. [Mar2005]

KEIMBLATT OEKODORF

Altenmarkt 95
Riegersburg, 8333
AUSTRIA

+43-(0)676-601-56-47
dialog@oekodorf.or.at

http://www.oekodorf.or.at

Began: 2001 | Pop. 2 | Forming
Rural | Diet: Primarily vegan

We are a group of people who aim to make the dream of an ecovillage in Austria come true. Our goal is to create a community of 150 to 300 people living together on the path to peaceableness, sustainability and self-development.

It is our vision to live with love and peace amongst ourselves and within nature. We strive to be aware of our social and ecological responsibility and to create space for each individual's personal development. In order to make this vision come true, a welcoming and open-minded village is being founded in which all generations, forms of life, and convictions can find their place within a context of sustainability and peacefulness.

The ecovillage will encompass 30–50 hectares and provide living space for 150–300 people. This large size requires precise long-term planning. The timeframes given (see www.oekodorf.or.at in English and German) are approximated using the experiences of other ecovillages and are meant as reference points. Our project aims to achieve the maximum of transparency and acceptance. Therefore it is important to make clear and emphasize the benefits the ecovillage brings to the region and its people.

Of utmost importance for such a large (and for Austria so unique) project is symbiosis on all levels. During the entire process everyone affected will be invited to work with us. The realization of this project will bring a great many benefits to the region.

Visitors Accepted: Check out our website (English and German) then contact us and coordinate a suitable time. Bring with you: toothbrush, sleeping bag, camping mat, clothes, musical instrument (if possible), good mood. [Mar2005]

KERALA COMMUNE

keralacommune@yahoo.com
http://www.sahjivan.org

Forming

Objectives: organic farming, solar power for lighting, bio-gas produced at the commune

---

Scissors [✂] at the end of a listing indicate that it was edited for length by the Directory *editors and a longer description can be found at* directory.ic.org.

for cooking, teaching how to be energy efficient, gender equality, common property, struggle against globalization, saying "No" to corporate funding, and teaching how to treat oneself when one gets ill (by using a natural raw diet and not to depend on drugs at heavy costs).

Kerala Commune, situated on a bank of a beautiful river called Bhavani, in the valleys of Mallisswara Mudi, a great mystic mountain, in a serene, pleasant atmosphere. The temperature is cool because of the high altitude. The commune is in south India, in the state of Kerala.

Mostly we are vegans, but we are not fanatic about eating fresh or cooked veggies alone. One can have fish or meat at times. We have fruits (including bananas) and legumes and coconuts produced at the commune.

Visitors from Europe or from the US will have to pay to stay at the commune. We follow organic farming, natural pesticides, and teach farmers around the commune to get out of using the chemical fertilizers and poisonous pesticides that have been proven dangerous to all kinds of life forms on this planet. We are advocates of alternate energy resources. We teach people to be self-sufficient in energy, and to take care of oneself when one gets ill. A society like India is male dominated in its fascist sense. We teach and practice gender equality and adult relationships in a democratic and free spirit.

Visitors Accepted [Jan2005][✂]

KHULA DHAMMA

+27-(0)83-354-8321
khuladhamma@mtnice.co.za

Began: 2003 | Pop. 4 | Forming | Spiritual
Rural | Diet: Vegetarian only

Five friends purchased land near the coastal village of Haga Haga in the eastern cape of South Africa in 2000. Since then five other members have joined and three have moved on. The land is just over 300 hectares of rolling "bush veld" with lush greenbelts, bordered by the Quko river.

Although all residents meditate and study the Teachings of the Buddha, the community is open to all seeking peace of mind and a harmonious environment congenial for the pro-active quest of ego dissolution. We, therefore, kindly request that all visitors and guests refrain from bringing any non-vegetarian food, weapons or intoxicating substances to Khula Dhamma.

Our shared vision for the future:
A balanced synthesis between a vibrant self-sufficient community and a retreat for silent meditation. Bringing together simple, natural and creative living into a sensitive and supportive environment for a diverse, yet attuned, tribe.

The community is a village-style set-up, with each family, couple or individual enjoying their own private space, but all contributing to the "greater whole." Without sacrifice or compromise we are naturally able to combine the greater good of the tribe with our own, understanding that they are ultimately one and the same.

Although some rays of our vision are starting to shimmer, many will take time and loving, energetic dedication to manifest. In all humility we hold no attachment to our dreams. Indeed we honour the journey itself as the goal.

Visitors Accepted: Please contact us via email at least one month before intended visit. [Mar2005][✂]

KIBBUTZ LOTAN

Mark Naveh
DN Hevel Eilot 88855
ISRAEL
+972-(0)8-6356888,
+972-(0)8-6356935
lotan-ecocenter@lotan.ardom.co.il
lotan-office@lotan.ardom.co.il
http://www.kibbutzlotan.com

Began: 1983 | Pop. 100 | Spiritual
Rural | Diet: Kosher

Kibbutz Lotan is situated in the Arava Desert in Israel's south, established in 1983 by graduates of the Reform Jewish youth movements from Israel and overseas. We came together to create a community based on a modern liberal approach to Judaism that strives to fulfill values of equality between the sexes, equality in work, and genuine communication between people. Lotan's population is equally divided between native-born Israelis and immigrants from all over the world. Hebrew is the commonly used language but English is also spoken. Our economy is based on date plantations, dairy, tourism, holistic health center, field crops, mariculture and professions held by members working outside the kibbutz. Presently we number 50 adult members and 50 children. We maintain a cooperative lifestyle with shared means of production and resources.

Lotan's Center for Creative Ecology was established as an expression of our Progressive Jewish and Eco-Zionist orientation. Rooted in "Tikun Olam," the Jewish concept for repairing and transforming the world, the Center began with a small desert organic garden, and expanded to include an ecological theme park, migratory bird reserve, nature trails, alternative building construction, and an ecological education center that combines hands-on, experiential environmental education with Jewish values within the framework of a living community.

Kibbutz Lotan is actively seeking new members, particularly single people and couples between the ages of 25-35.

Visitors Accepted: Please contact Mark Naveh at lotan-ecocenter@lotan.ardom.co.il. [Mar2005]

KIBBUTZ MIGVAN

Hashaked St
Sderot, 87013
ISRAEL

nomika@migvan.co.il
http://www.migvan.org.il

Began: 1987

The idea of the "urban kibbutz" was born in 1987, when some young adults, mostly kibbutzniks, looked for ways to influence Israeli society. The desert development town of Sderot was chosen as a place where a small community could carry out significant work. The original group included six members, but today has 60 adults and children.

At Migvan, the individual is the focus. The goal is to allow members to develop according to their needs and desires, as far as personal, social involvement, family, education, and professional aspects are concerned—a definite shift from the traditional kibbutz concept.

Migvan's finances operate communally, salaries being pooled and monthly personal/family budgets allotted to kibbutz members. The main income sources are the Gvanim Association for Education and Community Involvement (including welfare, immigrant absorption and services to the disabled) and Migvan Effect, a high tech company.

The children, an important part of the community, are enrolled in local or regional schools, depending on the choice of the parents. Some members have become active, along with local parents, in creating an alternative school setting.

Cultural activities are of major importance. Sabbath, holidays, family and community events are organized by members, creating ceremonies which integrate Jewish tradition with modern and humanistic val-

Additions and corrections: email: directory@ic.org, web: directory.ic.org, mail: RR 1 Box 156-D, Rutledge MO 63563, USA.

171

ues. The adults have a fortnightly study day framework covering various subjects. [Mar2005]

THE KIBBUTZ MOVEMENT

13 Leonardo Da Vinci St
Tel Aviv, 61400
ISRAEL

+972-(0)3-6925258,
+972-(0)3-6951195 (fax)
ran@kba.org.il
solrene@tzora.co.il

International Communes Desk
Yad Tabenkin
Seminar Efal
Ramat Efal, 52960
ISRAEL

+972-(0)2-9908365,
+972-(0)3-5346078
solrene@tzora.co.il
yaakovsy-t@bezeqint.net

http://www.kibbutz.org.il/eng/
welcome.htm

Approaching its centennial year, the Israeli kibbutz movement—despite crises and changes—is still the largest communitarian movement in the world. The 279 kibbutzim include about 115,600 souls, close to 2% of the population. Each kibbutz is a social-economic autonomous unit. Most kibbutzim are rural, multi-generational, combine agriculture and industry, are at least 50 years old, and range in size between 150 and 600 souls. Since kibbutzim have always been an integral part of the country, kibbutzniks participate significantly in almost all spheres of life. Three kibbutz members sit in the Israeli parliament and one of them, a woman, is a deputy-minister.

The great majority of kibbutzim belong to the Kibbutz Movement (KM), the remaining 16 forming the Religious Kibbutz Movement. The pluralistic KM includes some kibbutzim that are religious (from ultra-orthodox to reform), spiritualistic, anarchist, educational or ecological. All are more or less politically left-wing.

Originally each kibbutz lived by the maxim, "From each according to his ability, to each according to his need." Over the years, more money has been allocated to personal budgets in most kibbutzim. Various factors have created in many a lack of confidence in the future of the classic kibbutz way of life. (For analyses of this crisis, see our website.) Many kibbutzim now exemplify, "From each according to his ability, to each according to his contribution."

Since "kibbutz" is a legal entity in Israel, two kinds of kibbutzim are about to be legally defined: "Communal Kibbutzim," in which only minimal changes from the original principles have been made; and "New-style/Changing Kibbutzim," in which considerable changes are being/have been made.

Even the "New-style Kibbutz," taking responsibility for its weaker members, will be at least as economically communal as most intentional communities around the world.

The kibbutz has always invested much in education and almost all sons and daughters finish high school and go on to tertiary education. Informal education has received a high priority, especially in the arts and sports. The kibbutz movement has established a number of high-level academic institutions and artistic projects.

Associated with the KM is a growing number of urban communes, dedicated to bettering Israeli society, and linked to four new education-geared kibbutzim. Similarly, the four urban kibbutzim concentrate on social work and education. [Mar2005]

KIBBUTZ TAMUZ

Hanan Cohen
Beit Shemesh, 99000
ISRAEL

+972-(0)2-9900125
info@tamuz.org.il
hanan@info.org.il

http://www.tamuz.org.il

Began: 1987 | Pop. 61 | Spiritual
Urban | Diet: Omnivorous

Kibbutz Tamuz is located in the city of Beit Shemesh, Israel, which is approximately 30 minutes west of Jerusalem. The kibbutz was founded in the summer of 1987 by nine people who had previously been active in the kibbutz movement on other kibbutzim but had been disillusioned with the traditional kibbutz. The kibbutz belongs to the United Kibbutz Movement and is one of three urban kibbutzim in the country.

Kibbutz Tamuz is an urban kibbutz, a small Jewish community, and like the traditional kibbutz, Tamuz is a collective. Its 33 members function as a single economic unit, expressing the socialist ideals of equality and cooperation, ideas and praxis. However, unlike the traditional kibbutz, we are located in an urban environment, keeping us in tune with what is happening in society around us.

Equality and collectivism, like in the traditional kibbutz, are expressed through financial, social, and culture cooperation. All salaries and incomes are given to the kibbutz, and the members receive a budget according to the size of their family. The kibbutz covers all housing, health, transportation, and joint cultural expenses, and the personal budget covers the rest (unlike on most traditional kibbutzim, food and utilities are paid for by the member's personal budget). Any jobs or activities that need to be done around the kibbutz are done by members volunteering at weekly general assembly meetings, which also deal with decisions that have to be made by the group.

Visitors Accepted [Mar2005]

KINDNESS HOUSE

PO Box 61619
Durham, NC 27715

919-304-2220, 919-304-3220 (fax)

http://www.humankindness.org

Began: 1993 | Pop. 14 | Spiritual
Rural | Diet: Primarily vegetarian

Kindness House is a rural interfaith spiritual community that revolves around service. Our main work is to run the Human Kindness Foundation and its long-standing Prison-Ashram Project, which keeps us in touch with tens of thousands of people around the world.

If you are familiar with Bo Lozoff's writings or talks, you already have some idea of our lifestyle: a threefold focus of simple living, committed spiritual practice, and a dedication to service. If you are not familiar with his work, you may visit our website or order materials from our catalog in order to get a basic feel for the views and evolution of our organization and community.

We believe that in order to be of service to others, we must always continue to deepen our own spiritual realization. Our community life emphasizes work, practice, and study in a spirit of simple joy, mindfulness, and quietude; seeing every task equally as spiritual practice; every moment worthy of equal respect and attention.

There are several ways to join us in our work and community life—as a visitor, an intern, a parolee, or a member of our staff. If you wish to visit Kindness House, please contact us for information at least a month in advance, with your preferred dates clearly noted.

Visitors Accepted: Call or write, giving us your snail-mail address, and request our visitor information/application form. For

Scissors [✂] at the end of a listing indicate that it was edited for length by the Directory *editors and a longer description can be found at* directory.ic.org.

brief visits (not overnight), it's OK just to call and ask for a time to come out—no mailed info needed. [Feb2005]

KING EDWARD HOUSE

2822 W King Edward Ave
Vancouver, BC V6L 1T9
CANADA

604-731-2370
info@
    vancouvercooperativehouse.com
http://www.vancouvercooperative
    house.com

Began: 1974 | Pop. 6
Urban | Diet: Primarily vegetarian

For over 30 years King Edward House has been a cooperative household in Vancouver, British Columbia. We share vegetarian meals, social gatherings, environmental consciousness, ideas and laughter. Our household is usually made up of six people. This is a special place to live, and enriches the lives of those that live here.

We buy our groceries primarily from local organic suppliers. Each member of the community cooks one vegetarian dinner per week, and we share food shopping and household chores.

King Edward House regularly hosts members of our extended community as dinner guests, party guests, and for special events (such as book club meetings, intentional community study groups and lantern-making workshops). Our community extends to many people who have touched our lives as past housemates, or simply as regular visitors to our home.

We have more composters per capita than any place that we know of, and gargoyles abound in our yard. This is a home where you can hear live classical music while acupuncture takes place upstairs. We have a wildlife tree in our backyard that lists the varieties of bird life that we have counted in our natural habitat. We have created a front yard that is filled with plant life indigenous to the Pacific Northwest. Our large, character-filled home has hardwood floors, a fireplace, big trees and a great view of the mountains and the city. We are close to two major bus routes, and we have great storage for bicycles.

Visitors Accepted: Contact us in advance via email or by phone. We prefer to choose a time when many of us are here to meet our visitors and exchange information and ideas. [Mar2005]

KING HOUSE

803 E Kingsley St
Ann Arbor, MI 48104

http://www.icc.coop

Pop. 8 | Urban

King House is a nonsmoking apartment cooperative with six units.

Current ICC members have priority for signing contracts. King contracts are for 12 months, September 1–August 31. Apartments are not furnished. However, kitchen appliances, washer and dryer, and on-site parking are available. King is required to contribute to the ICC governance structure by electing a president to sit on the ICC board. King also encourages members to either sit on an ICC committee or provide ICC office labor. Other house jobs include yard maintenance, serving as maintenance manager, purchasing supplies, and acting as treasurer.

Visitors Accepted: Contact House President. [Mar2005]

KINGMAN HALL

House Manager
1730 La Loma Ave
Berkeley, CA 94709

510-841-6455

http://kingmanhall.org

Began: 1977 | Pop. 50
Urban | Diet: Primarily vegetarian

The essence of our former identity, the Living Love Center, permeates the wandering nooks and spaces in this house; be it in ephemeral murals found up here or behind there or within the constant flux of kindred spirits. Smile, smile, smile.

Although just one block from the UC Berkeley campus, our serene backyard features a stream, a huge redwood tree, a hot tub, and a natural ampitheater.

"Kingman has a giant amoeba-shaped dining room table that everyone can sit around and face each other while enjoying good food and gooder conversation." —Zak (English major)

It is a really social place here and great for networking.

Kingman Hall is above all a home for 49

Additions and corrections: email: directory@ic.org, *web:* directory.ic.org, *mail:* RR 1 Box 156-D, Rutledge MO 63563, USA.

students who get to experience communal living with all its benefits and all its drawbacks.

"Indeed, Kingman surpasses all expectations." —Half-Fish.

We are one of 17 co-ops associated with the University Students Cooperative Association (usca.org).

Visitors Accepted [Mar2005]

KIPLING CREEK

Frances or Michael Wirth
PO Box 123
Kipling, NC 27543

919-810-5019, 919-810-4810
wirth@peoplepc.com

http://mypeoplepc.com/members/
wirth/kiplingcreekcohousing

Began: 2005 | Forming

Conveniently located near Research Triangle Park/Raleigh, North Carolina, Kipling Creek has a 110 acre parcel of rolling forest, fields and streams. The old Strawberry Hill farm has approximately 32 acres of fields, 65+ acres of mature pines and hardwood forests and the remainder in streams/wetlands/riparian buffer zones... complete with beaver dams and abundant wildlife.

We envision interconnected clustered village pods that will produce a small human footprint on the land. The remainder is to be managed by a proper conservation plan/measures that will promote a sustainable community through organic farming, and plenty of open space for horses/llamas/goats. We are on the grid, DSL is available, county water is available now, and sewer service will be in about a year.

We are within 5-6 minutes of some of North Carolina's best rated schools, 30 minutes to downtown Raleigh, and 45 minutes to RTP (Reseach Triangle Park). Nearby Raven's Rock State Park has miles of hiking/equestrian trails and rock climbing. The Cape Fear River is a stone's throw away for the pleasures of canoeing, kayaking and water sports.

Bring your planning ideas, conservation skills, and, most importantly, visions of a dynamic community.

Presently one of the most important issues being dealt with is land use planning with county authorities. This in itself is not a casual feat, so a professional planner/architect is in the process of being selected.

Visitors Accepted: Please call the listed number to arrange a visit. [Mar2005]

KITEZH CHILDREN'S ECO-VILLAGE COMMUNITY

Kaluzhskaya Oblast
249650 Baryatinsky
RUSSIAN FEDERATION

+7-(0)8454-23224
kitezh@kaluga.ru
ecoliza@rmplc.co.uk

http://www.kitezh.org

Began: 1992 | Pop. 55 | Spiritual
Rural | Diet: Omnivorous

Kitezh is an exciting place, one of a kind in Russia, a community of happiness and joyful refuge for abandoned or orphaned Russian children. Kitezh is a new way of looking at life: it is a living, working community, a spiritual movement of people who build their lives on the principles of harmony, peace, and love. Kitezhans aim to live in harmony with nature. They are warm, openhearted. By serving others, they serve themselves.

Since 1992 Kitezh has functioned as a community of foster families who offer secure homes and schooling for orphaned Russian children. At present seven families with 30 children live 300 km south of Moscow in Kaluga region on 90 hectares of land, and Kitezh is growing fast. They have already built 10 houses, a school, a church, and an organic farm. The Kitezh school is recognized by the state.

Every summer volunteers and students from all over the world come to Kitezh to help: building, gardening, and working with the children. You're welcome!

The Kitezh way of fostering and educating children has already proved a real alternative to state orphanages. One day communities based on the Kitezh model will replace all orphanages in Russia. This is our dream, to give loving homes and a future to **all** orphan children.

Visitors Accepted [Mar2005]

KNOWLEDGE FARM

38211 Union St
Willoughby, OH 44094

301-395-0541
thefarm@idontknowdude.com

http://farm.idontknowdude.com

Began: 2004 | Forming | Rural

Knowledge Farm is the name of the farm community we would like to develop. There is no actual farm or property yet. Right now there is just an idea with interest from many people. We are basically in Phase I,

which involves finding 10 to 15 people interested in purchasing land or just living on it with the intent of developing this idea.

Knowledge Farm will be located on a yet undetermined plot of land (hopefully 75+ acres) somewhere in Ohio. Our current plan is to meet with those interested and begin finding a proposed location. If necessary, there is an individual prepared to purchase the land on their own under the nonprofit organization which will encompass the Knowledge Farm.

Visitors Accepted: Send email. [Jan2005]

KOINONIA

Volunteer Coordinator
1324 Georgia Hwy 49 S
Americus, GA 31719

229-924-0391
volunteer@koinoniapartners.org

Products Department
products@koinoniapartners.org

http://www.koinoniapartners.org

Began: 1942 | Pop. 33 | Spiritual
Rural | Diet: Omnivorous

We are an intentional Christian community welcoming people of all faiths. Koinonia was founded in 1942 by farmer and theologian Clarence Jordan, survived persecution in the 1950s-1970s for its interracialism and pacifism, and went on to become the birthplace of Habitat for Humanity International and other social justice organizations. To us, following the teachings of Jesus means treating neighbors equally, loving our enemies as well as our friends, and living a simple, shared life. We seek a daily balance between work, service, prayer and play.

Our 573 acres of land in rural Georgia are home to pecan orchards, fields of crops, an organic garden, a museum, woodshop, dining hall, chapel, residences and two neighborhoods of Partnership Housing, and wooded areas including a Peace Trail. Our ministries include a community outreach center with programs for youth and elders; a local home-repair partnership; hospitality to visitors; a volunteer program; and education on peace and justice, religious faith, Koinonia history, etc. To support our community we sell books, community-made arts and crafts, treats made from the pecans we grow, baked goods, etc., through our store and catalog. We are also sustained by donations, farm revenues, and the labor and prayers of our community and its supporters.

We welcome visitors and volunteers. We have guest housing as well as RV

Scissors [✂] at the end of a listing indicate that it was edited for length by the Directory editors and a longer description can be found at directory.ic.org.

accessibility and are working on a campground. Please contact us for information about our volunteer program, which is the first step towards membership in our community.

Visitors Accepted: Please contact us to fill out an application so that we may reserve housing for you. We can accommodate individuals and groups. Most come to volunteer, but some use our space as a retreat/sabbatical space/conference center. We have suggested donations, but we are open to anyone. [Mar2005]

KOMAJA

Komaja Meditationsschule and Foundation
Mittelurmi
6442 Gersau, Schwyz
SWITZERLAND

+41-(0)41-397-05-50,
+41-(0)41-397-05-51
info@komaja.org

http://www.komaja.org

Began: 1978 | Pop. 300 | Spiritual
Diet: Vegetarian only

"Komaja" means "radiant love." It describes a spiritual-philosophical system, as well as an international spiritual community founded in 1978 by the well-known tantric master Aba Aziz Makaja. Komaja offers a deep and non-dogmatic access to spirituality with a complete system of spiritual schooling.

Komaja is a specific form of tantric kundalini yoga, developed by Makaja, who as spiritual master is at the core of Komaja's life and development. Knowledge is Komaja's connecting spiritual thread, radiant love its principal virtue. The seven main activities of the community are: meditation, theoretical studies, development of community consciousness, Karma Yoga, spiritualization of sexuality (via asceticism or by being sexually active; original methods of realization are given for both paths), spiritual singing, and spiritual sport.

Today Komaja has more than 300 members and many friends who draw inspiration from its model of living. They live all over Europe, in Australia, and North America. Makaja and his community are socially involved in many countries, with humanitarian and ecological activities, scientific and educational/therapeutic activities, etc. Komaja is a member of the World Association for Sexology. Komaja's Love-Erotic Therapy (LET) for overcoming different kinds of addictions is privately and state

financed. Komaja is an example of how new forms of intimate relationships can be lived successfully: many people practise the zajedna, an original form of polyamory.

Visitors Accepted: Please write to us well ahead to arrange your visit. During the visit, the consumption of drugs, alcohol and nicotine, as well as animal carcasses, is not permitted. [Mar2005]

KOMUN

Istanbul
TURKEY
nothingized@yahoo.com

Began: 2001 | Pop. 14 | Urban | Diet: Other

An alternative life practice, in the name of equality, love and freedom.
An idea of sharing the life's itself.
Visitors Accepted: Email us. [Nov2004]

KOOKABURRA PARK ECO-VILLAGE

Grant Davies
3 Kookaburra Park Eco-Village
M/S 368
Gin Gin, Queensland 4671
AUSTRALIA

+61-(0)7-41-572759,
+61-(0)7-41-544178
grant@davies.id.au
grant@ic.org

http://kookaburra.eco-village.com.au

Began: 2003 | Pop. 80 | Forming
Small Town | Diet: Omnivorous

Kookaburra Park Eco-Village is situated just 2.5 km from a small township called Gin Gin on the main highway north (Bruce Highway) in Queensland. We are about 360 km north of Brisbane and the closest major city is Bundaberg (about 48 km away). Kookaburra Park has been developing for the past 10 years in stages. The concept is that the 485-acre parcel has a potential of 124 one-acre lots owned as freehold within the surrounding land, which is owned in common by the lot holders. The design and layout of the lots in the Park has been done using permaculture principles, and it runs under a piece of legislation in Queensland called the Body Corporate and Community Management Act. (If you know Crystal Waters Permaculture Village then you will understand the concept.) Kookaburra Park Eco-Village was designed by Max Lindegger and his staff, the same people who designed Crystal Waters. We created Kookaburra Park as a form of sustainable development that

we hoped would appeal to mainstream people who want to belong to a community and have some ecological awareness. So far we have developed some 80 or so lots and have 38 homes built. We have a real cross-section of people living at the Park at present with lots of kids. If you would like to join us please don't hesitate to contact us.

Visitors Accepted: Contact us. Mainly WWOOFing, working for accommodation and board. [Oct2004]

KVUTSAT YOVEL

everyone@kvutsatyovel.com
http://www.kvutsatyovel.com

Began: 1999 | Spiritual | Urban

Kvutsat Yovel is an intimate group that lives in the northern Israeli town of Migdal Ha'Emek. We are six new immigrants from the UK and North America who, after spending three and a half years living as a community in Jerusalem, moved to Migdal Ha'Emek in order to join with four other intimate groups of native Israelis. Together, there are 45 of us here in five small groups, building our own new community in a model which is perhaps best described as an urban kibbutz of groups. The age range amongst our members is 24-35, with all of the Israelis having finished in the army, and all of the Anglos having finished their first degrees. There are many long-term couples, several of whom are married. There are three children and one more on the way.

Visitors Accepted [Jan2005]

L'ACADEMIE YNYS WYTH

J. D. Snetselaar
Ynys Wyth
2072 E Bennett, C-7
Springfield, MO 65804

417-890-1554
Brijdrix@webtv.net
Mr_Snetselaar@webtv.net

http://community.webtv.net/
Brijdrix/LACADEMIEYNYSWYTH

We are a Blue Star Pagan academic circle with many community-based projects including the Pagan school for all ages and for all walks of life. One of our projects is

Additions and corrections: email: directory@ic.org, *web:* directory.ic.org, *mail:* RR 1 Box 156-D, Rutledge MO 63563, USA.

175

publishing of genealogical and metaphysical publications including the serial and subscription based newspaper/magazine, *The Coligny*.

Our primary goal, however, is using the diverse talents that are available out there, nurturing those talents, and providing internal validation and accreditation for the purpose of obtaining Sanctuary Land(s) to engage in Nature Preservation Project(s).

By design we are able to nurture growth perpetually. [Mar2005]

L'ARCHE MOBILE

Amy Stenson
151 S Ann St
Mobile, AL 36604

251-438-2094
larchmob@hotmail.com

http://www.larcheusa.org

Began: 1974 | Pop. 44 | Spiritual
Urban | Diet: Omnivorous

L'Arche Mobile is a Christian community that provides family-like homes for people with a mental handicap and assistants who choose to live in our community homes. Our life consists of creating authentic relationships with each other as well as trying to meet the needs of each person who lives in our homes.

The fundamental aspects of L'Arche are as follows: (1) Recognition of the unique value of a person with a developmental disability to reveal that human suffering and joy can lead to growth, healing, and unity. (2) Life sharing, where persons with a developmental disability and those who assist them live, work, and pray together. (3) Relationships of mutuality in which people give and receive love. (4) Based on the Gospel and dependent on the spirit of God where faithful relationships, forgiveness, and celebration reveal God's personal presence and love.

Our mission is: (1) to create homes where faithful relationships based on forgiveness and celebration are nurtured; (2) to reveal the unique value and vocation of each person; (3) to change society by choosing to live relationships in community as a sign of hope and love.

Visitors Accepted: Please contact us and we can set up a time that works for both you and the community. [Mar2005]

LA FLOR DEL AGUA COMMUNITY

Dennis James
542 Hartnell Pl
Sacramento, CA 95825

916-929-1978
stonejug@hotmail.com

http://www.laflordelagua.com

Began: 1982 | Pop. 4 | Forming
Rural | Diet: Omnivorous

We are located on the Macal river in the Cayo District of Belize. Our mountain property, situated on the edge of a Mayan village, has tropical fruit trees, electricity, and piped water from the village, plus the wonderful water from the river itself. The property is close to the main road and only 10 minutes from San Ignacio town. There are six of us in the group. We are a strictly organic, health conscious retreat and eco-community. Some of us go back and forth to the US part of the year, and others stay mainly in Belize.

We have small organic gardens and orchards, live a simple, peaceful life, and we especially love the tropical, relaxed lifestyle in Belize.

Visitors Accepted: New members are welcome. Please email or phone if you are interested in knowing more and/or visiting. [Feb2005]

LA'AKEA COMMUNITY

Attn: Membership
PO Box 1071
Pahoa, HI 96778

808-965-0178
info@permaculture-hawaii.com

http://www.permaculture-hawaii.com

Began: 2005 | Pop. 7
Rural | Diet: Primarily vegetarian

We dedicate ourselves to each other's long-term health and well being. We honor and work in harmony with the land we own and steward. We commit to nurturing our connection with the people of the bioregion in which we live by encouraging cooperative endeavors and building friendships.

Our land is blessed with lots of sun and rain, has native Ohi'a forest, orchards, ponds and a magical cinder cone.

Members are encouraged to build and

Scissors [✂] at the end of a listing indicate that it was edited for length by the Directory *editors and a longer description can be found at* directory.ic.org.

maintain personal structures that are as simple as possible, and to meet as many needs as possible through community owned structures and systems (water, electrical, phone, computer, kitchen, etc.).

We are dedicated to making full, voting membership possible for anyone who shares our values and works well with us, regardless of the amount of wealth she/he has.

We value relationships and sexuality as an important part of individual's lives and a powerful energy that nourishes ourselves and our community. We do not elevate one sexual relationship model (monogamy, polyamory) over another but place emphasis on healthy, positive relating.

We are living together out of choice and from joy, not out of scarcity, fear, or ideology.

We place a high value on people who are dedicated to working on themselves and who welcome community support and feedback as part of their growth/healing processes.

Visitors Accepted: Please email or write to us and let us know about yourself and when you would like to visit. [Mar2005]

LAMA FOUNDATION

PO Box 240
San Cristobal, NM 87564

505-586-1269
info@lamafoundation.org

http://www.lamafoundation.org

Began: 1968 | Pop. 10 | Spiritual
Rural | Diet: Vegetarian only

Lama Foundation aims to serve as a sustainable spiritual community and educational center dedicated to the awakening of consciousness, service, spiritual practice with respect for all traditions, and stewardship of the land. Community life is viewed as a school of practical spirituality whose focus is individual and collective spiritual growth through service to others, simplicity of lifestyle, self-awareness, and commitment to daily spiritual practice in some form. Members have an opportunity to learn mindfulness and responsible stewardship as well as skills such as natural building and permaculture, gardening, cooking, carpentry, and silk-screen printing. Community-building skills are a continuing focus. The community works together as a circle in caring for the foundation and strives for consensus in decision making. Summers are an out breath with many visitors and a public program of workshops, retreats, and hermitages. We also operate a cottage industry for producing prayer flags and other items.

Winters are an in breath where members continue to serve and strive to take more time for intensive contemplative practice and study. The fire of 1996 offered an opportunity to explore a more sustainable lifestyle utilizing green building and permaculture techniques. Life is rustic, but very beautiful at an elevation of 8600 feet. Come and visit!

Visitors Accepted: Call or email ahead of time to arrange a visit. [Mar2005]

LAND LIFEWAYS FARM

Danny Heim
PO Box 218
Pinehill, NM 87357

505-240-2649
dannyheim@hotmail.com

http://www.webspawner.com/
users/danheim

Began: 2003 | Pop. 2 | Forming
Rural | Diet: Omnivorous

This community has only one goal, to live from the land and to sever its ties from the system to the furthest extent possible. There are no paths to follow, no community mindset to adhere to, no programs of any kind except that which will enable us to live from the land and be as self-sufficient as possible. At the same time there are no restrictions on practicing whatever belief system you are endeared to. Members can have gatherings of their individual liking as long as it does not interfere with the operation of the farm nor infringe on any member's right to privacy. We hope that you have an interest in earth-based spirituality, but it is not at all required.

In this regard, Land Lifeways Farm hopes that if one learns to survive directly from the earth, then it is likely one will also learn to know the earth. This, in a nutshell, is what the desired result will be for the member. By creating an absolute life dependence on the earth, a relationship is formed out of need rather than ego. Once that relationship has taken hold, the meaning of this community becomes self-explanatory.

Drugs and alcohol are prohibited on the property, but off the land no one will judge you. Work is the word here. Work hard and eat well. Farming is the main source of food via crops and livestock. Hunting and gathering are also practiced but not mandatory for those who oppose.

Visitors Accepted: Email or call (you will have to leave message and your phone number). Food and lodging will be provided for two days. [Mar2005]

THE LAND STEWARDSHIP CENTER

PO Box 225
Columbiaville, MI 48421

810-793-5303
ctibbits@main.nc.us

http://glblc.lapeer.org/tibbits.htm

Began: 1991 | Pop. 3
Rural | Diet: Primarily vegan

The Land Stewardship Center in Columbiaville, Michigan, was formed to help revitalize and maintain the Tibbits farm as a demonstration of good land stewardship practices. There are currently two households at the center that live and work cooperatively to demonstrate and promote good land stewardship practices. Our goal is to learn to live more in harmony with the rest of nature. Community activities include gardening, reforestation, wetland and animal habitat restoration, vegan potluck meals, and having fun together. We welcome casual, day visitors as well as extended stays by apprentices, interns and other people who think they might be interested in working and living with us on a long-term basis.

Visitors Accepted: Contact us (Clark, Adam or Crystal) by phone, letter or email. [Mar2005]

Listings

Additions and corrections: email: directory@ic.org, web: directory.ic.org, mail: RR 1 Box 156-D, Rutledge MO 63563, USA.

177

LANDARC

Paula Harrison
407 Princeton St
Jefferson, MA 01522

508-579-9093
harrisog@mac.com

http://www.landarcvillage.org

Began: 2003 | Forming
Rural | Diet: Omnivorous

LandARC is a group of families and individuals planning to purchase land in central Massachusetts. We will have a common house for community activities such as meals, along with 10-15 private homes. We are currently seeking new members.

Our Vision:

LandARC is a multigenerational activist community, education center, and organic farm being planned for the central Massachusetts area. We are a diverse group dedicated to supporting each other in a life based on land stewardship and activism. We apply direct democracy, each person contributing equally in terms of resources, work, and decision making. As a collective homestead, we practice skill-sharing and non-exploitative economics. Creative expression permeates our space and time. We also function as a model of sustainable living that welcomes activists, learners, and travelers seeking to share ideas and work. We live simply and share resources so as to contribute to a global vision where the necessities of life are available for humans and other living beings. Our power as a group enables us to achieve what we couldn't do individually. We create radical systemic change through the arts, education, and service. We joyously defy the isolation of the modern mainstream.

Visitors Accepted: Our meetings are open to the public on the 2nd Sunday of each month. Meetings start at 4pm and are followed by a potluck dinner. Please call for more information. [Feb2005]

LANDELIJKE VERENIGING CENTRAAL WONEN

Korte Elisabethstraat 13
Utrecht, 3511 JG
NETHERLANDS

+31-(0)30-2612585
info@lvcw.nl

http://www.lvcw.nl

The LVCW is the national association of cohousing in The Netherlands. [Feb2005]

LAUGHING DOG FARM AND CSA

Daniel Botkin
398 Main Rd
Gill, MA 01376

413-863-8696
dbotkin@valinet.com

http://laughingdogfarm.com

Began: 2000 | Pop. 5 | Forming
Rural | Diet: Primarily vegetarian

Laughing Dog Farm is a small acreage, market garden and CSA situated on an historic hilltop which was once a famous commune. Our nine acre homestead, surrounded by natural woodlands, is comprised of two acres of constructed raised beds, fruit trees, berries, goats, and a solar greenhouse, managed by traditional, labor-intensive methods. We've been fortunate to have live-in seasonal interns for five years. We are now also actively seeking serious, longer-term comrades/co-"owners" who believe in sustainable agriculture, food activism and community. We have a large, versatile home to retrofit and share, as well as ample resources and ideas for building a long term, sustainable, family-oriented micro-community. We are a middle aged couple (teacher, counselor, athlete, body worker, singer...), with a vivacious, precocious seven year old. We seek a serious-minded, committed individual, couple or small family to join our venture this year, with the possibility of eventual partnership, co-ownership or land trust establishment with the right person(s). Our long term vision includes: organic growing and land stewardship skills, a sustainable home economy, a food literacy and garden mentoring program, heirloom and heritage food crop varieties, seed saving, homeschooling resource exchange, and educational programs for children.

Visitors Accepted: Get in touch by email and describe why you want to visit. We especially welcome visitors who are willing to pitch in and get involved on the farm. [Jan2005][✂]

LEBENSRAUM

Hochwaldstrasse 37/5
Gaenserndorf, 2230
AUSTRIA

+43-(0)676-523-89-44
kontakt@derlebensraum.com

http://www.derlebensraum.com

Began: 2001 | Pop. 76
Small Town | Diet: Primarily vegetarian

Austria's first cohousing project, the eco-settlement Lebensraum is situated in an agricultural area north-east from Vienna. Intended common activities: mutual babysitting, common meals, growing your own vegetables, work parties, bulk-purchasing, sharing of resources and equipment, as well as singing, dancing and celebrating. We have democratic structure, make decisions on a majority basis, and jointly ensure maintenance of the settlement. As in other cohousing communities, there is no shared community income.

Lebensraum (living space) consists of 31 clustered houses, each with private terrace and small garden. There are vast common facilities: kitchen, dining room, laundry, childrens' playgrounds and large pedestrian meeting areas. In the next stage we plan a health food shop with Café, offices and ateliers. The settlement is car-free and a fine place for children, with secure and safe surroundings and lots of green space. The building is ecologically constructed in passive house standard, equipped with alternative energy sources, effective water management and land use due to higher-density sustainable development, which ensures extremely low energy costs.

Part of the construction has been finished and occupied in winter 2004/5. The whole building will be finished and inaugurated in June 2005. Our residents are people of all ages and a wide variety of talents, interests and professions. We aim at pro-environmental behavior and interaction with other communities. We hope that the "living space" will prove to be a place to feel at home.

Visitors Accepted: There is no process established yet, everything is still so very new! Best is to send an email to show interest and we shall figure out how to proceed. [Mar2005]

LESTER HOUSE

House President
900 Oakland Ave
Ann Arbor, MI 48104

734-996-5970

http://www.icc.coop

Pop. 15 | Diet: Vegetarian only

If you love local, organic, vegan/vegetarian food and good company, then you will fall in love with Lester House. Six nights a week, you, your housemates, your pals from our sister co-op—Debs House (who all board here), or our outside boarders will prepare a vegan/vegetarian feast that will rival your mom's cooking! No meat is allowed in the house. Our parlour includes the famous waterbed; books, board games, and encyclopedias will also be at your disposal, but television will not. You can connect your own computer to the wireless inter-

Scissors [✂] at the end of a listing indicate that it was edited for length by the Directory *editors and a longer description can be found at* directory.ic.org.

net, or go downstairs to use the two computers and the Mother of All Laser Printers. You'll be surrounded by people who love you, themselves, and the world. You'll hear their thoughts, dreams, and ideas, and you'll also learn to hear your own.

Visitors Accepted: Contact House President. [Mar2005]

LIBERTY VILLAGE

9137 Liberty Village Way
Union Bridge, MD 21791

301-898-7654
info@libertyvillage.com

http://www.libertyvillage.com

Began: 1989 | Pop. 39
Rural | Diet: Omnivorous

Liberty Village is a rural cohousing community for all ages, accessible to metropolitan Washington and Baltimore. We have 18 completed homes of a planned 38. Due to unexpected county sewer restrictions our building program was halted at about the halfway point. In 2006 we expect to start building again towards our goal of 38 homes and our Common House.

The homes are mostly semi-custom duplexes, clustered on 8 of the 23 acres around a green, pedestrian common area. Six of the units, closest to the community building, are designed to be handicap / elderly friendly.

The remaining 15 acres are a mix of fields, woods, gardens, orchards, and wetlands. We have a 105-acre public park next door with soccer and softball fields, tennis and basketball courts, a children's play area, hiking and biking trails, fields and woods. On another side is a horse farm and, on another, 5-acre farmettes.

We are located in rural Maryland, 10 miles from Frederick, and about 50 miles from downtown Washington, DC and Baltimore, MD.

Visitors Accepted: Email us. [Mar2005]

LIFESEED

Fred Boshardt and Karen Lovelien
43900 Hwy 160
Mancos, CO 81328

970-533-9040, 970-759-4637
withease@earthlink.net

http://www.lifeseed.net

Began: 1999 | Forming | Rural

Lifeseed is an intentional community dedicated to the discovery and full expression of each individual's creative gifts. Located on 350 acres surrounded on all sides by national forest, the community will anchor an Eco-Lodge, Emergent Life Center, Center for the Arts, and Global Center for Peace. The Eco-Lodge and Emergent Life Center are under the name Ahtonawah. Integral in nature, Lifeseed supports individuals in moving forward on their own paths. The Lifeseed Vision: Lifeseed is the conscious expression of Love expressed as a community living in a rich energetic and sustainable environment, where the unique creative expression of each individual is discovered, nurtured and shared. By continually creating through unified consciousness, the community aligns in a single harmonic, while opening to the flow of infinite possibilities, inspiring individual and collective transformation, and creating pathways leading to profound universal peace.

Visitors Accepted: Contact us to make arrangements. [Feb2005]

LIFESHARE COMMUNITY

Ms. C. M. Smith
4221 Brownsboro Rd, Apt 7
Winston-Salem, NC 27106

ismenefox@yahoo.com
michellekarman@excite.com

Began: 2005 | Pop. 1 | Forming | Spiritual
Diet: Primarily vegetarian

[Mar2005]

LIGHT AS COLOR FOUNDATION

Lelia Saunders
PO Box 2947
Pagosa Springs, CO 81147

970-264-6250
lightascolor@frontier.net

http://www.swicc.org/las.html

Began: 1997 | Pop. 2
Rural | Diet: Primarily vegetarian

A spiritually conscious group of neighbors in south Colorado, attuned to nature, holism, and the visual arts. Modeled somewhat after Findhorn University of Light in Scotland. An educational retreat and conference center, small but networked. Pristine natural environment with gardens beside river and national forest. We are developing studios for multiple media: pottery, photography, stained glass, painting, weaving, dyeing, etc. Emphasis on freedom of creative flow through visual and tactile arts and the useful power of color to balance, heal, and uplift. We offer multitradi-tional shamanic journeys, spirit walks, and ceremonies. Apprentice programs in all the above. Organic process in new membership and a centering conduit for those who want to try living at 7,000 feet in a river valley. Our community of neighbors interacts with similar holistic focus. General ambience of peace and upliftment, natural serenity, and quiet industry. Individual development supported. Self-responsibility for livelihood. Focused organic process without rigid preconceptions for growth. Guests welcome with advance notice. Mature, responsible folks interested in both community and privacy most welcome. Excellent hot springs in town.

Visitors Accepted: Call or email. [Nov2004]

LIGHT MORNING

http://lightmorning.org

Began: 1973 | Pop. 11 | Spiritual
Rural | Diet: Vegetarian only

Light Morning is a small community of diverse folks who share meals, work together, and hold a common vision. Since our arrival in the Blue Ridge Mountains of Virginia in 1974, we have been striving to embody the beliefs that good health and self-esteem deserve cultivation; that a simpler lifestyle will enable us to live closer to the Earth; and that the Earth itself is a living creature.

We likewise believe that we are collectively ripening into an awareness that our personal and world circumstances are co-created, and that a new kind of family can facilitate this ripening. We choose to view our daily life, moreover, as the proving ground for these hypotheses.

Visitors, interns, and residents come to Light Morning to experience our emerging lifestyle and to develop practical skills for a sustainable future. These include homesteading skills such as four-season organic gardening, living off-the-grid, and building alternative structures; interpersonal skills such as conscious projection and creative problem-solving; and the more inward arts of meditation, dream-work, and prayer.

Light Morning also provides fellowship and support for those navigating transitions in their lives. And doesn't this increasingly mean all of us? For the urgent need of these times is to shake free of our slumberous self-absorption in order to become more truly responsive. In this context, Light Morning is a vortex that encourages transformational awakenings.

Visitors Accepted: Visit our home page on the internet. If you're moved by what you find there, contact us via email to set up a visit or an internship. [Mar2005]

Listings

Additions and corrections: email: directory@ic.org, *web:* directory.ic.org, *mail:* RR 1 Box 156-D, Rutledge MO 63563, USA.

179

LIGHT OF FREEDOM

**1257 Moles Rd SW
Willis, VA 24380**

**540-593-2169
lightoffreedom2001@yahoo.com**

Began: 1993 | Pop. 6 | Forming | Spiritual
Rural | Diet: Omnivorous

Light of Freedom is located near the beautiful Blue Ridge Parkway in southern Virginia. We are a community dedicated to truth—all is one. In oneness we see our equality as God created us. Our relationships with each other, nature, and God are derived from the principles of *A Course in Miracles,* which we highly value as a guide for a happy life. Everyone has their own chosen work and interests including horticulture, art, crafts, architecture, aquaculture, and writing, on land owned by the community. Individuals live in a community house or build their own sustainable homestead. Alternative building methods are encouraged. We live off the grid, preferring to catch and use the sun, wind, water, and earth given us, returning them naturally to the life cycle. We maintain our quiet enjoyment of organic gardening, ponds, and orchard with future vineyard plans. We give workshops on *A Course in Miracles* and alternative building methods. We meet as a community on a regular basis, and decisions are made by consensus. Meetings begin with our acknowledgment of peace as our one goal, and in peace, understanding comes, allowing us to perceive solutions to community problems. We recognize we share one spirit and one life, and all decisions are given to spirit for guidance, directions, and resolution.

For our community, living by the "Golden Rule" is to perceive in others what you would have them perceive in you. Our vision at Light of Freedom is, and will be, a happy gathering of equals.

community made .com

Crafts and Creations from U.S. Intentional Communities

Visitors Accepted: We welcome visitors—call or write for directions and availability of accommodations at least two weeks before you want to visit. [Nov2004]

LINDER HOUSE

**House President
711 Catherine St
Ann Arbor, MI 48104**

734-761-5043

http://www.icc.coop

Began: 1989 | Pop. 20 | Diet: Omnivorous

Check out Linder House! We have a living room with hardwood floors, ornate woodwork and a beautiful fireplace. We also have a cozy kitchen, spacious porch with porch swing, pool table, TV, VCR, Macintosh computer, laser printer and modem. What's more, we're non-smoking, the neighborhood is quiet, and the parking is ample. We eat dinner at nearby Vail House. We do not allow cats. Need we say more?

Visitors Accepted: Contact House President. [Mar2005]

LITTLE FLOWER CATHOLIC WORKER FARM

**16560 Louisa Rd
Louisa, VA 23093**

540-967-5574

littleflowercw@wildmail.com

**http://www.catholicworker.org/
communities/Commdetail.cfm?
Community=176**

Began: 1996 | Pop. 8 | Spiritual
Rural | Diet: Primarily vegetarian

Little Flower is a small Catholic Worker homestead/farm. We are committed to helping create a nonviolent, just world in harmony with the land. We share our lives and resources with each other and with those in need. We live as simply as we can; we organize and engage in nonviolent direct action against systemic violence; we try to enflesh the Gospel mandates to love God, one another, and our enemies.

Our daily life includes unschooling with three children, caring for our animals and gardens, and building and repairing our farm structures. We meet weekly as a community, share most meals, and have a liturgy together on Sundays. When we can, we also participate in Charlottesville Food Not Bombs on Sundays. We organize vigils, protests, and direct actions together with Catholic Worker houses in Washington, DC

and Norfolk, and with other groups in the Charlottesville/Richmond area. Our focus also includes nuclear weapons, nuclear power, the School of the Americas, and war.

Some of us work part-time. We also receive some donations to support our work.

Visitors Accepted: Give us a call or email. [Feb2005]

LOFSTEDT FARM COMMUNITY

**Bridget and George Baumann
5795 Kaslo S Rd
PO Box 1270
Kaslo, BC V0G 1M0
CANADA**

**250-353-7448, 250-353-7441 (fax)
lofstedtfarm@look.ca**

**http://mypage.direct.ca/l/
lofstedtfarm**

Began: 1984 | Pop. 9 | Spiritual
Rural | Diet: Omnivorous

Sixty-acre biodynamic-farm-based community located in the beautiful Kootenay mountains. Pleasant climate, mild summers and cool winters. The farm, surrounded by Crown Forests, is located five minutes south of Kaslo. The three main businesses are: Lofstedt Farm, Lofstedt Gardens CSA, and Lofstedt Farm Forestry Society (LFFS). The latter is a 1500-acre government-owned woodlot in our watershed, managed by Peter Van Allen. Besides the recently added biodiesel production plant, there is another project initiated by Filip Vanzhof, MD: a holistic retirement lodge and spa, for people wanting to remain in good health by taking part in farming and gardening activities and eating the healthy food they help produce. A capital input of some $50,000—is expected from interested retirees, with part ownership in the lodge. Over the last 20 years, many volunteers have participated in our internship program to practice ecological sustainable organic farming. The elderly Swiss owners want to retire and preserve the farm as a biodynamic learning center. We are looking for a number of enterprising, health-conscious retirees as well as younger trainees eager to learn and to help with: hay-making, grain growing, gardening and greenhouse work, washing and marketing produce, building, animal husbandry, beekeeping, working with tractors and draft horses, logging and surveying, dairying, and food processing, and doing some old-fashioned crafts in the bargain.

Visitors Accepted: Ask for an interview. [Mar2005]

Scissors [✄] at the end of a listing indicate that it was edited for length by the Directory *editors and a longer description can be found at* directory.ic.org.

LOS ANGELES ECO-VILLAGE

117 Bimini Pl #221
Los Angeles, CA 90004

crsp@igc.org

Lois Arkin
213-738-1254
lois@ic.org

Lara Morrison
213-383-8684
laraeco@hotmail.com

http://www.ic.org/laev

Began: 1993 | Pop. 36
Urban | Diet: Primarily vegetarian

The Los Angeles Eco-Village (LAEV) was founded in 1993 in the two-block neighborhood of Bimini and White House Place in the intensely urban Wilshire Center/Koreatown area of Los Angeles. Started as a project of the nonprofit Cooperative Resources & Services Project (CRSP) after the 1992 civil uprisings, our purpose is to demonstrate the processes of becoming a healthy and sustainable neighborhood socially, ecologically and economically.

We are still working toward a common vision among the very diverse intentional and pre-existing neighbors who live here. Overall, the founding vision included demonstrating lower-impact and higher-quality living patterns among newly arriving Eco-Villagers and pre-existing neighbors drawn to that vision.

There are about a dozen proactive Eco-Villagers within the current 35-person intentional community. There are approximately 500 residents in the two-block neighborhood. The vision for some of us is that someday all or most who live in the two blocks will manifest Eco-Village values.

Over the past decade, CRSP has purchased two apartment buildings (48 units of housing, including two common units) which we are slowly eco-retrofitting and plan to put in a land trust and preserve as affordable housing. We have a number of organic gardens in the neighborhood and have regular community dinners open to other neighbors, friends and relatives. Although many Eco-Villagers are child-friendly, we do not currently have policies or rules for children.

We provide regular tours, urban-sustainable-community workshops, public talks on a variety of related topics, and affordable accommodations for short stays.

Visitors Accepted: Email to let us know how many people, for how long, the purpose of your visit, and when you'd like to

come. Keep after us if we don't get back to you right away. Availability of and type of accommodations varies greatly. [Feb2005][✂<]

LOS VISIONARIOS

Fundacion Ecologica Condorhuana
Correo Central Loja
Loja
ECUADOR
uevn_private@uevn.org

http://www.uevn.org/Ecuador
http://groups.yahoo.com/group/
  uevn-discussion

Began: 1996 | Pop. 3 | Spiritual
Rural | Diet: Primarily vegetarian

We are an intentional community located 10 minutes from the world famous valley of longevity—Vilcabamba, Ecuador. We are founders and members of the Utopian EcoVillage Network Federation. We are seeking people who have a strong desire to live communally. We are part of a worldwide network of intentional communities with similar values, linked to support each other for the creation of a new society. The basic intention of our community is to be a pilot model demonstration of how to live in a real New World consciousness of sharing on all levels: financially, spiritually, mentally, emotionally and physically.

Visitors Accepted: Kindly read thoroughly our two websites, join our discussion forum, and send an introduction letter to be considered for visiting. [Mar2005]

LOST VALLEY EDUCATIONAL CENTER

81868 Lost Valley Ln
Dexter, OR 97431

541-937-3351
lvec@lostvalley.org

http://www.lostvalley.org

Began: 1988 | Pop. 24
Rural | Diet: Primarily vegetarian

Lost Valley Center has recently completed 15 years of experimentation and growth. We are 18 adults/6 children (ages 3 to 63) living and working together on 87 beautiful acres of gardens, meadows, forests, and creek, 18 miles southeast of Eugene, Oregon.

We live in cabins, yurts, and a six-plex. We serve organic vegetarian meals partly grown in our gardens or purchased bioregionally. We hope to start our own school

Listings

Additions and corrections: email: directory@ic.org, web: directory.ic.org, mail: RR 1 Box 156-D, Rutledge MO 63563, USA.

181

in the near future; our children now attend public school or are taught at home.

We run a nonprofit retreat and conference facility with 150 beds plus camping, and also organize our own workshops in areas such as Ecovillage and Permaculture Design, Heart of Now (personal growth), and yoga. We publish a magazine called Talking Leaves: A Journal of Our Evolving Ecological Culture ($20/year).

We offer longer-term learning experiences through our intern program. People wishing to apply for community membership first take part in Community Experience Week.

Some adult members work as Lost Valley staff; others work independently on- or off-site. Members keep their personal assets and pay their own bills, including a monthly room-and-board fee.

One of our unique gifts is to create and offer a balance between a strong ecological focus and a deep commitment to communication and to the functional extended family that we are cultivating. We strive to be creative, caring, embracing of change, eclectic in our approach, and open to diversities in age, race, spirituality, and sexuality.

Visitors Accepted: Check our website for a schedule of tours, visitor days, Community Experience Weeks, and workshops or programs. Contact us if available dates don't work for you; we may be able to arrange something else. [Mar2005]

LOTHLORIEN CO-OP

244 W Lakelawn Pl
Madison, WI 53703

608-256-2051
eli@phoenixegg.org
thatguy018@yahoo.com

**http://www.madisoncommunity.coop/
house.cfm?HouseID=5**

Began: 1973 | Pop. 32
Urban | Diet: Vegetarian only

We are a community of 32 people (both students and workers) and 5 cats (neither students nor workers) who share a large yellow castle on the shore of Lake Mendota. Since our founding in 1973, Lothlorien Co-op strives to provide a welcoming and supportive atmosphere for people of all ages, sexes, races and sexual orientations. Many of our housemembers are politically active in queer rights, labor rights, environmental and feminist movements, and our home is an open resource to activist groups like: Food Not Bombs, Stop the War, Radical Cheerleaders, and the Madison Art Collective. We often host events, providing the city of Madison w/good times. Based in egalitarian ideals, house decisions are made through modified consensus at weekly house meetings.

House Features: a huge living room and library w/hardwood floors, four fireplaces distributed throughout the house, multiple decks, two pianos. Our backyard has terraced gardens, a lakeshore fire pit, a dock, and two canoes. All but one of our 31 bedrooms are singles. We have a great location within walking distance of the Capitol, UW-Madison and MATC campuses, and bus lines. Additional fun fact: Loth has one of the largest solar hot water systems in Madison.

Summer Rent Rate: $195-245/mo, Fall-Spring Rate:~$310—includes all utilities and toiletries—Food: $90/mo.

We cook vegetarian meals with a vegan option nightly. Nearly all food at Loth is organic and most produce is also locally grown.

Visitors Accepted: Visitors are welcome to join us for dinner: Sunday–Friday at 6 pm, or brunch Sunday at noon. Advance arrangements are not necessary if you'd like to stay overnight, but are appreciated.

CRASHING: We accept short-term crashers pending a meeting with members of the house. Crashing fees are $7/night, including all-you-can-eat food; there is possibility for partial work-job payment as well. [Mar2005][✂]

LOTHLORIEN FARM

H. Forsey
RR 1
Ompah, ON K0H 2J0
CANADA

613-479-2453

Began: 1972 | Pop. 6
Rural | Diet: Omnivorous

Lothlorien Farm is a rural cooperative in the forest and lake country of eastern Ontario, founded in 1972. Our 700 acres of land is almost all bush (not really a "farm") but we do have gardens and a few fields. Our buildings include residences, workshops, and outbuildings, and there are several other approved house sites.

Currently we are a small, loose-knit but stable group of six resident members (all

Scissors [✂] at the end of a listing indicate that it was edited for length by the Directory editors and a longer description can be found at directory.ic.org.

adults) in four households, as well as several non-resident members, linked by various long-term friendships and a love for this piece of land. Our adult children stay connected but none are living here now.

Resident members work in individual home businesses (woodworking, weaving, writing and translating) and in part-time jobs (education, social services) in the area. Incomes are separate and houses are individually owned, while the land itself is owned collectively.

We don't do a whole lot together as a group, but we take care of each other's animals and houses if someone is away, and generally look after each other as good friends and neighbours. We are quite involved in the local community, through the volunteer fire department, the community choir, the library and other activities.

We are open to inquiries, especially from younger people who live within a few hours' drive and would like to get to know us gradually through a series of short visits.

Visitors Accepted: Contact us, explain your interest, see if a short visit makes sense. We don't have a visitor program as such; any arrangement would depend on circumstances and a rapport established over the phone. [Oct2004]

LOTHLORIEN NATURE SANCTUARY

PO Box 1082
Bloomington, IN 47402
elf@kiva.net

http://www.elflore.org

Began: 1983

Lothlorien Nature Sanctuary is a cooperatively owned and operated haven in Lawrence County, Needmore, Indiana, USA. Participation is welcomed and encouraged.

Monthly Councils occur on the second Sunday in or near the Radiance Hall at 1:00 pm (subject to change).

Full Moons are celebrated openly each month. Email Jef and Vic (with "Attn: Jef and Vic" in the subject line) for details.

Earth Steward Weekends occur throughout the camping season. These present wonderful opportunities for hands-on involvement. Contact Larry (with "Attn: Larry" in the subject line) for details.

We also hold several larger events throughout the year. Visit us online for complete information and maps.

Visitors Accepted [Jan2005]

LOVE & NONVIOLENCE COMMUNE

London, England
UNITED KINGDOM

revolutionaryanarchopacifist@
yahoo.com

http://www.aeinstein.org

Pop. 1 | Forming | Spiritual
Urban | Diet: Vegetarian only

"Forget everything you've been taught. Start by dreaming."
Visitors Accepted [Feb2005]

THE LOVE ISRAEL FAMILY

Serious Israel
The Camp of the Saints
3718-D Vineyard Way
Kettle Falls, WA 99141

509-732-6162, 425-481-3536
serious@loveisraelfamily.com

http://www.loveisraelfamily.com

Began: 1968 | Pop. 13 | Forming | Spiritual
Rural | Diet: Omnivorous

We live in a time of revelation. The truth about our higher nature is being revealed to us in a myriad of wonderful ways. It is now possible to know what is true, not just believe what we hope is true.

The Love Israel Family is made up of those who have received this knowledge through revelation. At last, we have been shown the common ground that makes peace and unity possible. Stated simply, it is reflected in these three truths:
• We are all one.
• Love is the answer.
• Now is the time.

Our lives are now dedicated to creating a culture that embodies these truths.

God calls this culture "Israel."

We each have a unique and invaluable role in creating this culture. These roles are being defined and refined through our daily lives together. Our lives are a witness to what we know to be true.

We have been shown that there are many more of us waking up all around the world. It is our intent to provide encouragement and focus for the gathering of our people. We are the first fruits of Jesus Christ.

"When the seers come together
then the watchers will see."
Visitors Accepted: Make contact first by phone, letter or email. [Mar2005]

LUTHER HOUSE

House President
1510-1520 Hill St
Ann Arbor, MI 48104

734-662-3735

http://www.icc.coop

Pop. 50 | Diet: Omnivorous

Situated a few minutes walk from central campus, Luther Co-op is comprised of two old Victorian houses, each over a hundred years old. The houses are close to convenience stores, coffee shops and city buses. Though able to house 50 people, the houses are very spacious with plenty of room in the common areas to sit, watch TV or talk. Dinners, held at 6pm Sunday through Friday, are a huge part of the social life at Luther, providing an occasion where the housemates can meet up and chat after a long day at school or work. For those not wanting to feel cooped up, we have (count them) three porches—including one with a porch swing—to hang out on. We also have a huge backyard with a fire pit (which is very popular during the summer), a basketball court, bike racks, and plenty of parking. The house is currently adding wiring to provide Ethernet to all its rooms. And to top it all off, Luther is also well known for hosting a huge Halloween party.

Visitors Accepted: Contact House President. [Mar2005]

LYONS VALLEY VILLAGE

Wonderland Hill
Development Company
4676 Broadway
Boulder, CO 80304

303-449-3232 ext 216
michelle@whdc.com

http://www.lyonsvalleyvillage.com

Began: 2004 | Forming | Small Town

This community will be located on a 2-acre parcel of land in the beautiful mountain town of Lyons, Colorado. It is bordered on one side by a public park with a river running through it and another by dedicated open space. Lyons is minutes from Boulder in one direction and Rocky Mountain National Park in another. We anticipate breaking ground in early Summer 2005.

Visitors Accepted: Please call or email Michelle at Wonderland Hill Development Company for more information. [Jan2005]

Additions and corrections: email: directory@ic.org, web: directory.ic.org, mail: RR 1 Box 156-D, Rutledge MO 63563, USA.

MA YOGA SHAKTI INTERNATIONAL MISSION

114-41 Lefferts Blvd
South Ozone Park
New York, NY 11420

718-641-0402
info@yogashakti.org

3895 Hield Rd NW
Palm Bay, FL 32907
321-725-4024

http://www.yogashakti.org

Began: 1979 | Diet: Vegetarian only

The Yogashakti Mission was started by Maha Mandaleshwar Shakti Sant Shiromani Ma Yogashakti Saraswati to further the spiritual development of humankind through the practice of yoga based on the techniques of highest values and truth embodied in the Upanishads, Geeta, and other scriptures.

The Yogashakti Mission is an international family dedicated to serving God and humanity in order to bring about a revival of spirituality through yoga.

The registered office of the mission is at 11, Jaldarshan, Nepean Sea Road, Mumbai 400 026, India. The mission also has centers at Gondia (Nagpur), Calcutta, New Delhi, New York, and Florida. Regular yoga classes are conducted by trained disciples at these centers.

The mission publishes a brief monthly journal, in English and Hindi, keeping the devotees in touch with the activities of the mission. Mataji has also published several books on yoga and allied subjects in Hindi and English that are available from Yogashakti Mission. If you are interested in learning the higher values of life, keeping your body and mind healthy, and assisting humanity toward spiritual growth, you are welcome to join the Ashram. Age, religion, caste, or creed are no barriers.

Visitors Accepted [Jan2005]

MA'AGAL HAKVUTZOT

http://circle.kibbutz.org.il

The Ma'agal Ha'kvutzot ("Circle of groups") is the umbrella organization of the renewed communal groups in Israel. The organization's membership is comprised of urban kibbutzim, groups consisting of graduates of youth movements and others, numbering today over 1000 adults all over Israel. The aims of the organization are to support the expansion of the communal idea in Israel, to nurture solidarity between groups, to promote important educational projects, and to work towards an Israeli society, both on an economic and political level, based on social democratic values. Additional information, in both English and Hebrew, can be found at the following websites:

- Kibbutz Bet Yisrael: http://www.reut.org.il
- Kvutzat Hemshech:
    http://hemshech.habonimdror.org.il
- Kibbutz Migvan: http://www.migvan.org.il
- Kibbutz Na'aran: http://www.naaran.org
- Kibbutz Tamuz: http://www.tamuz.org.il
- Kvutsat Yovel: http://www.kvutsatyovel.com

Other groups currently without websites include Kiryat Shalom, Kibbutz Pelech and the Jaffa commune of the Hashomer Hatzair youth movement, groups of the Kvutsot Habechira youth movement in Migdal Ha'emek and Nazareth Ilit, the Be'er Sheva group, a group in Jerusalem of the Machanot Ha'olim and scouts movement, a group in Haifa and another in Jerusalem of the Habonim-Dror youth movement. [Mar2005]

MADISON COMMUNITY COOPERATIVE

1201 Williamson St
Madison, WI 53703

608-251-2667
services@madisoncommunity.coop

http://www.madisoncommunity.coop

Began: 1968 | Pop. 215
Urban | Diet: Other

Madison Community Cooperative (MCC), founded in 1968, is a "co-op of co-ops." We provide affordable shared housing and food for about 200 students, workers, parents and children living in 12 houses. Each house of 6–32 members maintains a high level of autonomy by controlling its own membership process, setting its own annual budget (including room and food charges), and developing house policies according to its own culture. Some houses buy meat while others offer only vegetarian and/or vegan meals; some allow pets; one includes child care in its work system; one provides women's housing; one observes Shabbat and Jewish high holy days.

MCC's role is to provide stability, support self-management by the houses, and further the cooperative movement. Our board of directors, officers, committees and staff train and work with house members so that each house has the needed skills.

Every month, each house adds money to the collective MCC purse, which is disbursed to pay for major maintenance, insurance and mortgages; maintain an office; educate the membership; promote cooperative living to the larger community; continue to remove housing from the speculative real estate market; and more.

MCC is run by members of all the houses. Houses have board representatives, and most send reps to the various committees as well. General Membership Meetings, where we elect officers, are held three times a year. We invite you to visit our houses and see if one of them is a good fit!

Visitors Accepted: Please contact each house individually (preferably in person). Some co-ops allow only guests (visitors with a sponsor within the house). [Oct2004][✀]

MADRE GRANDE MONASTERY

18372 Highway 94
Dulzura, CA 91917

619-468-3006
info@madregrande.org

http://www.madregrande.org

Began: 1975 | Pop. 2 | Spiritual
Rural | Diet: Primarily vegetarian

As an eclectic monastery, we have monks who are men and women, of any spiritual persuasion so long as they follow a positive path to spiritual perfection. Membership in the monastery is necessary for permanent residence. The members are monks who make all decisions and set community goals and who are highly skilled in their abilities. Leadership in the monastery is by annual election among the monk community. Students are studying for friar or monk status in the Paracelsian Order. Students and retreat guests take limited part in community functions according to their skills and conditions of residence. The ability to work cooperatively on group goals is valued above all else. Special skills are needed, especially organic gardening, vegetarian cooking, maintenance, and a willingness to do even the menial to manifest our goals. For further information please see our website.

Visitors Accepted: Call or email first and set up an agreed upon date and length of stay. The monastery at times is closed for private groups or inside events. [Mar2005]

Scissors [✀] at the end of a listing indicate that it was edited for length by the Directory *editors and a longer description can be found at* directory.ic.org.

MAGIC

magic@ecomagic.org

http://www.ecomagic.org

Began: 1972 | Pop. 17 | Spiritual
Diet: Primarily vegetarian

Residents of Magic operate a nonprofit pub-lic-service organization with the same name, through which we demonstrate how people may live better by learning to see self and surroundings more accurately.

Core themes in our community life and in the programs we offer the general public are: (1) clarify values; (2) improve health; (3) increase cooperation; and (4) steward the environment.

Our activities include lectures and semi-nars about the nature of value; life-planning workshops; swimming, running, bicycling, and hatha yoga instruction; youth mentor-ing; mediation; community organizing; planting and caring for trees and other veg-etation; water- and land-management plan-ning; neighborhood design; and publishing. Several of our programs have been awarded national and international recognition for excellence.

We aim to strike a balance between utiliz-ing the diverse resources of our Stanford University/Silicon Valley surroundings and maintaining contemplative, modest lives. We welcome opportunities to meet new people and to explore how we may interact to mutual benefit. When writing us we request $1 or more to defray costs.

Visitors Accepted [Jan2005]

MAISON EMMANUEL

1561 Chemin Beaulne
Val Morin, QC J0T 2R0
CANADA

819-322-7014, 819-322-1166
inge.sell@maisonemmanuel.org

http://www.maisonemmanuel.org

Began: 1982 | Pop. 50 | Spiritual
Rural | Diet: Omnivorous

Maison Emmanuel Inc. is an intentional, life sharing community based on Anthroposophy, and modeled on the Camphill Communities existing worldwide. We are approx. 50 people (including 24 children, adolescents and adults in need of special care) living and working together in the beautiful Laurentian mountains, 100 km (60 miles) north of Montreal.

House parents, together with their chil-dren and young coworkers, live in family-like settings. The rhythmic structure of the household, school, workshops (bakery, can-dle-making, small farm, garden, weaving, woodwork) and therapies creates the warm, supportive environment of community liv-ing. Shared meals, seasonal festivals, plays, birthday celebrations and outings, help cre-ate bonds of friendship and responsibility where everyone learns to care and provide for the need of the others.

A program of expansion and integration has started in the center of a nearby town with two adult residences and our bakery with a boutique for Maison Emmanuel's crafts.

Training for new coworkers and a founda-tion course is provided. Many people from different countries live at Maison Emmanuel. The languages spoken within the community are about ²/₃ English and ¹/₃ French. The surrounding community speaks mostly French.

Visitors Accepted: Visitors are welcome. Prior appointment is requested, stating the length of stay and the date of arrival. [Feb2005]

MALU 'AINA

PO Box 489
Kurtistown, HI 96760

808-966-7622
info@malu-aina.org
aloha@gaiayoga.org

http://www.malu-aina.org

Began: 1979 | Pop. 4
Rural | Diet: Omnivorous

Malu 'Aina (Land of Peace) is the Hawaiian name given to the Center for Nonviolent Education and Action located 10 miles south of the city of Hilo on the island of Hawaii. We are a small-scale 22-acre agricul-turally based spiritual community commit-ted to justice, peace, and preserving the environment. Established as a nonprofit organization in 1979, permanent residency at Malu 'Aina Farm began in 1981.

Malu 'Aina is located on the slopes of the world's most active volcano. The climate is wet, averaging 175 inches of rain annually. Temperature is normally mild: 75–85° F day-time and 60–70° F nights, although some winter nights can be quite cool with tem-peratures dropping into the 50s.

Life on the farm involves physical labor and simple living. Our water supply is rain-catchment tanks. We have small-scale solar power and use composting toilets.

At Malu 'Aina we try to live a life of com-munity service by helping people in need of food and through our work for peace, jus-tice, and the environment. We are inter-ested in people who want to make life changes for justice.

Visitors Accepted: Call or email to sched-ule visit. [Mar2005]

MANITOU ARBOR ECOVILLAGE

PO Box 113
Kalamazoo, MI 49074

info@manitouarbor.org

http://www.manitouarbor.org

Forming

[Feb2005]

MANZANITA VILLAGE

258 Benjamin Dr
Prescott, AZ 86303

928-445-3015
contact@manzanitavillage.com

Joan Burrell
928-443-0397
bljoan@msn.com

Polly Hoover
928-541-9883
benpolly@mac.com

http://www.manzanitavillage.com

Began: 1994 | Pop. 24 | Diet: Omnivorous

A diverse, multi-generational cohousing community of caring neighbors in a tran-quil, safe environment within city limits of Prescott (off Bradshaw Drive).

There will be 36 homes when complete, of which 22 are now built and occupied. See our website for further information.

Visitors Accepted [Mar2005]

MAPLE RIDGE BRUDERHOF

http://www.mapleridgebruderhof.com

Maple Ridge was founded in October 1985. The Bruderhof movement had outgrown its then-current locations and it was time to start looking for a place to start a new Bruderhof. We looked for a property near Woodcrest, the first Bruderhof in the US, so the two communities could work closely together and support one another. The property, initially called Pleasant View, was found eight miles from Woodcrest Bruderhof.

The first families moved into Pleasant View on October 17, 1985. In spite of the cold winter weather, renovating and build-ing projects provided for joyful teamwork,

Additions and corrections: email: directory@ic.org, *web:* directory.ic.org, *mail: RR 1 Box 156-D, Rutledge MO 63563, USA.*

185

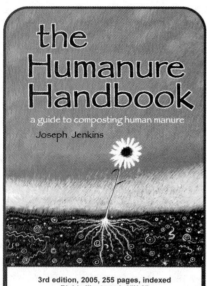
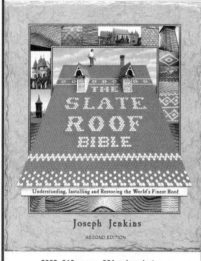
with young people from the Bruderhof working alongside young people from Hutterite colonies in Canada and the Dakotas, Amish barn-raising crews from Lancaster County, Jewish youth groups, and many others.

Formerly a small family resort, Pleasant View made a beautiful community. Best of all, at least for the children, was the ridge that towered in back of their new home, with rugged terrain to explore and panoramic views of Ulster County, Kingston, the Catskills, the Hudson River Valley and on into the Berkshires. On October 26, 1997 Pleasant View changed its name to Maple Ridge. [Feb2005]

MARATHON CO-OP

**732 Maltman Ave
Los Angeles, CA 90026**

**323-661-1398
apiser@earthlink.net**

Began: 1988 | Urban

We are a housing cooperative consisting of members of all ages, religious persuasions, and political beliefs. We have a seven-member board of directors serving alternate two-year terms. There are three committees: membership, building and grounds, and finance.

Visitors Accepted [Mar2005]

MARIPOSA GROUP

**FM 1841
Bivins, TX 75555**

**903-799-6161
MariposaGroup@Netscape.net**

**Eric Best
ericatn@pngusa.net**

http://www.mariposagroup.org

Began: 1984 | Pop. 8 | Spiritual | Rural
1. Physical and financial security—Our land is paid for, and houses will be paid for as they are built. Develop ways in which time, personal energy, and financial resources can be brought together so as to minimize the personal risk that any individual may experience in the areas of physical and financial security.
2. Personal and interpersonal comfort and self-esteem—Emphasize and practice methods of self-knowledge, friendship, intimacy, interpersonal communication, and interaction that promote respect, comfort, and trust between individuals, such that relationships have their basis in these qualities.

3. Freedom for higher levels of personal development and expression—Explore, develop, and promote ways of joyfully enhancing fully free personal development.

In short, to create a community space in a loving, supportive, free, and responsible environment where there is more opportunity for people to truly and fully enjoy life.

Visitors Accepted: Please call. [Jan2005]

MARIPOSA GROVE

**Oakland, CA 94608
mariposa@ic.org**

**http://www.healthyarts.com/
mariposagrove**

Began: 1999 | Pop. 12
Urban | Diet: Primarily vegetarian

Mariposa Grove is an activism and arts community in north Oakland, organized as cohousing. The three adjacent houses contain seven apartments as well as shared space for many meals, creative pursuits and collaborations, office space, workshop, gardens, etc. We've rebuilt severely deteriorated houses into a place where creativity inspires social change, activism inspires creative collaboration, and everyone is actively engaged in the urban fabric we inhabit. We engage in art parties, theater, fire performance, singing, and community organizing, sometimes together at home, sometimes separately with others in the broader community. We'd also love to build social and economic links with a rural community in our region. [Jan2005]

MASALA CO-OP

**744 Marine St
Boulder, CO 80302**

**303-443-8178
lincolnisaac@hotmail.com**

http://www.masalacoop.org

Began: 1999 | Pop. 11
Urban | Diet: Primarily vegetarian

Masala Community Housing is a nonprofit, vegetarian, consensus-driven, environmentally focused housing cooperative. We are part of the first community co-op system in Colorado. We are owned by the Boulder Housing Coalition, a nonprofit organization currently providing affordable housing to the Boulder area. The co-op is a mix of students and nonstudents, we purchase food cooperatively and eat five meals a week together.

Visitors Accepted [Mar2005]

Scissors [✄] at the end of a listing indicate that it was edited for length by the Directory *editors and a longer description can be found at* directory.ic.org.

MAXWELTON CREEK COHOUSING

6037 Cascara Way
Clinton, WA 98236

360-321-5206
heidim@whidbey.com

Began: 1992 | Pop. 19
Rural | Diet: Primarily vegetarian

We are eight households, each having built our own homes within the larger 20+ acre community. We finally have a complete community and are in the process of building our common house. We are located in rural south Whidbey Island amongst cedars and meadows.

One home available for short-term rentals.

Visitors Accepted: Visitors are welcome when we have community workdays. Please contact us by email in advance to find out what weekend we will be working and what time of day makes sense to have visitors (sometimes we are in a meeting). [Mar2005]

MEADOWDANCE COMMUNITY GROUP

Amanda Walden
2078 Vt Rte 15
Walden, VT 05873

802-563-3099, 802-563-2105
info@meadowdance.org

http://www.meadowdance.org

Began: 1997 | Pop. 13
Rural | Diet: Omnivorous

Meadowdance is a group in the process of building an intentional community in Vermont. We began the process by email and physical gatherings and came together to live in Springfield in 2000. We now live in Walden and own a property in Marshfield, where we hope to build our final community.

Our vision encompasses:
• a supportive and socially cohesive environment;
• ecological sustainability;
• an economic model that uses a base work requirement to secure the necessities of living for all members, while not restricting individuals' other financial activities;
• financial stability;
• working primarily within the community;
• diversity of ages, ethnicities, religions, and lifestyles in an egalitarian community;
• developing a rich, nurturing, challenging environment for children;
• a secular community that is supportive of individuals' spiritualities;
• music and fun in day-to-day life.

Housing options are based on individual preference. There are no fees or dues. Investment is suggested where possible, but we have no minimum investment requirement. Investment is secured by the land, buildings, businesses, and other major assets of the community. Monetary investments carry no additional decision-making power.

We use formal consensus for decision making and are committed to egalitarian, participatory, respectful, and constructive governance.

Visitors Accepted: Feel free to email Amanda about visiting Meadowdance. We like to get to know people who are interested in visiting first before scheduling a visit. [Jan2005]

MELBOURNE COHOUSING NETWORK

Melbourne, Victoria
AUSTRALIA

Hans Tilstra
+61-(0)3-95979904
tilstra@smartchat.net.au

http://home.vicnet.net.au/~cohouse

Forming

An informal network of people interested in making cohousing happen in south eastern Australia. [Oct2004]

MELE NAHIKU

PO Box 922
Hana, HI 96713

808-248-8023
zac13_us@yahoo.com
forestgod@hotmail.com

Began: 2001 | Pop. 6 | Spiritual
Rural | Diet: Primarily vegetarian

Visitors Accepted: Please call or email us first. [Mar2005]

MERIDIANA

Thorsten Krüger
Sjökvarteret
Mariehamn, 22100
ÅLAND ISLANDS

+358-(0)457-3425916
projekt@meridiana.info

http://www.meridiana.info

Began: 2004 | Forming

Our project: an ecovillage on the Åland Islands, where 6500 islands and skerries are situated in the beautiful archipelago between Sweden and Finland. The varied nature is an effervescent source of life quality and inspiration.

The ecovillage promotes a lifestyle which unites tradition and future in the spirit of Agenda 21: The knowledge of life close to nature, developed over centuries in the archipelago, meets present day possibilities for sustainable ecological development based on local activities.

By a high level of self-sufficiency and the use of regional products, we want to minimize transport needs we consider to be ineffective and damaging to the environment.

Instead, cyclic thinking and ecological principles are key for our personal development towards "creative simplicity."

In the present "age of information" we find new possibilities to unite the places of work and living, thus combining life in the breathtakingly beautiful Åland landscape with widespread income sources. One's own estimation of life quality is deciding on one's settlement—that is a great chance to keep the archipelago alive!

We warmly welcome all people who want to join us and/or support this project. Our aim is a wide and balanced variety in sex, age, culture and qualification. Currently especially welcome are those who want to help in planning and building up the ecovillage. [Mar2005]

MERRY FOX COMMUNITY

Dan Boss
2265 7th St NW
Grand Rapids, MI 49504

616-453-4682, 989-983-4107
danbosscom@yahoo.com

http://www.geocities.com/
merryfoxcommunity

Began: 1999 | Pop. 6
Suburban | Diet: Vegetarian only

The Merry Fox Community is located in Grand Rapids, Michigan. We are dedicated to a spiritual, sustainable, and vegetarian lifestyle. Our house is set on a 2.2 acre plot in the city. Currently six people live at the house and we plan to add a bedroom that will allow for an extra person.

The next step for us is to purchase a much larger plot of land (50-200 acres) in the southeast US. Ultimately we would like to have at least two thousand acres to support a community of about a thousand people.

Visitors Accepted: Email or call us; we'll begin a dialogue and go from there. For any

Listings

Additions and corrections: email: directory@ic.org, *web:* directory.ic.org, *mail: RR 1 Box 156-D, Rutledge MO 63563, USA.*

visit beyond a couple days it would be best to visit us in the summer, when it is feasible to sleep in a tent. [Nov2004]

METHOW CENTER OF ENLIGHTENMENT

PO Box 976
Twisp, WA 98856

509-997-2620
cosmicrose@nwi.net

http://www.angelfire.com/
scifi/acosma

Began: 1990 | Pop. 1 | Rural

The Holy Wise Ones have designated Methow as a major spiritual center in development upon this planet. It is the responsibility of each spiritual group upstairs to position their ground ambassadors, aligning them with their spiritual center of choice. It is unfortunate that so few can actually align with these centers and ironic that the future of humankind lies in backcountry rural areas where natural, uncontaminated resources are plentiful. Our interdimensional celestial project in north-central Washington is designed to be a major communications command post and cultural-development learning and healing center for all who have access to it. Space people (UFO intelligences) from all dimensions will come and go freely from this celestial-city location.

We are reaching out to gather as many as divine guidance and time allow (Earth and economic changes); our goal is 2,000 settlers. At Methow there are no rules or regulations of any kind, since the whole valley is our spiritual center, including everybody in it. It is a clean, simple plan, approved by the Holy Wise Ones, and allows for everyone to do their thing naturally, finding their way in their own time. [Mar2005]

METRO COHOUSING AT CULVER WAY

3965 Westminster Pl
St. Louis, MO 63108

Tom and Carol Braford
314-534-4780, 314-753-3374
braford@sbcglobal.net

http://www.CulverWayCohousing.com

Began: 1999 | Forming
Urban | Diet: Primarily vegetarian

Metro Cohousing at Culver Way is the first cohousing community in the Culver Way Ecovillage. We are renovating three turn-of-

the-last-century commercial buildings and building three new buildings in the Central West End in the City of St. Louis. The first of our 44 units will be ready for move-in by the end of 2005.

Visitors Accepted: We have potluck dinners twice a month for prospective members. Call or email for dates, times and locations. [Feb2005]

MICCOSUKEE LAND CO-OP

9601 Miccosukee Rd #23A
Tallahassee, FL 32309
edde@nettally.com

Began: 1972 | Pop. 179 | Rural | Diet: Other

The Miccosukee Land Cooperative (MLC) is a community of 100 families and individuals who together own 344 acres situated east of Tallahassee. Co-op members privately own their own homesteads, which range in size from one acre to several acres each. Over 90 acres are preserved in their natural state as common land, owned collectively and enjoyed by the entire membership.

MLC members are drawn together by a common desire to live in a rural environment where the land/environment is respected and interaction between neighbors is a sought-after experience. All activities (other than paying assessments for necessities such as taxes and insurance) are purely voluntary, allowing each person to choose the level of sharing and socializing they prefer. While we are a diverse group in age, occupation, and religious practice, many adults are in the prime years of their careers. Despite a busy pace, we make time to celebrate the milestones of our lives and to support one another in times of sickness or tragedy. Many of us carry the vision of more time for shared meals and sitting on the porch shelling peas, gossiping, and singing. In the meantime we walk more separate paths but always give thanks for our land and precious neighbors.

Visitors Accepted: Please email to arrange a visit. [Mar2005]

MICHIGAN HOUSE

House President
315 N State St
Ann Arbor, MI 48104

734-996-5952

http://www.icc.coop

Began: 1932 | Pop. 19 | Urban

Founded in 1932, Michigan House is the oldest co-op in Ann Arbor, and is indeed

believed to be the oldest student housing co-op in North America. We have a very strong community and a healthy sense of house pride. Our common areas are rarely empty, and members can often be found discussing politics or culture over the bustling dinner table. We offer vegetarian options at every meal while also providing for our meat-eating brethren. Members of the big purple house next door (Minnie's) also board at Mich and are treated as full-fledged Mich Housers themselves (except for the occasional Mich v. Minnie's bowling match). On a sunny day, you're sure to find us hanging out on the comfortable porch. Stop by sometime and see what it's all about!

Visitors Accepted: Contact House President. [Mar2005]

MICHIGAN WOMYN'S MUSIC FESTIVAL

PO Box 22
Walhalla, MI 49458

231-757-4766, 510-652-5441

http://www.michfest.com

Began: 1976 | Rural | Diet: Primarily vegetarian

Michigan Womyn's Music Festival is a crucible for womyn's culture; a place to get your opinions stretched and your senses rocked. We build this community anew every year and take with us the inspiration, power, and hope that it ignites in each of us. The experience? Truly extraordinary...

Situated on 650 acres of secluded forest and meadows, Michigan is home to 5,000-6,000 womyn from around the world. We are communally run by each womyn who attends—all participate in two- to four-hour work shifts in addition to the efforts of hundreds of womyn who work to create and maintain the festival space.

Three meals a day are served of wood-fire-cooked vegetarian specialties. There is a full peer-support system for all needs: medical, emotional, disability, sober support, and childcare.

There are over 300 workshops offered and nightly screenings of womyn's film works. The massive and wonderful crafts bazaar features the work of over 130 craftswomyn.

And the music... The multiple stages serve for both day and night shows, acoustic as well as loud and funky. The gathering of eclectic womyn's music spans the globe: rock, classical, percussion, folk, African, punk, a cappella, Latin, gospel, jazz, and pop—it's all here!

Scissors [✂] at the end of a listing indicate that it was edited for length by the Directory editors and a longer description can be found at directory.ic.org.

Please write, visit us on the Web, or call for more information.

Visitors Accepted [Mar2005]

MIDCOAST COHOUSING COMMUNITY

PO Box 262
Damariscotta, ME 04543

David Pope
207-563-3494
pope@maine.edu

Grace Goldberg
207-529-5386

http://www.midcoastcohousing.com

Began: 2003 | Pop. 15
Rural | Diet: Omnivorous
[Oct2004]

MIDDLE ROAD COMMUNITY, THE

3140 The Middle Rd
Nelson, BC V1L 6M3
CANADA

Gary Ockenden
250-825-9497
ockenden@netidea.com

http://www.cohousing.ca/
detailed.htm#middle

Began: 1994 | Pop. 46
Rural | Diet: Omnivorous

The Middle Road Community is a cohousing community in south eastern British Columbia. We live on 21 hectares (52 acres) of land about 11 kilometres (7 miles) from the lovely art and ski community of Nelson (population 10,000) in the Selkirk Mountains. The land, which includes a mixture of forest, wetland and fields, is situated on an open bench overlooking the west arm of Kootenay Lake. The natural habitat is home to a variety of birds and wildlife. Half of the land is taken up by privately owned home sites and the other half is held in common. (Title for private land is tied legally to the community lands.)

The common land includes forested areas, streams, a playing field, a root cellar, a large community fire pit, and a two-and-a-half acre fenced area containing organic gardens, a small orchard and a chicken coop. The Common House, a converted hay barn, is at the heart of the community—consisting of a large kitchen and dining area, a games area, a quiet room, an activity room, a ping-pong room, an exercise/weight room, a guest room and bathrooms. The wood

floors, fireplaces, and magnificent views make it a cozy and welcoming place. In warm weather, the large deck extending into the garden is popular.

Community decisions are made by consensus.

While the community is currently at capacity, we have a "waiting circle" and welcome serious enquiries regarding future membership. We have no formal visitor or internship program.

Visitors Accepted: Contact in advance to explore arrangements. [Mar2005]

MILAGRO COHOUSING

3057 N Gaia Pl
Tucson, AZ 85745

520-743-2097
info1@milagrocohousing.org

http://www.milagrocohousing.org

Began: 1994 | Pop. 56
Rural | Diet: Omnivorous

Milagro Cohousing, a community in balance with nature, is a multigenerational neighborhood of 28 families clustered on 8 of our 43 acres in the Tucson Mountains. Our mission is to create community living that values consensus decision making in a nurturing environment, encouraging the contribution and growth of each individual. We have built our homes and operate our community in a way that honors the sacredness of the earth. We are a demonstration of ecological community living.

Visitors Accepted: Email or call: two weeks notice increases the likelihood of a tour, which includes our Common House, common landscaped areas, sewerage treatment wetlands and the interior of a home. If weather permits, a walk of the 43-acre property perimeter is a possibility. [Mar2005]

MILLSTONE CO-OP

102 Morrison Ave, Apt 2
Somerville, MA 02144

617-718-9285
millstone@bostoncoop.net
bcc-housing@bostoncoop.net

http://www.bostoncoop.net/
millstone

Began: 1999 | Pop. 9
Urban | Diet: Vegetarian only

Millstone is a community and a housing cooperative, a group of 8-10 individuals living and struggling together, organized around a set of principles: vegetarianism,

environmental sustainability, open communication, communal ownership, creativity, and social justice.

These core values underlie our shared vegetarian meals, our weekly housemeetings, our chore systems, and our collective purchases. They're tucked away in our conversations over dinner. They're clear in the support we give one another for our outside lives.

Millstone is a community in active struggle. You may see us in public clamoring for a cause, but there's more to it. We are working to strengthen cooperatives in greater Boston. As our current focus, we have established and are building Boston Community Cooperatives, Inc. (http://bostoncoop.net/bcc), a nonprofit corporation that will develop cooperatively owned, affordable housing. Through BCC, we are working to purchase a property for ourselves. BCC is also working to buy currently existing housing cooperatives from their owners. They will become member-controlled.

We're looking for people with common interests. You don't need to be able to make a large financial commitment to join us, just have energy and enthusiasm!

Visitors Accepted: Please give us as much notice as possible. Contact us by phone or email. We will assign a sponsor who will show you around, answer any questions, and coordinate plans. If no one is available, or we have many other guests staying with us, we may not be able to house you, but can put you in touch with other BCC houses or co-ops in the area. [Mar2005]

MINNIE'S HOUSE

House President
307 N State St
Ann Arbor, MI 48104

734-996-5950

http://www.icc.coop

Began: 1970 | Pop. 24
Urban | Diet: Omnivorous

Minnie's is our warm purple house located in the relaxed and historic North State neighborhood. Members enjoy our comfortable living room complete with a brand new TV and VCR. We have parking, a bike shed, and free laundry. We eat dinner at Michigan Co-op next door; however, we have our own small kitchen convenient for late-night chats and early morning breakfast. We do not allow cats. There's no smoking allowed in our house, but our inviting porch will suit any smoker's needs.

Visitors Accepted: Contact House President. [Mar2005]

Additions and corrections: email: directory@ic.org, web: directory.ic.org, mail: RR 1 Box 156-D, Rutledge MO 63563, USA.

189

MONAN'S RILL

Santa Rosa, CA
kavinoks@pacbell.net

Began: 1972 | Pop. 33
Rural | Diet: Omnivorous

The goal of Monan's Rill is having a balanced and diverse community reflecting a variety of ages, occupations, marital status, and family structure (some households have children; others do not). Our ages range from young children to people in their sixties.

We work as teachers, psychotherapists, administrators, nurses, medical technologist, cabinetmakers/contractors, artists, social activists, and parents. Our legal structure is a general partnership, and as such none of us hold individual title to the houses or land. Each member contributes an initial monetary investment and a monthly fee. Each family or individual lives in their own home.

Additionally, we share an organic garden and orchard, a large community center, a play area, a woodworking and maintenance shop, and a small barn and stables. Twice a month we gather for a community potluck dinner, business meeting (consensus decisions), and workday; however, informal smaller gatherings occur frequently. We try to recognize and cherish the different skills and insights of each individual and are committed to helping and encouraging one another.

Visitors Not Accepted [Dec2004]

MONKTON WYLD COURT

Charmouth, Bridport
Dorset DT6 6DQ England
UNITED KINGDOM

+44-(0)1297-560342
Monktonwyldcourt@btinternet.com
info@monktonwyldcourt.org

http://www.monktonwyldcourt.org

Began: 1982 | Pop. 16
Rural | Diet: Vegetarian only

Monkton Wyld Court is an educational charity run by a resident community of about a dozen adults, plus children and animals. The eleven-acre grounds include a fifteen bedroom Victorian rectory, a converted stable block and other outbuildings, a large organic vegetable garden, terraced lawns, fields, woods and stream. Facilities include a library, meditation hut, art hut, pottery, workshop, healing room and piano room. Living at Monkton is a full-time commitment. Each morning, we meet together to talk and plan the day. Cooking, cleaning, milking the cows, etc. is organised by rota, but each resident is also responsible for specific areas of work, from gardening to admin. We generate income through a programme of educational courses and other events, and also run a kindergarten for the local community. Our weekly community meetings alternate between "business" meetings where we make decisions by consensus, and "communication" meetings, where we address (inter) personal issues. We are committed to making continual improvements to our levels of ecological sustainability, and usefulness to the wider community as an educational resource. We welcome volunteers to work with us for one week initially. Volunteers often return for longer visits, and sometimes end up living here.

Visitors Accepted: Apply to come as a volunteer, either in writing or through our website. [Mar2005]

MONTEREY COHOUSING

2925 Monterey Ave S
Minneapolis, MN 55416

952-930-7554

Mike Malone
952-926-3872
MikeJoTodd@mn.rr.com

Karmit Bulman
kbulman@mn.rr.com

http://www.jimn.org/mococo

Began: 1991 | Pop. 31
Urban | Diet: Omnivorous

We are a unique, small community, located on 2.5 acres of partly-wooded land near the Minneapolis city limits. We value diversity, and have varying incomes. Our 15 households currently include ages 8 through 77, and singles and couples, both with and without children.

Occupations include computer programmers, artists, teachers, therapists, caregivers, scientists and more. We follow diverse spiritual and secular paths; among our traditions are driving each other to the airport and ER, parties, and monthly events, which have included singalongs, games, house concerts, benefit auction, etc.

Community meals and "co-chats" (spontaneous conversations) are the glue that hold the community together. Maintaining our 1924 building (part Common House, part residences) also gives opportunities to work together.

Homes include eight retrofit apartment-style homes in an Edwardian mansion and seven newly constructed townhouses, connected by underground walkway, and ranging from 400-1600 sq ft. Central courtyard and play area are separated from the driveway, the parking areas, and the large front lawn, which includes a community garden and picnic area. The grounds near the homes are lovingly landscaped, and we often see wildlife.

The community also has an abundance of interior common space, with new kitchen, three-season porch, elevator, three working fireplaces, a workshop, a laundry room, a children's playroom, and an office.

Our community grows from working together and shared experience.

Visitors Accepted: Please call our voicemail (952-930-7554) to arrange a visit. [Mar2005]

MONTPELIER COHOUSING

Montpelier, VT

Lexi Shear
802-229-9810

Frosty Ohlson
802-522-3234

info@montpeliercohousing.org

http://www.montpeliercohousing.org

Began: 2004 | Forming

We are a diverse group committed to creating a cohousing neighborhood that fosters a cooperative sense of community, shares and conserves resources to live lighter on the earth, and supports each other's growth, well-being and joy. We hope to create a neighborhood of about 15 families in Montpelier; currently we have 8 member households. We envision owning our own homes and sharing a central common house. We use a consensus decision making process and are currently investigating appropriate legal structures for our organization and looking for land.

Visitors Accepted: Currently, we meet every other week. Call us to find out when the next meeting is. [Mar2005]

MOONSHADOW

RR 1 Box 304
Whitwell, TN 37397

423-949-3021
mediarights@bledsoe.net

http://www.svionline.org

Began: 1971 | Pop. 17
Rural | Diet: Primarily vegan

Moonshadow is in a forested Appalachian valley with caves, creeks, and bluffs. Our

Scissors [✂] at the end of a listing indicate that it was edited for length by the Directory editors and a longer description can be found at directory.ic.org.

deliberate existence has a minimum impact on the forest ecosystem. We combine traditional knowledge with appropriate scientific methods to interact intelligently with nature. Our handcrafted buildings are made of natural materials. Our energy is from the sun and the forest. Trees and shrubs are integrated with food crops and herbs for self-sufficiency. We experiment with native and exotic plants for nutrition and medicine. Artistic expression fulfills personal, functional, and political needs. As organizers in the environmental and social-justice movements, we network with other groups and individuals.

We are striving to facilitate an evolutionary process that will radically change the system—the dominant paradigm—to ensure a sustainable future and equality for all life. We have created a solar-powered office space where the Sequatchie Valley Institute, a nonprofit educational organization, is based. Our major goal is to share our collectively gained wisdom through workshops, tours, publications, video, audio, computer networking, and gatherings. The mission of the Sequatchie Valley Institute is to offer society an opportunity to experience and learn about living in harmony with nature by providing: education, art and research opportunities; land conservation and restoration; a dynamic model residence and learning center; and a vision for attaining a sustainable future.

We hope that sharing our experience and vision will help people move more gently on the Earth. Ecology!

Visitors Accepted: Visitors or potential interns should contact us through our website, please. [Feb2005][✄]

MORNINGLORY

RR 4
Killaloe, ON K0J 2A0
CANADA

Began: 1969 | Pop. 14
Rural | Diet: Omnivorous

We are a village of separate households of single people and families, scattered over 100 hilly acres. We homestead in varying degrees, use only solar electricity and wood heat, and grow organically most of our fruits and veggies. We've spent 30 years learning how to be good neighbors, which has been a worthwhile process.

Most of our children were home birthed; some are homeschooled; ages 10 to 18. Swimming and skating on our pond, trampolining, tobogganing, snowshoeing, full-moon drumming, and song circles are some of the things we do for fun. We all share a love of nature and musicmaking.

Guests are welcome if they arrange in advance and help out while they're here.

May all people find harmony with Earth and each other!

Visitors Accepted: Please write us describing who you are, why and when you would like to visit, what skills and experience you would like to contribute to the community, and what you would like to learn here. [Mar2005]

MOSAIC COMMONS

MetroWest, MA 01740

508-453-0446
info@mosaic-commons.org

Catya Belfer-Shevett
catya@homeport.org

http://www.mosaic-commons.org

Began: 2000 | Pop. 46 | Small Town
Mosaic Commons is a cohousing community soon to complete a land purchase (with Camelot Cohousing) in Berlin, Massachusetts.

Visitors Accepted: Contact info@mosaic-commons.org, or call. [Mar2005]

MOUNT MADONNA CENTER

445 Summit Rd
Watsonville, CA 95076

831-847-0406
personnel@mountmadonna.org
programs@mountmadonna.org
webmaster@mountmadonna.org

http://www.mountmadonna.org

Began: 1971 | Pop. 96 | Spiritual
Rural | Diet: Vegetarian only

We are a spiritual community, focused on yoga and service, with some 100 members living on 355 mountaintop acres, operating a conference center and a children's school. Our larger fellowship also operates a yoga and conference center in Santa Cruz, and a metaphysical bookstore. We share in work, meals (vegetarian), spiritual practices, rituals, and play, and strive to live by positive values. Our teacher, Baba Hari Dass, embodies and teaches the classical Ashtanga (eight-limbed) yoga, with all its vital relevance to our lives today. Our fellowship started in 1971, and our resident community in 1978. Primary criteria for membership are good work, positive attitude, and interest in spirituality. Our conference center hosts about 14,000 peo-ple each year, our children's school has 195 students from preschool through high school, and our town center and bookstores are successful. Most work is done on a volunteer basis. Many members also hold outside jobs. Visit our website or send for information.

Visitors Accepted: Please send email to personnel@mountmadonna.org. [Jan2005]

MOUNTAIN HOME

95245 Rink Creek Ln
Coquille, OR 97423

541-396-4764
chipnclara@earthlink.net

Began: 1989 | Pop. 8
Rural | Diet: Omnivorous

Mountain Home is a developing off-grid ecovillage located on 360 acres in the Coquille River watershed and is a prototype for ecological forest management based on resident stewardship. Ecoforestry, the restoration of forest health, guides our practices, which are certified by Smartwood. A conservation easement protects the natural values of the land in perpetuity. We own $2/3$ of the Walker Creek watershed and are trying to buy the remaining $1/3$ from the timber company neighbor.

We have year-round apprentices and are open to other permanent resident stewards. Cob Cottage Company (www.cobcottage.com) has held Natural building workshops here since 2001, swelling the population for half the year. "Cobville" now includes 6 cob/hybrid structures, walled courtyard and year-round, fenced gardens.

Permaculture guides landscape use decisions. Consultants Tom Ward and Toby Hemenway have helped design our 4-acre homestead combining drainage, erosion control, fencing, access, and gravity flow water as the framework for an evolving solar bowl/food forest. Design is based on supporting a dozen people and buildings are made of mostly recycled or natural materials. Systems include photovoltaics, gravity flow water, wood-fired/solar hot water, wood heat, composting latrine, and greywater biofilters. We eat together once a day and share cooking. Cooperation is the key to land-based self reliance: thus, we increasingly barter and work trade with Cobville and other neighbors.

Demonstrating ecological culture is part of our mission, so call or email for a visit!

Visitors Accepted [Mar2005][✄]

Listings

Additions and corrections: email: directory@ic.org, *web:* directory.ic.org, *mail: RR 1 Box 156-D, Rutledge MO 63563, USA.*

191

MUIR COMMONS

2244 Muir Woods Pl
Davis, CA 95616

Info@muircommons.org

http://www.muircommons.org

Began: 1991 | Suburban

Muir Commons was the first cohousing community newly constructed in the United States and was modeled after communities in Denmark. After several years of planning, groundbreaking took place on November 1990, with the residents moving in during the summer of 1991. Most of the homes were constructed as affordable housing. [Mar2005]

MULVEY CREEK LAND CO-OPERATIVE

Sandy Blaikie Anderson
PO Box 286
Slocan, BC V0G 2C0
CANADA

250-355-2947,
250-355-2393 ext 1421
sandylee@telus.net
twinlarches@hotmail.com

Began: 1993 | Pop. 10
Rural | Diet: Primarily vegan

MCLC is situated on 240 acres in the spectacular wilderness of British Columbia. The land has an abundance of delicious creek water, two acres of fenced co-op garden space, over five acres of rich arable garden or crop lands, magical campgrounds and forest reserves, and is adjacent to Valhalla Park with its hiking trails and glacial lakes.

We have one area of about 25 acres on a ridge that is set slightly apart from the rest of the 240 acres, which currently has two developed and three undeveloped sites and would be an ideal location for a mini ecovillage.

We are open to new people, families, children, and new ideas.

Members may purchase 4-acre lots, and/ or cabins. Rentals are available to non-members.

We are looking for new co-creators/land partners who are committed to and are excited about sharing skills in sustainable life support systems: holistic diets, alternative energy, ecovillage/permaculture design, natural building construction.

Other interests: living more with less, ethical and creative income generation, cottage industry, eco-tourism, communication skills (conflict resolution, mediation, anger management), meditation and other healing practices and therapeutic arts, and local/global service work in the areas of environmental protection and human rights (battered women's shelter, single mom-and-child respite/haven).

Visitors Accepted: Contact Sandy Blaikie Anderson (250-355-2947 or sandylee@telus.net) or Keith Newberry (250-355-2393 ext 1433). [Mar2005][✂]

N STREET COHOUSING

724 N St
Davis, CA 95616

Kevin Wolf
530-758-4211
kjwolf@dcn.org
kevin@wolfandassociates.com

Perry Poe
papoe@mother.com

http://www.nstreetcohousing.org

Began: 1986 | Pop. 55
Small Town | Diet: Omnivorous

N Street is a cohousing group that was started in 1986 when two tract homes built in the early 1950s took down their side fences. N Street continues to grow slowly, adding one house at a time. We currently have expanded to 17 houses, ten homes on N Street that back up to seven homes on the adjacent street. (Two of the homes on N Street are across the street from the community but are active members.) The removal of fences has created a beautiful open-space area that includes vegetable, flower, and water gardens; a play structure; a hot tub; a sauna; and a chicken coop, large grassy area, pond and more.

We enjoy sharing community meals in our common house 3-4 times per week and work parties once a month. Informally, people get together to share dinners at home, a soak in the hot tub, a game of cards, or just a nice cup of tea. We are a mixed community of half renters and half home owners of around 18 kids and 40 adults.

Visitors Accepted: Contact kevin@wolfandassociates.com. [Jan2005]

NAHZIRYAH MONASTIC COMMUNITY

Rev. Nazirmoreh K B Kedem
PO Box 1280
Yellville, AR 72687

870-449-4381
carrier@nmcnews.org
eemeht@thepurplepeople.com

http://www.nmcnews.org

Began: 1970 | Spiritual
Rural | Diet: Vegan only

Rev. Nazirmoreh, founder, director, and spiritual head of Nahziryah Monastic Community, and the Nazir Order of the Purple Veil, (also known as "The Purple People") is our spiritual teacher and guide. Rev. Nazirmoreh teaches that there are many paths, one goal; many names, one Divine Creator. The Nazir community is monastic, abiding by rules, order, and disciplines. The monastery includes men, women, and children. Resident members live a simple, monastic, communal life. We work hard, meditate, study, and strive daily to overcome the lower ego.

At the Nahziryah Monastic Community, Retreat for Meditation and Wholistic Living, we do organic gardening to help sustain the community's dietary needs (vegan). To support the community and the effort toward consciousness expansion and further spiritual development, we make and sell art crafts, as well as metaphysical/esoteric/spiritual literature of all faiths, recordings, essential and essence oils, incense, and meditation supplies.

Nahziryah Monastic Community sustains itself through its own laborious efforts, except for occasional donations given by the few who are sympathetic with the Nazir way of life and are willing and able to help, financially and otherwise, to support the service. The Nazir path is for those who hear the call and come to give their All in All... Behold the One in All.

Visitors Accepted: All visits must be pre-approved by the Rev. Nazirmoreh. Request a visitation questionnaire, then fill out and return it, that the Reverend may review and approve of according to time requested and reason for requested visit. [Jan2005]

NAKAMURA HOUSE

Ann Arbor, Michigan
http://www.icc.coop
Urban

We provide an extremely friendly and memorable cooperative experience. Combining

Scissors [✂] at the end of a listing indicate that it was edited for length by the Directory editors and a longer description can be found at directory.ic.org.

modern amenities (Macintosh computer, TV/VCR/cable, piano, and new stereo system) with a strong sense of tradition, a weird house culture, and fierce Nak pride, this co-op operates with abundant comfort and mirth. We provide a stable balance for students of all persuasions, including smokers/nonsmokers, cat lovers/haters, and vegetarians/carnivores. All your vices can be satisfied due to our prime location, proximate to campus (wake up five minutes before class), several eateries (fight the munchies), and three party stores (get your "pop and pretzels"). Our front porch, the best in all of Ann Arbor and the source of countless escapades, is marked by a beloved Pteranodon. Adept at throwing major parties as well as quieter social gatherings, Nakamura welcomes diverse students of all backgrounds. Stop by and check us out! We house 47 in 13 singles, 15 doubles, and 2 suites and seven more members in the Kagawa Annex.

Visitors Not Accepted [Mar2005]

NAMASTÉ GREENFIRE

373 Peacham Rd
Center Barnstead, NH 03225

603-776-7776
nhnamaste@yahoo.com

Forming | Spiritual | Rural

We see intentional community as a focused spiritual practice (not at all religious). The "reason for being" in circle is to perfect one's loving capacity inside wisdom, trust, respect, open sensitivity, integrity. This leads to cooperation, synergy and creativity without limits. Loving nature/loving each other is the means to empowering personal and group transformation. It is clearly our intention and it is done in circles.

We have gorgeous land, simple living structures, a vision of ecovillage and a need for committed partners. This is for anyone who wishes to rise above mind and body games to the 3rd Dimension; spirit and truth. We are into cultural evolution (a sane and sustainable future). We envision many such communities, community pods, communes (groups sharing and servicing together) that are vitally connected as a real means to global social justice. Learning how to perfect our capacity to love, trust and synergize is what we think of as permacultural relationships. This is done best inside safe circles of trusted friends. We are working on being

one such group. Join us. Free thinkers/activists always welcomed.

Social evolution is now.

Visitors Accepted [Mar2005]

NAMASTÉ... MULTI-CULTURAL, SUSTAINABLE LIVING COMMUNITY OF BELIZE C.A.

Michael James Taylor
228 Commercial St #107
Nevada City, CA 95959

530-559-9697
mjt_4u@hotmail.com

Began: 2005 | Pop. 95 | Forming | Spiritual Rural | Diet: Primarily raw foods

The intention of our community is that of being completely self-sustainable. As part of this community there is a yoga and raw food retreat, and special events center for visitors internationally alike. This retreat center is centrally located as part of the common area of the community and includes a sanctuary, community dorm, multi-purpose room (for yoga, prayer, education, arts, drumming, etc.), a kitchen, laundry, bath house, sauna, sweatlodge, and fenced common garden areas to support ongoing community conscious living.

This community is approximately 500 acres of a 4100-acre farming ranch with a major river running through it in the heart of the country of Belize's fertile, rich savannas. We hope to grow soy beans for a biodiesel pilot program, okra and other produce, and raise organically fed, hormone free livestock for international export.

This community is designed to be entirely financially sustainable with employment opportunities as part of the community, the ranch, and in town. The founder also hopes to open a "green" restaurant and health food store in town near the tourism hub of Belize, Belize City.

NAMASTÉ... Community will likely be cooperatively owned and operated. There will be approximately fifty 1-acre (+/-) lots available for purchase that can be legally deeded to the rightful owner on approval of application by elected elders of the community.

Visitors Accepted: Registered community members may have visitors (with creditable references) staying with them in their own home at any time. Other visitors may apply for temporary employment in exchange for staying in community. Yoga Masters and other teachers of various healing arts are welcome with notification. [Mar2005]

NANISH SHONTIE

Mala Spotted Eagle
PO Box 17
Blachly, OR 97412

541-925-3777
nanish@peak.org

http://www.nanish.org

Began: 1997 | Pop. 6 | Spiritual Rural | Diet: Omnivorous

Nanish Shontie is a native-guided nonprofit intertribal, interracial community in Western Oregon. It is a place where people have an opportunity to learn from traditional native people about the native way of living with Mother Earth. Nanish Shontie is helping to build a bridge between the modern world and indigenous world so that we may work together for the healing of Mother Earth.

Nanish Shontie is sharing the teachings of the ways that were taught to us from Mother Earth.

Visitors Accepted: Please contact us first and be open to a different culture. [Dec2004]

NARROW WAY CHRISTIAN COMMUNITY

1909 Saint Paul Church Rd
Chapin, IL 62628

Forming | Rural

"Enter ye in at the narrow gate; for wide is the gate, and broad is the way, that leadeth to destruction, and many there be which go in thereat; Because straight is the gate, and narrow is the way, which leadeth into life, and few there be that find it." Matthew 7:13–14 King James Version

A Christian Celibate Community forming on a 46 acre farm, in central Illinois, three houses. Mature Christian celibate men and women, desiring to live the teachings of Jesus, are welcome, as visitors and/or potential members.

"For thus saith the Lord unto the eunuchs that keep My Sabbaths, and choose the things that please Me; and take hold of My covenant, even unto them will I give in Mine house and within My walls a place and a name better than of sons and of daughters, I will give them an everlasting name, that shall not be cut off." Isaiah 56:4–5 King James Version

"There are eunuchs born that way from their mother's womb, there are eunuchs made so by men, and there are eunuchs who have made themselves that way for the sake of the Kingdom of Heaven. Let anyone

Additions and corrections: email: directory@ic.org, web: directory.ic.org, mail: RR 1 Box 156-D, Rutledge MO 63563, USA.

193

Listings

accept this who can." Matthew 19:12 Jerusalem Version

"I would like you to be free from worry. An unmarried man concerns himself with the Lord's work, because he is trying to please the Lord; but a married man concerns himself with worldly matters, because he wants to please his wife, and so he is pulled in two directions. An unmarried woman or a virgin concerns herself with the Lord's work, because she wants to be dedicated both in body and spirit; but a married woman concerns herself with worldly matters, because she wants to please her husband. I am saying this because I want to help you. I am not trying to put restrictions on you. Instead, I want you to do what is right and proper, and give yourselves completely to the Lord's service without any reservation." I Corinthians 7:32–35 Today's English Version

Visitors Accepted: Write for information. [Mar2005]

NASALAM

864 N Ranch Rd
Fair Grove, MO 65648

417-759-7854
nasalam@aol.com

http://www.nasalam.org

Began: 1984 | Pop. 2 | Spiritual
Rural | Diet: Vegetarian only

Nasalam is a tantric spiritual community dedicated to the spiritual unfoldment of humankind. Our lifestyle is designed to assist us in that goal by being gentle to the planet and all living things, made easier by living in the country on sacred land. We will develop a tribal lifestyle to provide the physical and emotional support needed by all humans. As a tantric community we believe in enjoying life to the fullest but within the context of spiritual growth. For that reason, we abstain from consuming animal protein and strive to be free of substances that pollute the body or enslave it through addiction. We employ daily practices to regulate the spiritual life of the community, and as we believe that sexual energy is a primary tool for realization of the divine we employ erotic interaction as part of our spiritual practice. Because of our erotic orientation we are primarily interested in gay/lesbian/bisexual members.

The more complete vision of Nasalam, its spiritual beliefs and social philosophy, can be found on our webpage.

Visitors Accepted: Read visitor information on webpage and contact us. [Jan2005]

NATURE'S PACE SANCTUARY

http://www.Back40Books.com

Began: 1995 | Pop. 5 | Spiritual
Rural | Diet: Omnivorous

Nature's Pace Sanctuary is located on 180 secluded, scenic, rolling acres in Southeast Missouri. Our Sanctuary is divided between forest and farm lands and fronts on the Current River.

Living in tune with Nature is important to us. We grow, forage, hunt and preserve our own food; heat with wood; work hard; and feel a spiritual connection with the Great Spirit and all the beings in the universe. We are wary of technology and continue to evaluate just what items are appropriate for us to use. Right now, we heat with wood (cut with chainsaws), light our homes with oil lamps (but use electricity in our business area), and operate an online store, but restrict the use of the computer, radio, television and recorded music. In the near future we plan to begin using horses for farm work, but presently use conventional transportation and tillage methods.

It is our desire to live an ascetic life apart from contemporary society and demonstrate through daily life the satisfaction and necessity of living within nature's laws. We prepare all foods from scratch and eat an omnivorous diet including wild game and edible plants.

We are organized as a 501(d) communal religious organization. Members receive food, clothing, shelter and a small discretionary allowance in exchange for their labor, with major property owned by the community. We are governed by a group of Elders chosen from the full members of our community.

If you are willing to live extremely close to the land and are a dedicated "child of the Earth," send $2.00 for information packets. Singles, couples, families welcome.

Visitors Accepted: Contact our visitor coordinator Linda Lee. Agree to pitch in and help do what needs to be done. Let us know in advance what skills you can add to our community and what your dreams are. [Oct2004][✂]

NEO COHOUSING

c/o Kip and Beth Gardner
426 Schneider St SE
North Canton, OH 44720

330-494-1775
kipandbeth@earthlink.net

Began: 2003 | Diet: Omnivorous

NEO Cohousing formed in late 2003, and is currently re-forming after undergoing some

membership attrition. We now have about 25 interested households.

Our group exists for two primary reasons: to promote the idea of intentional living arrangements throughout the northern Ohio region through outreach and education and to establish our own ecovillage-style community near Akron, Ohio.

This community may or may not be a formal cohousing community, as we are still discussing ownership and development models.

In September 2004 we adopted the following draft vision statement:

"We are striving to create an intentional community, designed by the residents to encourage social interaction between neighbors in daily life. We intend to promote and embody the restoration of healthy and balanced relationships among people, land and resources."

Briefly, we aim to develop a community of 6-15 households on 20-40 acres of rural land, featuring clustered village-style housing, as well as a mix of recreational and agricultural land. All land use decisions will be based on sound ecologically-integrated design principles (Permaculture). Our ownership model preference would be a land trust with individual equity ownership of dwellings and improvements. We have done a fair amount of planning with regard to a general vision for the community, core values, ownership models, and decision-making processes, but there is more to be done as we reorganize with new people.

Visitors Accepted: We hold planning meetings twice a month, and welcome all interested people to contact us for information on how to become involved. [Mar2005][✂]

NEO HIPPIE HAVEN

California
freedom_958@hotmail.com

Forming

I don't have any land but please contact me if you are interested in nature-living, sustainable, very cheap or free living. I like the old hippie vision minus the drugs. I think our American and global society is going downhill and I really want to find/create a pocket of good people living in harmony with each other and nature—growing our own stuff, maybe fishing or hunting with renewable supplies. Old Native American traditions and that lifestyle also resonates with me. I am a homeless-by-choice person who hangs out in parks and enjoys nature. I like the wilderness but it gets lonely. Seeking other like-minded people. Again, I don't have any money but I can work very well and I'm pretty smart. You need to

Scissors [✂] at the end of a listing indicate that it was edited for length by the Directory editors and a longer description can be found at directory.ic.org.

embrace the vision which is pretty simple (outlined above: freedom, simple, harmony). And I really try to stay away from drugs. As for a location to call our home, there is more than one option: one is to network and join other communities; another option is to find our own land. The most important reason I'm posting this is to get in contact with some other people who want to bring back the communal, sustainable, free, happy, harmonious-with-nature culture that was growing in the 70s—but preferably minus the drugs. Please email me if you are interested. Thanks.

Visitors Accepted [Nov2004]

NEVADA CITY COHOUSING

near W Broad St and Chief Kelley Dr
Nevada City, CA

info@nccoho.org

http://www.nccoho.org

Began: 2003 | Pop. 86

We are 84 (+2) people altogether—56 adult members, 30 kid members (+2 part timers). This includes: 17 elder members (55+), 12 single adult households, and 19 households with kids.

Construction has begun, and if all goes as planned, we will be moved in by Fall 2005. All of our houses are sold and we are not accepting new members at this time.

Email us if you would like to be on an interest list for possible openings. [Mar2005]

NEVE SHALOM/WAHAT AL-SALAM (OASIS OF PEACE)

Public Relations Office
Goodwin Dr
Doar Na Shimshon 99761
ISRAEL

+972-(0)2-9915621, +972-(0)2-9912222
pr@nswas.com

The American Friends of Neve
Shalom/Wahat al-Salam
4201 Church Rd, Ste 4
Mt. Laurel, NJ 08054
856-235-6200

The American Friends of Neve
Shalom/Wahat al-Salam
12925 Riverside Dr, 3rd Fl
Sherman Oaks, CA 91423
818-325-8884
afnswas@oasisofpeace.org

http://nswas.com

Began: 1970 | Pop. 200
Rural | Diet: Omnivorous

Neve Shalom/Wahat al-Salam (pronounced

nevey shalom/wahat as-salaam) is a cooperative village of Jews and Palestinian Arabs of Israeli citizenship. Situated equidistant from Jerusalem and Tel Aviv-Jaffa, Neve Shalom/Wahat al-Salam was founded in 1972 on 100 acres of land leased from the adjacent Latrun Monastery. The first families came to live in the village in 1977. By 2004, 50 families had settled there. Eventually, the population is expected to reach 140 families.

The members of Neve Shalom/Wahat al-Salam are demonstrating the possibility of coexistence between Jews and Palestinians by developing a community based on mutual acceptance, respect, and cooperation. Democratically governed and owned by its members, the community is not affiliated with any political party or movement.

Neve Shalom/Wahat al-Salam gives practical expression to its vision through its various branches:

- The bilingual, bi-cultural school, founded in 1984, educates some 300 children from the area, and works to establish this form of education as a viable model.

- The School for Peace, founded in 1979, conducts courses and seminars for Arab and Jewish youth and adults in Israel and from the Palestinian Authority.

- "Doumia-Sakinah," the Pluralistic Spiritual Center, provides a framework for exploring religious, cultural and spiritual resources that may be drawn upon in working and educating for peace.

- A hotel, with dining facilities and conference halls, offers comfortable accommodation and a variety of educational programs.

Visitors Accepted: Individual visitors should contact the public relations office at pr@nswas.com.

Group visitors should contact the group visits coordinator at rita@nswas.com.

Those wishing to stay at the guest house should contact the guest house directly at hotel@nswas.com. [Oct2004]

Listings

Additions and corrections: email: directory@ic.org, *web:* directory.ic.org, *mail: RR 1 Box 156-D, Rutledge MO 63563, USA.*

195

NEW CREATION CHRISTIAN COMMUNITY

Nether Heyford
Northampton NN7 3LB England
UNITED KINGDOM

+44-(0)1327-344500,
+44-(0)1327-344521 (fax)
info@jesus.org.uk

http://www.newcreation.org.uk

Began: 1974 | Pop. 680 | Spiritual
Diet: Omnivorous

The New Creation Christian Community is part of the Jesus Fellowship Church, which is also known as the Jesus Army. The fellowship is an evangelical Christian church with a contemporary charismatic emphasis. It is orthodox in doctrine, upholding the universally accepted Christian creeds.

The church numbers around 2,500, about 600 of whom live in Christian Community in 60 or so houses around the United Kingdom. Each community house consists of anything between 6 and 60 people, who live as a large "family."

The businesses, community houses, and other community assets are owned by the members and held in a legally constituted noncharitable trust fund. Within the community, each house has a "common-purse" arrangement, with members pooling their income to meet all personal and household expenses.

Community houses are open to receive visitors on a temporary basis for up to six months (which can be extended to up to 12 months). If visitors' stay is longer than a week, they pay a board-and-lodging charge, but the remainder of their income is at their disposal.

Visitors Accepted: Please contact us by email at our Central Offices if you would like to visit one of our community houses. [Oct2004]

NEW EARTH COOPERATIVE

Hawaii
Triaka@webtv.net

http://groups.yahoo.com/group/uniteddiversity

Forming

Aloha! For a peaceful, harmonious moral and ethical world, and the "highest good of all," we propose reorganizing existing political structures in accordance with the Constitution of United Diversity, "The New Earth Cooperative" as detailed on our website.

Goodwill to all,
Triaka [Dec2004]

NEW ENVIRONMENT ASSOCIATION

270 Fenway Dr
Syracuse, NY 13224

315-446-8009
hs38@mailbox.syr.edu

http://web.syr.edu/~hs38/neaindex.htm

Began: 1974
Urban | Diet: Primarily vegetarian

The association, begun in 1974, provides a framework and process for people to come together in order to create a sustainable society—a "New Environment"—through raising awareness, modifying lifestyles, developing a sense of community, and taking part in cooperative activities. A wide range of topics gets addressed at our general meetings and study groups, from organic gardening and holistic health to new economics and alternative education.

Activities vary and depend on members' interests. Currently, we operate a large CSA project in the Syracuse area, have published a "Steps to Sustainability" calendar, and are looking for land to create an educational center, possibly with a small community. The long-range goal is new communities that are humanly and environmentally sound. Members gather periodically for weekend retreats and pursue specific projects in small working groups. Our monthly newsletter reaches readers across the United States and in several other countries. Send for a free sample copy! [Mar2005]

NEW GOLOKA

1032 Dimmocks Mill Rd
Hillsborough, NC 27278

919-732-6492
bkgoswami@compuserve.com
lilasuka97@yahoo.com

http://www.newgoloka.com

Began: 1982 | Pop. 24 | Spiritual
Rural | Diet: Vegetarian only

New Goloka is a beautiful rural Radha-Krishna temple located 20 minutes from Chapel Hill, North Carolina. Our property is 16 acres surrounded by lush forest and large streams. The atmosphere is tranquil and spiritually uplifting. We have daily temple services and meditation. Our philosophy stresses that eating is a spiritual process, and so we cook and offer many sumptuous preparations daily.

Scissors [✂] at the end of a listing indicate that it was edited for length by the Directory editors and a longer description can be found at directory.ic.org.

We have flower and vegetable gardens that we use for temple worship and cooking.

We do have a guest facility, but one must make arrangements in advance and there is a screening process.

Our founder, His Divine Grace AC Bhaktivedanta Swami Prabhupada, said we should make a life of simple living and high thinking, so we hope to imbibe this mood here at New Goloka.

We daily study the Bhagavad-Gita as well as the Srimad Bhagavatam.

Visitors Accepted: Please call for directions or visit any Sunday at 5:00 pm for open house. This open house program is available worldwide in all of our 350 centers of the International Society for Krishna Consciousness. [Mar2005]

NEW HORIZONS

J. Fulkerson
Phoenix, AZ 85027

623-492-9965
jfulkerson@gaiagate.com
jdfulkerson@go.com

http://www.gaiagate.com/
newhorizons

Began: 1990 | Forming | Spiritual
Diet: Omnivorous

We are a group of like-minded people who enjoy getting together for family-friendly activities.

We have interests in community, sustainable living, Gaia, and having fun.

We are based in Phoenix, but if you can come on down for getting together every now and then, you are welcome.

Visitors Accepted: Contact by email with approximate dates you would be in Phoenix. If something is going on, we will respond with information. [Feb2005]

NEW MEADOW RUN BRUDERHOF

http://www.newmeadowrunbruderhof
.com

In 1957, the Bruderhof needed to establish a new community in the United States to accommodate members moving from Bruderhofs in the backwoods of Paraguay, where they had been eking out a meager existence for fifteen years since fleeing Europe during World War II. On June 2, 1957 the papers for the purchase of Gorley's Lake Hotel were signed. This property was located in the wooded foothills of Chestnut Ridge in southwest-

ern Pennsylvania, a lakefront hotel along US Route 40 (known as the "National Pike") near Fort Necessity National Battlefield.

New Meadow Run Bruderhof (formerly Oak Lake) has been in existence since July 1957. [Feb2005]

NEW VIEW COHOUSING

Steve Hecht
6 Half Moon Hill
Acton, MA 01720

978-635-1145
steve_hecht@newview.org
webmaster@newview.org

http://www.newview.org

Began: 1989 | Pop. 83
Suburban | Diet: Omnivorous

Suburban cohousing: basically families and individuals who want to share meals, child rearing, joys and sorrows, taking care of the land, and creating beauty; and who want a balance of privacy and community in their lives.

Visitors Accepted: Contact Nola@newview.org to set up a time for a tour. [Mar2005]

NEW WORLD RISING

nwrfred
PO Box 27773
Providence, RI 02907

401-942-6694
NWRfred@yahoo.com

http://www.newworldrising.org

Began: 1986

The focus of New World Rising is to develop networks of cooperative consciousness, communications, connections and communities. Our primary focus is developing a national and international network of communities. We are developing connections thru our forum at *http://groups.yahoo.com/ group/newworldrisingforum*. Our primary means of developing funding is thru renovating houses for sale in Rhode Island. We are also developing a bakery and awareness center and will be reactivating our cooperative living project here. We currently also have cooperative projects developing in Crestone, CO, New Paltz, NY, Gainesville, FL, and potentials developing in Texas and California and Brazil among other places. [Mar2005]

NEWBERRY PLACE: A GRAND RAPIDS COHOUSING COMMUNITY

719 Livingston Ave NE
Grand Rapids, MI 49503
steve@grandrapidscoho.org

Steve Faber
616-456-0485
steve@cityvisioninc.org

http://www.grandrapidscoho.org

Began: 2002 | Pop. 27 | Forming
Urban | Diet: Omnivorous

Newberry Place will be a development of an urban cohousing neighborhood of 15-20 units. We have purchased three parcels of land for a total of one acre in a residential neighborhood overlooking downtown. We are currently beginning the site design process which will help to determine the allowable density and total units available. Our core values are: Urban Location, Innovative Design, Community, Diversity, and Stewardship. We host Informational Meetings every month, so please contact us or visit our website if you are interested in learning more.

Visitors Accepted: If you're in Grand Rapids and want to visit with us, email steve@cityvisioninc.org. [Jan2005]

NEXT STEP INTEGRAL

Stephan Martineau
G 4 C17 RR#1
Winlaw, BC V0G 2J0
CANADA

250-355-2206
star@netidea.com
info@integrallife.org

http://www.integrallife.org

Began: 1992 | Pop. 13 | Spiritual
Small Town | Diet: Primarily vegetarian

Next Step Integral, formerly Morning Star Community, is an integral* community founded in 1992. (* integral: to integrate, to bring together, to join, to link, to embrace. Not in the sense of uniformity, but in the sense of unity-in-diversity.)

We are an international body of individuals touched at a core level by a call to come together in service to the work of consciousness evolution. As we deepen our understanding of the next step in consciousness evolution, we place a primary focus on actually applying our discoveries to our lives. We are awed, fascinated and humbled by the potential breadth and depth of human life. We are aware of a real need for integral exam-

Additions and corrections: email: directory@ic.org, *web:* directory.ic.org, *mail: RR 1 Box 156-D, Rutledge MO 63563, USA.*

197

Listings

ples of life to find expression here and now on earth. Our main emphases are: personal and global transformation, research, education, collective intelligence and networking.

Our vision is that we be, above all, a living body that will continue to grow, mature, expand and diversify, continuously re-examining, staying on the edge of the unknown, not settling, but being shaped by the call of the future and by the many parts that form the whole. We seek to respond wholeheartedly, seriously and joyously to the predicament of our times. To listen to the whisperings of Spirit that invite us to full Union, to communion, where the One and the Many are present and alive.

The vision of Next Step Integral arises from the knowledge that a quantum leap in consciousness is possible and necessary — one that will balance our awakened authentic individual self with the communion that is inherently possible between humans.

Visitors Accepted: Only with prior arrangement in writing. [Jan2005]

NICHE / TUCSON COMMUNITY LAND TRUST

1050 S Verdugo Ave
Tucson, AZ 85745

520-882-0985

Began: 1992 | Pop. 4
Urban | Diet: Primarily vegetarian

Niche is a cooperative house held in trust, located on two acres. It is currently primarily engaged in social justice activities, including promoting the community land trust model, helping neighbors mitigate the negative effects that greedy speculators are having on the area, and working with a youth service group. Occasional "Women Build Houses" activities still occur on the site. Se habla español.

Visitors Accepted: Write or call first. [Mar2005]

NIEDERKAUFUNGEN

Kirchweg 1
D-34260 Kaufungen
GERMANY

+49-(0)5605-80070
info@kommune-niederkaufungen.de

http://www.kommune-niederkaufungen.de

Began: 1986 | Pop. 76 | Diet: Omnivorous

Kommune Niederkaufungen, Germany's largest secular income-sharing commune, is

an undogmatic, left-wing project; non-religious and non-spiritual. The main focuses are a fully socialized economy, consensus decision making, collective work, reduction of patriarchal structures, and an ecological approach to work and lifestyle. We try to satisfy as many of our own basic needs as possible, and also to offer ecological products and social services to the local population. Where possible we consume organic, regional and seasonal products, and fair trade goods. We use renewable fuel resources for a major part of our heating (wood) and for part of our motor vehicle pool (rape seed oil).

We run 12 commune-owned collectives:
• carpentry and joinery shop
• seminar center, courses on commune themes and nonviolent communication
• building firm, interior and exterior construction, metal-workshop
• kitchen/catering firm
• Bioland certified organic market-garden, farm shop
• EU certified organic dairy farm, cheese making
• leather workshop
• kindergarten
• solar electricity production, consultancy, planning
• administration/consulting group
• physiotherapy practice, acupuncture massage
• a day care center for old people is now being built.
Some people work externally.

We live in 11 living groups with a men's group and two women's/lesbian groups, share all our meals, and have weekly general meetings. Newcomers go through a three- to six-month trial period. We frequently offer orientation weekends and weeks for interested people.

Visitors Accepted: Please contact us well in advance; include information about yourself, your reasons for wanting to visit, and the date and length of the visit. We will tell you whether a visit is possible. Please leave pets at home. [Mar2005]

NINTH STREET CO-OP

1714 9th St
Berkeley, CA 94710
ricklewis@california.com

http://barringtoncollective.org/housing/view.php?house_id=12

Began: 1993 | Pop. 7
Urban | Diet: Omnivorous

Ninth Street Co-op is a limited-equity housing cooperative owned by the residents. The

co-op consists of two duplexes and one cottage with a common area, four garages, fruit trees, an organic garden and chickens. We are in an urban, working-class neighborhood that is ethnically diverse. Members are low to moderate income. All members serve on the board of directors that meets monthly to discuss co-op business. Members share maintenance tasks. Ninth Street Co-op is self-managed. We have owned the property since 1986 and became a co-op in 1993. [Jan2005]

NOMAD COHOUSING

1460 Quince Ave #102
Boulder, CO 80304

Arthur Okner
303-442-3038
ArtOkner@att.net

Vinc Duran
vincd@frgcentral.net

http://www.nomadcohousing.org

Began: 1994 | Pop. 24
Urban | Diet: Omnivorous

Nomad Cohousing is an 11-unit urban community on one acre two miles from beautiful downtown Boulder. Our common dining area is attached to a 50-year-old community playhouse (The Nomad Theater) that we share with them in a relationship where they hold opening-night receptions for their plays in our common house and we use the theater for philanthropical passions, i.e., benefits for affordable housing agencies and the Sierra Club. We are adjacent to a small shopping center (supermarket, two restaurants, video rental, liquor store, cafe, diner and dry cleaners) and within a couple of minutes walk of the foothills to the Rockies and Boulder Mountain open space. As if this is not enough we are a block off of Boulder's bus route.

Visitors Accepted: Contact Arthur [Feb2005]

NOMENUS RADICAL FAERIE SANCTUARY

PO Box 312
Wolf Creek, OR 97497

541-866-2678
nomenus@budget.net

Began: 1984 | Pop. 12 | Spiritual
Rural | Diet: Omnivorous

The Wolf Creek Sanctuary is the manifestation of Nomenus' statement of purpose to "create, preserve, and manage places of

Scissors [✂] at the end of a listing indicate that it was edited for length by the Directory editors and a longer description can be found at directory.ic.org.

cultural/spiritual sanctuary for Radical Fairies and their friends to gather in harmony with nature for renewal, growth, and shared learning." Nomenus is incorporated as a church under section 501(c)3 of the tax code and is a resource for issues concerning the connections between gay men's sexuality and spirituality. The land is also available to outside groups as a rustic gathering/retreat center with primitive campsites and limited indoor lodging, and supports a small group of residents who are members of, and in service to, Nomenus.

Visitors Accepted [Mar2005]

NORTH MOUNTAIN COMMUNITY LAND TRUST

154 Hayslette Rd
Lexington, VA 24450

540-463-1760
mirabai888@yahoo.com

Began: 1972 | Pop. 5
Rural | Diet: Primarily vegetarian

North Mountain began in 1972 as a rural commune. We have a beautiful piece of land—130 acres, mostly hilly woods, about 10 of it tillable. We are located in a valley encircled by the ancient Allegheny Mountains.

The commune continued with many comings and goings through the 1970s and into the mid-1980s. As our membership grew older and most began having families, the need for individual housing grew. In 1990 we changed our structure to that of a land trust.

The land is owned by the community with members having lifetime leases to individual 2-acre plots. Homes are owned by the members. There is a work commitment each month as well as a monetary one. We have meetings monthly, potlucks regularly, and labor exchanges among us.

We now consist of five members—two homes, three adults, two teens, various dogs, cats, chickens, a barn, a shop, and a granary. We do some gardens together, others individually. We have hopes to grow in the future but no desire to grow too quickly or too large, remaining at six to eight households at most.

Visitors Accepted: If interested, please write to schedule a visit. We want to ensure that you know us and we know you and we all know what's involved when we join together in the dance of community living. Come dance with us at North Mountain Community. [Feb2005]

NORTHERN SUN FARM CO-OP

PO Box 71
Sarto, MB R0A 1X0
CANADA

204-434-6887, 204-434-6143

Began: 1984 | Pop. 11
Rural | Diet: Omnivorous

Northern Sun Farm Co-Op is a rural community with the land being cooperatively owned by all members. We have both resident and nonresident members. Our focus is on alternative energy, appropriate technology, simple lifestyles, and self-reliance. We live in family groups, and we promote individual responsibility for life choices. Northern Sun Farm is always open to visitors.

Visitors Accepted [Oct2004]

NYLAND

http://www.nylandcohousing.org

Began: 1990 | Pop. 140
Rural | Diet: Omnivorous

The Nyland CoHousing Community is one of the first completed cohousing communities in the United States. Nyland began as Colorado CoHousing in 1988 after a few friends got together to talk about the new book *CoHousing* by McCamant and Durrett. In May of 1990 we optioned the land; in August 1992 we began moving in; and all residents were in by May of 1993.

Our community of 122 people includes 87 adults, 6 teens, and 29 kids—with an assortment of visiting children and friends of the community. We own 42 acres of land, annexed by the town of Lafayette, in a rural area just outside the city of Boulder. There are 42 homes, a 6,000-square-foot common house, a 860-square-foot shop building, and a 600-square-foot greenhouse. Houses are individually owned, and common properties are being held in unison through a homeowners association. All properties are maintained and managed by the residents of Nyland.

Our decision-making structure consists of committees and consensus. We meet two times a month in general gatherings, and smaller work groups handle the tasks of managing the land and community affairs. Day care is provided during the day, and we generally have shared meals four nights a week in the common house. Tours of the community are available at 11:00 am the last Sunday of each month.

Visitors Accepted: Email info@nylandcohousing.org. [Jan2005]

O'KEEFFE HOUSE

House President
1500-1510 Gilbert Ct
Ann Arbor, MI 48105

734-930-2755

http://www.icc.coop

Pop. 85 | Urban | Diet: Omnivorous

The North Campus co-ops are divided into two co-op houses: Renaissance and O'Keeffe. Each co-op is further divided into suites with four in Renaissance and five in O'Keeffe. Within each suite approximately 18 members share a small kitchen and living room and a cable TV lounge. Each suite is further divided so that only four or five people share a telephone and a bathroom. Member rooms are primarily large or small singles, but our doubles provide some of Ann Arbor's most affordable housing. To ensure quality and balanced meals, the houses have hired a professional chef.

In addition to the house kitchens, the basement contains many common areas shared by both houses. These include a study lounge, recreation room (with a ping-pong table, pool tables and a "honky tonk" piano), music room (with a baby grand piano), laundry room (detergent and bleach provided), and a darkroom (supplies not included).

Visitors Accepted: Contact House President. [Mar2005]

OAK GROVE

16170 Mountain Orchard Ln
Round Hill, VA 20141

Began: 1993 | Pop. 1 | Forming | Spiritual
Rural

The Oak Grove Foundation, a Blue Ridge Mountain center/farm, emphasizes Earth mystery traditions, harmony and peace with the Earth, simplicity, and spiritual development—in workshops, seminars, research, and writing, as well as in ceremonies/celebrations.

Established in 1993, it includes the Earthpeace Center for workshops; the beginnings of a small, model 8–12-house ecovillage—emphasizing simplicity, sustainability, and alternative living and building—and a fledgling press.

The 82-acre center in a low gap in the

Additions and corrections: email: directory@ic.org, *web:* directory.ic.org, *mail:* RR 1 Box 156-D, Rutledge MO 63563, USA.

199

Blue Ridge, 60 miles from Washington, DC, is traditionally viewed as a Native American "place of peace" and a ceremonial ground for Native Americans living at the foot of the ridge along the Shenandoah River. Numerous medicine people are attracted to the land to give ceremonies, workshops, and vision quests.

Part of the land is an ancient mountain farm with venerable trees, stone walls, and lanes; views over three states; an old mountain dancing ground; the mystery and beauty of the Blue Ridge—the world's oldest mountains; and many ley lines.

Currently, one writer (Quaker/Buddhist) lives in a passive solar house, while tipis and a trailer house participants and guests. At this early stage, the center can accommodate only experienced or semiprofessional organic farmers/gardeners and builders.

Visitors Accepted [Mar2005]

OAKLAND ELIZABETH HOUSE

Director
6423 Colby St
Oakland, CA 94618

510-658-1380
oakehouse@oakehouse.org

http://www.oakehouse.org

Began: 1991 | Pop. 21 | Spiritual
Urban | Diet: Omnivorous

Elizabeth House is a cooperative living residence for women and children in transition from homelessness to independence. Peer and staff support, educational programming, and cooperative living are at the heart of the Elizabeth House experience. Two residential volunteers, along with non-residential staff, run the overall program. Women and children in need of housing, as well as volunteers interested in supporting families in need, are invited to apply for residency in our community.

Visitors Accepted [Mar2005]

OBERLIN STUDENT COOPERATIVE ASSOCIATION (OSCA)

135 W Lorain St
Oberlin, OH 44074

440-775-8108
osca@oberlin.edu

http://www.oberlin.edu/~osca

An association of nine self-managed student-run housing and dining cooperatives at Oberlin College.

OSCA, est. 1950, is a unique co-op in that it houses and feeds 175 student owners and feeds an additional 455 student owners in dining facilities. Individual houses are self-managed, and decisions for the association are made democratically, with representation from all of the individual units. Some decisions are by simple majority; most are by consensus. OSCA buys food from local farms as much as possible; special provisions are made for members with vegan, vegetarian and kosher dietary preferences. The co-op owns some of its facilities, and leases most from the University. [Mar2005]

OCEANIC ECOVILLAGE

P. Sonnier
iirick@yahoo.com

http://groups.yahoo.com/group/OceanicEcovillage

Began: 2004 | Forming | Diet: Omnivorous

This group is for persons interested in the formation of an underwater ecovillage. Technology has finally developed where underwater habitats are both possible and economically feasible. Persons interested in either becoming a member of the ecovillage or donating should post to the group. More information about the specifics of the habitat are available on request.

I have done research on the costs of materials involved in the construction of the domes. www.monolithic.com will answer many questions.

Monolithic.com specializes in construction of dome type housing, and has many characteristics of interest to the ecological minded person, such as energy efficiency, natural building materials, and ease of construction.

The purpose of the ecovillage is to allow study of oceanic life, and aquaculture.

I am posting this here, because I would like to hear ideas and discussion of starting an ecovillage, and am opening membership in the actual ecovillage. The actual ecovillage will begin construction when we have enough members and funds to begin construction.

It is an intentional community of persons who care about preserving our environment, especially marine life.

Visitors Accepted: When formation is complete, contact us and include time and date desired to visit, purpose of visit, and estimated time you would like to stay. Also include any special requirements, such as medical needs or disabilities. [Oct2004]

Scissors [✂] at the end of a listing indicate that it was edited for length by the Directory *editors and a longer description can be found at* directory.ic.org.

OLYMPUS

Mel Frizzell
PO Box 41462
Norfolk, VA 23541
knightsofmatrix@yahoo.com

Began: 2005 | Pop. 2 | Forming | Spiritual
Rural

Looking to form a Pagan Men's community in or near Charlottesville, Virginia. SCA, sci-fi, and fantasy types also would be welcome. Currently researching suitable real estate to build on in the area and seeking potential members to help form the community.

Would like to combine both Pagan beliefs and technology to form a simplistic yet progressive community. Most likely will start as communal living space, and community will be supported by renting out space for retreats and camping. Most community members will have independent finances and rent living space within the community. Living, dining, and recreational areas would be the first things built, but would like to add library, fitness room, and other amenities as community grows. [Feb2005]

OMEGA HOUSE

2412 First Ave S
Minneapolis, MN 55404

612-871-8431
omegahouse@earthlink.net

**http://www.home.earthlink.net/
~omegahouse**

Began: 1968
Urban | Diet: Primarily vegetarian

The Omega House is a unique co-op located south of downtown Minneapolis, Minnesota. Our co-op, short for cooperative, is an intentional community of adults striving to live well together. Omega House has been a co-op since 1968.

We share maintenance responsibilities and costs, collectively buy organic food, and operate according to flexible principles of consensus.

Residents must be at least 25 years old, financially able to contribute equitably, willing to take on a share of home-ownership responsibilities, and willing and able to engage with others in meetings and in a living situation.

Residents have private bedrooms and all other rooms and spaces are shared.

Visitors Accepted: Call and make an appointment. [Feb2005]

THE OMEGA INSTITUTE FOR HOLISTIC STUDIES

People and Culture
150 Lake Dr
Rhinebeck, NY 12572

845-266-4444 ext 304,
845-266-8691 (fax)
pac@eomega.org

http://www.eomega.org

Began: 1977 | Pop. 200 | Rural | Diet: Other

The Omega Institute is a nonprofit, holistic learning center. Since our founding in 1977, we have been at the forefront of personal and professional development.

More than 12,000 workshop participants come to our campus and our off-site conferences each year to take workshops and professional trainings in such diverse areas as psychology, health, spiritual studies, the arts, communication, sports, the environment and social action.

Our 195-acre campus is located in the beautiful Hudson Valley, two hours north of New York City.

Each year, hundreds of staff join Omega to be a part of something larger than themselves and to work and grow alongside like-minded people. A season at Omega offers a unique opportunity to contribute to Omega's goal of raised consciousness.

Omega is committed to staff diversity. We encourage service-oriented people of any age (18 and over), gender, national origin, race, sexual orientation and spiritual belief to apply.

Omega employs over 200 full-time and part-time staff from April through October. Seasonal staff works in exchange for room, board, a stipend and educational classes. Please visit our website to read in detail about our work exchange program or contact us for an application packet.

Visitors Accepted: Omega runs catalog workshops from April through October. During this time, visitors must check in at either the Main Office or Guest Services. We are open 7 days a week from 9am-5pm. From November through March visitors must check in at the Main Office, Monday through Friday, 9am-5pm. [Jan2005]

Listings

Additions and corrections: email: directory@ic.org, *web:* directory.ic.org, *mail:* RR 1 Box 156-D, Rutledge MO 63563, USA.

201

ONE COMMON UNITY

Trustee
161 Todd Place NE
Washington, DC 20002

202-529-2125
onecommonunity@earthlink.net
OCU@onecommonunity.be

http://www.onecommonunity.be

Began: 2000 | Urban | Diet: Primarily vegan

One Common Unity is an inter-generational community of healing artists, spiritual warriors, and peace workers dedicated to giving voice to the progressive spirit of humanity through a variety of community arts services, public events, and youth-led entrepreneurial projects.

Visitors Accepted: Walk through the door... [Oct2004]

ONE WORLD FAMILY COMMUNE

535 Spencer Ave
Santa Rosa, CA 95404

707-527-8380
owfc@sonic.net

http://www.galactic.org

Began: 1967 | Pop. 8 | Spiritual
Urban | Diet: Primarily vegetarian

At this time, there are seven older members in the One World Family Commune. We came together 30-36 years ago when we recognized the truth of the messages coming through Allen Michael from Galactica. Beginning in San Francisco's Haight/Ashbury, we operated our natural-food restaurant, The Here and Now, then in Mill Valley and on to Berkeley, where we numbered 75-80, and from there to Stockton. As Starmast Publications and Productions, we published Cosmic Cookery, our natural food cookbook, and five books of the Everlasting Gospel series, channeled from Galactica through Allen Michael. Our books are given freely, or with donation. We publish our Galactic Messenger Newsletter and produce videos shown on public-access TV in Santa Rosa, Sacramento, Los Angeles, Santa Monica and Malibu.

Allen Michael is a high galactic being in a body at this "time of the end" to channel the plan, the worldwide work stoppage/karma yoga exercise and 30/30 plan to end the money system and begin the world-sharing society of God consciousness. We use autonomous self-government, led by wisdom in our decisions by consensus. We share our energies in providing for our daily needs, communications, and producing videos. We welcome the donation of a large facility and property so that we may expand our New World demonstration in an environment that includes our many "Schools of Creative Experiences" for people to experience the magic of sharing and forgiveness.

Visitors Accepted: Call first. [Mar2005]

OPEN GATE FARM & RETREAT

Open Gate (Steenwyk)
4336 W Chapman Rd
West Chapman, ME 04757

207-764-3158
needup@ainop.com
trudie.steenwyk@maine.edu

Began: 2004 | Forming | Spiritual
Rural | Diet: Omnivorous

Open Gate, which is still in its forming stage, will evolve into an altruistic community which emphasizes brotherly love and forgiveness. A non-judgmental attitude is essential.

Open Gate will serve the larger community by offering retreat for those in need of quiet reflection and guidance from their Creator. A homeless shelter is also in the plans as is an alternative school setting for all grade levels.

Milking goats will serve as a community enterprise to benefit all. Fresh milk, yogurt, and cheeses will be available to surrounding towns.

Creativity will be nurtured by offering a variety of media at the Open Gate Art Facility.

Open Gate will further serve the community as a model for animal-assisted therapy in a farm setting. Those who desire a closer relationship with God and long to serve in the helping profession will find fulfillment at Open Gate.

Visitors Accepted [Mar2005]

ORAN MÓR

Pearl
HC 2 Box 363
Squires, MO 65755

417-265-3753
oranmor@speedymail.org

http://www.geocities.com/
   oran_mor_community/
   index.html

Began: 2003 | Pop. 2 | Spiritual
Rural | Diet: Omnivorous

We are a small egalitarian community and organic farm established in June 2003 and located on 110 acres in the hills of Ozark County, Missouri. Two of the six founding members have managed to survive the strenuous start-up period.

We raise dairy goats, egg chickens, and various vegetables using local organic inputs and no-till design. We work to put the principles of Permaculture into daily practice, using clean and renewable energy resources and recycling our waste as best we can. For example, we run our motor vehicles off of used cooking oil from local restaurants; we compost our human manure; we use a windmill to pump our well water.

We offer a wide range of work experiences in gardening, food processing, construction, milking, cheesemaking, forestry, salvage, maintenance and diesel mechanics.

We envision and work for a community which embraces the following values:

• Living simply in harmony with our environment, considering sustainability, ecology and the effect of our actions on the next seven generations;

• Living with a positive, loving focus, resolving our differences non-violently, valuing cooperation and sharing, and fostering respect, honesty and responsibility in all relationships;

• Encouraging and supporting individual creative expression and spiritual development, enjoying each other and celebrating each person's unique contribution to community.

Visitors Accepted: Contact us by email or telephone a week or two in advance of your visit. Please plan to work while you are here. [Mar2005]

ORANGE TWIN CONSERVATION COMMUNITY

Athens, GA

706-543-0672
village@orangetwin.com

Laura Carter
orangetwin@yahoo.com

http://www.orangetwin.com/village

Began: 2000 | Forming | Suburban

Visitors Accepted: Make a request to the people on the contact list. [Dec2004]

Scissors [✂] at the end of a listing indicate that it was edited for length by the Directory editors and a longer description can be found at directory.ic.org.

ORCA LANDING

Bert Bradley
731 N 96th St
Seattle, WA 98103

206-789-2540, 206-915-2535
orcaland@comcast.net

Began: 1990 | Pop. 9
Urban | Diet: Primarily vegetarian

Orca Landing is an urban cooperative in Seattle, Washington. We've been in our current location since 1990. Composed of six adults and three children, we operate by consensus even though two of us actually own the property. We've nearly finished enlarging our home, researching land trusts, and investing in our relationships as we grow a neotribal extended family.

As a community we've chosen not to embrace any specific political, environmental, or religious causes but to encourage individuals to pursue their own paths. There is, for example, a variety of spiritual beliefs in our household. In lieu of any official overriding agenda, all of us on different levels are involved in networking with our neighbors and various local organizations, including Northwest Intentional Communities Association (NICA), on the board of our Community Council, and more. We are interested in fostering communication across whatever divides people from one another. Most of us, for example, have been through Landmark Education's Curriculum for Living, including the Forum. We use the distinctions of the Landmark Forum to empower the dynamic community conversation we live in as we focus on what's possible. While we are not egalitarian, we practice voluntary simplicity, enjoy the arts and music and other creative pursuits, and share a love of outdoor adventure and wilderness.

Visitors Accepted: Call or write to the provided contact above. [Dec2004]

ORDER OF SAINT BENEDICT

http://www.osb.org/index.html

Began: 530 | Pop. 35 | Spiritual
Diet: Omnivorous

The international Benedictine monastic order of sisters and brothers was founded by Saint Benedict of Nursia, Italy (480-547), the Patriarch of Western Monasticism. In the sixth century A.D., he wrote what we know as the Rule of Benedict or Regula Benedicti.

The website features: Rule of Benedict (Latin and modern translations), geographic database of houses, advanced search, what's new, election results, international institutions, general information, texts and articles, habit, saints, etc.

Visitors Accepted: Contact the Guestmaster of the house. Accommodation for guests is often limited or booked. Priority is given to those visiting for a religious purpose: day of reflection, retreat, prayer, etc. [Jan2005]

OSHO MEVLANA RESIDENTIAL COMMUNITY

Lot 26
Bilin Rd
Myocum, NSW 2482
AUSTRALIA

+61-(0)2-6684-4091
melaleuca@linknet.com.au

http://www.mevlana-community.com

Began: 1996 | Pop. 19 | Spiritual
Rural | Diet: Primarily vegetarian

Osho Mevlana is an open residential community that has been created as an integrated experiment in living, inspired by the vision of Osho. The community welcomes people from any background or walk of life.

We are joined together by a common desire to wake up and create the space in which an Osho buddhafield can happen, to promote personal growth and creative expression.

We do this by sharing ownership of common areas for meditations, meals, workshops, healing, visitors, etc. We also aim to create viable businesses and jobs, either linked to the meditation center or otherwise.

We own individual houses and respect individual privacy. The residents are varied in nationality, age, and occupation; some work in the center, while others earn a living outside. We are trying to provide a variety of housing options and costs. Some residents are shareholders; others rent.

We are rural, in rolling hills near Bryon Bay, but just 10 minutes from town, beaches, and several other communities. The nature on the property of Osho Mevlana itself is abundant and typical of Byron Shire: hillside rain-forest pockets, large wetland forests, koalas, wallabies, many different birds, and beautiful views.

Visitors Accepted [Jan2005]

OSTERWEIL HOUSE

House President
338 E Jefferson St
Ann Arbor, MI 48104

734-996-5956

http://www.icc.coop

Began: 1946 | Pop. 13
Urban | Diet: Omnivorous

Osterweil Co-op is a member of the ICC. It is geared at providing affordable housing to students who attend colleges and universities in the area.

We are primarily a vegetarian house though we do serve meat and nonveggie dishes. Meals are made by the members five nights a week.

Members share rooms with like-sexed members. We have five double rooms and three singles. Rooms are distributed on a seniority list determined by the number of semesters a person has lived in Osterweil.

The Osterweil house is a quaint three-story brick-and-stucco building that dates back to post-World War II. It is located only two minutes from the University of Michigan.

Members are expected to give five or six hours of their time per week back to the house in the form of officer positions and other house works.

Visitors Accepted: Contact House President. [Mar2005]

OTAMATEA ECO-VILLAGE

Oneriri Road, RD 2
Kaiwaka
NEW ZEALAND

+64-(0)9-431-2577,
+64-(0)9-431-2656
daniel.tohill@actrix.gen.nz
thefarside@clear.net.nz

http://www.otamatea.org.nz

Began: 1996 | Pop. 27 | Forming
Rural | Diet: Omnivorous

The land was purchased in 1996 when founders sought a site suitable for cooperative permaculture development. Resource Consent was granted, and the purchase and legal process of subdividing 251 acres into 15 five-acre lots with individual titles, plus 176 acres of commonly-owned land was completed. An access road was built in 1998.

All 15 lots have sold but two properties have come up for sale again and information is available from the owners. One is bare land and the other has a house and

Listings

Additions and corrections: email: directory@ic.org, *web:* directory.ic.org, *mail: RR 1 Box 156-D, Rutledge MO 63563, USA.*

203

some gardens already established. Thus we are still in search of some new members. Our motivating philosophy is permaculture, commitment to organics, and movement towards self-sufficiency. Monthly meetings are held, plus the occasional facilitated community-building meeting, also shared meals and celebrations. Consensus is used for the decision-making process. Shareholders commit to do four hours community work weekly, including grazing projects, regenerating native bush, weed control, and administration.

Visitors Accepted: Annual residential Permaculture Design Courses are held, plus other workshops, and Open Days. WWOOFers (Willing Workers on Organic Farms) and visitors are welcomed, by arrangement. [Nov2004]

O.U.R. ECOVILLAGE

Box 530
Shawnigan Lake, BC V0R 2W0
CANADA

250-743-3067
our@pacificcoast.net
info@ourecovillage.org
http://www.ourecovillage.org

Began: 1990 | Pop. 8 | Spiritual
Rural | Diet: Primarily vegetarian

O.U.R. Ecovillage is a sustainable land-stewardship community that endeavors to foster the interconnectedness between all things. Support of individual, family, intentional community, and wider community. Appropriate/green/natural building, permaculture design training and gardens, deep-ecology, social-justice, and community building. All this on a beautiful, private, organic farm-based setting complete with farm animals, a lake, and eagles! O.U.R. Ecovillage now has an onsite ecological education school—TOPIA: The Sustainable Learning Community Institue (check the website for ongoing summer residential programs and short workshops). We are intercultural, interfaith, and intergenerational.

Visitor Accepted: Please email or phone two weeks in advance to arrange visit or tour. We have an eco-B & B, a dorm yurt, and camping, plus onsite outdoor food services (in the summer). Please propose dates and type of stay you are requesting and someone will email to confirm your visit. [May05]

OWEN HOUSE

House President
1017 Oakland Ave
Ann Arbor, MI 48104

734-996-5973

http://www.icc.coop

Pop. 24 | Diet: Omnivorous

Owen houses 24 people in three singles, nine doubles, and one spacious triple. Our boarders come from Stevens and the neighborhood. We boast a nicely inviting fireplace, a state-of-the-art VCR, a piano and an organ, a spacious bike shed and a freshly refurnished porch with an elegant porch swing.

We eat meat sometimes but always have vegetarian alternatives. All in all, Owen has been and continues to be a great house.

Visitors Accepted: Contact House President. [Mar2005]

OXFORD COMMUNITY

KA Hamberg
City Centre
Oxford England
UNITED KINGDOM
OxfordCommunity@sassafras.org

http://www.sassafras.org/oxford

Began: 2004 | Pop. 2 | Forming
Urban | Diet: Vegetarian only

Can one woman start a community in a country not her own? Here's to that eternally springing hope. I'd like to begin by finding a few like-minded folks to share a house from January 2005. Communal suppers, living simply, no television, vegetarian diet, support of nonviolence, organic outlook, and mutual respect are key attractive elements. I'm a fiction writer, nonprofit administrator, and Quaker. My husband is a postgrad political philosophy student of no organized religion. Wookie is the dog. If you're serious, positive, and mature, please get in touch.

Visitors Accepted: Please contact me via email. [Oct2004]

OZARK AVALON

Rose Wise
Ozark Avalon, Church of Nature
26213 Cumberland Church Rd
Boonville, MO 65233

660-882-6418

http://www.ozarkavalon.net

Forming | Spiritual
Rural | Diet: Omnivorous

Church of nature and nature Sanctuary near the Missouri River and Columbia in central Missouri.

The board is currently considering plans to develop a community of like-minded people building on parcels within the property.

Visitors Accepted: Call or email at least a week ahead of time. There are camping facilities available. [Jan2005]

PACIFIC GARDENS COHOUSING COMMUNITY

PO Box 207
Station A
Nanaimo, BC V9R 5K9
CANADA

250-754-3060, 250-754-3034 (fax)
cohousing@pacificgardens.ca

http://www.pacificgardens.ca

Began: 1998 | Forming | Diet: Other

As this is written, Pacific Gardens Cohousing expects to begin construction shortly. We are still looking for families.

We have 4.37 acres on the Chase River in Nanaimo, Vancouver Island, British Columbia. With a view of Mount Benson (and sunsets), the property is a delightful piece of "country in the city" covered with trees, an old orchard, seasonal pond and wildflowers.

Our 25-unit building is designed to maximize green space and provide the best opportunities for social interaction. Our common house will include a kitchen, dining room, lounge, teen room, office, children's play room, craft room, woodworking shop, and "soundproof" room for music practice and film screenings.

Each unit will be self-contained (you will have your own kitchen) and individually

---

Scissors [✂] at the end of a listing indicate that it was edited for length by the Directory editors and a longer description can be found at directory.ic.org.

owned (strata-titled condo). The price (ranging from approx. CDN $119,000 for a 1-bedroom to $299,000 for a 4-bedroom) includes shared ownership of the land and common amenities.

Down by the river in the forest of fir trees, you can imagine yourself far away from civilization; yet we are within a block of the bus and are minutes by car or cycle from downtown and local shopping. An elementary school, a high school, and Malaspina University-College are within easy reach.

We are committed to non-toxic products and will use the best available green building technology. Pacific Gardens Cohousing will be multi-generational and inclusive of all people who genuinely care about living in harmony with the earth and each other.

Visitors Accepted: Contact us for a land tour, info package, and a visit with our marketing staff. The next step is to be a guest at a Members' meeting and join us for a potluck. Our office location is in Port Place Mall opposite the Green Store. [Mar2005]

PAGAN INTENTIONAL COMMUNITY

703 S Norwood Ave
Tulsa, OK 74112
waterspryt@aol.com

**http://members.aol.com/
WaterSpryt**

Began: 1997 | Forming | Spiritual | Rural

Pagan Intentional Community (PIC) is a growing group of Earth-centered families, working toward forming our dream village in the tropics. We will live by sustainable farming and fishing in a rural setting. We want to raise our kids in peace, health, and simplicity. We seek new members who can help our effort succeed. People do not have to be wealthy to join us, as long as they can provide essentials for themselves and any dependents.

We are not a traditional commune. We will have our own homes and possessions but work together on a communal farm and share a town center. We will form our community guidelines and deal with problems in an open egalitarian forum, reaching decisions by consensus.

We hope to establish a free learning center, in which people of all ages will be able to learn about whatever interests them, unfettered by the constraints of a traditional school system.

We seek an island or large tract with fertile soil and a strong ecosystem where we may live lightly, gently finding our place in the existing food chain. Our family is headed down to Panama during the winter of 2005/06 to scout out possible community sites for our project. We prize diverse, creative, free thinkers who will make our village strong and viable. We are currently seeking grant money, and those who can help us obtain it. If you wish to join our email list, please email me at WaterSpryt@aol.com.

Brightest blessings!

Visitors Accepted: Contact us by email to find out where we are, and at what stage of development the community project is now. [Jan2005]

PAGANO

raxivar
611 16th
Sparks, NV 89431
raxivar@yahoo.com

**http://groups.yahoo.com/group/
Pagano**

Began: 2005 | Pop. 4 | Spiritual
Rural | Diet: Omnivorous

This is a virtual IC, allowing people to role-play themselves and explore IC issues. Though virtual and focused mainly on pagans, there will be no simulations of how well or ill any prayers, rituals, or uses of magick work out—this is mostly about the physical and psychological challenges inherent in forming an IC together.

Visitors Accepted: Go to the Yahoo website, join, look over the messages in the archive, decide if you want to participate. [Nov2004]

PANGAIA

RR 2 Box 3311
Pahoa, HI 96778

808-965-9988
pangaia@pangaia.cc
bamboo@pangaia.cc

http://www.pangaia.cc

Began: 1991 | Pop. 8 | Spiritual
Rural | Diet: Omnivorous

We are a piece of land, a group of people, a common vision.

Our vision is of unity with Gaia, the Earth mother, and with each other. Our most fundamental goals are to move toward sustainability, well-being, and harmony with our bodies and environment; discovering who we are by cultivating intimate rela-

Additions and corrections: email: directory@ic.org, *web:* directory.ic.org, *mail: RR 1 Box 156-D, Rutledge MO 63563, USA.*

tions with the land as well as our human and social landscape.

Inspired by those goals, we are a mostly raw-food community and are living active permaculture everyday. We are not dogmatic about being "raw-foodists." Some of us are close to 100% raw, while others are on the "substrate-diet."

We cater to eco-tourists and people seeking health and diet-related retreats. (See our website.)

We also create income from other sources, including the local farmer's market, and direct sales of agricultural and nursery products.

We are from very different backgrounds with a wide spread of ages (0–60).

We are also going through a major reorganization of ownership. We have found that owner/non-owner stratification is challenging and non-sustainable. Thus we are open to new part owners who want to create a home and community. Interested people can contact us first through email: bamboo@pangaia.cc.

Visitors Accepted: We welcome guests, visitors, interns, friends, and potential long-term residents who are sincerely interested. See our website; send email of introduction. [Mar2005][✄]

PANTERRA

Michael E. Woltz
8579 Hardscrabble Rd
Westfield, NY 14787

716-326-3993
Coros9@yahoo.com

Began: 1992 | Pop. 2 | Spiritual
Rural | Diet: Primarily vegetarian

Panterra is a community dedicated to personal enrichment through increased awareness. Currently, we use our relationships with ourselves, with others, and with all aspects of life to evaluate and foster personal change and understanding. Our hope is to create an environment where each person may achieve some degree of personal enhancement with support from the community.

We conduct classes and workshops designed to promote self-esteem and self-awareness. The "Studio at Panterra" is our private business where we offer yoga classes, movement therapy, and other sessions centered on the transformation of consciousness as a way to serve the local community. Although we are primarily a community of two, we have had individuals stay for periods of time with set purposes. We are will-

ing to share ideas and resources with others to encourage self-empowerment and community improvement.

In part, our intention is to reduce suffering where and when we can. We do not claim to have answers, but we do offer possibilities. We do not declare universal truths, but we do advance the search for personal current truth and its understanding. We honor the story of individuals and avoid adherence to dogmatic forms. Artistic and creative expression are actively supported, but we reserve the right to exclude expressions of violence within the community.

Visitors Accepted: Please contact us by mail well in advance. If you expect to visit for an hour or so contact us one to two weeks in advance. Longer visits, up to four hours, will require three to four weeks notice and is dependent on available time. No overnight guests. [Mar2005]

PARADISE VILLAGE

Ed Haggard
4208 Burton Hollow Rd
Whites Creek, TN 37189

615-317-3117
ed@thelovedrums.com
edhaggard@mindspring.com

http://thelovedrums.com

Began: 2002 | Pop. 7 | Spiritual
Suburban | Diet: Omnivorous

Paradise Village is just a bit northwest of Nashville on 27 acres in a hollow. Six multi-talented adults, two children, big stone house, fire circle, barn, shops, pond, hill, field, drums, dance, art, goats, chickens, horses, cats, dog. Green, Libertarian, activist, mulifaceted spirituality, pagan, polyamorous, Interplay, healer, auto repair, stone masonry, yard games and art.

Visitors Accepted: Email Ed and say whasup witcha :-) [Jan2005]

PARKER STREET CO-OP

Ken Norwood
2337 Parker St, Apt 9
Berkeley, CA 94704

slrcnorwood@earthlink.net

Began: 1987 | Pop. 33
Urban | Diet: Primarily vegetarian

We are a Limited Equity Housing Cooperative (LEHC) living in 22 one-bedroom units, 2 two-bedroom units, and 2 studios in two three-story buildings near UC Berkeley and two BART stations. There are

34 adults and one child. We have no shared kitchen and dining area yet, but we have two large common rooms, with adjacent laundries and large view decks, on the fourth floor of each building. There is a large tool- and work-shop under a portion of one building and a large storage basement under the other. We share a potluck supper meeting and several committee meetings each month.

On the grounds the ivy and asphalt are giving way to garden plots with edible plants, flowers, grape, berry, and kiwi vines, 15 fruit trees, and a large strawberry patch. There is a class-A compost bin and a full scale recycling program. The exterior of the building's stucco and three trim colors were repainted in 2004 with four months of decisions done by consensus by over 15 members involved—miraculous!

The state law for a LEHC limits the selling price of a person's unit (share) when that person moves out, which keeps housing affordable. Our units are now below market rate for the San Francisco Bay Area.

We are self-managed and do much better at consensus decisions. Over half of the members are active but that doesn't cause too many problems. However when a vacancy occurs we select for people who want to get involved.

Visitors Accepted: Contact Ken Norwood or call 510-548-6608. [Mar2005]

PATHWAYS COHOUSING

Julie Feinland
1 Mountain Laurel Path
Florence, MA 01062

413-587-0768
feinland@comcast.net

http://members.aol.com/pathways5

Began: 1995
Small Town | Diet: Omnivorous

Visitors Accepted [Mar2005]

PENINSULA PARK COMMONS

Eli Spevak
6325 N Albina Ave #6
Portland, OR 97217

503-289-3311
eli@aracnet.com

http://www.penparkcommons.org

Began: 2004 | Pop. 8 | Urban

Over five years ago, a group of folks first got together in a living room in North Portland and talked about what it would be like to

Scissors [✄] at the end of a listing indicate that it was edited for length by the Directory *editors and a longer description can be found at* directory.ic.org.

206

have a shared housing situation, where everyone had his or her own space but also access to common outdoor and indoor spaces and amenities. We wanted the best of cohousing—fun, community, low-impact living, and shared resources—combined with the advantages of privacy and individual homeownership. Eli Spevak and Jim Labbe never let go of the idea, and in January 2003 they purchased Peninsula Park Commons, a 7-unit courtyard apartment building in the Piedmont neighborhood, across the street from Portland's original rose garden.

In the summer of 2004 we converted the property to 6 condominiums and one common unit. Since then all the units have sold and planning is underway to construct 3-4 more units on the site. We have filled our courtyard with vegetable gardens, berries, fruit trees and flowers. Our common unit has been used for board games, meetings, dinner parties, shared newspapers, movies, and overnight guests.

Peninsula Park Commons is founded in the belief that the health and enrichment of individuals, communities, and the places in which they exist are inextricably linked. At the Commons, we have established a cooperatively governed community where a fun and energetic group of people share physical and social space, and where the development, decision making and day-to-day operations of the community reflect our core shared values. [Jan2005][✂<]

PENNINE CAMPHILL COMMUNITY

Steve Hopewell
Boyne Hill Chapelthorpe,
Wakefield
W Yorkshire WF4 3JH England
UNITED KINGDOM

+44-(0)1924-255281
enquiries@pennine.org.uk

http://www.pennine.org.uk

Began: 1977 | Pop. 40 | Spiritual
Suburban | Diet: Omnivorous

Pennine is part of the Camphill movement. The Camphill movement creates community settings in which children, young people, and adults, many with learning difficulties, can live, work, and learn with others in healthy social relationships based on mutual care and respect. Pennine's main activities are supporting a college for those with learning difficulties.

Most coworkers live within the 35-acre site, working on a voluntary basis and receiving no wage or salary but with their daily needs being met by the community. There is always an international flavor to the community, with usually half the coworkers coming from other countries, often as a gap year after or before college or university.

Our small farm and vegetable gardens are worked biodynamically and provide for much of the community's needs. There are several craft workshops and a riding school run jointly with the Riding for Disabled Association.

We are always open to inquiries; our usual request is that a potential coworker has a year free of commitments and would be prepared to live, work, and learn alongside others in the community. Many people come to help at the Pennine Community for about a year at a time. There are often places available, so please get in touch.

Visitors Accepted: Email is probably the best way to contact us. [Oct2004]

PEOPLE ON THE WAY

Matta and Zazi
HC 74 Box 660
Brandywine, WV 26802

mattawazaz@yahoo.com

Began: 2001 | Pop. 3 | Forming | Spiritual
Rural | Diet: Omnivorous

We began as a homesteading couple who learned how important it is to share our lifestyle with like-minded people. Our intention is to take part in the creation of a seasonal intentional community. Our goals are self-sustainability: growing good foods suited to the area, and making a living using the resources the land and community has to offer. We also feel it is our wish and duty to communicate and share our experiences with the larger community, including students, travelers, and members of other communities, as well as those interested in being more permanently involved.

The inspirations and skills of all involved shall affect the development of the community.

Our current projects include the establishment of blueberries and other fruits, and the low scale organic propagation of native brook trout.

We have 350 mountainous acres with several pure springs, some of which flow into a year round stream with a waterfall. We live near the Virginia border less than an hour away from Harrisonburg, a large college town. The Mountain Institute and the Lightstone Foundation are nearby sources of friends and resources.

We are currently searching for any good people to add their inspiration and companionship for any length of time during May through October. Please get in touch to find out more!

Visitors Accepted: Contact us via email or postal mail (the latter might be the best bet). Be patient with email because we have to go use a friend's computer. [Feb2005]

THE PHOENIX CO-OP

Membership Coordinator
636 Langdon St
Madison, WI 53703

608-256-1770, 608-256-3131
phoenixco-op@mail.com

http://www.madisoncommunity.coop/house.cfm?HouseID=11

Began: 1996 | Pop. 25
Urban | Diet: Omnivorous

Phoenix Co-op is located across the street from the Memorial Library of the University of Wisconsin campus and is one block from both the Memorial Union and beautiful Lake Mendota. The spacious mansion houses about 25 members, a mixture of both students and professionals. The house is beautified by decorative faces, a spiral staircase, fireplaces and a lovely courtyard with fountain. We have large, comfortable common spaces, a TV room with a large selection of videos and DVDs and a small workout area. High-speed internet access is available on two house computers and high speed wireless access is available on all floors. Delicious meals are prepared in a large, professionally equipped kitchen where members often gather socially. The food co-op is designed for both meat eaters and vegetarians and is also available to non-residents. Phoenix provides a relaxed environment for members to share their outside interests. It uses a modified-consensus decision-making process.

Visitors Accepted [Oct2004]

PHOENIX GAY CHUB MUSIC/ART COMMUNITY

BGM
PO Box 505
Mesa, AZ 85211

http://groups.yahoo.com/group/pgcmac

Began: 2004 | Pop. 1 | Forming | Spiritual
Urban

Brand new group to facilitate development of communal work and/or live spaces and be

Additions and corrections: email: directory@ic.org, *web:* directory.ic.org, *mail: RR 1 Box 156-D, Rutledge MO 63563, USA.*

207

Listings

involved in (but not limited to) the Roosevelt/Grand Art/Music scenes by gay (but not necessarily restricted to) overweight men.

Only professional musicians and artists and support people allowed.

Main reason: Downtown Phoenix Music and Art Cooperatives

Secondary reason: Gay Chub Polyfidelitous Communal Family (The second part requires sero-negativity.) [Dec2004]

PINE STREET

155 Pine St
Amherst, MA 01002

Bruce Coldham
413-549-3616
Bruce@ColdhamArchitects.com

http://www.coldhamarchitects.com/
cohousing/Pine_Street/
pine_street.htm

Rural

Pine Street Cohousing was formed during the summer of 1990 by a group intending to be residents, to develop a small community on a 5.3 acre site in Amherst, Massachusetts. Each of eight families has its own smaller-than-usual private house, as well as a share in a common house. The houses are clustered closely together to maximize the usefulness of the shared common house—a community space which effectively enlarges the living area of each house. To achieve this compactness, vehicles, parking, and roadway have been squeezed to the periphery. Pedestrian circulation predominates. [Feb2005]

PIONEER TRAILS INSTITUTE

David McKibbin
pioneertrails@usa.com

http://www.pioneertrailsinstitute.org

Began: 2004 | Pop. 3 | Forming
Small Town

Pioneer Trails Institute is established for the purpose of providing a facility that will serve as a center for the research, development, and implementation of affordable, efficient, and ecologically sound methods of building construction and renovation that include, but are not restricted to: energy generation from earth, solar, wind, and water sources; energy conservation; sewage and waste disposal; and the recycling of existing materials in unusual and creative ways. These purposes shall be attained by utilizing the building for various research laboratories, holding seminars, publishing newsletters, and serving as a prototype for the implementation of the various technologies developed.

Visitors Accepted: Please contact us before so we can arrange for your visit. [Dec2004]

PIONEER VALLEY

120 Pulpit Hill Rd
Amherst, MA 01002
rebecca@cohousing.com

Rebecca Reid
120 Pulpit Hill Rd #13
Amherst, MA 01002
rreid@the-spa.com

Josh Hornick
jhornick@k12.oit.umass.edu

http://www.cohousing.com

Began: 1989 | Pop. 68
Rural | Diet: Omnivorous

The Pioneer Valley Cohousing Group has created a style of housing that encourages a strong sense of community, supports our need for privacy, makes life affordable, and provides a secure and enriched setting for children and adults. We have a place where people know their neighbors in a meaningful way, a neighborhood where different traditions and values are respected and where we can all have a sense of security and belonging.

Our group purchased a 25-acre meadow site in north Amherst where we built 32 units and a large common house, moving in June–September 1994. We built a clustered mix of single, duplex, and triplex buildings on seven of those acres. The rest is field and woods, surrounded by town lands.

Residents own their own homes, as well as a share of the land and the common house. The common house is a place for community dinners, meetings, entertainment and other public and private functions. It includes a large kitchen/dining hall, children's playrooms, guest rooms, laundry facilities, library, and recycling center. Optional dinners three nights a week, gardens, play and work spaces, hiking trails, and other shared amenities chosen by residents have social and economic advantages.

The community is a short walk from a municipal lake; a recreation park with tennis, swimming, and playing fields; a small shopping center; a library; the university; and public transportation.

Visitors Accepted: First email Rebecca Reid (rebecca@cohousing.com) for information on the community, then contact Henry Lappin (413-549-3722) for a community tour. [Feb2005]

PLAIN ANABAPTIST COMMUNITY

http://groups.yahoo.com/group/
Natural_Lifestyle_Community

Began: 2005 | Forming | Spiritual
Rural | Diet: Omnivorous

This is for those who want to live a natural lifestyle, but are alone in their quest and are looking for other like-minded souls. We will eventually create our own real community. This is for those who feel like outcasts in their surroundings and yet cannot find a place to live with those who share our beliefs. The community will have the following characteristics:

• RELIGIOUS (Christian, preferably Anabaptist leanings—or if you are not Anabaptist but agree with their main principles)
• Bible literalists
• live COMPLETELY natural
• NO electricity
• NO cars
• NO other modern "conveniences"
• organic farming/foods
• we do NOT support slaughter houses (all meat comes from the community itself from humane methods)
• modesty
• men and women wear old-fashioned clothes (men wear slacks, button-up shirts, etc. Women wear long, plain dresses and will wear prayer coverings full-time as it tells us to in the Bible)
• barefoot freedom for all
• non-materialistic
• men are providers
• women take care of the home/children
• children are raised lovingly and with discipline
• unschooling/homeschooling is the norm
• community church/worship
• main language is English (doesn't have to be your first language)

I know I am not alone in my goal, and I pray other people out there will see how vital a community like this can be to the world!

Visitors Accepted [Jan2005]

Scissors [✂] at the end of a listing indicate that it was edited for length by the Directory *editors and a longer description can be found at* directory.ic.org.

PLANET EARTH 11

John Johnson
1021 Webster St
Traverse City, MI 49686

231-392-5711
tutbrotherwind@yahoo.com

Began: 2005 | Pop. 1 | Forming | Spiritual
Small Town | Diet: Omnivorous

A loving, caring community, utilizing Mother Earth's resources for best use and minimum impact. Currently forming and seeking like-minded people. Greenhouse, grounds, additional land all available for right people. Limited room and high standards.

Visitors Accepted: Call, email or regular mail note and particulars. [Feb2005]

PLANTS FOR A FUTURE

1 Lerryn View
Lostwithiel
Cornwall PL22 0QJ England
UNITED KINGDOM

+44-(0)1208-873554
+44-(0)1208-872963
webmaster@pfaf.org
kenfern1@btinternet.com
pfaf@scs.leeds.ac.uk

http://www.pfaf.org

Began: 1986 | Pop. 5 | Forming
Rural | Diet: Primarily vegan

Plants for a Future is a resource center for rare and unusual plants, particularly those that have edible, medicinal, or other uses. We practice vegan-organic permaculture with emphasis on creating an ecologically sustainable environment and the use of perennial plants.

We have two pieces of land, in Devon and Cornwall, where we demonstrate our agricultural principles and carry out research into interesting plants. We are in the process of constructing an ecovillage.

The project consists of a registered charity and a workers' cooperative. Many volunteers also help in the project.

There are still long term plans to create an ecovillage, but a lot of work with planning permission needs to happen first.

Yes, the workers' co-op is still going. We are still looking for people who want to join the community at both of our sites. It's just that we are more focused on the objectives of the community.

Visitors Accepted: Phone first. [Feb2005]

PLEASANT HILL COHOUSING

2200 Lisa Ln
Pleasant Hill, CA 94523

Susan Hedgpeth
510-642-8093
hedgpeth@berkeley.edu

http://phch.org

Began: 1997 | Pop. 71
Suburban | Diet: Omnivorous

We are a suburban cohousing community on 2.2 acres in Pleasant Hill, California (near Walnut Creek, east of San Francisco) next door to an elementary school. We have 32 self-sufficient townhouse-style units along with a common house (kitchen/dining room, sitting room, laundry, kids room), workshop, organic garden, and a pool. We used "green" building features in our design and added photovoltaic solar panels after move-in. Our vision is to create and live in a community that fosters harmony with each other, the larger community, and nature. We moved in Fall 2001.

Visitors Accepted: We usually have tours on the first Sunday of the month. If you are interested, contact us at 925-685-6877 or the email address above. [Feb2005]

PLOW CREEK

Louise Stahnke
19183 Plow Creek Rd
Tiskilwa, IL 61368

815-646-4851, 815-646-6600
stahnke@plowcreek.org

http://www.plowcreek.org

Began: 1971 | Pop. 46 | Spiritual
Rural | Diet: Omnivorous

We are an intentional Christian community associated with the Mennonite Church. Located in rural Illinois, we are part of Shalom Mission Communities, with involvement especially in Central America. We welcome those who acknowledge Jesus as Lord of their lives and wish to share in our life together as a part of discipleship.

Values of mutual respect, justice, compassion for the poor, fidelity in marriage, and pacifism form the core of our life together. Hospitality and being connected with other cultures through personal relationships are also important in our shared life.

Some of our members work at a variety of jobs in the larger community, while others help in the farming, growing fruits and vegetables using methods that are environmentally friendly.

As a church we have both communal and noncommunal members. The Fellowship is communal and has 14 adults and 6 kids; the noncommunal church includes 13 adults and 13 children (numbers as of November 04).

For further information, please contact Louise Stahnke at address above.

Visitors Accepted: Check our website first if you can. Email, call 815-646-6600 or write. Let us know something about yourself (and family if applicable) and why you desire to visit. [Jan2005]

THE POINT OF INFINITY RETREAT CENTER AND COMMUNITY

Kenneth Pollinger, PhD
PO Box 33
101 Red Star Rd
Greenfield Park, NY 12435

845-647-8834, 845-358-6448
newagectr@earthlink.net
mizellegreen@aol.com

New Age Center
1 South Broadway
Nyack, NY 10960

http://www.NewAgePointofInfinity.com

Began: 1998 | Pop. 5 | Forming | Spiritual
Rural | Diet: Primarily vegetarian

We are an emerging community interested in expressing enlightenment through everyday life. The Point of Infinity Retreat and community is located on a magical 38 acre wooded parcel in the astonishingly beautiful Catskill Mountains near Ellenville, New York. A peaceful atmosphere and an enchanted, mystical, natural mountain top plateau ideal for ceremonies, rituals, retreats, health programs and more. Only a two hour driving distance from New York City. Offering potentialities for all spiritual paths in holistic health, spiritual growth and alternative living. We are interested in making a transition to a more sustainable way of living through permaculture, organic gardening, wild food foraging and alternative energy. Seeking individuals, partnerships or families willing to be self motivated, aware and creative. Those with open minds, ready to share talents, gifts and points of view and to be sacred mirrors for one another are most welcome.

Visitors Accepted: Send for application form or contact us. [Mar2005]

Additions and corrections: email: directory@ic.org, *web:* directory.ic.org, *mail:* RR 1 Box 156-D, Rutledge MO 63563, USA.

POLY, PAGAN, NUDIST COMMUNITY

Drostan Barclay
15315 Blacksmith Ter
Woodbridge, VA 22191

703-447-1231
drostan@livenaked.net
http://www.livenaked.net

Began: 2005 | Pop. 4 | Forming | Spiritual
Rural | Diet: Omnivorous

We are a polyamorous, pagan, nudist community looking to start up somewhere in the western United States. We are currently focused close to Denver, Colorado. We want to purchase 40–100 acres of land to create a sanctuary for Pagans and followers of Earth-based religions. We want to grow many of our vegetables year round, to be a center for the healing-arts, and to be an educational facility for self-sustainable skills and Pagan/Earth-based religion workshops.

We embrace polyamory in all of its forms and seek bisexuals, gay, lesbian, transgender, and all other people who are comfortable in their own skin and committed to building a safe, loving, intimate, and intentional family. A family where nudity is the accepted norm and clothes are used only for their intended purpose—protection against the elements. A family where intimate touch is differentiated from sexual touch and intimate touch is not only openly accepted, and welcomed, but embraced by all as a healthy expression of love.

We will share food, utilities, rent, and work equally and practice consensus decision making, complete honesty, and the expression of vulnerability.

Freedom of expression, creative, emotional, sexual, spiritual, etc., as weird and different as it may be, is welcome and warmly encouraged. People on an intense spiritual path, people who seek to be naked and open with their body and emotions, creative artists, healers, masters, shaman, and simply sensitive individuals looking for a safe environment are all welcome. Nonviolence, respect of others, non-wastefulness, and open, honest, truthfulness are a must.

Please, no recreational drugs except for natural plants and used only in ritual.

Visitors Accepted: Please email us with your interest in joining us. Tell us about yourself, your passions and dreams, and if we all feel a connection, we'll invite you to come visit for a couple of days, then take it from there. [Mar2005][✂]

PORT TOWNSEND ECOVILLAGE

510 35th St
Port Townsend, WA 98368

360-379-4858
kkolff@olympus.net

http://porttownsendecovillage.org

Began: 2004 | Pop. 4 | Forming | Spiritual
Small Town | Diet: Omnivorous

Do you want to build a small ecological home and share so many facilities you may need little private space? Are you willing to help in a group effort to measure and reduce our ecological impact? Do you want to walk, bike or bus to beaches, a food co-op, and the heart of a cultural and historic small town?

Port Townsend EcoVillage is a community of people dedicated to living in harmony with each other and with the earth. Our cooperative will have 27 households on seven acres sharing a sanctuary, common house, bathhouse, barn, shop, playground, greenhouses, tools, cars and more. A land trust may hold title to the underlying land.

We are committed to consensus, NonViolent Communication (NVC) and living more simply and justly. We seek and embrace diversity in all its forms. We revere nature and celebrate the seasons and life events together. We integrate people and the land using permaculture principles to enhance the natural fertility of the earth, raise animals and grow some of our own organic food on three acres.

We encourage green cottage-industries on-site, offer educational opportunities, model ways to live more sustainably, and welcome innovative ideas as we continue to evolve.

We hope to finish infrastructure in 2006, followed by common buildings and homes shortly thereafter. We seek singles, families and elders to join us in our vision.

Visitors Accepted: Contact Kees "Case" Kolff, preferably at kkolff@olympus.net, or by phone. [Mar2005]

PRAG HOUSE

Seattle, WA
prag_house@riseup.net

http://www.nas.com/riverfarm/evglt.htm

Began: 1970 | Pop. 13
Urban | Diet: Omnivorous

Established in 1972, we are an urban housing cooperative that seeks to foster community and sustainable lifestyles. We are adults and children with ages ranging from 4 to 60. We live in a large 15-bedroom house built in the early 1900s.

We share organic vegetarian food, although none of our current members are vegetarian. We have at least one scheduled communal meal a month. Currently we practice a moderate form of income sharing in which members pay a portion of their income to the community in addition to payments for base dues and food.

We seek to live a more environmentally sustainable and communitarian lifestyle. Title to our property is held by the Evergreen Land Trust.

Visitors Accepted: We are not normally open to visitors. Potential visitors should send a written request in advance. We occasionally have open houses, fundraisers, or other special events that are open to people interested in the community. Please email to request more information. [Oct2004]

PRAIRIE ONION COHOUSING

JoLynn Doerr
6436 N Hamilton
Chicago, IL 60645

773-764-4914
info@prairieonioncohousing.org
prairieonioncoho@mac.com

http://www.prairieonioncohousing.org

Began: 2003 | Forming | Urban

Prairie Onion Cohousing will create and sustain an intergenerational, cooperative urban community and living environment that is healthful and nurturing for its residents, connected with the larger community, and respectful of the earth's resources which we all share.

We intend to build a cohousing community within the city of Chicago. We are currently looking for a site of about two acres of land (about one city block) that is easily accessible to the Loop and within walking distance of public transportation. We anticipate a community of

Scissors [✂] at the end of a listing indicate that it was edited for length by the Directory editors and a longer description can be found at directory.ic.org.

210

about 25 households who will share green space and a common house, with parking located at the edge of the site. [Jan2005]

PRAIRIE SKY COHOUSING COOPERATIVE

100-403 31st Ave NE
Calgary, AB T2E 9B3
CANADA

403-289-7179
info@prairiesky.ab.ca

Susan Stratton
susan@prairiesky.ab.ca

Kathleen Ryan
403-276-4296

http://www.prairiesky.ab.ca

Began: 1995 | Pop. 50
Urban | Diet: Omnivorous

We are an urban community of 18 households: singles, couples, and families. We completed Alberta's first cohousing project in May 2003. Prairie Sky is on $3/4$ of an acre $2^1/_2$ miles from downtown Calgary in three buildings that mix townhouses and apartments around a courtyard. We have a 3400 sq ft Common House that extends our private living spaces with a large kitchen and dining room, lounge, playroom, bathrooms, laundry, craft room, studio, rec room, guest room and office, and parking underground.

We have chosen to live where our actions reflect our commitment to our Prairie Sky neighbors and to social and environmental responsibility. We built for energy efficiency and water conservation—and for minimum sound transmission, so we'd stay friends in close quarters. We make decisions by consensus at monthly business meetings, and we divide responsibilities among six teams: Coordination, Building Care, Community Care, Landscape and Gardening, Social, and Common House.

We value diversity and community involvement. We do not share any ideology beyond the belief that living more closely with our neighbors enriches our lives. Sharing resources (a second car, magazines and newspapers, gardening and workshop tools, pet care, child care, rides to the airport) reduces our expenses. Sharing fun (common meals, movies, hiking, skiing, canoeing, guitar playing, dance lessons, music events—whatever comes up) increases the joy in our lives.

Visitors Accepted: Contact by email or

phone, explain purpose or circumstance and hoped-for length of stay. [Mar2005]

THE PRIORITIES INSTITUTE

Logan Perkins
1565 California St Apt 607
Denver, CO 80202

303-777-5511
Logan@priorities.org

http://www.priorities.org

Began: 1995 | Pop. 3 | Forming
Urban | Diet: Omnivorous

We run an educational nonprofit focusing on moral evolution, current events, governmental structure, land use planning and car-free city designs. We create models for autoless, livable cities for up to 90,000 people. Offering free design work for eco-cities, intentional communities and cohousing for select groups. Ideally, we'd love to have investors to create a development. We're also open to join a community, preferably an Ithaca-Ecovillage-type development. We're not egalitarian, vegetarian, New Age yuppies, or biblical, but we are tolerant. We love reading, designing sustainable communities, well-behaved pets and kids, research and writing, visiting hip communities, educational programs, homeschooling, history, gardening, light partying, controlled drinking, silly humor, tasty foods, lotsa friends, meeting interesting folks, music, living in the here and now while reflecting on the past and planning a better future.

Visitors Accepted: Contact Logan. [Mar2005]

PROJETORGONE

ACOR-ASBL
29 Rue Des Glycines
Neuilly Sur Marne, F-93330
FRANCE

+33-(0)143-086-800
projetorgone@free.fr
acor1901@free.fr

http://projetorgone.free.fr

Began: 2004 | Pop. 7 | Forming
Rural | Diet: Other

Projetorgone is a forming utopian project of intentional community life, in accordance with the research of W. Reich, to live together a conviviality for every days, the greeting, the freedom to be, the personal development, the natural love, the political and practical ecology, the polyamour and

political sexuality, soon in ecovillage, ecolieu, or elsewhere...

Projetorgone aims at recreating a microclimate where the natural love could again found the bonds between the human ones working to get rid of their essential neuroses and pollution by including/understanding the orgone better, our vital energy.

Projetorgone draws its raison d'étre in the report of an egoistic, sick world, perverted and without future, in the report which any revolutionary project must find and counter the source even neuroses of the system of company that it calls in question. After Wilhelm Reich and David Cooper, we blame the sexual repression generalized, though camouflaged well, applied to a whole population by a system repressive, capitalist, family, school, religious.

Projetorgone works for the blooming of the individual as a whole, including emotional, sexual, spiritual dimensions. This blooming appears to us, obviously doomed to failure in the current context, of a company based on the dough, sexual morals, the power, the mercantile mercantile, the emotional plague, it to appear, the possessivity, the jealousy, and etc.

To recreate a way of life together where each one can leave their isolation, discover their bodies and their capacity for natural love and contact, build a respectful environment for the life and planet, find the simplicity of natural love; such is the direction of our endeavour.

Visitors Accepted: It is necessary to study the website and agree with it. [Mar2005]

PROVIDENCE COHOUSING

Shirley DiMatteo
198 University Ave
Providence, RI 02906

401-861-1537
shelly-dimatteo@cox.net

Sara/Don Slate
401-435-2039
sslate@cox.net

Libby Edgerly
401-274-1597
ledgerly@cox.net

Began: 2004 | Forming

We are a group of people interested in developing an intergenerational intentional community here in Providence, Rhode Island.

Visitors Accepted: Contact Shirley DiMatteo. [Jan2005]

Additions and corrections: email: directory@ic.org, *web:* directory.ic.org, *mail: RR 1 Box 156-D, Rutledge MO 63563, USA.*

Listings

PRUDENCE CRANDALL HOUSE

438 66th St
Oakland, CA 94609

510-652-7600
springfriedlander@yahoo.com

Began: 1972 | Pop. 9
Urban | Diet: Omnivorous

Our two adjacent separately owned single family homes are far more than good neighbors. We built and use a bicycle shed and a bridge for the wheelchair ramp. We share our rear gardens and produce, pick up stuff for each other when shopping, move our cars and our garbage, etc. Lately we have shifted away from partying and eating together but still interact several times per week.

Prudence Crandall House, PCH, has one of the original owners from 1972 who is now 61, three women who are 54, 36, and 30 years old, plus a 3 year old daughter and a 31 year old man. The 3,000 sq ft house has been improved to better accommodate collective living by adding a full second bathroom, a real staircase between the two floors, pantry space and a guest room, and by opening up the kitchen to the dining and living room, and improving sound insulation between the floors and between the rooms. Green features include more insulation, a wood burning stove with a catalytic converter, and solar hot water and electric panels on the roof. Also we have composted and used drip irrigation for the vegetable beds for 32 years and now use a worm bin.

Anna Barnard bought the neighboring house eight years ago with hopes of doing incremental cohousing. Unfortunately we have been unable to find other cohousers to purchase adjacent homes when they became available. Anna shares her house with two renters who are not involved with PCH or the neighborhood. She has improved the temperature and sound insulation, does French intensive gardening in raised beds and commutes by bicycle. Anna edits the newsletter for our active neighborhood group of four adjacent streets with 148 households.

Visitors Accepted: It is easiest for us to accommodate you if you arrange it about two weeks before you arrive. We welcome visitors to join us for dinner and/or stay overnight. [Mar2005]

PUGET RIDGE COHOUSING

7020 18th Ave SW
Seattle, WA 98106

Ed Fischburg
206-763-3450
sharlaed@hotmail.com

Ivan Miller
206-762-7301
imiller@psrc.org

http://www.scn.org/
pugetridgecohousing

Began: 1988

[Feb2005]

PUMPKIN HOLLOW COMMUNITY

1467 Pumpkin Hollow Rd
Liberty, TN 37095

615-536-5022
community@pumpkinhollow.net
thebarn@pumpkinhollow.net

http://www.pumpkinhollow.net

Began: 1996 | Pop. 6
Rural | Diet: Omnivorous

The first residents of Pumpkin Hollow Community moved onto this rustic and remote land in late November 1996 and now own it cooperatively with a mutual benefit nonprofit. Everyone on the land participates in the financial obligation to pursue communal ownership.

Our mission originally included: "maintaining a rural, residential community for the practice of sustainable agriculture, ecological living, art, and education." Over the years, we've added doing radical activism, practicing earth-based spirituality, and throwing transformative, carnivalesque festivals to our mission.

Since 2002, Pumpkin Hollow has been home base for the editorial collective of Fifth Estate, North America's oldest anti-authoritarian publication.

The first residents chose this region for the wild (and relatively affordable) land in proximity to already established intentional communities. (see Short Mountain, IDA, etc.)

The values of equality, diversity, and tolerance have been combined with a visionary, down-to-earth, DIY culture. While some communities have the resources to provide an open gate to any and all who come, we wish to be more cautious, to create a voluntary association that carefully welcomes visitors and fairly selects new members.

Many of us feel an affinity for anarchism and paganism but decades of combined experience in community living have taught us that open communication, transparent agreements, honest disclosure, and mutual respect are required to seed the context where freedom might bloom.

Visitors Accepted: Telephone and email. Be patient and persistent. Don't show up unannounced. Be prepared to contribute. [Mar2005][✀]

PURPLE ROSE COLLECTIVE

1531 Fulton St
San Francisco, CA 94117

Began: 1978 | Pop. 11
Urban | Diet: Primarily vegetarian

Collectively owning our old Victorian house means freedom from landlord-imposed restrictions, but also means more responsibility for maintenance. We take turns cooking dinner, and have weekly house meetings. We share the evening meal, which is primarily vegan and organic. We compost all kitchen waste in our lovely little garden, share appliances and tools, and are a bike-friendly household. We also value being open and honest. [Mar2005]

QUAKER HOUSE

1416 Hill St
Ann Arbor, MI 48104

734-761-7435
qhrc_apply@umich.edu

734-846-6545
davcar@isr.umich.edu

Pop. 6 | Small Town | Diet: Primarily vegetarian

[Feb2005]

QUMBYA CO-OP

5130 S University Ave
Chicago, IL 60615

773-684-2536, 773-955-9293
qumbyamc@qumbya.com
concordmc@qumbya.com

http://www.qumbya.com

Began: 1991 | Pop. 51
Urban | Diet: Primarily vegetarian

We're a group of students, artists, community organizers, and others who share food,

---

Scissors [✀] at the end of a listing indicate that it was edited for length by the Directory editors and a longer description can be found at directory.ic.org.

fun, and friendship in our three old houses. We cook vegetarian/vegan homemade food and dine together most nights. Members participate by cooking (once every few weeks), by doing a chore (from shopping for organic produce to vacuuming), and by coming to weekly meetings. We also work on the house together, doing minor maintenance with our own people power.

Our houses are great for people new to the area—or anyone sick of the apartment blues. We are a diverse community accepting of many different lifestyles. It's a terrific situation for those seeking community, a chance to gain new skills and to share with others. We are in Chicago, near the U of Chicago, and close to the downtown loop.

If you're interested, give a call or write us an email. We'd love to have you over for dinner!

Visitors Accepted: Visitors should email membership coordinators of the house they want to visit to schedule a dinner visit. Dinners start at 7pm and 7:30pm, depending on the house. Contact the membership coordinators: concordmc@qumbya.com, bowersmc@qumbya.com, haymarketmc@qumbya.com. [Mar2005]

RACCOON CREEK COMMUNITY

Indiana

317-259-4417, 812-336-4486
rcc@netdirect.net

http://raccooncreek.blogspot.com

Began: 2004 | Forming
Rural | Diet: Omnivorous

Raccoon Creek Community is being formed on a wooded 154-acre site in Owen County, Indiana. Fewer than 30 acres will be used for the community. The remainder is now in Indiana's classified forest program and ultimately will be left to a land trust or the Nature Conservancy.

We have formed to demonstrate to the larger community that one can live in community, lightly on the land, and still have a comfortable life using the cohousing model. We will generate electricity with photovoltaics, grow much of our own food, build "green" homes and a community house, and ultimately establish an education center

for schools and other groups. We are receiving help in planning and design from state university departments.

Like-minded individuals and families of all ages are encouraged to consider joining us.

Visitors Accepted: Prospective members who attend at least one community meeting may be invited to visit the property. Call one of the numbers above for information. [Mar2005]

RAINBOW FAMILY GATHERINGS

rob@welcomehome.org
agr@agr.welcomehome.org

http://www.welcomehome.org/rainbow.html

Began: 1972
Rural | Diet: Primarily vegetarian

Some say we're the largest nonorganization of nonmembers in the world. We have no leaders and no organization. To be honest, the Rainbow Family means different things to different people. I think it's safe to say we're into intentional-community building, nonviolence, and alternative lifestyles. We also believe that peace and love are a great thing and there isn't enough of that in this world. Many of our traditions are based on Native American traditions, and we have a strong orientation to take care of the Earth. We gather in the national forest yearly to pray for peace on this planet.

Visitors Accepted: Plan on primitive camping conditions, and to really enjoy the community, working as a volunteer in one of the group kitchens—it is always a fun experience, and a good way to make friends. [Mar2005]

RAINBOW FARM

3801 S County Rd 575 E
Selma, IN 47383

765-747-7027,
765-282-0484 (kitchen)
rainbowfarm3801@earthlink.net

http://www.oakwoodretreatcenter.org

Began: 1974 | Pop. 16 | Spiritual
Rural | Diet: Omnivorous

Rainbow Farm is an International Emissary Community dedicated to the spiritual regeneration of humankind and stewardship of the earth. It is located in east-central Indiana on 276 acres of forest and field. The current focus is the provision and creation

of sacred space for healing and transformational work. The community operates a year round full service retreat facility (Oakwoood Retreat Center at Rainbow Farm) and hosts a wide variety of events and visitors. Please call ahead to visit.

Visitors Accepted [Mar2005]

RAINBOW HEARTH SANCTUARY AND RETREAT CENTER

1330 Waterway Ln
Burnet, TX 78611

512-756-7878
info@rainbowhearth.com

http://www.rainbowhearth.com

Began: 1986 | Pop. 2 | Spiritual
Rural | Diet: Primarily vegetarian

Rainbow Hearth is an ecospiritual center based on permaculture, interspecies communication, music, arts, and life skills to stay healthy, viable, and in balance with the Earth. Our commitment is to live with dignity, comfort, purpose, delight, and integrity and in heart space.

Rainbow Hearth's nine acres rise from lakeshore to 180 feet above the lake through woods, organic gardens, orchards, and meadows. Our 30-acre neighborhood of private landholders is bordered by enormous ranches recognized as critical for water quality and wildlife habitat. A 900-acre state park is nearby.

Members and neighbors are self-employed in teaching, holistic health, writing, entertainment, landscaping, building, and business consulting. We combine simple lifestyles with high-tech capabilities. The neighborhood children are wise to the ways of nature, and they roam freely and safely.

Interested persons may rent available rooms or houses or purchase lots in the immediate neighborhood. Rainbow Hearth is now devoted to providing retreat space for individuals, couples, families, and small groups.

The Whole Works! Institute—a nonprofit corporation—sponsors an Earth-keeper internship program of particular interest to persons committed to exploring powerful and effective alternatives to mainstream living options. Spiritual and physical regeneration retreats are available.

See website for details.

Visitors Accepted: Review our website, and/or the "Intern Application" in the Whole Works! Institute section, then email us. [Oct2004]

Additions and corrections: email: directory@ic.org, *web:* directory.ic.org, *mail:* RR 1 Box 156-D, Rutledge MO 63563, USA.

213

RAINBOW PEACE CARAVAN

AP 111
Tepoztlan, Morelos 62520
MEXICO
info@lacaravana.org

http://www.lacaravana.org

Began: 1995 | Pop. 13
Diet: Primarily vegetarian

We are an international group of artists and ecologists traveling since 1996 from Mexico to Tierra del Fuego (Firelands), South America, in our own converted buses. By networking with indigenous, ecological, and alternative groups we create bridges and plant seeds. Multimedia theater, workshops and courses, conferences, audiovisuals, bioregional gatherings, and ceremonial villages are the means by which we promote our message of peace, hope, unity, and harmony with la Madre Tierra. We are a mobile ecovillage experiment, bringing practical solutions to people interested in creating more sustainable lives. We learn, teach, motivate, share, and inspire. We live simply, communally, and joyfully, and we are dedicated to communal and personal growth in our journey.

Visitors Accepted: Email a brief description of yourself and your intended visit.

We ask for daily or weekly donation to help with our daily costs. Also we expect that a visitor will participate in group work and group play! We ask that illegal substances, pets, and weapons not be brought to our group.

We are always happy to meet new people! [Mar2005]

RAINBOW VALLEY

PO Box 108
Takaka, Golden Bay 7172
NEW ZEALAND

+64-(0)3-525-8209
trcw@xtra.co.nz
tonyclearwater@hotmail.com

Began: 1974 | Pop. 20
Rural | Diet: Omnivorous

A community of individuals. Our 100 hectares is an open valley between forest-covered hills. The Anatoki River leads up to wilderness and down to the wider community of Golden Bay. Community is first and foremost about people, not land. The people cooperate and share in different ways and at different levels. Differences are respected. Communication is recognized as vital. We want the community to be an environment that encourages cooperative work in all its forms, self-expression, and self-exploration.

We aim to follow the path of nonviolence (physical and emotional) in conflict resolution. Affairs pertaining to the whole community are resolved through meetings, with consensus always the aim. A company structure represents us legally, in which all members are entitled to equal shares. Children play an important part in our community, helping us achieve a sense of extended family. Our community house has a vital role as the heart place, channeling communication, social life, and community spirit. The farming/gardening/conserving of communal land is a strong focus, while various arts and crafts manifest another dimension. All residents are responsible for their own income. Produce is sold for agreed purposes or is shared. Visitors are welcome when there is space.

Visitors Accepted: Xmas and January are the only times when our main house may not be available as friends and family often stay. Most other times of the year there is always accommodation and we are open to visitors. Booking is preferred by phoning but not essential. [Feb2005]

RAINBOW WAY STATION

Zen c/o: James W. Bush
General Delivery
Kurtistown, HI 96760

wambatron@yahoo.com
wambatron@hotmail.com

http://members.fortunecity.com/
fbush2/rainbow.html

Began: 2004 | Forming
Rural | Diet: Primarily vegetarian

The Rainbow Way Station is on three acres of undeveloped land deep in the Hawaiian rain forest. Located 3-5 miles off the main highway, a vehicle is recommended. Though we are quite remote we are also only 15 miles from Hilo, HI. There is no infrastructure, but roads run along two sides of the land. There is no budget for paid labor, but work/camp space exchange is possible.

The intent is to form a small core group (8-10), having space left over for visitors and travelers. We are in the process of building a botanical "Eco-Ark" as a tourist attraction, thus providing a source of future funding.

While striving to be spiritually centered individuals, our community is not affiliated with any religion or specific spiritual practice.

The initial land base is privately "owned" (land trust pending) and is being made available as a stepping stone toward the growth of a community of private "owners" with a community vision. It IS hoped that you will join in with like-minded individuals in obtaining neighboring parcels. Making your own rules, following your own beliefs and focuses. Instead of one large, jointly owned (or lost) parcel where everyone has to fit into the same box, this is a vision of many smaller, diversely focused, privately owned boxes working cooperatively. We are NOT a commune. You are not required to give all your assets to an organization. Nor are you expected to work all week for the organization. You are expected to be self sufficient AND contribute to the common good in return for the common benefit.

Visitors Accepted: See website for instructions and contact info. Small deposit required (refundable). [Oct2004][✄]

RAPHA COMMUNITY

1420 Salt Springs Rd
Syracuse, NY 13214

315-449-9627
jsketcha@syr.edu

Began: 1971 | Pop. 31 | Spiritual | Urban

Rapha (from the Hebrew word for healing) began in the late 1960s as a small house church. We are nonresidential, making decisions by consensus. We function through shared volunteer leadership. For charitable giving we are registered as a not-for-profit corporation.

Our purpose is to take questions of faith seriously, to support and accompany members on both the inner and outer journey, and to be an extended family, caring for one another, having fun together, sharing joys and sorrows, eating, singing, and praying. We strive to challenge each other to identify, bless, and use our gifts in the world, to reach beyond ourselves to the needs of others.

Since we own no communal property, we meet in homes, churches, recreation centers, and the like. We gather once a month for worship, alternating times with children included and times for adults only. We celebrate traditional holidays together as well as personal events like weddings, house blessings, or children's graduations. We meet informally in times of personal crisis or need. We meet twice a year for evaluation and visioning about our life together. We meet in small groups, or

Scissors [✄] at the end of a listing indicate that it was edited for length by the Directory *editors and a longer description can be found at* directory.ic.org.

"cells," committed to mutual support, study, or projects.

We are open to new members—families with children, couples, and singles. Some members identify themselves as Christian, but many wisdom traditions have enriched our faith journey since our founding—for example, Judaism, Roman Catholicism, Quakerism, Buddhism, and well as Native American, goddess, and creation spirituality.

Visitors Accepted [Feb2005]

RAVEN ROCKS

54118 Crum Rd
Beallsville, OH 43716
chris@ravenrocks.org

http://www.ravenrocks.org

Began: 1970 | Pop. 11 | Rural

Raven Rocks, established in 1970, is a small rural project in the northern edge of Ohio Appalachia. The community has found focus in the effort to pay for, restore, and set aside for permanent preservation more than 1,000 acres of hill and ravine lands. The original environmental concern—to rescue the property from strip mining for coal—has grown to include a variety of member-financed projects, including several structures above and underground that utilize conservation techniques and solar strategies. One underground building was designed for public demonstration and will incorporate seven solar strategies, as well as a biointensive garden. All agricultural projects—including our Christmas-tree operation, grass-fed cattle, and gardens at all the homes—are organic. Most of our acreage has been set aside for natural restoration of the native hardwood forest. The entire property, including the homes and other improvements, is designed as permanent preserve and hence not available for sale or development.

Members earn their own livings, then volunteer the time required (about 7,000 hours annually) to raise Christmas trees that pay for the land and to do the work of the corporation.

Education has been a fundamental interest of this group. We are striving to get more of our multifaceted public statement and demonstration in place and fear that the effort could be jeopardized by too much premature publicity and traffic. Hence, for the immediate future we are withholding our phone number. [Mar2005][✂<]

REBA PLACE FELLOWSHIP

727 Reba Pl
Evanston, IL 60202

847-328-6066 (office 8am-5pm),
847-475-8715 (home)
R_P_F@juno.com
rpfcana@earthlink.net

http://www.rebaplacefellowship.org

Began: 1957 | Pop. 50 | Spiritual
Urban | Diet: Omnivorous

Reba Place Fellowship began in 1957 in what has become an ethnically diverse neighborhood in south Evanston. Its fortysome members and children now live in large multifamily homes and apartment buildings in Evanston and in Rogers Park, in north Chicago. Reba sponsors affordable housing for many low-income families. Fellowship members work in shared community ministries and in "outside" earning jobs, mostly in the service professions.

Reba Place Fellowship's long-term commitment to its local neighborhoods has encouraged the formation of two congregations and given life to a couple of cooperative "villages" within the city. In recent years Reba has worked to review its structures, to become a more reconciling and empowering presence within its racially diverse neighborhoods. After 42 years of community experience, Reba is still under construction. Interns and visitors welcome.

Visitors Accepted: Contact RPF at the office phone or by email. [Dec2004]

RED EARTH FARMS

Alyson Ewald
1 Woehrle Rd
Rutledge, MO 63563

660-883-5330
redearth@galatea.org

http://redearth.galatea.org

Began: 2005 | Pop. 4 | Forming
Rural | Diet: Primarily vegan

Red Earth Farms is dedicated to developing sustainable lifestyle choices. We enjoy our close relationship with the planet that sustains us, and we do our best to honor our nonhuman friends. We believe in taking care of each other as well; our guiding principle is "Love the land; love your neighbors." In our actions we endeavor to do to others as we would have them do to us. This means a deep support for cooperative projects and a growing gift culture.

It also means we respect the diversity among us. We hope this freedom of implementation will result in a number of different models of sustainable systems. Though we encourage cooperation, it will rarely be obligatory. Individuals, families, and income-sharing communities make decisions about their own land, and everyone can participate in decisions affecting the wider Red Earth Farms community. The issues upon which we will seek full community agreement will likely be few.

We are aiming to generate a high percentage of our own food, as well as shelter, fuel, clothing, tools, and other essentials. Nonviolence, permaculture, feminism, and our personal spiritual paths are important to us.

We are negotiating for 40-80 acres less than a mile from Dancing Rabbit Ecovillage and about three miles from Sandhill Farm. We have neighborly relationships with these communities; we share potluck dinners, frisbee games, and gardening tips. We are open to visitors and we welcome children, families, and those of nontraditional lifestyles.

Visitors Accepted: Contact us (email preferred). [Mar2005]

REDFIELD COMMUNITY

The Secretary
Buckingham Road
Winslow
Buckinghamshire MK18 3LZ England
UNITED KINGDOM

+44-(0)1296-713661
info@redfieldcommunity.org.uk

http://www.redfieldcommunity.org.uk

Began: 1978 | Pop. 24
Small Town | Diet: Primarily vegetarian

Redfield was founded in 1978, and now has 15 adult members and 9 kids. We share a Victorian mansion and stable block in 17 acres of pasture, woodland, gardens and orchards. The land and the ground floor of the house are communal, with individual units and rooms on the first and second floors. We don't income-share, but we income-pool, as we are a registered housing co-op, and all members pay a monthly rent to the co-op (part per capita, and part floor space occupied). Members tend to work part-time in paid jobs, and are expected to put two days a week into Redfield. This could be in the garden, on maintenance, cooking, cleaning, admin, splitting logs (we have wood-burners in all our rooms) or looking after the animals (we have sheep, pigs, chickens and bees). We eat our evening meals together, and people sign up

Additions and corrections: email: directory@ic.org, *web:* directory.ic.org, *mail: RR 1 Box 156-D, Rutledge MO 63563, USA.*

215

to cook (which means we each cook about once every two weeks). We have weekly consensus decision-making meetings; no capital is needed to join; we are secular and don't have a particular group philosophy, although we tend to have a 'green' outlook; we recycle; our land is organic; we have solar hot water, compost toilets, and eco-paints; and there is an environmental organisation called LILI based here (in the stable block) which employs three members, and runs courses, provides information and undertakes projects and installations. We are a WWOOF host, have visitor days, and run Living in Communities weekends twice a year. We welcome enquiries about visiting and membership.

Visitors Accepted: Check our website for information on ways to visit Redfield and then email or write to us. [Feb2005]

REEVIS MOUNTAIN SCHOOL OF SELF-RELIANCE

**HC-02 Box 1534
Roosevelt, AZ 85545**

**928-467-2675 (messages only; remote phone)
reevismountain@starband.net
bigfoot@reevismountain.org**

http://www.reevismountain.org

Began: 1979 | Pop. 3 | Spiritual
Rural | Diet: Omnivorous

We are a spiritually oriented, self-reliant, wholesome natural-foods farm family. Our vision is to raise awareness of our eternal divinity by living what we love and seeking truth each day.

Our 12-acre homesite is a remote, high-desert, riparian valley in the Superstition Wilderness. Access is an 8-mile hike or a 4x4 drive to highway; 10 miles to the nearest "outside" socializing/telephone opportunity.

Our lifestyle is rustic as well as junk food and media free. We began as a New Age community focused on self-sufficiency and survival skills. Today we're a family/sanctuary, an organic farm, and a classroom. Funding sources: class fees, donations, an herbal remedies mail-order business.

We accept a small number of students for 30 days of "learning by doing" and a $350.00 tuition. This fee and work exchange provide room and board, a peaceful, healing environment, and a mentor who has enriched the lives of many. Longer-term residency is open to those who complete their 30-day stay harmoniously. We do not accept children/pets. Opportunities for outside employment are

nil as our access road makes commuting a real challenge.

We have classes open to the public on Stone Masonry, Meditation, Herbal Medicine, Survival Skills, and Oriental Touch Healing. Please visit our website for current information on classes and herbal remedies.

Visitors Accepted: Please email or call to schedule a visit. Email is usually the quickest way to schedule something. Visitors are welcome for varying lengths of time at variable costs, depending on what level of participation or room and board are desired while visiting. [Jan2005]

THE REFUGE

**Jeanne Elder
PO Box 9342
Pueblo, CO 81008
healingcommunities@comcast.net**

http://www.healingcommunities.org

Began: 2004 | Pop. 1 | Forming | Spiritual
Rural | Diet: Omnivorous

A healing community is a community of God's people, dedicated to Him and one another in love, who express that love by bringing healing of body, soul and spirit to their communities.

We are forming a community that will bring Christians together in Unity to bring healing Spirit, soul and body to those in the community and the communities in which we live.

Visitors Accepted: Please email for information. [Mar2005]

REGENERATIVE CO-OP OF POMONA

**Pomona, CA
RegenPomona@gmail.com**

http://www.regen.org

Began: 1999 | Pop. 16
Suburban | Diet: Primarily vegetarian

The Regenerative Co-op of Pomona, Regen, is an intentional community located in a quiet suburb east of Los Angeles. Founded by graduates of Cal Poly Pomona's Center for Regenerative Studies in 1999, we strive to incorporate sustainable and regenerative principles in our urban/suburban environment.

The food in the co-op is vegetarian, although the co-op includes residents who are non-vegetarian away from home. Community meals occur five nights a week and always include a vegan option. We use

solar power, maintain a gray water system, edible landscaping and organic gardening. Community decisions use a consensus model in weekly community meetings.

We organize a Sustainability Seminar every February with workshops and speakers on topics from solar power to activism in the media (topics change each year). We host the local Food Not Bombs chapter every Sunday which provides vegetarian meals to the local homeless. In addition we host various workshops of social and environmental interests throughout the year.

Currently we can accommodate up to 20 residents distributed between three homes. Some of us are very active in local peace and environmental activism; others have never been to a protest. We have had residents from as far away as Germany and as local as Orange County. We are organizers, teachers, technicians, students, business people, philosophers, artists, and many other things. We do have openings from time to time. If you are interested in applying please contact us.

Visitors Accepted: Send an email to the listed address and we will be happy to invite you to dinner generally. [Mar2005]

RENAISSANCE HOUSE

**House President
1512-1520 Gilbert Ct
Ann Arbor, MI 48105**

http://www.icc.coop

Pop. 66 | Diet: Omnivorous

The North Campus co-ops are divided into two co-op houses: Renaissance and O'Keeffe. Each co-op is further divided into suites with four in Renaissance and five in O'Keeffe. Within each suite approximately 18 members share a small kitchen and living room and a cable TV lounge. Each suite is further divided so that only four or five people share a telephone and a bathroom. Member rooms are primarily large or small singles, but our doubles provide some of Ann Arbor's most affordable housing. To ensure quality and balanced meals, the houses have hired a professional chef.

In addition to the house kitchens, the basement contains many common areas shared by both houses. These include a study lounge, recreation room (with a ping-pong table, pool tables and a "honky tonk" piano), music room (with a baby grand piano), laundry room (detergent and bleach provided), and a darkroom (supplies not included).

Visitors Accepted: Contact House President. [Mar2005]

Scissors [✂] at the end of a listing indicate that it was edited for length by the Directory *editors and a longer description can be found at* directory.ic.org.

RÉSEAU DES ÉCOHAMEAUX ET ÉCOVILLAGES DU QUÉBEC

Lucie Lemelin
783 Gervais
Wotton, J0A 1N0
CANADA

819-828-0367, 514-256-6381
respir@aei.ca

http://ecohameau.tripod.com/
index.html

Began: 2003 | Forming

Organisme québécois dont la mission est d'aider au démarrage d'Écohameaux en milieu rural.

Vous pouvez nous rejoindre soit par courriel our par téléphone 819-828-0367. [Feb2005]

RETIREMENT COMMUNITIES

MLM Spohr
301 N Ninth St
Kenilworth, NJ 07083

908-397-0974
spohr@cocmast.net

http://retirementcommunities.us

Began: 2003 | Pop. 4 | Forming | Urban

The city can be a good place to grow old, and many people are interested in moving back to urban centers, as long as they are safe and affordable. Lower crime rates have made downtowns more appealing, and theories like Creative Capital offer exciting insights into the value of city life.

Pedestrian-friendly, urban cooperative communities near colleges, universities, or cultural centers attract independent, interesting people who want alternatives to traditional retirement lifestyles. More and more, sophisticated retirees want a more cosmopolitan lifestyle, but so far, most affordable developments are in isolated rural or suburban areas, and only the wealthy can afford a townhouse in Manhattan or a charming cottage in Princeton. These options are perfect for many, but what about the rest of us?

The Square at Kean represents a small group who want to retire in metropolitan New Jersey, and who are looking for like-minded people to join with us.

Visitors Accepted: Contact us to find out about upcoming meetings. [Jan2005]

REWILDING COMMUNITY

Sky and Griffin
PO Box 1404
Twain Harte, CA 95383

800-471-5403
feralhuman@ziplip.com

http://www.rewild.org

Began: 2004 | Pop. 2 | Forming | Spiritual
Rural | Diet: Omnivorous

We're forming a tribe of aspiring hunter/gatherers with an emphasis on emotional healing and direct communication. We expect this to be a lifelong transition. We wish to exclude gardens, electricity of any kind, pets, livestock, etc. We want to gather all our food, shelter materials, clothing, etc. from the local wild land.

Visitors Accepted: Write us an email or letter or voicemail and let us know when, why, for how long. While transient we are open to meeting up with folks on the road. [Jan2005]

RIPARIA

PO Box 4812
Chico, CA 95927

530-895-8786
RTrau77613@aol.com

Began: 1987 | Pop. 25
Rural | Diet: Primarily vegetarian

Riparia is an intentional community on 12 acres. Riparia has nine homes, a year-round creek, organic gardens, and orchards. There are 25 people presently living in our community. We have a good mix of ages with both young people and elders.

We interact with the greater Chico area, including sponsoring fund-raisers and other events at Riparia to benefit local organizations. Our focus is right livelihood and working on environmental, peace, and social justice issues. We are learning to live cooperatively yet retaining a strong commitment to individuality.

Visitors Accepted [Mar2005]

RISE AND SHINE

Kristina
2205 N New Jersey
Indianapolis, IN 46205

embraceresistance@hotmail.com

Forming

We are currently in the process of looking for a location (and are flexible about where

that may be), more specifically some land to share. Our goal is to have an animal sanctuary with accompanying facilities for humane education. We would like to practice and teach sustainable agriculture, solar technology and other sustainable power, and strawbale or other regionally appropriate building methods. If you have a section of your land to share, lease, sell, negotiate, etc., please contact us via email. Also, if you are interested or have any suggestions for us, please let us know.

We hope to be incorporated as a non-profit within a couple of years. [Nov2004]

RIVER CITY HOUSING COLLECTIVE

Summit House
200 S Summit St
Iowa City, IA 52240

319-337-5260

Anomy House
802 E Washington St
Iowa City, IA 52240

319-337-8445

http://www.river-city-housing.org

Began: 1977 | Pop. 26
Urban | Diet: Primarily vegetarian

Our collective currently consists of two large houses close enough to walk to the university or downtown. We own both houses, and are planning to buy another. We each pay a share slightly below the average cost to rent in the area but we require each member to work a minimum of 16 hours a month for the collective. This work includes cooking, shopping, maintenance, management, meetings, and committees such as newsletter, education/ cultures, membership, work credit, recycling, and food club. We especially need individuals skilled in plumbing, electrical, and carpentry. We also appreciate skills such as cooking/baking, music, and teaching.

This is a consensus community, so we are learning about tolerance, teamwork, real-estate management, and group process. We interview people who want to live here as a group, usually over dinner, and then make a group decision on membership/boarding privileges.

If you live here you must like children, pets, and composting. Success is a process, not a destination. We need hardworking, friendly people who appreciate diversity.

Visitors Accepted: Please make arrangements in advance via phone or postal mail. [Feb2005]

Listings

Additions and corrections: email: directory@ic.org, web: directory.ic.org, mail: RR 1 Box 156-D, Rutledge MO 63563, USA.

217

RIVER FARM

3231 Hillside Rd
Deming, WA 98244

360-592-5222,
360-592-2716 (Holly)
riverfarm@nas.com

http://www.nas.com/riverfarm

Began: 1984 | Pop. 15
Rural | Diet: Omnivorous

We live in the Pacific Cascadia bioregion in the northwest corner of the United States and are one of the five communities in the Evergreen Land Trust. We are eleven adults and four children. We now have openings.

Our community is maintaining wildlife areas, practicing ecologically-based farming and forestry, and hosting educational events for the community and each other. The farm is a mixture of forests, gardens, fields, a marsh, several streams, a river and a mountainside. We value independence and practical homesteading and practice consensus decision making. We work to improve our communication skills and to widen our views. We are open to written correspondence and endeavor to network with similar folks.

We are active in our local watershed and practice sustainable forestry.

Please, mail inquiries only.

Visitors Accepted: Send a letter.
[Mar2005]

RIVER HAYVEN

N9562 County Rd G
Colfax, WI 54730

715-632-2610
woods@organic.org

http://www.riverhayven.org

Began: 1992 | Pop. 8
Rural | Diet: Primarily raw foods

Our village is a home for people who seek the companionship and support of others who care about living ecologically, and evolving spiritually. We have no particular spiritual orientation, and welcome a diversity of viewpoints. We support members moving toward a living/raw foods lifestyle.

We have large organic gardens, 7 miles of trails, and a 5000 square foot common house that is a monolithic dome. Common meals are held here. The dome has five rooms/suites to provide lodging to people as they are building their homes.

We are planning businesses that include a raw foods/alternative healing retreat center and options for elder care. We have state-approved plans for our commercial build-

ings, and 20 acres of our land have been rezoned to commercial.

Our 250 acres of beautiful land are varied, with rolling hills covered by oak woods, white pine, jack pine, maple, and reemerging prairie. We have a mile and a half of frontage on the Hay River, including a few ponds. Eagles, otter, deer, beaver, and turkey are a few of the animals abundant on this land.

Our community is organized as a cooperative, and we have memberships available for residential or seasonal living. Our membership fees vary according to the use level desired.

Visitors Accepted: We have monthly potlucks May through October. Contact us to get on our email list that announces these potlucks. If you are unable to come to a potluck, email or telephone us to arrange a visit. [Mar2005]

RIVER ROCK COMMONS

520 N Sherwood St #3
Fort Collins, CO 80521

Linda L. B. Albright
lindaba@riverrock.org

http://www.riverrock.org

Began: 1997 | Forming

[Mar2005]

ROCKY HILL COHOUSING

Northhampton, MA
rockyhillcohousing@mail.com

Marsha Leavitt
mleavitt@email.smith.edu

Dorothy Riehm Entin
entin@attglobal.net

http://www.rockyhillcohousing.org

Began: 2001 | Pop. 83.5 | Forming

Our dream is to create a neighborhood that recaptures the essence of community: To create a human environment that fosters interconnectedness, safety, growth, and meaningful lives. To create physical aspects that serve the needs and enhance the well-being of the individuals and the community. To live in harmonious relationship to our place on the earth.

Our cohousing neighborhood will include 28 homes (mostly duplexes) clustered around a common house. There will also be five "associate member" (privately-owned) houses built along the road leading into Rocky Hill Cohousing.

We have begun the building process and expect to begin moving in spring of 2005.

Visitors Accepted: Email rockyhillcohousing@mail.com. [Jan2005]

ROSE CREEK VILLAGE

Hannah Pavao
999 Lola Whitten Rd
Selmer, TN 38375

888-849-5344, 731-645-9833
hannah@rosecreekvillage.com
shammah@rosecreekvillage.com

http://www.rosecreekvillage.com

Began: 1989 | Pop. 195 | Spiritual
Rural | Diet: Omnivorous

Our desire is simply to be the church of Jesus Christ, whom we call by his Hebrew name Yahshua. But what makes us different than so many others with the same desire?

Our test of truth is not Scriptural interpretations that we think are accurate. Our test of truth is results. "A good tree cannot bear bad fruit, nor can a bad tree bring forth good fruit." We are not satisfied with theories or unrealized hopes. Yahshua said, "They will know you are my disciples by your love for one another." Can this be real?

It can. Every day we get to prove that Yahshua is faithful to his word. Without a lot of rules, based completely on the desire for love and holiness that the Spirit of God puts in the heart of all his disciples, we live the most extraordinary and joyful life that we have ever heard of.

As of 2004, we are 35 families and 200 people living together in a village on 100 acres in West Tennessee. Most of the men work in village-run businesses. We simply get up every day to devote ourselves to our Master's wishes. We sing, dance, work, and play together. We have a Celtic band, a dance troupe, a drum corps, a horsemanship team, and now even a Tae Kwon Do demonstration team.

In everything we do, we seek to demonstrate a life that is based on love and relationships. We believe in hammering out differences and living in honesty and freedom. Our goal is that every person is completely submitted to God, but that they be free, vibrant, strong, creative, courageous, and kind.

Visitors Accepted: Please contact us so we know you are coming. Often, we can make arrangements for you to stay at the village, although at festival times we sometimes run out of room. Our whole village has a family atmosphere, so visits are han-

Scissors [✂] at the end of a listing indicate that it was edited for length by the Directory *editors and a longer description can be found at* directory.ic.org.

dled somewhat informally, although we will meet you and be glad to give you a tour and introductions. [Jan2005][⸂✁]

ROSEWIND COHOUSING

Lynn Nadeau
3221 Haines St
Port Townsend, WA 98368
inquiry.welcome@olympus.net

http://www.rosewind.org

Began: 1989 | Pop. 50
Small Town | Diet: Omnivorous

RoseWind Cohousing is a community of people who want fairly frequent and positive interactions with their neighbors. We would like to live a little more lightly on the land by sharing, by preserving green space, and by practicing a bit of sustainable agriculture within our small-town community. We want to live and learn, work and play together. We want to learn to function as a group that is respectful of individuals, using consensus to make decisions and set policies.

We have designed a neighborhood that includes a central commons with a vegetable garden, playground, grassy fields, and wild-rose thickets. Our privately-owned lots show our individuality in the diversity of building styles. Our common house (community hall) is frequently used, for meals, meetings, concerts, and other gatherings.

We continue to evolve our group process and sometimes stumble, but through it all we maintain our friendly connections with one another. We look out for each other in many ways large and small.

The town of 8000 where we are located is Port Townsend, on the NE corner of Washington's Olympic Peninsula. Seattle is about three hours away. PT has Victorian history, boats, lots of art and music, liberal politics, a moderate climate and seasonal festivals. It's a great town for children and families, especially.

Visitors Accepted: Please email well ahead of time. Getting to know if we'd be a good fit for you takes time, and the infrequent resales can go quickly, so you want to already know enough to make an informed choice. We have no guest room, but www.ptguide.com has details on other accomodations. [Mar2005]

ROSNEATH FARM

Dunsborough
AUSTRALIA

+61-(0)4-1231-8385
enquiries@rosneath.com.au

http://www.rosneath.com.au

Began: 1994 | Pop. 19 | Forming | Spiritual
Small Town | Diet: Omnivorous

Our ecovillage project is three hours drive south of Perth in Western Australia. We have 50 strata title lots for sale. They average 1700 sq m so we preserve 60 hectares each of forest and farming land. We have started conversion to intensive, organic, permaculture-guided, autonomous microenterprises. Autonomous: individuals or families will run their own farming operation, be it beekeeping, wine making, marron farming, orchards, or vegetable gardens, with licenses to use land and facilities of the strata company.

Rezoning has been achieved for the residences, the farming activities, and two special development nodes. Tourism activities in 4 hectares in the northwest corner will have buffers to protect privacy. We have a biodynamic wood-fired bakery there now. The village center on the east side will meet residents' needs. There we will build a laundry, a store, an office, a library, a computer room, workshops, a freezer room, and meeting rooms. Our first building was a guest house. We will provide a range of facilities so well that people feel no need to duplicate them at home. Rosneath Farm's unique feature is that the houses are totally independent, through the use of solar power, dry composting toilets, and water tanks. We have no bills. We raise free-range kids, not battery kids, in the cleanest air and water on the planet.

Visitors Accepted: Check website, email or phone. [Mar2005]

ROSY BRANCH FARM

320 Stone Mountain Farm Rd
Black Mountain, NC 28711

828-687-6571
pst63@aol.com

Began: 1987 | Pop. 18 | Rural | Diet: Other

Rosy Branch Farm is a neighborhood community focused on stewarding our land and ourselves in a cooperative ecological and peaceful manner. Begun in 1985, we currently have eight families living on the land (50 acres).

Listings

Additions and corrections: email: directory@ic.org, *web:* directory.ic.org, *mail: RR 1 Box 156-D, Rutledge MO 63563, USA.*

219

Each family is deeded approximately 3/4 acre and has an equal share in the remaining community property (44 acres). Economically each family is independent, and we collectively contribute to community property needs through quarterly dues. We have monthly work days, land meetings and potluck get togethers. Our land neighbors two other communities, Earthaven Ecovillage and Full Circle.

We are not actively seeking new members, but we're into cooperation and sharing information—including labor exchange, trading visits, etc. Occasionally members sell or rent their property interests.

Visitors Accepted: Please write, email or phone first. [Mar2005]

ROWE CAMP & CONFERENCE CENTER

Office Manager
PO Box 273
22 Kings Highway Rd
Rowe, MA 01367

413-339-4954
retreat@rowecenter.org

http://www.RoweCenter.org

Began: 1973 | Pop. 15
Rural | Diet: Primarily vegetarian

Rowe Camp and Conference Center is located in the beautiful Berkshires of Massachusetts, three miles from Vermont. Since 1924 we have run a small creative summer camp for teenagers. In 1974, our conference center was founded. We offer weekend and weeklong retreats for adults

and families on a wide variety of religious, political, psychological, and health issues.

Our work-study program is a chance for people who want to slow down, take stock, explore new directions, engage in creative and meaningful work, and be a part of a value-based, supportive community. Work-study participants work 33 hours a week in exchange for room, board, and the opportunity to participate in many of our programs. The stay lasts anywhere from six weeks to a year, and work is arranged by matching your skills and preferences with Rowe's needs, which may include housekeeping, maintaining our buildings and grounds, office work, and more. Our cooking internship is an opportunity to learn vegetarian cooking and bread baking from our wonderful cooks.

The study portion is self-directed and includes personal study, group work, attendance at conferences, individual meetings with a mentor, the experience of living in community, and the opportunity to practice new skills.

Rowe Camp and Conference Center balances a respect for the integrity and freedom of each person with the needs of the community and the organization. We are dedicated to fostering a new society that can nurture the best in each of us, reward idealism and caring, and expand hope and vision.

Visitors Accepted: We welcome visitors anytime, but request that they call ahead to arrange a visit. There is a small fee charged for overnight stays, but we are always happy to barter. Please call or email us to arrange a visit. [Feb2005]

RUTHS' HOUSE

House President
321 N Thayer St
Ann Arbor, MI 48104

734-827-8146

http://www.icc.coop

Began: 1993 | Pop. 12
Urban | Diet: Omnivorous

Ruths' is located five minutes from both central campus and the Medical Center. Ruths' is a beautiful Victorian house with huge windows and lots of hardwood floors. We have two kitchens, three refrigerators and four bathrooms. We also have a microwave, a TV and a VCR, and some limited parking. Our house is a great community! Please, visit anytime.

Visitors Accepted: Contact House President. [Mar2005]

SACRAMENTO COHOUSING

4252 Aubergine Way
Sacramento, CA 95655

916-369-2245
cohousing@sbcglobal.net

http://cohousing.hopto.org

Began: 2000 | Forming | Urban

The mission of Sacramento Cohousing is to

Scissors [✂] at the end of a listing indicate that it was edited for length by the Directory *editors and a longer description can be found at* directory.ic.org.

develop an affordable cohousing neighborhood in the Sacramento area based upon the following values:

• Community. A desire to live in a supportive community respectful of varying individual needs for privacy and interaction.

• Sharing. An interest in sharing, cooperating, and working together for the fun and the efficiency of it.

• Diversity. An openness to individual differences and a desire to create a welcoming environment to people of all ages and backgrounds, including children.

• Respect. A concern for the opinions of others and a commitment to treat each other with respect, especially when making decisions that will affect the whole group.

• Ecology. An interest in incorporating environmentally-friendly design elements in order to create a lower-impact and more ecologically sound living environment.

Visitors Accepted: We are working to build a cohousing community in the Sacramento area. Email to get on our Yahoo! group to learn more about us and be invited to meetings, beginning with an orientation meeting. You can also learn about us and our project schedule at our public website. Thank you for your interest! [Mar2005]

SACRAMENTO SUBURBAN COHOUSING

Marty Maskall
8456 Hidden Valley Circle
Fair Oaks, CA 95628

916-967-2472
mmaskall@pacbell.net

Began: 2005 | Forming | Suburban

Looking for site in the Eastern half of Sacramento County, probably in Fair Oaks, Orangevale, Citrus Heights, or Rancho Cordova. Planning 25 to 35 townhomes on three to five acres. For info, contact Marty Maskall. [Mar2005]

SACRED SUENOS

Yves Zehnder, Chrystel Murphy-Starr
Cassilla 1101 812
Loja
ECUADOR
sacredsuenos@wildmail.com

http://www.sacredsuenos.com

Began: 2001 | Pop. 2 | Forming
Rural | Diet: Primarily vegetarian

We are a newly forming organic farming community located in southern Ecuador,

believing in blending personal happiness with ecological and social responsibility. We make our decisions through consensus, practice voluntary simplicity and permaculture. We enjoy sharing, not only between ourselves, but also outside of our community through agricultural and social outreach.

We purchased undeveloped land in June 2004. Our population as of yet is usually made up of one or two cos living full-time on the farm and another one to three cos living here seasonally. In addition, we often have one to six visitors/volunteers learning and helping on the farm.

Visitors Accepted: Please email us far in advance if you would like to visit. We almost always accept visitors, especially if they want to stay and help out. [Mar2005]

SAGE VALLEY

http://www.earthloving.com

Forming

Sage Valley, located in the high desert of central Nevada, is a "Gathering Place for Elders." Everyone will own their own land within a community association based on the Peace Principles, sustainable living and spiritual growth. Forty acre plots will be available in January of 2005. See website for details. [Nov2004]

SAINT JUDE CATHOLIC WORKER HOUSE COMMUNITY

317 S Randolph St
PO Box 1612
Champaign, IL 61820

217-355-9774, 217-398-3413
cwh-stjude@prairienet.org

http://www.prairienet.org/
cwh-stjude

Began: 1980 | Pop. 3 | Forming | Spiritual
Urban

St. Jude Catholic Worker House, a house of hospitality for single women and families. Our noon soup kitchen is open to anyone in need seven days a week. Live-in volunteer community practices works of mercy by serving the poor by managing the house of hospitality. Weekly roundtable discussion on practical aspects of managing the house, application to faith, social justice, etc.

Volunteers other than live-ins coordinate soup kitchen and help with other household tasks. Prefer applicants who have some experience ministering to the poor, 1+ year commitment, and a desire to put Gospel

values into practice through ministry to the poor. Room and board, small monthly stipend provided. Send inquiries to the address listed.

Visitors Accepted [Mar2005]

SAINT MARTIN DE PORRES HOUSE

26 Clark St
Hartford, CT 06120

860-724-7066
doucot@sbcglobal.net

Began: 1992 | Pop. 6 | Spiritual
Urban | Diet: Omnivorous

St. Martin's core community is a young couple with two grade-school-age boys, an older gentlemen, and two young women. There is no boss. Our common work includes: Monday: food co-op; Tuesday: housecleaning; Wednesday: furniture pantry; Thursday: furniture gathering; Saturday: children's work. Ongoing work includes newsletter, peace work, wood gathering for heat, activities with neighborhood children. During the summer we host a summer camp. Much of our time is unstructured. We usually eat dinners together, and we feel our work together is our form of prayer.

Visitors Accepted [Mar2005]

SALAMANDER SPRINGS

Bob Burns or Jill Shealy
178 Hitchcock Rd
Milledgeville, GA 31061

478-932-5552
adiantum61@yahoo.com
sunshineangel822@yahoo.com

http://salamandersprings.tripod.com

Began: 1998 | Pop. 3 | Rural | Diet: Other

This community is not seeking new members at present.

Visitors are still welcome to see a permaculture homestead in the making, and spring, summer and fall interns are needed to help run the organic gardens and other aspects of the farm. We offer our knowledge in exchange for food and a place to sleep, for one week up to three months.

Visitors Accepted: Please email or call us, to be sure we have space and to be sure we can accommodate you.

Once you make preliminary arrangements, call back one week before you come, and just before you arrive. We will give directions on the last call. [Mar2005]

Listings

Additions and corrections: email: directory@ic.org, *web:* directory.ic.org, *mail: RR 1 Box 156-D, Rutledge MO 63563, USA.*

SAMENHUIZING WEST-BRABANT

Alsembergsteenweg 1117
Beersel B1650
BELGIUM

+32-(0)2-380-24-62
L.Jonckheere@scarlet.be

http://www.lagrandecense.be

Began: 2000 | Pop. 41 | Forming
Rural | Diet: Primarily vegetarian

We aquired a large farm near Brussels to be transformed into an ecological cohousing community for 20 units. The group has grown to 16 households (as of January 05). [Feb2005]

SAN ANTONIO COHOUSING

Patrick Shearer
PO Box 15039
San Antonio, TX 78212

210-833-5815
cohousing@consultability.org

Began: 2005 | Forming | Urban

We are working to develop a cohousing community in San Antonio. Currently we are identifying potential sites and organizing other potential residents.

We are currently focusing on neighborhoods near downtown, such as the Southtown area.

Visitors Accepted [Jan2005]

SAN FRANCISCO COHOUSING

Johann Zimmern
3841–23rd St
San Francisco, CA 94114

415-269-4150
johann@kindermind.com

Began: 2004 | Pop. 28 | Forming | Urban

We are a group of SF families with small children in search of a co-op housing arrangement. All of us would like to continue to live in the city and we have started a small group to explore options. There's a possibility for additional families to join us and we are looking for people with ideas and resources to help out. [Dec2004]

IC Web Site
Intentional Communities on the Web
Your home for community.
www.ic.org

SAN MATEO ECOVILLAGE

3329 Los Prados St
San Mateo, CA 94403
sanda@greensolutions.org
sanda@cohousing.org

http://www.greensolutions.org/smcc.htm

Began: 1998 | Pop. 10 | Forming
Suburban | Diet: Primarily vegetarian

We are forming a small urban community facing a lagoon between San Mateo and Foster City. We purchased a four-unit building and expect to purchase a second soon. We have planted fruit trees and extensive organic gardens. We are seeking other "families" to co-own and/or rent in some form of a cooperative—something between intentional community and cohousing. (It looks like we will be using the legal structure called Tenants in Common.) We have worked to help develop more of a community within the local neighborhood. The location is wonderful: lots of birds, sunrise over the water, nearby biking/walking path, park with playground, tennis/basketball courts, and city amenities of proximity to freeway and public transportation, etc.

Values we would like to see "grow" on this site can be summed up in the concept of sustainable development: growing some of our own food; supporting local organic farmers in farmers' markets or in a community-supported agriculture (CSA); reducing, reusing, recycling; avoiding buying food and other items that contribute to the destruction of local economies and the environment. We want to share time in the garden and at the dinner table with the people we live with as well as other activities. We seek open communication and a deep expression of feelings. We expect those wishing to join us to have a commitment to these values and goals as well.

Visitors Accepted: Please send an email. [Feb2005]

SANDHILL FARM

Attn: Kathe
RR 1 Box 155
Rutledge, MO 63563

660-883-5543
sandhill@ic.org

http://www.sandhillfarm.org

Began: 1973 | Pop. 6
Rural | Diet: Primarily vegetarian

We are a family of five adults and one child, living on 135 acres in NE Missouri. We grow our own organic food and share income, meals, vehicles and other resources. The land includes gardens, orchards, woods, cropland, bee yards and pasture.

Our income is derived from foods we produce (sorghum, tempeh, honey, garlic and condiments), activist administrative work, group process consulting and organic-farm inspection.

We tend to work hard and get satisfaction from providing for ourselves as much as we can while maintaining close ties with neighbors, friends and other communities.

Core values include cooperation, nonviolence, honesty, and working through conflict. We hold meetings once or twice a week and make decisions by consensus. We are eager for new members—including children—and are especially interested in adults under 40 who are drawn to the prospect of stepping into a thriving 31-year-old community and co-creating its next generation.

Our vision is to grow to 12 adults plus kids. Children are fully integrated into everyday life. People with good communication skills, both one-on-one and in group, tend to do well here. Initiative, organization and the ability to see the broader needs of the whole group are also prized.

A visit for up to one week can be arranged most times of the year. Please write and introduce yourself. Extra hands are appreciated during our growing season, especially at sorghum harvest (mid-September to mid-October).

Visitors Accepted: Write, call or email, attention "Kathe;" include self introduction and what you are seeking from your visit. [Feb2005]

SANKOFA

Stuart Kunkle
PO Box 209
Ester, AK 99725

907-479-4712
bythedeepwaters@yahoo.com

Began: 2004 | Pop. 4 | Forming
Rural | Diet: Omnivorous

We are a family that is looking to create an intentional community in Alaska. Our desire to do this is guided by our wishes for a healthy, productive lifestyle for us and our children. We are also acting with an eye towards peak oil and, in North America, peak natural gas.

Peak oil is here now. We want to create a community that is increasingly reliant on our local surroundings for all our needs. We want to network with other communities.

Scissors [✂] at the end of a listing indicate that it was edited for length by the Directory editors and a longer description can be found at directory.ic.org.

With the onset of energy shortages and rapidly increasing energy expense, we want to be as prepared as we can for anything (the supply lines to go down?), and still be able to live well. We seek to empower ourselves, and our children, with useful skills and knowledge so we can all continue to prosper into the future. We are building a lifeboat, while at the same time reaching out to others and linking these life rafts together so as to help each other. We seek others with the desire to learn and teach (or share) what they know to those who want to face the imminent energy shortages and all of the repercussions of these events. We have a strong desire to build a tribe and work together for the survival of the group. Most activity occurs between May and September. We are looking for like-minded folk and would need to go through an arduous interviewing process before anything is set in stone. We are hoping to coordinate the purchase of land either in the Interior or down south on the Kenai Peninsula.

Visitors Accepted: People are welcome to visit us where we are living now. Visits in the warmer months would entail taking part in the work we are doing gardening, turkey, chicken and rabbit raising, and just general building and "putzing around" projects. [Mar2005]

SANTA CRUZ COUNTY COHOUSING

Santa Cruz, CA

831-425-3994
info@sc-cohousing.org

Randa Johnson
randa@labyris.com

Lynn Welter
Lynn.Welter@scccc.org

http://www.sc-cohousing.org

Forming

[Mar2005]

SASSAFRAS RIDGE FARM

HC 77 Box 350
Hinton, WV 25951

304-466-4022
farmhouse@mountain.net

Began: 1972 | Pop. 24 | Spiritual | Rural

Sassafras Ridge Farm, founded in 1972 by three young adults sharing an old shack, has evolved. Our intentional neighborhood, with boundaries greatly expanded by friends' purchases of adjacent farms and forest, grew from 240 to over 400 acres. Ten households shelter one to five people each (children included) in solo, partner, and one- and two-parent families. Households are economically autonomous and privately owned. Half the land and most farm equipment are jointly owned by three partners.

Many may join in preparation and celebration of Earth holidays with the broader community, with religious freedom. We share and center in and by a half-acre pond.

The mountainous, wooded farm includes 20 acres of hay, 40 of pasture, creeks, and two ponds. A clean canoeable river, kayaking, and white-water rafting are near.

Activities include gardening, animal care, building fences, gathering firewood, and construction. Equal access and responsibility are fundamental to our cooperative intent.

Within Sassafras, one household is occasionally willing to trade two to four days' room and vegetarian meals for labor. Written prearrangements required. No space available for new residents!

Visitors Accepted: One household is occasionally willing to host work trade visitors. Contact by email or postal mail two weeks to two months in advance. [Mar2005]

SBSHC: SANTA BARBARA STUDENT HOUSING COOPERATIVE

6503 Madrid Rd
Suite J
Isla Vista, CA 93117

805-685-6964
info@sbcoop.org

http://www.sbcoop.org

Began: 1976 | Pop. 71
Urban | Diet: Omnivorous

The Santa Barbara Student Housing Cooperative (SBSHC) provides students democratic control; community ownership; safe, inexpensive housing; and greater social interaction. A wide range of students from a variety of backgrounds and countries is attracted to our student housing co-ops. We own three group houses and one apartment building located near the University of California, Santa Barbara campus.

SBSHC has an open membership policy. Not only do we not discriminate in any way, but we actively encourage diversity among our groups in order to stimulate education and awareness.

Members must attend house meetings two to three times per academic quarter and complete at least five hours of co-op work duties per quarter, in addition to normal house chores and maintenance. Members own and operate the co-op. Rent charges reflect the costs of running and maintaining the co-ops. No profits are made; income goes toward paying off loans as well as paying staff salaries, with surplus earnings being reinvested in the buildings, the residents, and further co-op expansion. A portion of the budget is assigned to member-education programs and workshops.

SBSHC is committed to environmentally responsible living. We are also affiliated with the North American Students Cooperative Organization (NASCO).

Visitors Accepted: Please email or call for a request to visit our co-op. [Mar2005]

SEADS OF TRUTH, INC.

PO Box 192
Harrington, ME 04643

207-483-9763, 207-483-2764
seads@mainline.net

http://mainesolar.org

Began: 1979 | Pop. 3 | Forming
Rural | Diet: Omnivorous

Solar Energy Awareness and Demonstration Seminars is a not-for-profit group establishing a self-sufficient alternative-energy community and seminar center on 60 acres in rural Maine. We hold solar workshops on a wide range of topics, including photovoltaic panel construction, hydroponic-grow systems, and lifestyle counseling. We are using a community land trust model and stress voluntary cooperation and mutual aid—working with others, using group consensus, and sharing. We promote and participate in peace activism and activities, stressing a renewable energy future. After a provisional period, families will have an opportunity for individual, limited-equity home ownership on common land. Members will share responsibilities and benefits of operating the solar-powered seminar center and traveler hostel in our common building, which has been in operation for 18 years. Greenhouse, gardens, and independent solar electric utility are our step toward self-sufficiency as well as world peace. We are still in the formative stages and need "real" people and families to continue the process into the twenty-first century. Please write or email.

Visitors Accepted [Mar2005]

Additions and corrections: email: directory@ic.org, *web:* directory.ic.org, *mail: RR 1 Box 156-D, Rutledge MO 63563, USA.*

223

7TH MILLENNIUM COMMUNITY

S. V. Mercado
svm7m@hotmail.com
svm7thmil@yahoo.com

http://www.geocities.com/
sm7thmil/index.html

Began: 1992 | Spiritual
Small Town | Diet: Primarily vegetarian

The 7th Millennium Community is the proposed self-sufficient cooperative composed of a Christian camp, conference/retreat center, kibbutz, cottage industry and general consulting enterprise. Christians ought to be the creators of jobs and suppliers of goods and services, rather than mere employees and consumers. They ought to be working for God rather than for the material-oriented society.

First, we are going back to the early Messianic era by emulating some of the living and working practices of the New Testament Church (Acts 2:44-45; 4:32-35). Second, we are going to follow the excellent examples of the self-sufficient communes of the Hutterian Brethren, Mennonites, Amish and other groups. We are also going to follow the successful kibbutzim in Israel. Third, we are striving to live our daily lives in preparation for our Messiah's seocnd coming.

Conceived as the ideal solutions to the problems of the Sabbath-observing and other Christians, we in the 7th Millennium Community will pursue the establishment of the self-sufficient cooperative so as to provide an alternative homeland to live in for safety, and to create job opportunities to the students and graduates. The proposed site would be somewhere in Maasin City.
Visitors Accepted [Mar2005][✂]

SHADOWLAKE VILLAGE

Mark Davis
1731 Sage Ln
Blacksburg, VA 24060
540-552-1035

Muriel Kranowski
1713 Ginger Ln
Blacksburg, VA 24060
540-552-2888

slv_coho@yahoo.com

http://www.shadowlakevillage.org

Began: 1998 | Pop. 63 | Diet: Omnivorous

We are a cohousing community of 33 households, located on 33 acres in a beautiful natural setting in the town of Blacksburg, in the mountains of southwest Virginia on a ridge between the Blue Ridge and the Appalachians.

Most members moved in during 2002-2004. Our Common House is built. We include families with young children and/or teenage children, couples, and singles. Membership has been by self-selection.

Our guiding values include:

- a commitment to have a supportive and enriching community that fosters connection with each other, the larger community, and the Earth;
- living in harmony with ecological systems;
- creating a balance between private life and community life;
- encouraging diversity in membership;
- working to create and maintain creative and positive relationships through consensus decision making, open dialogue, and creative conflict resolution.

In addition to our own 17 acres of undisturbed woods, we're adjacent to a 169-acre park that is an old farmstead, and we're near a walking/biking trail into a National Forest.

As we develop our policies, guidelines, and norms, we strive for mutually respectful ways towards consensus, and we also remember to have fun and enjoy the rewards of living in community.

Visitors Accepted: Contact us by phone or email and arrange a mutually convenient time to come. [Feb2005]

SHAMBALA ECO-RESORT & ECOVILLAGE COMMUNITY PROJECT NEW ZEALAND

Varcha Silke Ahnefeld
service@
shambala-resort-newzealand.com
andrewblake2012@yahoo.de

http://www.shambala-resort-
newzealand.com

Began: 2004 | Forming
Rural | Diet: Vegetarian only

Wanted: practical dreamers.

Are you someone who thinks big, loves to co-create with like-hearted others? Are you interested in holistic lifestyles, alternative healing, free energy, wellness, vegetarian cuisine, ayurveda, permaculture?

Then why not join us in co-creating paradise on a beautiful south Pacific island...

Why not join us and help pioneer this new intentional ecovillage community and

Scissors [✂] at the end of a listing indicate that it was edited for length by the Directory editors and a longer description can be found at directory.ic.org.

eco-resort, incorporating the best in alternative technologies...

Share... harmonious living in peace and joy, with like-minded souls from around the world...

Keywords: permaculture, wellness, self-sufficient, free energy, practical spirituality, raw food, vegetarian, peaceful, drug free, alternative schooling, organic agriculture, song, self-realization, dance, meditation...

Visitors Accepted: Visit our website then contact us, introduce yourself, share how you see yourself getting involved in the vision. [Feb2005]

SHANNON FARM COMMUNITY

Jenny Upton
130 Catbrier Circle
Afton, VA 22920

434-361-1417
jennyup@cstone.net

http://www.ic.org/shannonfarm

Began: 1972 | Pop. 93
Rural | Diet: Omnivorous

Shannon is a cooperative intentional community, home to over 60 adults who range in age from the 20s to the 70s and over 30 children from infants to teenagers. Together, we share 520 acres of mountain forests, pastures, and river-bottom hayfields at the base of the Blue Ridge Mountains, located 27 miles west of Charlottesville.

The purpose of Shannon Farm is to be a residential intentional community where people share land, encourage member-managed businesses and agriculture, and support cooperative living situations here and in the larger world.

No overall belief system, other than a commitment to cooperative living, has defined our community since moving onto the land in 1974. Different lifestyles coexist at Shannon, and we seek new members of diverse races, ages, and adult sexual orientations.

The community is a private, non-speculative land-and-housing trust that owns the land and all buildings. Shannon members finance their personal homes and own long-term leases that may be transferred to other members at a fixed maximum price.

Monthly membership dues finance Shannon Farm Community. There is no joining fee, but personal assets are necessary to finance house construction or purchase an existing leasehold. Expectations of members include participation in building community through physical, organizational or social work, paying dues, and involvement in community events.

People who wish to explore Shannon may start by visiting on monthly meeting day, held on the first Saturday of each month. We welcome those who share a commitment to the values of our community—those who want to help build Shannon and the global intentional communities movement.

Visitors Accepted: Call Jenny Upton or Dan Questenberry at the number listed. [Feb2005]

SHARING COMMUNITY

24370 Brown Rd
South Bloomingville, OH 43152

740-332-0205
sf@bright.net
deye@bright.net

Began: 1999 | Pop. 5
Rural | Diet: Omnivorous

Sharing Community is a rural intentional community located 60 miles southeast of Columbus, Ohio in the foothills of the Appalachian Mountains. Our immediate area includes numerous artisans and fun-loving, educated households. We are located less than one hour from the university town of Athens, Ohio, and near several towns where employment is available. The community is composed of 60 acres of wooded hillsides and rolling meadows with abundant wildlife; each family owns its own land so in that sense we are not a typical intentional community. Currently we are two households, with one other person exploring membership.

Goals: stewardship of the land and the environment, sustainable lifestyles, consensus-based decision making, respect for individual diversity, caring for fellow members, and charitable works. Members live in individual energy-efficient houses they have designed and built themselves. Members are self-supporting; no employment is available at the community.

We consider ourselves to be self-aware, lifelong learners who are seeking the best ways to live out our values. We all relocated to this area several years ago while we explored membership in another community nearby that did not work out but which served to bring us together. We explore ways to share simpler, cooperative, sustainable lifestyles in a rural setting and feel like we are trying to live in a future that is not yet a path in mainstream society. So we do our best—and we hope. [Mar2005]

SHARINGWOOD COHOUSING

22116 E Lost Lake Rd
Snohomish County, WA 98296
360-668-1439

Rob Sandelin
360-668-2043
floriferous@msn.com

http://sharingwood.org

Began: 1984 | Pop. 85
Rural | Diet: Omnivorous

We live on 39 forested acres in south Snohomish County, about 25 miles northeast from Seattle. Sharingwood is a lot-development cohousing model, where members buy lots and build their own homes to meet individual budgets and tastes. There is a mixture of owners and rental spaces and while most homes are pretty middle-class standard we have a small number of alternative dwellings including a cob/strawbale home. We share meals on a regular and ongoing basis and have a bulk food purchasing program that is available to residents.

We use a variety of decision-making approaches, although consensus is the goal on most issues. We empower small groups to make specific decisions that do not really require the input of the entire membership.

In addition to a monthly meeting, we have found that sharing circles can play an important role in nurturing a deeper sense of trust within the community. Here members find an opportunity to come together and share honestly and openly in a safe space.

Initiated by individuals, people do things together like homeschooling, yoga, meditation, sharing resources, organic gardening, work parties, hot tub, campfires, playfield, concerts, and children's activities. There are a large number of children in the community so they initiate many of their own games and play events.

The "enchanting" nature of the native forests and the many trails that surround the community define a village-like setting. Wilderness to some, sanctuary to others, for most it offers a comforting contrast to our workaday world.

Visitors Accepted: Visit our website for information on how to contact us for tours. [Oct2004]

Additions and corrections: email: directory@ic.org, *web:* directory.ic.org, *mail: RR 1 Box 156-D, Rutledge MO 63563, USA.*

225

SHEPHERDSFIELD

777 Shepherdsfield Rd
Fulton, MO 65251

573-642-1439

Began: 1979 | Pop. 95 | Spiritual | Rural

Shepherdsfield is a Christian fellowship that tries to live as the early Christians did and as recorded in the Acts of the Apostles, including the "sharing of all things in common." We have accepted Jesus Christ as the way, the truth, and the life. Through Him we have found answers to the many questions that arise in trying to live together and in reaching out to others.

We earn our living through an organic bakery, a wallpapering and window-washing company, and several cottage industries. We have a large ministry that reaches over the world in studies of Scripture and principles of life. We operate our own school for our children and take seriously the task of raising children in an environment of "purity and childlikeness."

Our desire has been to show others that Christianity is not limited to the institutional forms that have so disenchanted many people and led them to reject the claims of our master, Jesus of Nazareth. We would not want to mislead anyone by claiming our life is a utopia that requires little or no effort for the individual. Quite the contrary, true peace and brotherhood can only be accomplished when the utmost of diligence is applied in living out and promoting the necessary qualities. That requires a struggle. However, we find great joy in living for God in the present and seeing ourselves and others changed from day to day.

Visitors Accepted: If you would like to visit us, please write or call in advance. [Mar2005]

SHERWOOD CO-OP

4746 18th Ave NE
Seattle, WA 98105

206-524-1958, 206-522-7872
sherwoodcoop@riseup.net

Began: 1935 | Pop. 14
Urban | Diet: Primarily vegetarian

The Sherwood Co-op is the last organizational remnant of the Students' Cooperative Association started in the 30s by University of Washington students, which at its high point was on a level with the Ann Arbor and Berkeley campus co-op systems. The SCA sold off all of its holdings in the late 50s.

Sherwood rented our current house from the late 70s to 2001, when we bought it on short-term owner financing. Our debt is due back in full May 1, 2006, and we are currently in the arduous process of securing a mortgage. If you or anyone you know has experience or information (or half a million dollars :) that could help us with this project, please get ahold of us.

Presently, we are a 14-member student cooperative living in a large 1911 house in the University District of Seattle. We support each other. We share vegetarian food and each cook dinner twice a month. We each have a cleaning chore and are part of a work team—food, finance, logistics, maintenance, or membership. We have quarterly work parties where we do projects around the house.

We are members of North American Students of Cooperation (NASCO), and are close to membership in the Evergreen Land Trust (ELT). Our mission is to provide low-cost housing for students, so that students can focus on their studies, contribute to their community, and have more time to be active and creative in life. We emphasize sustainable living and introducing cooperative living as a lifestyle choice beyond school. Our long term goal is for Sherwood to act as an economic and organizational engine for the development of other coops.

Visitors Accepted: Visitors are great! Give us a call, or email (phone is a more reliable way to reach us). Please give us a few days notice so we all know you're coming, especially if you'll need to stay overnight. We generally have couch space for overnight visitors. [Mar2005]

SIDHEFIRE

Phoenix
phoenix@sidhefire.com

http://www.sidhefire.com

Began: 2002 | Pop. 3 | Forming | Spiritual
Rural | Diet: Primarily vegetarian

Small intentional community located outside Yelm, Washington. Our focus is on permaculture, organic sustainability, spirituality and quality of life.

Visitors Accepted: Our schedule is posted on the website. We are open to visitors during scheduled visitation times (RSVP required). Other visitation subject to approval. [Feb2005]

SILVER SAGE VILLAGE

Wonderland Hill Development
Company
4676 Broadway
Boulder, CO 80304

303-449-3232 ext 215
sharon@whdc.com

Annie
303-449-3232 ext 115
annie@whdc.com

http://www.silversagevillage.com

Began: 2003 | Pop. 12 | Urban

Silver Sage Village is a 16-home community being built in Boulder, Colorado and is designed specifically for proactive adults. This community is near open space trails, two bus routes, community gardens, shops and restaurants. It is also right across the street from Wild Sage Cohousing, an intergenerational community.

Visitors Accepted: Please call Wonderland Hill at 303-449-3232 ext 215 or email annie@whdc.com to schedule an appointment to look at floor plans and/or a walk of the site. [Jan2005]

SIRIUS COMMUNITY

72 Baker Rd
Shutesbury, MA 01072

413-259-1251
info@siriuscommunity.org

http://www.siriuscommunity.org

Began: 1978 | Pop. 38 | Spiritual
Rural | Diet: Primarily vegetarian

Sirius is a spiritual community, educational center, and ecovillage founded in 1978 by former members of the Findhorn Community in Scotland. It is one part of an expanding network of light, working to increase the consciousness of humanity.

Sirius is a demonstration center of spiritual principles based on respect for the individual and cooperation with nature, seeing the divinity in all life. We are committed to living our lives with spiritual integrity recognizing that we are all in a process of growth with every experience in our life offering valuable lessons. We honor the highest truths common to all religions, and our unity in diversity is a source of inspiration for visitors and members. Meditation and attunement are central to our life together.

Sirius also demonstrates ecological ways of living, including organic food production, solar and environmentally friendly

---

Scissors [✄] at the end of a listing indicate that it was edited for length by the Directory editors and a longer description can be found at directory.ic.org.

building practices, and electrical generation using solar, wind, and vegetable oil. We recycle waste materials, build and use composting toilets, collect and filter used vegetable oil for operating our vegetable-oil burning cars and trucks, and choose to live less polluting, less consumptive lifestyles. Healing of the planet is of primary importance to us, and we are members of the Global Ecovillage Network.

As a nonprofit educational corporation, Sirius offers workshops and seminars and hosts programs for the public. Day and overnight visitors are also welcome; please call to make arrangements.

Visitors Accepted: If interested in visiting or attending any of our programs please contact the office. [Mar2005]

SIVANANDA ASHRAM YOGA RANCH

Raghu Rama
PO Box 195
Budd Rd
Woodbourne, NY 12788

845-436-6492, 845-434-9242
YogaRanch@sivananda.org

http://www.sivananda.org/ranch

Began: 1974 | Pop. 15 | Spiritual
Rural | Diet: Primarily vegetarian

The Sivananda Ashram Yoga Ranch is a secluded haven of 77 acres of hilly woodland in the New York Catskills, and part of an international organization of yoga schools and retreats. We are an intentional community that both teaches and practices a spiritual lifestyle of self-mastery of body and mind, selfless service, devotion, and philosophy. Our daily schedule is based on these five principles:
1) Proper Exercise (asanas)
2) Proper Breathing (pranayama)
3) Proper Relaxation (savasana)
4) Proper Diet (vegetarian)
5) Positive Thinking and Meditation
    (vedanta philosophy and dhyana).
Residents participate in daily meditation, prayer, and study; yoga asana classes, selfless service, and vegetarian meals. The ashram also holds workshops and has a Teen Camp, hiking and ski trails, cooking courses and an Ayurvedic consultation and Body Treatment Center available to guests. A sauna and swimming pond are also available. Our meals are wholly vegetarian. We grow much of our food in our organic garden and greenhouse. and most purchased food is also organic. The community welcomes serious aspirants to participate in our

Work-Study Program and possibly stay on as staff. A four-week Yoga Teachers Training Course is offered every June and September. The ashram is a nonprofit spiritual/educational corporation run and maintained by an all-volunteer staff, work-study residents, and other helpers. Please feel free to call or look at our website for more in-depth information on our various programs or to request a brochure.

Visitors Accepted: Contact us by phone or email for reservations and information. [Mar2005][✄<]

SKYHOUSE COMMUNITY

2 Dancing Rabbit Ln
Rutledge, MO 63563

660-883-5881
skyhouse@ic.org

http://www.skyhousecommunity.org

Began: 1996 | Pop. 5
Rural | Diet: Primarily vegan

As part of Dancing Rabbit Ecovillage (see separate listing), Skyhouse strives to be a model of ecological living. We are an income-sharing community, and our money and resources are held in common. Members do a variety of tasks, and new folks are plugged in to existing projects and businesses or can bring jobs and ideas with them. We are committed to nonviolence, egalitarianism, and the breakdown of culturally constructed gender roles. We meet as a group to make decisions by consensus, resolve conflicts, and help each other work through life's challenges.

On a summer evening you might find us coming together after a hard day's work. Some folks come in from the gardens, while others have been building our strawbale homes, doing computer work, or giving a tour of our village. Members, friends, and visitors gather at the community table, while the day's cook puts the finishing touches on dinner. After a delicious meal offering homemade bread and tofu, home-grown veggies, and home-brewed beer, folks gather for a sing-along or sit and joke about the day's events. The end of the day brings another brilliant sunset shining its golden light over the nearby pond and far-off rolling hills.

Does this sound too good to be true? Arrange a visit to see for yourself. We are actively seeking new members, so come add your unique perspective and energetic pioneering spirit to our tight-knit group.

Visitors Accepted: Skyhouse doesn't currently have its own visitor program. People

interested in coming to visit our community should go through the Dancing Rabbit Visitor Team and let them know that they are particularly interested in Skyhouse. [Mar2005]

SOCIETY FOR THE PROMOTION OF CREATIVE INTERCHANGE

Ray Anderson
Wichita, KS 67203
ourgreatestproblem@lycos.com

http://members.tripod.com/~aranders

Began: 1987 | Pop. 2 | Spiritual
Urban | Diet: Vegetarian only

As an extended family or tribe, we are seeking a few more members and doing our best to function as the model of an alternative social, economic, and political order, one that has the promotion of what we call "creative interchange" as its ruling and guiding concern.

By "creative interchange" we refer to a transformative process that can be described as "the coming to see the world through the other's eyes, to feel it with the other's feelings, and—as a result—being changed by that so that one can understand and appreciate what she or he couldn't understand or appreciate before."

We are looking for new members with the following qualifications:
- They believe, as we do, that every human being deserves to have a real say in all the decisions that affect their daily life.
- They believe, as we do, that we live in a social, economic, and political system that makes it very difficult for people to share as equals in making the decisions that shape their daily lives.
- They are ready, willing, and eager to seriously consider membership in our Society and our extended family by spending time with us becoming familiar with the way in which we: 1) try to discover and provide better social and economic conditions for creative interchange, and 2) resolve whatever differences arise among us strictly on the following basis: after listing all the alternatives of which we are aware, we postpone taking action until we identify one that we all wholeheartedly agree is more likely than any other to promote creative interchange.

If you fit the above description, please get in touch with us right away.

Visitors Accepted: Please contact us at our email address to make arrangements. [Oct2004][✄<]

Additions and corrections: email: directory@ic.org, *web:* directory.ic.org, *mail: RR 1 Box 156-D, Rutledge MO 63563, USA.*

227

SOJOURNER TRUTH HOUSE

House President
1507 Washtenaw Ave
Ann Arbor, MI 48104

734-668-9064
marwan456@hotmail.com

http://www.icc.coop

Pop. 53 | Urban | Diet: Omnivorous

We are a friendly, non-smoking house which generally attracts a diverse mix of graduate, international, and undergraduate students. Truth is located just minutes from Central Campus and quite close to the North Campus bus stop. We have a beautiful sunny living room, big screen TV, DVD player, VCR, pool table, ping pong table, soda machine, piano, fireplace, an exercise room, two computers, a laser printer and a spacious parking lot. We allow up to six cats which must be kept in member's rooms. All of the bedrooms are spacious with a jack for active cable and high speed internet. There is also a jack for optional private phone installation in each room. Come talk and dine with us—dinner is at 6:00 pm.

Visitors Accepted: Contact House President. [Mar2005]

SOLSTICE DAWN

Roy Guisinger
RR 1 Box 4
Belgrade, NE 68623

308-357-1000
roy@designinsight.net

http://www.solsticedawn.org

Began: 1999 | Pop. 3 | Forming | Spiritual
Rural | Diet: Omnivorous

Solstice Dawn is so called for the returning of Light after the long night.

We work for a fully sustainable world in which competition has given way to cooperation and every part of the system contributes to the greatness of the whole. We endeavor to live and promote a sustainable lifestyle as we seek to create greater harmony in the four pillars of our personal beings (mental, physical, spiritual, and social).

Our approach is based upon scientific principles, with the awareness that there are greater truths than science alone can realize. We choose to be politically, environmentally, and socially active, and we are involved with many state and national organizations that promote positive change.

We are committed to truth, health, integrity, and harmony. With the many social ills present in our society today, we spend a lot of energy on creating awareness

and making a difference. We value our work and we work hard. Anyone who shares those values might find a home here. Inquiries are welcome; deadbeats are not. Please call ahead before visiting. [Mar2005]

SOLTERRA

98 Solterra Way
Durham, NC 27705

Nancy Leinbach
919-493-7030
nyleinbach@aol.com

http://www.solterra.net

Began: 1993 | Pop. 75
Urban | Diet: Omnivorous

Solterra is a passive-solar cohousing community nestled in a semirural area but close to the amenities of several major universities, including Duke University and the University of North Carolina, Chapel Hill. Our 20 acres are open and wooded, and the single-family homes and sites are privately owned. Each home is car accessible.

Members share ownership in the common lands, paths, play spaces, common house, roads, and common gardens. One side of our property abuts forestland owned by Duke. We enjoy Durham city services and close-by excellent public and private schools. Our eclectic members come from every part of the country and range in age from 0 to 110. Our interests are broad, and our consensus form of management includes committees to oversee all phases of the development and social life of Solterra.

We share meals weekly, usually a potluck and a cooked meal. Eating styles vary, from meat eaters to macrobiotics, and our common meals reflect these tastes. There are 30 resident families; we'll have 39 when Solterra is built out. All of our lots have been sold. We also have a few resale lots, and we're actively seeking new members, adults and children. We welcome visitors; just let us know when you can come.

Visitors Accepted: Call Nancy Leinbach if you wish to visit Solterra. [Nov2004]

SOMA – THE SOMA PROJECT

Kevin
California
somacommunity@yahoo.com

http://geocities.com/somacommunity

Began: 2004 | Pop. 2 | Forming | Spiritual
Rural | Diet: Other

Welcome to the ultimate vision for community.

Are you tired of the Rat Race? Do you feel that there must be a better way of life? Are you ready to find true happiness? If Yes, you are invited to join the great social experiment known as The SOMA Project.

The goal of TSP is to build the society of tomorrow, today. And do so with the best methods and ideas available. More than just a community, TSP is a gathering of people, and ideas, from all over the world, who want a stake in planning the future of humanity.

Some areas of focus...
• Harmony – we shall all pursue peace and love.
• Nutrition – we shall eat life-giving foods.
• Spirituality – we shall pursue the path of enlightenment.
• Fitness – we shall maintain a healthy body.
• Family – we shall protect and care for one another.
• Architecture – we shall build green.
• Land – we shall take care of the earth.
• Resources – we shall use them efficiently.
• People – we shall treat all equally.
• Animals – we shall respect every creature.
• Ritual – we shall embrace global experiences.
• Growth - we shall always be making improvements.
• Pioneers – we shall boldly lead the way.
And more...

To learn more and find out how you can get involved, please visit our website. Namaste. "Making the future of tomorrow, a reality for today!"

Visitors Accepted: Email request. [Jan2005]

SOMERVILLE ECOVILLAGE

Enquiries
PO Box 147
Chidlow, Western Australia 6556
AUSTRALIA

+61-(0)8-9572-3225
enquiry@ecocom.org

http://www.ecocom.org
http://www.greenedge.org
http://www.somervilleecovillage
.com.au

Began: 2000 | Forming | Diet: Other

Somerville Ecovillage is in Chidlow in the Perth Hills in Western Australia.

The land (399 acres) was purchased by the community in 2002 and the process of rezoning the land is underway.

Subject to government approval, it is anticipated that lots will go on sale late in 2005 or early in 2006.

The Somerville Vision: "A village where

Scissors [✂] at the end of a listing indicate that it was edited for length by the Directory editors and a longer description can be found at directory.ic.org.

community flourishes, in which every person's needs are supported, in balance with a sustainable ecological ethic."

Visitors Accepted: Visitors should check the website for current visiting arrangements: http://www.greenedge.org/viewing.htm [Jan2005]

SONGAIA COHOUSING COMMUNITY

22401 39th Ave SE
Bothell, WA 98021
info@songaia.com

Carol Crow
425-486-5164
carol@songaia.com

http://www.songaia.com

Began: 1987 | Pop. 36 | Spiritual
Suburban | Diet: Other

Songaia is a semi-rural cohousing community located on 11 acres of wooded hillside, gardens, orchard, and meadow. Our 15 homes include studio rentals, and both one and three bedroom duplexes. The homes are arranged around a green village-like commons.

Songaia: "Song of the Living Earth" is named for our love of singing and celebration and our connection to the earth.

Our shared community life at Songaia is active: members gather frequently for meals, singing, work parties, celebrations, men's and women's circles, and social activities. The connections we continue to form are creating a strong network of friends and caring neighbors, a safe, supportive environment where children, elders, and families of all types can live more lightly on the land.

Members and non-member renters share the use of our common facilities and grounds. Our common house includes a large dining/meeting room, kitchen and pantry, laundry, play room, living room, office, and two guest rooms. Our barn includes a greenhouse, larger pantry, shop, and ceramics room, as well as storage. The homes are clustered near the center of the community, so there are almost five acres of natural forest.

While valuing simplicity, cooperation and an Earth-conscious, sustainable lifestyle, we continue to evolve a rich, active life together on a beautiful piece of property close enough to Seattle, Bellevue, and Redmond to enjoy the benefits of city. We are very fortunate.

Visitors Accepted: We are not actively recruiting for additional membership. We are, however, open to visitors. Visiting Songaia requires a resident to sponsor your visit who would host you during your stay.

Email us to learn about options. [Jan2005][✄✂]

SOPHIA COMMUNITY

Don Wedd
5615 S Woodlawn Ave
Chicago, IL 60637

773-955-1325
don_wedd@excite.com
becky_032000@yahoo.com

http://www.geocities.com/
sophiacommunity

Began: 1993 | Pop. 8 | Spiritual
Urban | Diet: Primarily vegetarian

Sophia Community is an intentional community living in a lovely big house in Hyde Park, near the University of Chicago. Four young women who had all spent a year doing volunteer work in inner-city Chicago neighborhoods founded Sophia Community in 1993.

We live in Quaker House, where we manage the house and guest business on behalf of the 57th Street Meeting of Friends. Usually we have 6-7 adults in the community, aged 25-50; in 2005 there is one married couple with a young child.

Our key values are:

• Simple living – communal chores, mostly organic food, shared community space, common household fund
• Presence to each other – commitment to relationships, shared meals
• Social Justice – most of us work for non-profits or social service
• Spirituality – diverse, but we share spirituality together twice weekly
• Hospitality – we run a small guest business for traveling Quakers and others

Visitors Accepted: Phone to make arrangements. We have few visitors, so there is no set process. We may have guest rooms available. [Mar2005]

SOUTHERN CALIFORNIA NATURE SANCTUARY PROJECT

Michael Walker
c/o Triskelion Crafters
3824 Ray St
San Diego, CA 92104
SoCalNatureSanctuary-
owner@yahoogroups.com
maristo@cox.net

http://groups.yahoo.com/group/
SoCalNatureSanctuary

Began: 2004 | Forming | Spiritual

The goal of the Southern California Nature

Sanctuary Project is to form an interfaith cooperative and create a community and nature sanctuary, sponsoring spiritual retreats in Southern California. Members could include (but would not be limited to) Buddhists, Pagans, Eco-spiritualists, Taoists, Gnostics, Naturists, Pantheists, or other diverse and life-affirming, earth-loving spiritual paths.

Our working group currently consists of approx. 50 interested individuals. We are currently (late 2004, early 2005) working on organizational structure, bylaws, creating a fundraising plan.

Assistance is desired. [Dec2004]

SOUTHERN CASSADAGA SPIRITUALIST CAMP

PO Box 319
Cassadaga, FL 32706

386-228-3171, 386-228-2880
info@cassadaga.org

http://www.cassadaga.org

Began: 1894 | Spiritual | Rural

Designated as a historic district on the National Register of Historic Places, the Southern Cassadaga Spiritualist Camp Meeting Association is a unique religious community founded in 1894. We are located on a 55-acre tract of land, off I-4, midway between Daytona Beach and Orlando, Florida. While members may own the homes they live in, the association retains ownership of the land and offers lifetime leases. We also own and manage two apartment buildings.

The purpose of our community is to promote the understanding of the religion, science, and philosophy of spiritualism and to offer a nurturing environment for like-minded people. We have ongoing educational programs for those wishing to develop their mediumship and/or healing abilities, and we also offer ministerial courses. A number of mediums, healers, and ministers live and work on the grounds. Our unique offerings attract many visitors to our church services, our spiritual/metaphysical bookstore, and our counselors. Seminars and workshops are also offered frequently, and the public is invited to attend all activities. Please write for our Annual Program, enclosing $1 to cover shipping and handling.

Visitors Accepted [Mar2005]

Listings

Additions and corrections: email: directory@ic.org, *web:* directory.ic.org, *mail:* RR 1 Box 156-D, Rutledge MO 63563, USA.

229

SOUTHWEST SUFI COMMUNITY

Rabiya Lila Forest
PO Box 373
Silver City, NM 88062

505-534-0431
rabiya@zianet.com
rashadwilson@mac.com

http://www.ruhaniat.com/about/
SSC.php

Began: 1995 | Pop. 3 | Spiritual
Rural | Diet: Primarily vegetarian

The Southwest Sufi Community (SSC), located near Silver City, New Mexico, is first and foremost a spiritually oriented community, promoting understanding of the Sufi message but open to students of all inclusive spiritual paths. We learn through experience, and eat, dance, and pray together. The community, begun in June 1995, is establishing a retreat center, a nature preserve, and a residential village on 1500 acres along Bear Creek.

People interested in residency at the Southwest Sufi Community need to have the pioneer spirit, be financially self-sufficient, and in good health. People in their 20s and 30s are especially welcome. The SSC is located in a county with limited employment prospects. Since the land is remote from town, it is not practical to commute. People should expect to support themselves in creative ways. Those interested in establishing cottage industries on the land are especially encouraged to come and check us out.

The best way to get to know the community is to attend our annual Meeting of the Ways retreat in August. The day rate is $50/day or $290/week and includes limited indoor accommodations, camping, vegetarian meals, classes, and time in nature. We welcome visitors at other times, too, especially on weekends. Please write or email before planning a visit and tell us you saw this listing in the Communities Directory.

Visitors Accepted: Start with an email or letter or phone call; we'll arrange a time that suits you and us. [Feb2005]

SOWING CIRCLE

15290 Coleman Valley Rd
Occidental, CA 95465

707-874-2441

http://www.oaec.org

Began: 1994 | Pop. 19
Rural | Diet: Primarily vegetarian

Sowing Circle is an intentional community set on 80 acres outside Occidental in

---

Scissors [✂] at the end of a listing indicate that it was edited for length by the Directory editors and a longer description can be found at directory.ic.org.

Sonoma County, California. The land was formerly the home of the Farallones Institute (1974–1990), which educated thousands of people about appropriate technologies and biointensive organic gardening. In 1994, Sowing Circle created the Occidental Arts and Ecology Center (OAEC), a nonprofit organization, to expand upon the Farallones Institute's good work.

OAEC offers residential workshops in permaculture, forming intentional communities, organic gardening and seed saving, "corporations and democracy," the fine arts, starting school gardens, and horticultural therapy. Call for a catalogue of programs.

While Sowing Circle and OAEC are two distinct legal and financial entities, we share the responsibilities of communal living, including cooking, cleaning, gardening, and facility maintenance. We are committed to exploring new approaches to sustainability, both in terms of low-impact living and of community building. We seek to help reverse current social and economic patterns that create hyperindividualism, consumerism, and alienation from nature. We strive to create a practice of right livelihood. [May05]

SPARROW HAWK VILLAGE

22 Summit Ridge Dr
Tahlequah, OK 74464

800-386-7161, 918-458-0063 (fax)
lccc@sanctasophia.org

http://www.sanctasophia.org/
village/index.html

Began: 1981 | Pop. 80 | Spiritual | Rural

Sparrow Hawk Village, an intentional spiritual community, was established in 1981. We are nestled among 440 acres of gently rolling Ozark forest filled with abundant wildlife and natural, serene beauty. Organic community gardens, orchards, horse pastures, hiking trails, springs, and over a mile of river frontage, bordered by 700 acres of primitive state forest, significantly add to our quality of life.

Sparrow Hawk Village is open to members of all faiths. While many villagers are esoteric Christian, we are blessed with members of various western and eastern practices, which create a diverse spiritual experience.

Village life is enriched by a constant stream of international guests and students who participate in classes and workshops offered by accredited programs of Sancta Sophia Seminary. The campus includes a beautiful church, an esoteric library, a bookstore, a gift shop, a Wellness Center, and administrative offices. Daily meditations,

Sunday services, and other spiritually oriented gatherings are available. Many villagers participate in a weekly meditation for world peace.

Sparrow Hawk Village is located at the end of a county road 5 miles off Oklahoma State Scenic Highway 10 and approximately 11 miles from Tahlequah, Oklahoma, capital of the Cherokee Nation and location of Northeastern State University.

If interested in visiting, guest rooms and a campground are available depending on Sancta Sophia's schedule. Homes and homesites are for sale with a few rentals.

Visitors Accepted: Find out more at www.sanctasophia.org. Email, fax or call for more information. [Mar2005]

SPIRIT COVE

Sherry Carter
37 Grouse Hollow
Murphy, NC 28906

828-342-8838
sherplans@aol.com

http://www.spiritcoveproperties.com

Began: 2004 | Forming | Spiritual
Diet: Omnivorous

Spirit Cove is a nature lover's refuge, where every effort is being made to preserve the natural beauty of the land and the natural habitat, while providing choice opportunities for homeowners to live in a peaceful setting, hike through hardwood forest, gather with neighbors at the pond or follow the footsteps of the Cherokees to the National Forest. There are 13 one-acre-plus lots, all wooded, with views; underground utilities, and a community well.

There is a 5.2 acre preserve of pristine forest backing up to the National Forest Service. There are also 3.3 acres with a large (3/4–1 acre) pond with a community area. Walking and hiking trails will run to the pond and through the preserve to the Nantahala National Forest.

Restrictions protect the natural setting, the quiet environment and homeowner values. Community activities are optional and will hopefully include potlucks, trail building, a community garden, environmental education, yoga, meditations and any quiet activity planned by residents.

All finances are independent and there are no requirements to participate in community activities. Suitable for full-time or seasonal residents. Seven lots currently for sale, $27,900–39,900.

Visitors Accepted: Contact by phone. [Jan2005]

SPIRIT DANCE CO-OPERATIVE COMMUNITY

http://www.spiritdance.net

Began: 2000 | Pop. 11 | Forming | Spiritual
Rural | Diet: Omnivorous

Visitors Accepted: Send us an email first. [Feb2005]

SPRING LANE FARMS

Guy Holt
5016 NE 59th Ter
Kansas City, MO 64119

816-560-1858
holt_guy@yahoo.com

Began: 2004 | Forming | Small Town

Spring Lane Farms is a new community nestled among the rolling hills NW of Kansas City, Missouri. Currently in the planning stages, this development will feature passive solar homes, healthy interiors and traditional architecture. The site is located adjacent to a historic farmstead along with a natural spring, wells, cisterns, windmills and outstanding water features. Amenities will include sustainable biomass plantings, permaculture design, alternative energy, gardens, silviculture and rainwater catchment. The housing will be clustered and surrounded by a private conservation area.

Visitors Accepted: Please contact Guy Holt. [Feb2005]

SPRING VALLEY BRUDERHOF

http://www.springvalleybruderhof.com

Spring Valley Bruderhof is an intentional community in southwestern Pennsylvania. We have our own school up to the 10th grade, a daycare, laundry, kitchen, and an organic garden where we grow most of our vegetables.

Spring Valley is home to the Peace Barn, a project of the Spring Valley Bruderhof school children. They are remodeling an old barn into a sanctuary for peace and justice worldwide. [Feb2005]

Listings

Additions and corrections: email: directory@ic.org, web: directory.ic.org, mail: RR 1 Box 156-D, Rutledge MO 63563, USA.

231

SPRINGHILL COHOUSING COMMUNITY

Stroud England
UNITED KINGDOM
info@cohouses.net

David Michael
16 Springhill Cohousing, Uplands
Stroud England
UNITED KINGDOM

+44-(0)1453-766466
david@ic.org

http://www.cohouses.net

Began: 2000 | Pop. 79 | Forming
Small Town | Diet: Vegetarian only

Springhill Cohousing Community is the first new-build cohousing community in Britain. There are 20 houses and 15 apartments and of course a large common house (3500 sq ft). The two acre site is very close to the centre of Stroud, a town of 25,000 with a Green mayor and four organic cafes. The train station is a short walk away; trains take 90 minutes to London.

The project was 90% pre-sold even before legal completion (ownership) of the site and before building permission had been granted.

Building work was done in phases, starting in 2003 and was 98% complete by February 2005. The last residents have now moved in and the first house is for re-sale.

We used a £4M facility from the Coop Bank to pay for the building phase.

The Common House is on three stories. We are decorating it and beginning to fit the kitchen. We are just starting to use it for meetings.

We are committed to setting up a Disputes Committee and are looking for consensus decision making training. Most residents have been working together on the project for at least three years.

We have the largest solar PV generator in Britain (49KWp), newspaper insulation, triple glazing, car share, etc.

Visitors Accepted: Email first to arrange a time and see if someone can host you. [Feb2005]

SPRINGTREE COMMUNITY

Tom
268 Springtree Ln
Scottsville, VA 24590

434-286-3466

Began: 1971 | Pop. 4
Rural | Diet: Vegetarian only

We are two married mid-age couples. Our commune (established in 1971) is on 120 rural acres. We share income, eat meals together, organize work by preference. We are eclectic, independent, and frugal. While we are aging, this is not a retirement community (!). Our group goals are often expressed through work—gardening, orcharding, and tree planting; keeping chickens; maintaining our two houses. We support ourselves with income from outside jobs.

We intend to remain a small, close group. We strive to keep the community flexible in meeting our changing needs for stability and adventure, individual activity and group cohesiveness. We value commitment and compatibility.

Visitors are welcome by prior arrangement. In season, we can have apprentices for one to six months learning and practicing ecological gardening, community, and country-living skills. For more information, write and tell us about yourself.

Visitors Accepted: A letter of introduction and a request works best for us. As a last resort, phone, telling us who you are and why you are interested in Springtree. [Feb2005]

SRI AUROBINDO SADHANA PEETHAM

2621 W Hwy 12
Lodi, CA 95242

209-339-1342 ext 5, 209-339-3710,
909-629-0108
SASP@lodinet.com

http://sasp.collaboration.org

Began: 1993 | Pop. 4 | Forming | Spiritual
Rural | Diet: Primarily vegetarian

Sri Aurobindo Sadhana Peetham is a small ashram for the practice of Sri Aurobindo's Integral Yoga. We provide residential facilities and work activities as a field for the Sadhana (spiritual practice). The basic needs of the members are provided for, and the collective work supports the financial expenses of the ashram. The rules of the Sri Aurobindo Ashram in Pondicherry, India: no drugs/alcohol, no smoking, no sex, and no politics are followed here, and an atmos-

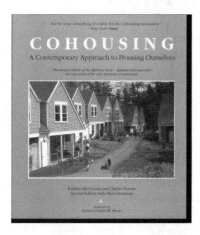
Scissors [✂] at the end of a listing indicate that it was edited for length by the Directory editors and a longer description can be found at directory.ic.org.

phere is attempted to be cultivated and maintained that honors and reflects the Divine Presence. Collective meditations are held daily, as well as a weekly study group and monthly retreats that are attended by friends and visitors from the regional area. A vegetarian diet is observed. No member plays the role of the spiritual leader of the ashram. The cultivation of the inner guru and reliance on the divine force of Sri Aurobindo and Mother's presence and teachings are the guiding principle. Practical direction of the day-to-day operations is overseen by a board of directors. Sri Aurobindo Sadhana Peetham is registered as a nonprofit religious corporation. Our main purpose is to provide a collective environment for one-pointed concentration on the Sadhana.

Visitors Accepted: First contact us by phone or email and give a brief background of yourself. [Feb2005]

STELLE COMMUNITY

815-256-2204
csc@stelle.net

http://www.stellecommunity.com

Began: 1963 | Pop. 90
Rural | Diet: Omnivorous

Stelle began as an intentional community in 1973 based on the book *The Ultimate Frontier*. In 1982, Stelle became an open community. Over the years, many residents have built aspects of sustainable living, such as green technologies and organic food production, into their lifestyles. Stelle residents comprise a diverse group although the common threads of responsible, conscious and courteous living are visible.

Visitors Accepted: Contact Center for Sustainable Community by phone or email. Open houses are held the first Sunday of every month. Visit www.centerforsustainablecommunity.org for more information. [Jan2005]

STEWARDSHIP INCORPORATED

PO Box 1159
Mountain View, HI 96771

808-965-8821, 808-938-4844 cell
mail@stewardshipincorporated.org

Forming

Stewardship Incorporated is a nonprofit community initiative dedicated to implementing sustainable systems on private and public lands. We intend to transform an unutilized

agricultural experiment farm into a research and demonstration center for enlightened living practices. Malamaki Experiment Farm is located on 189 acres in the Malamaki Rainforest Reserve on the Big Island of Hawaii. Stewardship Inc. is a very young effort. We are currently recruiting a permanent board of directors who will also be the resident, working staff. These positions will require people of extraordinary integrity, initiative, courage, and freedom from other obligations (minimum 1 year commitment). Anyone joining us, at this stage, is committing to intense personal involvement with a small core group of initiators. Effective stewardship is conscious awareness of present, physical reality and is manifest through intelligent, strenuous labor. Most of the people who come to us are so caught up in idealistic, intellectual concepts, spiritual quests and utopian fantasies that they are unable to function effectively in any context, let alone the highly challenging circumstances of this project. Be aware: rainforest living is often dirty, wet, and isolated. Be prepared to face many challenges that might not support your current perception of reality. Aloha. Please get in touch and communicate your intention. We are not operating a hippy tourist facility. We are only interested in communicating with people who are: 1. emotionally-stable; 2. self-supporting and living in the real world; 3. ready and able to make a long-term commitment. [Oct2004][⌘<]

STONE CURVES COHOUSING

4133 N Stone Ave
Tucson, AZ 85705

520-293-5290
info@StoneCurves.com

Christine Johnson
520-207-8718
ManzJohnson@netzero.net

Carlos Nagel
520-887-1188
closfree@aol.com

http://www.StoneCurves.com

Began: 2001 | Forming | Urban

Stone Curves Cohousing is an urban infill community. We are pleased to be working with the city of Tucson in both making our community pedestrian friendly and offsetting our power usage costs through the Tucson Electric Power rebate program.

We have integrated into our team the foremost permaculturist of our area. He will help us create one of the best native plant and water usage environments in Tucson. It

is envisioned to be a demonstration model of what can be done in and for our desert.

We will be composed of 48 households, all of which will share in the use of a 16-room common house, a 1200 sq ft shop, gardens, pool and multiple play areas for kids and adults.

Visitors Accepted: By appointment: email or telephone. [Oct2004]

STONE SOUP COOPERATIVE

Mark Fick
1430 W Leland
Chicago, IL 60640

773-878-3225

Began: 1997 | Pop. 39
Urban | Diet: Primarily vegetarian

Stone Soup is an urban intentional community dedicated to joy and justice. Our members are organizers, teachers, social workers, students, artists, and others doing creative work for social change. We support each other's commitment to social justice with a caring, creative, and fun living environment.

Stone Soup is made up of 39 members in three properties. Two houses are in Chicago's Uptown neighborhood and the third is in the McKinley Park neighborhood. Communal dinners are held five nights a week, including a weekly Tuesday potluck that is open to the public (please call ahead). We accommodate short-term visitors who make arrangements in advance.

Visitors Accepted: Call ahead to reserve guest space. [Jan2005]

STORYBOOK SHIRE

Kerry McClure
102 Longleaf St
Pickerington, OH 43147

614-837-5319
kerryandtonymcclure@yahoo.com

Began: 2004 | Forming
Rural | Diet: Omnivorous

We are in the intital stages of beginning a community near Columbus, Ohio that will be comprised of cottages and gardens, with common structures, as well. There will be a focus on healthy building practices, self-sustainability—off-gridding, but also thinking of ways to make a living, to profit off the land—llamas, alpacas, open farmers and artisan markets, small theatre, etc. Please email if you are interested in helping to form a beautiful, enchanted village.

Visitors Accepted [Dec2004]

Listings

Additions and corrections: email: directory@ic.org, *web*: directory.ic.org, *mail*: RR 1 Box 156-D, Rutledge MO 63563, USA.

233

STUDENT COOPERATIVE ORGANIZATION (SCO)

Recruitment Coordinator or Secretary
ACME Co-op
23 Elliott St
Athens, OH 45701

740-589-6979, 740-589-2600
acmecoop@yahoo.com

Began: 1990 | Pop. 8 | Small Town

We are a consensus based organization. Our focus is, traditionally, on university and college students in the Athens County area, although we do have non-students living in the house (most were students when they first lived here).

We are, primarily, a learning ground for young people new to the concepts of intentional community and cooperatives.

Visitors Accepted: If you would like to come to Athens for a visit, please send us an email or contact us by phone at least one week before your expected visit, especially if you would like to stay overnight. [Nov2004]

STUDENTS' COOPERATIVE ASSOCIATION

1648 Alder St
Eugene, OR 97401

541-683-1112
asuosch@gladstone.uoregon.edu

http://gladstone.uoregon.edu/~asuosch

Began: 1935 | Pop. 74 | Urban | Diet: Other

The Students' Cooperative Association is a student-owned and student-operated housing organization in Eugene, Oregon. Our primary purpose is to provide cooperative, affordable housing to college students. We achieve this by buying our food in bulk and cooking our own meals, as well as doing most of the maintenance and all of the general cleaning.

The co-ops strive to foster diversity as well as create a strong sense of community. The members run the houses, so there is no landlord making a profit from their home. This also means the members have the responsibility to keep food on the table and the house in order.

Founded in 1935, we are one of the country's oldest student co-op associations. We now have three houses along tree-lined Alder Street across from the University of Oregon campus. Lorax Manner houses eco-friendly students who cook vegan meals. We use the word manner instead of manor to signify living in an environmentally sustainable way. The Campbell Club houses an eclectic mix of vegetarian-cooking students and two cats. We are turning the Janet Smith House into a home exclusively for graduate students.

Visitors Accepted: Call, email, write, or just drop by to make an appointment for a tour and to have dinner. [Mar2005]

THE SUDANESE CHADIAN COMMUNITY IN NE INDIANA

Zakaria Idriss
1402 E Wayne St
Fort Wayne, IN 46803

260-385-1253, 260-385-0852
zakaria@suchadian.com
idrisseimo@yahoo.com

http://www.suchadian.com

Began: 2003 | Pop. 428 | Forming | Diet: Kosher

The mission of The Sudanese Chadian Community of Northeast Indiana is to assist refugees, immigrants and multi-ethnic communities to develop self-sufficiency and cultural awareness.

Visitors Accepted: Our door is open to visitors. [Mar2005]

SUGAR MOUNTAIN

Missouri
communityinfo@sugarmountainhome.com
homesteading@sugarmountainhome.com

http://www.sugarmountainhome.com

Began: 1998 | Pop. 28
Rural | Diet: Omnivorous

Sugar Mountain is a homesteading community of like-minded individuals, practicing skills of self-sufficiency, homesteading, and striving towards independence, preparedness, and survival, with an eye toward preserving old-time skills that might otherwise be lost. Members are carefully selected, and only 1-2 family units are added per year. Over 5 years time, we have gone from one founding family unit to a total of 10 family units. Contact by email. [Jan2005]

SUMMERGLEN FARM AND HOMESTEAD

Katie Gwinn
736 Rock Hill Church Rd SE
Floyd, VA 24091

540-745-6868

http://summerglenhomestead.com

Began: 1999 | Pop. 2 | Forming | Spiritual
Rural | Diet: Omnivorous

We are a developing homestead community focusing on sustainable living close to nature. Our goals are 1) to create community based on the principles of giving more to the land than we receive through better-than-organic practices; 2) to nurture the Summerglen School of Homesteading wherein we teach essential, primitive living and farming skills; 3) to create a spiritual retreat where folks may come to find quiet, peace and an opportunity for deep introspection.

We offer 110 acres of beautiful land, hardwood forests abounding with springs and creeks, cultivated and wild foods, domestic and wild animals. We are off-grid and use no combustion machines for gardening or building.

Our farm is isolated but very accessible to the wonderfully eclectic little town of Floyd, Virginia. The gardens are our main focus. We eat a well-rounded diet rich in raw foods, but are not vegetarians. We have milk goats and chickens, but do not slaughter our animals, but barter with neighbors for organic meats. All of the animals here, from the food animals to the pets, are rescued. Love of animals is a must for a happy life here.

The land is privately owned but ready to be shared with like-minded and like-spirited individuals. Decisions are typically made on a consensus basis. Expenses and activities are shared on a collective give/give basis, working together to accomplish our obligations and goals.

We welcome you as a guest (please call first) to come and explore our place, our philosophy, and the art of living here on this dynamic homestead.

Visitors Accepted: Please call first. If we seem to have similar values, beliefs and ways of operating, we would love to have you come for a short initial visit. A small donation of cash and/or help with the gardens or projects is appreciated in exchange for food and accommodations. [Oct2004][✂]

SUMMIT AVE COOPERATIVE

1820 Summit Ave
Madison, WI 53726

608-238-3441
summitavecoop@sbcglobal.net

Began: 1970 | Pop. 17 | Urban

We are an 17-member, independent, self-sustaining housing cooperative on the near west side of Madison, Wisconsin. The co-op was formed in 1970 when we obtained ownership of a large, three-story house from an agricultural fraternity at the University of Wisconsin–Madison.

Scissors [✂] at the end of a listing indicate that it was edited for length by the Directory editors and a longer description can be found at directory.ic.org.

The membership has gone through many changes since then, but the goal has always been to provide affordable housing in a friendly, family-like community environment. Our current membership is very diverse (both students and professionals from all walks of life, ranging in age from 20 to 55), and we share no particular political or ideological bent. We all share the duties of running the house (from cooking to cleaning to keeping the books) through a five-hours-per-week work-job system.

The heart of our community life revolves around the delicious, vegetarian-option house meals served Sunday–Thursday at 6 pm. We make decisions (usually by simple majority) at mandatory house meetings held every 2½ weeks. Ad hoc committees are regularly created to handle specific projects such as financial planning or landscape planning.

What makes us so unique? We're a bunch of quirky, unrelated folks who manage to operate almost like a family and run a clean, friendly *home*. It works!

Visitors Not Accepted [Mar2005]

SUNHOUSE CO-OP

Ann Arbor, MI

734-763-2177
sunhouse@sunward.org

**http://www.sunward.org/
sunco-op.html**

Began: 1997 | Pop. 3
Suburban | Diet: Primarily vegetarian

Sunhouse is one of 40 households comprising Sunward, an intentional community where resources are shared, the Earth is respected, diversity is welcomed, children play together in safety, and living in community comes naturally. We live on 20 beautiful acres of woods, ponds, organic gardens, playfields, with an antique barn, and more.

Diversity of background and interests enrich our experience while common threads tie us together for a rewarding living environment. Cooperative living experience is a must along with a sincere desire to live in a consensus-based community. We love the land and thrive in village life. Keeping clean and neat common areas and sharing in the upkeep of the house are priorities, especially in the kitchen! Laughter, art, and music highlight our home. We do not smoke, use drugs, or have TV in the house. We enjoy cooking organic vegetarian cuisine for each other and for community

meals in the Common House. We share a commitment to open, honest communication and good group process. A common kitchen pantry, shared chores, utilities, broadband, and phone enhance our experience. We are fun-loving, progressive professionals and grad students. We have extensive organic garden space to practice that art. Participating in the life of the wider Sunward Community is a big part of our experience.

If this is in line with your values and lifestyle and you can make at least a one year commitment, please begin a dialog with us today.

Visitors Accepted: Please read our website first and contact us well in advance. We cannot well accommodate drop-in visitors. [Mar2005]

SUNRISE RANCH

Cliff Penwell
5569 N County Rd 29
Loveland, CO 80538

970-679-4200, 970-679-4229
sunrise@emnet.org

http://www.sunriseranch.org

Began: 1945 | Pop. 98 | Spiritual
Rural | Diet: Omnivorous

Sunrise Ranch is an Emissary community founded in 1945, and located about 10 miles west of Loveland, Colorado (a little over an hour and a half north of Denver). The Emissaries (also known as Emissaries of Divine Light) are a worldwide spiritual organization and, in the United States, a registered nonprofit charity dedicated to the spiritual regeneration of humankind. The demonstration of practical spirituality in each aspect of living is one of the Emissaries' main concerns.

Sunrise Ranch has about 100 residents—85 adults and 15 children. The community has weekly worship services, an elected governing board, regular community meetings, internship and visitor programs, and a retreat and conference business handling groups up to 200.

Work opportunities include support of most of the functions required for a busy, well-established community to flourish. All community members are required to contribute some time to community tasks. Because Sunrise Ranch is the international headquarters of the Emissary program, much administrative work takes place on-site.

While external changes have their ebb and flow, there is a firm commitment to our spir-

itual heritage and a strong, focused intent on the radiant expression of the divine.

Becoming a community member involves several stages ranging from a few days' visit to participation in a two-year internship program.

Visitors Accepted: Contact us at 970-679-4200. We welcome visitors. We ask that you please call before arriving. Some work-share arrangements are available from time to time. [Mar2005]

SUNSET HOUSE

Jeff Markwardt
915 16th Ave
Seattle, WA 98122

206-323-9055
jrmarkwardt@netscape.net

**http://www.nas.com/riverfarm/
evglt.htm**

Began: 1978 | Pop. 6
Urban | Diet: Primarily vegetarian

Sunset House is an intentional community that is affiliated with the Evergreen Land Trust. We live in a 6-bedroom, purple house in the Central District of Seattle near a food co-op and Seattle University. We are six socially conscious musicians, students, activists, organizers, and nonprofit workers living out progressive, engaged, and enthusiastic lives. We share a commitment to positive social change, keeping our home beautiful, and cooperative living.

House perks: Lots of common space, view of city skyline and Olympic Mountains, affordable living, shared food system, shared responsibility for house upkeep, large back deck and front porch, veggie/ queer/vegan friendly, and large garden spaces.

Principles of Sunset House: To steward our house responsibly, keeping it beautiful, safe, and well-maintained. To build strong relations with each other, formally, and informally. To cultivate an intentional community of mutual aid, generosity, and laughter. To create a household that feels alive, full, active, and welcoming, strengthening the web of family, friends, and extended community. To support environmental and social change by practicing what we preach, encouraging each other in this work, and supporting other groups in these efforts.

Evergreen Land Trust's mission: Take land and housing out of the marketplace to promote community development in harmony with the environment.

Visitors Accepted: Call, email, or write. [Nov2004]

SUNTOADS FARM COMMUNITY OF NEW MEXICO

PO Box 153
Elida, NM 88116

505-274-6440
jfeb@yucca.net

Began: 1999 | Pop. 6
Rural | Diet: Omnivorous

SunToads is a small rural farm community (presently 6 adults) in southeast New Mexico. We seek mentally healthy, reliable singles and couples. You can live rent-free on our land in exchange for a little help. You pay for your utilities, food and personal needs.

Be as modern or primitive as you wish. On-grid or off-grid to the extent that you desire. We have RV hookups and abundant free adobe, cob, concrete, and limestone materials. Rural, quiet, serene. Temperate climate. Independent, privacy-conscious lifestyle. Personal responsibility, cooperativeness, honesty, respect of others, and water conservation are expected. Organic food garden.

In general, SunToads is 100% free of: problematic alcohol, illegal items and substances, and smoking. Pets are subject to numerous restrictions. No particular mind-set, philosophical orientation, religion, or diet is mandated. Certain disabilities and all ages are OK. We are accommodating to people with multiple chemical sensitivities, allergies, fibromyalgia, chronic fatigue, Lyme disease, etc. Our community is ideal for people with a fixed income, though not a requirement.

We will gladly send you much more detail via email (not postal mail). In the subject line, write "detailed community description" and/or "unpaid position details." We get 100+ spams per day that we delete without reading, but when we recognize the subject we don't delete the email.

Visitors Accepted: Contact us before a desired visit. Prior arrangements must be made. No walk-ins or surprise visits. No pets. [Nov2004][✂<]

SUNWARD COHOUSING

Ann Arbor, MI 48103

734-663-5516
info@sunward.org
http://www.sunward.org

Began: 1994 | Pop. 88

We are a community of people dedicated to creating a place where resources are shared, the Earth is respected, diversity is welcomed, children play together in safety, growth is nurtured, and living in community comes naturally. Our core values and vision help to provide a common foundation for our decisions and our relationships with each other.

Around 90 people live at Sunward Cohousing, from wee ones to octogenarians. We have singles and couples, families and empty-nesters, and at least one household that functions as a cooperative. We have a diversity of backgrounds, occupations, spiritual and secular paths, and sexual orientations.

In our 6+ years together on the land, we have experienced births, deaths, weddings, partings, members joining and departing, and much more. Many of us were drawn to Sunward for the sense of community and for the opportunity to live more lightly on the land. We steward 20 beautiful acres—of woods, prairie, and ponds—one quarter of which contains our clustered private homes and common house.

Visitors Accepted: We look forward to meeting prospective members! Please contact us well in advance and please be patient. We cannot well accommodate drop-in visitors. Please read FIC's guide to visiting communities before your visit and thank you for respecting the privacy of our home. [Mar2005]

SUNWISE CO-OP

2535 Westernesse Rd
Davis, CA 95616

530-753-7657
disbean@hotmail.com
http://members.dcn.org/scha/intro.htm

Began: 1978 | Pop. 8
Small Town | Diet: Vegetarian only

Sunwise co-op is a 8-bedroom passive solar house in suburban Davis, California. It belongs to the larger organization of the Solar Community Housing Association. Our house is located on a green belt with a large garden and chickens. The members of our house are both students and professionals (all low income) who share the roles of maintaining the house, working together toward the goal of sustainable/environmentally conscious living, and educating others about cooperative living. We also share vegetarian/vegan meals, chores, toothpaste, and our time. We make consensus-based decisions during house meetings in order

Ann Arbor, Michigan

Caring for each other and our environment
Engaging in dialogue to seek clarity & build connections
Creating a beautiful legacy for future generations

www.sunward.org   info@sunward.org

Scissors [✂<] at the end of a listing indicate that it was edited for length by the Directory editors and a longer description can be found at directory.ic.org.

to ensure that all members of the household are heard and appreciated. The house welcomes applicants who are open to a diverse household working together to live consciously.

Visitors Accepted: Please call in advance of your proposed visit, as we must reach consensus if you wish to stay over. For day visitors less advance notice is required. [Mar2005]

SURREALESTATES

Sacramento, CA

feedyoureye@hotmail.com

http://www.surrealestates.org

Began: 1992 | Pop. 15 | Forming
Urban | Diet: Other

These are architecturally designed, lofted, small, single family houses. They will be built with SIPS panels, a high insulation pre-fabricated panel system that can be constructed quickly, and that provides great strength and R factor. The open living plan has a 20-foot height ceiling in the main room. The houses have three small bedrooms, however the two bedrooms in the loft can be easily changed to one open space. Houses have been engineered for solar, and may be fitted with a system later. The detached 800 sq ft studios have 12' high walls, a roll up and regular door, about three windows and two skylights. Studios are ~13-25 feet from the house. There is gated parking for each house.

Each lot has space for a small patio and the properties will pool their back sides to make a communal walkway and garden. We plan to open studios some of the time to become a destination for arts events, classes and such. There is however a restriction about posting regular open hours.

Light rail is a three minute walk, and there are bike trails into town through the Discovery Park area of the riverfront. Within walking distance there are coffee shops, galleries (http://www.sacforart.com/nsac.html), a hardware store, the arts commission, library, tennis court, ball park, boxing, kung fu, and a little theatre. A new children's gated "Tot Lot" just opened four blocks away.

Visitors Accepted: Contact us by email or visit our website to see when the next open studio or class is. [Jan2005]

SUSAN B. ANTHONY WOMEN'S LAND TRUST

**PO Box 5853
Athens, OH 45701**

**740-448-6424, 740-448-7285
ad965@seorf.ohiou.edu
freewimin@netzero.net**

http://www.frognet.net/~sbamuh

Began: 1979 | Pop. 5
Rural | Diet: Omnivorous

We are a community of five women residents—feminist, ecologically attuned, politically active—living in four dwellings. We share 150 acres 10 miles from Athens, Ohio, home of Ohio University (20,000 students) and Hocking Technical College (4,000 students).

Major decisions are made by consensus of residents and a nine-member board. We seek a balance between individual freedom and the welfare of the community. We have safe, congenial, inexpensive living space. After a one-year provisional membership, women can build a home, bring a mobile home, convert an outbuilding, or share space. The terrain is rugged—accessibility is problematic.

Susan B. Anthony Women's Land Trust is a nonprofit, tax-exempt women's outdoor education center. We host workshops on topics such as racism, nature and the arts, and practical skills for women. We have a campground for individuals and groups by advance reservation only. We are active in the women's community, which includes a feminist choir, women's herstory celebration, university LGBT Programs Center and Women's Studies Program. A farmer's market, public radio, worker-owned businesses, and many alternative projects enhance this scenic area in the Appalachian foothills.

Visitors Accepted: Inquiries, visitors, and exploring members welcome—contact us. [Mar2005]

SUSTAINABLE LIVING SYSTEMS

**Jill Davies
1993 Knightmare Dr
Corvallis, MT 59828**

**406-961-4419
info@wchi.net
jill@sustainablelivingsystems.org**

**http://www.sustainablelivingsystems
.org**

Began: 2000 | Pop. 13 | Forming
Rural | Diet: Omnivorous

The problem: The earth can no longer bear the true cost of our agriculture, shelter, and land use systems.

The solution is to create human living systems that are ecologically sound and economically viable, based upon whole systems thinking, and integrating care of the earth, care of people, and care of the community. Our mission is to:

1. facilitate access to environmentally responsible, off-the-grid, affordable housing;
2. preserve and refine traditional methods of food and seed production;
3. demonstrate and teach sustainable living;
4. contribute toward building a local, land-based economy.

Program areas:

1. Western Cultural Heritage Institute – an educational permaculture community demonstrating an environmentally responsible approach to shelter, energy, food production and collective living.
2. Education – on-site workshops with hands-on training, seminars addressing principles of sustainable living, hosting interns for various periods of time.
3. Seeds – breeding, sharing and maintaining a seed bank of native food and medicinal plants.
4. Shelter – "earthships," strawbale, cordwood, papercrete, and adobe construction methods, with off-the-grid energy systems, and innovations in no-discharge sanitation systems and water recycling.
5. Local Economy Enhancement – towards sustainable forms of prosperity for all, we are working on building a local food system in the Bitterroot Valley.

Visitors Accepted: First study our website, then if interested, call or email to express what your interest is and to set a time to visit. [Mar2005]

SVANHOLM

**Eberhard
Svanholm Allé 2
DK-4050 Skibby
DENMARK**

**+45-47566670, +45-47566633
eberhard@svanholm.dk**

http://www.svanholm.dk

Began: 1977 | Pop. 100
Rural | Diet: Omnivorous

The Svanholm Community consists of about 65 adults and 35 children aged from 0 to 80. We wish to expand by around 20 adults plus children.

Listings

Additions and corrections: email: directory@ic.org, *web:* directory.ic.org, *mail:* RR 1 Box 156-D, Rutledge MO 63563, USA.

237

We own an estate with 625 acres of farmland and 408 acres of park and woodlands.

When we bought the property in 1978 we wanted to live in a production collective based on shared work, shared economy, and shared decision making. We wanted whole lives, with influence on our work and daily living, and a place where our children would thrive, with animals and fresh air.

We live in smaller groups in some 12 different houses on and around the old estate, and these are the centers of daily social life. We are at the moment improving our main common kitchen and dining room.

Most of us work at home in one of the production areas or service areas; some 25 people have jobs outside the community. Until recently our main production has been organic farming.

We might develop new productions or have more people earn salaries outside in the future.

We pool all income in a common fund, and we each receive 20% of our individual salary for clothes, amusements, dentist, etc.

Our decision-making authority is the biweekly communal meeting, where we do not vote but discuss our way to agreement.

Working visitors are occasionally welcome (mostly around harvest).

Visitors Accepted: Please contact our guest group by email at: guestgroup@svanholm.dk before visiting. [Feb2005]

SWEETWATER COMMUNITY LAND TRUST

2435 Sweetwater Ln
Mansfield, MO 65704

417-741-7363 (JC)
jcutler@getgoin.net

Began: 1981 | Pop. 10
Rural | Diet: Omnivorous

We have 480 acres of rural land; 60 acres is farmable, the rest is hilly/wooded. Land is owned and managed by the trust, which gives 99-year leases for 10-acre home sites. Buildings, tools, vehicles, businesses, etc. are privately owned; individuals and families manage their own finances. We function as a "neighborhood" where members regulate their own community involvement (from totally private to cooperative housing, gardens, businesses, etc.). Sharing and mutual support are common. We manage Sweetwater by informal discussion and consensus and by cooperative arrangements among equals. Our focus is land stewardship and environmental quality, optimizing human well-being and relationships ("sustainable culture"). We are nondiscriminatory.

Visitors Accepted: Contact us to make arrangements. We can send you a brochure describing our community and our visitor policies. [Feb2005]

TACOMA ECO-VILLAGE

Peter Wilson
707 Spring St
Fircrest, WA 98466

206-683-8854
peter@effortlessliving.org

http://www.effortlessliving.org

Began: 2005 | Forming | Spiritual
Diet: Primarily vegetarian

The Society for Effortless Living is a free association of members with two common and vital explorations:
1) to know and live our true Essence-Being and
2) to co-create a true Eco-Village based on organic permaculture principles in Tacoma or Olympia, Washington.

Meetings are monthly and anyone who shares the above path will be welcome as an instant and equal member of the Society.

Visitors Accepted: Please visit our website for more information and the latest news, including upcoming meeting time and place. [Mar2005]

TAKOMA VILLAGE COHOUSING

6827 4th St NW
Washington, DC 20012

202-545-0130
info@takomavillage.org

Steve Pretl
202-413-8351
stevep@takomavillage.org

Anna Amato
202-726-0736
anna@takomavillage.org

http://www.takomavillage.org

Began: 1998 | Pop. 78
Urban | Diet: Omnivorous

Takoma Village is the first urban cohousing community in the greater metro Washington, DC area. We have forty-three attached flats, duplexes, and townhouses plus the common house. Units range from one bedroom with a den to four bedrooms with a basement. The common house includes two guest rooms, children's room, game room, office, living room, exercise room, dining room, and workshop.

Takoma Village is one and a half blocks from the Takoma Metro Station and easy walking to shopping on Georgia Avenue in DC and in Takoma Park, MD. Most residents commute by public transportation or bicycle. Many work at home, at least part-time. Residents range in age from 3 months to 83 years and are well-distributed across that range.

We have many energy-efficient systems and green materials. All units received the Energy Star rating.

We maintain a notification list and occasionally have units for sale or rooms for rent. If you are interested in living in our community, please contact us. We are always delighted to meet new friends.

Visitors Accepted: Please contact Steve Pretl and arrange a visit. We do fairly regular orientations for people who live in the area. [Jan2005]

TALKEETNA BLUEBERRY SANCTUARY

Gary Lawley
PO Box 651
Talkeetna, AK 99676

907-733-3596
marlee@cyberlynx.ak.net

Began: 2001 | Pop. 13 | Forming
Rural | Diet: Omnivorous

Our three-family group is actively seeking members. Ideally we would like five to seven families. 2003 was consumed mostly by road building to access the development site, and drilling a well. 2004 saw the construction of two houses and a generator shed. Situated on a 115-foot bluff in the middle of 240 acres with a sweeping view of the Alaska range and Denali, we have maintained ski trails, a 9-hole disc golf course, a small private lake for swimming and canoeing, and a hot tub. As a group, we are striving to foster ecological soundness, synergistic participation, and simplicity.

Visitors Accepted: Please arrange in advance by calling or emailing. [Feb2005]

Scissors [✄] at the end of a listing indicate that it was edited for length by the Directory *editors and a longer description can be found at* directory.ic.org.

TALKING CEDARS DEVELOPMENTS LTD.

Michael Poole
PO Box 372
Tofino, BC V0R 2Z0
CANADA

250-725-3718, 250-726-8330
freeminer@yahoo.com

**http://www.earthfuture.com/
econews/talkingcedars**

Began: 1988 | Pop. 6 | Forming | Spiritual
Small Town | Diet: Primarily vegetarian

Talking Cedars is an ecovillage that is being planned on 17 acres within the old-growth forest. We are two miles south of Tofino, close to the Pacific Ocean on the west coast of Vancouver Island, Canada. A Coho salmon stream is protected on the property.

A development plan is needed to create a cohousing-style ecovillage for about 80 people. Zoning for 13 homes is in place now. Rezoning is possible to allow for a total of 28 units of housing, cabins, campsites and uses for a bioregional permaculture of sustainability. Retreat center common buildings could allow the resident managers to offer year-round workshops and tours. Visitors are seeking energy and cultural alternatives. We also have begun an "ewok" canopy treewalk. We hope home construction will begin in 2005.

Prices of membership will probably range from $8 for a newsletter and day-trip tour, $20 per campsite and about $100 per cabin use. Management shareholders may join with $100,000 Canadian, or more, per home-site in a healthy corporation.

The ecovillage is hoped to be a pedestrian community, with parking separate, including car and boat share. Solar and sustainable tech houses can be built from environmentally sound materials.

M. Poole has a $50,000 mortgage that needs to be paid out by July. Loans to pay the mortgage and begin building will be secured on the title and receive first option for a home site according to legal agreements. A core of prospective co-owners is

---

**Online Communities
Directory**

Search our online database for new communities and the latest updates from communities listed here.

directory.ic.org

---

needed or the $2 million property will need to be sold on the open market.

Visitors Accepted: Just phone, write, email or drop in while in Tofino. We would like visitors to join our nonprofit society to support social change. [Feb2005][✄<]

TAMERA – HEALING BIOTOPE I

Monte do Cerro
P-7630 Colos
PORTUGAL

+351-283-635-306,
+351-283-635-484
tamera@mail.telepac.pt
igf@tamera.org

http://www.tamera.org

Began: 1995 | Pop. 105 | Spiritual
Rural | Diet: Primarily vegetarian

Tamera is a project for a future worth living, with a project site that comprises 331 acres, 30 km inland from the Atlantic coast. The project sees itself as a base and training camp for global peace work. The aim is to develop a cultural model of a nonviolent lifestyle for a couple of hundred people and the implementation of a "healing biotope." A "healing biotope" is a life community of people, animals, and plants whose life forces complement each other and are no longer blocked by each other through violence and fear. Between people the character of Tamera is guided by honesty in relationships, truth in love, transparency in the community, and above all taking on one's own responsibility and thus steering free of leadership cults. Currently 90 staff members live and work at Tamera, but during each summer there are many guests who like to help building up the project. A youth project and the "Youth School for Global Learning" as well as a Peace School for young adults has been founded. New ideas for professions and new commitments in political and humanitarian fields can be found here. Tamera is looking for support and cooperation with other committed peace workers and future-orientated communities. Our main "meeting point" for contact and network is the annual summer camp. Our next large step is the experiment "Monte Cerro," starting in 2006.

Visitors Accepted: Please contact us via phone or email to find out whether we are open for guests at the time you want to visit us. Please check our website for our current schedule and more information on how to visit Tamera. [Mar2005]

TANGUY HOMESTEADS

37 Twin Pine Way
Glen Mills, PA 19342

610-399-6724
raldred@comcast.net

Began: 1945 | Pop. 98 | Suburban

Tanguy Homesteads began in 1945 when six families bought a 100-acre farm for low-cost housing, cooperatively owned, open to all races and religions. We now have 38 families, varying in race, political perspective, religion, and job skills. Each member family owns a home on two acres, plus shares in Tanguy and the community center, ballfield, pond, and woods.

Tanguy is guided by a set of bylaws, but change is a source of constant renewal. Each resident adult is expected to attend our monthly membership meetings and serve on at least one committee, where most work is done. Committees include Activities, Community Building, Land, Pond, Finance, Homestead, New Members, Publications, and Tractor. Members elect new officers and the board of directors each year.

In the monthly meetings we make decisions as a community. No votes are taken ordinarily; decisions are reached through "substantial agreement." Workdays are important in getting many projects completed. Celebrations, holidays, an annual camping trip, ball games, fishing contests, singing, dances, and weekly potlucks all contribute to our community spirit.

We have a monthly assessment ($50), used to maintain road, building, and pond; to pay taxes and insurance; and to support activities. Prospective members are encouraged to attend meetings and community events to learn about Tanguy.

Visitors Accepted: Call or email. [Feb2005]

TAO BEAR RECOVERY COMMUNITY

Eric Greene
27710 Cordoba Dr #2306
Farmington Hills, MI 48334

734-812-5543
ericdgreene@comcast.net

Forming | Spiritual
Suburban | Diet: Omnivorous

Tao Bear Recovery Community is currently in the planning stages. Once established, it will be a contemplative, healing community located somewhere in the beautiful mountain west. At Tao Bear, open and honest communication will be encouraged, and

Additions and corrections: email: directory@ic.org, web: directory.ic.org, mail: RR 1 Box 156-D, Rutledge MO 63563, USA.

Listings

members will give and receive love, validation, support, and acceptance. We will be a peaceful and contemplative community, where one can engage in quiet meditation and introspection; a mindful community, where members are self-aware, courteous, and considerate of the needs of others; an eco-friendly community, where land stewardship, recycling, and sustainable gardening are practiced and alternative housing and energies are explored; a spiritual community, where we live simply and in harmony with the Tao.

If you are recovering from a dysfunctional childhood, alcoholism, addiction, or codependency, or just want to be involved in the creation of a unique healing community, please contact us for more information.

Visitors Accepted: Please contact Eric by email, phone or letter. [Nov2004]

TARARU VALLEY SANCTUARY

People Coordinator
PO Box 5
Thames, 2815
NEW ZEALAND
+64-(0)9-3531558,
+64-(0)7-8688988
ecovillage@tararuvalley.org
http://www.ecovillage.co.nz

Began: 2004 | Pop. 4 | Forming
Rural | Diet: Primarily vegetarian

Tararu Valley Sanctuary manages 600 hectares (1500 acres) of land which is the Valley watershed catchment. The majority of land is temperate rainforest with around 100 acres of open ground which has been farmed pastorally for many years. The Valley ecosystem has been classified as a Key Ecological Site.

Our vision is: "An educational community living sustainably while restoring the natural Mana of Tararu Valley." We seek up to five land partners for our small ecovillage who will share in protecting the Valley ecosystem and living sustainably.

Nontoxic and energy-efficient building materials and methods are encouraged with an internal building code in place. We are off the grid, so alternative energy sources are essential. Also alternative wastewater systems are required.

We are actively seeking foundation members as of October 2004. Purchasing a share entitles you to a two-hectare allotment on which to live and work. All members are entitled to access all common land and community facilities as they are developed.

Large communal buildings exist and a native tree nursery will be built soon.

Visitors Accepted: Please email us to arrange a visit and explain your intentions. [Oct2004]

TEACHING DRUM OUTDOOR SCHOOL

7124 Military Rd
Three Lakes, WI 54562
715-546-2944
balance@teachingdrum.org
http://www.teachingdrum.org

Began: 1989 | Pop. 8 | Spiritual
Rural | Diet: Omnivorous

We are first and foremost a teaching/learning community, dedicated to sharing the skills of truthspeaking, awareness, attunement, honor, respect, and being a social animal. The talking circle is our forum. The sweatlodge is our heart. The wild herbs are our healers. We live in wood-stove heated cabins, use electricity, computers, cars, and telephones, but our approach is to live as simply and closely to the Earth Mother as possible. We have no indoor toilets or bathing facilities, but we do have running water. We purchase local organic food, and forage for some of our summer greens.

We are a living-learning center, and others come to us to volunteer, take classes, and participate in our year-long program.

Our primitive camp, Nishnajida—a cluster of bark-and-thatch wigwams—lies 5 miles from our office center. There, we foster the year-long Wilderness Guide Program where students from all over the world come to make their clothing from skins; fish and forage for food; make craft items like bows, bowls, spoons, baskets; track; learn lodge construction and maintenance; and most of all learn about themselves and how to live in a community.

Everyone in our learning community is involved with the maintenance of this program, as well as with our own personal projects, passions, and growth. All are either staff or paying volunteers. Information about open positions, volunteer opportunities, classes, and the Wilderness Guide Program are available from our website.

We are a pet-free, alcohol/tobacco/drug-free atmosphere. We do welcome families.

Visitors Accepted: Please email, or call well in advance of your intended visit. We like to open a dialogue with potential visitors before they arrive. A half-day tour is available, by advance reservation, for $30.00. [Jan2005]

TEMESCAL COMMONS COHOUSING

Tom Garlick
480-D 42nd St
Oakland, CA 94609
tomgarlick@earthling.net

Began: 1996 | Pop. 25 | Spiritual
Urban | Diet: Omnivorous

Visitors Accepted: Contact Tom via email. The more advance notice we receive the more likely we will be able to accommodate tours. We are a small community that really enjoys meeting new people and sharing about life in cohousing. Please feel free to let us know of your interest. [Jan2005]

TERRA NOVA

Columbia, MO
573-443-5253
clairenova@juno.com

Began: 1995 | Pop. 3
Urban | Diet: Omnivorous

We're a stable, close-knit group of friends whose vision includes surrounding ourselves with even more friends in the houses in our neighborhood that border our 1.5 acres. As these come up for sale, we hope people with similar values will buy them. In what might serve as a common green space, we've planted fruit and nut trees and are slowly developing a wooded area, a wildflower meadow, and a large garden, part of which is set aside for use by others. Our location in town makes it easy to walk, bike, or bus, minimizing our auto use.

Our household is a mix of income sharers and expense sharers living in two small houses. We emphasize urban sustainability, lower-impact consumption, communication, and working through personal differences. We come together daily for the evening meal and (usually) weekly for meetings. Important decisions are made by consensus. We value learning about ourselves and each other and are creating deep friendships.

We are not currently seeking new members of our own household. Neighboring households that associate with us would be compatible but have their own personalities.

Most of us formerly lived at East Wind in southern Missouri and our wider circle of friends includes a number of others who did as well. Columbia itself has a lot to offer, with two colleges and a university and the attendant theater, concerts, and lectures. There are active groups working for peace, justice, the environment, and gay issues. A farmers' market is close by.

Scissors [✂] at the end of a listing indicate that it was edited for length by the Directory *editors and a longer description can be found at* directory.ic.org.

Visitors Accepted: Please contact us for more information or to arrange a tour. [Mar2005]

TERRASANTE VILLAGE

Bruce Scher
7678 S Avra Rd
Tucson, AZ 85735

520-822-2940, 520-403-8430
scher@ancientimages.com

Began: 2004 | Pop. 15 | Forming
Rural | Diet: Primarily vegetarian

Terrasante is an ongoing experiment in earth architecture, sculpture, permaculture, and community on 2+ acres of Sonoran desert about 25 miles SW of Tucson, AZ.

Third Jewel Land Trust

Join Us! Wild desert, clean ground water, electricity, organic architecture, 4-5 acre parcels. Interviewing now for spirited members: multi-faceted, friendly, green. We are capable, caring, solvent. Cottage industry, arts/crafts welcome.

Reserved as commons, five acres at the center of the trust will include a meeting hall and visitor parking, meditation dome, sweatlodge and fire ring, half acre fenced garden, outdoor kitchen and ramada.

Call us to see this special place. Come walk and talk with us. Join and help us build health, harmony, and a realized community that connects with the larger world.

Visitors Accepted: Call 520-822-2940 for specific directions. [Dec2004]

TERRAVIE

info@terravie.org

http://www.terravie.org

TerraVie is a nonprofit charitable organization that acquires, preserves and manages land for future generations which is made available for the development of viable communities.

TerraVie is devoted to scrupulously managing the land at their disposition in conformity with its charter and principles. TerraVie is committed to preserve its objectives, irrespective of the socioeconomic or political context.

This initiative is based on the principle that land is not a commodity, but a fundamental resource to be protected for the community as a whole.

It acts as a local economic development tool while informing the public about the various aspects of a lifestyle in harmony with nature. It emphases ecovillages and elimination of land speculation.

TerraVie is a nonprofit charitable organization, managed by an elected board of directors and made up of resident members, environmental organizations and individuals with the following common objectives:

• Acquire, hold and ecologically manage land, eliminating it from any real estate speculation.
• Preserve, protect and restore the environment, natural resources and any endangered species.
• Promote residential and agricultural sustainable development on 25% of the land.
• Ensure the construction of environmentally sound housing, available to all.
• Ensure that all activities taking place in the territory are environmentally friendly.
• Develop a model of viable communities inspired by ecological alternatives.
• Inspire the population to adopt a lifestyle that minimizes environmental impact. [Mar2005]

3CIRCLES COMMUNITY

Leroy E. Grey
PO Box 908
Shelbyville, TN 37162

703-621-6797
info@3circles.net
ThreeCirclesUSA@netscape.net

http://www.3circles.org/community

Began: 2005 | Pop. 2 | Forming
Rural | Diet: Omnivorous

The 3Circles Empowerment Principle:

"Whatever you put your time and money and resources into, that is what you empower and whatever you empower, you give power over yourself; It is now time to stop empowering the system that seeks to destroy you, and to empower one another instead."

The number three is foundational to the structure of the entire universe (proton, neutron and electron) and to all DNA (4 compounds organized in endlessly repeating units of three). For each 3Circles Community the number three represents our acknowledgement that spiritual growth is a process which we either deny (expecting others to be at our stage of awareness) or we embrace (providing a community infrastructure that promotes growth). We provide that growth infrastructure through 3 circles of spiritual training, assisting community members on their journey: from Spiritual Pilgrim to Life-Student to Spiritual Entrepreneur or Life-Manager.

The common thread that unites all 3Circles members is simple: we all believe in a "higher power," acknowledging that all of creation is encoded with an "intelligent design." Some of us call this God.

I am not so naïve as to believe that everyone who says they believe in God is a believer. I am also aware that spiritual growth is dynamic and fluid, that I was once blinded by so many of the beliefs I no longer hold. Given this understanding each 3Circles Community is formed of people who agree to let go of their traditions and their traditional beliefs in order to embrace something totally new, something not yet known in it's entirety.

Visitors Accepted: Please email and call. [Feb2005][⚥]

TIBETAN BUDDHIST LEARNING CENTER

93 Angen Rd
Washington, NJ 07882

908-689-6080

http://www.labsum.org

Began: 1958

The Tibetan Buddhist Learning Center (TBLC), Labsum Shedrub Ling, was founded in 1958 through the great efforts of Geshe Wangyal, a Kalmyk-Mongolian lama who received his Buddhist training in Kalmykia and in Tibet. Over the years, Geshe-la took on Western students who were interested in learning about Tibetan Buddhism. Before Geshe-la passed away in 1983, he appointed Joshua W. C. Cutler as director of the activities of the center, the main activity of which is teaching Tibetan Buddhism.

In summer, winter, and spring, TBLC gives weekend seminars intended as intensive instructions on specific topics for beginners and advanced students alike. Our primary aim: to develop a Buddhism that is culturally American and, at its heart, not different from the Buddhism that traveled from India through Tibet to TBLC's Tibetan monk-scholars and students in the United States.

TBLC also has a limited number of resident students who study Tibetan language and Buddhist philosophy for extended periods of time. Living in this Buddhist contemplative community gives them a unique opportunity to apply the Buddhist teachings in a practical way.

The Tibetan Buddhist Learning Center holds a weekly prayer and meditation session every Sunday beginning at 11 am in the main temple followed by a class on Buddhist philosophy and meditation in the School House beginning at 1:30 pm.

Visitors Accepted [Jan2005][⚥]

Additions and corrections: email: directory@ic.org, *web:* directory.ic.org, *mail: RR 1 Box 156-D, Rutledge MO 63563, USA.*

241

TOLSTOY FARM

**32404 Mill Canyon Rd N
Davenport, WA 99122**

**509-725-FARM
tim@tolstoyfarm.org
pete@tolstoyfarm.org**

http://www.tolstoyfarm.org

Began: 1963 | Pop. 48
Rural | Diet: Omnivorous

We are a decentralized rural community sharing 240 acres of canyon land in eastern Washington. The two main parcels are non-profit corporations with dweller-owned homes, some on and some off the grid. Five adjoining parcels are owned by alumni.

We are 50 people whose lifestyles and interests are varied, from seasonal laborers and weekenders to rural commuters to primitivists who rarely leave the canyon; from high-tech to no-tech; from carnies to vegans.

Our differing pursuits include growing organic food to eat and sell, self-sufficiency, potlucks, carpentry, quilting, computers, cooking, massage, herbs, mycology, art, seed saving, nature loving, volleyball, brewing, crafts, parenting, flowers, orchards, reading, relaxing, rebellion, rituals, music, and compost.

Farm-grown veggies sell in Spokane and through community-supported agriculture (CSAs). A limited number of apprenticeships are available yearly. Occasional openings occur when a member sells. Buyers must be approved through consensus meetings. We have one general meeting a year and weekly potlucks. We associate and/or disassociate with each other freely. In reference to our typical shortcomings, one member notes, "We are a microcosm of the outside world." Those wishing information should write or email and inspire us to respond. [Mar2005]

TOMORROW'S BREAD TODAY

**Don McCormick
301 E 26th St
Houston, TX 77008**

**281-733-3160, 281-481-6260
dhmccor@aol.com
charity@tbt.org**

http://www.tbt.org

Began: 1995 | Pop. 8 | Forming | Spiritual
Diet: Omnivorous

We have been given the opportunity and the means to help people live their lives more abundantly through sharing their works, their goods, their suffering, and their loves. We want to humbly follow our bliss and change the world so that sorrow is replaced by joy. We think that many others have done this and are doing this better than we can do it. We like what Dorothy Day said and did, and we like what the Bruderhof Communities say and do. Reading about them and watching their efforts help us do our work.

Visitors Accepted [Jan2005]

TORRI SUPERIORE ECOVILLAGE

**Via Torri Superiore 5
Ventimiglia, Imperia 18039
ITALY**

**+39-0184-215504, +39-0184-215290
info@torri-superiore.org
lucilla@gen-europe.org**

http://torri-superiore.org

Began: 1989 | Pop. 16
Rural | Diet: Omnivorous

The medieval village of Torri Superiore is situated in the Ligurian hinterland, close to the town of Ventimiglia (11 km away). Torri Superiore is an ecovillage and a member of the Global Ecovillage Network (GEN).

The village was abandoned by all original inhabitants, and progressively restored over the last fifteen years by a community of Italians and Germans. The village is made of 160 rooms, all built in local stone and lime, which still feature the traditional arches and vaults.

The Cultural Association that has been developing the project since 1989 also has non-resident members and owns about 50% of the village, while the other 50% is individually owned by ecovillage members. Only members of the association are allowed to buy property in Torri Superiore.

The restoration of the buildings respects the original characters of the beautiful hamlet while using ecological materials and appropriate technologies whenever possible. Courses and educational activities range from permaculture design to facilitation, consensus decision making, ecovillage creation, pottery and creative cuisine. Organic agriculture activities focus mainly on olive oil production, and vegetable gardens to supply the community centre.

The proximity to the beautiful river and the sea, the easily accessible walks on the surrounding mountains, and the mild climate make Torri Superiore an attractive location for ecologically sensitive people who appreciate the informal, friendly style of the group.

Visitors Accepted: Contact us by email or phone, and book accommodation at our ecological guesthouse. Volunteers and working guests are also accepted. Check our calendar for courses. [Jan2005]

TOUCHSTONE COHOUSING

**% Cohousing Development
Company
424 Little Lake Dr #18
Ann Arbor, MI 48013
touchstonecoho-
   owner@yahoogroups.com**

**Nick Meima
734 663 5516
nick@cohousingdevelopment.com**

http://www.ic.org/touchstone

Began: 2001 | Pop. 28 | Forming | Suburban

Touchstone is a neighborhood of forty-six households built on six acres in Scio Township. It is a community created and sustained by its residents with the intention of sharing the joys and challenges of life and appreciating each individual. Decisions are made using consensus. For more information, visit our website. [Oct2004]

TRES PLACITAS DEL RIO

**1710 West Alameda St
Santa Fe, NM 87501
info@tresplacitas.org**

http://www.tresplacitas.org

Began: 1996 | Pop. 22
Urban | Diet: Omnivorous

Tres Placitas Del Rio is a small-scale cohousing community. We live in an urban neighborhood with a rural feel along a tree-lined river. As of 1/05, we are 14 adults and 8 children, ages 3 to 74, in nine households. A maximum of 11 houses plus community structures is anticipated on 2.5 acres around a large open space. Pattern language, permaculture, and each member's uniqueness shape and enrich our community. Homes are owner designed and sometimes owner built. We love children, animals, gardens, and creativity. An attitude of resource consciousness and land stewardship is fostered. We operate by consensus and are striving to find the balance between community life and personal freedom. Our relationships are based on mutual respect between committed, caring, creative, and responsible individuals of all ages. We tend to engage actively in the social and political issues of our larger community and the planet. We are (extra)ordinary people from varied backgrounds living life in community without pretense. Tres Placitas is

---

Scissors [✂] at the end of a listing indicate that it was edited for length by the Directory *editors and a longer description can be found at* directory.ic.org.

a strong base for a healthy life—a place to settle in and call home.

Visitors Accepted: Please send an email expressing your interest in visiting and a tour will be arranged. [Jan2005]

TRIBE OF BLANK

Elisa Nuss
Stella, NE 68442
cuarrech@gmail.com

http://groups.yahoo.com/group/
tribe_of_blank

Began: 2004 | Pop. 3 | Forming
Diet: Omnivorous

We are currently a very small tribe of folks who wish to walk away from civilization and live independently as far as is possible, using tribal models of social organization and resource relationships as a guide. We will experiment and find what works best for us, as our tribe.

Our inspirations are the few existing hunter-gatherers, the Roma (gypsies), the Amish and others who live in tribes or successfully independent of civilization.

We're seeking others who are interested and will decide on where/how to live permanently when we have reached a critical mass or have waited long enough.

What we are not and do not want to be:

Full-scale farmers: we will acquire as much land as is needed to support us in a permaculture-modified hunter-gatherer lifestyle.

Religious: there is nothing wrong with humans, and no need to save them spiritually.

Vegetarian: we believe that meat is a healthful and necessary part of our diet.

Cultural impersonators/appropriators: we are not disrespectfully re-creating any sacred cultural aspect of past or existing tribes.

Enactors: while we may model some portion of our developing culture after fictional or romanticized cultures such as elves or Celts, we are not pretending to be them.

Visitors Accepted: Contact us through email and we'll discuss it. [Jan2005]

TRIBE OF DIRT

New Hampshire
tribeofdirt@gmail.com

http://www.geocities.com/dirtribe/
index.html

Began: 2001 | Pop. 3 | Forming
Diet: Omnivorous

Much of what we believe now about the world around us was influenced by the works of Jared Diamond (Guns, Germs & Steel), Joseph Campbell (Power of Myth), Daniel Quinn (Ishmael, Story of B, Beyond Civilization, etc.) but above all else, Life Experiences.

We are no longer interested in salvationist or agriculture-based religions. We do however believe ritual and tradition are important. We believe the two encourage group cohesion, help make our lives more real and allow us to slow down and focus. We do not believe humans are inherently flawed. We know that we are of the same material as the rest of the animals, vegetables, minerals, etc. of the world. We eat from the dirt, have sex, are born, die and turn to dirt to feed the rest with our bodies.

We are no longer interested in public institutions nor wage slavery. We believe in taking care of our own. We believe our energies (work, moneys, charity, happiness, etc.) should primarily stay within the tribe.

We are no longer interested in environmentalism. We believe there are just too many humans on the earth right now and no amount of control is going to fix our situation.

What we are interested in is uniting a group of people capable of adapting and surviving whatever may come as a result of the prolific human population. Something our children will want to continue to nurture and pass on to their children. We envision simply a committed extended family living together and making a living together.

Visitors Accepted: Email us to set up a time, date and meeting place. [Mar2005]

TRIBE OF LIKATIEN

Stamm der Likatier
Magnusplatz 6
87629 Füssen
GERMANY

+49-(0)8362-38993
viola@likatien.de
stamm-der-likatier@likatien.de

http://www.likatien.de

Began: 1974 | Pop. 253
Urban | Diet: Primarily vegetarian

The Tribe Füssen Eins is also known as Tribe of Likatien. Likatien means "residents at lik," which refers to the last ancient Celtic tribe, living at the river Lech.

One of our central visions is to become a tribe—in a modern meaning. For us that means a special quality of admitting with each other and getting close to our emotional and spiritual reality.

In the way people get involved with the tribe and each other the tribe becomes sustainable. In the inner circle the people swear to stay here for their whole lives.

We want to develop a culture of love and trust as a sign for mankind's original destiny. A culture which includes the consciousness of a balance in relationships—between people and nature but also between each other. So communication is very important for us.

The Tribe was founded in 1974 and in 2004 has more than 250 people, more than half of them children and youths. In the city of Füssen we own about 25 houses, where we live and work. We have an esoteric bookshop, a bio-shop, a computershop, a company which organizes esoteric fairs, internet shops, lawyers, a healer's school with holistic doctors. There is also a group of people doing agriculture for the tribe, trying to develop permaculture.

We make our community decisions by consensus. People in the inner circle meet every evening to discuss problems and work together.

There are also many festivities. The tribe loves good party spirit, because enthusiastic lively party elation creates a feeling of paradise. And that's a goal the tribe aspires to: to create a possibility for Paradise on earth.

Visitors Accepted: Guests are welcome any time. Please contact us beforehand. [Mar2005][⅌<]

TRILLIUM FARM COMMUNITY

PO Box 1330
Jacksonville, OR 97530

541-899-1696 (farm)
trillium@deepwild.org

http://www.deepwild.org

Began: 1976 | Pop. 2
Rural | Diet: Primarily vegetarian

A remote river canyon in the eastern Siskiyou mountains provides a spectacular wilderness setting for Trillium: 82 acres of conifer forest, oak woodland, chaparral along the banks of the Little Applegate River, with gorgeous meadows, several ponds and waterfalls along seasonal Birch Creek. Less than an hour from Ashland (theater, arts, college town) and Medford (regional commercial center), Trillium basks in a sunny rain shadow, a 3-hour drive to the Redwood coast.

We operate Birch Creek Arts & Ecology Center, hosting educational, cultural, and

Listings

Additions and corrections: email: directory@ic.org, *web:* directory.ic.org, *mail:* RR 1 Box 156-D, Rutledge MO 63563, USA.

243

spiritual programs. Our Dakubetede Environmental Education Programs provide academic credit for these and other programs, including the DEEP Ecostery, a 17-credit experience in community during 2 months in the spring or autumn. To protect the vibrant wilderness that surrounds us, we operate TELAV (Threatened & Endangered Little Applegate Valley) to work for watershed health.

For 30 years, Trillium has functioned as a village, with 8 privately situated rustic residential cabins with full solar access. A cluster of office, craft, and utility buildings surround the parking lot, just below the Mother Garden. We have a nice guest cottage, and a community house in the historic homestead cabin next to two ponds above the river. We preserve the river gorge as a wild sanctuary, free from any buildings. All of Trillium functions as a critical wildlife oasis sanctuary, thus we do not welcome dogs.

At this time, we are only 2 full-time residential land stewards, sharing Trillium with an ever-fluctuating number of university students, interns, and friends exploring community. We desire to expand into an ecovillage community of approximately 8-10 full-time residential members, and several non-residential members.

Visitors Accepted: Please call or write us to introduce yourself with at least two weeks advance notice of your arrival. [Mar2005]

TRILLIUM HOLLOW

9601 NW Leahy Rd
Portland, OR 97229

503-297-1696
info@trillium-hollow.org

http://www.trillium-hollow.org

Began: 1991 | Pop. 42
Suburban | Diet: Omnivorous

We are a suburban cohousing community nested in 3.6 acres of lush forested wildlife setting with a creek and evergreen firs. Located minutes from downtown Portland within walking/biking distance of mass transit, parks, schools (Beaverton school district), shops, and medical.

Our neighborhood is primarily made up of self-sufficient flats (studios, 1, 2, 3, 4 bedrooms) with one stand-alone unit owned as condominiums. There are generous common facilities, including a 3,600 sq ft Common House with guest rooms and generous dining/meeting spaces, indoor and outdoor child play areas, a woodshop, hot tub, 24/7 Internet, laundry facilities, native plant landscaping, and organic community garden.

Our shared community life at Trillium is active: members gather frequently for meals, work parties, celebrations, Qigong study group and social activities. Our regular celebrations include Solstices, Talent/No Talent show, Founder's Day, summer bash and New Years. We are a caring, supportive, consensus-based community, seeking to live lightly on the land, working cooperatively with our surrounding neighbors, valuing participation in our community, and sharing meals together available two to four nights a week.

Our vision is to create and live in a community that fosters harmony with each other, the larger community, and nature.

Visitors Accepted: Tours are scheduled at mutually convenient times. Email us to arrange for a tour. [Mar2005]

TRUTH CONSCIOUSNESS

Sacred Mountain Ashram
10668 Gold Hill Rd
Boulder, CO 80302

303-447-1637, 303-459-3833
info@truthconsciousness.org

Desert Ashram
3403 W Sweetwater Dr
Tucson, AZ 85745

520-743-0384, 520-743-8821
info@truthconsciousness.org

http://truthconsciousness.org/
TC_HomePage.htm

Began: 1974 | Spiritual
Diet: Vegetarian only

Truth Consciousness, founded in 1974 by Prabhushri Swami Amar Jyoti, maintains Ashrams and Spiritual Centers devoted to the principles of truth and dharma (righteousness) and the freeing of human consciousness into divine consciousness. Monastic disciples reside at the ashrams in Colorado and Arizona, and along with lay devotees gather twice weekly for satsang and daily for aarati, meditation, chanting and karma yoga (selfless service). Every facet of life is seen as part of spiritual practice.

The eternal wisdom of the Himalayan sages is embodied in the oral teachings and writings of Swami Amar Jyoti. Please visit our website to see our inspirational books, spoken-word audio satsangs, spiritual journals, *Prayer & Meditation* calendar and *Chants to the Divine* CDs.

While there is no fee for any programs other than retreats, donations are always welcome. Truth Consciousness is a non-profit, tax-exempt organization. Inquiries may be directed to either ashram.

Visitors Accepted: Please see our website for information for visitors. Make prior arrangements with the Center you wish to visit. [Oct2004]

TULLSTUGAN COLLECTIVE HOUSING UNIT

Dorjgrand 4
Stockholm, SE-11668
SWEDEN

+46-(0)706559483

Dick Urban Vestbro
+46-(0)8-6423233
dickurba@chello.se

http://www.tullstugan.org

Began: 1994 | Pop. 52
Urban | Diet: Omnivorous

The Tullstugan unit consists of about 40 adults and 17 children in 21 apartments on two staircases within a larger inner-city block of flats. It is based on the Swedish "self-work model" of collective housing (as distinct from the classical collective-housing unit, which was based on services through employed staff). Cooking in the central kitchen is a precondition for becoming a member. Also persons in the neighboring area can become members of the cooking teams providing dinners four evenings a week. The unit was originally built by the municipal housing company Familjebostäder, but was later sold to the residents. Common spaces consist of a dining room, a children's play room, a TV room and a small guest room.

Visitors Accepted: Contact the chairperson by email. [Feb2005]

TURN CEDARS

Abigail Brown
1315 Edgecliff Rd
Fort Worth, TX 76134

817-293-3445
abibrown@earthlink.net
brownway@mindspring.com

http://brownway.home.mindspring
.com/turncd

Began: 1980 | Pop. 2 | Spiritual
Suburban | Diet: Primarily vegetarian

Small Christian community (including one Quaker) seeks more good people as members here especially Jews, Christians,

Scissors [✂] at the end of a listing indicate that it was edited for length by the Directory *editors and a longer description can be found at* directory.ic.org.

Tribes

Who are these tribes? Where are they? What do they do? 1900 years ago the ancient tribal life of Abraham and his offspring, a life of hospitality and peace, vanished from the earth, but now is the time when they are being restored, the Twelve Tribes who "earnestly serve God night and day." (Acts 26:7)

The families, households, and clans that make up these communities are composed of people from every sort of background. But they now have a common character from a kindred spirit — brothers and sisters dwelling together in unity. Generations live together in a place where God dwells, where the lonely have a home, a place to belong that is blessed with life everlasting.

This commonwealth is a new spiritual nation made up of twelve tribes, which encircle the globe. There are no rich or poor among them, for these preserved ones are learning how to love one another, becoming a light to the nations.

In a modern world that has removed the ancient boundaries, we are restoring the age-old foundations, uniting the hearts of fathers and sons. It is good and pleasant, like the dew, like oil upon the head, like a watered garden, a place where God dwells...

We live a simple life in community working together, eating together, sharing all we have. The laws that govern us are being written on our hearts. Our aim is to love each other as our Master Yahshua (known to many as "Jesus Christ") loved us and to love our Creator with all our heart, soul, mind, and strength, and to love our neighbors as we love ourselves. Daily we gather in our households with singing and dancing to give thanks to the One who has saved us from an empty and hopeless existence. We have moved from the kingdom of darkness into the kingdom of his marvelous light... You are invited to come visit.

SOMETHING VERY OLD is being born.
The appointed time has come.
No longer strangers, no longer rootless,
a people is being gathered.
The prophetic voice of a new millennium
can be faintly heard.
No longer separated, no longer alienated,
A commonwealth is being formed...

Listings

In the USA and Canada:
☎ 1-888-TWELVE-T
(1-888-893-5838)

www.TwelveTribes.org
(English Español Français Deutsch Português)

Muslims, Skeptics, Whatever. Members here already belong to churches downtown and many other organizations. New members must be honest, trustworthy, peaceable, cooperative, and able to enjoy doing work. Must love nature, science, organic gardening, good food, good health, music and other arts. No tobacco, no substance abuse. Prefer vegetarians or modest users of animal products. At present we also participate in other communities' efforts to work for social justice, healthy environment, good health care systems, world peace, etc. We already have three dogs. Perhaps we want ducks for eggs, a cow or goat for milk. We are a small piece of countryside within an urban area. Newcomers should be able to buy or rent their own housing in nearby neighborhoods. More details upon request.

Primary Focus: Supporting one another fairly.

Visitors Accepted: Must call ahead to make arrangements. No drop-ins, please. [Mar2005]

TWELVE TRIBES

contact_us@twelvetribes.org

http://www.TwelveTribes.org

Began: 1972 | Spiritual | Diet: Other

The folks that you will meet in the communities listed below are part of a tribespeople. Our life is expressed through living together in community—a new social order. Our desire is to live as naturally as possible by being close to Creation and to people. Our vision: not a lifestyle, but the forming of a new nation—the twelve-tribed nation of Israel.

Although it is not a legal name or entity, we are known as the Twelve Tribes because we are organized as a tribal people in twelve different geographical areas (Northeastern, Southeastern, Midwest, and the West Coast of the United States, Canada, France, Spain, Germany, England, Brazil, Argentina, and Australia). In each tribal area there are a number of communities, depending on how long that tribe has been established. Each community consists of one or more households which all share a "common purse" in that location, funded by whatever industries that community has established. Some are farm communities, and some are urban. Some have cottage industries, some service industries, and many operate cafes and markets selling wholesome food at reasonable prices. In every community we live together, work together, teach our children

together, take our meals together, and worship together.

Our life is not "religious" in the conventional way of thinking (we don't "go to church"), but it is deeply "spiritual"—that is, we strive to maintain a heart-to-heart fellowship with one another, and with our Creator, at all times. To us, the only valid religion is one that expresses itself in daily, practical love and care for one another that overcomes economic, racial, social, and doctrinal divisions. We believe the Bible, living by the teachings of both the Old and New Testaments. We follow Yahshua, the Messiah, called "Jesus Christ" in most English Bibles. We prefer his original Hebrew name and title, because it connects us to his radical origins and mission - to restore the spiritual life that was supposed to characterize Israel. They were supposed to be a spiritual nation of twelve tribes whose life of love and unity was to be a light to the nations around them. But they failed.

So we have set our hearts to restore that life in a real and practical way, to carve out of this dying world places where children can grow up pure and undefiled, full of vision and purpose, and where weary damaged people can find healing and restoration. Together we can express the love of our awesome Creator!

Visitors Accepted [Mar2005]

TWELVE TRIBES COMMUNAUTÉ DE HEIMSBRUNN

**Communauté de Heimsbrunn
71 Rue Galfingue
68990 Heimsbrunn
FRANCE**

**+33-(0)3-89-81-90-80
Sus@DouzeTribus.com**

http://www. twelvetribes.org

Spiritual | Small Town | Diet: Omnivorous

Heimsbrunn is a small village close to the French city of Mulhouse, in Alsace, close to the border between Germany and France. A small Twelve Tribes community lives there. They are a group of around 50 wholehearted followers of the Messiah who live their faith, zealously laboring day and night on the many projects they have on their heart. Our goal is to practice obedience to the commandments of the Son of God, observing the Holy Scriptures and sharing our hearts. We gather together every morning and evening, to sing, to dance, to share our revelation and faith, concluding our gatherings with our prayers. Becoming

friends and increasing in our mutual love is the main purpose of our life… a life where forgiveness, patience, helping and encouraging each other daily are by far the most necessary and essential responsibilities of each member. We desire to come to know all who want to discover our life, and of course you are very welcome at any time to have a taste of our joy and peace. Come and share a few moments of our life, along with a cup of maté…and hear our story.

Visitors Accepted [Mar2005]

TWELVE TRIBES COMMUNAUTÉ DE SUS

**11 Route du Haut Béarn
64190 Sus-Navarrenx
FRANCE**

**+33-(0)5-59-66-14-28
Sus@DouzeTribus.com**

http://www.twelvetribes.org

Began: 1983 | Spiritual
Rural | Diet: Omnivorous

Near the southern border of France, in view of the Pyrenees Mountains, is the small village of Sus. Here are 140 people from many different backgrounds and nations who have been gathered together in the hope of demonstrating the life of love and peace that the Son of God came to establish on Earth. No longer lonely and alienated from one another in this society that holds up independence and materialism as its supreme gods, this little flock has become a tribe that works at different crafts and lives a simple life together, sharing all things in common just like the first disciples of Yahshua. Our community is made up of families with many children and single people who are living in two big houses on the same property. We earn our living making shoes, clothing, furniture and selling them at different markets and fairs in the whole of France. But besides running our businesses, our everyday life contains much activity: cooking, shopping, cleaning, and fixing houses and vehicles. We take to heart what God wanted for Abraham when He commanded Abraham to teach his children in the way of Yahweh. Therefore, parents teach their own children with the help of some friends who are gifted as teachers. They work together and help each other to raise children who will do what is right and just. We also do our best to include our children in our daily social life.

We are open to hearing from you by phone or letter, and we also invite people to come visit us. Our doors and our hearts are

Scissors [✂] at the end of a listing indicate that it was edited for length by the Directory editors and a longer description can be found at directory.ic.org.

open to you, so please come for a day or to stay …

Visitors Accepted [Mar2005][✄✂]

TWELVE TRIBES COMMUNITY AT PEPPERCORN CREEK FARM

1375 Remembrance Dr
Picton, NSW 2571
AUSTRALIA

+61-(0)2-46-772-668

http://www.twelvetribes.com/
whereweare/
peppercorncreekfarm.html

Began: 1987 | Pop. 51 | Spiritual
Rural | Diet: Omnivorous

Just one and a half hours south west of Sydney you'll come to our farm. We have 22 acres with a beautiful creek winding through it, and peppercorn trees dotted along the water's edge, hence the name Peppercorn Creek Farm. Eight families along with a number of single men and women live here.

The reason we are together is not to lead an alternative, self sufficient life in the country, but to simply be the way our God intended people to be, which is caring for and loving one another. We work hard with many building projects, but mostly we want to build up one another. That's our greatest project. We are thankful for the words our Master Yahshua spoke and the life He lived, and that we can be obedient to the things that have been recorded in the Bible. We are so grateful there is "a way" to follow, and that it works.

We gather twice a day where we play music, dance and speak what is on our heart. Then we always eat our meals together, and enjoy the fellowship that takes place.

If you were to walk around you may see goats being milked, chickens being fed, the garden being cared for, children swimming in the creek or being taught, the busy kitchen producing wholesome food and the endless pile of dishes, the firewood being cut, the lawns being mowed, etc.

There is so much that goes on as we lead our busy life, but we're never too busy to receive guests who desire to come and visit us. After all, that's why we're here. We're building our life so that many more who have the same heart and desires can come and be with us. We really would love to meet you.

Visitors Accepted: Please phone, write, email or just turn up. [Mar2005]

TWELVE TRIBES COMMUNITY AT STENTWOOD FARM

Dunkeswell (Near Honiton)
Devon EX14 4RW England
UNITED KINGDOM

+44-(0)1823-681155
community@stentwoodfarm.co.uk

http://www.twelvetribes.org/
whereweare/stentwoodfarm.html

Began: 1997 | Spiritual
Rural | Diet: Omnivorous

Since 1997 we have lived as a small community in the east of Devon on a little farm that needs a lot of restoration, just like our lives. We are here as a little light in the darkness, just beginning to shine here in Britain, a demonstration of God's kingdom on the Earth where human relationships are truly being restored. Living as one big family, we are learning to trust one another and be vulnerable, to share our hearts with one another and be personal. This is salvation to those of us who grew up in such a closed and hostile society as Britain. We are being healed of our hardness, learning to judge ourselves, and beginning to come back to being like we were created to be, to bear the likeness of our loving Creator, to love like he loves.

There are about eight families and several single people here, always busy fixing the house, caring for the chickens and goats, or working in our little bakery business, or getting on with the daily privileges around the house. You might meet us at one of the markets in the local towns around here or in the summertime at music festivals with our big mobile Café, called Common Ground, where we go looking to meet any others who are longing for a new, clean life free from compromise.

Please call, write, or feel free to visit.

Visitors Accepted: Contact us any way you can, or just turn up. We are always happy to have anyone come who would like to join in on our full time life to find out what it is all about. [Mar2005]

TWELVE TRIBES COMMUNITY AT STEPPING STONE FARM

Ben Shimon
RR 2 Box 55
Weaubleau, MO 65774

417-428-3251
benshimon@gmail.com

http://www.twelvetribes.org

Began: 2003 | Pop. 12 | Spiritual
Rural | Diet: Kosher

Here in southwest central Missouri, on the edge of the plains and the Ozarks, just outside of the small town of Weaubleau, you will find us living and working together on our small organic farm. We have the hope of establishing things the way they were meant to be, not just things like how to care for the sheep and goats and cows and chickens and geese and turkeys and bees or grow good food and pretty flowers in the greenhouse and gardens and orchard, but the really important things in life like how to be in our relationships. When it all comes down to it the most important things are our relationships with each other and with our creator, which is why we choose to live together. Our leader and teacher, the Son of God, went before us in this, showing us how to love by giving himself completely for our sake so that in following Him we could find the way. He is the center of our life together, where each individual is essential to form the whole. We are filled with vision for the life that is forming here, an organic life that fills our need for restored relations, because we need each other. This farm is not an end in itself, but rather a beginning. That is why we call it The Stepping Stone Farm, because we want what we build here to serve as a stepping stone for others and we are always glad when others are interested in participating in the rich life we share, or even just a visit to see. Our farm is also listed with the WWOOF program, so "WWOOFers" are always welcome.

Visitors Accepted: Just give us a call or email us ahead of time if possible, so we can give you directions and have a place prepared for you. [Mar2005]

TWELVE TRIBES COMMUNITY AT THE MORNING STAR RANCH

Dean Delozier
12458 Keys Creek Rd
Valley Center, CA 92082

760-742-8953, 760-742-0569
othniel1@earthlink.net
mevaser@earthlink.net

http://twelvetribes.com/
whereweare/morning-star-
ranch.html

Began: 2003 | Pop. 70 | Spiritual
Rural | Diet: Other

The entrance of the Morning Star Ranch is lined with palm trees, leading you through the persimmon orchard where the cows graze, past the goats and chickens to our red barn-shaped houses where you will find

Additions and corrections: email: directory@ic.org, *web:* directory.ic.org, *mail:* RR 1 Box 156-D, Rutledge MO 63563, USA.

247

us busily cleaning, cooking, sewing, teaching our children and watching the little ones, and washing the dishes. The road continues up the steep hill, past the pottery shop into the avocado grove where you will find the men working together under the trees or in the packinghouse sorting fruit for the market.

There are many different nationalities here sharing our home: French Canadian, Spanish, German, Mexican, Argentinean, all serving the same God with the same faith, in lasting friendships. In this new life the cultural barriers are being broken down. As the long-established cultures of the Earth are being left behind for the self-gratification of "Western culture," a brand new culture is emerging. Our common faith has brought us together to accomplish our Creator's work of restoration. The restoration of all things begins with this restoration of human relationships.

We would love to share our life with you. You can drop by for Friday night when we end our working week by bringing in the Sabbath with a festive meal, Israeli folk dancing, and singing with our whole hearts to the One who made us. Or come as a willing worker (a WOOFER). The gates of Morning Star Ranch are always open. Please come and see us!

Visitors Accepted: Please call, write or come by... [Mar2005]

TWELVE TRIBES COMMUNITY IN ARCADIA

601 W Oak St
Arcadia, FL 34266

863-494-3305, 888-893-5838
peaceriverfarm@commonsensecare
.com
aquila@commonsensecare.com

http://www.commonwealthofisrael.org

Began: 2002 | Pop. 24 | Spiritual
Small Town | Diet: Kosher

Nestled between the cattle ranches and citrus groves of southwest Florida is the quaintest little town called Arcadia. It's here that many people come to camp along the banks of the Peace River, whereas others like to canoe, meandering along as the river flows gracefully past cypress trees and oaks draped with Spanish moss. The beauty of our Creator is abundant here as one can appreciate His gift to man. As beautiful and wonderful as Arcadia is, especially along the Peace River, there are people who came here for more than enjoying the splendor of His creation. We have a community of people

here in Arcadia who live together for one common goal, to love our Creator and to love those created in His image. Our God has placed the Twelve Tribes communities all over the world and Arcadia happens to be one of the little spots chosen that means a lot to Him. He has chosen Arcadia to be one of His homes. And we of the community want to give ourselves to Him by loving those who seek Him and desire his life.

Visitors Accepted: Visitors are very welcomed. Please call or email ahead of time so arrangements can be made. Our gates are always open. [Mar2005]

TWELVE TRIBES COMMUNITY IN ASHEVILLE

Asheville, NC 28801

888-893-5838

http://www.twelvetribes.org

Began: 2005 | Pop. 20 | Spiritual
Diet: Kosher

We are currently in the process of getting a place in Asheville. In fact, by the time this goes into print, we will probably have a house there. Please check the website or call toll free to find out our current address. If you live in this area and would like to know more about our common life together, serving our Creator and one another, please contact us. We look forward to seeing you there.

Visitors Accepted: Please contact us. We always welcome visitors and love meeting new people. There is no time limit on staying with us. Come for a day or to stay. We just ask that our way of life is respected. We look forward to seeing you! [Mar2005]

TWELVE TRIBES COMMUNITY IN ASHLAND

Shemiah
Ashland, OR

760-295-3852, 760-631-1833
(Ask for Daveed)
david@parchmentpress.net

Began: 2004 | Pop. 10 | Spiritual
Diet: Omnivorous

We are forming a community after the pattern of the earliest believers in Acts 2 and 4; surrendering everything to the One who surrendered all for us, by coming together into a common life of love and unity. We have a small group of totally committed people already, and we are looking for those who hate their futile lives in this world, to

come into a new life with us in the Kingdom... a Kingdom ruled by love and unity through the power of the Spirit.

Visitors Accepted: Just call us and we will take great joy in hosting you! Please remember, though, that we are a community rooted in the ancient wisdom of the people of YHWH; visitors need to conduct themselves with respect for our life, faith, and traditions—modesty in dress, chastity outside of marriage, and one-man/one-woman, faithful, monogamous marriage are the norm here. Please come prepared to respect those boundaries. If you do, you can also expect to enjoy the standards of abundant hospitality common to ancient tribal cultures, after the model of our father Abraham. [Jan2005]

TWELVE TRIBES COMMUNITY IN BELLOWS FALLS

Ruth
PO Box 108
175 Basin Farm Rd
Bellows Falls, VT 05101

802-463-9264
basinfrm@sover.net

http://www.twelvetribes.org/
whereweare/bellowsfalls.html

Began: 1984 | Pop. 40 | Spiritual
Rural | Diet: Other

From nearby Fall Mountain overlooking Bellows Falls it's not hard to spot our farm—two green patches stitched together by a silver river onto the sleeve of town. We began as a small community in neighboring Westminster Station in 1984.

We are about 40 people, farming about 120 acres. We all live in a big farmhouse together, with plenty of room to share with you. We are growing and milling spelt (an ancient grain), vegetables (of all sorts), and some herbs. We love to work with the soil, the plants and animals, our greatest goal being to work in harmony with the Creator of all, knowing that what we do in cooperation with nature and her Maker will not cause harm, but bring healing to the land, and ultimately to the people who consume the fruit of the earth. We long to see restoration come about in all the aspects of life.

We welcome people of all ages, religions, and backgrounds to come visit. Our focus is our love for our God and our Master, Yahshua, and caring for people.

Visitors Accepted: If someone would like to visit they are welcome to call, write, email, or even stop by. We encourage visi-

Scissors [✂] at the end of a listing indicate that it was edited for length by the Directory *editors and a longer description can be found at* directory.ic.org.

248

tors to come and experience our life before becoming members. [Mar2005]

TWELVE TRIBES COMMUNITY IN BOSTON

92 Melville Ave
Dorchester, MA 02124

617-282-9876
bostoncommunity@verizon.net
commonsense.wfm@verizon.net

http://www.twelvetribes.com/
whereweare/boston.html

Began: 1981 | Spiritual
Urban | Diet: Omnivorous

Our growing community in Vermont had a hard time finding places to buy large quantities of food, so we sent people to Boston where the produce markets were bigger. We found that not only was food plentiful, so was the possibility of work. So, after taking council, we sent a delegation to the big city in hopes of starting a new community.

Eventually our community in Boston had doubled. We had 4 households and thriving construction, plumbing, and electrical businesses.

Living smack in the middle of the city, it was not hard to notice the many needy people around us. How we wanted them to understand the purpose of life on this planet, to know God's heart and experience a life of love and forgiveness. This inspired us to look for a place to open a restaurant where we could serve good, healthy food in a wholesome atmosphere and not only that, we could extend this marvelous life to all those on a quest for something more fulfilling than a mundane existence.

Eventually we found just the place on the edge of Lower Mills. Fathers and sons banded together to turn this old run down storefront into a beautiful Café and wholesome food market.

We are now only one household of about 25 people as many of the larger families were sent to more pleasant places for raising many children. After 20 years we still live in the original house we first had on Melville Avenue. We love working together in our Café and store, interacting with God's highest creation—human beings. We would be honored to host you! Come for a day, or to stay....

Visitors Accepted: Call and let us know when you would like to visit. Or you can just drop in at the Café in Lower Mills (2243 Dorchester Ave) to meet us where we work. [Mar2005][✂]

TWELVE TRIBES COMMUNITY IN BRUNSWICK

Maurice Welch
815 Albany St
Brunswick, GA 31520

912-267-4700, 912-399-3918
www.welmau@aol.com

http://www.commonwealthofisrael
.org

Began: 2001 | Pop. 40 | Forming | Spiritual

We are in search of the New Testament church. It is viewable in the book of Acts, chapters 2 and 4. Have you seen it? We believe it can be realized. Do you? If not, why? When the Son of God walked the earth he said to seek first His kingdom and his righteousness. We are a body of people who are doing this, with his help. Widows are cared for and the solitary are placed in families. In our life together we are seeing the things depicted in the pages of the New Testament come to life. Come and visit us for a short time or a lifetime.

Visitors Accepted: Just write us a letter or give us a call. [Mar2005]

TWELVE TRIBES COMMUNITY IN CAMBRIDGE

41 North Union St
Cambridge, NY 12816

518-677-5374

http://www.twelvetribes.com/
whereweare/cambridge.html

Began: 1997 | Spiritual
Rural | Diet: Omnivorous

We are a people who have fallen in love, having fallen in love with the one who is love... Yahshua, the Son of God. His love is contagious. When we heard the news of how he lived and died for us, it made us want to respond. We see that devoting our lives to him and his people is the appropriate response for what he did. We live together as a community of believers following his words and teachings daily. We are a part of a larger group of people, a spiritual nation, the Twelve Tribes. Our community in Cambridge, New York, is a farming community established in 1997. It is nestled in the rolling hills of the upper Hudson River Valley. It is called the Common Sense Farm, and here we support ourselves with a cottage industry that makes wholesome and practical personal-care products. This keeps our developing farm from coming under economic pressure to produce more than what is

normal and healthy—protecting our land and animals. We are young and old, families and single people, coming from different backgrounds, but we all have the same desire to love one another just as Yahshua loved us—caring for each other and giving up our time, our space, our belongings, even our own personal goals and ambitions. Whatever it will take to see his kingdom of peace and justice established here on Earth, now. Each new day is another opportunity to learn how to do this in our relationships with one another because that is where it all starts anyway, isn't it?

Please come visit us any time. You do not need to fill out an application. You do not need any money. Call, or write us a letter, or just drop in.

Visitors Accepted [Mar2005]

TWELVE TRIBES COMMUNITY IN CHATTANOOGA

316 North Seminole Dr
Chattanooga, TN 37411

423-698-6591

http://www.twelvetribes.org

Began: 1971 | Pop. 45 | Spiritual
Suburban | Diet: Kosher

In the summer of 2001, several families moved to Chattanooga from our New England locations in order to begin "again" here in this area. Chattanooga is actually the very location where our Community had its beginnings in the earlier 70s. Some remember us here as "The Yellow Deli people," because of the several restaurants we ran back then. Since our arrival back, other families as well as single people have moved here to increase our number as well as enhance our life. There are around 50 of us in number now, living in three houses, two with adjoining properties, on about 5 acres on Missionary Ridge. This is a historic ridge and over looks the city of Chattanooga.

We support ourselves by running several service-type industries including plumbing and electric, carpentry and landscaping.

We are part of the International group of The Twelve Tribes Communities.

You can find out more at our website.

Visitors Accepted: We welcome visitors and would love to correspond with those who are interested in our life. If you would like to visit, just call us or write, or even come by if you're in the area. [Mar2005]

Additions and corrections: email: directory@ic.org, *web:* directory.ic.org, *mail: RR 1 Box 156-D, Rutledge MO 63563, USA.*

249

Listings

TWELVE TRIBES COMMUNITY IN COXSACKIE

7 Ely St
Coxsackie, NY 12051

518-731-2181

**http://twelvetribes.org/
whereweare/coxsackie.html**

Began: 1997 | Spiritual
Urban | Diet: Omnivorous

Welcome to the sleepy village of Coxsackie. Preserved by neglect for 100 years, the old buildings stand tall just as in the yellowed postcards, frozen in time, waiting for loving hands to bring them to life again. Our community's vision is a long-term one, as we slowly fix up these buildings and restore their former glory.

As the buildings are slowly healed, we are also seeing healing in our personal lives and families, as we entrust ourselves to our Master Yahshua. Many of us had some major lacks in our foundations, but through the help of our brothers and sisters speaking the truth in love, we are being rebuilt into what we were created to be.

We own a beautiful but forlorn 3-story opera house called the Building Block next to the Hudson. The public will be able to travel up the river and dock their boat, and meander through waterfront gardens into the theater, where they will be inspired and enlightened by our own plays. For now, we endure the greater work of building patience in our hearts.

Next to this, a quaint building, formerly the Electric Co., now houses our print shop, which supplies printing to our industries and curricula for our children. There is also a 1850s storefront, once condemned, but now home to our families and our shoe store "Simon the Tanner."

Come by boat or by car. Our doors are always open. We love to share the hope we have. We're about 10 min. off the I-87 Thruway and the closest community to New York City. Come for a day or to stay!

Visitors Accepted: Give us a call at 888-TWELVE-Tribes or just show up! [Mar2005]

TWELVE TRIBES COMMUNITY IN HAMBURG

Eric Lansittle
2051 N Creek Rd
Lake View, NY 14085

716-627-2532, 716-649-2536

**http://www.twelvetribes.com/
whereweare/hamburg.html**

Began: 1993 | Pop. 36 | Spiritual
Small Town | Diet: Omnivorous

The life of the community in Hamburg

began in 1993 in East Aurora, New York, with a small household of people sent from Island Pond, Vermont. We have moved a few times since then and we settled in Lakeview, New York just outside Hamburg. As the early church did, our life centers around the one we follow, Yahshua, the messiah of the New Testament, and the love he gave us to pour out on each other. We devote our lives to him and to each other every day, sharing everything we have. All our time and energy are focused on caring for the community of those who believe in this love. In this same way the disciples our Master gathered lived and shared everything they had. They were set free to live this way after He rose victoriously over selfishness and its result, death. We have been set free to do the same. We have abandoned our individual lives and work together in various trades. We are about 50 people in one house and are always looking for ways to share the abundance of life that we have in our master. Many of us were searching for meaning to life and for real love. All of us needed to be forgiven and escape the trap of selfishness. We are thankful for the example our Master showed us. We know there are other people with the same heart, and we are looking to share what we have with them. This is a way of life that does away with the egocentricity of loneliness and arrogance of separation. We live a simple, normal, and uncommon life and wholeheartedly welcome anyone who wants to know their purpose.

Visitors Accepted [Mar2005]

TWELVE TRIBES COMMUNITY IN HYANNIS

Daniel MacAdam
14 Main St
Hyannis, MA 02601

508-790-1620

**http://www.twelvetribes.com/
whereweare/hyannis.html**

Began: 1991 | Spiritual
Urban | Diet: Omnivorous

Our family household has been here on the Cape, in Hyannis, Massachusetts, since 1991. We have numbered from about 80 people to less than 20 at times. It all depends on what is happening in our community as well as the many other communities of the Twelve Tribes to which we are vitally connected. You see, we live to meet the most pressing needs of the people we love, wherever they may be in our great Nation - The Commonwealth of Israel. We

live in a wonderful household where we share responsibilities and work together to meet the needs of the day. Our little restaurant, the Common Ground Café at 420 Main Street, is where we serve delicious, wholesome food and drink. We also have a tree care business we call Forest Keepers. This keeps us all very busy, but not so busy that we don't have time to take care of our goats and chickens. We are nothing fancy or showy, but we are so thankful to be alive and we love where we live. Our goal in life is to possess the substance of love so that we can lead a simple life of caring for our friends and in so doing serve our God, the God of Abraham, Isaac, and Jacob. We all have given up everything to do this and the result is the most challenging, satisfying, and fascinating life. We have life! We are part of an emerging culture, a Nation coming to birth that is a Nation of human relationships built on the solid foundation of selfless love. Please stop by.

Visitors Accepted: Call us. Or you can stop by our cafe or our household. We love having visitors and once we get to know each other a bit we can decide what would be best in terms of someone moving in. [Mar2005]

TWELVE TRIBES COMMUNITY IN IRÚN

Shimon
Caserío Barraca 88
20305 Irún
SPAIN

+34-(0)943632316
tribudeshimon@sentidocomun.net
shimon@docetribus.com

http://www.docetribus.com

Began: 1999 | Pop. 45 | Spiritual
Rural | Diet: Omnivorous

For ages, the Iberian Peninsula has been a bridge between cultures, continents, and seas. We are in the North in Guipuzcoa, Asturias and Burgos and in the South in Malaga. Our life in common unity has gone on well for many years because we have crossed a bridge. Loneliness lies behind; ahead is our future as one people sharing our lives together following the pattern of the first followers of the Messiah. (Acts 2 and 4 of The New Testament).

Yahshua is the bridge. In love with His message, each one of us has come out of the cultures, religions and traditions of whatever society we were a part of to form a new society where love rules and the restoration of basic human relationships is real. Love is

---

Scissors [✄] at the end of a listing indicate that it was edited for length by the Directory editors and a longer description can be found at directory.ic.org.

cleansing our hearts from their pollution. Our life together is the groundwork to put love into action caring for each other's needs.

You'll find us cultivating the land, fixing a windmill, baking pastries for a celebration, building a wooden cabin, preparing a skit, learning Hebrew dances, practicing music with our children or maybe selling organic maté and spelt bread at a market. Each busy "bee" buzzes around in the abundant activity of the beehive.

As the Friday evening shadows fall we gather to celebrate the Shabbat. Saturday we rest and keep on celebrating. Sunday we might have outdoor projects together and play volleyball if the weather is nice. If you wish to visit us don't hesitate to call or write. You won't have to pay to simply take part in our daily life. WOOFERS are welcome. Caserio Barraca is an organic farm 15 min. away from San Sebastian city. Welcome!

Visitors Accepted: Just come. [Mar2005]

TWELVE TRIBES COMMUNITY IN ISLAND POND

PO Box 449
Mountain St
Island Pond, VT 05846

802-723-9708

http://www.twelvetribes.org/ whereware/islandpond.html

Began: 1978 | Spiritual
Urban | Diet: Omnivorous

The Community in Island Pond began in 1978 and eventually we grew to 14 houses and over 300 people. We decided to spread out so over a period of time members were sent to different localities in New England and throughout the world. Presently we are two houses and about 40 people, ages ranging up to 82 years old. Island Pond is in a small valley surrounded by the beautiful green mountains of Vermont. Our main house is an old three-story railroad hotel that overlooks the town and a peaceful lake with an island in the center of it. We have a small business where we work together selling shoes and clothing. The primary purpose of our store is to create an environment where people can come and taste the love, the warmth, and the care of our master, Yahshua, by the way we serve them and by the way we relate to one another.

The purpose of our presence in Island Pond is to be a witness of the love and character of Yahshua the Messiah (Jesus Christ

of the Scriptures) by being of one heart and mind, working together to accomplish his will on this Earth. We live as one big family, sharing everything in common. We work for the common good rather than a paycheck. We submit to one another because the love of God has been poured into our hearts. We have abandoned our lives, as commanded in the Scriptures (our possessions, opinions, preferences, and independence), to do the will of God. We are not perfect, but we are growing in love for one another and Yahshua, who is the center of our life.

Visitors Accepted: Our doors are open 24 hours a day, and we invite you to come and visit us. [Mar2005][✂]

TWELVE TRIBES COMMUNITY IN ITHACA

Andrew Beeman
119 Third St
Ithaca, NY 14850

607-272-6915, 607-256-9770
yediydyah@tribaltradingcompany.com

http://www.twelvetribes.com/ whereware/ithaca.html

Began: 2001 | Pop. 55 | Spiritual
Suburban | Diet: Omnivorous

Ithaca is a multicultural hub in upstate New York. Within this "Melting Pot" there is a people who are forming a brand new culture. Stirring in their hearts is the desire to love as their Creator loves. This people live together in true community, learning to love, serve and forgive as a witness of the Creator's heart.

We here in the community in Ithaca are devoted to our Master Yahshua and to one another. We endeavor to show the care, warmth and hospitality of our Master. Although we do have shortcomings, we have hope to change, as we strive to properly represent the heart of our God.

Our large beautiful house is in restoration. Restoration is our Way, in all aspects of life. Our home and our lives are being restored. Because we love to work together, we have cottage industries, one of which is the Maté Factor, where we prepare a line of organic yerba maté tea. Another is our construction company, where we extend our restoration and building abilities to those in the surrounding area.

Our Café, located on the Ithaca Commons, is called The Maté Factor. Here we serve wholesome food and our favorite beverage in its various forms, and interact

with the local community, introducing them to our emerging culture.

We warmly invite you to come to our home any Friday at 6pm to celebrate the Sabbath with song and Israeli folk dancing, spontaneous expressions from our hearts, and a wonderful candlelit meal together. We also hold an open discussion "Rap Session" in our Café on Sunday nights at 8pm. We would love for you to come.

Visitors Accepted: Please call and let us know that you would like to come. We warmly invite any who are interested in our way of life and want to see what keeps us together! [Mar2005]

TWELVE TRIBES COMMUNITY IN KATOOMBA, BLUE MOUNTAINS

45 Waratah St
Katoomba
Blue Mountains
Sydney, NSW 2780
AUSTRALIA

+61-(0)2-47-82-9744

http://www.twelvetribes.org

Began: 2002 | Pop. 17 | Spiritual
Urban | Diet: Omnivorous

We are grateful to live in a World Heritage National Park near Sydney. It's very pretty up here... it's not hard to hear the voice of Creation when you visit the Blue Mountains. As you look into the valley at the beautiful blue haze or as you gaze at the cliff faces reflecting the sun—creation speaks. Many people come to the Blue Mountains to appreciate this voice—to wonder at the beauty in this unique area.

We too delight in this voice, and long to see the reputation of the One who created all of these things to be made right. We live our daily life in the small tourist town of Katoomba desiring that the Voice of our Creator be heard—through a people living together in a life of love and unity.

There are three families and a couple of single people. At present we're setting up our Café in the main street of town. It'll be called Common Ground. Our friends in the communities at Peppercorn Creek Farm and Oatlands support us for now. We are very grateful for them.

Our main desire is that we properly represent our Master Yahshua (the Hebrew name for Jesus), just like He perfectly represented His Father. Our goal is to love one another just as He loved us. We're not there yet, but we press on in the hope He has given us, judging our own selfish

Additions and corrections: email: directory@ic.org, *web:* directory.ic.org, *mail:* RR 1 Box 156-D, Rutledge MO 63563, USA.

Listings

Communities Directory

ways which come to divide us. His life and words were louder than that of the most beautiful sunset settling over the blue haze of the valley. We join in with the rest of Creation up here in the Blue Mountains proclaiming the goodness of our Creator—why don't you come and join us...

Visitors Accepted: Please phone, write or email us, or simply turn up. You are always welcome. [Mar2005]

TWELVE TRIBES COMMUNITY IN LANCASTER

12 High St
Lancaster, NH 03584

603-788-4376, 603-788-4379
lancaster@twelvetribes.com
lancaster@simonthetanner.com

http://www.twelvetribes.com/
whereweare/lancaster.html

Began: 1988 | Pop. 80 | Spiritual
Small Town | Diet: Other

Tucked away in the heart of the beautiful White Mountains of northern New Hampshire, you will find a cozy little town—Lancaster! Here within this town of about 2,000 people you'll find us—The Community in Lancaster! We are part of a new and emerging culture, The Twelve Tribes. Since we first moved to Lancaster in 1988, we have been slowly growing both in number and in our love for one another. We have nothing better to do than to love one another and care for each other's needs the same way that Yahshua, the Son of God did when he walked the earth. We are truly grateful for this abundant, rich life that he died to establish. In response to his great love for us, we spend our days together working, dancing, sharing, teaching, caring, playing music. Here in Lancaster we own and operate a shoe and clothing store by the name of Simon the Tanner. Nestled in one of the corners of the store you'll find one of our infamous Common Ground Cafés. Here, folks of all ages can come in for a wholesome sandwich, soup, salad or bread made fresh daily from wholesome ingredients. We also work together on construction crews—roofing, building, plumbing—you know, basic good, hard work. At home, you'll find us milking the goats, home-schooling our children, making cheese, renovating our houses, making quilts, washing lots of dishes, all with a thankful heart. Please, if you are ever in northern New Hampshire, stop by for a visit at the store or give us a

call at the house. We welcome you to come and witness the life that we speak of. We would love to get to know you!

Visitors Accepted: If you are interested in visiting, please give us a call, write us a letter or just drop in! [Mar2005]

TWELVE TRIBES COMMUNITY IN MANITOU SPRINGS, CO

966 Manitou Ave
Manitou Springs, CO 80829

719-573-1907, 719-685-5511
manitousprings@twelvetribes.com

http://www.twelvetribes.org

Began: 1972 | Pop. 40 | Spiritual
Small Town | Diet: Other

Ah, few things compare to the beauty of the towering and rugged Colorado Rocky Mountains. Although this land is rich in natural beauty and breath-taking views, even these highest mountains look on with envy at the majestic view of people living together actually loving one another. Our life is not free from problems, and we have our wrinkles to iron out, but the love of our Creator poured out into our hearts causes us to overcome what would separate us. We love our life of togetherness.

We are 8 families and about 15 single people. We train our children at home, cook meals for one another, work at our 24 hour Maté Factor Café, work on our Forest Keepers Tree Service, do construction work, and deliver organic produce. Above all, we strive to meet the pressing needs of one another.

We gather together morning and evening to sing, speak and worship. Our meals are taken together. We share all our finances, and work together. A priority is made of coming to a common understanding in areas where we may have problems with one another. We know that it is our unity that will prove to the world that the Father sent His Son. We are devoted to building each other up in love.

We love to have guests. We warmly invite you to visit us or to give us a call. Once we were alone, but now we are not. Once we were not a people, but now we are. Once we had not received mercy, but now we have mercy to give. Come visit us, where God's tender shoot is springing forth, becoming a mighty tree.

Visitors Accepted: Please contact us and get to know us. We would like to get to know you. Our foundation is friendship. We are here for you. [Mar2005]

TWELVE TRIBES COMMUNITY IN NELSON

202 Vernon St
Nelson, BC V1L 4E2
CANADA

250-354-2786, 250-359-6847
daveq@netidea.com

http://www.twelvetribes.com/
whereweare/nelson.html

Began: 2000 | Pop. 32 | Spiritual
Diet: Omnivorous

Beneath the beauty of Mt. Sentinel at the entrance to the Slocan Valley is the 130-acre farm where we are learning to cultivate right relationships between men and women, adults and children, us and the earth. Because of the love Yahshua the Messiah has shown us, we are experiencing the regeneration of our human purpose—to manifest the character of our Creator as a dwelling of His Spirit. The fruit of this is the expression of His heart; an environment that abounds with love, compassion, and understanding, allowing us to be healed in every aspect of our being.

Our desire is to see this life spread so that all who are seeking to find their "Ultimate Purpose" can have the opportunity to be joined to His people, where love loves, healing happens, and relationships grow deeper. You will be able to find us in the town of Nelson at our Cafe, The Preserved Seed, or at our farm, just outside of town. Please come to see us, or call for more information. We would love to share the life we have with you!

Visitors Accepted: Please feel free to call to arrange a visit. Or if coming to Nelson, visit our cafe, The Preserved Seed, at 202 Vernon Street to meet us in person. You can reach us at the cafe by calling 250-352-0325. [Mar2005]

TWELVE TRIBES COMMUNITY IN NORTHERN VIRGINIA

15255 Ashbury Church Rd
Hillsboro, VA 20132

540-668-7123, 540-668-7156
hillsborocommunity
@stoneybrookfarm.org

http://www.twelvetribes.org

Began: 2003 | Pop. 45 | Spiritual
Rural | Diet: Kosher

An hour west of Washington, DC, near the foothills of the Appalachian Mountains, our little farm sits peacefully along the twisting Catoctin Creek. Unless you walked through

Scissors [✂] at the end of a listing indicate that it was edited for length by the Directory editors and a longer description can be found at directory.ic.org.

the nearby town of Hillsboro during rush hour, you might not realize that the bustle and business of the nation's capitol continually pulses just a little more than an hour away.

As in all of the Twelve Tribes communities, we are a spiritual people. However, our emphasis is not on rites and rituals, but on love. To us, knowing God means walking in love. For this reason, we share all of our possessions in common and we choose to live together in households, where we can be in very close fellowship with one another.

Most everything we do, we do together. This includes working, eating, cleaning, and enjoying recreational activities. But we also hold on to traditional family values. We acknowledge the sanctity of marriage, and the proper rearing of our children as of the highest importance. We want our children to know that they are loved, and to understand the purpose for their lives.

Those of us here in the community share a very special life together as we are knitted together by a common cause: We fully believe in the goodness of our Creator, yet are persuaded that He deserves more than modern Christianity. However, our intention is not to be critical of the efforts of others, but to give ourselves to being a people who are full of life and care for their fellow man.

We have guests here often. We would love for you to come for a visit!

Visitors Accepted: If possible, please call or email first so as to help us be well-prepared with a place to stay, etc. [Mar2005]

TWELVE TRIBES COMMUNITY IN OAK HILL

Adam Mann
7871 State Rte 81
Oak Hill, NY 12460

518-239-4184, 518-239-8287
adam@twelvetribes.com
ammann58@gmail.com

http://www.twelvetribes.com/whereweare/oakhill.html

Began: 1997 | Pop. 80 | Spiritual
Rural | Diet: Omnivorous

Oak Hill is in eastern New York State in the northern foothills of the Catskill Mountains.

In the fall of 1997 a couple of families moved here with the vision of raising their children in a normal, healthy environment. We now number more than 80, inhabit three houses on the farm property and are

spilling over into others in the village. Our community is called Journey's End Farm.

Some of us work together on our farm, where our children are fully involved, planting and harvesting, caring for the animals, making cheese and yogurt. The "Wood Shop" is a cottage industry where we make custom doors, windows, molding, and furnishings. From this shop we also operate a construction industry. The most recent addition to our busy community is the newly renovated Oak Hill Kitchen, a Common Ground Café in the center of town, with a bakery, Café, and storefront for goods manufactured by our friends in some of our other communities.

The center of our life is our four households where we live together, eat together, praise together, and labor together. We maintain an environment where we can show hospitality to each other, care for and educate our children, and welcome visitors and guests.

Our future vision includes producing much more of the organic food we eat, developing alternative sources of energy, learning to make use of environmentally responsible and renewable sources, as well as recycling waste products as an energy source. We also plan to build a lodge for year-round festivals and celebrations.

Visitors Accepted: We love to have visitors and seekers spend time with us and we invite you to come and experience the rich life that we are experiencing every day. Please contact us by phone, email, or letter. [Mar2005][✂]

TWELVE TRIBES COMMUNITY IN OATLANDS

204 Pennant Hills Rd
Oatlands
Sydney, NSW 2117
AUSTRALIA

+61-(0)2-9630-9619

http://twelvetribes.org

Began: 2001 | Pop. 21 | Spiritual
Suburban | Diet: Omnivorous

We were sent out almost 4 years ago from what had been our home at Peppercorn Creek Farm in Picton, to establish another home closer to the city. Like a swarm of bees, we left the rolling hills of Picton to begin something new. We came here to establish a place just like the one we had left, where people could come and find a home, a family, a place to belong. Where they could be needed, loved, and taken care of, just as we had been.

We began as just one young family and a few single people, learning the value of hard work in establishing something new. Our Café in Rozelle and baking industry have steadily grown over the last 4 years, and so have we. We are now a young established community of two families with children and over a dozen single people who together cover the many needs of a Café, baking industry, and construction and demolition industry, as well as caring for the daily needs of the household and the children at home.

We are not many to meet so many needs, but this is teaching us to be flexible and to love one another in the midst of varying pressures, and most of all, to trust in our God who cares for us. In so many ways we see how our life together is perfectly designed by our God, not only to teach us invaluable lessons, but to heal and restore us back to being real human beings, who reflect the goodness and faithfulness of our wonderful Creator.

Our home is open to any who desire to see the life we live. That is the reason we are here. So, there is always room for more—just come and see!

Visitors Accepted: Please phone, write or email us, or simply turn up. You are always welcome. [Mar2005]

TWELVE TRIBES COMMUNITY IN PLYMOUTH

35 Warren Ave
Plymouth, MA 02360

508-747-5338
kharash@twelvetribes.com

Began: 1999 | Pop. 65 | Forming | Spiritual
Suburban | Diet: Other

On the coast of stony New England is the small town of Plymouth, MA. One of the oldest continuously inhabited towns in North America, it has never lost its small town identity. Out of respect for those early Separatists and their fellow settlers who came to build a new life for themselves in 1620, we in the Twelve Tribes seek to establish a true community of believers here.

We live in Plymouth as three households of around 75 people. Together we operate a wholesome food store and a busy construction firm that has us building and restoring homes and commercial properties all up and down the east coast. Soon we will begin renovations toward a Common Ground Café and Bakery in the heart of downtown Plymouth.

Our goal: to actualize the words of the

Additions and corrections: email: directory@ic.org, *web:* directory.ic.org, *mail: RR 1 Box 156-D, Rutledge MO 63563, USA.*

253

New Testament calling for a people devoted to loving others in word and deed. We base it all on the love of Yahshua the Messiah. Anyone coming through the area is invited to stop by for a visit, whether long or short.

Visitors Accepted: While advance notice is nice, it is not necessary. The richest aspect of our life happens on the weekends, but anyone can stay with us as long or as short as they like. [Mar2005]

TWELVE TRIBES COMMUNITY IN RUTLAND

134 Church St
Rutland, VT 05701

802-773-0160

**http://www.twelvetribes.com/
whereweare/rutland.html**

Began: 1993 | Pop. 45 | Spiritual
Urban | Diet: Omnivorous

Here in Rutland we are a small community nestled in the Green Mountains of Vermont. Rutland is a city that's just small enough to not lose touch with the natural beauty all around. Here in our community we have a Café and juice bar called the Back Home Again. This restaurant is the setting for us to work together and share our life with other interested people while at the same time providing good, health-giving food for our customers.

Upstairs we are opening a hostel to house hikers on the Appalachian Trail and Vermont's Long Trail, as well as other weary travelers. In this way many people will be able to stay with us, by working in our Café or paying a small fee.

Next door to the Café we are building a store to sell shoes and natural fiber clothing similar to some of our other communities.

Across town we have three houses where we all live together in harmony and grow vegetables in the summer in our terraced garden. Our houses adjoin in the back, giving us a very large backyard to gather together in and for our children to enjoy themselves in.

Feel free to visit us here in our "cluster," as we call it. Or come to our restaurant to see our community function together as a unit. The life we share is one of joy and purpose. As we see it, nothing else comes close. We would love to share our common life with you and tell you about the wonderful hope of a new start that we have found in Yahshua the Messiah. We are looking forward to meeting you!

Visitors Accepted: Call us to work out the details. [Mar2005]

TWELVE TRIBES COMMUNITY IN SAN SEBASTIAN

Eish
Paseo de Ulia 375
20013 San Sebastian
SPAIN

+34-(0)943-580029
ulia@docetribus.com
shimon@docetribus.com

**http://www.twelvetribes.com/
whereweare/spaincommunities.html**

Began: 1994 | Pop. 25 | Spiritual
Diet: Omnivorous

Our community of Mount Ulìa is located on the pilgrims' way called Camino de Santiago (St. James Way). We are a part of the Tribe of Shimon, one of the Twelve Tribes of Israel.

We enjoy our life together because we have been freed from worrying about our own needs. Now we live for a higher purpose: to bring our Saviour's kingdom on earth. We are no longer lonely but we are in a covenant of friendship, love and care, and we meet each other's needs. Our Master Yahshua makes it possible. We desire to live the way His disciples lived in the First Century. Now we share our lives together in obedience to His commandments, learning from the example of the early communities depicted in the Book of Acts.

The love of our Creator has set our hearts on fire to bring His rule of peace on the earth. We love our busy life where old and young alike are appreciated and necessary. You might find us doing our household chores, cooking, sewing, gardening or baking organic spelt bread and cookies that we sell in markets and at our "Common Sense" food store in downtown San Sebastian. We don't like rituals but we gather every morning and evening to dance and sing to our Creator, thanking Him for the restoration of our lives, which starts in our own hearts and extends to our marriages, families and friends.

You are really welcome here. Stay as long as you need to, to see if this is the life your heart has been longing for. Every Friday night at sunset we celebrate to welcome the Sabbath which is just a shadow of the age of peace that will come to the earth. You are invited.

Visitors Accepted: You are always welcome, night and day. It is better if you can phone us before you come. [Mar2005]

TWELVE TRIBES COMMUNITY IN SAVANNAH

223 E Gwinnett St
Savannah, GA 31401

912-232-1165, 912-232-9979

**http://www.commonwealthofisrael.
org**

Began: 2002 | Pop. 34 | Spiritual
Urban | Diet: Kosher

Under the shade of majestic live oak trees with spanish moss blowing gently in the breeze, is the beautiful historic downtown of Savannah, Georgia. Right on the coast, and very rich with history, many people visit here from all over the world. People look in awe at the beautiful Civil War-era mansions that line the streets. Right here, downtown, in one of these stately homes, lives a very humble and simple people. We are not the wealthy ones you might expect to find in such an area as this, but ones who have given up everything to live for and serve our Creator and one another.

We live downtown where our life can be seen by all, for we love this life we have been given and want to share it with all those seeking the real purpose for their lives. So here in this lovely home you won't find the rich and powerful, but you will find people loving one another, taking care of their children, cooking meals for each other, all working for the common good of all. We want people to see this life of love that is more amazing than anything else that has ever happened in this historic area. We want to invite you to come see for yourself. You are welcome to come visit anytime.

Visitors Accepted: Please contact us and let us know if you would like to visit. We love sharing our life with others. There is no time limit for staying as long as visitors are respectful of our way of life. We look forward to seeing you. [Mar2005]

TWELVE TRIBES COMMUNITY IN VISTA

Wade Skinner
2683 Foothill Dr
Vista, CA 92084

760-295-3852, 760-295-2177
mevaser@earthlink.net

**http://twelvetribes.org/whereweare/
vista.html**

Began: 2002 | Pop. 30 | Spiritual
Suburban | Diet: Omnivorous

Here we are in the town of Vista in a big house which is still under construction. We're

Scissors [✂] at the end of a listing indicate that it was edited for length by the Directory *editors and a longer description can be found at* directory.ic.org.

making the grass green and establishing a home for the lonely. If you come during the week you might work with us on getting our little garden planted, or fixing the fence the goats are always trying to knock down. For sure you would end up around the island in our kitchen, which seems to be the social center of our community.

We are so thankful to be together living to please our Creator. We like to play music and sing together. We like to have deep, meaningful conversations. What could be greater than connecting your heart to another? And we love our children! They are our future. They are involved in every aspect of our life.

Although our life has a deep spiritual foundation, you will not find it the least bit mystical. We are all engaged each day in meeting pressing needs. It could be cooking supper for our household, milking our goats, working on our construction crew, going to the farmers' markets to make friends and sell Yerba Maté, or working in our little print shop in our adobe building downtown. We plan to build a Café soon that will be a "Common Ground" where all will feel welcome to spend some time with us, eating good organic food and talking over a glass of Yerba Maté tea.

Visitors Accepted: Our doors are always open to visitors. We invite people from all walks of life to come for a visit or to stay. Please bring any of your friends or family. We hope that you will find what your heart has always longed for—a home and a purpose for your life. Give us a call or write, or just drop by... [Mar2005]

TWELVE TRIBES COMMUNITY IN WINNIPEG

**89 East Gate Dr
Winnipeg, MB R3C 2C2
CANADA**

204-786-8787

**http://www.twelvetribes.com/
whereweare/winnipeg.html**

Began: 1983 | Spiritual | Diet: Omnivorous

Our communal way of living is the result of obedience to the One who died and rose again to rescue mankind from their loneliness.

Day after day we work with each other in our industries and households, learning the practical application of love. One of our main industries here in Winnipeg is our machine shop. In this facility, we have built several portable Cafés for the many events we cater to in the summer.

We also own a Café in downtown

Winnipeg, a small but unique retreat from the city clamor, where people from all walks of life can enjoy the wholesome, organic food and peaceful atmosphere. That's why we call it The Common Ground.

We distribute herbal tea and natural body care products as well. The proceeds from our industries are used cooperatively to care for the needs of all. Our three large houses are located in a quiet residential area of Winnipeg known as the The Gates. In our homes we are always busy and we take all our meals together. Our children are the focus of our life. They are taught at home with those who are gifted teachers to make sure they get the academic training they need.

The hope we have received, and the healing we experience, compels us to extend it to others. For the lonely, dissatisfied or searching, there is a home in our midst and a family you can become a part of.

Visitors Accepted: We are most delighted to receive visitors at anytime whether in our homes or in our industries. Please call or visit us and we'll be glad to share more in detail of the life we live.[Mar2005][✂<]

TWELVE TRIBES COMMUNITY ON THE LAKE OF THE OZARKS

**Lev Zorav
1120 Lay Ave
Warsaw, MO 65355**

**660-438-4481, 660-438-3397
warsawed@earthlink.net
levzorav@parchmentpress.net**

**http://www.twelvetribes.com/
whereweare/warsaw.html**

Began: 1997 | Spiritual
Small Town | Diet: Omnivorous

In an unlikely town on the northern gateway to the Ozarks is a vibrant new life, community, culture. Here we are, a household of 40 or so; single people and families (children included). We live together out of our sincere trust and love for our Master Yahshua, the Son of the Living God, and for one another, valuing the pure and moral relationships that are the building blocks of enduring societies. How disappointed He would be to see the result of his life being just another religion, with just another church where people can go once a week to briefly acknowledge Him; but how enthralled he is to see a household full of friends, pouring our their energy every day, day after day, to care for one another in obedience to His commands.

We don't want to live with estrangement between us. Yes, there are problems, of

course there are when so many people live together, but one of the most important things that our Master said was to be in unity (Jn. 17:21), the one thing that so many intentional communities can't seem to attain. We strive for it. There is nothing more satisfying than sweet fellowship in enduring, life-long friendships. (Psalm 133)

Any time, any day, we would love to have you, for a short visit or to stay. It's up to you. I'm sure you will enjoy our household. This little town isn't big enough for our aspirations, it's just a springboard to the rest of the Midwest, from the Mississippi to the Rocky Mountains. We want to go everywhere with our Master Yahshua's life.

Visitors Accepted: Please call or write and let us know of your intention to visit. We welcome people to come and get to know us! [Mar2005]

TWELVE TRIBES COMUNIDAD EN BUENOS AIRES

**Batallon Norte 120 (esquina Mansilla)
General Rodriguez, Provincia de Buenos Aires CP: 1748
ARGENTINA**

**+54-(0)237-484-3409
sentidocomun@netpad.com.ar**

**http://www.twelvetribes.com/
whereweare/buenosaires.html**

Began: 1997 | Pop. 45 | Spiritual
Rural | Diet: Omnivorous

Our community here in Argentina began in 1997. We are a community of about 45 people and are located in a semirural environment, near the capital, Buenos Aires. Our main occupations are organic gardening, whole-wheat-bread making, and the development of alternative energy methods. We travel frequently to different parts of the country, selling wholesale natural foods and the products we make in our cottage industries at craft fairs. Our life together in community is a simple expression of the love we have for one another. The deep personal relationships we have with each other are being built daily through our common life in the community. Our community and our common life together are based on our obedience to the simple, clear teachings of our master, Yahshua, the Son of God. Our lives and relationships are being restored daily through our life of love.

Visitors Accepted: Please call or write or just come over. We invite and welcome all who are interested in our life and our community to come and visit. Our homes and our hearts are open to you. [Mar2005]

Additions and corrections: email: directory@ic.org, web: directory.ic.org, mail: RR 1 Box 156-D, Rutledge MO 63563, USA.

255

TWELVE TRIBES COMUNIDADE DE CURITIBA

Neriyah Nadiv
Rua Jornalista Caio Machado 291
Bairro Sta. Quitéria
Curitiba, Paraná 80310-430
BRAZIL

+55-41-555-2393, +55-41-274-8636
curitibacommunity@bsi.com.br
vrioverde@terra.com.br

http://www.twelvetribes.org

Began: 1997 | Pop. 47
Spiritual | Diet: Omnivorous

With the rooster's crowing and early morning bird songs, our farm community in the Curitiba area rises to meet the day, singing, dancing and harmonizing themselves with the One who created them. These "sons of God" are common folk who have left the ranks of the movie-minded, morally-decaying society, for the solid traditions of a culture designed by the God of Israel. Daily, with one mind, they strive to live out their ideals in the most practical way possible, cooking their food with wood fires, cultivating their fields with hoe and straw hat, and home-schooling their children. These are the people you would find at the farm, men and women of faith, full of hope for the future, trusting in their Creator for their daily bread and for the protection that comes from his hand.

Visitors Accepted: Please contact us to arrange a visit. We invite anyone interested in visiting or staying with us for awhile to please come. It's not an easy life we live, but our doors are open to all who have a sincere heart, looking for truth and true identity... [Mar2005]

TWELVE TRIBES COMUNIDADE DE LONDRINA

Ethan Meor
Rua Jayme Americano, 420
Jardim California
Londrina, Paraná 86040-030
BRAZIL

+55-43-3025-2066 (inside Brazil),
+55-43-3326-9664 (inside Brazil)
comunidadelondrina@dozetribos.com.br
ethanmeor@dozetribos.com.br

http://www.twelvetribes.com/
    whereweare/londrina.html

Began: 1989 | Pop. 100 | Spiritual
Diet: Omnivorous

Thirteen years ago, we left the declining social order of Brazil's northeastern coastal cities and its semi-arid plains to put down roots in rich soil and build a home in a land where we could practice what was in our hearts. So in the South, in a region of rich, red, volcanic soil, wide open valleys golden with wheat and rolling green hills fragrant with coffee blossoms, we began.

What started with fifty or so people has doubled into a farm community with its representation in the city. The well-established life of this community begins each day with an early-morning gathering, when we sing, dance and express what is in our hearts, having an open life with each other. We then work together in different areas of the farm, industry or commerce until the hour of our evening gathering, when we bring our day to a close. From dancing Israeli-style folk dances, making our own music, teaching children, working with the animals or in the field, to gathering wildflowers for our small beeswax candle industry, there is always lots of work to be done!

We are not perfect, but we're learning with our Creator, and the more we obey, the more is being revealed to us. In this very simple and pleasant life we live together, we are growing in respect and love for one another. We want to love like he, our Creator, loved us.

Come and visit us and spend a few days at our house! Contact us, and it will be a pleasure to receive you in our homes. We are always open and looking for the sons of God, those who will leave everything behind to follow Yahshua, the man today called Jesus.

Visitors Accepted: Anyone visiting the Community in Londrina would participate in the community's life, full time: wake-up time at 5:30 am, gathering, exercises, farming, candle-making, teachings, celebrations, Sabbath rest, etc. Anyone visiting should be a willing soul, indeed, because activities are non-stop until evening. [Mar2005]

TWELVE TRIBES COMUNIDADE DE OSÓRIO

Guidon Ben Naftali
Caixa Postal 95, Estrada do Mar,
Km 12,8
Osório, Rio Grande do Sul
95520-000
BRAZIL

+55-51-9817-3229 (cell phone)
comunidadeosorio@terra.com.br
guidon@dozetribos.com.br

http://www.twelvetribes.org

Began: 2004 | Pop. 17 | Spiritual
Rural | Diet: Omnivorous

Started just a year ago near the city of Osório, in the state of Rio Grande do Sul, our little community made up of three families, children and a few single people sits near a forest of tall, gnarled fig trees, windblown brambles and cactus.

We gather together with the rising of the sun and with its setting to sing, dance and hear the expression of each one's heart. Our daily lives are filled with the work of gardening, tending the sheep, milking Mimosa the cow, candle-making and leatherwork. On the very busy tourist highway that passes in front of our land we are setting up a kiosk as an outlet for our homemade products during the coming summer months.

Ever since we moved here, we have had the vision of living a self-sustaining lifestyle. We have planted a garden to grow our own vegetables and sown fields with various grains and manioc for our staples. For water, we drilled a well and are developing a Savonius wind pump to get the water up to our water box. Our house is illuminated at night by nine special neon bulbs fed by batteries charged with a solar panel, and our hot water comes from a coil built into our wood stove in the kitchen. Simple, but it all works...

But really, the true and amazing self-sustaining force that keeps us going is the love of God which was poured into our hearts. This energy is what gives us the inexhaustible courage to go on and build our community in love. All we really want is that others would experience and live out with us this wonderful life that we live. We wait for you, for a visit or to stay... all are welcome.

Visitors Accepted: You can just show up, or phone to tell us you are coming so we can make sure we have a place for you to stay... We love visitors, especially those with a heart to do what we are doing! [Mar2005]

TWELVE TRIBES GEMEINSCHAFT IN KLOSTERZIMMERN

Gemeinschaft in Klosterzimmern
86738 Deiningen, Bavaria
GERMANY

+49-(0)9081-290-1062

http://www.zwoelf-staemme.de

Pop. 120 | Spiritual | Rural
Diet: Primarily vegetarian

A very long time ago—so they say—a huge meteorite shot out of the universe, hit the earth, and through its impact created an amazing valley where our farming community is located: the Ries crater in Bavaria

Scissors [✂] at the end of a listing indicate that it was edited for length by the Directory *editors and a longer description can be found at* directory.ic.org.

with its rich soil. Before we came here we used to live like most everyone else: working, going to school, trying to make it in the system, trying to believe in a cause or in God. But whatever we did, it left us feeling empty, lonely, and searching for our purpose in life and for true love. When we almost despaired we met a people who lived a common life, who loved and encouraged one another daily, and forgave each other for their mistakes and shortcomings. Through the witness of this life of a true brotherhood God's love became tangible to us for the first time. Realizing His love for us had the impact of a meteorite on us and changed our lives completely: We left behind our old lives, careers, and our selfish ambitions in order to gain this new life that God was establishing on the earth.

Our days are now filled with caring for one another and for our children, cooking, sewing, working in the fields, and restoring this old farm estate. In the mornings and evenings, we gather to sing and dance, and to hear the prophetic word which inspires us to become closer friends with Him and one another. We would love to share our common life, our hope and vision with you and are looking forward to meeting you!

Visitors Accepted [Mar2005]

TWIN OAKS COMMUNITY

138 Twin Oaks Rd
Louisa, VA 23093

540-894-5126
twinoaks@ic.org

http://www.twinoaks.org

Began: 1967 | Pop. 100
Rural | Diet: Omnivorous

Twin Oaks is an income-sharing community of 100 people living on 450 acres of farm and forestland in Virginia. We were founded in 1967, and our lifestyle reflects our values of egalitarianism, ecology, and nonviolence. We welcome scheduled visitors throughout the year.

We are economically self-sufficient. Members work in our community businesses—making hammocks and chairs, indexing books and making tofu. These businesses provide about one-third of our work; the rest goes into the tasks needed to support a rural village of 100 people— organic gardening, milking cows, equipment and building maintenance, office work, and more. Our work schedules are very flexible.

Twin Oaks has an intricate community culture. Our everyday lives include many recreational activities—social and support groups, performances, music, games, dance, and art. Our culture values tolerance of diversity and sustainable living. We share our vehicles, we build our own buildings, and we share houses of 10-20 people. Some of us work actively for peace and justice, ecology, and feminism. Each summer we host a Women's Gathering and a Communities Conference; see our website for details.

We offer a three-hour tour on many Saturday afternoons; please call during business hours or email to reserve a place. Our three-week visitor program is a prerequisite for membership and must be arranged by letter or email well in advance of the proposed stay. Information about visiting is available on our website or by mail.

Visitors Accepted: Read our website visiting section and then correspond with us to arrange a Saturday tour and/or a 3-week visit. Arrangements must be made well ahead of any visit. [Feb2005]

TWO ACRE WOOD

680 Robinson Rd
Sebastopol, CA 95472

707-824-0830, 707-829-9191
martyr@sonic.net
maryru@sonic.net

Mary Ruthsdotter
707-824-6844

**http://www.cohousing.org/
    specific/two_acre_wood/
    welcome.html**

Began: 1994 | Pop. 35
Small Town | Diet: Primarily vegetarian

Two Acre Wood Cohousing is a community in the traditional cohousing mold. We are generally all politically progressive and environmentally conscious and interested in learning to live together in a supportive, loving community with lots of room for individual differences. We have no official philosophy.

We moved into our brand new homes in the summer of 1999. So far none of the units have been sold (Jan, '05). But we do have one or two possible rental homes. We will be maintaining a list of people who might be interested in purchasing or renting a unit should one become available.

Visitors Accepted: An email to one of the addresses given would be a good start. We are a small community and so far have had no homes up for sale, so we don't encourage a lot of visitors looking to live in cohousing, but are certainly open to visitors if you are interested. [Feb2005]

Additions and corrections: email: directory@ic.org, web: directory.ic.org, mail: RR 1 Box 156-D, Rutledge MO 63563, USA.

TWO ECHO COHOUSING

93 Echo Rd
Brunswick, ME 04011
info@two-echo.org

Enid Sharp
207-798-4823
enid@two-echo.org

Katie Clark and Rob Wiener
207-729-1071
karo@two-echo.org

http://www.two-echo.org

Began: 1991 | Pop. 80
Rural | Diet: Omnivorous

92 rural acres. 27 clustered lots surrounded by protected woods and fields. Singles, couples, children, seniors. Traditional New England village architecture, individually designed. 25 homes built, 1 starting, 1 lot for sale. Common House opens May 2005. 15 minutes from downtown Brunswick and Bowdoin College.
Visitors Accepted: Phone or email us. [Mar2005]

UFA-FABRIK

Sigrid Niemer
Internationales Kultur Centrum
Viktoriastraße 13
12105 Berlin
GERMANY

+49-(0)30-755-03-0,
+49-(0)30-755-03-116
info@ufafabrik.de
sigrid.niemer@ufafabrik.de

http://www.ufafabrik.de

Began: 1976 | Pop. 38
Urban | Diet: Omnivorous

In the summer of 1979, over 100 people took over the desolate grounds of the former UFA-Film studios, creating a comprehensive work and living project for innovative social, cultural, and ecological lifestyles. We now have 30 resident members (ages 1 month to 90 years) and about 160 employees. Our four-acre site, leased from the city, includes a bakery, an organic market, an international Café, two theaters and an open air stage in summer, a guesthouse, a neighborhood center, and an animal farm.

We host a wide variety of classes, a free school, a circus school, Germany's number one samba band "Terra Brasilis," an ongoing ecology exhibition, and an International Theatre Festival in alternate summers.

The urban village of 18,000 square meters (approximately four acres) is divided into various areas. The spirit of enterprise you can discover here encourages people's involvement and has inspired many to take chances in their lives. In 2004 the ufaFabrik was honoured by the UN-Habitat as one of 100 projects worldwide that got the status "Best Practice to Improve the Living Environment."
Visitors Accepted: We don't have a special programme for guests. If someone wants to visit us, he can book a room in the guesthouse and try to arrange an interview with one of the members. There is no possibility to work with us for a short time.

In general the area welcomes guests every day from 10 am up to the night (Café, theatre etc.). [Mar2005]

UNION ACRES

654 Heartwood Way
Whittier, NC 28789

828-497-2869, 828-497-4964/0060
swasapp@earthlink.net

http://www.unionacres.org

Began: 1989 | Pop. 34 | Spiritual
Rural | Diet: Omnivorous

In the mountains of Western North Carolina, Union Acres is one hour west of Asheville on 80 acres with views and streams—24 residential lots and 7 acres of common land. Union Acres is based on Earth stewardship with consensus decision making and community service. Our stated purpose is to live as neighbors in peace and ecological balance with respect to one another and all life. Our members are diverse in backgrounds, ages, occupations, and interests. We are building a community building and have a garden, picnic shelter and seasonal pool in our meadow.

Eclectic spirituality is accepted and expressed. We are family oriented with approximately 23 adults and 11 children. Interests and activities include a food co-op, gardening, potlucks, and homesteading. Some members horseback ride, kayak, canoe, hike, Peace Dance, contradance, and meditate.

Other members have plans to develop a nearby retreat center as well as a cohousing group within our community for retired individuals. A wonderful, creative Charter School has opened nearby for grades K-8th.

Visitors must email and/or call before coming. There are three lots for sale now. Interested people would need to be able to purchase a lot and build a home. Info packets $7.
Visitors Accepted: Email us and send a biography of you and your interest. Plan a visit by email and/or phone. [Nov2004]

UNIVERSITY STUDENTS' COOPERATIVE ASSOCIATION

2424 Ridge Rd
Berkeley, CA 94709

510-848-1936
housing@usca.org

http://www.usca.org

Began: 1933 | Pop. 1250
Urban | Diet: Omnivorous

The University Students' Cooperative Association (USCA) is the largest student housing cooperative in North America, housing over 1,200 people. Although a private nonprofit corporation, the USCA works in cooperation with the University of California to provide housing for its students.

About 900 of the USCA's members live in room-and-board houses scattered around the Berkeley campus, including 17 large houses that each function as a separate cooperative household with elected managers for room assignment, work organization (housekeeping, food service, etc.), and maintenance. A central support staff of about 25 nonmembers provides technical information to members and oversees day-to-day administration (such as housekeeping applications and organizational financing). We also provide warehousing and support services to individual house food programs. [Jan2005]

UPPER APPLEGATE COMMUNITY

Robert Murray
RR 1 Box 1824-1
Couch, MO 65690

417-938-4606
upperapplegateministries@yahoo.com

http://www.angelfire.com/mb2/
  radamacher

Began: 1998 | Pop. 20 | Spiritual
Rural | Diet: Primarily vegetarian

Upper Applegate Community is a Counter Culture Rainbow Christian Community located on 42 acres of land in Southern Missouri, 18 miles outside of Thayer in Oregon County. We are in the Ozarks and it

---

Scissors [✂] at the end of a listing indicate that it was edited for length by the Directory *editors and a longer description can be found at* directory.ic.org.

is very beautiful here. All are welcome to come and visit us and help us on the land. We are vegetarian and are very much into organic farming. We have a Biblical Hebrew School here and all are free to attend. We help the homeless with shelter and we provide food to the hungry. We provide help and counselling to anyone fighting to overcome an addiction and we do have a very high success rate in this area. We have several free campouts and gatherings every summer and they are alcohol free. For more information send us an email or give us a call. Feel free to contact us anytime. God Bless all of you and have a wonderful day. Peace be with you. Jesus Rules!!!!!

Visitors Accepted: Send us an email or give us a call and visit our website. [Jan2005]

UTAH UNITED ORDER

Bradley Anderson
unitedorder@thehomesteadresource
.com

http://www.thehomesteadresource
.com/custom.em?pid=225775

Began: 2005 | Forming | Spiritual
Rural | Diet: Omnivorous

Just a listing of a potential place to start a community in West Box Elder County where currently there are large tracts of land available cheaply.

I am thinking of developing something along the lines of the early Co-op, stewardships or Full United orders that Brigham Young established in Utah.

Visitors Accepted: We are still looking for people who want to help develop it. [Mar2005]

UTOPIAGGIA

Villa Piaggia
I-05010 Montegabbione (TR),
ITALY

+39-347-348-78-05
schibel@tin.it

Began: 1975 | Pop. 18
Rural | Diet: Omnivorous

We are an anarchic humanitarian commune living as ecologically as possible with the land. The community started in Lower Bavaria in 1975 and moved to central Italy in 1982. Many of the founding members came out of the movement of the 1960s. There are 15 adults and 3 adolescents and children living in three houses on 100 hectares of hilly land. A large flock of sheep

provides the basis for commercial cheese production. We keep horses and poultry, and among the activities we are engaged in, there are pottery and other handicrafts, as well as language courses (Italian, German, English). There are openings for new members. Visitors are always welcome but should write first.

Visitors Accepted: Write us well in advance and wait for our reply. [Mar2005]

UTOPIAN VISIONS

Ray Arrowood
arrowoody@yahoo.com

http://www.utopian.50megs.com

Began: 2004 | Pop. 1 | Forming

UV is an aquatic living experiment due to launch in the spring of 2005 on Lake Cumberland in Kentucky. The initial floatation platform will house 4 people, and be expanded as necessary as the community grows.

The goal is zero negative impact on the environment, and 100% self-sufficiency in food/power production. Vegetables will be grown in self-watering floating containers and protein supplied by fishing. Wastes will be minimized and 100% recycled on board. See the website for power production information.

Volunteers are needed for moving and assembling the modular floatation platform this coming spring. Volunteer and earn your place in the core group.

Visitors Accepted: Please write to make arrangements for visiting, and I will pick you up at the dock and transport you to the community floatation platform. [Nov2004]

THE V2B COOPERATIVE

Rob Martin
135 Wisconsin Ave
Waukesha, WI 53186

262-853-2339
info@v2b.org

http://www.v2b.org

Began: 2004 | Pop. 20 | Forming
Urban | Diet: Other

The v2b Cooperative is a project designed to encourage and support cooperative liv-

ing and working in SE Wisconsin. The cooperative is organized to provide the greatest positive effect on creating and maintaining living spaces that maximize quality-of-life and efficiency for Co-op members (housemates).

We're currently forming, but moving along quite nicely with an anticipated move-in date of fall 2005. As of the beginning of February, we have our legal documents in final draft form, and financing well organized; we're ready to make an offer on our building and approach the city for variances and approvals.

Visitors Accepted [Feb2005]

VAIL HOUSE

House President
602 Lawrence St
Ann Arbor, MI 48104

734-996-5960

http://www.icc.coop

Began: 1960 | Pop. 23
Urban | Diet: Omnivorous

Welcome to Vail, located in a 150-year-old adobe (Ask us about it!!!) Greek Revival house just five minutes from central campus, as well as near a North Campus bus stop. We have three porches, several computers, laser printer, cable TV and VCR, stereo, piano, one of the oldest oak trees in Ann Arbor, and hardwood floors. Outside we have a bike shed, basketball hoop, a clean compost pile, and a garden in our giant backyard. We serve meat meals 4 times per week and always have vegetarian alternatives. Stop by for dinner anytime at 6 pm!

Visitors Accepted: Contact House President. [Mar2005]

THE VALE

PO Box 207
Yellow Springs, OH 45387

937-767-1461, 937-767-1511
info@communitysolution.org

http://www.smallcommunity.org/
vale.asp

Began: 1960 | Pop. 40
Rural | Diet: Omnivorous

The idea for The Vale began in 1946 when Jane and Griscom Morgan invited a family to share their home on 40 acres of land two miles south of Yellow Springs. In 1950 the second house was built and more followed. Now there are 11 homes and 20 members. The group incorporated as The Vale in 1960.

Additions and corrections: email: directory@ic.org, *web:* directory.ic.org, *mail:* RR 1 Box 156-D, Rutledge MO 63563, USA.

Listings

Gris and Jane felt strongly that land should be shared, and not used as a commodity, so in 1980 they donated the land to the Community Service, Inc. Land Trust, from which it is leased by The Vale. Seventeen of its wooded acres were put into a conservation easement, so they would never be built upon. From the beginning, The Vale has had a strong interest in children, thus, after the founder's children left, new families with children joined. Each family lives in its own home, but many share space with additional people. Most families earn their livelihood outside the community. The land, woods and common areas, utilities, and a half mile gravel lane are managed together. Gardening is important to many members. Prospective members must live at The Vale for at least one year before applying for membership. At the moment The Vale has no openings for renting or for building.

Business is decided by consensus. Business meetings are usually every month, with the addition of seasonal get-togethers.

Visitors Accepted [Feb2005]

VASHON COHOUSING

10421 SW Bank Rd #20
Vashon, WA 98070
206-463-4053

Tim Morrison
206-463-2945
moday4@yahoo.com

http://www.vashoncohousing.org

Began: 1989

We are a cohousing community of 20 families occupying 18 detached residences (16 single-family units and 2 duplexes). We are located a quarter mile from the Vashon town center. Vashon is an Island in Puget Sound, and is about 40 minutes (by a combined bus or car and ferry trip) from Seattle.

Visitors Accepted: To arrange a visit, contact Tim Morrison at the email address given above. [Oct2004]

VENTANA VERDE

Cardie
1959 Estes Rd
Los Angeles, CA 90041

323-370-3250, 323-344-3967
info@oilcloth.com

Began: 2003 | Forming | Rural | Diet: Other

Lo de Marcos, Nayarit, Mexico - 5 partners, private homes to be built, common house

and shared infrastructure, community being formed. [Mar2005]

VILLAGE COHOUSING

1104 Mound St
Madison, WI 53715

Art and Sue Lloyd
608-256-7250
aslloyd@mailbag.com

Stephanie Fassnacht
608-262-5370
fassnach@ssc.wisc.edu

http://www.designcoalition.org/
    current/currentp/village/
    mm_wsj.htm

Began: 1992 | Pop. 35
Urban | Diet: Omnivorous

Village Cohousing is an urban infill community, built on 1/2 city block just south of the University of Wisconsin – Madison. Most of our 35 members moved in in 1999. Our ages span several generations, from 1 to 86 years old.

Visitors Accepted: Send email to fassnach@ssc.wisc.edu, aslloyd@mailbag.com, or amychris@merr.com [Nov2004]

VILLAGE OF HARMONY

Mike Jones
221 Juardo Ave
178 CR 51
Bosque, NM 87006

505-379-6208
voh4love@yahoo.com
villageofharmony@juno.com

http://www.geocities.com/voh4love

Began: 1993 | Pop. 8 | Spiritual
Rural | Diet: Omnivorous

We are a small community formed in 1995. Our focus is love, peace, harmony, seeking joy in all aspects of life. Village of Harmony is located 55 miles south of Albuquerque, NM on a desert mesa surrounded by mountains. We are five miles east of the Rio Grande River and a wetlands preserve. The weather is mild year round, sunny with low humidity. We build alternative houses and some of us live in small trailers, etc. Most use solar electricity and live very simply. At present we are all over 40 years old and have no children, but we are open to families and younger people. Some of us even grow some of our own food. We attempt to live in harmony with all things and strive to be debt free. Some of us work part-time

jobs and some of us are on disability. All of us are very independent and own our own places. We are open to new members and can help others find inexpensive building lots and achieve self-sufficiency. One of our members has just donated 2 acres that is community property and is open for someone to develop for their own house along with our new community center, etc. All of our members currently are on their own lots. Write for other information and directions.

Visitors Accepted: Email, write or call for directions and date of visit. [Mar2005]

VILLAGE TERRACES COHOUSING NEIGHBORHOOD

Lee Warren
Earthaven Ecovillage
1033 Camp Elliott Rd
Black Mountain, NC 28711

828-669-4328
villageterraces@earthaven.org
lewarren@buncombe.main.nc.us

http://www.earthaven.org/
    village-terraces

Began: 2000 | Pop. 9 | Spiritual
Rural | Diet: Omnivorous

Village Terraces is a neighborhood "pod" within Earthaven Ecovillage. Our vision is to create extended family and a deep connectedness to the earth, ourselves and each other. As the first cohousing group at Earthaven, we are building and living densely in order to share resources, including common space. We currently share living space in our first of four buildings, which house 9 adults and 4 children, a business and our spacious common spaces.

We will eventually share the neighborhood with 24-30 adults plus children. The cohousing style provides private "apartments" which can include private kitchenettes and baths, with the added benefit of shared common spaces such as a large common kitchen and bath, common gardens, orchards, and a goat yard. We also have access to Earthaven's Council Hall and other community facilities, as well as shared use of most of Earthaven's 325 acres.

We value:
• A deep respect for the land and each other, acknowledging the Oneness of all things.
• A desire to raise children together in a neighborhood and village context.
• Honest and responsible communication

Scissors [✂] at the end of a listing indicate that it was edited for length by the Directory *editors and a longer description can be found at* directory.ic.org.

and an active willingness to resolve conflicts in a healthy manner.

- A commitment to consciously and lovingly raising both plants and animals for food.
- Love and acceptance of our bodies.
- Cooperative living in common walled buildings built with materials from our land.

Visitors Accepted: Please visit Earthaven's website at www.earthaven.org and make sure that this sounds like a place you are interested in. Make an appointment to visit Earthaven through email to info@earthaven.org. If you are interested specifically in visiting Village Terraces please email or call us with the dates you are visiting Earthaven and we will make an appointment for a tour of Village Terraces Cohousing Neighborhood. [Mar2005]

VINE & FIG TREE CENTER FOR SUSTAINABLE CULTURE

11076 County Rd 267
Lanett, AL 36863

334-499-2380
vineyfig@mindspring.com

http://vineyfig.home.mindspring.com

Began: 1986 | Rural

The original Vine & Fig Tree was formed in 1986 as a land-based community in rural Alabama, with a vision of people living "in loving Gandhian nonviolence among ourselves and with all creation." Although this community was successful in many ways (11 adults and kids at peak, two home-birthed children, growing much of our own food, hosting peace/justice gatherings, etc), it dissolved in 2000. Two of us now plan to re-start the community, holding to that same vision but with a new emphasis on working toward a truly sustainable local economy, with both food and energy self-sufficiency. We believe that the impending peak of world oil production capacity, along with the ecological damage caused by our current culture's addiction to high-energy lifestyles, makes it imperative for us to learn how to live simply, on current solar income—which we believe can only be accomplished by committed people living together in a cooperative community. We want to do this not only for ourselves, but to serve as a model and demonstration/ learning and service center for the surrounding area. That is, to become a "preservationist community," not merely a "survivalist community." (See Richard Heinberg, Powerdown,

chapter 5.) Although our name comes from Scripture (Micah 4), we do not intend to be a "religious" community. However, we believe that celebrating authentic spiritual traditions and the arts are as important as (or inseparable from) sustaining physical life.

Visitors Accepted: Preferably, write us a longish letter explaining who you are, your background, skills, strengths and weaknesses, etc, along with why you think Vine & Fig Tree might be the place for you. At a minimum, call us ready to discuss the above. Thanks! [Mar2005]

VIVEKANANDA MONASTERY AND RETREAT CENTER

6723 122nd Ave
Fennville, MI 49408

269-543-4545
vedanta@datawise.net

Began: 1960 | Pop. 7 | Spiritual
Rural | Diet: Primarily vegetarian

Vivekananda Monastery is just two things. First, it's an ashram. Second, it's an educational institution dedicating to teaching what an ashram is all about: inner development aimed at discovering the Divine, within and without.

Visitors Accepted [Feb2005]

VLIERHOF

Mofwoofoo, Anatosh, Tarunai, Caroline, Tineke, Annalise, or Theo
Postbus 33
6566 ZG Millingen ad Rijn
NETHERLANDS
+49-(0)2821-970242
info@vlierhof.nl
bagelhole1@aol.com

http://www.vlierhof.nl

Began: 2002 | Pop. 10 | Spiritual
Rural | Diet: Primarily vegetarian

A farm, 3.7 hectares on the border of Germany and Holland, walking distance from the Rijn River, just inside Germany near the village Keeken and the border town Millingen in Holland.

We're interested in sustainability, wellness, artistic expression, relating compassionately, health, and organic living.

Currently, 10 people live here and we are working to make it available as a Care Farm for people who need the healthy environment of a farm to improve. We have an acre

to grow organic vegetables, currently 7 chickens, and about 11 sheep, an area for art projects, rebirthing, and massage.

Some of us are living in caravans and others in a large, old farmhouse. Most people are Dutch, with 3 Polish workers, and 1 American. Age ranges from 33 to 67.

We are studying nonviolent communication (cnvc.org) by Marshall Rosenberg, once a week.

We eat lunch and dinner together. We are now installing a heating system that involves burning huge amounts of firewood and heating water to flow thru the walls. There are other construction plans underway to create more living space and room to accommodate groups and festivals. We are also building a large greenhouse now, will have a duck garden, and eventually a heated pool.

Visitors and volunteers are welcome and those who would like to see if they would fit in here to live. We particularly could use someone musical for improv. singing, someone with computer knowhow, and maybe a ceramicist, or whatever.

Visitors Accepted: Please contact us by email, phone, or letter. [Jan2005]

VOICE FOR THE VOICELESS

Isaiah Micah Shiloh
IsaiahShiloh@yahoo.com

Began: 2005 | Forming | Spiritual
Small Town | Diet: Vegetarian only

Seeking to form a community of dedicated Christians committed to advancing a change in the human paradigm. Specifically, ending humanity's self-serving notion that exploitation of animals is acceptable in civilized society.

At various times in human history slavery was acceptable, females were considered second class citizens at best, and exploitation of children was routine. Not only was each injustice accepted by society, they were supported through misuse of the Scriptures, just as animal abuse enablers use the "God gave man dominion over the animals" defense to defend the indefensible. Yes, the word is "dominion" (as in good stewardship) not "domination."

Only idealistic workers who are driven by the dream please. One person of conviction is worth 99 who are merely intrigued by an idea.

How will our ideals be realized? Through activism directed toward educating the public about the cruelties animals silently endure at the hands of God's most violent creation—human beings. Leafleting,

Additions and corrections: email: directory@ic.org, web: directory.ic.org, mail: RR 1 Box 156-D, Rutledge MO 63563, USA.

261

Listings

protesting, writing, picketing and most importantly prayer. Prayer would be integral to the mission—the straw that stirs the drink.

Establishment of an animal rescue mission and sanctuary would also be a long term goal. Environmental and social justice issues will be addressed as the Holy Spirit leads.

So if you are tired of averting your eyes from the injustice and suffering that abounds all around us, and are being Holy Spirit led to do something about it, I would enjoy hearing from you. [Feb2005][✂]

THE VOL COMMUNITY

836 W Cleveland St
Fayetteville, AR 72701

479-575-0567
information@volcommunity.org
http://www.volcommunity.org

Began: 1978 | Pop. 4
Rural | Diet: Primarily vegetarian

The VOL Community is a spiritually oriented community whose emphasis is on self-realization and self-sufficiency, located on 49 acres in a secluded valley. Projected land use includes separate areas for community activity, residences, and cropland/pasture.

Goals: Create a time/space where the self-realization of each member is fully supported and nurtured. Live in harmony with each other and nature. Share spiritual life together. Flow with universal energy so all actions are appropriate. Become self-sufficient so that conditions "outside" have little effect on the community.

Notes: The community is egalitarian. The structure consists of goals, membership rights, and agreements. There is a three-month to one-year trial membership period (by consensus). The diet is basically vegetarian. Planned: homeschooling, cottage industries, separate sleeping quarters for each family: all other facilities are communal. The VOL Community is a "multi-spiritual path" community, open to all people regardless of age, sex, race, or ideol-

---

IC Web Site

Intentional Communities on the Web
Your home for community.

www.ic.org

---

ogy, according to consensus of current members.

Visitors Accepted: Read our website thoroughly, email us and talk to us, ask for the questionnaire, fill it out and return it, talk to us some more, and arrange a visit with us in advance. [Oct2004]

WALDEN TWO COMMUNITY CALIFORNIA

info@waldentwo.org
http://www.waldentwo.org

Began: 2005 | Forming
Rural | Diet: Omnivorous

A resource site dedicated primarily to creating a general, small set of instructions for creating a Walden Two community anywhere in the world.

Also, this is for discussing any Walden Two related issue including past and present Walden Two inspired communities, Walden Two related issues in economics, farming, behavior analysis, self-control, and so on.

Lastly, it is for the creation of a Walden Two community with a Planner-Manager system and a strong radical behaviorist/behavior analytic foundation here in California or on the west coast. There is no community yet. It's all in the planning stage. They might want to visit Twin Oaks in Virginia or Los Horcones in Sonora Mexico. [Feb2005]

WALKER CREEK FARM

Teresa Sequoyah Vaughn
The Abbey at Walker Creek
18318 Periwinkle Ln
Mount Vernon, WA 98274

360-422-5709
aviathar@yahoo.com

Began: 1975 | Pop. 14
Rural | Diet: Omnivorous

The 24-year-old Walker Creek community retains about half of its 20 acres in woodland and protects a salmon-spawning creek. The rest of the land includes private gardens, homes, communal roads, trails, lawns, orchards, and play equipment. Each home contains an independent family,

---

extended family or individual. The adult population, usually about 10 people, meets monthly to share a meal and reach consensus on issues facing the community. At this time, there is no room for new members, but we are in the process of converting a barn into a community center/guest house.

Visitors Accepted: We are more generally available on Sundays. Email if you are interested and we'll try to set up a time. We often have work parties you are welcome to join if you want to get to know people better! [Oct2004]

WALNUT STREET CO-OP

1680 Walnut St
Eugene, OR 97403

541-484-1156
walnut@ic.org
http://icetree.com/walnut

Began: 2000 | Pop. 9
Urban | Diet: Primarily vegetarian

Walnut Street Co-op is a social change oriented cooperative household in the friendly town of Eugene, Oregon. In September 2000 we moved into a large, rambling house together, seeking to build community. As housemates, that means eating dinner together, sharing chores, attending house meetings, and fulfilling a basic commitment to resolving any conflicts that arise. We trust that each person holds a piece of the truth, and we are committed to deep listening with each other even during hard conversations. Over time we're finding that our friendships are deepening, and a shared vision is emerging based on creating shifts in society toward dialogue, deliberation, and integration of diverse viewpoints.

Visitors Accepted: Phone or email us ahead of time. First visit usually consists of joining us for dinner and a tour. We don't have a real guest room, but can occasionally accommodate out-of-towners for a day or two. [Oct2004]

WATERLOO CO-OPERATIVE RESIDENCE INC.

http://www.wcri.coop

Waterloo Co-operative Residence Inc. provides quality affordable student housing through Member Co-operation.

WCRI is a dynamic student organisation providing housing for over 900 students in Waterloo, Ontario, Canada. We offer accommodations through communal living in our

---

Scissors [✂] at the end of a listing indicate that it was edited for length by the Directory editors and a longer description can be found at directory.ic.org.

three dormitories, or through 1,2,3 or 4 bedroom apartments. [Mar2005]

WELCOME HERE - CIRCLE OF LIGHT COMMUNITY NETWORK - RAINBOW TRIBES

Lookingheart (Focalizer)
2030 N Fremont St
Springfield, MO 65803

417-831-5570

http://welcomehere.org

Began: 1972 | Diet: Primarily vegetarian

Welcome Here Circle of Light is a loving effort of combined heartsongs dedicated to Spirit and the Children of the Rainbow Family Tribes and serves as a community network open and free to all.

The Rainbow Family has celebrated an annual gathering of the tribes within North America commencing around the 1st of July and progressing through the 7th since approximately 1972. Rainbow gatherings are attended by thousands of people from every corner of the globe and are comprised of many individuals, groups and non-groups, freely associating under the premise of harmony, coming together for a moment in time to pray in a circle for world peace.

This blessing occurs with the rising of the sun on the morning of July 4th in a sacred meadow until high noon. This silent meditative prayer and introspect of a world of harmony is a vibration shared by many world wide. We are all truly connected as a family of one. Rainbow Family Gatherings grow and become through autonomous participation that is egalitarian, based on mutual respect and has an open consensual counsel process that allows for all views and considerations.

Visitors Accepted: Check the website for local / annual / world gatherings and then come visit. All are welcomed freely. [Oct2004]

WELLSPRING

Mary Ann Ihm
4382 Hickory Rd
West Bend, WI 53090

262-675-6755
wellspring@hnet.net

http://www.wellspringinc.org

Began: 1982 | Pop. 5 | Spiritual
Rural | Diet: Primarily vegetarian

Wellspring's residential community is inte-grally connected to the garden program March thru November. Members from the larger community support Wellspring and its educational programs: wellness education, the arts, ecology and gardening, and personal-growth retreats. The retreat and conference center is open to the public as are its bed-and-breakfast and international hostel.

Local families subscribe to 25 weeks of organic produce each season. Volunteers help the community with the work.

Wellspring is an easy driving distance from Milwaukee yet is surrounded by nearly 1,000 acres of green space, a nature center, and country landscape. River frontage, meadows, woods, ponds, labyrinth and a restored prairie enhance the natural beauty of Wellspring.

Visitors Accepted: Make a reservation - call or email ahead and set an approximate arrival time. [Feb2005]

WESTMEREFOLC GEPÉODE

thunar_99@yahoo.com

http://www.geocities.com/thunar_99

Began: 1999 | Spiritual | Rural

Intentional tribal Heathen community based out of Oregon and eastern Washington. Still in the planning stages. Please contact by email. [Mar2005]

WESTWOOD COHOUSING

Jean Reese
jeanreese@charter.net

Paula Robbins
828-281-3253
paularww@bellsouth.net

http://www.westwoodcohousing.com

Began: 1992 | Pop. 50
Urban | Diet: Omnivorous

Westwood Cohousing Association is an intentional community in Asheville, North Carolina, nestled in a wooded setting with 24 clustered dwellings and a common house in the center of the community. The buildings have a central heat and hot-water system with solar collectors on the common house roof and radiant floor heating, and landscaping according to permaculture principles.

The community infrastructure has been completed since the summer of 1998, and everyone has moved in and is working together to create a pleasant living space and community. Dinners are held twice a week in the common house, with everyone participating in their creation. Work days are more infrequent, but with everyone helping, a lot gets done!

Visitors Accepted: Please call Audra at 828-255-7913 to schedule a tour. Donations of $5 per person are requested. [Jan2005]

WHITE BUFFALO FARM

Wayne Talmage
16877 Grange Rd
Paonia, CO 81428

970-527-3041
wltalmage@mail.tds.net

http://www.whitebuffalofarm.com

Began: 1975 | Pop. 18 | Spiritual
Rural | Diet: Omnivorous

White Buffalo Farm is an intentional Fifth World community dedicated to the manifestation of a higher spiritual vibration of love-light-wisdom on Mother Earth.

The community expresses itself spiritually in drum circles, dream circles, sweatlodge, vision quest, and Fifth-World rituals and ceremonies that enhance our connectedness to Mother Earth and all the planetary kingdoms.

We are dedicated to creating sanctuary from the main culture while working in spiritual service to heal Mother Earth and her kingdoms. We are dedicated to enlightening ourselves, the larger circle of humankind, and protecting Mother Earth from our ignorance. We are pioneers in organic farming and are major advocates of making the whole earth a place where all humans walk softly on the mother.

Visitors Accepted: Call Wayne. [Dec2004]

WHITE HAWK

Anna Stalter
110 Queen St.
Ithaca, NY 14850
ams15@cornell.edu

http://www.whitehawk.org

Began: 2004 | Pop. 10 | Forming | Rural

We are a newly forming group of people from all walks of life meeting/working to establish an ecological neighborhood on 120 acres near Ithaca, NY.

Visitors Accepted: Email to arrange a land tour. [Mar2005]

Listings

Additions and corrections: email: directory@ic.org, *web:* directory.ic.org, *mail: RR 1 Box 156-D, Rutledge MO 63563, USA.*

263

WHITEHALL CO-OP

2500 Nueces St
Austin, TX 78705

512-472-3329, 512-472-7382

http://www.whitehallcoop.org

Began: 1949 | Pop. 13
Urban | Diet: Primarily vegetarian

Founded August 6, 1949, Whitehall Co-op is Texas's oldest housing cooperative. The 13-member household includes a variety of ages and occupations, and everyone contributes equally to monetary costs and household labor. Whitehall is a nonsexist, nonracist, noncompetitive living environment. All decisions are made by consensus.

Our goals include obtaining intimate, meaningful tribal/familial bonds, emotional support, and spontaneous and planned creation and play. We are learning proper use of resources, noncompetitiveness, and communication skills. We want to be a part of a significant, nonexploitive socioeconomic movement.

The household is vegetarian, though not all members are completely vegetarian. Dinners that include fish or turkey have sometimes been prepared for special occasions with a full consensus agreement by all members. No smoking of any sort is allowed in Whitehall. All members have individual rooms with a shared or semiprivate bathroom. Whitehall was the first Texas recipient of funds from the National Co-op Bank (Washington, DC) in 1979 for use in construction of a professional-grade kitchen, which has been enjoyed by many a great cook over the years.

Visitors Accepted: To visit Whitehall, contact us in advance with some references of people who know you who we can call. We have a guest room and like to have visitors. We live under one roof and want to open our home to community minded folks while making sure our home is a safe place for us. [Mar2005]

WHOLE HEALTH FOUNDATION

William
1760 Lake Dr
Cardiff by the Sea, CA 92007

760-753-0321
developtrust@cox.net

http://www.wholehealthfound.com

Began: 1972 | Pop. 12
Urban | Diet: Primarily vegetarian

Whole Health Foundation is a holistic residential opportunity, one mile from the Pacific Ocean in southern California, 20 miles north of San Diego. We are all non-smokers and mostly vegetarian with occasional seafood or poultry preparation. We share a 13-bedroom eight-bath home with a year-round edible organic garden, outdoor solar shower, Jacuzzi, sauna, laundry, both filtered and distilled drinking water, whole-house filtration for ideal shower and bathing water, air purifier for kitchen and common areas to create negative ions and low-level ozone to eliminate airborne material, Norwalk juicer, electric wheatgrass juicer, and food dehydrator. No meat preparation, drugs, or alcohol abuse are permitted. We offer community-making workshops and residential fasting and rejuvenation programs for between $550 and $395 per week, depending on the level of supervision. Short-term visitors are welcome with prior notice for $50 per day and/or work in the organic garden. Longer-term residential housing is available from $550 to $750 per month. This opportunity is available to provide optimum health support for established vegetarians and others who want to live full-time in a holistic-health-community setting. Most residents have stayed for several years and some for only a few months. Contact William Polowniak at the above address. For information and personal reply send $5.

Visitors Accepted: Call to make an appointment and describe your intentions. Only potential residents are permitted to visit. Casual visitors or sight seeing is discouraged. [Jan2005]

WHOLE VILLAGE

20725 Shaws Creek Rd
Alton, ON L0N 1A0
CANADA

519-941-1099
info@wholevillage.org

Jeff Gold
519-941-9199
jgold@netrover.com

Mary MacEachern
marymace21@yahoo.ca

http://www.wholevillage.org

Began: 1995 | Pop. 28 | Forming
Rural | Diet: Omnivorous

Whole Village is located on two hundred acres near Orangeville, Ontario. Some of the members live on the site. The remainder will move into a new residence now under construction. Whole Village members pledge to operate a biodynamic farm as an integral part of the community, and to achieve these goals consistent with principles of sustainable land stewardship.

We are creating an ecologically sustainable and environmentally sensitive community. We protect and enhance the natural habitat through a system of land stewardship embracing the unique geographical, historical, cultural, and biological attributes of the land.

Whole Village is intended to be a solution for two difficult problems: the steady loss of farmland to urbanization and the devastating effects of low commodity prices on farmers and the rural communities that they belong to. Through a comprehensive conservation easement, all of the WV property, except for the compact housing cluster, is preserved for 999 years as farmland, managed forest, or natural areas. Each member is included in the community supported agriculture venture, where the farmers growing food for WV on the land are guaranteed a living wage and the respect and support they deserve.

Visitors Accepted: Please call or email at least one week in advance of your intended visit. No pets please, we have free range chickens. [Jan2005]

THE WILD HUMAN INITIATIVE

Kiyonah Thundersong
550 West Queen St
Boone, NC 28607

828-263-9403
wildhumaninitiative@yahoo.com
http://groups.yahoo.com/group/
WildHumanInitiative

http://www.wildhumaninitiative.
villagevisionaries.net

Began: 2004 | Pop. 36 | Forming | Spiritual
Small Town | Diet: Omnivorous

We are a tribe of free-minded, wild-hearted individuals and families.

We are creating grassroots community networks online, and we are searching for land and a suitable homestead in the areas north and west of Asheville, NC.

We have two main purposes as a nonprofit organization—to build grassroots community and to provide charitable relief to the travelling poor.

We also seek to build bridges of skill and understanding between ancient and contemporary lifeways (blending computer technologies with wilderness survival skills, for example).

We offer experiential social and educa-

Scissors [✂] at the end of a listing indicate that it was edited for length by the Directory *editors and a longer description can be found at* directory.ic.org.

tional opportunities in the form of potlucks, parties, workshops, field trips, seminars, websites with informative newsletters, and more.

We are seeking people with the following interests to brainstorm and vision with us about forming community on the land this summer:

- unschooling and radical homelearning
- vegetarianism and healthy gardening
- natural construction, including treehouses, springhouses, rope bridges, rock walls, and more
- musical talents and equipment.

We are primarily Rainbow people, although our friends fit all descriptions. We have no rules or regulations, except that a person take good care of themselves, respect and treat everyone with love and compassion, and take care of others and the Earth too. We truly believe that we are all in this together, and we are all family, and we can make our dreams come true now, by working, living, and loving together...

Visitors Accepted: Please go to our cyberhomes and check us out. Then communicate with us directly, either by email or by posting on the forums. Thank you so much. We really appreciate your interest. [Feb2005]

WILD SAGE COHOUSING

Boulder, CO
information@wildsagecohousing.org
http://www.wildsagecohousing.org

Began: 2000 | Urban | Diet: Omnivorous

Wild Sage Cohousing is a 34-home community in Boulder, CO. Construction was completed in 2004 in the new Holiday Neighborhood, an urban infill site in North Boulder. Many environmental features and materials were used in the construction of Wild Sage.

Visitors Accepted: Contact via email. [Jan2005]

WINDHAVEN

Tony Beauregard
482 Deer Valley
Canyon Lake, TX 78133

830-227-5097
tonybeau@cajunbro.com
http://www.theclans.org

Began: 2005 | Forming
Rural | Diet: Omnivorous

This is a community that will focus on both sustainability and healing of the

mind and spirit. The members of this community will support an Assisted Living Facility in an effort to help people heal and return to society (psychological research).

Visitors Accepted: Currently our community is still forming. If you would like to visit with us, contact us and we will let you know our meeting schedules, etc. [Feb2005]

WINDSONG

20543 – 96th Ave #27
Langley, BC V1M 3W3
CANADA

Alan Carpenter
604-882-5337

Valerie McIntyre
604-888-3831
valerie333@windsong.bc.ca

http://www.windsong.bc.ca

Began: 1996 | Pop. 90
Suburban | Diet: Omnivorous

WindSong Cohousing in Langley, British Coulmbia, is about 40 km east of Vancouver in the southwestern corner of Canada. The surrounding area, formerly a farming community, is now a residential suburb laced with many creeks and streams flowing into the nearby Fraser River.

WindSong has 34 townhomes along a pedestrian street covered by glass, making it ideal for easy access to the common house and for neighbourly interaction in all kinds of weather. Our 5,500-square-foot common house includes underground parking, a large kitchen and dining room, a performance stage, fireside lounge, and patio. Other spaces are dedicated for guests, teens, play, arts and crafts, laundry, office, consultation, washrooms, multi-purpose use, and workshop. WindSong is well-served by schools, parks, walking trails, public transportation, and nearby commercial amenities.

Our site includes 4 acres of undeveloped forest, field, and wetland including a salmon-bearing stream. Our surrounding shared gardens include organic lawns, flowers, fruit trees and raised vegetable beds, a fire pit, children's swings, and secluded reading areas. Our property is also home to a wide variety of birds, squirrels, and raccoons. About half of our homes have small private yards.

We are a mixed community of families, singles and seniors with a diversity of income levels. We do most of our commu-

nity administration, cleaning, and maintenance through a participatory Community Contribution System and we make our decisions by consensus. For more information contact Alan Carpenter.

Visitors Accepted: See Tour information at our website for current contact information. [Mar2005]

WINDSPIRIT COMMUNITY

4514 E Dripping Springs Rd
Winkelman, AZ 85292
info@windspiritcommunity.org

http://www.windspiritcommunity.org

Began: 1993 | Pop. 8
Rural | Diet: Primarily vegetarian

We are a 10-year-old community that encourages spiritual (non-religious) development among its members. Each day brings new opportunities to cast the ego aside in order to work toward our common good as caretakers of this planet in transition, and to further explore our true individual roles as sacred players.

We are located 80 miles north of Tucson, AZ on land that was once part of the Christmas Star Community (1979-1994). At this time, we have seven permanent community members with the potential to provide lifetime leases for three to five more in the coming years. Our base membership is small, however we have several long term associate members living here as well. Over the years we have created a successful visiting/intern program, which brings in pre-approved community participants to live on the land with us and join in on community projects and celebrations.

Currently, we are creating the roots for small cottage industries as well as building more infrastructure. Classes are offered on a regular basis on subjects such as permaculture, healing work, music, organic gardening, building, etc. We are blessed with an amazing landscape with over 1000 organic mature fruit, nut, and native trees with many varieties. This combined with gardens, a greenhouse, xeriscape plants, cacti and countless native plants help create our magical food forest village, a Sonoran desert oasis. We invite you to explore our website for further information. Blessings!

Visitors Accepted: Look over our website to see if you are compatible with our vision. Contact one of the members listed on the site via email or letter and then call for a brief interview. [Mar2005]

Additions and corrections: email: directory@ic.org, web: directory.ic.org, mail: RR 1 Box 156-D, Rutledge MO 63563, USA.

265

WINDTREE RANCH

Jacquie or Don Mackenzie
4200 E Summerland Rd
Douglas, AZ 85607

520-364-4611
windtreeranch@direcpc.com

http://windtreeranch.org

Began: 1989 | Pop. 3 | Spiritual
Rural | Diet: Vegetarian only

Building ecosustainable lifestyles and educating children about them. We prepare delicious, colorful vegetarian meals of organically grown fruits and veggies and eggs raised on this tobacco-free and drug-free ranch. All is prepared in strawbale hall. Weaving recycled treasures into gnomelike homes made from paper and stone; snuggled into majestic red-rock mountains with breathtaking views and abundant wildlife: cougar, wolf, fox, deer, and bird sanctuary.

Developing spiritual peace through connecting with Mother Earth in daily activities: caring for horses, alternative construction, gardening, community service, teaching children, and other right-livelihood undertakings we need to be teaching our young. We love and emotionally support each other's joys, gifts, and sorrows by following a path of tolerance and acceptance of Personal Choices. By willingly sharing finances, knowledge, and labor within a barter system we work to sustain this nonprofit-oriented, non-ownership-oriented lifestyle for generations to come.

By example we teach those children who share this sacred space with us. We live each day with the ever-present goal of ecosustainable, off-grid, freedom from consumerist lifestyles as our way of quietly preparing for the Earth changes in a positive, cooperative, enlightening chance for us to heal ourselves physically, emotionally, and spiritually while our Mother Earth heals herself.

We welcome like-minded inquiries from those who are healthy, whole, financially secure, and devoted to helping children by answering questions in their eyes, minds, and dreams with truth and wisdom.

Visitors Accepted: Get form off the website. [Mar2005]

WINDWARD FOUNDATION

55 Windward Ln
Klickitat, WA 98628

509-369-2000
windward@gorge.net

http://www.windward.org

Began: 1977 | Pop. 12 | Spiritual
Rural | Diet: Omnivorous

Windward is about sustainable, self-reliant

living that combines stewardship, entrepreneurial skills, and artistic expression. It's a pursuit of independent projects within a framework of cooperative association and mutual support.

Our fiber sheep and dairy goats set the rhythm of an intellectually dynamic and physically active life. On our 111-acre site, we're interweaving the skills of the past with appropriate technology to create a hands-on, back-to-basics way to practice right livelihood.

Our criteria: (1) we have to be better off with you than without you; (2) say what you mean and mean what you say; and (3) take it seriously or take it somewhere else.

If you can handle that, please visit our website. If you like what you see, the next step would be to send a letter introducing yourself to our email address.

Visitors Accepted [Jan2005]

WINSLOW COHOUSING GROUP

Roberta Wilson
353 Wallace Way NE
Bainbridge Island, WA 98110

206-780-1323
bertaw@bainbridge.net

Marci Burkel
mburkel@winslowcohousing.org

Audrey Watson
audrey@galisteo.com

http://www.winslowcohousing.org

Began: 1989 | Pop. 78
Small Town | Diet: Omnivorous

Winslow Cohousing is located on Bainbridge Island in Puget Sound, 35 minutes west of downtown Seattle by Washington State ferry. Tours are scheduled at mutually convenient times. Email Roberta at bertaw@bainbridge.net to set up a tour.

We are organized as a stock cooperative with 30 dwelling units and a common house on 6 acres with woods and gardens, within walking/biking distance of schools, shops, library, medical. Unit types range from studios to four bedrooms. All units are self-sufficient, with kitchens, dining areas, living rooms, bedrooms, and bathrooms. The group formed in 1989, started construction in 1991, and moved in early in 1992.

We are a caring, supportive, consensus-based community, seeking to live lightly on the land, valuing participation in our community and meals together available five nights a week. We are putting our forest in a

conservation easement. A subset of our group is exploring a car co-op.

Visitors Accepted: Please set up a tour, rather than just showing up. Ask tour person about picture taking—some people who live here don't want to have their pix taken. Tours take about an hour, so please come when you have the time. And please cancel if you're not going to come. Otherwise, we'll be waiting for you! Unless a home is for sale and is being shown, tours will not include private homes. [Jan2005]

WISCOY VALLEY COMMUNITY LAND COOPERATIVE

Bill Carter/Tony Brown
31783 Bur Oak Ln
Winona, MN 55987

507-452-4990, 507-454-8021
bill@prairiemoon.com

Began: 1975 | Pop. 26
Rural | Diet: Omnivorous

We are a land cooperative of around 25 adults and 1 teenager living on 358 acres in southeast Minnesota.

We share the land in common, but housing, incomes, diet, schooling, etc., are each individual's responsibility.

We have very little turnover at our land co-op and find replacements by word of mouth.

Visitors Accepted: Contact Bill or Tony with your request and dates of visit. At a Sunday meeting, the request will be discussed and approved, etc. Extended visitors need a sponsor and may pay a fee of $47.50/mo. [Feb2005]

WISE WOMAN CENTER/ LAUGHING ROCK FARM

PO Box 64
Woodstock, NY 12498

845-246-8081

http://www.susunweed.com/ Wise-Woman-Center.htm

Began: 1982 | Pop. 9 | Forming | Spiritual
Rural | Diet: Omnivorous

Goddesses, goats, and green witches gather at the Wise Woman Center to reweave the healing cloak of the ancients. Community members of Laughing Rock Farm prepare organic wild-food meals including fresh goat cheeses for the guests, who come to study herbal medicine with Susun S Weed, and spirit healing with Vicki Noble, Z Budapest, Whitefeather, and many others.

Scissors [✂] at the end of a listing indicate that it was edited for length by the Directory *editors and a longer description can be found at* directory.ic.org.

Community members have time to attend all workshops and weekday goat walks plus plant talks with Weed. There is an emphasis on the Green Nations: herb gardens and herbal remedies for people and animals—we have goats, geese, rabbits, cats, ducks—and herbal wild-food good cooking. We forage for mushrooms in our rocky magical forest where fairies play with us, the turtles swim with us in the river and ponds, and the owl's cry soothes our hearts. Life in our community is based on speaking your truth every morning at talking stick. We seek to love all parts of ourselves compassionately. Personal time is encouraged—women are paid a day's wage to take a "moon day" once a month. Personal responsibility is absolutely required of all members, as is participation in simple ceremonies celebrating life and the seasons. Our days and nights are rich with experience and learning.

Visitors Accepted [Mar2005]

WISTERIA

Pomeroy, OH 45769
info@wisteria.org
http://www.wisteria.org

Began: 1996 I Pop. 38
Rural I Diet: Omnivorous

Wisteria is located in Southeastern Ohio, near the city of Athens. We are organized as a corporation. Decisions are made at monthly meetings by a super majority vote but we attempt to meet everyone's needs in our decisions. All members are shareholders who elect a Board of Directors. Members are organized by households, and each household owns and votes shares.

At Wisteria we value our independence and individuality. Thus, we function more as a cooperative of homesteaders than as a commune. Our homes are widely spaced to allow for maximum privacy. Currently not all members are residential. We have a community building, which serves as a place for us to gather.

Wisteria's land is an important part of our community. The land is in the process of healing and on-going reclamation after strip mining. Part of our guiding principle is to honor and nurture the land and ecosystems that we are a part of. Approximately one third of our land is a nature preserve. Some members utilize solar power and other environmental innovations in their private homes.

Some of the reclaimed fields are used as an event campground. There we offer rustic space for gatherings of all types. We specialize in alternative events ranging from 20-1000 people. We both host and sponsor concerts, festivals, weddings, retreats, and we are open to many other group uses. We strive to create a highly developed educational event site, which brings people closer to nature. Drop-in visitors are never accepted. If you are interested in meeting us and would like to become a volunteer for our organization, please email us to get your name on our Work Day mailing list. If you are a prospective client interested in our event campground or stage please contact us via email. [Jan2005]

WOODBURN HILL FARM

**27290 Woodburn Hill Rd
Mechanicsville, MD 20659**

**301-884-8027, 301-472-4279
ff725@yahoo.com**

http://www.soundzimpossible.com/whf

Began: 1975 I Pop. 13
Rural I Diet: Omnivorous

Woodburn Hill Farm was founded on a formerly Amish farm in 1975. At present, we are a co-op model with family units more independent, with 14 adults and 2 teens on our 128 acres.

The place is owned by our corporation of 28 shareholders, a multiracial group, all connected with the farm over the years. Decisions are made by consensus. Residents can be shareholders or not, but both types pay rent to the corporation to cover expenses. We have one Main House with common areas and three living spaces; four separate family houses (the newest one with a geothermal heat pump); assorted barns; and a modular-built house with four living spaces, a large meeting room, and a geothermal heat pump. The rest of our heat is mostly from wood stoves.

We work locally in education, the arts, helping professions, and organic agriculture. We try to "live lightly" here: gardening organically, recycling, composting. We tend toward vegetarian and are loosely committed to holistic health and nonsexist working. All adult residents share in the upkeep, with seasonal workdays and rotating chore sign-ups. We celebrate earth cycles like equinox, solstice, full moon, etc. Some of us practice yoga and Tai Chi. Music is an important part of our lives.

Our preference is for creative, stable people who value cooperative living, ecological and social justice, spirituality, and celebrations.

Visitors Accepted: Those interested should contact us in advance of a visit. Send us an email or call. If you haven't seen our website, check it out. [Feb2005]

WOODCREST BRUDERHOF

http://www.woodcrestbruderhof.com

Woodcrest, the Bruderhof movement's first American settlement, was founded in 1954 in a small town called Rifton, NY, two hours north of New York City. In the preceding years, several members had been sent to North America from the Bruderhofs in Paraguay in order to contact interested seekers and to raise funds for a mission hospital. In the United States they met many people interested in living in intentional community and eager to hear about life at the Bruderhof. Several made the long trip down to Paraguay to visit the Bruderhofs there.

At a July 1953 conference in Paraguay, the Bruderhof decided to start a new branch in North America. Woodcrest was purchased in June 1954, and was immediately flooded with guests and new members. Many came from Quaker and Brethren backgrounds; others were agnostics, atheists, or of other non-religious backgrounds. People from intentional communities like Koinonia (founded by Clarence Jordan), Macedonia Cooperative, Kingwood, and Celo joined Woodcrest too. [Feb2005]

WOODFOLK HOUSE

**912 Woodfolk Dr
Charlottesville, VA 22902**
i_gnomon@excite.com

Began: 1999 I Pop. 8
Urban I Diet: Primarily vegetarian

Woodfolk House (also known as Woodfolk Asylum) is a group house in the town of Charlottesville, Virginia. We have been in Cville since May of 1999. We have two rules (no damn tv, no TV damn it). This is based on the understanding that TV shuts down communications, while rules tend to filter individuals out of our life and society.

Our vision revolves around three essential elements. We are supportive of activism and while activism is not a requirement we have a history of activism within our membership. We are an environmental model house (1st strawbale house in Cville, solar heated and more). Finally, we are accepting of people within their struggles (what we sometimes describe as accepting of high functioning

Additions and corrections: email: directory@ic.org, *web:* directory.ic.org, *mail: RR 1 Box 156-D, Rutledge MO 63563, USA.*

267

Listings

crazy people). During our first year the most common element of our demography were members who had been rejected from other communities because of stigmas related to mental health conditions that in most cases did not directly limit their ability to contribute, but rather reflected the unresolved and unacknowledged fears, prejudice or pain in those labeled normal. We are almost never seeking members (the last open room was filled within 6 hours), but are always interested in getting to know folks who will fit when space is open and like to get the word out about our flavor of community. If you are visiting other communities in central Virginia please consider contacting us.

Visitors Accepted: We have no formal visitor program. Most folks guest a week to ten days before or after their visits to other nearby communities. Contact us (by email if possible) and arrange a host. [Dec2004]

WOODLAWN TOWNHOME COOPERATIVES

Chicago, IL

773-288-5124

Jesse Bacon
trayf@redconcepts.net

Began: 2004 | Forming

[Mar2005]

WYGELIA

2919 Monocacy Bottom Rd
Adamstown, MD 21710

301-831-8280
wygelia@erols.com

Began: 1985 | Pop. 6
Rural | Diet: Omnivorous

There are 6 of us now, all wonderful people, and we have an inquiry from a possible seventh.

We have cleared land for a garden—ground that has never been farmed before. In the process, we harvested saw timber to use on the garage, and firewood.

We have started building a 1250-sq-ft garage, octagonal in shape.

We remain dedicated to the empowerment of creativity, to grow and nurture each one's special ability and talent. [May05]

YALAHA COMMUNITY NETWORK

Tom and Beverley
8039 Sunset Dr
Yalaha, FL 34797

407-758-1378, 352-324-3822
hovendick@comcast.net

Began: 2003 | Forming
Rural | Diet: Omnivorous

Visitors Accepted: Contact Bev or Tom at 352-324-3822. Accommodations are limited. [Nov2004]

YARROW ECOVILLAGE

42312 Yarrow Central Rd
Chilliwack, BC V2R 5E2
CANADA
info@yarrowecovillage.ca

http://www.yarrowecovillage.ca

Began: 2002 | Pop. 27
Rural | Diet: Primarily vegetarian

The twenty-five acre (10 hectare) former dairy farm in Chilliwack, BC, consists of two hectares (five acres) zoned Rural Residential and eight hectares (twenty acres) of agricultural land.

We are creating an ecovillage of up to 35 homes with stores, cottage industries and an organic farm. Ownership and governance is through a cooperative known as the Yarrow EcoVillage Society. Decisions are made by consensus.

The plan is to build an environmentally sustainable community based on cohousing and permaculture principles. Funds will be raised through membership equity, investment shares, and revenue from on-site activities. Costs will be met through sweat equity and cash payment. Part of the equity will be shared between members and the rest will form a development fund.

The members are a diverse group with many skills. There are now over 25 members and associates.

Members make decisions on all aspects of the ecovillage. A membership share is $1,000. Individuals not yet in a position to become members may become associates ($200 fee). This fee can later be put toward full membership. Members contribute $20 per month to a maximum of $300. Members may purchase investment shares in increments of $100. Investment shares are the primary means of building equity in the project. Members may also earn sweat equity credits towards a future home or business in the community.

The cooperative is open to new members.

Visitors Accepted: Contact us via email to arrange a time to visit. [Mar2005]

YELLOW PLUM COMMONS

2021 W 19th Ave
Kennewick, WA 99337

509-585-2558
info@yellowplum.org

http://www.yellowplum.org

Began: 2001 | Pop. 40 | Forming | Suburban

Visitors Accepted: Email or phone Scott or Bobi Wilson to set up a time. [Jan2005]

YOGAVILLE / SATCHIDANANDA ASHRAM

RR 1 Box 1720
Buckingham, VA 23921

800-858-9642
arc@yogaville.org

http://yogaville.org

Began: 1966 | Pop. 230 | Spiritual
Rural | Diet: Vegetarian only

Satchidananda Ashram-Yogaville is a thriving yogic community located on 700 acres of wooded property with 150 full time residents, an elementary school and The Light of Truth Universal Shrine which honors all the world's religions.

Yogaville is the international headquarters of Integral Yoga which conducts numerous trainings in basic, intermediate and advanced Hatha Yoga as well as a wide variety of specialized teacher trainings, such as Cardiac Yoga, Yoga for People with Cancer, Prenatal and Postnatal Yoga, and many more.

Yogaville also offers weekend workshops and retreats on many topics pertaining to health and spirituality. A sampling of these programs are "Osteoporosis, Yoga and Bone Building," "Transcending Fear, Anger and Depression," "Vegetarian Cooking for the Holidays," and "Kabbalah and Yoga."

The Living Yoga Training (LYT) is a work/study program designed to introduce people to the daily benefits of the yogic

Scissors [✂] at the end of a listing indicate that it was edited for length by the Directory editors and a longer description can be found at directory.ic.org.

lifestyle. Classes on the rich elements of yoga are combined with work opportunities.

As you can see there are many avenues in which to come and visit or live and serve as part of the Yogaville community.

Visitors Accepted: Visitors are always welcome for the day or overnight. Call or email for arrangements, or visit our website. [Feb2005]

YONDERFAMILY HOUSING AND LAND TRUST, INC

6500 Yonders Farm Rd
Jeffersonville, GA 31044

912-945-6078, 206-600-6399
learnmore@yonderfamily.org

http://yonderfamily.org

Began: 1967 | Spiritual | Rural | Diet: Other

Yonderfamily began in 1967 as a bus caravan of young hippies traveling across the country seeking peaceful adventure. A sign was put in the destination window above the driver saying "Yonder" as that was where we where headed.

We supported ourselves by farm labor and forest work planting trees, etc. As time went on and children were born on the bus, our priorities changed to seeking land and community.

In 1988 we bought a farm in middle Georgia to be held in trust for the preservation of sustainable living resources and education. It is the mission of the Yonderfamily Council, living by example, to provide ecologically minded, life sustaining education and resources in benefit to all—and to use, teach and learn via a network of community based programs promoting the perpetual integration of social ecological harmony. We honor and respect the diversity that makes us all rainbow and have found home and community by aspiring to live by example upholding our mission.

For the past 30 years Yonderfamily's dedication to sustainable green lifestyles combined with an open arms philosophy has led to providing society with a unique approach to renewal of the spirit and transitional life skill training. Our EcoVillage Project is bio-diversity in peaceful action.

Visitors Accepted: All you have to do to be here is just show up. To stay you must sign and agree to our Tuit policy which is a community contribution of: no less than 3 hours a day and at least 2 days per week OR the land share fee of $30 per week. [Feb2005][✂]

YORK CENTER COMMUNITY CO-OP

Marvin Holt
800 E 13th St
Lombard, IL 60148

630-629-0555
mholt15520@comcast.net

Ms. Marchese
630-629-6441

http://www.yorkcentercoop.org

Began: 1944 | Small Town

The York Center Community, Inc., is an over 50-year-old housing cooperative consisting of 78 individual homes, each on up to one acre of land in the suburban (DuPage County) Chicago area. The housing cooperative was founded upon Rochdale principles, which include a nondiscriminatory clause, a rarity in the 1940s! Historically, it was a catalyst for President Truman's executive order outlawing discriminatory practices in Federal Housing Administration (FHA) financing. Its structure has been upheld by the Illinois Supreme Court (1960). In terms of demographics and lifestyles, it generally reflects those of the middle-class suburban United States but with a professional population a bit skewed toward, not limited to, human-service professions. We value people of goodwill who wish to become a part of our community. [Feb2005]

YULUPA COHOUSING

Alexandra Hart
PO Box 1938
Sebastopol, CA 95473

707-829-8586
YulupaCoho@aol.com

http://www.yulupacoho.com

Began: 2000 | Forming | Urban

Yulupa Cohousing is a 29-unit urban-infill cohousing community in Santa Rosa, CA, an hour north of San Francisco in Sonoma County—an area known for its wine and liberal politics. The project is currently under construction, with scheduled move-in for late spring 2005. As of January 2005, there are still a few units available on the 1.65 acre site—we are especially looking for families with children.

We are a diverse, intergenerational community. Excerpts from our Vision and Values include: "Our community's spirit grows out of profound respect for the natural world and our human connection to it.... We seek to provide mutual support, inspiration, warmth and openness to each member in a way that nourishes many generations." Other values include diversity, tolerance, privacy, learning, growth and innovation, communication, and environmental and ecologic consciousness.

No risk money is required from participants beyond low monthly dues to cover basic operating expenses. After an orientation, potential members may attend group meetings, and make a deposit on a unit.

This is a developer-driven cohousing development with Michael Black, architect.

Homes range from studios to a four bedroom, with prices from $170,000 to $475,000. Common areas include a large common house with kitchen, dining room/multipurpose room, kids' room, laundry room, and lounge, as well as a guest room, exercise room, and a workshop. Gardening area is also available.

Check our website to view project design, floor plans, and to read current members' bios, our values statement, and more. [Jan2005][✂]

Listings

Additions and corrections: email: directory@ic.org, web: directory.ic.org, mail: RR 1 Box 156-D, Rutledge MO 63563, USA.

269

ZEN PEACEMAKER CIRCLE

Margi Gregory
177 Ripley Rd
Montague, MA 01351

margigregory@comcast.net
margigregory@peacemakercircle.org

http://www.zpf-motherhouse.org/
zpc-overview.htm

Began: 2003

We are a network of interlocking circles located in the US and Europe that provides a container for people from various contemplative traditions who wish to integrate spirituality with social action. We are dedicated to the realization and actualization of the oneness and interdependence of life, using as our guide the Three Tenets of Not Knowing (thereby giving up our fixed perspectives), Bearing Witness to the joy and suffering of our world, and Loving Action. We come together in contemplative practice and to study, to receive support from one another and to engage in actions arising from our deepening understanding of the oneness of life. We offer support to people who wish to begin circles wherever they might live, as well as advanced trainings for coordinators and ongoing circles. Trainings include processes for developing inclusivity, decision making, and shared participation and ownership within the group. Our co-founders are Roshi Bernie Glassman and Roshi Sandra Jishu Holmes.

Visitors Accepted: There are currently circles in San Francisco and Los Angeles, CA; Boulder, CO; Albuquerque, NM; Wycoff, NJ; and Western Massachusetts. Contact Margi Gregory for information on how to contact coordinators for those circles. [Feb2005]

THE ZEN SOCIETY

Ninshin Rachel McCormick
Pine Wind Zen Center
863 McKendimen Rd
Shamong, NJ 08088

609-268-9151
ninshin@jizo-an.org
seijaku@jizo-an.org

http://www.thezensociety.org

Began: 1985 | Pop. 4 | Spiritual
Rural | Diet: Primarily vegetarian

"Community is the spirit, the guiding light, whereby people come together to fulfill a purpose, to help others fulfill their purpose, and to take care of one another."

The Zen Society is a nonprofit grassroots organization, founded in 1985 to support growth towards a deepening spiritual awareness and appreciation of life in all its myriad of forms.

You are invited to experience a unique kind of spirituality. One without borders—an expansive spiritual journey, where the insights of Zen and Buddhism mix with faith-based religions and other wisdom traditions.

Zen-Life is about being human, about the human heart, the human experience, and the pure human potentiality inherent in each of us.

It is an essential spiritual practice designed to enliven the body, the mind, the emotions, and the soul.

Whether you come to learn about Zen, or are beginning your spiritual search; or are simply looking for retreat, rest and relaxation, and the nurturing energies of a mature community; or just continuing your growth on a well-traveled path; your visit to The Zen Society will certainly prove to be inspiring, welcoming, and—an experience which you will never get over.

Visitors Accepted: Please call or email ninshin@jizo-an.org. [Feb2005]

ZEPHYR VALLEY COMMUNITY CO-OP

Greg Smith
RR 1, Box 121E
Rushford, MN 55971

507-454-5587
smithgjo@hbci.com

http://www.hbci.com/~zephyr/
zephyr.html

Began: 1993 | Pop. 23
Rural | Diet: Omnivorous

Zephyr Valley Community Co-op is a rural cohousing community with 13 adults and 10 kids on 550 acres of stunningly beautiful land in southeast Minnesota. The land, purchased in '94, is owned collectively. There are seven existing homes owned individually by members, which occasionally become available for resale to new members or rental to prospective members, plus more homesites. We have a community center (for community meals, parties, meetings, guests, laundry, etc.) as well as a spring fed swimming pond, a soccer/baseball field, trails for walking and skiing, and barns for animals and storage.

The values that hold us together can be summed up in the word Respect—respect for the land, for each other, for ourselves. We live lightly on the land, caring for it consciously. Decisions about the land and community are made by consensus, all others are individual.

We are involved in the larger rural community here. Zephyr is in the country but close to several cities and universities.

Our children are growing up with an intimate knowledge of the natural world—where the biggest tadpoles are in the creek, what ice is best for skating, which bluff has the coolest sand outcroppings, what the air tastes like in the different seasons.

About 50 acres are in organic vegetables, plus many acres of restored wetlands, pastures, woodland, bluff lands, high grass meadows, ponds, creeks and a trout stream. This is a wonderful place to live! Please feel free to contact us and arrange a visit.

Visitors Accepted: Contact Zephyr in advance. [Mar2005]

ZIM ZAM

362 London Rd
Asheville, NC 28803

828-277-0758
ab414@seorf.ohiou.edu
clafey@yahoo.com

http://www.seorf.ohiou.edu/~ab414

Began: 1996 | Pop. 4 | Forming
Urban | Diet: Primarily vegan

ZimZam expresses our desire for vibrant physical, mental and emotional health. We strive to be connected and in tune with the earth. Here eco-consciousness is the norm and shared food is vegan. We examine our lives and challenge each other to be ever more earth friendly.

We work to create a place where we feel safe and respected. All sexual orientations, genders, cultural backgrounds and ages are welcome. We envision a space which includes children, while adults choose to

---

Scissors [✂] at the end of a listing indicate that it was edited for length by the Directory *editors and a longer description can be found at* directory.ic.org.

restrain their own procreation. Another founding vision is that all animals have the right to be free, therefore we don't own animals either as livestock or as pets.

Currently we have a 3 bedroom house on an acre of land 3 miles from downtown. The city bus goes by our front door. The land is managed as evolving edible forest garden. We are activists: creating, promoting and manifesting visions of sustainable culture utilizing models of non-authoritarian democracy.

Possible directions for growth: adding a rural component; adding adjacent properties; working toward an eco-neighborhood/village/city. We're open to inclusion of neighboring households, some of which might not be vegan nor exclude animal ownership. The most likely way for you to become a part of ZimZam is to buy an adjacent house or to help fund the construction of additional bedroom spaces in our current house. Those without that much financial ability could live nearby and help, through work, to create more living spaces within the community.

Visitors Accepted: Calling us on the phone is the most likely way to reach us. We will gladly call you back if you leave a message. Email often gets lost. Visitors must have a genuine interest in possibilities of future participation. As a Servas host we host occasional visits from people of other countries. Also, we will sometimes host eco/peace/justice activist(s) passing through who need a place to stay a night or two. We don't usually have the time or resources to accommodate the needs of people who are touring communities in a general way. [Mar2005]

ZUNI MOUNTAIN SANCTUARY

PO Box 636
Ramah, NM 87321

505-783-4002
dbalsam@prodigy.com
zunimtn@cia-g.com

http://www.zms.org

Began: 1995 | Pop. 8 | Spiritual
Rural | Diet: Primarily vegetarian

Zuni Mountain Sanctuary is a Radical Faerie community dedicated to providing an environment for spiritual growth and renewal of its stewards, Radical Faeries, and those of like minds and spirits. The Sanctuary is situated on a land trust of 320 acres in the Zuni Mountains of western New Mexico.

The Sanctuary is home to six resident-stewards who maintain the Sanctuary and are devoted to promoting a sustainable lifestyle, based upon principles of Permaculture and Holistic Management. To this end, the stewards are responsible for land and water conservation, organic gardening, recycling efforts, solar powered electricity, passive solar heating, and the like.

Each of our buildings have used traditional techniques including adobe, pressed brick, strawbale, and cob construction.

The Sanctuary hosts a number of small mini-gatherings throughout the year. The annual Qweer Shamanism Gathering is held the last week in August into September bringing over 100 visitors in a ten-day period to explore spiritual aspects of the sacred.

The Sanctuary is an omnivorian and gender inclusive community that fosters respect and honors individual nature and the diversity of our shared humanity.

Visitors Accepted: Visitors may camp during the warmer months and are provided indoor space during the cooler months. Visitor donation request is to contribute ten dollars per day to offset food costs but "nobody will be turned away for lack of funds." [Feb2005][✂✄]

Listings

Additions and corrections: email: directory@ic.org, web: directory.ic.org, mail: RR 1 Box 156-D, Rutledge MO 63563, USA.

271

About the Short Community Listings

This section contains listings from previous editions and updates of the *Directory* for communities that did not update their listings on our website during the short time allotted for this edition of the book. We felt that it would be useful to our readers to provide contact information for these communities, but felt uncomfortable printing their old descriptions and survey answers, given that they are generally five years old at this point. To the best of our ability, we have kept area codes and addresses up to date and have removed communities that seemed unlikely to still be in existence.

Please check our website *directory.ic.org* for potential updates for these communities, or to see if they have been removed from our database. We apologize for any inaccurate information.

A note on telephone numbers

For communities outside the US and Canada, phone numbers are listed such that they can be called from any country. An example for a German community would be +49-(0)1234-56789. The plus sign indicates that one must start with your country's International Direct Dialing (IDD) prefix for any call abroad (011 is the IDD for the US and Canada). The next numerals (up to the dash) are the country code, which is also necessary for international calls (in the example 49 is the country code for Germany). In parenthesis, you will find the National Direct Dialing (NDD) prefix which is the number one would dial within the country before dialing the actual phone number (in the US and Canada the NDD is 1; in Germany it is 0) and which is not necessary when dialing from outside the country. After that is the complete phone number including any area, region, or city codes. Thus for the above example, if calling from the US one would dial 011-49-1234-56789 but if calling within Germany one would dial 0-1234-56789.

ACME ARTISTS COMMUNITY

Acme Artists Community
2418 W Bloomingdale Ave
Chicago, IL 60647

773-278-7677
nnwac@nnwac.org
http://www.nnwac.org

ADIDAM

12040 N Seigler Springs Rd
Middletown, CA 95461

707-928-1100
correspondence@adidam.org
http://www.adidam.org

AEIROUS / YEWWOOD

93640 Deadwood Creek Rd
Deadwood, OR 97430

541-964-5341
marygold@aerious.org
humnbyrd@aerious.org
http://www.aerious.org

AGAPE LAY APOSTOLATE COMMUNITY

1401 W Birch St
Deming, NM 88030

505-546-4940, 505-546-8281
http://www.zianet.com/agape

ALCHEMY FARM

237 Hatchville Rd
East Falmouth, MA 02536

Karen Schwalbe
508-564-4325
kschwalbe@whrc.org

ALESKAM

Loudmila Ignatenko
60 Let Oktyabra Str 1, Apt 17
684020 Razdolny Setl, Kamchatka
RUSSIAN FEDERATION

+7-(0)415-31-97-1-40,
+7-(0)415-31-93-5-13
yupik@elrus.kamchatka.su

ALIANTHA

548 Windover Ave NW
Vienna, VA 22180

703-242-6072 ext 7
info@aliantha.org
http://aliantha.org

AMATA COMMUNITY

317 Nelms Ave NE
Atlanta, GA 30307

404-378-3954
noahglassman@yahoo.com
http://www.geocities.com/
noahglassman/amatacom.html

AMERICAN IDEAL

RR 1 Box 169
Golden Eagle, IL 62036

618-883-2225
aipu2@yahoo.com
http://groups.yahoo.com/group/
amidl

ANANDA KANAN OZARK RETREAT CENTER

3157 County Rd 1670
Willow Springs, MO 65793

417-469-5273
dadaik@anandakanan.com
http://www.anandakanan.com

ANANDA VILLAGE

14618 Tyler Foote Rd
Nevada City, CA 95959

530-478-7500
sangha@ananda.org
http://www.ananda.org

ANDELSSAMFUNDET I HJORTSHØJ

Gl. Kirkevej 56
DK-8530 Hjortshøj
DENMARK

+45-86-22-21-24
Myattpeter@hotmail.com
http://www.andelssamfundet.dk

AQUARIUS NATURE RETREAT

PO Box 69
Vail, AZ 85641

ARCOBALENO FIAMMEGGIANTE (TRIBE)

Vico S Pietro a Majella 6
Bioregione Partenopea
I-80138 Napoli
ITALY

+39-(0)81-455026

ASSOCIATION FOR THE EARTH

Dabrówka 30
24-134 Staroscin
POLAND

+48-(0)83-65-40-91 ext 360
DLaZiemi@dlaziemi.most.org.pl
http://www.most.org.pl/las

ATLANTIS RISING, INC.

PO Box 154
Bradford, NH 03221

ATMASANTULANA VILLAGE

Near MTDC Holiday Resort
Karla 410 405
Maharashtra
INDIA

+91-(0)2114-282232,
+91-(0)2114-282291,
+91-(0)2114-282261
info@ayu.de
http://www.ayu.de

AUROVILLE

PO Box 1534
Lodi, CA 95241

831-425-5620, +91-(0)41386-2227
info@aviusa.org
http://www.auroville.org

ও B ঞ

BACKYARD TECH

Cone St
Macleay Island, Queensland Q-4186
AUSTRALIA

+61-(0)74-095-100

BEAL COOPERATIVE

525 Mac Ave
East Lansing, MI 48823

517-332-5555

BEANNACHAR CAMPHILL COMMUNITY

South Deeside Rd
Banchory-Devenick
Aberdeen AB12 5YL Scotland
UNITED KINGDOM

+44-(0)1224-869251
richard.beannachar@talk21.com
http://www.beannachar.co.uk

BELLINGHAM COHOUSING

2614 Donovan Ave
Bellingham, WA 98225

360-935-2614
info@bellcoho.com

Edwin Simmers
360-734-2677
EdwinSimmers@bellcoho.com

David Longdon
360-671-6802
david@bellinghamcohousing.org
http://www.bellinghamcohousing.org

BIRCHWOOD HALL COMMUNITY

Storridge Malvern
Worcs WR13 5EZ England
UNITED KINGDOM

bfromer@netcomuk.co.uk

BLACK WALNUT COOPERATIVE

1353 Rutledge St
Madison, WI 53703

608-257-5949

BREAD AND ROSES – BASE COMMUNITY

Fabriciusstrasse 56
D-22177 Hamburg
GERMANY

+49-(0)40-69-70-20-85
jens.schild@weitblick.de
http://www.brot-und-rosen.de

BRIGID COLLECTIVE

2012 10th St
Berkeley, CA 94710

brigidcollective@yahoo.com

BUDDHIST SOCIETY OF COMPASSIONATE WISDOM

1214 Packard St
Ann Arbor, MI 48104

734-761-6520
a2buddha@provide.net
http://users.rcn.com/chicagobuddha/
   locations/annarbor

ও C ঞ

CANBERRA COHOUSING

http://www.canberracohousing.com

CARPENTER VILLAGE

PO Box 5802
Athens, OH 45701

740-593-6562

CASA AMISTAD

2615 N 4th St
Philadelphia, PA 19133

215-423-7465
Cityquake@aol.com
AmigoJorge@aol.com

CASA MARIA CATHOLIC WORKER COMMUNITY

1131 N 21st St
Milwaukee, WI 53233

414-344-5745

CATHOLIC WORKER COMMUNITY OF CLEVELAND

3601 Whitman Ave
Cleveland, OH 44113

440-631-3059, 216-631-3059

CAVE CREEK

23780 Cave Creek Rd
Boonville, MO 65233
kfrueh@mail.coin.missouri.edu

CEDAR HOLLOW COMMUNITY

590 Pleasant Ridge Rd
Edmonton, KY 42129

CELO COMMUNITY

Attn: Walters
7965 White Oak Rd
Burnsville, NC 28714

CENNEDNYSS COMMUNITY

PO Summertown
South Australia 5141
AUSTRALIA

+61-(0)8-8390-3166
dlg@adelaide.dialix.oz.au

CENTER OF UNITY SCHWEIBENALP

+41-(0)33-951-2001
info@schweibenalp.ch
http://www.schweibenalp.ch

CENTRE FOR ALTERNATIVE TECHNOLOGY

Machynlleth
Powys SY20-9AZ Wales
UNITED KINGDOM

+44-(0)1654-702400
community@cat.org.uk
http://www.cat.org.uk

CHESTER CREEK HOUSE

1306 E 2nd St
Duluth, MN 55805

218-728-5468

CHICKEN SHACK HOUSING COOPERATIVE

Brynllwyn
Rhoslefain, Tywyn
Gwynecki LL36 9NH Wales
UNITED KINGDOM

+44-(0)1654-711655
pcbritain@gn.apc.org

CIRCLE OF DIVINE UNITY

736 Fred Burr Rd
Victor, MT 59875

406-961-0007,
406-777-6961
marioncantwell@msn.com

CLANABOGAN CAMPHILL COMMUNITY

15 Drudgeon Rd
Clanabogan, Omagh
County Tyrone BT78 1TJ N Ireland
UNITED KINGDOM

+44-(0)1662-256111
http://www.camphill.org.uk/guide/
    clanabog/clanabog.htm

CO-ORDINATION CO-OP

CMB Upper Tuntable Falls Rd
Near Nimbin, NSW 2480
AUSTRALIA

+61-(0)66891005

COHOUSING RESEARCH AND EDUCATION

Brisbane, Queensland
AUSTRALIA

+61-(0)7-38642535
http://www.grahammeltzer.com/
    cohousing/index.htm

COHOUSING.BE

Gent
BELGIUM

+32-(0)9-342-06-41
Federico_Bisschop@hotmail.com
http://www.cohousing.be

COLUMBANUS COMMUNITY OF RECONCILLATION

683 Antrim Rd
BT 154EG Belfast N Ireland
UNITED KINGDOM

+44-(0)2890-778009
columbanus@cinni.org

COMMUNAUTÉ DE L'ARCHE

La Borie Noble
F-34650 Roqueredonde
FRANCE

+33-(0)67-44-09-89

COMMUNAUTÉ DE LA VIEILLE VOIE

Vieille Voie de Tongres 33
B-4000 Liège
BELGIUM

+32-(0)41-266077

COMMUNAUTE DU PAIN DE VIE

9 Place Verte
F-59300 Valenciennes
FRANCE

+33-(0)2-31925419

COMMUNITY AND RETREAT FOR MINDFUL LIVING

2304 N Abbott Ln
Fayetteville, AR 72703

COMMUNITY HOUSE

1757 Mills Ave
Cincinnati, OH 45212

513-396-7202 ext 201

COOPER STREET HOUSEHOLD

5003 E Cooper St
Tucson, AZ 85711

CREEKSIDE COMMUNITY

119 Warrington St, St Albans
Christchurch
NEW ZEALAND

+64-(0)3853646

CROSSROADS MEDIEVAL VILLAGE

+61-(0)2-6288-0743
crossroads@crossroads.org.au
http://www.crossroads.org.au

DAMANHUR

via Pramarzo 3
I-10080 Baldissero Canavese
Torino
ITALY

+39-(0)124-502193,
+39-(0)124-512226
locusta@damanhur.it
welcome@damanhur.it
http://www.damanhur.it

DANDELION COMMUNITY CO-OP, INC.

194 Jackson Rd
RR 1
Enterprise, ON K0K 1Z0
CANADA

613-358-2304
dlion@kingston.net

DAYTON HOUSE

1034 Dayton Ave
Saint Paul, MN 55104

651-644-7439
ccrawford@isd.net

DE HOBBITSTEE

Van Zijlweg 3
NL-8351 HW Wapserveen
NETHERLANDS

+31-(0)521-321324,
+31-(0)521-321328
hobbitherberg@ddh.nl
t.r.@koster2.fol.nl

DE REGENBOOG

Norbert Gillelaan 20
B-1070 Brussels
BELGIUM

+32-(0)2-520-6586

DEARBORN COMMONS COHOUSING

Seattle, WA

Carmelita Logerwell
425-822-6557
CLogerwell@bdo.com
http://www.dearborncommons.com

DELAWARE STREET COMMONS

PO Box 1153
Lawrence, KS 66044

785-550-0163
info@delaware-street.com
http://www.delaware-street.com

DOROTHY DAY CATHOLIC WORKER HOUSE

503 Rock Creek Church Rd NW
Washington, DC 20010

202-882-9649

DOWNEAST FRIENDS COMMUNITY

122 Cottage St
Bar Harbor, ME 04609

207-288-2152 (machine)

DOWNIE STREET COLLECTIVE

459 Downie St
Peterborough, ON K9H 4J6
CANADA

705-742-7621

EARTHEN SPIRITUALITY PROJECT

Loba & Jesse Wolf Hardin
PO Box 516
Reserve, NM 87830

earthway@concentric.net
http://www.concentric.net/
  ~earthway

EARTHSEA

Box 95
Riverport, NS B0J 2W0
CANADA

902-766-4129
info@earthsea.ca
http://home.tallships.ca/earthsea

EARTHSONG ECO-NEIGHBOURHOOD

Waitakere, Auckland
NEW ZEALAND

+64-(0)9-832-5558
http://www.ecohousing.pl.net

EARTHWORM HOUSING CO-OP

Dark Ln
Leintwardine
Shropshire SH7 0LH England
UNITED KINGDOM

+44-(0)1547-540461

EDENVALE

4330 Bradner Rd
Abbotsford, BC V4X 1S8
CANADA

604-856-3388
office@edenvaleretreat.ca
http://www.edenvaleretreat.ca

EKOBYN BÅLARNA

Bergsjö
SWEDEN

Seija Viitamäki-Carlsson
+46-(0)652-71269
seija@bdab.se
http://www.bdab.se/ekobyn

EL BLOQUE

Apartado 51
E-03530 La Nucia
SPAIN

+34-6-5870175
elbloque@usa.net

ELDERWOOD FARM

15210 Schleweis Rd
Manchester, MI 48158
ferguson@wunderground.com

ELOHIM CITY

RR 3 Box 293
Muldrow, OK 74948

918-427-7739

ELSWORTH COOPERATIVE

711 W Grand River Ave
East Lansing, MI 48823

517-337-3236
http://www.msu.edu/user/coop

EMMAUS HAARZUILENS

Eikstraat 14
NL-3455 SJ Haarzuilens
NETHERLANDS

+31-(0)30-677-1540
emmaus@emmaus.nl

EMMAUS HOUSE

PO Box 1177
New York, NY 10035

212-410-6006

ERETZ HACHAIM

Sunderland, MA 01375

413-549-4094
info@thelivingland.org

Yosef Lifchitz
413-549-8404
http://www.thelivingland.org

ETERNAL CAUSE SOCIETY

1652 Ridge Ave
Philadelphia, PA 19130

FAERIE CAMP DESTINY

PO Box 531
Winooski, VT 05404

802-257-4871
info@faeriecampdestiny.org
http://www.faeriecampdestiny.org

FAIRVIEW HOUSE

1801 Fairview St
Berkeley, CA 94703

510-658-3899
http://barringtoncollective.org/
housing/view.php?house_id=27

FAMILIEN-GEMEINSHAFT RAT & TAT

Haus Benediktus
A-3710 Frauendorf 76
AUSTRIA

+43-(0)663-9223711,
+43-(0)WIEN-4935055

FAN LAKE BRETHREN

9036 N Mexican Sage Pl
Tucson, AZ 85742

509-292-0502

FAR VALLEY FARM

12788 New England Rd
Amesville, OH 45711

740-448-4894

FATHER DIVINE'S PEACE MISSION MOVEMENT

1622 Spring Mill Rd
Gladwyne, PA 19035

610-525-5598
http://www.libertynet.org/fdipmm

FERENCY HOUSE

146 Collingwood Dr
East Lansing, MI 48823

517-332-0846, 517-332-0847
coop@pilot.msu.edu
http://www.msu.edu/user/coop

FREIE CHRISTLICHE JUGENDGEMEINSCHAFT

Altenaer Strasse 45
D-58507 Lüdenscheid
GERMANY

+49-(0)23-51-35-80-39
stadtmission@fcjg.de
http://www.fcjg.de

FRIENDS CO-OP

437 W Johnson St
Madison, WI 53703

608-251-0156
friends_coop@hotmail.com
http://www.madisoncommunity.coop/
house.cfm?HouseID=9

FUN FAMILY FARM

2127 205th St
Robinson, KS 66532

785-544-6700

GINGER RIDGE FARMS

RR 2 Box 4051
Pahoa, HI 96778

808-965-7622

THE GRAIL COMMUNITY

125 Waxwell Ln
Pinner
Middx HA5 3ER England
UNITED KINGDOM

+44-(0)181-866-2195,
+44-(0)181-866-0505
waxwell@compuserve.com
grailcentre@compuserve.com

GREATER WORLD COMMUNITY

PO Box 1041
Taos, NM 87571

505-751-0462
biotecture@earthship.org
http://www.earthship.org

GREENHOUSE

716 N 63rd St
Seattle, WA 98103

206-781-9110

GREENWOOD

258 W Greenwood Ave
Lansdowne, PA 19050

610-623-5656

GRIMSTONE COMMUNITY

Grimstone Manor
Horrabridge, Yelverton
Devon PL20 7QY England
UNITED KINGDOM

+44-(0)822-854358
101653.2176@compuserve.com
GrimstoneManor@compuserve.com

GRISHINO COMMUNITY

http://www.grishino.ecology.net.ru

GUAYRAPÁ

C/Estragón s/n
E-43364 Montral (Tarragona)
SPAIN

+34-977-846-887, +34-977-760-156
guayrapa@jazzfree.com

HAIRAKHANDI LOVE CENTER

Vocabolo Villarosa 56
Localita Corniole
I-06026 Pietralunga (PG)
ITALY

+39-(0)75-933074
ommacho@libero.it
http://digilander.libero.it/
Hairakhandi/

HEARTWOOD COMMUNITY INCORPORATED TE NGAKAU O TE RAKAU

51 Browns Rd
Christchurch 8001
NEW ZEALAND

+64-(0)3-355-4746 (city),
+64-(0)3-312-3058 (rural)
katet@ihug.co.nz
http://www.converge.org.nz/evcnz

HENDERSON COOPERATIVE HOUSE

1330 Hill St
Ann Arbor, MI 48104

734-995-0123
http://www.housing.umich.edu/
residencehalls/henderson

HESBJERG

Hesbjergvej 50
DK-5491 Blommenslyst
DENMARK

+45-6596-7505,
+45-2121-4533
hesbjerg@post5.tele.dk
andpa@post5.tele.dk

HET HUIS VAN ANTONIA

info@hethuisvanantonia.nl
http://www.hethuisvanantonia.nl

HIGH FLOWING COMMUNITY

261 Milky Way Ln NW
Riner, VA 24149

540-763-2651

HOLDEN VILLAGE

HC00 Stop 2
Chelan, WA 98816
http://www.holdenvillage.org

HORIZONS ECOVILLAGE

1900 Rio Hill Ctr #113
Charlottesville, VA 22901

434-361-1212

HOUSE OF PEACE CATHOLIC WORKER

838 Princeton St
Akron, OH 44311

330-834-1112

HUEHUECOYOTL

A. P. 111, Tepoztlán
Morelos 62520
MEXICO

+52-(01)739-39-52021,
+52-(01)739-39-52022
sircoyote@aol.com
huehue@laneta.apc.org
http://www.laneta.apc.org/rem/
   huehue.htm

HUNTINGTON OPEN WOMYNS LAND (HOWL)

PO Box 53
Huntington, VT 05462

802-434-3953
wehowl@juno.com

ISHAYAS

254 Burke Dr
Stanwood, WA 98282

mandytarrant@yahoo.com
http://www.ishaya.org

ISLE OF ERRAID

Findhorn Foundation
Fionnphort, Isle of Mull
Argyll PA66 6BN Scotland
UNITED KINGDOM

+44-(0)1681-700384
bookings@erraid.fslife.co.uk
http://www.erraid.com

ITTOEN

8 Yanagiyama-cho
Shinomiya
Yamashina-ku, Kyoto 607-8025
JAPAN

+81-(0)75-581-3136,
+81-(0)75-581-3139 (fax)
http://www.ittoen.or.jp

JESUIT VOLUNTEER CORPS (DC)

PO Box 3756
Washington, DC 20027

202-687-1132
jvi@jesuitvolunteers.org
http://www.JesuitVolunteers.org

JESUIT VOLUNTEER CORPS (NW)

PO Box 3928
Portland, OR 97208

503-335-8202
jvcnw@jesuitvolunteers.org

JESUS PEOPLE USA

920 W Wilson Ave
Chicago, IL 60640

ljackson@jpusa.org
jpusa@jpusa.chi.il.us
http://www.jpusa.org

JUBILEE PARTNERS

PO Box 68
Comer, GA 30629

706-783-5131
http://www.jubileepartners.org

KADESH-BIYQAH

Box 120
S-671 23 Arvika
SWEDEN

+46-(0)570-42001
nccg@nccg.org
http://www.nccg.org/Kadesh.html

KANA-GEMEINSCHAFT

Mallinckrodtstr 108
D-44145 Dortmund
GERMANY

+49-(0)2311839853

KANATSIOHAREKE (GA NA JO HA LAY GAY)

Place Of The Clean Pot
4934 State Hwy #5
Fonda, NY 12068

516-673-5692

Short Listings

279

KEVERAL FARM COMMUNITY

Tristan Dorling
St Martins by Looe
Looe
Cornwall PL13 1PA England
UNITED KINGDOM
rainbow@argonet.co.uk
http://www.keveral.org

KIBBUTZ KETURA

IL-88840 DN Eilot
ISRAEL

+972-(0)3-527-8874,
+972-(0)3-524-6156
ketura-
    volunteers@ketura.ardom.co.il
http://www.ardom.co.il/heilot/ketura

KIBBUTZ NEOT SEMADAR

Alon Shemi or Anat Ganor
IL-88860 DN Eilot
ISRAEL

+972-(0)7-6358111
ikc@ilhawaii.net
http://www.kinfonet.org/
    Community/centres/
    Neot_Semadar

KYNHEARTH

1398 Cox Store Rd SW
Floyd, VA 24091

pat@swva.net

L'ARCHE – HOMEFIRES

10 Gaspereau Ave
Wolfville, NS B4P 2C2
CANADA

902-542-3520
larchehomefires@ns.sympatico.ca
http://www.larchehomefires.org

LA SENDA ECOVILLAGE

Apdo 595
San Miguel de Allende, GTO 37700
MEXICO

+52-(01)415-35161
romance@mpsnet.com.mx
juliettesanchez@hotmail.com

LAKE CLAIRE COHOUSING

258 Connecticut Ave NE
Atlanta, GA 30307

John Greene, Nancy Lowe
404-687-0179
greenelowe@mindspring.com

LAKE VILLAGE

7943 S 25th St
Kalamazoo, MI 49048

269-327-0614, 269-387-8134

LAURIESTON HALL

Laurieston
Castle Douglas DG7-2NB Scotland
UNITED KINGDOM

+44-(0)1644-450-263
david@lauriestonhall.demon.co.uk

LE NOVALIS

810 boul. des Mille – îles
Auteuil, Laval, QC H7L 1K5
CANADA

514-278-3020
flemire@cam.org
http://www.cam.org/~flemire/
    novalis/fr/novalis.htm

LEARNERS TREK

138 Twin Oaks Rd
Louisa, VA 23093
LearnersTrek@yahoo.com
http://www.twinoaks.org/members-
    exmembers/members/felix/
    learnerstrek.html

LEBENSGARTEN STEYERBERG

Ginsterweg 3
D-31595 Steyerberg
GERMANY

+49-(0)57-64-23-70
lebensgarten@gmx.de
elsafrajo@compuserve.de
http://www.lebensgarten.de

LEE ABBEY ASTON HOUSEHOLD COMMUNITY

121 Albert Rd
Aston
Birmingham B6 5ND England
UNITED KINGDOM

+44-(0)1598-752621,
+44-(0)121-326-8280
jim@leeabbey.org.uk
http://www.leeabbey.org.uk

LICHEN

PO Box 25
Wolf Creek, OR 97497

541-866-2665 (7–9am best)
licheneers@yahoo.com
http://www.communitymade.com/
    communities/lichen-more.html

LIFE CENTER ASSOCIATION

4722 Baltimore Ave
Philadelphia, PA 19143

jimba@aol.com

LINDSBERGS KURSGÅRD

Lindsberg 10
S-79191 Falun
SWEDEN

+46-(0)23-43030
http://www.lindsberg.net

LITTLE GROVE COMMUNITY

Grove Ln
Chesham
Bucks HP5 3QQ England
UNITED KINGDOM

+44-(0)1494-778080
nick.weir@btinternet.com
N.Mackeith@ich.ucl.ac.uk

LIVING ROCK COOPERATIVE

803 E Grand River Ave
East Lansing, MI 48823

517-332-1437
licavol1@msu.edu

LONG BRANCH ENVIRONMENTAL EDUCATION CENTER

PO Box 369
Leicester, NC 28748

828-683-3662
paulg@buncombe.main.nc.us
http://main.nc.us/LBEEC

LOSANG DRAGPA BUDDHIST CENTRE

Dobroyd Castle
Pexwood Rd
Todmorden OL14 7JJ England
UNITED KINGDOM

+44-(0)1706-812247,
+44-(0)1706-815236
losangD@aol.com

LOTHLORIEN – CENTRO DE CURA E CRESCIMENTO

Caeté - AÇU
46-940-000 Palmeiras, BA
BRAZIL

+55-75-344-1129
centro@lothlorien.org.br
http://www.lothlorien.org.br/
portugues

MAAT DOMPIN

Charlottesville, VA 22906

540-992-0248, 804-969-2674

MARSH COMMONS

101 South G St
Arcata, CA 95521

Joyce Plath
joyceplath@aol.com

Peter Starr
startrak@northcoast.com
http://www.MarshCommons.org

MAXWORKS COOPERATIVE

716 W Maxwell St
Chicago, IL 60607

MOLINO CREEK FARMING COLLECTIVE

PO Box 69
Davenport, CA 95017

MOLLOY ASHRAM RETREAT

Frazer Rd
Mount Molloy, Queensland 4871
AUSTRALIA

+61-(0)70-40-941168

MONTE VUALA

CH-8881 Walenstadtberg
SWITZERLAND

+41-(0)81-735-1115
montevuala@frauenhotel.org
http://www.frauenhotel.org

MOURNE GRANGE CAMPHILL VILLAGE COMMUNITY

Newry Rd, Kilkeel
Co Down BT34 4EX N Ireland
UNITED KINGDOM

+44-(0)1693-76-22-28,
+44-(0)1693-76-01-28
100653.2371@compuserve.com
http://www.camphill.org.uk/guide/
mourne/mourne.htm

MT. MURRINDAL COOPERATIVE

W Tree Via Buchan, Victoria 3885
AUSTRALIA

+61-(0)51-550-218 (or 225 or 222),
+61-(0)3-5155-0279

MØRDRUPGÅRD

Mørdrupvej 7
DK-3540 Lynge
DENMARK

+45-48187007
korn@moerdrupkorn.dk
http://www.moerdrupkorn.dk

NESS

Ed or Chelle
381 Hewlett Rd
Hermon, NY 13652

315-347-4097
chellel@usa.net

NEW COMMUNITY COOPERATIVE

425 Ann St
East Lansing, MI 48823

517-351-3820
http://www.msu.edu/user/coop

NEW HUMANITY CENTRE

2001 Eleonon Rd
Akroyali Avias
GR-24100 Kalamata
GREECE

+30-721-58172,
+30-721-58035 (fax)
http://users.belgacom.net/grenade/
new_humanity_center.html

NEW JERUSALEM COMMUNITY

745 Derby Ave
Cincinnati, OH 45232

513-541-4748, 513-541-2377

NEW VRINDABAN

RR 1 Box 319
Moundsville, WV 26041

304-843-1600
mail@newvrindaban.com
http://www.newvrindaban.com

NOAH PROJECT OF ASHEVILLE

PO Box 1173
Leicester, NC 28748

828-683-5739, 828-NOAH-316
noahproject@earthling.net
http://www.noahproject.com

NOMADELFIA

CP 178
I-58100 Grosseto, GR
ITALY

+39-(0)564-338243,
+39-(0)564-338244
nomadelfia@gol.grosseto.it
popolo@nomadelfia.it
http://www.nomadelfia.it

NWA COHOUSING

1215 S Dunn Ave
AR 72701

http://groups.yahoo.com/group/
NWAcohousingcommunity

O'BRIEN LAKE HOMESTEADERS

PO Box 38
Eureka, MT 59917

406-889-3452

OAK CREEK COMMONS

1323 Stoney Creek Rd
Paso Robles, CA 93446

800-489-8715
info@oakcreekcommons.org

Mike Swettenam
805-239-4597
mikesw@oakcreekcommons.org
http://www.oakcreekcommons.org

OAK VILLAGE COMMONS

Oak Village Commons
Austin, TX

512-301-9563

Cat Barron
512-301-9917
ccbarron@io.com
http://www.oakhillcohousing.org

OFEK SHALOM CO-OP

Madison, WI 53703

608-257-8880, 608-442-8649
services@madisoncommunity.coop
http://www.madisoncommunity.co
op/house.cfm?HouseID=10

OHIO BIO-ENVIRO SETTLEMENTS, INC.

contact@obes.itgo.com
http://www.obes.itgo.com

OJAI FOUNDATION

9739 Ojai Santa Paula Rd
Ojai, CA 93023

contact@ojaifoundation.org
http://www.ojaifoundation.org

OLIVE BRANCH COMMUNITY

PO Box 73497
Washington, DC 20056

202-682-9056
olivemoss@aol.com
http://www.olivebranchcommunity.org

ÖKOLEA – KLOSTERDORF

Hohensteiner Weg 3
D-15345 Klosterdorf
GERMANY

+49-(0)3341-35-939-30,
+49-(0)3341-35-939-0
info@oekolea.de
http://www.oekolea.de

OLYMPIA HOUSING COLLECTIVE

129 Percival St NW
Olympia, WA 98502

360-352-2401

OSHO MIASTO

I-53010 Frosini Siena
ITALY

+39-(0)577-960124
oshomiasto@oshomiasto.it
http://www.oshomiasto.it

THE OTHONA COMMUNITY

East Hall Farm, East End Rd
Bradwell-on-Sea
Essex CM0 7PN England
UNITED KINGDOM

+44-(0)1621-776-564
webmaster@othona.org
http://www.othona.org

PADANARAM SETTLEMENT

RR 1 Box 478
Williams, IN 47470

812-388-5571

PALMGROVE CHRISTIAN COMMUNITY

PO Box 455, Utu-Abak
Abak AKS
NIGERIA

+234-(0)11-085-501-022

PARADISE GARDENS

808-934-9516
http://www.angelfire.com/pq/
paradisegardens

PARNASSUS RISING

PO Box 33681
Phoenix, AZ 85067

PATHFINDER FELLOWSHIP

Bickersteth House
25 Sheffield Terrace
London W8 7NQ England
UNITED KINGDOM

+44-(0)171727-5586,
+44-(0)171-229-6943

PEACE FARM

188 US Highway 60
Panhandle, TX 79068

806-341-4801
peacefarm@arn.net
http://users.arn.net/~peacefarm

PEOPLE HOUSE

3035 W 25th Ave
Denver, CO 80211

303-480-5130, 303-237-5049
PeopleHouse@mindspring.com
http://www.peoplehouse.com

PEOPLE OF THE LIVING GOD

RR 2 Box 423
McMinnville, TN 37110

931-692-3236, 931-692-3730
cook@people-livinggod.org
potlg@blomand.net
http://www.people-livinggod.org

PIÑON ECOVILLAGE

PO Box 3537
Santa Fe, NM 87501

505-455-2595
pinon_ecovillage@yahoo.com
pinon@ic.org

Sean Knight
sean@ic.org
http://www.pinon-ecovillage.org

PIONEER CO-OP

340 Parkway Cir
Davis, CA 95616

530-757-2015

POD OF DOLPHINS

185 Dolphin Ln NE
Check, VA 24072

540-651-3040
dolphins@swva.net

POTASH HILL COMMUNITY

9 Frazier Ln
Cummington, MA 01026

413-634-0181

PRO-FEM

tan@pobox.com
http://www.profem.com

PROJEKT EULENSPIEGEL

Modell Wasserburg e.V.
Gasthof
Dorfstraße 25
D-88142 Wasserburg/Bodensee
GERMANY

+49-(0)8382-89056
+49-(0)8382-887875
eulenspiegel.wasserburg@
   t-online.de
http://www.eulenspiegel-
   wasserburg.de

PROWOKULTA

info@prowokulta.org
http://www.prowokulta.org

PUMPKIN HOLLOW FARM

1184 Route 11
Craryville, NY 12521

518-325-3583, 1-877-325-3583
pumpkin@taconic.net
http://www.pumpkinhollow.org

THE QUARRIES

434-831-1020
quarries@aol.com
quarries@earthlink.net
http://www.thequarries.com

RACHANA RETREAT

23301 NE Redmond Fall City Rd
Redmond, WA 98053

425-868-8118

RAINBOW HOUSE

1115 Tennessee St
Lawrence, KS 66044

785-843-3704

RENAISSANCE VILLAGE

19393 Sanctuary Rd
Penn Valley, CA 95946

RIDGE HOUSE

2420 Ridge Rd
Berkeley, CA 94709

510-548-9722
http://www.usca.org/coops/rid.htm

RIVER SPIRIT COMMUNITY

PO Box 173
Mad River, CA 95552
wildriver@saber.net

RIVERSIDE COMMUNITY

R D 2 Upper Moutere
Nelson, South Island LMO-805
NEW ZEALAND

+64-(0)3-5267-805,
+64-(0)3-5267-033 ext 30
michel@riverside.org.nz
robert@riverside.org.nz
http://www.nelson.planet.org.nz/
   riverside

ROBERTS CREEK COHOUSING

Box 152
Roberts Creek (Sunshine Coast),
BC VON 2WO
CANADA

Gary Kent
604-885-2971
garykent@uniserve.com

Carol Shoji
604-885-2198
cshoji@dccnet.com
http://www.cohousing.ca/robertscreek

Short Listings

SACRED MOUNTAIN RANCH

PO Box 90763
Phoenix, AZ 85066
janiece@differentway.net
http://differentway.net/smr

SAINT FRANCIS & THERESE CATHOLIC WORKER HOUSE

52 Mason St
Worcester, MA 01610

508-753-3588, 508-753-3089

SAINT FRANCIS CATHOLIC WORKER

4652 N Kenmore Ave
Chicago, IL 60640

773-561-5073

SALT CREEK INTENTIONAL COMMUNITY

585 Wasankari Rd
Port Angeles, WA 98363

360-928-3022
thenwhat@olypen.com
Janevavan1@aol.com

SANTA CRUZ STUDENT HOUSING COOPERATIVE

316 Main St
Santa Cruz, CA 95060

831-426-2667

SANTA ROSA CREEK COMMONS

887 Sonoma Ave
Santa Rosa, CA 95404

707-523-0626

SEATTLE'S INTENTIONAL COMMUNITY PROGRAM

4540 15th Ave NE
Seattle, WA 98105

206-524-7301 ext 214

SENECA FALLS CO-OP

2309 Nueces St
Austin, TX 78705

512-477-2052
seneca@iccaustin.coop
http://www.iccaustin.coop/houses/
seneca.html

SHADY GROVE

PO Box 688
Penngrove, CA 94951

707-792-9825
http://mythicimages.com

SHAMBALA

PO Box 10
Bellingen, NSW 2454
AUSTRALIA

+61-(0)2-6655-1367,
+61-(0)2-6655-1826
tazo007@hotmail.com

SHILOH COMMUNITY

PO Box 97
Sulphur Springs, AR 72768

479-298-3299, 479-298-3297
shilohf@nwark.com
800-374-4564
http://www.users.nwark.com/
~shilohf/community.htm

SHIVALILA

PO Box 1966
Pahoa, HI 96778

808-965-9371
shivalila@aol.com

SHORT MOUNTAIN SANCTUARY, INC.

247 Sanctuary Ln
Liberty, TN 37095

615-536-5176, 615-563-4397 (msg)
http://www.radfae.org/sms.htm

SICHLASSENFALLEN

1139 N 21st St
Milwaukee, WI 53233

414-933-2063
ky24003@yahoo.com

SIMON COMMUNITY

PO Box 1187
129 Malden Rd
London NW5 4HW England
UNITED KINGDOM

+44-(0)20-7485-6639
info@simoncommunity.org.uk
communityoffice@
simoncommunity.org.uk
http://www.simoncommunity.org.uk

SONG OF THE MORNING

9607 Sturgeon Valley Rd
Vanderbilt, MI 49795

989-983-4107
guestsrv@goldenlotus.org
office@goldenlotus.org
http://www.goldenlotus.org

SOUTHERN OREGON WOMEN'S NETWORK

2000 King Mountain Trl
Wolf Creek, OR 97497

ST. JOHN'S ORDER

642 Myrtle Ave
South San Francisco, CA 94080

650-615-9529, 650-255-9225
anama@jps.net
http://quietmountain.org/
dharmacenters/st_johns/
st_johns.htm

STARLAND RANCH

56925 Yucca Trl #355
Yucca Valley, CA 92284

760-364-2069
http://www.starlandretreat.com

STARSEED COMMUNITY

672 Chapel Rd
Savoy, MA 01256

413-743-0417
starseed@bcn.net
http://www.massretreats.com

STEPPING STONES HOUSING CO-OP

154 Stiby Rd
Yeovil BA21 3ER England
UNITED KINGDOM

+44-(0)1654-712538
highburyfarm@hotmail.com
sasandalex@gn.apc.org
http://www.highburyfarm.freeserve.
   co.uk/homepage.htm

STEWART LITTLE CO-OP

211 Stewart Ave
Ithaca, NY 14850

607-273-1983, 607-273-2218
stewart_little@cornell.edu

STIFTELSEN STJÄRNSUND

+46-(0)225-80001,
+46-(0)225-80210
fridmail@tiscali.se
http://frid.nu

STORYBOOK GLEN

PO Box 95
Pettigrew, AR 72752

479-677-2679, 479-677-3070

STRANGERS & GUESTS CATHOLIC WORKER COMMUNITY

108 Hillcrest Dr
Blockton, IA 50836

SU CASA CATHOLIC WORKER COMMUNITY

5045 S Laflin St
Chicago, IL 60609

773-376-9263
danieldlp@aol.com

SUNFLOWER CO-OP

1122 S 3rd St
Austin, TX 78704

512-447-1268

SUNNYSIDE FARM

9101 Holiness Hwy
Mokane, MO 65059

573-676-5609

SUNRISE FARM COMMUNITY

W Tree Via Buchan, Victoria 3885
AUSTRALIA

+61-(0)3-5155-0336,
+61-(0)3-5152-0276

ஐ T ஐ

TACOMA CATHOLIC WORKER

1417 S G St
Tacoma, WA 98405

253-572-6582
guadalope@juno.com

TAIZÉ COMMUNITY

F-71250 Taizé
FRANCE

+33-(0)385-50-30-30,
+33-(0)385-50-30-02
community@taize.fr
meetings@taize.fr
http://www.almac.co.uk/taize/
   taize.html

TEN STONES

463 Ten Stones Circle
Charlotte, VT 05445
802-425-2931

Joan White Hansen
802-425-7145
perofjs@together.net
http://www.sover.net/~dogstar/
   10stones.html

TERRA FIRMA

172 Drummond St
Ottawa, ON K1S 1K4
CANADA

Anthony Leaning,
Rebecca Aird
613-233-6286
raird@magma.ca

THINC

Tasmania
AUSTRALIA

+61-(0)3-6295-0774
info@togetherhousing.com.au
http://www.togetherhousing.org.au

THREE SPRINGS

58920 Italian Bar Rd
North Fork, CA 93643
farm@sierranet.net

TONANTZIN LAND INSTITUTE

PO Box 7889
Albuquerque, NM 87194

505-277-5465
atila@unm.edu

TORONTO CATHOLIC WORKER

5 Close Ave
Toronto, ON M6K 2V2
CANADA

416-516-8198

TOWN HEAD COLLECTIVE

Town Head Cottages
Dunford Bridge
Sheffield S36 4TG England
UNITED KINGDOM

THE TRIBE

21010 N Old Highway 89
Paulden, AZ 86334

TRIFORM CAMPHILL COMMUNITY

20 Tri Form Rd
Hudson, NY 12534

518-851-9320
info@triformcamphill.org
http://triformcamphill.org

TROUBADOUR MÄRCHENZENTRUM

Bretthorststraße 140
D-32602 Vlotho
GERMANY

+49-(0)5733-10801
info@maerchen-zentrum.de
http://www.maerchen-zentrum.de

TUI LAND TRUST

RD 1 Wainui Bay
Takaka
NEW ZEALAND

+64-(0)3-525-9654,
+64-(0)3-525-751
kayawayne@mandalabook.com

TURTLEDOVE POND

9274 Whippoorwill Trl
Jupiter, FL 33478

561-746-7245
turtledovepond@webtv.net
http://community-2.webtv.net/
turtledovepond

TURTLES ISLAND

PO Box 616
Pine Hill, NY 12465

TWO PIERS

14 Oriental Pl
Brighton BN1 2LJ England
UNITED KINGDOM

+44-(0)1273-739-779,
+44-(0)1273-772-682
twopiers@co-op.org
info@twopiers.co-op.org
http://easyweb.easynet.co.uk/
~twopiers/twopiers/welcome.html

UDGAARDEN

Udgaarden 24
DK-8471 Sabro
DENMARK

+45-86-94-96-18, +45-86-94-91-17
Udgaarden@lading.dk
kaj.larsen@adr.dk

UNKNOWN TRUTH FELLOWSHIP WORKERS

342 Garnet Lake Rd
Warrensburg, NY 12885

VALSØLILLEGÅRD

Knud Lavard Svej 94
DK-4174 Jystrup
DENMARK

+45-57-528777
heinerg@post3.tele.dk

VARSITY HOUSE

119 NW 9th St
Corvallis, OR 97330

541-758-7216

VIALEN

http://hem.passagen.se/vialen

VILLAGE COMMUNITY

Perth
AUSTRALIA
villagecommunity@yahoo.com.au
http://au.geocities.com/
villagecommunity

VIVEKANANDA VEDANTA SOCIETY

5423 S Hyde Park Blvd
Chicago, IL 60615

312/773-363-0027
Info@VedantaSociety-Chicago.org
http://www.vedantasociety-
chicago.org

WAIUA ASHRAM KAUAI

Sri Mario`ja
PO Box 1892
Kapaa, HI 96746
mario_ja@hotmail.com

WALDEN COMMUNITY

Madrid
SPAIN
kapok1@wanadoo.es
http://perso.wanadoo.es/waldencm
/home.htm

WALNUT HOUSE COOPERATIVE

1740 Walnut St
Berkeley, CA 94709

510-549-3140

WATERMARGIN COOPERATIVE

103 Mcgraw Pl
Ithaca, NY 14850

607-272-9441
http://www.watermargin.org

WATERSMEET HOMES

S93W27685 Edgewood Ave
Mukwonago, WI 53149
krogstad@netzero.net
http://www.angelfire.com/wi/
watersmeet

WAWAVOX

Kastanienalle 77
10435 Berlin
GERMANY

+49-(0)30-443-587-86
k77projects@gmx.de
http://www.k77.org

WE'MOON LAND

PO Box 1395
Estacada, OR 97023

503-630-7848
matrix@wemoon.ws
http://www.teleport.com/~wemoon

THE WELL AT WILLEN

bookings@thewellatwillen.org.uk
http://www.thewellatwillen.org.uk

WESTSIDE COMMUNITY

12479 Walsh Ave
Los Angeles, CA 90066

310-827-3618, 323-823-0287,
323-823-784
fsotcher@aol.com

THE WEYST

P. Peterusstraat 21
NL-5423 SV Handel
NETHERLANDS

+31-(0)492-322509

**WILLIAM STRINGFELLOW
CATHOLIC WORKER**

2130 N Linn St
Peoria, IL 61604

309-681-9892, 309-686-2887

**WISE ACRES COOPERATIVE
ASSOCIATION**

PO Box 490
Indianola, WA 98342
http://www.wise-acres.org

WOGENO MÜNCHEN EG

WOGENO München eG
München, Barvaria
GERMANY

+49-(0)89-721-17-05
info@wogeno.de
http://wogeno.de

WOMANSHARE

1531 Grays Creek Rd
Grants Pass, OR 97527

541-862-2807

WOMEN'S ART COLONY FARM

20 Old Overlook Rd
Poughkeepsie, NY 12603

845-473-9267, 212-473-2546
http://www.katemillett.com/pages/
1/index.htm

WÄXTHUSET VÄDDÖ

Fjäll 6908
S-76040 Väddö
SWEDEN

+46-(0)175-31290,
+46-(0)175-31097
waxthuset@waxthuset.se
lena.kristina@waxthuset.se
http://www.waxthuset.se

YAHARA LINDEN GATHERING

1038 Williamson St
Madison, WI 53703

608-249-4474

YAMAGISHI-KAI

Gip Code 519-1424
555 Kawahigashi Iga-cho
Ayama-gun Mie Prefecture
JAPAN

+81-(0)5954-5-4594
yoshihikotomio@yahoo.co.jp

**YOGODA COMMUNITY
PROJECT**

8217 Ardleigh St
Philadelphia, PA 19118
yogoda@wj.net

Z

ZACCHAEUS HOUSE

89 Pine St
Binghamton, NY 13901

607-773-0246

**ZEGG – CENTRE FOR
EXPERIMENTAL CULTURAL
DESIGN**

Rosa-Luxemburg-Strasse 89
D-14806 Belzig,
GERMANY

+49-(0)33841-59510
zeggpol@zegg.de
empfang@zegg.de
http://www.zegg.de

**ZENDIK FARM ARTS
FOUNDATION**

HC 82 Box 217A
Marlinton, WV 24954

304-799-7281
mail@zendik.org
info@zendik.org
http://www.zendik.org

ZENTRUM WALDEGG

CH-3823 Wengen
SWITZERLAND

+41-(0)33-855-44-22
enfo@waldegg.ch
http://www.Waldegg.ch

ZEPHYR

180 Zephyr Cir SE
Floyd, VA 24091

540-745-3474

**THE ZION UCC INTENTIONAL
COMMUNITY**

435 1st St #437
Henderson, KY 42420

270-826-0605, 270-826-0281

Short Listings

287

From 1972 to the present, Communities magazine has consistently offered excellent information, stories, and community wisdom to the movement. Here is a list of recent back issues, which the Fellowship for Intentional Community is proud to make available.

#112 Multigenerational Community
To the Ecovillage!; It Takes All of Us; Elder Leadership in Cohousing; What Can You Expect of Me as a Community Elder?; Seriously Seeking Community, Part II; Myths About Intentional Community. (*Fall '01*)

#113 Communication & Process
Getting Real--Ten "Truth Skills"; Birthing Co-Creative Community; Towards Clarity & Honesty; True Consensus, False Consensus; Agenda Planning-Making Meetings Flow; The Fine Art of Giving & Receiving Feedback. (*Win. '01*)

#114 What Do Children Learn in Community?
Community-Based Education: Superior to Public Schools? Self-Reliance, Self-Esteem, and Social Confidence; A Place in the Tribe; Low-Cost "Health Insurance" for Communities--Or Anyone Else. (*Spr. '02*)

#115 The Heart of Sustainability
Portland's Natural Building Convergence; Many Hands Make Sustainability Work; Sustainability in the City of the Angels; "More Sustainable Than Thou," An Eco-Communitarian's Recovery; The Haybox Cooker; Everybody Loves Strawbale. (*Sum. '02*)

#116 Can We Afford to Live in Community?
Inventing a Rural Community Economy, Business by Business; The Making of a Community Entrepreneur; Developing a Hybrid Economy; "Family Style" Income-Sharing; No Funds? How One Community Did It. (*Fall/Win. '02*)

#117 Ecovillages: What Have We Learned?
What is an Ecovillage; Creating "Ecovillage Zoning" with Local Officials; Why Urban Ecovillages are Crucial; A 73-Year-Old Ecovillage in the Land of Ice and Fire; Accountability and Consequences. (*Spr. '03*)

#118 Lovers in Community
Make It or Break It; Breaking Up (While Staying in Community); Living Outside the Box; Relationships in the Crucible; Lovers, Friends, and Parents; I Can't Live Without Women; Relationship by Consensus. (*Sum. '03*)

#119 Right Livelihood in Community
Recipe for a Thriving Community; Findhorn's Village Economy; An Honest Day's (Village) Work; Healthy & Unhealthy Communal Economies; Right Livelihood in a Camphill Village; Redwoods, Rugged Cliffs, & Mineral Baths; Developing Trust in Communities. (*Fall '03*)

#121 Thriving in Community
Still Thriving After All These Years; Where There Are Cooks, There's Good Morale; Finding My Heart at Camphill Soltane; Ecology in Community: Commitment to Place; Living the Spiritual Quest of Elder Years. (*Win. '03*)

#122 Community Seeker's Guide
My Marathon Tour of Communities; From a Community Seeker's Journal; Planning a Community Visit; Tips for Guests & Hosts; When and Why to Block Consensus; Seeking Community in New York City. (*Spr. '04*)

#123 A Day in the Life
By the Plume of Popocatepetl; A Spring Day in Portugal; La Caravana Arcoiris por la Paz; Pilgrimage in a Desert Monastery; How to Really Support Ecovillages (Not Just Hugs and Theories). (*Sum. '04*)

#124 Spiritual Community
Avoiding Spiritual Community; Rocky Mountain High; Why I'm Moving to Findhorn; On the Edge of the Abyss; Spiritual Beings, Material World; Do we Really Value "Diversity"? (*Fall '04*)

#125 Life After Student Co-ops
What I Learned Last Summer; Ruined for American Culture; Now I Want to Join a Community (or Maybe Start My Own ...); The Toughest Issue We Ever Faced (*Win. '04*)

#126 The Arts in Community
101 Art Projects Your Community Can Do; Painting and Dancing for Community; Creativity as "Learning Game"; Confessions of a Process Warrior (*Spr. '05*)

Purchase online at store.ic.org
or see order form on page 312.

Tony Sirna – Dancing Rabbit Ecovillage

About the Appendix

The Appendix, coming last but certainly not least, contains elements (such as the Indexes) that can greatly enhance your use of this book, and also provides information about FIC membership and an order form for FIC products.

Helping you find all the information you're looking for in the *Directory* is very important to us, so we've done our best to create useful indexes to aid you in your search.

Article Index

The article index is a traditional index of the articles that make up the first section of the *Directory*.

Community Listings Keyword Index

The Community Listings Keyword Index, though by no means exhaustive, is a vital tool for rooting out some of the information packed between the covers of this book. To get the most out of your *Directory*, use this index in conjunction with the Maps and the Cross-Reference Charts.

This index is based on the listing and questionnaire each group provided about itself. If a community is not indexed under a particular keyword, that does not necessarily mean that the group does not practice or pursue that particular value—it may mean only that they did not mention that aspect in their description.

We tried to index groups based on the areas of focus they offer our readers, and on those recurring questions we hear from people searching for their ideal community.

Realizing that vocational and spiritual considerations often play a major role in community searches, we also indexed many businesses run by communities (restaurants, woodworking shops, conference centers, etc.) and certain spiritual paths (Catholic Workers, Zen Buddhists, Twelve Tribes, Quakers, etc.).

Communities in grey do not have full descriptions, as they did not fill out a questionnaire in time for this edition, and are found in the Short Community Listings section on page 273. Communites in black have full descriptions and are found in the Communites Listing section and in the Cross-Reference Charts.

Both of the indexes were prepared by Twin Oaks Indexing, a professional book indexing business of Twin Oaks Community in Virginia.

Article Index

Community Listings Keyword Index

Wyld Court, Moonshadow, Omega Institute for Holistic Studies, One Common Unity, Open Gate Farm & Retreat, Panterra, Paradise Village, Phoenix Gay Chub Music/Art Community, Pumpkin Hollow Community, Qumbya Co-op, Rainbow Hearth Sanctuary and Retreat Center, Rainbow Peace Caravan, Rainbow Valley, Sowing Circle, SurrealEstates, Susan B. Anthony Women's Land Trust, Trillium Farm Community, UFA-Fabrik, The v2b Cooperative, Vlierhof, Wellspring, Windward Foundation, Women's Art Colony Farm, Zendik Farm Arts Foundation.

ASHRAMS
Kashi Ashram, Kindness House, Ma Yoga Shakti International Mission, Molloy Ashram Retreat, Sivananda Ashram Yoga Ranch, Sri Aurobindo Sadhana Peetham, Truth Consciousness, Vivekananda Monastery and Retreat Center, Waiua Ashram Kauai, Yogaville/Satchidananda Ashram.

AUSTRALIA
Backyard Tech, Canberra Cohousing, Cascade Cohousing, Cennednyss Community, Central Coast Community, The Change, Co-ordination Co-op, Cohousing Research and Education, Crossroads Medieval Village, Crystal Waters Permaculture Village, Danthonia Bruderhof, Earth First Australia, Freestone Hill Community, Gondwana Sanctuary, Hope Hill Community, Jesus Christians, Jindibah, Komaja, Kookaburra Park Eco-Village, Melbourne Cohousing Network, Molloy Ashram Retreat, Mt. Murrindal Cooperative, Osho Mevlana Residential Community, Rosneath Farm, Shambala, Somerville Ecovillage, Sunrise Farm Community, THINC, 12 Tribes Peppercorn Creek Farm, 12 Tribes Katoomba, 12 Tribes Oatlands, Village Community.

AUSTRIA
Familien-Gemeinshaft Rat & Tat, Keimblatt Oekodorf, Komaja, Lebensraum.

BED AND BREAKFASTS/GUEST FACILITIES
Abode of the Message, Bartimaeus Community of Meadow Wood, Berkeley Cohousing, Crystal Waters Permaculture Village, Earthaven Ecovillage, Edges, Gaia Grove Ecospiritual Community & Ecoretreat, Neve Shalom/Wahat al-Salam, O.U.R. Ecovillage, SEADS of Truth Inc., Sophia Community, Torri Superiore Ecovillage, Trillium Farm Community, 12 Tribes Rutland, UFA-Fabrik, Walker Creek Farm, Wellspring, WindSong, Yulupa Cohousing.

BEHAVIORISM
Comunidad Los Horcones, Walden Two Community California.

BELGIUM
Cohousing.be, Communauté de la Vielle Voie, De Regenboog, Samenhuizing West-Brabant.

BELIZE
La Flor del Agua Community, Namasté...Multi-Cultural Sustainable Living Community.

BOLIVIA
Comunidad Planetaria Janajpacha.

BRAZIL
Lothlorien—Centro de Cura e Crescimento, 12 Tribes Curitiba, 12 Tribes Londrina, 12 Tribes Osório.

BRUDERHOF
Beech Grove Bruderhof, Bellvale Bruderhof, Bruderhof Communities, Bruderhof-Haus Holzland, Bruderhof-Haus Sannerz, Catskill Bruderhof, Danthonia Bruderhof, Darvell Bruderhof, Fox Hill Bruderhof, Maple Ridge Bruderhof, New Meadow Run Bruderhof, Spring Valley Bruderhof, Woodcrest Bruderhof.

BUDDHISM
American Buddhist Shim Gum Do, Buddhist Cohousing, Buddhist Society of Compassionate Wisdom, Dharma House Community Project, Khula Dhamma, Losang Dragpa Buddhist Centre, Osho Mevlana Residential Community, Tibetan Buddhist Learning Center, The Zen Society.

BUILDING, ALTERNATIVE
Beaver Creek, Dancing Rabbit Ecovillage, The Domes, EarthArt Village, Kibbutz Lotan, Light Morning, Light of Freedom, Sharingwood Cohousing, Springhill Cohousing Community, Tao Bear Recovery Community, Village of Harmony, Windtree Ranch.

BUILDING, GREEN
Agape, Attachment Parenting Village, Awaawaroa Bay Eco-Village, Berea College Ecovillage, Dayspring Circle, Dragon Belly Farm, Eastern Village Cohousing, Echollective Farm, Ecovilla Asociación Gaia, Ecovillage Sieben Linden, Emerald Coast Village, Fordyce Street Cohousing, Freedom-Universe, GaiaYoga Gardens, Garden O' Vegan, Great Oak Cohousing, H.O.M.E. Heaven on Mother Earth, Higher Ground Cohousing, Jamaica Plain Cohousing, Lama Foundation, Lebensraum, Light of Freedom, O.U.R. Ecovillage, Pacific Gardens Cohousing Community, Pioneer Trails Institute, Pleasant Hill Cohousing, Raccoon Creek Community, Rise and Shine, Sirius Community, Soma, Storybook Shire, Sustainable Living Systems, Takoma Village Cohousing, TerraVie, Torri Superiore Ecovillage, Village Terraces Cohousing Neighborhood, The Wild Human Initiative, Wild Sage Cohousing, Woodfolk House, Zuni Mountain Sanctuary.

BUILDING, NATURAL
Beaver Creek Homestead, Emerald Earth, Hudson Valley Ecovillage, Lama Foundation, Moonshadow, Mountain Home, Mulvey Creek Land Co-operative, O.U.R. Ecovillage, Oceanic Ecovillage, WhiteHawk.

CAMPING
7th Millennium Community, Camp Sister Spirit, Center of Light Spirituality Center, Common Ground (VA), Comunidad Los Horcones, Dragonfly Farm, Earthaven Ecovillage, Eden Ranch Community, Enota Mountain Village, Franciscan Workers/ Companions in Community, Koinonia, Lost Valley Educational Center, Mulvey Creek Land Co-operative, Nomenus Radical Faerie Sanctuary, O.U.R. Ecovillage, Olympus, Ozark Avalon, Rainbow Family Gatherings, Rainbow Way Station, Rowe Camp & Conference Center, Saint Martin de Porres House, Sivananda Ashram Yoga Ranch, Southwest Sufi Community, Sparrow Hawk Village, Susan B. Anthony Women's Land Trust, Talking Cedars Developments Ltd., Tamera—Healing Biotope I, Teaching Drum Outdoor School, Upper Applegate Community, Wisteria, Zuni Mountain Sanctuary.

CANADA
AAAA Community for Tender Loving Care, Azania Alliance, Beaver Creek Homestead, Big Rock Farm, Cranberry Commons, Dandelion Community Co-op Inc., Downie Street Collective,

Dragonfly Farm, Drumlin Co-operative, Earthsea, Edenvale, Headlands, Kakwa Ecovillage, King Edward House, L'Arche —Homefires, Le Novalis, Lofstedt Farm Community, Lothlorien Farm, Maison Emmanuel, Middle Road Community, Morninglory, Mulvey Creek Land Co-operative, Next Step Integral, Northern Sun Farm Co-op, O.U.R. Ecovillage, Pacific Gardens Cohousing Community, Prairie Sky Cohousing, Réseau des ÉcoHameaux et ÉcoVillages du Québec, Roberts Creek Cohousing, Spirit Dance Co-operative Community, Talking Cedars Developments Ltd., Terra Firma, TerraVie, Toronto Catholic Worker, 12 Tribes Nelson, 12 Tribes Winnipeg, Waterloo Co-operative Residence Inc., Whole Village, WindSong, Yarrow Ecovillage.

CATHOLIC

Abbey of the Genesee, Agape, Casa Maria Catholic Worker Community, Catholic Worker Community Cleveland, Denver Catholic Worker, Dorothy Day Catholic Worker House, Dorothy Day Cohousing, House of Peace Catholic Worker, Karen Catholic Worker House, Little Flower Catholic Worker Farm, Saint Francis & Therese Catholic Worker House, Saint Francis Catholic Worker, Saint Jude Catholic Worker House Community, Strangers & Guests Catholic Worker Community, Su Casa Catholic Worker Community, Tacoma Catholic Worker, Toronto Catholic Worker, William Stringfellow Catholic Worker.

CELIBACY

Narrow Way Christian Community, Sri Aurobindo Sadhana Peetham.

CHILDREN-ORIENTED

AngelsValley, Camphill Special School, Clare's House of Hospitality, Eden Project, Everett, Federation of Arts for the Youth of Our Nation Foundation, Franciscan Workers/Companions in Community, Freeland Community, Garden O' Vegan, Karen Catholic Worker House, Kitezh Children's Eco-Village Community, Meadowdance Community, Oakland Elizabeth House, Saint Martin de Porres House, The Vale, Windtree Ranch.

SEE ALSO YOUTH.

CHRISTIAN

7th Millennium Community, Agape Community, Agape Lay Apostolate Community, Alpha Omega Christian Communities, ARC Retreat Center, Ashram Community, Bruderhof Communities, Bruderhof-Haus Sannerz, Cambridge Terrace Community, Camphill Village Kimberton Hills, Camphill Village Newton Dee, Catskill Bruderhof, Christ of the Hills Monastery, Danthonia Bruderhof, Darvell Bruderhof, Elim, Elmendorf Christian Community, Family, The Family, Fox Hill Bruderhof, Greenhaus Community, Hutterian Brethren, Iona Community, Jesus Christ's Community, Jesus Christians, Koinonia, L'Arche Mobile, LittleFlowerCatholicWorker, Narrow Way Christian Community, New Creation Christian Community, Palmgrove Christian Community, Plain Anabaptist Community, Plow Creek, Refuge, Shepherdsfield, Turn Cedars, Upper Applegate Community, Voice for the Voiceless.

SEE ALSO NAMES OF SPECIFIC DENOMINATIONS.

CLASS

Azania Alliance, Free State Community.

CO-COUNSELING

Du-Má, Finca Luna, Hidden Valley.

CO-CREATION

CedarSanctum, Hummingbird Community, Light Morning, Mulvey Creek Land Co-operative.

COHOUSING

Albuquerque Urban Ecovillage, Altair Cohousing, Anarres Ecovillage, Aprovecho Research Center, Arcadia Cohousing, Awakening to Grace, Azania Alliance, Bartimaeus Community of Meadow Wood, Berea College Ecovillage, Berkeley Cohousing, Blue House, Blue Ridge Cohousing, Blueberry Hill, Buddhist CoHousing, Burlington Cohousing, Cambridge Cohousing, Camelot Cohousing, Camp Sister Spirit, Cantine's Island Cohousing, Casa Verde Commons, Cascade Cohousing, Cascadia Commons, Catocton Creek Village, Center for Purposeful Living, Center of Light Spirituality Center, Central Austin Cohousing, Central Florida Cohousing, Champlain Valley Cohousing, Coastal Cohousing, Coastal Cohousing (Maine), Cobb Hill, CoFlats Stroud, CoHo Cohousing, Cohousing Bristol, Cohousing for San Diego!, Commons on the Alameda, Community Project, Concord Village, Coyote Crossing, Cranberry Commons, CW Lismortel, Dapala Farm, Davis Square Cohousing, Denver Urban Cohousing, Detroit Cohousing, Dorothy Day Cohousing, Doyle Street, Dragon Belly Farm, Duwamish Cohousing, Earthswell Farm, East Bay Cohousing, East Lake Commons, East Ventura/West Valley CoHousing, Eastern Village Cohousing, EcoVillage at Ithaca, EcoVillage of Loudoun County, EdlerSpirit Community at Trailview, Empty Nest Cohos, Eno Commons, Enota Mountain Village, Eugene Cohousing, Everett, The Farm, Fellowship Community, Fordyce Street Cohousing, Free State Community, Fresno Cohousing, Friends and Neighbors, Frog Song, Garden State Cohousing, Gemeenschappelijk Wonen Nieuwegein, Genesee Gardens Cohousing, Grace, Great Oak Cohousing, Gricklegrass, Hanoar Haoved Vehalomed, Harmony Village, Hearthstone, Heartwood Cohousing, Het Carre, Higher Ground Cohousing, Highline Crossing, Homewood Cohousing, Hope Hill Community, Hudson Valley Ecovillage, Hundredfold Farm, Ibsgården, Jackson Place Cohousing, Jamaica Plain Cohousing, Kakwa Ecovillage, Karen Catholic Worker House, Kipling Creek, Komaja, Komun, Landelijke Vereniging Centraal Wonen, Lebensraum, Liberty Village, Los Angeles Eco-Village, Lyons Valley Village, Manitou Arbor Ecovillage, Manzanita Village, Mariposa Group, Mariposa Grove, Maxwelton Creek Cohousing, Melbourne Cohousing Network, Metro Cohousing at Culver Way, Midcoast Cohousing Community, Middle Road Community, Milagro Cohousing, Monterey Cohousing, Montpelier Cohousing, Mosaic Commons, Muir Commons, N Street Cohousing, NEO Cohousing, Nevada City Cohousing, New View Cohousing, Newberry Place, Nomad Cohousing, Nyland, Oxford Community, Pacific Gardens Cohousing Community, Pathways CoHousing, Peninsula Park Commons, Pennine Camphill Community, Pine Street, Pioneer Valley, Planet Earth11, Pleasant Hill Cohousing, Poly Pagan Nudist Community, Prairie Onion Cohousing, Prairie Sky Cohousing Cooperative, Providence Cohousing, Prudence Crandall House, Puget Ridge Cohousing, Raccoon Creek Community, Rainbow Hearth Sanctuary and Retreat, Retirement Communities, River Rock Commons, Rocky Hill Cohousing, RoseWind Cohousing, Rosneath Farm, Sacramento Cohousing, Sacramento Suburban Cohousing, Samenhuizing West-Brabant, San Antonio Cohousing, San

Mateo Ecovillage, Santa Cruz County Cohousing, Shadowlake Village, Shambala Eco-Resort & EcoVillage, Sharingwood Cohousing, Silver Sage Village, Solstice Dawn, Solterra, Songaia Cohousing Community, Springhill Cohousing Community, Stewardship Incorporated, Stine Curves Cohousing, Sunward Cohousing, Sunwise Co-op, Takoma Village Cohousing, Talking Cedars Developments Ltd., Temescal Commons Cohousing, Touchstone Cohousing, Tres Placitas del Rio, Tribe of Blank, Tribe of Likatien, Trillium Hollow, Tullstugan Collective Housing Unit, Turn Cedars, Two Acre Wood, Two Echo Cohousing, Utopian Visions, Vashon Cohousing, Village Cohousing, Village Terraces Cohousing Neighborhood, Westwood Cohousing, Whole Village, Wild Sage Cohousing, WindSong, Winslow Cohousing Group, Woodlawn Townhome Cooperatives, Yarrow Ecovillage, Yellow Plum Commons, Yulupa Cohousing, Zen Society, Zephyr Valley Community Co-op.

COLOMBIA
Atlantis.

COMMUNICATION
Acorn Community, AinaOla, Camphill Communities California, Chacra Millalen, Colibri Urban Housing Collective, Du-Má, Ecovillage Sieben Linden, Firetender, Friends and Neighbors, GaiaYoga Gardens, Ganas, Glen Ivy, Heartsong, Kibbutz Lotan, Lost Valley Educational Center, Mariposa Group, Millstone Co-op, Monkton Wyld Court, Mulvey Creek Land Co-operative, New World Rising, Niederkaufungen, Omega Institute for Holistic Studies, Orca Landing, Port Townsend Ecovillage, Pumpkin Hollow Community, Rainbow Hearth Sanctuary and Retreat Center, Rainbow Valley, Rewilding Community, River Farm, San Mateo Ecovillage, Sandhill Farm, Shadowlake Village, Sharingwood Cohousing, Tao Bear Recovery Community, Terra Nova, Tribe of Likatien, Village Terraces Cohousing Neighborhood, Vlierhof, Walnut Street Co-op, Whitehall Co-op, Yulupa Cohousing.
SEE ALSO CONFLICT RESOLUTION.

COMPOSTING
Berea College Ecovillage, City of the Sun Foundation Inc., Dedetepe Eco-Farm, Jamaica Plain Cohousing, King Edward House, Parker Street Co-op, Prudence Crandall House, Purple Rose Collective, River City Housing Collective, Vail House, Woodburn Hill Farm.

COMPOSTING TOILETS
Agape, Beech Hill Community, Berea College Ecovillage, Dayspring Circle, Malu 'Aina, Mountain Home, Oran Mór, Redfield Community, Rosneath Farm, Sirius Community.

CONFERENCES/EVENTS
Abode of the Message, Breitenbush Hot Springs, Brynderwen Vegan Community, Camp Sister Spirit, Earthseed, Edges, The Farm, Harbin Hot Springs, The Hermitage, IDA, Kalani Oceanside Retreat, Koinonia, Light As Color Foundation, Lost Valley Educational Center, Lothlorien Co-op, Lothlorien Nature Sanctuary, Michigan Womyn's Music Festival, Monkton Wyld Court, Moonshadow, Mount Madonna Center, Namasté...Multi-Cultural Sustainable Living Community, One Common Unity, Rainbow Peace Caravan, Riparia, River Farm, Rowe Camp & Conference Center, Sunrise Ranch, Twin Oaks Community, UFA-Fabrik, Upper Applegate Community, Wellspring, Wisteria, Zuni Mountain Sanctuary.

CONFLICT RESOLUTION
Colibri Urban Housing Collective, Dolphin Community, Higher Ground Cohousing, Light Morning, Oran Mór, Rainbow Valley, Sandhill Farm, Shadowlake Village, Skyhouse Community, Society for the Promotion of Creative Interchange, Village Terraces Cohousing Neighborhood, Walnut Street Co-op.
SEE ALSO COMMUNICATION.

CONSERVATION
Adirondack Herbs, Awaawaroa Bay Eco-Village, Bryn Gweled Homesteads, Common Ground Community, Crystal Waters Permaculture Village, ECLIPSE, Eden Ranch Community, Enota Mountain Village, The Farm, Green River Community Land Trust, Harmony Village, Hudson Valley Ecovillage, Jamaica Plain Cohousing, Kipling Creek, Montpelier Cohousing, Moonshadow, Orange Twin Conservation Community, Pioneer Trails Institute, Prairie Sky Cohousing Cooperative, Rainbow Valley, Raven Rocks, SunToads Farm Community of New Mexico, The Vale, Whole Village, Winslow Cohousing Group, Zuni Mountain Sanctuary.

COSTA RICA
H.O.M.E. Heaven On Mother Earth.

COTTAGE INDUSTRIES
7th Millennium Community, Adirondack Herbs, Alpha Farm, Blackberry, Camphill Village Kimberton Hills, Camphill Village Minnesota Inc, Camphill Village Newton Dee, Camphill Village USA Inc., Cerro Gordo Community, Crystal Waters Permaculture Village, Dapala Farm, Dayspring Circle, Dragonfly Farm, Earthaven Ecovillage, East Wind Community, Edges, Federation of Arts for the Youth of Our Nation Foundation, Gaia Grove Ecospiritual Community & Ecoretreat, GaiaYoga Gardens, Ganas, Garden O' Vegan, Hudson Valley Ecovillage, Koinonia, Lofstedt Farm Community, Niederkaufungen, Port Townsend Ecovillage, Rose Creek Village, Shannon Farm Community, Shepherdsfield, Southwest Sufi Community, 12 Tribes de Sus, 12 Tribes Community at Stentwood Farm, 12 Tribes Boston, 12 Tribes Cambridge, 12 Tribes Chattanooga, 12 Tribes Coxsackie, 12 Tribes Island Pond, 12 Tribes Ithaca, 12 Tribes Oak Hill, 12 Tribes Oatlands, 12 Tribes San Sebastian, 12 Tribes Winnipeg, 12 Tribes Comunidad en Buenos Aires, 12 Tribes Londrina, 12 Tribes Osório, Twin Oaks Community, The The VOL Community Community, Windspirit Community, Yarrow Ecovillage.

CRAFTS
Acorn Community, Anahata Community, Angels Valley, Camphill Soltane, Camphill Special School, Camphill Village Kimberton Hills, Camphill Village Minnesota, Inc., Crystal Waters Permaculture Village, Dunmire Hollow Community, Emerald Coast Village, Everett, The Hermitage, In Planning Ecovillage, Koinonia, Lofstedt Farm Community, Maison Emmanuel, Nahziryah Monastic Community, Pennine Camphill Community, Rainbow Valley, 12 Tribes de Sus, Utopiaggia.

CREATIVITY
Bear Creek Farms, Cedar Sanctum, Hermitage, Innisfree Village, LandARC, Lifeseed, Mariposa Grove, Meridiana, Millstone Co-op, Namasté Greenfire, Rowe Camp & Conference Center, Society for the Promotion of Creative Interchange, Terrasante Village, Tres Placitas Del Rio, Wygelia.

CROATIA
Komaja.

CSAS (COMMUNITY-SUPPORTED AGRICULTURE)

Birdsfoot Farm, Camphill Village Kimberton Hills, Dapala Farm, Grace, Hundredfold Farm, Laughing Dog Farm and CSA, Lofstedt Farm Community, New Environment Association, Tolstoy Farm, Whole Village.

CULTURE, ALTERNATIVE

AbundantFreek, Comunidad Los Horcones, Dreamtime Village, Embassy of the Heavens, Emma Goldman Finishing School, Franciscan Workers/Companions in Community, Gaia Grove Ecospiritual Community & Ecoretreat, Kakwa Ecovillage, The Love Israel Family, Methow Center of Enlightenment, Michigan Womyn's Music Festival, Namasté Greenfire, Nanish Shontie, New Environment Association, Tamera—Healing Biotope I, Tribe of Blank, Tribe of Likatien, Trillium Farm Community, 12 Tribes Morning Star Ranch, 12 Tribes Hyannis, 12 Tribes Ithaca, 12 Tribes Lancaster, 12 Tribes Community on the Lake of the Ozarks, UFA-Fabrik, ZEGG—Centre for Experimental Cultural Design.

CULTURE, SUSTAINABLE

Abundant Dawn Community, EarthavenEcovillage, LostValleyEducationalCenter, Sweetwater Community Land Trust, Vine & Fig Tree Center for Sustainable Culture, Zim Zam.

SEE ALSO LIVING, SUSTAINABLE; SUSTAINABILITY.

DENMARK

Andelssamfundet I Hjortshøj, Hertha, Hesbjerg, Ibsgården, Mørdrupgård, Svanholm, Udgaarden, Valsolillegård.

DISABILITIES, PEOPLE WITH

AAAA Community for Tender Loving Care, Angels Valley, The Bruderhof Communities, Camphill Communities California, Camphill Soltane, Camphill Special School, Camphill Village Kimberton Hills, Camphill Village Minnesota Inc., Camphill Village Newton Dee, Camphill Village USA Inc., Christ of the Hills Monastery, East Lake Commons, Fox Hill Bruderhof, Innisfree Village, Kibbutz Migvan, L'Arche Mobile, Maison Emmanuel, Pennine Camphill Community, Village of Harmony.

DIVERSITY

Acorn Community, Ambrosia Housing Cooperative, Awaawaroa Bay Eco-Village, Beech Hill Community, Blue Ridge Cohousing, Blueberry Hill, Bosch Co-op, Breitenbush Hot Springs, Bryn Gweled Homesteads, Cambridge Cohousing, Collegiate Living Cooperative, Common Place Land Cooperative, Concord Village, Debs House, Du-Má, Dunmire Hollow Community, Duwamish Cohousing, East Lake Commons, East Wind Community, Ecotopia Romania, EcoVillage Detroit, Eden Ranch Community, El Semillero, Emerald Coast Village, Enota Mountain Village, Ganas, Harmony Village, Hillegass House, Hummingbird Community, Jamaica Plain Cohousing, Los Angeles Eco-Village, Lost Valley Educational Center, Manzanita Village, Malu 'Aina, Meadowdance Community Group, Miccosukee Land Co-op, Monan's Rill, Monterey Cohousing, New Earth Cooperative, Newberry Place: A Grand Rapids Cohousing Community, Omega Institute for Holistic Studies, Pagan Intentional Community, Parker Street Co-op, Port Townsend Ecovillage, Prairie Sky Cohousing Cooperative, Pumpkin Hollow Community, Qumbya Co-op, Reba Place Fellowship, River City Housing Collective, River Hayven, Sacramento Cohousing, SBSHC: Santa Barbara Student Housing Cooperative, Shadowlake Village, Shannon Farm Community, Sharing Community, Sirius Community, Stelle Community, Sunhouse Co-op, Sunward Cohousing, Sunwise Co-op, Tanguy Homesteads, Twin Oaks Community, Union Acres, Walnut Street Co-op, WindSong, Yulupa Cohousing, Zuni Mountain Sanctuary.

EARTH-CENTERED

Barking Frogs Permaculture Center, Earthen Spirituality Project, Earthseed, Hidden Valley, Land Lifeways Farm, Milagro Cohousing, Nanish Shontie, New Horizons, Oak Grove, Pacific Gardens Cohousing Community, Pagan Intentional Community, Pangaia, Pumpkin Hollow Community, Rainbow Family Gatherings, Sassafras Ridge Farm, Songaia Cohousing Community, Southern California Nature Sanctuary Project, Sunward Cohousing, Teaching Drum Outdoor School, Village Terraces Cohousing Neighborhood, White Buffalo Farm, The Wild Human Initiative, Windtree Ranch, Wise Woman Center/Laughing Rock Farm, Woodburn Hill Farm, Zim Zam.

ECOLOGICAL

AAAA Community for Tender Loving Care, Abundance Farm, Abundant Dawn Community, Acorn Community, Albuquerque Urban Ecovillage, Anarres Ecovillage, Aprovecho Research Center, Arcosanti, Atlantis, Attachment Parenting Village, Beaver Creek Homestead, Berea College Ecovillage, Blackberry, Blue Crane, Central Coast Community, Cerro Gordo Community, Chacra Millalen, Co-operative Effort, Colibri Urban Housing Collective, Common Ground Community, Common Ground VA, Comunidad Los Horcones, Comunidad Planetaria Janajpacha, Crystal Waters Permaculture Village, Dancing Rabbit Ecovillage, Dedetepe Eco-Farm, Dharma House Community, Du-Má, EarthArt Village, Earthaven Ecovillage, Earthsong Eco-Neighbourhood, East Wind Community, Ecotopia Romania, EcoVillage at Ithaca, Ecovillage Sieben Linden, Egrets' Cove, Emma Goldman Finishing School, The Farm, Firetender, Footprint Ecovillage, Fox Housing Cooperative, Gaia Grove Ecospiritual Community & Ecoretreat, Gesundheit! Institute, Grail Ecovillage, Great Oak Cohousing, Greenplan, Harmonious Earth Community, Harmony Village, Hearthaven, Heathcote Community, Het Carre, Hidden Valley, Hopewell Community, Humanity Rising, IDA, In Planning Ecovillage, Julian Woods Community, Jump Off Community Land Trust, Jupiter Hollow, Keimblatt Oekodorf, Kibbutz Lotan, Komaja, La'akea Community, Lifeseed, Lofstedt Farm Community, Los Angeles Eco-Village, Lost Valley Educational Center, Magic, Meadowdance Community Group, Meridiana, Milagro Cohousing, Monkton Wyld Court, Moonshadow, Mountain Home, NEO Cohousing, Niederkaufungen, O.U.R. Ecovillage, Oceanic Ecovillage, Oran Mór, Plants for a Future, Port Townsend Ecovillage, Priorities Institute, Projetorgone, Providence Cohousing, Pumpkin Hollow Community, Rainbow Hearth Sanctuary and Retreat Center, Rainbow Peace Caravan, Rainbow Way Station, Raven Rocks, Red Earth Farms, Redfield Community, River City Housing Collective, River Farm, River Hayven, Rosy Branch Farm, Sacramento Cohousing, Sacred Suenos, Samenhuizing West-Brabant, Shadowlake Village, Sirius Community, Skyhouse Community, Solterra, Somerville Ecovillage, Sowing Circle, Springtree Community, Susan B. Anthony Women's Land Trust, Sustainable Living Systems, Svanholm, Talkeetna Blueberry Sanctuary, Talking

Cedars Developments, Tao Bear Recovery Community, Tararu Valley Sanctuary, Terrasante Village, TerraVie, Torri Superiore Ecovillage, Trillium Farm Community, Twin Oaks Community, UFA-Fabrik, Union Acres, Utopiaggia, Wellspring, White Hawk, Windtree Ranch, Woodburn Hill Farm, Yalaha Community Network, Yonderfamily Housing and Land Trust Inc., Yulupa Cohousing, Zim Zam.

ECOVILLAGES

AAAA Community for Tender Loving Care, Albuquerque Urban Ecovillage, Berea College Ecovillage, Big Rock Farm, Breitenbush Hot Springs, Center of Light Spirituality, Cohousing Bristol, Dancing Bones, Dancing Rabbit Ecovillage, Dolphin Community, Dreamtime Village, Earth First Australia, Ecovilla Asociación Gaia, EcoVillage at Ithaca, EcoVillage Detroit, Ecovillage of Loudoun County, Ecovillage Sieben Linden, Eden Project, Everett, The Farm, Findhorn Foundation and Community, Footprint Ecovillage, Fox Housing Cooperative, Greenplan, Hudson Valley Ecovillage, Hummingbird Community, In Planning Ecovillage, Infinite Star Light Offering Visionary Ecovillages, Kakwa Ecovillage, Keimblatt Oekodorf, Kookaburra Park Eco-Village, La Flor del Agua Community, La Senda Ecovillage, Lebensraum, Los Angeles Eco-Village, Los Visionarios, Lost Valley Educational Center, Manitou Arbor Ecovillage, Meridiana, Metro Cohousing at Culver Way, Mountain Home, Mulvey Creek Land Co-opera-tive, Namasté Greenfire, NEO Cohousing, O.U.R. Ecovillage, Oak Grove, Oceanic Ecovillage, Otamatea Eco-Village, Pagan Intentional Community, Piñon Ecovillage, Plants for a Future, Port Townsend EcoVillage, Projetorgone, Rainbow Peace Caravan, Réseau des ÉcoHameaux et ÉcoVillages du Québec, San Mateo Ecovillage, Shambala Eco-Resort & Ecovillage Community, Sirius Community, Somerville Ecovillage, Tacoma Eco-Village, Talking Cedars Developments Ltd., Tararu Valley Sanctuary, TerraVie, Torri Superiore Ecovillage, Trillium Farm Community, Whole Village, Yarrow Ecovillage, Yonderfamily Housing and Land Trust Inc.

ECUADOR

Hospital Comunitario Waldos, Los Visionarios, Sacred Suenos.

EDUCATION

Abundance Farm, Agape, Aprovecho Research Center, Beacon Hill Friends House, Beaver Creek, Beech Hill Community, Berea College Ecovillage, Blue Crane, Boston Community Cooperatives, Camp Sister Spirit, Camphill Village Kimberton Hills, Center for Purposeful Living, Central Coast Community, Cohousing Research and Education, Cold Pond Community Land Trust, Common Ground VA, Comunidad Los Horcones, Crystal Waters Permaculture Village, Dancing Rabbit Ecovillage, Dapala Farm, EarthArt Village, Ecovilla Asociación GAIA, Ecovillage at Ithaca, Eden Project, El Semillero, Enota Mountain Village, The Farm, Findhorn Foundation and Community, Franciscan Workers/Companions in Community, Freestone Hill Community, Friends and Neighbors, Gaia University, Gentle World Inc., Gesundheit! Institute, Grail Ecovillage, H.O.M.E. Heaven on Mother Earth, Hanoar Haoved Vehalomed, Harmonious Earth Community, Healing Grace Sanctuary, Heartwood Institute, The Hermitage, Himalayan Institute, Hummingbird Community, Jump Off Community Land Trust, Kalani Oceanside Retreat, Kashi Ashram, Kibbutz Lotan, Kibbutz Migvan, The Kibbutz Movement, Knowledge Farm, Koinonia, Komaja, Lama Foundation, Land ARC, Laughing Dog Farm and CSA, Light As Color Foundation, Ma Yoga Shakti International, Ma'Agal Hakvutzot, Malu 'Aina, Monkton Wyld Court, Moonshadow, Neve Shalom/Wahat, New Environment Association, Next Step Integral, Oakland Elizabeth House, Poly Pagan Nudist Community, Port Townsend Ecovillage, Priorities Institute, Pumpkin Hollow Community, Raccoon Creek Community, Raven Rocks, Rise and Shine, River City Housing Collective, River Farm, SBSHC: Santa Barbara Student Housing Cooperative, SEADS of Truth Inc, Sirius Community, Sivananda Ashram Yoga, Southern Cassadaga Spiritualist Camp, Sowing Circle, Spirit Cove, Sunwise Co-op, Susan B. Anthony Women's Land Trust, Sustainable Living Systems, Tararu Valley Sanctuary, Torri Superiore Ecovillage, Trillium Farm Community, Vivekananda Monastery and Retreat Center, Voice for the Voiceless, Wellspring, Windtree Ranch, Wisteria, Yonderfamily Housing and Land Trust Inc.

SEE ALSO HOMESCHOOLING; LEARNING; SCHOOLS; UNSCHOOLING; WORKSHOPS/COURSES.

EDUCATION, ALTERNATIVE

Egrets' Cove, The Farm, Shambala Eco-Resort & Ecovillage Community.

EGALITARIANISM

Acorn Community, AinaOla, Blackberry, Cantine's Island Cohousing, Carrowmore Community, Cascadia Commons, Chippenham Community, Community Planet Foundation, Comunidad Los Horcones, Du-Má, Emma Goldman Finishing School, Freedom-Universe, Hospital Comunitario Waldos, Kerala Commune, Kibbutz Lotan, Kibbutz Tamuz, Komun, Light of Freedom, Lothlorien Co-op, Meadowdance Community Group, Moonshadow, Oran Mór, Pagan Intentional Community, Phoenix Co-op, Pumpkin Hollow Community, Sandhill Farm, Skyhouse Community, Soma, Sweetwater Community Land Trust, Twin Oaks Community, Utopiaggia, The VOL Community, Welcome Here Circle of Light Community Network—Rainbow Tribes, Whitehall Co-op.

ELDER CARE

The Bruderhof Communities, Fellowship Community, Fox Hill Bruderhof, Gaia Grove Ecospiritual Community & Ecoretreat, Niederkaufungen, River Hayven.

ELDERS

Catholic Worker Community, ElderSpirit Community at Trailview, Sage Valley.

SEE ALSO RETIREMENT.

ENERGY, ALTERNATIVE/RENEWABLE

AAAA Community for Tender Loving Care, Adirondack Herbs, Awaawaroa Bay Eco-Village, Berea College Ecovillage, Blue Moon Cooperative, Breitenbush Hot Springs, City of the Sun Foundation, Inc., Common Place Land Cooperative, Dancing Rabbit Ecovillage, Dunmire Hollow Community, EarthArt Village, Edges, Hudson Valley Ecovillage, In Planning Ecovillage, Kakwa Ecovillage, Kerala Commune, Lebensraum, Mulvey Creek Land Co-operative, Northern Sun Farm Co-op, Oran Mór, Point of Infinity Retreat Center and Community, Rise and Shine, SEADS of Truth Inc., Shambala Eco-Resort & Ecovillage Community, Skyhouse Community,

Spring Lane Farms, Sunwise Co-op, Sustainable Living Systems, Tao Bear Recovery Community, Tararu Valley Sanctuary, 12 Tribes Oak Hill, 12 Tribes Comunidad en Buenos Aires, Utopian Visions, Vine & Fig Tree Center for Sustainable Culture, Woodburn Hill Farm.

ENERGY-EFFICIENCY
Arcosanti, Awaawaroa Bay Eco-Village, Center of Light Spirituality Center, Cohousing Bristol, EarthArt Village, ECLIPSE, Ecovillage at Ithaca, Egrets' Cove, Harmony Village, Heathcote Community, Highline Crossing, Hockerton Housing Project, Hudson Valley Ecovillage, Jump Off Community Land Trust, Kerala Commune, Nomad Cohousing, Oceanic Ecovillage, Pioneer Trails Institute, Prairie Sky Cohousing Cooperative, Sharing Community, Takoma Village Cohousing, Tararu Valley Sanctuary.

ENVIRONMENTAL PRESERVATION/PROTECTION
Awaawaroa Bay Eco-Village, Cerro Gordo Community, Dancing Rabbit Ecovillage, Duwamish Cohousing, EarthArt Village, East Lake Commons, EcoVillage of Loudoun County, Mulvey Creek Land Co-operative, Oceanic Ecovillage, Raven Rocks, River Farm, RoseWind Cohousing, Spirit Cove, Tararu Valley Sanctuary, TerraVie, Trillium Farm Community, Whole Village.

ENVIRONMENTAL RESTORATION
Awaawaroa Bay Eco-Village, Moonshadow, Mountain Home, Raven Rocks.

ENVIRONMENTALIST
Adirondack Herbs, Anarres Ecovillage, Association for the Earth, Beech Hill Community, Berea College Ecovillage, Breitenbush Hot Springs, Carrowmore Community, Cascade Cohousing, Cascadia Commons, Champlain Valley Cohousing, Cobb Hill, Cold Pond Community Land Trust, CoLibri Urban Housing Collective, Common Ground Community, Common Ground VA, Concord Village, Cranberry Commons, Dancing Rabbit Ecovillage, Dayspring Circle, The Deliberacy, Detroit Cohousing, Dunmire Hollow Community, East Bay Cohousing, Ecovillage at Ithaca, EcoVillage Detroit, EcoVillage of Loudoun County, El Semillero, ElderSpirit Community at Trailview, Emerald Coast Village, Freedom-Universe, Fresno Cohousing,

Gaia Grove Ecospiritual Community & Ecoretreat, Gaia University, The Gathering, Genesee Gardens Cohousing, Gentle World Inc., Grail Ecovillage, Gricklegrass, Hearthaven, Hei Wa House, Hockerton Housing Project, Jindibah, Jump Off Community Land Trust, Kibbutz Lotan, King Edward House, Lebensraum, Lothlorien Co-op, Masala Co-op, Millstone Co-op, Moonshadow, New Environment Association, New View Cohousing, Northern Sun Farm Co-op, Ohio Bio-Enviro Settlements Inc, Omega Institute for Holistic Studies, Oran Mór, Pacific Gardens Cohousing, Pangaia, Plants for a Future, Plow Creek, Prag House, Prairie Onion Cohousing, Prairie Sky Cohousing Cooperative, Projetorgone, Redfield Community, Regenerative Co-op of Pomona, Riparia, Rocky Hill Cohousing, San Mateo Ecovillage, SBSHC: Santa Barbara Student Housing Cooperative, SEADS of Truth Inc, Sharing Community, Solstice Dawn, Soma, Sunset House, Sunwise Co-op, Sustainable Living Systems, Sweetwater Community Land Trust, Trillium Farm Community, Turn Cedars, 12 Tribes Oak Hill, Two Acre Wood, Voice for the Voiceless, Wellspring, Wild Sage Cohousing, Woodfolk House, Yarrow Ecovillage, Yulupa Cohousing.

SEE ALSO ANIMAL RIGHTS; ANIMAL SANCTUARIES; CONSERVATION; ENERGY, ALTERNATIVE/RENEWABLE; ENERGY-EFFICIENCY; FORESTRY, ECOLOGICAL; FUEL, ALTERNATIVE; LAND PRESERVATION; LAND RESTORATION; NATURE SANCTUARIES; SOLAR POWER; STEWARDSHIP; SUSTAINABILITY; WATER PROJECTS, ALTERNATIVE; WASTE DISPOSAL, ALTERNATIVE; WIND POWER.

EVANGELISM
Elim, Elmendorf Christian Community, The Family, New Creation Christian Community.

FAERIE
Nomenus Radical Faerie Sanctuary, Zuni Mountain Sanctuary.

FAMILY-ORIENTED
Ambrosia Housing Cooperative, Ashland Vineyard Community, Attachment Parenting Village, Cambridge Terrace Community, Empty Nest Cohos, Laughing Dog Farm and CSA, Mele Nahiku, Middle Road Community, Namasté Greenfire, Saint Jude Catholic Worker House Community, Talkeetna Blueberry Sanctuary, WindSong.

FARMING
AAAA Community for Tender Loving Care, Abbey of the Genesee, Atlantis, Attachment Parenting Village, Beaver Creek, Birdsfoot Farm, The Blue Crane, Blueberry Hill, Camphill Village Newton Dee, Camphill Village USA Inc., Canon Frome Court Community, Central Coast Community, Cerro Gordo Community, Cold Pond Community Land Trust, Common Ground Community, Common Place Land Cooperative, Dedetepe Eco-Farm, Earth First Australia, Earth Re-Leaf, Earthright Farms, Echollective Farm, Ecovillage at Ithaca, Eden Project, Eden Ranch Community, Fledgling Community, Fox Housing Cooperative, Garden O' Vegan, Greening Life Community, Gricklegrass, Headlands, The Hermitage, Hudson Valley Ecovillage, Kakwa Ecovillage, Kerala Commune, Kipling Creek, Kitezh Children's Eco-Village Community, Koinonia, Land ARC, Land Lifeways Farm, The Land Stewardship Center, Laughing Dog Farm and CSA, Little Flower Catholic Worker Farm, Lofstedt Farm Community, Malu 'Aina, Namasté...Multi-Cultural Sustainable Living Community, Nature's Pace Sanctuary, O.U.R. Ecovillage, Oak Grove, Open Gate Farm Retreat, Oran Mór, Pagan Intentional Community, Pennine Camphill Community, People on the Way, Plain Anabaptist Community, Rainbow Valley, Reevis Mountain School of Self-Reliance, River Farm, Rosneath Farm, Sacred Suenos, Sassafras Ridge Farm, Summerglen Farm and Homestead, SunToads Farm Community of New Mexico, Svanholm, Tanguy Homesteads, Tolstoy Farm, 12 Tribes Community at Stepping Stone Farm, 12 Tribes Cambridge, 12 Tribes Nelson, 12 Tribes Northern Virginia, 12 Tribes Oak Hill, 12 Tribes Curitiba, 12 Tribes Londrina, Twin Oaks Community, Upper Applegate Community, Vlierhof, Walden Two Community California, White Buffalo Farm, White Hawk, Whole Village, Yarrow Ecovillage.
SEE ALSO AGRICULTURE; HOMESTEADING.

FEMINISM
Acorn Community, Lothlorien Co-op, Reba Place Fellowship, Susan B. Anthony Women's Land Trust, Twin Oaks Community, Wise Woman Center/Laughing Rock Farm.

FOODS, NATURAL/WHOLE
Ashram Community, The Christine Center, Dragon Belly Farm, Everything

Is Related, GaiaYoga Gardens, Reevis Mountain School of Self-Reliance, 12 Tribes Comunidad en Buenos Aires.

FOOD, ORGANIC

AAAA Community for Tender Loving Care, AinaOla, Anarres Ecovillage, Aprovecho Research Center, Aquarian Concepts Community, Arcadia Cohousing, Atlantis, Attachment Parenting Village, Awaawaroa Bay Eco-Village, Awakening to Grace, Bear Creek Farms, Beaver Creek, Beech Hill Community, Birdsfoot Farm, Black Elk House, Bosch Co-op, Bower House, Carrowmore Community, CedarSanctum, Cerro Gordo Community, Chacra Millalen, Chaneeg Channesch, Co-operative Effort, Common Ground VA, Common Place Land Cooperative, Commons on the Alameda, Corani Housing and Land Co-op, Dancing Rabbit Ecovillage, Dapala Farm, Debs House, Dedetepe Eco-Farm, Dragon Belly Farm, Dragonfly Farm, Dunmire Hollow Community, Earth Re-Leaf, Earthright Farms, East Lake Commons, Echollective Farm, Ecovillage at Ithaca, El Semillero, Embassy of the Heavens, Emerald Coast Village, Enchanted Garden, Eno Commons, Enota Mountain Village, Everything Is Related, Fox Housing Cooperative, Freedom-Universe, Freeland Community, Gaia Grove Ecospiritual Community & Ecoretreat, GaiaYoga Gardens, Glenwood House, Grail Ecovillage, Greening Life Community, Heathcote Community, Hockerton Housing Project, Hudson Valley Ecovillage, Humanity Rising, Hundredfold Farm, Jamaica Plain Cohousing, Kakwa Ecovillage, Kerala Commune, Kibbutz Lotan, King Edward House, Kipling Creek, Kitezh Children's Eco-Village Community, Koinonia, La Flor del Agua Community, LandARC, Laughing Dog Farm and CSA, Lester House, Light Morning, Light of Freedom, Lofstedt Farm Community, Los Angeles Eco-Village, Lost Valley Educational Center, Lothlorien Co-op, Madre Grande Monastery, Middle Road Community, Monan's Rill, Monkton Wyld Court, Morninglory, Nahziryah Monastic Community, Namasté...Multi-Cultural Sustainable Living Community, New Environment Association, Niederkaufungen, Ninth Street Co-op, O.U.R. Ecovillage, Omega House, Oran Mór, Otamatea Eco-Village, Oxford Community, People on the Way, Plain Anabaptist Community, Plants for a Future, Pleasant Hill Cohousing, Point of Infinity Retreat Center and Community, Port Townsend Ecovillage, Prag House, Purple Rose Collective, Rainbow Hearth Sanctuary and Retreat Center, Raven Rocks, Redfield Community, Reevis Mountain School of Self-Reliance, Regenerative Co-op of Pomona, Riparia, River Hayven, Rosneath Farm, Sacred Suenos, Salamander Springs, San Mateo Ecovillage, Sandhill Farm, Shambala Eco-Resort & Ecovillage Community, Sharingwood Cohousing, Shepherdsfield, Sidhefire, Sirius Community, Sivananda Ashram Yoga Ranch, Sophia Community, Sowing Circle, Sparrow Hawk Village, Spring Valley Bruderhof, Stelle Community, Sunhouse Co-op, SunToads Farm Community of New Mexico, Svanholm, Tacoma Eco-Village, Teaching Drum Outdoor School, Torri Superiore Ecovillage, Trillium Hollow, Turn Cedars, 12 Tribes Community at Stepping Stone Farm, 12 Tribes Irún, 12 Tribes Manitou Springs, 12 Tribes Oak Hill, 12 Tribes San Sebastian, 12 Tribes Vista, 12 Tribes Winnipeg, 12 Tribes Comunidad en Buenos Aires, Twin Oaks Community, UFA-Fabrik, Upper Applegate Community, Vlierhof, Wellspring, White Buffalo Farm, White Hawk, Whole Health Foundation, WindSong, Windspirit Community, Windtree Ranch, Wiscoy Valley Community, Wise Woman Center/Laughing Rock Farm, Woodburn Hill Farm, Yarrow Ecovillage, Zephyr Valley Community Co-op, Zuni Mountain Sanctuary.

FOODS, RAW

AAAA Community for Tender Loving Care, AinaOla, Earth Re-Leaf, The Freeland Community, Kerala Commune, Namasté...Multi-Cultural Sustainable Living Community, Pangaia, River Hayven, Shambala Eco-Resort & Ecovillage Community.

FORESTRY, ECOLOGICAL

Aprovecho Research Center, Cerro Gordo Community, Mountain Home, River Farm, Whole Village.

FOSTER CARE

Angels Valley, Kitezh Children's Eco-Village Community.

FRANCE

Communauté de L'Arche, Communaute du Pain de Vie, Dharma House Community Project, Projetorgone, Taizé Community, 12 Tribes Heimsbrunn, 12 Tribes de Sus.

FUEL, ALTERNATIVE

Agape, Beaver Creek, Dancing Bones, Dancing Rabbit Ecovillage, Emerald Coast Village, Kerala Commune, Lofstedt Farm Community, Namasté... Multi-Cultural, Sustainable Living Community, Niederkaufungen, Oran Mór, Reba Place Fellowship, Sirius Community.

SEE ALSO RENEWABLE ENERGY.

GARDENING

Agape, Angels Valley, Aprovecho Research Center, Aquarian Concepts Community, ARC Retreat Center, Arcadia Cohousing, Awakening to Grace, The Barn, Bear Creek Farms, Beaver Creek, Berea College Ecovillage, Black Elk House, The Blue Crane, The Blue House, Bosch Co-op, Bower House, Bryn Gweled Homesteads, Brynderwen Vegan Community, Burlington Cohousing, Camphill Communities California, Camphill Soltane, Camphill Village Kimberton Hills, Camphill Village Minnesota Inc, Camphill Village Newton Dee, Camphill Village USA Inc., Canon Frome Court Community, Carrowmore Community, Cascade Cohousing, CedarSanctum, Center of Light Spirituality Center, Chacra Millalen, Champlain Valley Cohousing, Chaneeg Channesch, Colibri Urban Housing Collective, Common Ground VA, Common Place Land Cooperative, Commons on the Alameda, Corani Housing and Land Co-op, Cornerstone Housing Cooperative, Dancing Waters Permaculture Co-op, Denver Space Center, Detroit Cohousing, The Domes, Dragonfly Farm, Du-Má, Dunmire Hollow Community, Duwamish Cohousing, Earthaven Ecovillage, Earthright Farms, East Lake Commons, Edges, Egrets' Cove, El Semillero, ElderSpirit Community at Trailview, Embassy of the Heavens, Emerald Coast Village, Emerald Earth, Enchanted Garden, Eno Commons, Enota Mountain Village, Everything Is Related, Fordyce Street Cohousing, Freestone Hill Community, Gaia Grove Ecospiritual Community & Ecoretreat, Ganas, Garden O' Vegan, Gentle World Inc., Green River Community Land Trust, Greening Life Community, Greenplan, Harmony Village, Hearthstone, Heathcote Community, Higher Ground Cohousing, Highline Crossing, Hillegass House, Hockerton Housing Project, Hope Hill Community,

IDA, Innisfree Village, Jamaica Plain Cohousing, Julian Woods Community, Jump Off Community Land Trust, Kibbutz Lotan, Kitezh Children's Eco-Village Community, Koinonia, La Flor del Agua Community, Lama Foundation, The Land Stewardship Center, Laughing Dog Farm and CSA, Lebensraum, Liberty Village, Light As Color Foundation, Light Morning, Light of Freedom, Little Flower Catholic Worker Farm, Lofstedt Farm Community, Los Angeles Eco-Village, Lost Valley Educational Center, Lothlorien Co-op, Lothlorien Farm, Madre Grande Monastery, Magic, Mariposa Grove, Middle Road Community, Monan's Rill, Monkton Wyld Court, Monterey Cohousing, Moonshadow, Morninglory, Mountain Home, Mulvey Creek Land Co-operative, N Street Cohousing, Nahziryah Monastic Community, Namasté...Multi-Cultural Sustainable Living Community, Nature's Pace Sanctuary, New Environment Association, New Goloka, Niederkaufungen, Ninth Street Co-op, North Mountain Community Land Trust, O.U.R. Ecovillage, Oran Mór, Otamatea Eco-Village, Peninsula Park Commons, Pennine Camphill Community, People on the Way, Pioneer Valley, Pleasant Hill Cohousing, Plow Creek, Point of Infinity Retreat Center and Community, Poly Pagan Nudist Community, Port Townsend Ecovillage, Priorities Institute, Prudence Crandall House, Purple Rose Collective, Raccoon Creek Community, Rainbow Hearth Sanctuary and Retreat Center, Rainbow Valley, Raven Rocks, Reba Place Fellowship, Redfield Community, Regenerative Co-op of Pomona, Riparia, River Farm, River Hayven, RoseWind Cohousing, Rosneath Farm, Salamander Springs, San Mateo Ecovillage, Sandhill Farm, Sankofa, Sassafras Ridge Farm, SEADS of Truth Inc., Sharingwood Cohousing, Sivananda Ashram Yoga Ranch, Solterra, Songaia Cohousing Community, Sowing Circle, Sparrow Hawk Village, Spirit Cove, Spring Lane Farms, Spring Valley Bruderhof, Springtree Community, Stelle Community, Stone Curves Cohousing, Storybook Shire, Summerglen Farm and Homestead, Sunhouse Co-op, SunToads Farm Community of New Mexico, Sunwise Co-op, Surrealestates, Tao Bear Recovery Community, Terra Nova, Terrasante Village, Torri Superiore Ecovillage, Tres Placitas Del Rio, Trillium Farm Community, Trillium Hollow, 12 Tribes Community at Peppercorn Creek Farm, 12 Tribes San Sebastian, 12 Tribes Vista, 12 Tribes Comunidad en Buenos Aires, 12 Tribes Osório, Twin Oaks Community, Union Acres, Vail House, The Vale, Village Terraces Cohousing Neighborhood, Walker Creek Farm, Wellspring, Whole Health Foundation, The Wild Human Initiative, WindSong, Windspirit Community, Windtree Ranch, Winslow Cohousing Group, Wise Woman Center/Laughing Rock Farm, Woodburn Hill Farm, Wygelia, Yulupa Cohousing, Zim Zam, Zuni Mountain Sanctuary.

GERMANY

Bread and Roses—Base Community, Bruderhof-Haus Holzland, Bruderhof-Haus Sannerz, Dolphin Community, Ecovillage Sieben Linden, Freie Christliche Jugendgemeinschaft, Kana-Gemeinschaft, Komaja, Lebensgarten Steyerberg, Niederkaufungen, Projekt Eulenspiegel, ProWoKultA, Tribe of Likatien, Troubadour Märchenzentrum, 12 Tribes Klosterzimmern, UFA-Fabrik, Wawavox, WOGENO München eG, ZEGG—Centre for Experimental Cultural Design, Ökolea—Klosterdorf.

GREECE
New Humanity Centre.

HEALTH/HEALING
AAAA Community for Tender Loving Care, Adirondack Herbs, Alpha Omega Christian Communities for the Chemically Injured, Angels Valley, Aquarian Concepts Community, Bartimaeus Community of Meadow Wood, Blackberry, Breitenbush Hot Springs, Cambridge Terrace Community, Camphill Special School, Camphill Village Minnesota Inc., The Center of Light Spirituality Center, The Christine Center, City of the Sun Foundation Inc., Common Place Land Cooperative, Dolphin Community, EarthArt Village, Earthseed, Edges, El Semillero, Embassy of the Heavens, Everything Is Related, Finca Buena Vida, Firetender, Franciscan Workers/Companions in Community, Free State Community, Freestone Hill Community, Gaia Grove Ecospiritual Community & Ecoretreat, GaiaYoga Gardens, Genesee Gardens Cohousing, Gentle World Inc., Gesundheit! Institute, The Glenwood House, Goodenough Community, Grace, H.O.M.E. Heaven on Mother Earth, Harmonious Earth Community, Heartsong, Heartwood Institute, Himalayan Institute, Hospital Comunitario Waldos, Humanity Rising, Hummingbird Community, Infinite Star Light Offering Visionary Ecovillages, Kalani Oceanside Retreat, Kashi Ashram, Kerala Commune, Kibbutz Lotan, La Flor del Agua Community, La'Akea Community, Light Morning, Lofstedt Farm Community, Ma Yoga Shakti International Mission, Magic, Methow Center of Enlightenment, Mulvey Creek Land Co-operative, NEO Cohousing, New Environment Association, Niederkaufungen, Omega Institute for Holistic Studies, One Common Unity, Osho Mevlana Residential Community, Pagan Intentional Community, Pangaia, Peninsula Park Commons, Point of Infinity Retreat Center and Community, Poly Pagan Nudist Community, Prairie Onion Cohousing, Rainbow Farm, Rainbow Hearth Sanctuary and Retreat Center, Reevis Mountain School of Self-Reliance, Refuge, Rewilding Community, River Hayven, Rowe Camp & Conference Center, Salamander Springs, Sankofa, Shambala Eco-Resort & Ecovillage Community, Sivananda Ashram Yoga Ranch, Solstice Dawn, Soma, Southern Cassadaga Spiritualist Camp, Tamera—Healing Biotope I, Tao Bear Recovery Community, Terrasante Village, Tres Placitas Del Rio, Tribe of Likatien, Turn Cedars, 12 Tribes Stentwood Farm, 12 Tribes Coxsackie, 12 Tribes Nelson, 12 Tribes Oatlands, 12 Tribes Rutland, 12 Tribes Winnipeg, Vlierhof, Wellspring, Whole Health Foundation, The Wild Human Initiative, Windhaven, Windspirit Community, Windtree Ranch, Wise Woman Center/Laughing Rock Farm, Yogaville/Satchidananda Ashram, Zim Zam.

HOLISM
BBES (Bible Belt Exodous Society), Bear Creek Farms, Beaver Creek, Breitenbush Hot Springs, EarthArt Village, Ecovillage Sieben Linden, Finca Buena Vida, Gaia Grove Ecospiritual Community & Ecoretreat, GaiaYoga Gardens, The Glenwood House, Heartsong, Himalayan Institute, Kibbutz Lotan, Light As Color Foundation, Lofstedt Farm Community, Monkton Wyld Court, Mulvey Creek Land Co-operative, Nahziryah Monastic Community, New Environment Association, Omega Institute for Holistic Studies, Point of Infinity Retreat Center and Community, Shambala Eco-Resort & Ecovillage Community, Stelle Community, Tribe of Likatien, Whole Health Foundation, Zuni Mountain Sanctuary.

HOMELESS CARE

Blue House, Clare's House of Hospitality, The Gift of a Helping Hand, Karen Catholic Worker House, Oakland Elizabeth House, Open Gate Farm & Retreat, Regenerative Co-op of Pomona, Upper Applegate Community.

HOMESCHOOLING

Attachment Parenting Village, Bear Creek Farms, Blackberry, The Blue Crane, Common Place Land Cooperative, The Family, Fox Housing Cooperative, Hidden Valley, Laughing Dog Farm and CSA, Morninglory, Plain Anabaptist Community, Priorities Institute, Sharingwood Cohousing, 12 Tribes de Sus, 12 Tribes Community at Peppercorn Creek Farm, 12 Tribes Community at the Morning Star Ranch, 12 Tribes Coxsackie, 12 Tribes Lancaster, 12 Tribes Manitou Springs, 12 Tribes Winnipeg, 12 Tribes Curitiba, 12 Tribes Londrina, The VOL Community.
SEE ALSO UNSCHOOLING.

HOMESTEADING

Agape, AinaOla, Beaver Creek, Beaver Creek Homestead, Common Ground (VA), Common Place Land Cooperative, Earthright Farms, The Eden Project, The Homestead at Denison University, Jump Off Community Land Trust, Light Morning, Little Flower Catholic Worker Farm, Morninglory, Mountain Home, Nature's Pace Sanctuary, O'Brien Lake Homesteaders, People on the Way, River Farm, Salamander Springs, Sugar Mountain, Summerglen Farm and Homestead, Tanguy Homesteads, Union Acres, The Wild Human Initiative, Wisteria.
SEE ALSO AGRICULTURE; FARMING.

HOSPITALITY

ARC Retreat Center, Clare's House of Hospitality, Denver Catholic Worker, Dorothy Day Cohousing, Ecovillage Sieben Linden, Franciscan Workers/Companions in Community, Hearthaven, Karen Catholic Worker House, Oakland Elizabeth House, Plow Creek, Saint Jude Catholic Worker House Community, Sophia Community, 12 Tribes Ithaca.

HUNTING/GATHERING

Rewilding Community, Tribe of Blank.

INCOME SHARING

Abbey of the Genesee, Acorn Community, Alpha Farm, Angels Valley, Atlantis, Beech Grove Bruderhof, Camphill Soltane, Camphill Special School, Camphill Village Newton Dee, The Change, Christ of the Hills Monastery, Comunidad Los Horcones, East Wind Community, Ecovilla Asociación Gaia, El Semillero, Elim, Elmendorf Christian Community, The Family, Freedom-Universe, Hanoar Haoved Vehalomed, Hope Hill Community, Hutterian Brethren, In Planning Ecovillage, Jesus Christ's Community at Hebron, Jesus Christians, Keimblatt Oekodorf, Kibbutz Lotan, Kibbutz Tamuz, Kitezh Children's Eco-Village Community, Kvutsat Yovel, LifeShare Community, Little Flower Catholic Worker Farm, Love Israel Family, Mele Nahiku, Nasalam, Nature's Pace Sanctuary, Neo Hippie Haven, New Creation Christian Community, Niederkaufungen, Oran Mór, Order of Saint Benedict, Pangaia, Pennine Camphill Community, Reba Place Fellowship, Saint Martin de Porres House, Sandhill Farm, Shepherdsfield, Sivananda Ashram Yoga Ranch, Skyhouse Community, Solstice Dawn, Springtree Community, Tomorrow's Bread Today, Tribe of Dirt, Twelve Tribes, 12 Tribes Stentwood Farm, 12 Tribes Stepping Stone Farm, 12 Tribes Community the Morning Star, 12 Tribes Arcadia, 12 Tribes Asheville, 12 Tribes Ashland, 12 Tribes Bellows Falls, 12 Tribes Boston, 12 Tribes Brunswick, 12 Tribes Chattanooga, 12 Tribes Coxsackie, 12 Tribes Hamburg, 12 Tribes Irún, 12 Tribes Island Pond, 12 Tribes Ithaca, 12 Tribes Katoomba, 12 Tribes Lancaster, 12 Tribes Manitou Springs, 12 Tribes Nelson, 12 Tribes Northern Virginia, 12 Tribes Oak Hill, 12 Tribes Oatlands, 12 Tribes Plymouth, 12 Tribes Rutland, 12 Tribes San Sebastian, 12 Tribes Savannah, 12 Tribes Vista, 12 Tribes Winnipeg, 12 Tribes Lake of the Ozarks, 12 Tribes Comunidad en Buenos Aires, 12 Tribes Curitiba, 12 Tribes Osório, 12 Tribes Gemeinschaft Klosterzimmern, Twin Oaks Community, Voice for the Voiceless, Wygelia, Zuni Mountain Sanctuary.

INDIA

Atmasantulana Village, Auroville, Kerala Commune.

INDIGENOUS

CambridgeTerraceCommunity, Healing Grace Sanctuary, Nanish Shontie, Neo Hippie Haven, Rainbow Peace Caravan.
SEE ALSO NATIVE AMERICAN.

INTERGENERATIONAL

Azania Alliance, Blue Ridge Cohousing, Ecovillage at Ithaca, The Eden Project, Federation of Arts for the Youth of Our Nation Foundation, Fellowship Community, Garden State Cohousing, Goodenough Community, Grace, Great Oak Cohousing, Hearthstone, Jamaica Plain Cohousing, LandARC, Manzanita Village, Milagro Cohousing, O.U.R. Ecovillage, One Common Unity, Pacific Gardens Cohousing Community, Pleasant Hill Cohousing, Prairie Onion Cohousing, Providence Cohousing, Yulupa Cohousing.

INTERNSHIPS

Agape, Aprovecho Research Center, Arcosanti, Birdsfoot Farm, Emerald Earth, Goodenough Community, Healing Grace Sanctuary, Laughing Dog Farm and CSA, Light Morning, Lost Valley Educational Center, Rainbow Hearth Sanctuary and Retreat Center, Reba Place Fellowship, Rowe Camp & Conference Center, Salamander Springs, Sunrise Ranch, Sustainable Living Systems, Trillium Farm Community, Windspirit Community.

IRELAND

Komaja.

ISRAEL

Hanoar Haoved Vehalomed, International Communes Desk, Kibbutz Ketura, Kibbutz Lotan, Kibbutz Migvan, The Kibbutz Movement, Kibbutz Neot Semadar, Kibbutz Tamuz, Kvutsat Yovel, Ma'agal Hakvutzot, Neve Shalom/Wahat al-Salam.

ITALY

Arcobaleno Fiammeggiante—Tribe, Damanhur, Hairakhandi Love Center, Nomadelfia, Order of Saint Benedict, Osho Miasto, Torri Superiore Ecovillage, Utopiaggia.

JAPAN

Ittoen, Yamagishi-kai.

JESUIT

Jesuit Volunteer Corps DC, Jesuit Volunteer Corps NW.

JESUS

3Circles Community, Aquarian Concepts Community, Bellvale Bruderhof, The Bruderhof Communities, Danthonia Bruderhof, Elmendorf Christian Community, Fox Hill Bruderhof, Greenhaus Community, Jesus Christ's Community at Hebron,

Jesus Christians, Jesus People USA, The Love Israel Family, Narrow Way Christian Community, New Meadow Run Bruderhof, Plow Creek, Rose Creek Village, Shepherdsfield, 12 Tribes, 12 Tribes Londrina, Upper Applegate Community, Woodcrest Bruderhof.

JUDAISM
AAAA Community for Tender Loving Care, Kibbutz Lotan, Upper Applegate Community.
SEE ALSO KIBBUTZIM; ISRAEL.

JUSTICE
Bosch Co-op, Dorothy Day Cohousing, Emerald Earth, Emma Goldman Finishing School, Emma Goldman's, Franciscan Workers/Companions in Community, Gaia Grove Ecospiritual Community & Ecoretreat, Gesundheit! Institute, Grail Ecovillage, Gricklegrass, Hei Wa House, Iona Community, Koinonia, Little Flower Catholic Worker Farm, Malu 'Aina, Millstone Co-op, Moonshadow, Namasté Greenfire, Niche/Tucson Community Land Trust, O.U.R. Ecovillage, Plow Creek, Port Townsend Ecovillage, Riparia, Saint Jude Catholic Worker House Community, Sophia Community, Spring Valley Bruderhof, Stone Soup Cooperative, Turn Cedars, 12 Tribes de Sus, 12 Tribes Cambridge, Twin Oaks Community, Voice for the Voiceless, Woodburn Hill Farm.

KENYA
Jesus Christians.

KIBBUTZIM
7th Millennium Community, Hanoar Haoved Vehalomed, International Communes Desk, Kibbutz Ketura, Kibbutz Lotan, Kibbutz Migvan, The Kibbutz Movement, Kibbutz Neot Semadar, Kibbutz Tamuz, Kvutsat Yovel, Ma'Agal Hakvutzot.

KOSHER
12 Tribes Asheville, 12 Tribes Chattanooga, 12 Tribes Northern Virginia, 12 Tribes Savannah, 12 Tribes Stepping Stone Farm, AAAA Community for Tender Loving Care, Kibbutz Lotan, Oberlin Student Cooperative Association, Sudanese Chadian Community, 12 Tribes Arcadia.

LAND
Anarres Ecovillage, Green River Community Land Trust, Greenplan, Heathcote Community, Land Lifeways Farm, Miccosukee Land Co-op, Oran Mór, Priorities Institute, Raccoon Creek Community, Rainbow Valley, Rewilding Community, TerraVie, Tonantzin Land Institute, Wind Tree Ranch, Wisteria.
SEE ALSO STEWARDSHIP.

LAND PRESERVATION
Common Ground Community, Enota Mountain Village, L'Academie Ynys Wyth, Malu 'Aina, Nomenus Radical Faerie Sanctuary, Raven Rocks.

LAND RESTORATION
Edges, Hudson Valley Ecovillage, The Land Stewardship Center.

LEARNING
Adelphi, Beaver Creek Homestead, Birdsfoot Farm, Earthaven Ecovillage, Gaia University, Learners Trek, Nanish Shontie, Pagan Intentional Community.
SEE ALSO EDUCATION; SCHOOLS.

LIVESTOCK
The Barn, Bear Creek Farms, Beech Hill Community, Bryn Gweled Homesteads, Camphill Village Minnesota Inc., Canon Frome Court Community, Chaneeg Channesch, Cohousing Bristol, Earthaven Ecovillage, Earthswell Farm, Enota Mountain Village, Headlands, The Hermitage, Hockerton Housing Project, Land Lifeways Farm, Laughing Dog Farm and CSA, Lofstedt Farm Community, Middle Road Community, N Street Cohousing, Namasté...Multi-Cultural Sustainable Living Community, Ninth Street Co-op, North Mountain Community Land Trust, O.U.R. Ecovillage, Open Gate Farm & Retreat, Oran Mór, Paradise Village, People on the Way, Port Townsend Ecovillage, Raven Rocks, Redfield Community, Sankofa, Sassafras Ridge Farm, Springtree Community, Storybook Shire, Summerglen Farm and Homestead, Sunwise Co-op, 12 Tribes Community at Peppercorn Creek Farm, 12 Tribes Community at Stentwood Farm, 12 Tribes Community at Stepping Stone Farm, 12 Tribes Community at the Morning Star Ranch, 12 Tribes Bellows Falls, 12 Tribes Cambridge, 12 Tribes Hyannis, 12 Tribes Lancaster, 12 Tribes Oak Hill, 12 Tribes Vista, 12 Tribes Londrina, 12 Tribes Osório, Twin Oaks Community, UFA-Fabrik, Utopiaggia, Village Terraces Cohousing Neighborhood, Vlierhof, Whole Village, Windward Foundation, Wise Woman Center/Laughing Rock Farm.

LOW-IMPACT
Aprovecho Research Center, Breitenbush Hot Springs, Dancing Bones, Earth Pod, Emerald Earth, Hudson Valley Ecovillage, Los Angeles Eco-Village, Moonshadow, Peninsula Park Commons, Planet Earth 11, Port Townsend Ecovillage, Raccoon Creek Community, Sacramento Cohousing, Sowing Circle, Sunward Cohousing, Terra Nova, TerraVie, Trillium Hollow, Utopian Visions, Winslow Cohousing Group, Zephyr Valley Community Co-op.

MACEDONIA, THE FORMER YUGOSLAV REPUBLIC OF
Komaja.

MALTA
Komaja.

MEDIA
Dreamtime Village, Moonshadow.

MEDITATION
American Buddhist Shim Gum Do Association, The Barn, Chacra Millalen, The Christine Center, ElderSpirit Community at Trailview, Franciscan Workers/Companions in Community, Gaia Grove Ecospiritual Community & Ecoretreat, Gondwana Sanctuary, Himalayan Institute, Julian Woods Community, Kashi Ashram, Khula Dhamma, Komaja, Light Morning, Monkton Wyld Court, Mulvey Creek Land Co-operative, Nahziryah Monastic Community, New Goloka, Osho Mevlana Residential Community, Reevis Mountain School of Self-Reliance, Shambala Eco-Resort & Ecovillage Community, Sharingwood Cohousing, Sirius Community, Sivananda Ashram Yoga Ranch, Sparrow Hawk Village, Spirit Cove, Sri Aurobindo Sadhana Peetham, Tao Bear Recovery Community, Terrasante Village, Tibetan Buddhist Learning Center, Truth Consciousness.

MEN
Easton Mountain, The Hermitage, International Puppydogs Movement, Niederkaufungen, Nomenus Radical Faerie Sanctuary, Olympus, Phoenix Gay Chub Music/Art Community.

MEXICO
Comunidad Los Horcones, Huehuecoyotl, La Senda Ecovillage, Rainbow Peace Caravan, Ventana Verde.

MONASTERIES
Christ of the Hills Monastery, Madre

Grande Monastery, Nahziryah Monastic Community, Order of Saint Benedict, Truth Consciousness, Vivekananda Monastery and Retreat Center.

MULTICULTURALISM
Acorn Community, The Blue Crane, Ella Jo Baker Intentional Community Co-op, Hidden Valley, Kakwa Ecovillage.

MUSIC
Atlantis, Blue Moon Cooperative, Camphill Communities California, Common Place Land Cooperative, Dunmire Hollow Community, Emerald Coast Village, Gaia Grove Ecospiritual Community & Ecoretreat, Michigan Womyn's Music Festival, Morninglory, Phoenix Gay Chub Music/Art Community, Rainbow Hearth Sanctuary and Retreat Center, Wild Human Initiative, Windspirit Community, Wisteria.

NATIVE AMERICAN
Nanish Shontie, Rainbow Family Gatherings, Teaching Drum Outdoor School.

NATURE
Abundance Farm, Alpha Farm, Chacra Millalen, Dancing Bones, EarthArt Village, Enota Mountain Village, Findhorn Foundation and Community, Gentle World Inc., Healing Grace Sanctuary, Heartwood Cohousing, Jupiter Hollow, Kalani Oceanside Retreat, Keimblatt Oekodorf, Kitezh Children's Eco-Village Community, Light As Color Foundation, Lothlorien Nature Sanctuary, Meridiana, Morninglory, Namasté Greenfire, Neo Hippie Haven, Oak Grove, Pleasant Hill Cohousing, Point of Infinity Retreat Center, Port Townsend Ecovillage, Sirius Community, Southern California Nature Sanctuary, Spirit Cove, Summerglen Farm and Homestead, Susan B. Anthony Women's Land Trust, Trillium Hollow, 12 Tribes Bellows Falls, The VOL Community, White Buffalo Farm, Wisteria, Yarrow Ecovillage, Yulupa Cohousing.

NATURE SANCTUARIES
Crystal Waters Permaculture Village, Earth Re-Leaf, Lothlorien Nature Sanctuary, Nature's Pace Sanctuary, Nomenus Radical Faerie Sanctuary, Ozark Avalon, Southern California Nature Sanctuary Project, Southwest Sufi Community, Trillium Farm Community, Wisteria.

NETHERLANDS
CW Lismortel, De Hobbitstee, Dutch Cohousing Association, Elim, Emmaus Haarzuilens, Gemeenschappelijk Wonen Nieuwegein, Het Carre, Het Huis van Antonia, In Planning Ecovillage, Komaja, Landelijke Vereniging Centraal Wonen, Vlierhof, The Weyst.

NETWORKING
Cerro Gordo Community, Cohousing for San Diego!, Dunmire Hollow Community, GreenPlan, Hanoar Haoved Vehalomed, Infinite Star Light Offering Visionary Ecovillages, Light As Color Foundation, Melbourne Cohousing Network, New World Rising, Next Step Integral, Rainbow Peace Caravan, Sankofa, Welcome Here Circle of Light Community Network— Rainbow Tribes, The Wild Human Initiative, Yalaha Community Network.

NEW ZEALAND
Anahata Community, Awaawaroa Bay Eco-Village, Cambridge Terrace Community, Creekside Community, Earthsong Eco-Neighbourhood, Gricklegrass, Heartwood Community Inc., Otamatea Eco-Village, Rainbow Valley, Riverside Community, Shambala Eco-Resort & EcoVillage Community, Tararu Valley Sanctuary, Tui Land Trust.

NICARAGUA
Abundance Farm.

NIGERIA
Federation of Arts for the Youth of Our Nation, Palmgrove Christian Community.

NONVIOLENCE
Agape, AinaOla, Attachment Parenting Village, Blackberry, Earth Re-Leaf, East Wind Community, Emma Goldman Finishing School, The Farm, Franciscan Workers/Companions in Community, Freedom-Universe, GaiaYoga Gardens, Grace, Hearthaven, Infinite Star Light Offering Visionary Ecovillages, Karen Catholic Worker House, Little Flower Catholic Worker Farm, Love & Nonviolence Commune, Malu 'Aina, Niederkaufungen, Oran Mór, Oxford Community, Panterra, Poly Pagan Nudist Community, Port Townsend Ecovillage, Rainbow Family Gatherings, Rainbow Valley, Reba Place Fellowship, Sandhill Farm, Shambala Eco-Resort EcoVillage, Skyhouse Community, Tamera—Healing Biotope I, Twin Oaks Community, Vine & Fig Tree Center for Sustainable Culture, Vlierhof.

NUDIST/CLOTHING-OPTIONAL
GaiaYoga Gardens, Poly Pagan Nudist Community.

OFF-THE-GRID
Bear Creek Farms, City of the Sun Foundation Inc., Dancing Rabbit Ecovillage, EarthArt Village, Earthaven Ecovillage, Emerald Earth, GaiaYoga Gardens, Healing Grace Sanctuary, The Homestead at Denison University, Light Morning, Light of Freedom, Mountain Home, Plain Anabaptist Community, Skyhouse, Storybook Shire, Summerglen Farm and Homestead, Sustainable Living Systems, Tararu Valley Sanctuary, Windtree Ranch.

PACIFISM
Comunidad Los Horcones, Greenplan, Koinonia, Plow Creek.

PAGANISM
L'Academie Ynys Wyth, Olympus, Pagan Intentional Community, Pagano, Paradise Village, Poly Pagan Nudist Community, Pumpkin Hollow Community, Rainbow Way Station, Westmerefolc Gepéode.

PANAMA
Finca Buena Vida.

PEACE
Adirondack Herbs, Beech Grove Bruderhof, Chacra Millalen, Community of Light, Dunmire Hollow Community, The Farm, Father Divine's Peace Mission Movement, Genesee Gardens Cohousing, H.O.M.E. Heaven on Mother Earth, Hei Wa House, House of Peace Catholic Worker, Hummingbird Community, Iona Community, Keimblatt Oekodorf, Khula Dhamma, Koinonia, Lifeseed, Light of Freedom, The Love Israel Family, Malu 'Aina, Neve Shalom/Wahat al-Salam, New Earth Cooperative, Oak Grove, One Common Unity, Pagan Intentional Community, Peace Farm, Rainbow Family Gatherings, Riparia, Rosy Branch Farm, Sage Valley, Saint Martin de Porres House, SEADS of Truth Inc., Shambala Eco-Resort & Ecovillage Community, Solterra, Sparrow Hawk Village, Spring Valley Bruderhof, Summerglen Farm and Homestead, Tacoma Eco-Village, Tamera—Healing Biotope I, Turn Cedars, 12 Tribes de Heimsbrunn, 12 Tribes de Sus, 12 Tribes Cambridge, Twin Oaks Community, Union Acres, Village of Harmony, Welcome Here

Circle of Light Community Network—Rainbow Tribes, Zen Peacemaker Circle.

PEOPLE OF COLOR
Azania Alliance.

PERMACULTURE
AinaOla, Albuquerque Urban Ecovillage, Barking Frogs Permaculture Center, Beaver Creek, Big Rock Farm, The Blue Crane, The Change, Crystal Waters Permaculture Village, Dancing Waters Permaculture Co-op, Dreamtime Village, Earth Re-Leaf, Earthaven Ecovillage, Earthright Farms, Ecovilla Asociación GAIA, The Eden Project, Edges, Emerald Earth, Finca Luna, Freedom-Universe, GaiaYoga Gardens, Grace, H.O.M.E. Heaven on Mother Earth, Heathcote Community, Hudson Valley Ecovillage, Hummingbird Community, Kookaburra Park Eco-Village, Lama Foundation, Lost Valley Educational Center, Mele Nahiku, Mountain Home, Mulvey Creek Land Co-operative, Namasté Greenfire, NEO Cohousing, O.U.R. Ecovillage, Oran Mór, Otamatea Eco-Village, Pangaia, Plants for a Future, Point of Infinity Retreat Center and Community, Port Townsend Ecovillage, Rainbow Hearth Sanctuary and Retreat Center, Reba Place Fellowship, Rosneath Farm, Sacred Suenos, Salamander Springs, Shambala Eco-Resort & Ecovillage Community, Sidhefire, Sowing Circle, Spring Lane Farms, Stone Curves Cohousing, Sustainable Living Systems, Tacoma Eco-Village, Talking Cedars Developments Ltd., Terrasante Village, Torri Superiore Ecovillage, Tres Placitas Del Rio, Tribe of Blank, Tribe of Likatien, Westwood Cohousing, Windspirit Community, Yarrow Ecovillage, Zuni Mountain Sanctuary.

PERSONAL GROWTH
Acorn Community, Adelphi, AinaOla, Albuquerque Urban Ecovillage, Aquarian Concepts Community, Ashland Vineyard Community, Bartimaeus Community of Meadow Wood, Breitenbush Hot Springs, Bright Morning Star, Cambridge Terrace Community, Camphill Village USA Inc., Carrowmore Community, Center for Purposeful Living, Chacra Millalen, Comunidad Los Horcones, Du-Má, Earthseed, EcoVillage Detroit, El Semillero, Firetender, GaiaYoga Gardens, Glen Ivy, Greening Life Community, Heartsong, Higher Ground Cohousing, Himalayan Institute, Keimblatt Oekodorf, Komaja, L'Academie Ynys

Wyth, L'Arche Mobile, La'Akea Community, Lost Valley Educational Center, Mariposa Group, Montpelier Cohousing, Next Step Integral, Omega Institute for Holistic Studies, Osho Mevlana Residential Community, Panterra, Projetorgone, Rainbow Peace Caravan, Rocky Hill Cohousing, Rowe Camp and Conference Center, Soma, Teaching Drum Outdoor School, VOL Community, Wellspring.

PHILIPPINES
7th Millennium Community.

POLAND
Association for the Earth.

POLITICS
Azania Alliance, Breitenbush Hot Springs, Emma Goldman Finishing School, Greenplan, Hei Wa House, Kansas City Project, Lothlorien Co-op, Ma'Agal Hakvutzot, Michigan House, Moonshadow, Projetorgone, Rowe Camp & Conference Center, Society for the Promotion of Creative Interchange, Solstice Dawn, Susan B. Anthony Women's Land Trust, Tres Placitas Del Rio, Two Acre Wood.

POLYAMORY
Azania Alliance, Komaja, Paradise Village, Phoenix Gay Chub Music/Art Community, Poly Pagan Nudist Community, Projetorgone.

PORTUGAL
Chumbaria, Tamera—Healing Biotope I.

PREPAREDNESS
Bear Creek Farms, Sugar Mountain.

PROCESS, GROUP
Acorn Community, Alpha Farm, Healing Grace Sanctuary, Hillegass House, River City Housing Collective.

PSYCHOLOGY
Abundance Farm, Adelphi, Angels Valley, Azania Alliance, Himalayan Institute, Humanity Rising, Omega Institute for Holistic Studies, Pagano, Rowe Camp & Conference Center, Windhaven.

PUBLISHING
Catholic Worker Community, Gentle World Inc., Himalayan Institute, Iona Community, L'Academie Ynys Wyth, Lost Valley Educational Center, Ma Yoga Shakti International Mission, Magic, Moonshadow, Oak Grove,

One World Family Commune, Pioneer Trails Institute.

QUAKER
Ashland Vineyard Community, Beacon Hill Friends House.

QUEER
Azania Alliance, Colibri Urban Housing Collective, Debs House, Hei Wa House, The Hermitage, IDA, International Puppydogs Movement, Lothlorien Co-op, Nasalam, Niederkaufungen, Nomenus Radical Faerie Sanctuary, Phoenix Gay Chub Music/Art Community, Poly Pagan Nudist Community, Sunset House, Zuni Mountain Sanctuary.

RADICAL
Ashram Community, Azania Alliance, Corani Housing and Land Co-op, LandARC, Little Flower Catholic Worker, Nomenus Radical Faerie Sanctuary, Pumpkin Hollow Community, Reba Place Fellowship, Walden Two Community California, Zuni Mountain Sanctuary.

RAINBOW
Earthsky Tribe, Rainbow Family Gatherings, Welcome Here Circle of Light Community Network—Rainbow Tribes.

RECOVERY
Angels Valley, Humanity Rising, Tao Bear Recovery Community.

RENEWABLE ENERGY
Beaver Creek, Coflats Stroud, Dancing Rabbit Ecovillage, The Eden Project, Freedom-Universe, Gaia Grove Ecospiritual Community & Ecoretreat, Hudson Valley Ecovillage, Pioneer Trails Institute.
SEE ALSO SOLAR POWER; WIND POWER; FUEL, ALTERNATIVE.

RETIREMENT
ElderSpiritCommunity, Free State Community, Lofstedt Farm Community, Retirement Communities, Union Acres.

RETREAT FACILITIES
Abbey of the Genesee, Abode of the Message, Agape, Ananda Kanan Ozark Retreat Center, Aquarian Concepts Community, Aquarius Nature Retreat, ARC Retreat Center, The Barn, Breitenbush Hot Springs, Camp Sister Spirit, Chacra Millalen, The Christine Center, Community of Light,

Appendix

303

Community Retreat Mindful Living, Dreamtime Village, Easton Mountain, Enota Mountain Village, The Farm, Finca Buena Vida, Gaia Grove Ecospiritual Community & Ecoretreat, Goodenough Community, Grail Ecovillage, Harbin Hot Springs, Himalayan Institute, Hudson Valley Ecovillage, Hummingbird Community, Kalani Oceanside Retreat, Kashi Ashram, Koinonia, La Flor del Agua Community, Lama Foundation, Light As Color Foundation, Lost Valley Educational Center, Madre Grande Monastery, Molloy Ashram Retreat, Namasté...Multi-Cultural Sustainable Living Community, Nomenus Radical Faerie Sanctuary, Olympus, Open Gate Farm & Retreat, Order of Saint Benedict, Pangaia, Point of Infinity Retreat Center and Community, RachanaRetreat, Rainbow Farm, Rainbow Hearth Sanctuary and Retreat Center, River Hayven, Rowe Camp & Conference Center, Sivananda Ashram Yoga Ranch, Southern California Nature Sanctuary Project, Southwest Sufi Community, Sri Aurobindo Sadhana Peetham, Summerglen Farm and Homestead, Sunrise Ranch, Talking Cedars Developments Ltd., Truth Consciousness, Union Acres, Vivekananda Monastery and Retreat Center, Wellspring, Wisteria, Yogaville/Satchidananda Ashram, The Zen Society.

REVOLUTION
Atlantis, Beech Grove Bruderhof, IDA, Love & Nonviolence Commune, Spring Valley Bruderhof.

RIGHT LIVELIHOOD
Community of Light, Earthaven Ecovillage, Ganas, Kakwa Ecovillage, Riparia, Sowing Circle, Windtree Ranch, Windward Foundation.

ROMANIA
Ecotopia Romania.

RUSSIAN FEDERATION
Aleskam, Grishino Community, Kitezh Children's Eco-Village Community.

SCHOOLS
Abode of the Message, Birdsfoot Farm, Camphill Special School, The Farm, Freestone Hill Community, Gaia University, Heartwood Institute, Hummingbird Community, Kitezh Children's Eco-Village Community, L'Academie Ynys Wyth, Lama Foundation, Maison Emmanuel, Monkton Wyld Court, Mount

Madonna Center, Neve Shalom/Wahat al-Salam, Niederkaufungen, O.U.R. Ecovillage, Open Gate Farm & Retreat, Pennine Camphill Community, Sivananda Ashram Yoga Ranch, Spring Valley Bruderhof, Summerglen Farm and Homestead, Tamera—Healing Biotope I, Teaching Drum Outdoor School, Tibetan Buddhist Learning Center, UFA-Fabrik, Upper Applegate Community.

SEE ALSO EDUCATION; LEARNING.

SELF-SUFFICIENCY
7th Millennium Community, Angels Valley, Atlantis, The Barn, Beaver Creek Homestead, The Blue Crane, Cerro Gordo Community, City of the Sun Foundation Inc, Common Place Land Cooperative, Comunidad Los Horcones, Dapala Farm, Earth Re-Leaf, EarthRight Farms, Ecovillage Sieben Linden, The Eden Project, Eden Ranch Community, Garden O' Vegan, Gricklegrass, Hidden Valley, Hockerton Housing Project, In Planning Ecovillage, Kerala Commune, Khula Dhamma, Land Lifeways Farm, Meridiana, Moonshadow, Namasté...Multi-Cultural Sustainable Living Community, Northern Sun Farm Co-op, Otamatea Eco-Village, People on the Way, Poly Pagan Nudist Community, Rainbow Way Station, Reevis Mountain School of Self-Reliance, Sankofa, SEADS of Truth Inc., Shambala Eco-Resort & Ecovillage Community, Storybook Shire, Sudanese Chadian Community, Sugar Mountain, Summit Ave Cooperative, Tribe of Blank, Trillium Hollow, 12 Tribes Osório, Twin Oaks Community, Utah United Order, Utopian Visions, Village of Harmony, Vine & Fig Tree Center for Sustainable Culture, The VOL Community, Windward Foundation, Yalaha Community Network.

SERBIA AND MONTENEGRO
Komaja.

SERVICE
Abode of the Message, Alpha Farm, Aquarian Concepts Community, Breitenbush Hot Springs, Camphill Soltane, Center for Purposeful Living, Clare's House of Hospitality, Denver Catholic Worker, Dolphin Community, Du-Má, ElderSpirit Community at Trailview, Findhorn Foundation and Community, Firetender, Franciscan Workers/Companions in Community, Gesundheit!Institute, H.O.M.E. Heaven on Mother Earth, Healing Grace Sanctuary, Kashi Ashram, Kibbutz

Migvan, Kindness House, Kitezh Children's Eco-Village Community, Koinonia, Lama Foundation, LandARC, Magic, Mount Madonna Center, Mulvey Creek Land Co-operative, Nahziryah Monastic Community, Niche/Tucson Community Land Trust, Niederkaufungen, Omega Institute for Holistic Studies, Reba Place Fellowship, Sivananda Ashram Yoga Ranch, Truth Consciousness, Union Acres, Village Cohousing, Windtree Ranch.

SIMPLICITY
Agape, Aprovecho Research Center, ARC Retreat Center, Ashland Vineyard Community, Beacon Hill Friends House, Blue Moon Cooperative, Champlain Valley Cohousing, Common Place Land Cooperative, Dancing Bones, Denver Catholic Worker, EarthArt Village, Earthaven Ecovillage, El Semillero, Emerald Earth, Emma Goldman Finishing School, Everything Is Related, Fox Housing Cooperative, Franciscan Workers/Companions in Community, GaiaYoga Gardens, Garden O' Vegan, Green River Community Land Trust, Gricklegrass, Healing Grace Sanctuary, The Homestead at Denison University, Humanity Rising, Infinite Star Light Offering Visionary Ecovillages, Jindibah, Khula Dhamma, Kindness House, La'Akea Community, Lama Foundation, LandARC, Light Morning, Little Flower Catholic Worker Farm, Malu 'Aina, Meridiana, Morninglory, Nahziryah Monastic Community, Namasté Greenfire, Neo Hippie Haven, New Goloka, Northern Sun Farm Co-op, Oak Grove, Olympus, Oran Mór, Orca Landing, Oxford Community, Pagan Intentional Community, Port Townsend Ecovillage, Projetorgone, Rainbow Hearth Sanctuary and Retreat Center, Rainbow Peace Caravan, Sacred Suenos, Sharing Community, Songaia Cohousing Community, Sophia Community, Talkeetna Blueberry Sanctuary, Teaching Drum Outdoor School, 12 Tribes de Sus, Village of Harmony, Vine & Fig Tree Center for Sustainable Culture.

SOCIAL CHANGE
Aquarian Concepts Community, Bright Morning Star, Common Ground Community, Cornerstone Housing Cooperative, Dancing Rabbit Ecovillage, Du-Má, Emma Goldman Finishing School, Fox Housing Cooperative, Healing Grace Sanctuary, Kansas City Project, Kerala Commune,

Mariposa Grove, New Environment Association, Niederkaufungen, San Mateo Ecovillage, Skyhouse Community, Solstice Dawn, Stone Soup Cooperative, Sunset House, Talking Cedars Developments Ltd., Tomorrow's Bread Today, Walnut Street Co-op, Zen Peacemaker Circle.

SEE ALSO ACTIVISM.

SOCIAL RESPONSIBILITY

Beacon Hill Friends House, Breitenbush Hot Springs, Sacred Suenos.

SOCIALISM

Hanoar Haoved Vehalomed, Kibbutz Tamuz, Niederkaufungen.

SOLAR POWER

Agape, Arcadia Cohousing, Bear Creek Farms, Beaver Creek, Beaver Creek Homestead, Berea College Ecovillage, Blue Moon Cooperative, Cerro Gordo Community, City of the Sun Foundation Inc., Coflats Stroud, Common Ground Community, Cranberry Commons, Dancing Rabbit Ecovillage, Dedetepe Eco-Farm, Eclipse, Ecovillage at Ithaca, The Eden Project, Emerald Coast Village, Emerald Earth, Fordyce Street Cohousing, Gaia Grove Ecospiritual Community & Ecoretreat, Grace, Green River Community Land Trust, Hockerton Housing Project, The Homestead at Denison University, Hypatia Housing Cooperative, Kerala Commune, Light of Freedom, Lothlorien Co-op, Malu 'Aina, Moonshadow, Morninglory, Mountain Home, Niederkaufungen, Pioneer Trails Institute, Pleasant Hill Cohousing, Prudence Crandall House, Raccoon Creek Community, Raven Rocks, Redfield Community, Regenerative Co-op of Pomona, Rise and Shine, Rosneath Farm, Sirius Community, Skyhouse Community, Solterra, Spring Lane Farms, Springhill Cohousing Community, Sunwise Co-op, SurrealEstates, Trillium Farm Community, 12 Tribes Osório, Village of Harmony, Vine & Fig Tree Center for Sustainable Culture, Westwood Cohousing, Whole Health Foundation, Wisteria, Woodfolk House, Zuni Mountain Sanctuary.

SEE ALSO RENEWABLE ENERGY.

SOUTH AFRICA

The Blue Crane, Khula Dhamma.

SPAIN

El Bloque, El Semillero, Finca Luna, Guayrapá, 12 Tribes Irún, 12 Tribes San Sebastian, Walden Community.

SPIRITUALITY

3Circles Community, AAAA Community for Tender Loving Care, Abbey of the Genesee, Abode of the Message, Agape Community, Aquarian Concepts Community, Ascension Point, Atlantis, Awakening to Grace, The Barn, Bartimaeus Community, Blackberry, Blue Crane, The Bruderhof Communities, Cambridge Terrace Community, Camp Sister Spirit, CedarSanctum, Center for Purposeful Living, Center of Light Spirituality, The Change, City of the Sun Foundation, Clare's House of Hospitality, Common Place Land Cooperative, Dancing Waters Permaculture Co-op, Dolphin Community, Earth Re-Leaf, EarthArt Village, EarthSky Tribe, Easton Mountain, Eden Project, Embassy of the Heavens, Enota Mountain Village, Everett, Everything Is Related, The Farm, Fellowship Community, Findhorn Foundation and Community, Fox Housing Cooperative, Freedom-Universe, Freeland Community, Freestone Hill Community, Friends and Neighbors, Gaia Grove EcoSpiritual Community & Ecoretreat, GaiaYoga Gardens, The Gathering, Gentle World Inc., Glen Ivy, Gondwana Sanctuary, Goodenough Community, Harbin Hot Springs, Healing Grace Sanctuary, Hearthaven, Hertha, Hidden Valley, Hope Hill Community, Humanity Rising, Hummingbird Community, Infinite Star Light Offering Visionary..., Iona Community, Jindibah, Khula Dhamma, Kibbutz Lotan, Kibbutz Tamuz, Kindness House, Kitezh Children's Eco-Village Community, Koinonia, Komaja, Kvutsat Yovel, Lama Foundation, LifeShare Community, Light Morning, Light of Freedom, Lofstedt Farm Community, Los Visionarios, Love & Nonviolence Commune, Love Israel Family, Ma Yoga Shakti International Mission, Magic, Maison Emmanuel, Mariposa Group, Mele Nahiku, Methow Center of Enlightenment, Mount Madonna Center, Namasté Greenfire, Namasté...Multi-Cultural Sustainable..., Nanish Shontie, Nasalam, Nature's Pace Sanctuary, Neve Shalom/Wahat al-Salam, New Goloka, New Horizons, Next Step Integral, Nomenus Radical Faerie Sanctuary, O.U.R. Ecovillage, Oak Grove, Oakland Elizabeth House, Omega Institute for Holistic Studies, One Common Unity, One World Family Commune, Open Gate Farm & Retreat, Oran Mór, Order of Saint Benedict, Osho Mevlana Residential Community, Ozark Avalon, Pagano,

Pangaia, Panterra, Paradise Village, People on the Way, Phoenix Gay Chub Music/Art Community, Planet Earth11, Point of Infinity Retreat Center & Community, Port Townsend EcoVillage, Pumpkin Hollow Community, Rainbow Farm, Rainbow Hearth Sanctuary and Retreat, Rainbow Way Station, Rapha Community, Reba Place Fellowship, Reevis Mountain School of Self-Reliance, The Refuge, Rewilding Community, River Hayven, Rosneath Farm, Rowe Camp & Conference Center, Sacred Suenos, Sage Valley, Saint Martin de Porres House, Sassafras Ridge Farm, 7th Millennium Community, Shambala Eco-Resort & Ecovillage Community, Sidhefire, Sirius Community, Society for the Promotion of Creative..., Solstice Dawn, Soma, Songaia Cohousing Community, Sophia Community, Southern California Nature Sanctuary..., Southern Cassadaga Spiritualist Camp, Sparrow Hawk Village, Spirit Cove, Spirit Dance Co-op Community, Summerglen Farm and Homestead, Sunrise Ranch, Tacoma Eco-Village, Talking Cedars Developments Ltd., Tamera—Healing Biotope I, Tao Bear Recovery Community, Teaching Drum Outdoor School, Temescal Commons Cohousing, Tomorrow's Bread Today, Tribe of Likatien, Trillium Farm Community, Truth Consciousness, Turn Cedars, Union Acres, Utah United Order, Village of Harmony, Village Terraces Cohousing Neighborhood, Vlierhof, Voice for the Voiceless, The VOL Community, Wellspring, White Buffalo Farm, Wild Human Initiative, Windspirit Community, WindTree Ranch, Windward Foundation, Wise Woman Center/Laughing Rock Farm, Yonderfamily Housing and Land Trust Inc., Zen Peacemaker Circle, Zen Society, Zuni Mountain Sanctuary.

SEE ALSO ASHRAMS; CHRISTIAN; JESUS; MONASTERIES; PAGANISM; CAMPHILL COMMUNITIES; 12 TRIBES COMMUNITIES; NAMES OF SPECIFIC RELIGIONS/SPIRITUAL PATHS.

STEWARDSHIP

Abundant Dawn Community, Blackberry, Blue Moon Cooperative, Breitenbush Hot Springs, Common Place Land Cooperative, Dancing Rabbit Ecovillage, Dayspring Circle, Dunmire Hollow Community, EarthArt Village, The Eden Project, Eden Ranch Community, Edges, Heartwood Institute, Jump Off Community Land Trust, Jupiter Hollow, La'Akea Community, Lama Foundation, Land

Stewardship Center, LandARC, Laughing Dog Farm and CSA, Lothlorien Nature Sanctuary, Lothlorien Farm, Magic, Mountain Home, Newberry Place: A Grand Rapids Cohousing Community, North Mountain Community Land Trust, O.U.R. Ecovillage, Rainbow Farm, River Farm, Rosy Branch Farm, Sharing Community, Stewardship Incorporated, Sunward Cohousing, Sweetwater Community Land Trust, Tao Bear Recovery Community, Tres Placitas Del Rio, Trillium Farm Community, Union Acres, Whole Village, Windward Foundation, Wisteria.

STUDENT HOUSING
Bower House, Brown Association for Cooperative Housing, CHUVA, Collegiate Living Cooperative, The Domes, ECLIPSE, Gregory House, The Homestead at Denison University, Inter-Cooperative Council (Michigan), Inter-Cooperative Council (Texas), Jones House, Kingman Hall, Michigan House, Nakamura House, O'Keeffe House, Oberlin Student Cooperative Association, Osterweil House, Renaissance House, Ruths' House, Santa Cruz Student Housing Co-op, SBSHC: Santa Barbara Student Housing Cooperative, Sherwood Co-op, Sojourner Truth House, Student Cooperative Organization, Students' Cooperative Association, University Students' Cooperative Association, Vail House, Waterloo Co-operative Residence Inc.

SUFISM
Abode of the Message, Southwest Sufi Community.

SUSTAINABILITY
Acorn Community, Awaawaroa Bay Eco-Village, Beaver Creek Homestead, Beech Hill Community, Berea College Ecovillage, Bible Belt Exodus, Blackberry, Burlington Cohousing, Cerro Gordo Community, Champlain Valley Cohousing, Cobb Hill, The Community Planet Foundation, Cranberry Commons, Dancing Bones, Dancing Rabbit Ecovillage, Domes, Dragon Belly Farm, Earth Re-Leaf, EarthArt Village, Earthaven Ecovillage, Earthsky Tribe, Earthswell Farm, East Bay Cohousing, East Wind Community, Echollective Farm, Ecotopia Romania, Ecovillage at Ithaca, EcoVillage Detroit, Eden Project, Forming Intentional Community, Fox Housing Cooperative, Free State

Community, Freedom-Universe, GaiaYoga Gardens, Grail Ecovillage, Greenplan, Gricklegrass, H.O.M.E. Heaven on Mother Earth, Harmonious Earth Community, Harmony Village, Heathcote Community, Hei Wa House, The Homestead at Denison University, Hopewell Community, Jindibah, Jump Off Community Land Trust, Kakwa Ecovillage, Karen Catholic Worker House, Keimblatt Oekodorf, Kipling Creek, LandARC, Lifeseed, Light Morning, Light of Freedom, Lofstedt Farm Community, Los Angeles Eco-Village, Los Visionarios, Meadowdance Community Group, Meridiana, Merry Fox Community, Millstone Co-op, Monkton Wyld Court, Moonshadow, Namasté Greenfire, NEO Cohousing, New Environment Association, O.U.R.Ecovillage, Oak Grove, Oran Mór, Pangaia, Plants for a Future, Priorities Institute, Regenerative Co-op of Pomona, Salamander Springs, San Mateo Ecovillage, Sidhefire, Somerville Ecovillage, Sowing Circle, Stewardship Incorporated, Sunwise Co-op, Talking Cedars Developments Ltd., Tao Bear Recovery Community, Terra Nova, Torri Superiore Ecovillage, Tribe of Likatien, Vlierhof, Whole Village, Wild Sage Cohousing, Windhaven, Windward Foundation, Yalaha Community Network, Yarrow Ecovillage.
SEE ALSO CULTURE, SUSTAINABLE; SUSTAINABLE LIVING.

SUSTAINABLE DEVELOPMENT
Albuquerque Urban Ecovillage, Earth First Australia, Hockerton Housing Project, Kookaburra Park Eco-Village, Lebensraum, San Mateo Ecovillage, TerraVie.

SUSTAINABLE LIVING
Abundance Farm, AinaOla, Aprovecho Research Center, Cobb Hill, Earthswell Farm, ECLIPSE, Ecovillage Sieben Linden, Edges, Emerald Earth, Enota Mountain Village, Footprint Ecovillage, Forming Intentional Community, GaiaYoga Gardens, Harmony Village, Healing Grace Sanctuary, Hertha, Hockerton Housing Project, Hudson Valley Ecovillage, Jump Off Community Land Trust, Lama Foundation, LandARC, Mulvey Creek Land Co-operative, Neo Hippie Haven, New Horizons, Point of Infinity Retreat Center and Community, Port Townsend Ecovillage, Prag House, Rainbow Peace Caravan, Reba Place Fellowship, Red Earth Farms, Sacred Suenos, Sage Valley, Sharing

Community, Sherwood Co-op, Solstice Dawn, Songaia Cohousing Community, Spring Lane Farms, Stelle Community, Summerglen Farm and Homestead, Sunwise Co-op, Sustainable Living Systems, Tararu Valley Sanctuary, TerraNova, Twin Oaks Community, Windtree Ranch, Yonderfamily Housing and Land Trust Inc., Zuni Mountain Sanctuary.
SEE ALSO CULTURE, SUSTAINABLE; SUSTAINABILITY.

SWEDEN
Ekobyn Bålarna, Kadesh-biyqah, Lindsbergs Kursgård, Stiftelsen Stjårnsund, Tullstugan Collective Housing Unit, Vialen, Wäxthuset Väddö.

SWITZERLAND
Center of Unity Schweibenalp, Komaja, Monte Vuala, Zentrum Waldegg.

TECHNOLOGY, ALTERNATIVE/APPROPRIATE
AAAA Community for Tender Loving Care, Aprovecho Research Center, Centre for Alternative Technology, Dapala Farm, Ecovilla Asociación Gaia, Egrets' Cove, Northern Sun Farm Co-op, Windward Foundation.

TRIBE
AinaOla, Arcobaleno Fiammeggiante (Tribe), The Tribe, Tribe of Blank, Tribe of Dirt, Tribe of Likatien, Westmerefolc Gepéode.

TURKEY
Dedetepe Eco-farm, Komun.

UNITED KINGDOM
Anarres Ecovillage, Ashram Community, The Barn, Beannachar Camphill Community, Beech Grove Bruderhof, Beech Hill Community, Birchwood Hall Community, Brynderwen Vegan Community, Camphill Village Newton Dee, Canon Frome Court Community, Centre for Alternative Technology, Chicken Shack Housing Cooperative, Clanabogan Camphill Community, CoFlats Stroud, Cohousing Bristol, Columbanus Community of Reconciliation, Community Forming, Community Project, Corani Housing and Land Co-op, Cornerstone Housing Cooperative, Darvell Bruderhof, Earthworm Housing Co-op, Findhorn Foundation and Community, Fox Housing Cooperative, Frankleigh Co-Flats, Grail Community, Grimstone Community, Gwerin

Housing Association, Hockerton Housing Project, Iona Community, Isle of Erraid, Jesus Christians, Keveral Farm Community, Komaja, Laurieston Hall, Lee Abbey Aston Household Community, Little Grove Community, Losang Dragpa Buddhist Centre, Love & Nonviolence Commune, Monkton Wyld Court, Mourne Grange Camphill Village Community, New Creation Christian Community, Othona Community, Oxford Community, Pathfinder Fellowship, Pennine Camphill Community, Plants for a Future, Redfield Community, Simon Community, Springhill Cohousing Community, Stepping Stones Housing Co-op, Town Head Collective, 12 Tribes Stentwood Farm, Two Piers, The Well at Willen.

UNSCHOOLING
Little Flower Catholic Worker Farm, The Wild Human Initiative.
SEE ALSO HOMESCHOOLING.

VEGAN
AAAA Community for Tender Loving Care, Brynderwen Vegan Community, Earth Re-Leaf, Eden Project, Garden o' Vegan, Gentle World Inc., Infinite Star Light, Nahziryah Monastic Community, Plants for a Future, Skyhouse Community.

VEGETARIAN
Awakening Grace, Black Elk House, Carrowmore Community, Chrysalis Co-op, Cooperative Roots, Dedetepe Eco-Farm, Dharma House Community, Dolphin Community, Ecovilla Asociación GAIA, Emma Goldman Finishing School, Emma Goldman's, Grace, Kashi Ashram, Khula Dhamma, Komaja, Lama Foundation, Lester House, Light Morning, Lothlorien Co-op, Love & Nonviolence Commune, Ma Yoga Shakti International, Merry Fox Community, Millstone Co-op, Monkton Wyld Court, Mount Madonna Center, Nasalam, New Goloka, Oxford Community, Regenerative Co-op of Pomona, Shambala Eco-Resort & EcoVillage, Society for the Promotion of Creative Interchange, Springhill Cohousing Community, Sunwise Co-op, Truth Consciousness, Voice for the Voiceless, Wind Tree Ranch, Yogaville/Satchidananda Ashram.

WASTE DISPOSAL, ALTERNATIVE
Beech Hill Community, Berea College Ecovillage, Crystal Waters Permaculture Village, Dayspring Circle, EarthArt Village, Eclipse, Pioneer Trails Institute, Sustainable Living Systems, Tararu Valley Sanctuary, Utopian Visions.

WATER PROJECTS, ALTERNATIVE
Berea College Ecovillage, Crystal Waters Permaculture Village, EarthArt Village, Julian Woods Community, Light of Freedom, Malu 'Aina, Mountain Home, Pioneer Trails Institute, Regenerative Co-op of Pomona, Rosneath Farm, Spring Lane Farms, Stone Curves Cohousing, Sustainable Living Systems, Tararu Valley Sanctuary.

WIND POWER
Beaver Creek, Blue Moon Cooperative, Dedetepe Eco-Farm, Emerald Coast Village, Gaia Grove Ecospiritual Community & Ecoretreat, Hockerton Housing Project, Light of Freedom, Oran Mór, Pioneer Trails Institute, Sirius Community, 12 Tribes Osório.
SEE ALSO RENEWABLE ENERGY.

WOMEN
Clare's House of Hospitality, The Eden Project, Grail Ecovillage, Huntington Open Womyns Land, Karen Catholic Worker House, Michigan Womyn's Music Festival, Mulvey Creek Land Co-operative, Niche/Tucson Community Land Trust, Niederkaufungen, Oakland Elizabeth House, Saint Jude Catholic Worker House Community, Southern Oregon Women's Network, Susan B. Anthony Women's Land Trust, Twin Oaks Community, Wise Woman Center/Laughing Rock Farm, Womanshare, Women's Art Colony Farm.
SEE ALSO FEMINISM.

WORK-STUDY PROGRAMS
Abode of the Message, The Christine Center, Yogaville/Satchidananda Ashram.

WORKSHOPS/COURSES
Abode of the Message, Aquarian Concepts Community, Arcosanti, Barking Frogs Permaculture Center, The Blue Crane, The Center of Light Spirituality Center, The Christine Center, City of the Sun Foundation, Inc., Dedetepe Eco-Farm, Dreamtime Village, Ecovilla Asociación Gaia, Ecovillage at Ithaca, Edges, El Semillero, Emerald Earth, Finca Buena Vida, Goodenough Community, Harbin Hot Springs, Heartwood Institute, The Hermitage, Himalayan Institute, Hockerton Housing Project, Hudson Valley Ecovillage, Iona Community, Jump Off Community

Land Trust, Kalani Oceanside Retreat, Kashi Ashram, Lama Foundation, Light of Freedom, Los Angeles Eco-Village, Lost Valley Educational Center, Magic, Michigan Womyn's Music Festival, Moonshadow, Mountain Home, Niederkaufungen, Oak Grove, Omega Institute for Holistic Studies, Osho Mevlana Residential Community, Otamatea Eco-Village, Panterra, Pioneer Trails Institute, Rainbow Peace Caravan, Redfield Community, Reevis Mountain School of Self-Reliance, Regenerative Co-op of Pomona, SBSHC: Santa Barbara Student Housing Cooperative, SEADS of Truth Inc., Sirius Community, Sivananda Ashram Yoga Ranch, Southern Cassadaga Spiritualist Camp, Sowing Circle, Sparrow Hawk Village, Susan B. Anthony Women's Land Trust, Sustainable Living Systems, Talking Cedars Developments Ltd., Teaching Drum Outdoor School, Tibetan Buddhist Learning Center, Torri Superiore Ecovillage, UFA-Fabrik, Whole Health Foundation, The Wild Human Initiative, Windspirit Community, Wise Woman Center/Laughing Rock Farm, Yogaville/Satchidananda Ashram.

YOGA
Atlantis, Dedetepe Eco-Farm, Earth Pod, Emerald Coast Village, GaiaYoga Gardens, H.O.M.E. Heaven on Mother Earth, Harbin Hot Springs, Himalayan Institute, Julian Woods Community, Kashi Ashram, Komaja, Lost Valley Educational Center, Ma Yoga Shakti International Mission, Magic, Mount Madonna Center, Namasté...Multi-Cultural Sustainable Living Community, One World Family Commune, Panterra, Sharingwood Cohousing, Sivananda Ashram Yoga Ranch, Spirit Cove, Sri Aurobindo Sadhana Peetham, Truth Consciousness, Yogaville/Satchidananda Ashram.

YOUTH
Camphill Soltane, Franciscan Workers, Healing Grace Sanctuary, Hummingbird Community, Iona Community, Magic, Niche/Tucson Community Land Trust, One Common Unity, Rowe Camp & Conference Center, Sivananda Ashram Yoga Ranch, Tamera—Healing Biotope I.

Communities Magazine Back Issues

$\mathcal{F}$ROM 1972 TO THE PRESENT, *Communities* magazine has consistently offered excellent information, stories, and community wisdom to the movement. Here is a list of all those back issues, which the Fellowship for Intentional Community is proud to make available. See order form on page 312.

Communitas #1*: A New Community Journal; Virginia communities; Philadelphia Life Center; Alpha Farm. (Jul '72)

Communitas #2*: Country life; conferences; Meadowlark therapeutic community; School of Living; Mulberry Farm; Arthur Morgan. (Sep '72)

#1 Directory '72: Membership selection; Camphill Village; Twin Oaks; women and communal societies. (Dec '72)

#2 Law, Communes, Land Trusts: Rural poverty; Open Gate; Papaya; Changes Therapeutic Community. (Feb '73)

#3 Community Market Development: Ananda; economic Clearinghouse. (Spr '73)

#4 Schools and Community: The Vale School; The Farm; community heritage. (Sum '73)

#5 Personal Change/Social Change: Community culture; Boston co-op houses; group relationships. (Oct '73)

#6 Overseas Community: May Valley Co-op; Christian communes; back-to-the-land. (Jan '74)

#7 1974 Directory: Women in community; Prisoners' struggles; People of Color and community. (Mar '74)

#8 Individuality and Intimacy: Jealousy, open relationships, couples, singles; Christian homesteading. (May '74)

#9 Children in Community: Iris Mountain; Twin Oaks; Ananda; children's books. (Jul '74)

#10 Work: Labor credit systems; Times Change process. (Nov '74)

#11 Land Reform: Ownership and use; planning; living on the land; Paolo Soleri; energy. (Dec '74)

#12 Directory '75: Karum; networking; building new society. (Jan '75)

#13 Spiritual Life in Community: Christian, ashrams, secular, atheist, ritual; composting. (Mar '75)

#14 Therapy: encounter groups; spiritual therapy; overcoming jealousy; The Farm. (May '75)

#15 Research and Education in Community: Survival schools; martial arts; Paolo Soleri interview. (Jul '75)

#16 Planning: Ecology and economics; short and long-range contingencies; why plan?; land use; alternative energy. (Sep '75)

#17 Family, Sex, and Marriage: Gay relationships; gender roles; childrearing; spiritual marriage; German communes. (Nov '75)

#18 Directory '76: Government; Twin Oaks; Project Artaud; East Wind. (Jan '76)

#19 Urban Communities: New Haven; Twin Cities; Phil. Life Ctr; take back the night; structure and decision making. (Mar '76)

#20 Middle Class Communes: How to start; interpersonal skills; teenagers in communes; sharing housework. (May '76)

#21 Kibbutzim: Local relations; Ananda Co-op Village; social planning; food co-ops. (Jul '76)

#22 Networking in the Ozarks: Kibbutz family; norms vs. rules; community market; Findhorn. (Sep '76)

#23 Women and Work in the Kibbutz: Rainbow Family; leaving community; Project America. (Nov '76)

#24 Building Community: Physical design; culture; decentralized politics; Directory '77; Another Place Farm. (Jan '77)

#25 Don't Start a Commune in 1977: ... join an existing one instead; Neighborhood Planning Council in DC; first FEC assembly, international communities. (Mar '77)

#26 Rebuilding the City: Urban co-ops: Austin, NY, DC, Greenbriar Community. (May '77)

#27 Movement for a New Society: Social class; long-range planning; older women; Plowshare Community. (Jul '77)

#28 Seabrook: A political community; middle-aged men in community; ex-Twin Oakers. (Sep '77)

#29 Democratic Management: Consensus; leadership; group consciousness; The Ark. (Nov '77)

#30 Directory '78: School of Living and Deep Run Farm; financing; Roger Ulrich interview. (Jan '78)

#31 Learning in Community: Teaching and learning for all ages; spiritual abortion. (Mar '78)

#32 Future of Community: FEC; Cerro Gordo; Karass; The Community Soap Factory. (May '78)

#33 A Woman's Issue: Mothers and daughters; Virginia Blaisdell interview; feminism in MNS; nontraditional work. (Jul '78)

#34 West Coast Communal Movement: Hoedads, Alpha Farm, co-op grocery, salvage biz, other activities in CA and OR. (Sep '78)

#35 Consumer Co-op Bank: Income and resource sharing; Utopian heritage. (Nov '78)

#36 Kerista: British Columbia; Circle of Gold. (Jan '79)

#37/38 Guide to Cooperative Alternatives: Double issue on community participation, social change, well-being, appropriate technology, networking; *Directory of Intentional Communities*; resource listings. $15, 184 pgs. (Sum '79)

*Communitas was a predecessor to *Communities* that ran for two issues.

#39 Federation Women: The Hutterites; travel ashram community; Healing Waters; Industrial Co-op Assoc. (Aug '79)

#40 Worker-Owned Businesses: Community development; urban ecology; feminist credit union; trusteeship. (Oct '79)

#41 Relationships: Friendships, family, sexuality; Renaissance Community. (Dec '79)

#42 Regionalism—The Southeast: Another Place; Co-op Anti-nuke; community resources. (Feb '80)

#43 Health and Well-Being: Massage; setting up a tofu kitchen; feminist retreat; radical psychiatry; cmty health clinic. (Apr '80)

#44 Consumer Cooperative Alliance: Housing; food; arts; energy. (Jun '80)

#45 Art Collectives: Freestate Anti-nuke; Rainbow Family; women in Oregon communities. (Oct '80)

#46 Directory '81: Culture; pregnancy; econ.; potlatch. (Dec '80)

#47 Stories: Community organizing; economics and work; culture. (Feb '81)

#48 Communities Around the World: Cuba, China, Israel, India, Spain, El Salvador, England. (Apr '81)

#49 Tempeh Production: Overcoming masculine oppression; social change; credit unions; insurance. (Jun '81)

#50 Dying: Hospice, grieving, death in community, rituals, practical guide to home death. (Oct '81)

#51 Political Paradigms for the '80s. (Dec '81)

#52 Barter Network: Santa Cruz Women's Health Collective; worker-owned businesses. (Feb '82)

#53 Spiritual Communities: Lama, Sirius, The Farm, Renaissance, Abode of the Message, Shambhala. (Apr '82)

#54 Peace: Bright Morning Star interview; social activism; community land trust; Meg Christian; kibbutz. (Jun '82)

#55 Building Economic Democracy: Co-op Bank; legal network; worker buyout; unions. (Oct '82)

#56 10th Anniversary Issue and Directory '83: best of *Communities*. (Dec '82)

#57 Women in Business: Feminist therapy; Audubon Expedition; Women's Resource Distribution Company; science fiction; peace movement. (Feb '83)

#58 Co-op America Debut: Catalog; Sisterfire; Consumer Co-op Bank. (Apr '83)

#59 Computers: Arab/Jewish settlement; holistic living; growing pains. (Jul '83)

#60 Gatherings '83: Michigan public schools; Solidarity. (Oct '83)

#61 Parenting, Childcare, and Education: Co-op housing; Syracuse Cultural Workers; planning. (Win '84)

#62 Progressive Economics and Politics: Co-op housing; new ideas for your community and kibbutz society. (Spr '84)

#63 Living in Community: Stelle, Emissaries of Divine Light; peace efforts in Nicaragua; women's peace camp; democratic management. (Sum '84)

#64 Social Notes: The Great Alternative Life Group; old folks in a future world; case against consensus; kibbutz and educ. (Fall '84)

#65 Greenham Women's Peace Camp: The Farm; educ. for cooperation; justice in India; spiritual fraud; Jubilee Partners. (Win '84)

#66 Directory '85/'86: Builders of the Dawn; Rainbow Gathering. (Spr '85)

#67 Technology in Community: Sunrise Ranch, Ponderosa Village, Windstar. (Sum '85)

#68 Historic Communal Societies: Shakers; Harmony; Zoar; Amana; Icarians, Fourierists, and Llano. (Fall '85)

#69 South Africa: Appropriate technology for developing countries; community homes for the mentally disabled; Windstar Foundation. (Win '86)

#70 San Francisco Bay Area: Co-ops, clinics, housing, the Cheeseboard Collective. (Spr '86)

#71/72 Model Communities: Past, present, future; historic future cities; Kerista: polyfidelity. (Sum/Fall '86)

#73 FEC—10 Years: Social, gender, political, organizational issues. (Win '87)

#74 Urban Middle-Class Communes: Sirius; Clairemont Project; Ozark Regional Land trust; Aprovecho and End of the Road; alternative special education; Findhorn. (Sum '87)

#75 Planetization: Gaian politics, faith for the planetary age, Green movement, eco-feminism, deep ecology, Christian stewardship. (Sum '88)

#76 Education in Community: Cooperative alternative education, Twin Oaks, Stelle, Mt. Madonna School, Centrepoint, Camphill Villages, The Farm School. (Spr '90)

#77/78 1990–91 Directory of Intentional Communities: All feature articles in first edition of *Directory*. 129 pgs. (Nov '90)

#79 We're Back(!): FIC Highlights; Directory update. (Win '93)

#80/81 Vision and Leadership: Buddhist community, What happened to Kerista?, the URI split up, Sunflower House, Co-op America, collaborative decision making. (Spr/Sum '93)

#82 Women in Community: Women at Twin Oaks, The Farm; Women in Bruderhof, Hutterite, Shaker, Oneidan communities; Maggie Kuhn. (Spr '94)

#83 Celebration of Community: Highlights of the Aug '93 gathering: Kirkpatrick Sale/Bioregionalism, Dorothy Maclean/ Findhorn, Corinne McLaughlin/leadership, Gordon Davidson/spiritual economics, Noel Brown/environment; founders panels. (Sum '94)

#84 Growing Up in Community: Idyllic, nurturing, humorous, confusing, and frightening aspects of community childhood—in commune, kibbutz, The Farm, Christian, Bruderhof, activist, and secular egalitarian communities. (Fall '94)

#85 What We Have Learned: The Transition at King View Farm, Co-op Wars; A Closer Look into "Cults." (Win '94)

#86 Nurturing Our Potential: "We Have to Keep Growing?", Toward Gender Harmony, Conflict, Multiple Parenting. (Spr '95)

#87 Love, Romance and Sex: Community Ideals and Personal Loves; Re-Sacralizing Marriage; ZEGG; Healing from Abuse in Community; Spiritual Growth and Multiple Relationships. (Sum '95)

#88 Intentional Communities and "Cults": What Really Happened at Waco?; Religious Intolerance; Deprogramming Our Members. (Fall '95)

#89 Growing Older in Community: Choosing to Age in Community; Supporting the Aging Process in Community; Listening to the Wisdom of Our Elders; Stephen Gaskin on Rocinante; "Benevolent Dictators" in Community? (Win '95)

#121 Thriving in Community: Still Thriving After All These Years; Where There Are Cooks, There's Good Morale; Finding My Heart at Camphill Soltane; Ecology in Community: Commitment to Place; Living the Spiritual Quest of Elder Years. (Win '03)

#122 Community Seeker's Guide: My Marathon Tour of Communities; From a Community Seeker's Journal; Planning a Community Visit; Tips for Guests & Hosts; When and Why to Block Consensus; Seeking Community in New York City. (Spr '04)

#123 A Day in the Life: By the Plume of Popocatepetl; A Spring Day in Portugal; La Caravana Arcoiris por la Paz; Pilgrimage in a Desert Monastery; How to Really Support Ecovillages (Not Just Hugs and Theories). (Sum '04)

#124 Spiritual Community: Avoiding Spiritual Community; Rocky Mountain High; Why I'm Moving to Findhorn; On the Edge of the Abyss; Spiritual Beings, Material World; Do we Really Value "Diversity"? (Fall '04)

#125 Life After Student Co-ops: What I Learned Last Summer; Ruined for American Culture; Now I Want to Join a Community (or Maybe Start My Own...); The Toughest Issue We Ever Faced. (Win '04)

#126 The Arts in Community: 101 Art Projects Your Community Can Do; Painting and Dancing for Community; Creativity as "Learning Game"; Confessions of a Process Warrior. (Spr '05)

Benefits of FIC Membership

Why we want you to be an FIC member

You are us.

FIC members are the lifeblood of our organization. It's the time, skills, connections, dollars, and faith of our members that keep the Fellowship nourished and our efforts circulating.

Without our members and their support, we would be unable to create this Directory, generate the online data it's based on, publish Communities magazine, host and co-sponsor events that highlight cooperative living, offer Community Bookshelf, operate our website, or answer the many emails and phone calls we receive every day from the press and the public.

Why you want to be an FIC member

You know the importance of making available to the world the ideas and inspiration of community. In addition to the satisfaction of knowing you're helping make that happen, members get:

- A subscription to our newsletter.
- A 10% discount on many of our publications and products.
- A discount on advertising in Communities magazine.
- Invitations to our semi-annual meetings, and notices about conferences on community that may interest you. (We also send out monthly email messages with more news and special offers—please drop us a line at order@ic.org to get on the list.)
- Eligibility to join Sunrise Credit Union, the only US credit union based in an intentional community. See www.sunrisecreditunion.org for more information, or call 888-871-3482.

If you live in a community and join as a community member, then everyone living with you can receive these benefits.

If you're interested in involvement beyond membership—perhaps because of particular skills or contacts you have—we'd love to hear from you. There's a list of possibilities posted on the web at fic.ic.org/getinvolved.html; you can also contact our Inreach Committee by email at inreach@ic.org, or call the main office (# below).

How to join now

To become an FIC member, use the order form on the following page, or go to store.ic.org and click on Membership, or call us at 800-995-8342. You can also reach us by mail at Fellowship for Intentional Community, RR 1 Box 156, Rutledge, MO 63563, USA.

We look forward to hearing from you!

FIC Order Form

The FIC offers a number of products and services to help you find and create community. You can become an FIC member or order our products using this form. All of these and a wide selection of books from Community Bookshelf are also available at store.ic.org

FIC Membership   ❑ New member   ❑ Renewal   *See page 311 for more information.*

Choose a category of membership:

Individual:	❑ Basic: $30	❑ Low income: $15	❑ Organizational: $50
Community:	❑ under 10 members: $40	❑ 10–40 members: $75	❑ Over 40 members: $100
Donor:	❑ Supporting: $100	❑ Sustaining: $250	❑ Sponsoring: $500+

Here is my contribution to the FIC Directory Endowment!   *See page 35 for more information.*

❑ $500   ❑ $250   ❑ $100   ❑ $50   ❑ Other $_____

FIC Publications

❑ Communities Directory	*circle one* $24	❑ Building United Judgment	$16
❑ Visions of Utopia Video (DVD or VHS)	$30	❑ A Manual for Group Facilitators	$16

Communities Magazine:
Pricing for subscriptions and sample issues include standard/surface mail shipping; prices in parentheses are for First Class mail in US and Air Mail internationally. *See ads on inside front and back cover.*

	US	Canada	Other
❑ 1 year subscription (4 issues):	$20 ($30)	$24 ($34)	$26 ($50)
❑ 2 year subscription (8 issues):	$34 ($54)	$42 ($62)	$46 ($94)
❑ 3 year subscription (12 issues):	$45 ($75)	$57 ($87)	$63 ($135)
❑ Sample issue:	$6 ($8)	$7 ($10)	$8 ($14)
❑ Back issue (*see page 308*): #_____	$4 each (any 3 counts as 1 item for shipping)		

Shipping

Destination–Method	1st item	Add. items
US–Periodical/Standard Mail	$3.00	$1.00/each
US–First Class/Priority Mail	$5.00	$2.50/each
Canada–Surface Mail	$5.00	$3.00/each
Canada–Air Mail	$6.00	$4.00/each
Other–Surface Mail	$8.00	$4.00/each
Other–Air Mail 3–10 days	$12.00	$8.00/each

The above shipping charges apply to all items except FIC memberships and Communities magazine samples and subscriptions.

Shipping Charges Calculation

Shipping Method:_____ 1st item $_____

Number of additional items ____ x $____ = $_____

Total $_____

Order Information

Total for selected items $_____

–10% FIC Member discount $_____
(not applicable for shipping or discounted quantity orders)

Subtotal $_____

Shipping $_____

Total $_____

❑ Check enclosed (payable to FIC). Foreign checks must be paid in US dollars and have corresponding US bank printed on the check.

❑ Visa   ❑ M/C   ❑ Discover

Card # _____ Exp. _____

Contact Information

_____   _____
NAME OF INDIVIDUAL OR CONTACT PERSON   PHONE

_____   _____
GROUP NAME OR AFFILIATION (IF APPROPRIATE)   EMAIL

_____
STREET ADDRESS

_____
CITY/TOWN   STATE/PROVINCE   COUNTRY   ZIP/POSTAL CODE

❑ Add me to your monthly email announcements list.
We send occasional promotional emails to our customers but do not share emails with other organizations.
   ❑ Please, don't use my email for promotional mailings.
   ❑ Please, don't share my name or postal address with like-valued organizations.

**To order, mail this form to: FIC, 138 Twin Oaks Road, Louisa, VA 23093, USA;
call 800-462-8240 (US & Canada); email order@ic.org; or use our secure website at store.ic.org.**